Volume 1   Issue I

Back in THE BRONX

Celebrating the experience of growing up and living in the Bronx

Remembering Jahn's

by Berton M. Miller (Clinton '57)

For a 16 year old in the Bronx in the late 1950's. there were three kinds of weekend evening hang-outs.

There were the "no-date" places, which included the likes of Tommy's candy store; Tony's Pizza on Featherbed Lane & Macombs Road and Nat's pool room located on Burnside Avenue.

There were "after-date" meeting places where you went to schmooze, brag and commiserate with the gang. The quintessential "after-date" destination was the open-all-night 167th Street Cafeteria.

And then there were the "with-date" places you went to when the movie was over but you didn't want the evening to end. At or near the top of any "with-date" list was always Jahns Old Fashioned Ice Cream Parlour.

Jahns was situated where Kingsbridge Rd. joined East Fordham Rd., by the Valentine Theater, within walking distance of the legendary Paradise, adjacent to the Castro Convertible showroom and across the street from Bond's clothing (where I got my first suit with pegged pants).

Jahns attraction wasn't great ice cream. Most people thought Addie Vallins on 161st Street, or Rushmeier's (later Luhr's) on University Ave. just south of Tremont, to name a couple, were better in this department.

Continued on page 2

A Village Called the Bronx

By Susan Thayler

Glen Rock, N.J They say that home is where the heart is. But you won't find my heart anywhere among the sad wrecked buildings that line the street where I once lived. My heart is with the Bronx of memory, a Bronx that even then we knew was just a stepping stone to Bigger and Better.

Even before the early 1960's when the influx of minority groups to our neighborhood spurred what surely must have been one of the more rabid episodes of white flight in the history of urban breakdown, our folks were preoccupied with Getting Out.

Mothers spent whole afternoons sitting outside on folding chairs (this was pre-lib, when it was possible to do such things without guilt) having conversations that went something like this:

"We drove out to Merrick last week to look." "Oh yeah? Did you find anything?" "Well, we saw some nice possibilities, a very nice cape with an expandable attic on a corner lot." "Yeah? So–when are you moving already?" (Pause.) "We'll see."

Most of this time amounted to wishful thinking. A fortunate few might actually make it to a garden apartment in Flushing or Bayside, but for those of us whose dreams could not stretch even as far as Queens, we could always hope for this: A sunny, roomy four with a sunken living room in one of those sedate buildings on the Grand Concourse.

While Davidson Avenue was never exactly the Concourse, at least it was part of what we referred to with (misguided) pride as the West Bronx, as distinguished from the

Continued on Page 13

From the Editors...

CLINTON '61

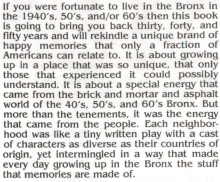

TAFT '62

If you were fortunate to live in the Bronx in the 1940's, 50's, and/or 60's then this book is going to bring you back thirty, forty, and fifty years and will rekindle a unique brand of happy memories that only a fraction of Americans can relate to. It is about growing up in a place that was so unique, that only those that experienced it could possibly understand. It is about a special energy that came from the brick and mortar and asphalt world of the 40's, 50's, and 60's Bronx. But more than the tenements, it was the energy that came from the people. Each neighborhood was like a tiny written play with a cast of characters as diverse as their countries of origin, yet intermingled in a way that made every day growing up in the Bronx the stuff that memories are made of.

This book represents four years and sixteen issues of **Back In THE BRONX** magazine. It contains over 180 stories including countless vintage photographs and more than 1500 classified ads that are for the most part, written not by professional writers or authors, but by people like yourself who want to share their experiences with fellow Bronxites. We began publishing **Back In THE BRONX** in 1992, and since our first issue, we have brought back memories of hot August nights at Freedomland; summer dances under the stars at Poe Park; shopping at Alexander's; having a sundae at Krum's or Jahn's; experience a day at Orchard Beach or cheering at Yankee Stadium. Share a Bronxite's description of the essence of "The Egg Cream Mystique" or "Bronx Style Fishing" that describes 'fishing' for coins below a subway grating. The stories go on and on.

Do you often think of friends that you had thirty and forty or more years ago and wonder where they are today and how to get in touch with them? Each issue contains hundreds of ads that subscribers have placed in **Back In THE BRONX** in hopes of finding their long lost friends or neighbors. Chances are that this book will contain many classifieds that in some way relate to you, your friends, or your neighborhood.

Should you find much enjoyment reading through this 16 issue book and wish to continue receiving **Back In THE BRONX** on a quarterly basis, you may join the more than 10,000 subscribers who are currently receiving our magazine. Become a subscriber today. Your subscription is your passport to travel back in time, back to the old neighborhood, and back to good times with great people. This wasn't your life, it IS your life because all those formative years are what made us what we are today. The ups and downs, the hopes and dreams .... It's all there for you to keep forever.

So don't delay. Fill out the order form or call our toll free #: **1-800 7 BRONX-5.**

Sincerely Yours,
Stephen M. Samtur
Susan J. Samtur
Editors

Back In THE BRONX

A number of the photographs in **Back In THE BRONX** are courtesy of and are available from the Bronx Historical Society.

Publishers & Editors	Stephen M. Samtur	Clinton '61
	Susan H. Samtur	Taft '62
Contributing Editors	Barbara Fasciani	Roosevelt '65
	Martin Jackson	Science '58
	Sandra Zuckerman	Jefferson '57
	Al Zuckerman	New Ultrecht '50
Art & Production	Ellen Grodjesk	
Printed By:	Trunbell Printing, Trumbell, CT	

Jahn's (Continued from page 1)

But the size of the ice cream desserts at Jahns, no doubt helped boost its popularity. Who can ever forget the volume or variety of "The Kitchen Sink" or the "Banana Boat," two of Jahns favorite fabled menu options.

More than anything, the popularity of Jahns was based on its atmosphere. Jahns was festive, as if there was always a party going on. It was loud, with laughter in the air bouncing off the fake Tiffany hanging lamps over each wooden booth.

And for entertainment, there was always the "Stump the Server" game in which **you** tried to trick the waiter into serving the wrong order to the **wrong** person at your table. Despite the fact that no matter how large your party was and how complicated you made your order (hot fudge sundae with one scoop of black raspberry, one scoop of vanilla fudge, chopped walnuts, not peanuts, whipped cream on the side, no cherry; one chocolate ice cream soda with a scoop of cherry vanilla, one scoop of chocolate, no whipped cream, glass of water on the side; and so on for 10 people); and despite the fact that they never wrote down a word of your order, they always got it right, thereby happily disproving what all your teachers always tried to drill into your head: "If you want to remember it, YOU MUST WRITE IT DOWN!"

Jahns was a place that was innocent; as innocent as the times themselves. Jahns was the place to which you took a girl you cared about.

Jean Stasio - Alumni President, Evander Childs 1950 with another Evanderite, Red Buttons.

Bronx Honor Roll
Those Who Have Achieved

Bronx Science

Edgar Doctorow
Bobby Darren
Stokely Carmichael

Cardinal Hayes

George Carlin
Regis Philbin
Rocky Colovito
Kevin Loughery

DeWitt Clinton

James Baldwin
Paddy Chayefsky
Daniel Shore
Neil Simon
Richard Rodgers
Fats Waller
Don Adams
Martin Balsam
Judd Hirsch
Stubby Kaye
Robert Klein
Burt Lancaster
Avery Corman
Ed Lopat
Jan Murray
Jimmie Walker
Nate Archibald
Dolph Shayes
James Caan
A.M. Rosenthal

Evander Childs

Red Buttons
James Coco
Carl Reiner

Monroe

Hank Greenberg
Ed Kranepool
Jules Pfeiffer

Morris

Gabe Pressman
Angel Cordero

Roosevelt

June Allison

Taft

Eydie Gorme
Stanley Kubrick
Sanford Brown
Mal Z. Lawrence

Other notable folks with ties to the Bronx

Charles Osgood
Vic Damone
Bess Myerson
Dennis Day
Dion DiMucci
Jonas Salk
Roberta Peters
Jerry Vale
Jake LaMotta
Dianne Carroll
Ron Liebman
Gary Marshall
Al Pacino
Rob Reiner
Eli Wallach
Corazon Aquino
Edward Koch
Vin Scully
Joey Adams
Danny Aiello
Ellen Barkan
Alan Alda
Armand Hammer
Theodore Kheel
George Steinbrenner
Don Criqui
Lauren Bacall

Tony Curtis
Hal Linden
Sal Mineo
Charles Nelson Reilly
Isabel Sanford
Vanessa Williams
Herman Badillo
Ted Kennedy
George Burns
Norman Cousins
Edgar Alan Poe
Geraldo Rivera
Pat Summerall
Herman Wouk
Teresa Brewer
Cab Calloway
Joey Bishop
Joe Franklin
Penny Marshall
Carroll O'Connor
Connie Selleca
Cardinal Cooke
E. Colin Powell
Robert Kennedy
Anne Bancroft
Ralph Lauren
Eddie Pinckney
Mario Merola
Robert Abrams
Calvin Klein
Bobby Bonilla
George Cukor
Avery Fisher
Leon Cooper
Rosalyn Yallow

...Nobel Prize Winners

Gertrude Elio
Robert Hofstadter
Herman J. Muller
Melvin Schwartz
Steven Weinberg
Gerald Edelman

You Can Go Home Again

by Alan S. Gordon, DeWitt Clinton '61

Thomas Wolfe was wrong...you can go home again. At the least, you can go back to your old building and see who lived there when you were young.

The New York Public Library's Microfilm Division is the guardian of the past. It stocks a series of books known officially as The Address Directories and known unofficially as the backwards phone book. These directories, available for all five boroughs for most years after 1920, list residents by street and building address.

Located on the third floor of the Library's main branch at Fifth Avenue and 42nd Street, the microfilmed Directories are a complete record of the Bronx that was. Microfilm readers and microfilm photocopy machines are available, but change is not, so bring rolls of quarters if you plan to make copies. Arrive early. The Microfilm Division opens at 11 AM on Tuesdays and Wednesdays, 10 AM on Thursday through Saturday and gets crowded early.

When I went, I looked first

245 E. Gunn Hill, circa 1970

Alan Gordon & Andrew Diamond, PS 94 Graduation 1956

4

at the listing for my old building at 245 East Gun Hill Road. I picked the directory for 1956, the year I graduated from Public School 94, around the corner on Kings College Place. There they all were, listed as if no time at all had passed: My grandparents in 5E, my cousin Gene in 4J, my aunt Marilyn in 3K, my aunt Bev in IC, my parents and my sister and me in 4D, a one bedroom apartment with a view of "the lot." Originally tennis courts in 1925 when 245 was built, and later two "fancy" new buildings, in 1956 this empty lot was our jungle to be explored, full of fireflies and butterflies on warm summer evenings .

And there too were all of my relatives and the three teachers and 6 cousins and two dozen friends and schoolmates who lived in one or another of 245 East Gun Hill Road's 62 apartments.

Building numbers in the Directory are listed in numerical sequence, so across the street and on the next page were Lou's Candy Store in 215 and Chasin's Deli in 250. A comic book from Lou's or

a bag of hot french fries were each a dime, and either one was good for a half hour's enjoyment. Down the block was the Oval Pharmacy, where my first job ever paid 50 cents an hour to deliver orders.

A lifetime later, when Penny Marshall (who grew up on the Parkway) directed the movie "Awakenings", she shot several key scenes in the Oval and on Bainbridge Avenue. My children and my wife had parts in the film and, as I stood in the background and looked down at them all playing on the field, it seemed as if I were caught in a time warp...and if I waited just a moment longer I might get to see one of my neighbors from

245 come walking through the park, enjoying the forsythia in bloom on a beautiful spring day.

Gone now are the forsythia and the monkey bars, and the "parkies" pushing 5432876their yellow trucks selling peanuts, crackerjacks and sodas.

That was Gun Hill Road in 1956... For me, Junior High School 80 lay ahead, and then De Witt Clinton, all before the name of John Fitzgerald Kennedy was heard even for the first time on the streets of Bronx. But part of it's all still there, year by year, in the Library's Address Directories. ■

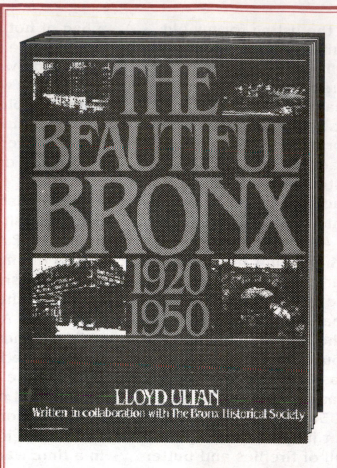

LOST

&FOUND

Oh... for the Good Ole Days!

by Carol Ball-Teplin (Class of '58)

I've always heard the expression "You can't go home!" Well, after spending the weekend at the Taft Reunion, I can honestly dispute that statement. For three days I felt as if I were transported back to the Bronx. I met people from my past – not just classmates, but friends who lived in my building at the corner of 173rd Street and Topping Avenue, and around the corner from Topping Avenue, Mt. Eden Avenue. and Monroe Avenue. People who I would recall from time to time in my memory bank of childhood experiences, suddenly came so life. They even looked better than they did as children - more mature, more worldly and "all growed up."

The conversations took me back to 1947. There was a terrific snow storm that stopped the city in its tracks. Stores and schools were closed and I remember sled riding in Claremont park with my friends down the "big hill" ending on Clay Avenue, and walking back up the steps to Mt. Eden.

My father was upset because he couldn't find his car. The snow had completely covered everything. I helped him dig out around the corner from the plumbing shop where he worked on Teller Avenue and 169th Street. As a child I couldn't understand his lack of joy and excitement; as an adult I can completely relate!

We had three candy stores in my immediate area. One was on 173rd Street and Topping Avenue, but we didn't hang out there. Then there was a long narrow candy store owned by the Barr's on Monroe and 173rd Street which was too small to congregate The one we all loved was Gellers, on Monroe Avenue near Mt. Eden. It was a big store that you had to walk down a flight of stairs to get into. We were thrown out of Geller's on more than one occasion for loitering or reading the comics, but we had lots of fun, and you always met someone you knew there. Leta Goldman, Barry Meyers, Bruce Greenberg, Joe Lovaglio, Sheila Alexander, Harvey Wasserman, Jimmy Solo, Marty Shisrin, Marvin Alsman, Murray Chances, Marvin Berger, Phyllis Shifser, Linda Bale, Judy Modell, Lenny Horowitz, Joel Glick, Stanley Feld, Michael & Freddy Etkin, Edra Kleinman, Cynthia Greenberg, to name just a dozen or two, could all be found at Geller's (maybe not at the same time)!

Looking back at the late 1940's and early 1950's there were no malls or supermarkets in my neighborhood, except for the A&P on 174th and Monroe Avenue. My mother only shopped at the A&P "when all else failed." Instead, we would traipse to the mecca for shopping - Bathgate Avenue. We would shop for fruit and vegetables from open stands; my mother knew all the merchants and would hondle with them for the best apples "from the back." We would get Sunday morning breakfast from Hal & Sids appetizing, who would give us extra onions with the pickled herring, with a wink to my mother. There was a Woolworth on Bathgate Avenue where I would get a taste of heaven in the form of a Root Beer Float, while shopping for Carnation Pink lipstick by Tangee.

The shop that intrigued me the most was the kosher butcher. We got our chickens from Gedalye. I would watch as he

plucked the chickens and burned the pin feathers off over a fire he built in the back. When he was in a particularly good mood, he would throw in some chicken legs for the soup, and once in a blue moon we would find unhatched eggs, which was a great delicacy, packed with the giblets. Of course my siblings and I would fight over them!

We bought our rye bread, rolls and challah from Beeberman's bakery, and for a treat, If we were good, mama would buy us Charlotte Russe! I don't even know if they still make them anymore, but I remember how delicious the whipped cream was and how we made a contest of who could lick it the slowest to make it last the longest.

I remember walking to the library on Washington Avenue near Tremont. We'd walk down 173rd Street and walk along Webster Avenue. Passing the live chicken market my friends and I held our breath against the smell which emanated from the open doors. We saw crates upon crates filled with chickens about to meet their maker and we would dream up stories of running in and setting them free.

Riding bikes, roller skating, climbing the rocks, playing land or stoop-ball and watching the boys play softball were fun things to do as a kid. My friends, Elaine Manos, Sheila Spindel, Linda Shapiro and I would love to follow the "Parkies." God only knows what would have happened if we ever caught one, but it sure was fun tailing them as pre-pubescent children of the Bronx. When we reached our teens we graduated to smoking cigarettes on "tar beach" and "make-out" in Linda's house when her parents were out for the evening. Talk about your "group-grope" in the dark!

Saturdays in the Bronx would be the most fun of all. We'd go to the movies for the matinee. Sometimes we went to the Kent on 167th Street, or the Luxor on 170th, or the Mt. Eden or the Surrey on Mt. Eden Avenue.. We almost always walked, but sometimes we would take the bus to the Paradise or Valentine theaters on the Concourse or Fordham Road.

Elaine, Linda, Sheila and some of the other girls would save our money and go to Tom's Inn, the Chinese Restaurant on the Concourse off Mt. Eden Avenue. We would order soup, and Fried Rice and fill up on noodles and tea, and usually we each had to pay around 75 cents, for this exotic feast.

A special treat for us on Saturdays was Ladies Day at the Polo Grounds or Yankee Stadium. I seem to recall 25 or 50 cents admission, and a quarter for a frank. The very best time was when the Giants played the Brooklyn Dodgers at the Polo Grounds! Once, Elaine and I travelled all the way into that scary, dark continent of our arch rivals and we rooted for the Giants in Ebbets Field! I'll never forget the feelings of pride mixed with terror and fear-for-our-lives when we visited enemy territory - Brooklyn!

When I was in Joseph H. Wade Jr. High School, my favorite school of all time, I got a job after school and on Saturdays, working at Dr. Katz's the optometrist office on Third Avenue,

Continued on Page 12

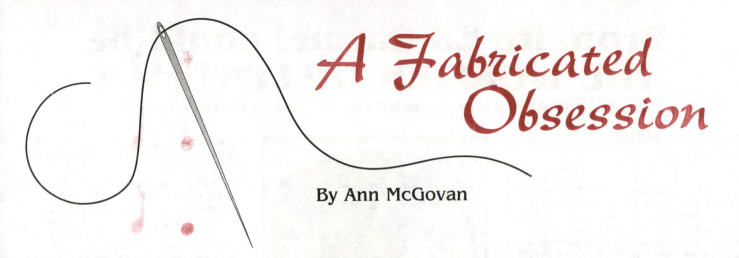

A Fabricated Obsession

By Ann McGovan

Our third grade class lined up outside St. Margaret's Catholic Church in Riverdale in the Bronx, and when Sister Ellen graced us with her expansive smiles, we proceeded into the Church, down the isle and into the pews, accompanied by Ms. Eleanor Lanning's rousing organ music. Gail Minogue sat two rows behind me; I turned my head just a bit, and strained my eyes to take in every detail of her new Fall outfit. When she returned to her seat from Communion, I was able to get a better look; gaping at her tan, soft, wool, fitted coat, I watched the hem sway gently with each of her measured steps. Of course we were much too young for the 'new look', but the latest rage in color combinations was apropos-chartreuse and tan-and Gail's hat was precisely that, a petite velvet confection of curved ostrich plumes in these striking colors. I had no thought of the Mass, but only of her breathtaking outfit and committed every detail to memory. Gail set the standard, it was the leftover Shirley Temple look and she had precisely twenty-five spiral curls which her mother laboriously set every Saturday night and rearranged every day. When she was little, Gail had been a model and with her savings from this enterprise, her Mother brought her the latest fashions from Saks Fifth Avenue. The all-time stopper was on Easter Sunday, when Gail entered St. Margaret's wearing a glen plaid suit with a bolero jacket and a huge tan felt hat that resembled one worn by a cowboy in a Life magazine photo. The kicker was that her ringlets were gone and she sported a new hairdo, a 'poodle cut'. Yes, a 'poodle cut,' something I'd never heard of before. This outfit was overwhelming and I could not take my eyes off her.

I survived with hand-me-downs, not so much from my oldest sister Maureen because she was much larger than I but from neighbors, thriftshops and even Aunt Wilma, who gave me her elegant, out-of-style castoffs. I simply could not be seen wearing out of style garments, so Aunt Wilma's giant shouldered, off-white wool jacket became my first project. I struggled in vain; but not even the best tailor could have done anything to rectify the immense armholes. In a rage of fury and despair, I savagely attacked the garment and tore it to shreds. Our cramped bedroom became a seething blizzard of ivory fluff. Immobile by the time the last particle settled, I was crushed by the futility of my effort and the vision of myself walking down the isle wearing last year's worn, outgrown coat; if I didn't have the right clothes, I would not be accepted, I would remain an outsider, a martyr.

Shortly thereafter, I had another opportunity to redeem myself. Mrs. Hickey, the dressmaker who lived up the hill, gave me some well made, but out of fashion outfits from some of her wealthy clients. Two of the suits had strange puffed sleeves which seemed childish, so I removed them altogether since 'sleeveless' was the latest style, and my solution for the short skirts was to lengthen them with ruffles. My confidence grew as I became adept in the art of salvaging. A plaid wool skirt with a tear in it came my way and gave me another occasion to test my skills. Since Bermuda shorts had become de riguer, it didn't take me long to slit open the seams, iron the fabric and cut out a McCall's pattern for the famed walking shorts. I stitched them up on Ma's foot treadle sewing machine, taking care to avoid the hole and making sure the lines in the plaid were all in perfect alignment. The finished product was very attractive indeed, my recovery activities were paying off!

Gail Minogue, Mary Dreiss, Sheila Burrows and other members of the clique hung out at the Riverdale Neighborhood House, and that is where I decided to give my latest sewing achievement a test run. Shyly, I approached the members of the gang who were sporting their "Bermas" and I noticed, first, Gail looking at me and then the gaze of the clique following in unison. When she complimented my creation, I was momentarily stunned and all I could do was utter some pleasantry, while deep inside I was ecstatic! My simple wool shorts triggered my peers' approval of me. I was accepted and I deliriously took a hard earned step into the circle of belonging. ■

Bronxite Ed Carmel could be THE WORLD'S TALLEST MAN

Reprinted From Bronx Westchester Magazine, January, 1958

By ROBERT C. ROMAN
Associate Editor

Just a few giant steps from Tremont and University Avenues lives Ed Carmel a young man who claims: "I'm the tallest man who ever walked the face of the Earth." Ed, who weighed 16 pounds at birth, now stands a shade over 8 feet 9 inches and weighs over 450 pounds. "At my last check~up the doctor said that I grew about one-quarter of an inch last year, and, who knows, maybe I've gained one-quarter of a ton!"

The son of Isaac and Miriam (Pines) Ha Carmeli, he was brought to the United States as an extra large two-year old ("The doctor picked me up and slapped me, so I slapped him right back!") from Tel Aviv Israel, where he was born some twenty-eight years ago "When I grew a bit my father gave me blocks to play with," Ed chortles, "Sixth Avenue Seventh Avenue . . . And trains, too— the New York Central, the Pennsylvania..." His father, an insurance salesman for Metropolitan Life ("My father is an insurance expert and has written numerous articles about his field."), is 5 feet 6, his mother, a secretary for the National Women's League of the Theological Seminary of America ("She's the sparkplug of the organization."), is 5 feet 5. But Ed's grandfather Isadore Carmeletzky, a rabbi in Warsaw, Poland, was 7 feet 5 and known as the tallest rabbi in the world. When Ed entered kindergarten, he was already taller than his teacher, and all through grade school (at eleven he was 6 feet tall) and high school (he was well over 7 feet when he graduated) he towered over everyone else. When the basketball coach at the Bronx's William Howard Taft High School saw him he supposedly proclaimed: "I've got the beginning of a championship team right there (pointing at Ed)!"

"I stopped playing when my head kept hitting the rim of the basket," Ed recalls, reflecting upon his brief basketball days. "My favorite memory of Taft was a fine teacher and person, Mrs. Greenwald, who was very helpful to me."

However, Ed admits that he had aready begun to neglect his studies. And at the City College of New York he spent most of his time in extra curricular activities. I guess I'm just a born extrovert," he admits). He was elected vice-president of the freshman class, was "almost

unanimously" elected Class Giant, and left the college after two years to enter show business.

He began nightclub work and called himself "The World's Tallest Comic-Poet." He also did extensive radio and television work as a folk singer, disc jockey, and in commercials. Because Ed has one of the lowest voices in the United States, he has recorded the bass parts in numerous commercials. He has also made two recordings: "The Happy Giant" and "The Good Giant,"

Brief experience as a wrestler ("I'd play the part of a monster, while my opponent died of fright) and appearances as a giant on scores of television shows, including those of Wendy Barrie, Robert Montgomery, Art Linkletter, Gary Moore, Perry Como, Dean Martin and Steve Allen ("He gave me a chance to do some of my comedy routines") helped to bring him to the attention of Nat Eagles, a man who assembles "unusual people" for circuses, carnivals, fairs and other theatrical enterprises.

Ed was hired to replace Ted Evans (a mere 8 feet 6 inches), who had died, as the giant for the Ringling Bros. Barnum and Bailey Circus ("They billed me as 'The Tallest Man on Earth"). He thus began a happy association and an assignment ("from the end of March to the middle of May") which he has held for eight years. He loves this work. "I love children," he says. It gives me a

great deal of satifaction to see them marvel at myself and the other side-show attractions.

Ed has also appeared in five films. He did a bit role in Alfred Hitchcock's "North By Northwest," did larger parts in three low-budgeters, "Trouble Makers," "I was a Nazi," and "50,000 B.C.," but was most noticeable in American-International's "The Brain That Wouldn't Die," made in 1962. He played the monster finally set free from a mad doctor's lab who escapes and sets fire to the building where he and others were held captive, kills the doctor, and thereby ends the suffering of the doctor's other victims. He also was hired to plug another TV chiller. "I had to dress as the Frankenstein monster and walk around giving out shrunken heads," he recalls. "Then I had to lug a coffin on my back around town. It had a mummy hanging out of it. Delightful, wasn't it?" He has no complaints about such work but implores: "Why do they always have to make a giant an idiot. Can't they give him average intelligence, at least?" He adds "I keep active, though, because I want to do roles I can do in order to pay the freight."

"I eat four times as much as the average man and steak is my favorite food (Bronx steak houses take note), And beds, clothing, and cars have always been my particular problems." He has to sleep diagonally on a special 8-foot bed. All of Ed's clothes except his handkerchiefs, must be custom made. His shirts are neck, 23; sleeves, 52; suits are 70 extra long and shoes are size 36 with an over TEN-E width ("they cost me over $150 a pair"). Tie buying, of course, becomes quite a chore. Ed must get the longest tie available and then he must use the full length instead of folding them double as most men do. He drives a car, which has had the front seat removed, from the back seat. When he gets into a car the front seat must be unoccupied. Ed sits in the back and stretches his feet over the front seat. He also can't get into a phone boot (the telephone doesn't reach both his ear or his mouth), can't sit in a movie or theatre seat (he has to crouch in the rear) and elevators and subways are constant hazard. "On the whole just about everything gets pretty cramped for a big guy like me," he says, good naturedly, referring to some of his plights in life."

Continued on Page 13

Coming your way... the new Ford THUNDERBIRD

Who Am I ?

Can you name these three famous Bronx high schools alumni?
You'll find out who they turned out to be on page 12.

Mystery Bronxite #1

Mystery Bronxite #2

Mystery Bronxite #3

Test Your Memory

Circle/Fill in Your Answer.

1. You've Just come out of the Loew's Paradise movie theatre in the Bronx in 1960 with your date and it's raining heavily. Which Ice cream parlor would you likely WALK to?
(A) Jahns
(B) Addie Vallens
(C) Krums

2. If you were making an egg cream, which chocolate syrup would you likely use?
(A) Hershey's
(B) Bosco
(C) U-Bet

3. The restaurant closest to Yankee Stadium that specialized in orange drinks in the 1950's was
(A) Chock Full-O-Nuts
(B) Nedick's
(C) Court Delicatessen

4. If you were traveling by train from the Bronx in 1955 to see the Yankees play the Brooklyn Dodgers in the World Series at Ebbetts Field, how much would you have paid for a subway token?
(A) ten cents
(B) fifteen cents
(C) twenty cents

5. A first class letter mailed from the Bronx In 1960 would cost
(A) four cents
(B) five cents
(C) eight cents

6. If you made a road test appointment for your driver's license in the Bronx in 1965, you could have easily walked there if you lived
(A) on the Concourse
(B) near Fordham Road
(C) in Parkchester

7. Match the Bronx H.S. with the following celebrities
(A) Regis Philbin   (I) Bronx Science
(B) Bobby Darren   (2) Cardinal Hayes
(C) Edye Gorme   (3) Wm. H. Tatt
(Fill in # below.)

A=   B=   C=

8. Match the movie theatre to the Street:
(A) Luxor   (1) 170th St.
(B) Kent   (2) 167th St.
(C) Earl   (3) 161st St.
(Fill in # below.)

A=   B=   C=

9. If you wanted soft custard-style ice cream and you heard music coming from an ice cream truck, which name would appear on the truck?
(A) Good Humor
(B) Bungalow Bar
(C) Mr. Softy

10. Which of these singing groups came from the Bronx?
(A) The Earls
(B) The Cadillacs
(C) Jay and the Americans

11. A game played in the Bronx in the 1950's and 60's involving eight boxes in a pattern that used a thick piece of wood and good balance, was called
(A) Skelly
(B) Marbles
(C) Potzie

12. Girls growing up in the Bronx would often play jump rope while chanting a rhythmic song. The very first name they would utter would be
(A) Alice
(B) Marilyn
(C) Susan

13. Girls would play a game that utilized a bouncing spaldeen and intricately crossed pieces of metal called
(A) Box Ball
(B) Jacks
(C) Potzie

14. The train system replacing the Sixth and Ninth Avenue Els and running from 205th Street and the Concourse in the Bronx to Coney Island was
(A) IRT
(B) BMT
(C) LSMFT
(D) IND

15. The section in the Bronx where Edgar Allen Poe's cottage still remains is
(A) Kingsbridge
(B) Morrisania
(C) Highbridge

16. Botanical Garden's main attraction was called
(A) Arbortorium
(B) Conservatory
(C) Green Tree

17. A very popular Swim Club on the order of the movie *The Flamingo Kid* located in the eastern part of the Bronx near the Throggs Neck Bridge was called
(A) Cascades
(B) Miramar
(C) Shorehaven

18. Which insurance company purchased land in the Bronx to build Parkchester?
(A) Metropolitan Life
(B) Prudential Insurance
(C) State Farm

19. The recommended sequence for making the best egg creams is?
(A) syrup, milk, club soda
(B) milk, syrup, club soda
(C) club soda, milk, syrup

20. The main General Post Office (GPO) in the Bronx is located at
(A) Pelham Parkway & White Plains Road
(B) Concourse & 149th Street
(C) East Tremont Avenue & Unionport Rd

Answers on page 26

If you have a test or questions for a test, do not hesitate to send them in. Please make sure that you also supply the correct answer. Please use a blank sheet of paper following the format above and enclose in the reader reply envelope.

Ole Days (Continued from Page 8)

under the El. I was then exposed to the Sugar Bowl on Claremont Parkway, and the best egg creams in the world, made by Howie or his brother Murray Messer. Did I ever have a crush on Howie! I soon found out that every other panting fourteen year old girl had a crush on him too! I remember Carole Terach, Cookie, Eleanore, and Millie Teplitsky as part of the Sugar Bowl crowd.

We had a grocery store just underneath our apartment. Whenever my mother needed something from the grocer she would send me downstairs. She seldom gave me money, instead she would say "Tell him to put it on the book." This was my first experience with "credit," and was the forerunner to Mastercard for me. Each week when dad would come home with his pay, he would go down to Horowitz the grocer to settle his account. Horowitz would take out the book and go over our page, and then we would start all over again for the next week. What fun it was to see Jack Horowitz at the reunion – without his book!

Another exciting experience which came with the thrill of living in a Bronx apartment building, was watching Eddie Martinelli shovel the coal into the furnace. I used to love to watch the magical, hypnotizing fire, and I would beg Eddie to let me shovel the coal. I'll never forget the time he let me, and how important, grown up and special I felt. Meeting Eddie and his wife Isabel at the reunion, was a very special treat for me.

I could go on recounting my memories of growing up in the Bronx, and the genuine pleasure it was to recall these memories, but it would probably fill a book. Hey, that's not a bad idea - I just might do that. Stay tuned for the further adventures of me as a kid!

We heartily encourage all our readers to send in short stories about their experiences in the Bronx, and we thank Carol for this issue's article. Back in the Bronx reserves the right to edit all submitted stories.

This issue's Mystery Bronxites

1. Robert Klein

2. Regis Philbin

3. Gary Marshall

Village (Continued from page 1)

East Bronx, where all our poorer relatives lived. Between Macombs Rd. and Tremont Avenue, we were situated just enough west of Jerome Avenue that we could turn a deaf ear to the rumblings of the elevated Woodlawn-Jerome Avenue line, the comings and goings of which laced our nights and days with numbing consistency.

What our parents failed to recognize in their eagerness to lead us on to greener pastures was that life in the Bronx had it's advantages. Not just the superficial kinds, such as the proximity of Yankee Stadium to our living rooms. What we had and what we took for granted was a sense of community. When you were born in the Bronx, you belonged not only to your parents but to the neighborhood as well.

Consider: There were 60 families in our buildings. Most had children. Therefore on any given day one could find upward of 50 children on the sidewalk in front of our building, ranging in age from infancy onward. Our building was one of many on the block, but because it had a commodious courtyard with spiked railings around it that it was useful for games such as iron tag, kids from up and down the block congregated there.

The noise we made drove the older tenants to stuff their ears with cotton, especially in spring and summer, when the crash of steel wheels against pitted concrete echoed raucously in the air. (No prissy polyurethane wheels for us; the noise our skates made was half the fun.)

The selection of playmates being limitless, we were never beggars and we were free to choose our friends from day to day. Our mothers, too, had a wide circle of confidantes. Since we were, by and large, of the same ethnic heritage (Jewish) and stratum (aspiring upwardly mobile), our needs, desires and frustrations were often common knowledge. Just as everyone knew the layout of everyone else's apartment, so they knew, to a sometimes unnerving degree, what went on inside that apartment. Pretensions fizzled under that kind of intimacy. If for no other reason than that they had no place else to go, our neighbors were always there. Money problems, the loss of a job, an unwanted pregnancy—nothing could be withheld for long. Crises came and went. When the throat of a child in apartment B-60 almost closed during a diphtheria attack, every mother in the building wrung her hands in worry; they put themselves on call, lending thermometers, hot water bottles,

consolations, until the doctor arrived. When the young girl in B-41 fell out of her crib onto the makeshift vaporizer, a pot filled with boiling water, and scaled her arm, a cadre of women was on the scene to distract the other siblings, to soothe the hysterical mother and child, to – and this is important – assuage feelings of guilt: "It wasn't your fault; how could you know she was going to fall out of the crib? You couldn't watch her every second!"

Now here we are, most of us, reaping the dreams sown by our parents. We have reached Bigger and Better. The suburbs we live in have well-defined property lines. Neighbors are people to whom one waves when one carries out the trash, people whose privacy must be preserved at all cost.

The cost to some of us is considerable.

Where is that company of women in whose relaxed reciprocity we might exercise our Bronx-bred need for "yenting," not to mention the leisure time this would necessitate?

Our children, who cannot miss what they never had, cannot understand what was so great about living there, in a slum. What do they know, these kids whose heads are into electronic invaders from space and other substitutes for human interaction, what do they know of the exhilaration of games such as ring-a-lievio, captain, double dutch salt-and-pepper, skelly, potsy and a hundred creations of our own imaginings?

While some of us already have begun to dribble back, there are not enough yet to turn the tide. Most often, we aim for Manhattan or Brooklyn when we flee the isolation of the suburban dream gone sour because, physically, we have no other option. One cannot live in an empty shell.

Perhaps someday those dead Bronx streets will resound again with the shouts of "Ready or not, here I come!" One day some smart developer will tap the vast areas waiting to be reclaimed. If I am still able to tote a folding chair to the sidewalk when that happens, save a place for me, if not on Davidson Avenue, then maybe in a sunny four with a sunken living room on the Grand Concourse. ▪

Susan Thaler who writes short stories, is author of "Rosaria," a novel for young adults.

Carmel (Continued from Page 10)

There are also advantages. "The polluted air problem of New York City doesn't affect me, "I'm above it, you're closer to it. When he leaves his home and goes into the street it's like a personal appearance. "Even before I went to school, I can remember going to a candy store to buy bubble gum, and a crowd of kids and grown-ups following me. I'm still the phenomenon — wherever I go, people by the thousands follow". Such an attraction is especially useful at special sales at shopping centers, business openings, political rallies, and Ed has been hired to promote such projects in various places —

from Pittsburg to Hong Kong (Bronx business leaders take note). Since Ed is also the World's Tallest Spontaneous Poet", this interviewer asked him to toss back a rhyme concerning our borough. He responded with this rhyming quip:

**"In this world which is sometimes bleak,
Life goes on from week to week.
I've performed for television, circus and honky tonks,
But my most pleasurable hours are spent in the Bronx."**

Stoop Sitting

The stoop attached to our houses was an institution.
It was here where you learned the facts of life, fell in love and made lasting friendships.

It was here you shared your innermost secrets...

It was here where you shared your innermost secrets, learned how to interact with girls (and boys) and moved fast when an adult or parent wanted to get through. It was here on a hot summer night where you could stay out long past your normal bedtime, as "long as you stayed on the stoop." It was here that you learned to greet another's passing mother with a courteous "hello Mrs." and a silent nod of the head to each passing father.

On a hot night you had to look hard to find a spot to squeeze into or to sit on. Our stoop only consisted of three or four small smooth concrete strips with one large area where a card game could be played by the boys or a game of jacks could be played by the girls. The side walls of the stoop were usually covered with small, low iron railings with pickets to discourage sitting on them. But these were more often broken or smoothed away, so you could sit there also.

On cold and snowy nights the stoop was deserted so you could stop and shake the snow off before going into the vestibule. On leaving the house, you could exit from the vestibule and stand on the stoop for a moment and survey the neighborhood. If you were all dressed up on a Sunday, you could pause and stand on the top step and be admired by all those passing below. When leaving with a date, you could pause and show him off while straightening your seams. Or when returning from a first date, the stoop was usually the limit a good Catholic young girl would allow. It was here where you sneaked your first kiss and made plans for the next date.

The stoop was also a favorite place to take a picture. Standing on the top step, being overshadowed by the arch of the two big doors must have been one of the better backdrops available in the neighborhood. The house number imprinted on the glass transom or nailed to the wooden foot frames must have lent some permanency to the resulting pictures. All the brides and the bridal parties wanted a last picture taken on the stoop. Maybe the arched doorways at the top of

showed off a date...

the stoop framed them and wrapped them in the warmth and permanency of cathedral-like arches.

There were several games that were played on our stoops. Besides the formations of lead soldiers playing war there was hour after hour of popular board games. Chinese checkers was played with sets of colored marbles, while for the more patient and careful there was Monopoly and Parchese. The early card games learned here included Go Fish and Steal the Old Man's Pack, but these quickly gave way to

Poker, Black Jack, Banker Broker and Pinochie.

Perhaps the most popular game played on the stoop was stoop ball. This was a game that had basic rules that probably were developed with the invention of the tenement and were understood by everybody who grew up in New York.

If you were lucky enough to live in a brownstone, you had a long steep multi-step stoop with a step at the second floor level. If you lived in a fancy apartment house with rugs in the lobby and big iron entrance doors, you had only a one-step stoop, where no one was allowed to play. If you lived over a store front on a busy shopping street, you probably had a very narrow entrance and also an unusable one-step stoop. But if you were in the majority and lived in a multistory tenement, you were rewarded with a stoop.

For those who didn't own a stoop, I wonder where they sat and read and traded their comic books. Where could they sit and lick an Italian ice, an ice pop or mellerole? Where could they learn to help mothers carry strollers, baby carriages or bicycles up and down steps? Where could they learn the rules of life and courtesy, by helping older people and mothers overburdened with groceries to negotiate the steps?

The stoop was also the neighborhood lending library, where you could sit for hours with your back against a wall and read a plethora of fantastic far-away adventures, without even missing a beat of what was happening on the street. The favorite reading materials were

...and fell in love.

usually G-rated juvenile novels read by the girls; comic books were preferred by the boys and sport pages of the Eagle, the News, the Mirror or the Journal American were preferred by the older folks. If you had waited late at night at the candy store for the pink editions, you could return to the stoop and sit and read by the dim light coming from the vestibule to see if your horse came in.

You could trade comic books after you read them and the stoop was ideal for this purpose. You could spread your comics out in piles and survey what was available from the competition. The piles would be arranged by popularity and condition of the comic books. The newer ones with their covers still attached would bring three or four older ones in trade. An enterprising and careful trader could build up his inventory quickly, especially if he was dealing with a younger and less sophisticated trader. All this would be part of the lessons to be learned on the stoop.

Who can say how long a slab of cold concrete can linger in the subconscious and still bring forth vivid pictures of childhood memories. These old stoops are silent

now, or are they? Do they again contain another new generation of young and innocent children who, with only limited play areas, make the best of the facilities at hand? Are they still playing ghost and trading comic books on the steps? Do they still eagerly run errands for people who lean out of third floor windows and toss down coins wrapped with paper instruc-

tions? Do they still use colored chalk to mark their initials and draw their heart shaped valentines, to the ever consternation of the supers?

There were many games played out on the stoops of the city, some athletic, some were emotional and some were adolescent, but all were part of a good life growing up in The Bronx.

Now and Then . . .

That was then - 1959-64	This now – 1989-1993
Top Television Family	
"Father Knows Best" 29.7 rating; 43 share	"Roseanne" 23.4 rating, 35 share
It's a bird, it's a plane, it's Superwoman	
• 33.9% of women worked in 1964. In 1959, 18.7% of married women in the labor force had children under age 8.	• Women comprise 46.8% of the work force and 57.1% of married women have children under age 6.
A penny saved...	
• The minimum wage was $1 an hour; the average hourly wage was $2.02; the average weekly salary was $78.78; the annual median household income was $5417.	• The minimum wage is $3.80; the average hourly wage is $9.84; the average weekly salary is $335.20; the median annual income is $28,600.
Whiz kids	
• 4.5% of all persons had four years of college education; 3.9% of women and 5% of men had four years of college. 11% of men have four years of college.	• 10.1% of the population has four years of college; 9.3% of women and 11% of men have four years of college.
That's Amore	
• The marriage rate was 8.5% per 1,000 population; the divorce rate was 2.2 per 1,000 population.	• The marriage rate is 9.7 per 1,000 population; the divorce rate is 4.7 per 1,000 population.

Sources: Center for Health Statistics, Scientific Technical Information Branch; U.S. Department of Labor, Bureau of Labor Statistics, U.S. Bureau of the Census; Nielsen Media Research

We Will Offer
$25⁰⁰
to the *Best* story for each issue.

All stories that are printed
will receive a *Free* one year subscription to
Back in the BRONX!

Personals

P 1 • A romantic, kind, considerate interesting male 40-65 who loves to travel, enjoys theatre, dine, and dancing and wants a loving romantic woman to enjoy all of the above.

P 2 • Zany female, offbeat, youthful, adventurous woman with a social conscience. Loves rock music, dancing 'til I drop, camping, outdoors and best of all - PEOPLE! Seeking man w/similarities and strong love of humankind.

P 3 • TAFT '48 You? Relative? Friend? Looking for a caring, fun-loving, healthy, marriage-minded male, 38-45, to introduce to a terrific, warm, romantic, family oriented, college grad sister.

P 4 • ROOSEVELT '59 – Italian, Catholic female, single, alive and well in NYC; wondering about you and how your life has developed since the threshold days of our youth. Interested in good conversation.

P 5 • Vivacious, warm, sensitive, intelligent, New York lady who loves life, laughter and love wants to share her life with equal counterpart .

P 6 • '57 Graduate (female) loves fishing, camping, boating and ballroom dancing. Petite 5'2" and a size 6. A non-smoker please.

P 7 • TAFT '52 widowed Jewish female looking for well-educated, fun-loving, conversationalist who also enjoys travel, theatre.

P 8 • I graduated TAFT in '57 and am fun-loving, honest and sincere. Looking for a Queens or L.I. resident who is also fun-loving, honest, and sincere non-smoker.

P 9 • Independent, caring, full-loving, great sense of humor, professional lady from Florida wants to meet tall, successful gentleman, ages 48-58. I'm recently divorced and have a joi de vivae. Believe it! I've never lied to you before!

P 10 • TAFT '54 – youthful, intelligent, independent, loving and witty divorced female seeking a fun-loving, sincere, secure and intelligent male. Single for 10 years, ready for a serious relationship.

P 11 • TAFT '59 – Very attractive interior designer, youthful, free spirited, loves to travel, enjoys photography, looking for intelligent spontaneous, multifaceted man who's happy with his life, enjoys people and loves to live.

P 12 • Daughter of TAFT graduate '60, attractive, professional, Jewish female, 25, looking to meet a son (25-30) of a former TAFT graduate to quench my thirst for happiness.

P 13 • EVANDER graduate single and living in who has achieved and doesn't have facades, contact me.

P 14 • TAFT '54 – well-educated, down-to-earth, pretty, chatty widow with eclectic tastes, talents and experiences seeks interesting, hamish man who enjoys films, theatre, music, art or just hanging out.

P 15 • TAFT '63 - Attractive, fun-loving, sincere, divorced female seeks warm, sincere, good humored NY or NJ male to enjoy conversation, dancing, quiet and happy times. Where are you?

P 16 • Walk this way: PS 104, JHS 82, TAFT HS, Bronx Community, Macombs Rd., Featherbed Lane, Harrison Ave. Kingsbridge Rd.; this tall thin, athletic, divorced male seeks ponytailable female for the right stoop, schoolyard, egg cream, pretzel, stickball game. Contact Kenny Fennessey.

P 17 • TAFT '68—Macombs Rd., Jesup Ave., Featherbed Lane; single gal, non-smoker, loves walking the outdoors, classical music. Live upstate (Rockland) but miss the homeland. Let's reminisce about PS 104, JHS 82, will answer all (male/female).

P 18 • TAFT '53, divorced, sincere people-minded, attractive slim professional. Looking for serious relationship. Loves films, music, dancing, dining out, art. Good sense of humor, non-smoker, Westchester resident.

P 19 • 1956 Bronx High School of SCIENCE – pretty, classy, warm, winsome woman seeks dynamic man (50's) to love.

Missing Persons

MP 1 • ROOSEVELT GARDEN BOYS-WHERE ARE YOU? Helen Kaplan Bender wants you to know that Beverly Gold, Suzanne Goldman, Helen Kaplan, Diane Billis, Dave Friedman, Stuart Ostrowsky and Betty Zimmerman are still alive. Where are you, Chucky Goodman, Leon Ruldolph, Jerry Sussman?

MP 2 • "What's playing at the Roxy?" Where are you, Ellen Resnick and the cast of Guys and Dolls? Anybody there from TMR Ranachqua Unit C1954-57?

MP 3 • CLINTON '66 - friends & acquaintances of David Heller - keep in touch and help me find Joel Bernstock CLINTON '66 or Les Bernstock CLINTON '64 .

MP 4 • ROOSEVELT '65, Barbara Kramer sure would love to know what happened to Beverly Glushakoff and Natalie Ginsburg. I'll pass your info onto Alison Robbins Levine; we're still friends after all these years.

MP 5 • EVANDER '63- Phyllis Melker Rothstein - where are you, Diane Miller? Remember Fordham Rd. and Orchard Beach? Anybody from the Eastchester Projects? (Bouck & Burke Avenues)

MP 6 • CLINTON '61 – Eddie Gookait, where are you? Remember CLINTON Pl. and Grand Ave. and Seymour's Candy Store? Contact Richard Rothstein .

MP 7 • Where are you, Carol Medina Bonilla and gang? Remember PS 82 and the Hill Top Candy Store on Macombs Rd

MP 8 • Lou Zabbia - CLINTON '51 would like to find Bob Hills of Olmstead Ave. near Quimby, early to mid 50's. Your brother Al attended All Hollows HS. Would love to hear from anyone who may know your whereabouts.

MP 9 • Ben Weissbach CLINTON '58 has been looking for twenty years to have a reunion with Jerry Kantor and Bruce Koyner. Can anybody help?

MP 10 • CLINTON '65 – looking for old friends from the 50's and 60's from PS 48 and the Hunts Point section of the Bronx.

MP 11 • CLINTON '58 - Gene Gold is looking for Joyce Levay TAFT '59 from Burnside and Aqueduct Avenues, also, John Erickson CLINTON '58 from 209th St. and Hull Ave.

MP 12 • TAFT '61 - Alice Neuman, Mike Stern, Music Class of JL Mott JHS '57-59. Where are you guys? Barbara Forman Iskowitz.

MP 13 • TAFT '58 – may Forman looking for former TAFT grads, JHS 22, PS 90 & 88, and people who lived on Marcy Pl.and Sheridan Ave.

MP 14 • TAFT '62 – regrets, I was unable to attend the Bronx HS Reunion at the Concord, but, would welcome contacts from old friends. Write me.

MP 15 • CLINTON '62 - Joel Goldberg looking to find Steven Trauman CLINTON '62 from Mt. Eden Ave. with whom he studied with at CCNY Library...also CLINTON '62. Alan Lutrin with whom he played stickball & cut classes for lunch at Schwellers Deli...

MP 16 • TAFT '61 Jeff Weinstein trying to locate Michael Sandler – TAFT '62 from Andrews Ave. Remember playing football on Andrews and making fun of your mother's hamburgers (hockey pucks).

MP 17 • Jeff Glatzer – TAFT '61 – and JHS 82. Remember stickball on the Concourse – where are you? Also, Steve Candell TAFT '61 contact Jeff Weinstein TAFT '61 ASAP.

MP 18 • David Laser - Stuyvesant '60 – we were both in the All City Chorus – contact Myrna Leavin Goldberg ROOSEVELT '62.

MP 19 • Victor 'Chick' DeVito – CLINTON '60 Myrna Leavitt Goldberg ROOSEVELT '62 would like to find him to talk about dancing to the American Bandstand when we were both in high school.

MP 20 • Warren Tockerman CLINTON '60 is looking for Enid Klein Schoen who graduated WALTON in 1958. Please contact.

MP 21 • TAFT '60 – Janet Goldeberg Auerbach who lived near Tremont would love to get reacquainted with her good friend Joan Leiss TAFT '60.

MP 22 • Sheldon Rambler CLINTON '62 wishes to find Stanley Rosen from Tiebout Ave. and CLINTON '62 and also wishes to find Susan Vassoff from Kingsbridge and

Concourse and Hunter '62.

MP 23 • Lou Zabbia – **CLINTON** '51 would like to find Bob Hills of Olmstead Ave. near Qukmby, early to mid 50's. Your brother Al attended ALL HOLLOWS HS. Would love to hear from anyone who may know your whereabouts.

MP 24 • Anyone that lived on Kingsbridge Terrace and went to PS 86 and **EVANDER**, please contact Carol Sutton Friedner. She would also like to find Frances Grecco last seen laughing with me in Mrs. Solomon's steno class.

MP 25 • Anita Kleinbaum **TAFT** '68 looking to find Wendy Sadovnick **ROOSEVELT** '68, Mark Holod **TAFT** '67 and Harriett Schwartz **TAFT** '68.

MP 26 • Marlorie Levy Roberts PS 70 - '58, JHS 22 '60, **TAFT** '63 and 167th St. & Concourse would love to find Lee Sanders, **TAFT** '65, last seen in 1970 in the Bronx. He may have moved to Yonkers and possibly to Virginia.

MP 27 • Looking for Tommy Kelly **TAFT** '59, contact Matthew Wallis, owner and developer of Reborn Maternity, NYC; Huntington; Manhasset; Paramus; Livingston, NJ; Westport, CT and Los Angeles.

MP 28 • Hal Levy **TAFT** '56 searching for Natalie Yagudnick last seen at Camp Emanuel summer of 1956.

MP 29 • Susan Amerling-Stern (Susan Oppenheimer) of Highbridge, **TAFT** '59 who is a full professor at BMCC (CUNY and a certified diver who got engaged 75 feet under the Caribbean is looking to find Lenore Auerback of Woodycrest/ Nelson Ave.

MP 30 • Myrna Gertler **TAFT** '59 – Michael Bruce Gold **TAFT** '59, where the heck are you? Everyone wants to know how and where you are, especially me. Please appear before our 40th Reunion.

MP 31 • Sarah Ball Cohen would like to find the following **TAFT** '62 friends: Ilene Shifrin, Sara Kaplan, Diane Grill, Sheryl Mazor, David Fenster, Barbara Ferrari, Marcia Levine, Karen Yanegida, Howard Shiller, Renee Turner, Phyllis Ustens, Millie Ross, Madeline Miller, and Diane Glassman.

MP 32 • Brenda Ball Levy is looking for Carole Unger, Margie Lucas, Lai Fong Dong, Jackie Brown, and Andy Stern.

MP 33 • Hi, remember Kathie Carr? If you do, I live in Ft. Lauderdale now and would love to hear from you.

MP 34 • Susan Adler is looking for '59 **WALTON** grads, Gail Stein (Loring Place), Karen Sesky, Maxine Cohen; Music & Art and/or Hunter HS grads, Gloria Spilkowik (Plimpton Ave.) and Janice Gutter (Davidson Ave.).

MP 35 • Gerald Sheindlin is looking for Patricia Myerson who lived on Sheridan Ave.

MP 36 • **ROOSEVELT** '69 – Ilana Zeev – where are you? Former teenage buddy, Barbara Kfefel Sylvester is wanting to make contact. Also, I would like to locate

David Adler. Many years have passed since I wore the red pants outfit on prom night. All is very well; hope you are too, friend.

MP 37 • **TAFT** '51 – where are Rita Webber and Phyllis Goldberg? Remember the hours spent doubting if we would ever marry and leave the Bronx? Write Karel of Walton Ave.

MP 38 • **TAFT** '62 – Anne Soskil Greenspan, now South Bay, CA (Silicon Valley) interested in finding out if any former **TAFT**ites are in the area.

MP 39 • Wade Jr. HS Hebrew class 53-55, also looking for Larry Levine, Stanley Orenstein, Marty Shifrin, Ceilla Weinstein, Linda Bale, Beth Levy, Esther Frank, and Rosemary Bardfeld – contact Carol Ball Teplin.

MP 40 • **TAFT** '56 – Joyce Amir Ben-Ezra looking to find Lola Schwartz, Carol Rosen, Mary Ellson **TAFT** '56. Where are you?

MP 41 • David Saltzman, where are you? I remember all the laughs we had and the party in your house. Please contact Linda Nadler Dreishpon, **TAFT** '56.

MP 42 • Judi Peskin, Macombs Rd. looking to find Marilyn Visconi Guberman last seen in 1964. Known to have moved to Princeton, NJ area.

MP 43 • **CLINTON** '56 – along with my brothers Alan and Dan, looking for Harrison Ave. stickballers from the 50's and early 60's. Remember PS 26, JHS 82, Park Plaza theatre. Contact Howard Silver.

MP 44 • **TAFT** '57 - where are you, Carol Feld, Wilma Mishkin, Dorothy Goldstein, Linda Wishnik, etc.? Remember great times at the 92nd St. Y? Rita Levy lives! Let's talk! Let's laugh! Let's complain!

MP 45 • I am seeking the whereabouts of Howard Negrin. He lived at 1411 Townsend Ave. and I believe went to **SCIENCE** in '52. Contact Joan Kaplan.

MP 46 • Bobby Nahama, **TAFT** '62 or '63, last seen in Fort Lee, NJ. Interested party, Jeff Heller.

MP 47 • Steven Kreiss is looking for the following: Steven Feldman **TAFT** '62 (basketball team), Harvey Castro **TAFT** '62 (went to CCNY), Ellen Jacobs **TAFT** '62 and Betty Ettman **TAFT** '64 or '65.

MP 48 • **TAFT** '65 – **ROOSEVELT** Garden Crowd. That was the place where we hung out. Looking for those who remember the great times. Contact Steve Bayern, Ricky Moldan.

MP 49 • **TAFT** '60 – Janet Goldenberg Auerbach looking for Joan Leiss. Lived near Tremont Ave. We were good friends. I would love to get reacquainted.

MP 50 • Class of **TAFT** '61. Susan Ehrenreich, where are you? We heard that you might be In Colorado, Anita Weiss **TAFT** '60.

MP 51 • **TAFT** '53 - Where is Marvin Zeichner? East or West coast? Barbara Salant is looking for former "Taft Review"

buddy, '63.

MP 52 • **TAFT** '51 – where are you, Rita Webber and Phyllis Goldberg? Remember the hours spent doubting if we would ever marry and leave the Bronx? Write Karel of Walton Ave.

MP 53 • Looking for former Bronxites or **TAFT**ites who are now living in Colorado. I'm near Denver. Also, I would like to find friends from **TAFT** '63, especially Michelle (Harris) Rosenthal, Helen (Waldman) Rummel, Gloria Krinsky, Francine Shuman. Contact Rosalie Paikin Richter.

MP 54 • Can anyone help me find Ivan Goldstein. Graduated **CLINTON** '57. Last seen living on Creston Ave. & Fordham Rd in 1962. Contact Goldie Rosner.

MP 55 • Anita Pomerantz Gore **TAFT** '60 looking for Marsha Fried **TAFT** '60 & Barbara Asch **TAFT** '59 .

MP 56 • Susan Goldman Schwartz **TAFT** '62 hopes to hear from Karen Lieb **TAFT** '62.

MP 57 • Marcia Grossman Fox **TAFT** looking for Rhoda Jaeger (Popham Ave.), Sheila Wittenberg (Macombs Rd.), Sandy Screiber (Davidson Ave. & Music&Art) and Julia Mitchell (Nelson Ave.).

MP 58 • **TAFT** '58 – Rosalind (Roz) Katz would enjoys hearing from the gang she lost touch with.

MP 59 • Steven Kreiss **TAFT** '62 is looking to find Neil Raphael (College & 171st), Betty Etman (170th & Concourse) Harvey Castro **TAFT** '62 last seen at CCNY.

MP 60 • **TAFT** '60 – Sheila Mencher has not seen Rita Fox from **TAFT** '62 and 167th off Concourse. Any help would be appreciated.

MP 61 • Where are you? Annene Weiss from Harrison Ave. **TAFT** '53, Audrey Engel, **TAFT** '53, Rhoda Silverstein, Annette, Evelyn Joseph from Morris Ave., Isaac Francis, originally from Grant Ave. Renee Weinberg Strauss wants to get in touch.

MP 62 • Does anyone know where the following people are? Bette Flaks, Marty Zafman, Hal Welner, Normy Schatzoff.

MP 63 • Joel Goldberg **CLINTON** '62 looking for Steve Taubman **TAFT** '62 from University Ave.

MP 64 • Desperately seeking Phil Winkler, Bobby Mazur, Marty Conkiel, and Joel the Lizard (Hunter-Lehman) – Student Freak Committee gathering the tribe- Contact Buck Paradise, Joan (Luca) Leibowik, Joan (Shirley Goodvibes) Lok, & Arthur Kushner.

MP 65 • Myron Buchman would love to find Marble Hill survivors Ira Shapiro, Linda Wolf, Elaine Mandel, Paula Goldberg, Helene Kursman. How many guys still have their Mr. Shea box?

MP 66 • Barbara Gurkin would love to hear from any graduates of Wade JHS '62 or **ROOSEVELT** '65 who remember how great it was growing up in the Bronx and would love to relive some of those times.

MP 68 • 181st St. Grand Concourse, Valentine Ave. & 182nd St. Leo's Candy Store, Ryer Ave 181st St. Did you spend time in my apartment? Girls? Please contact Howie Simon.

MP 69 • Norm and Shelli Giaser looking for Simone & Buddy to say thanks for bringing them together 9/14/57.

MP 70 • Phil Greenberg, **CLINTON** '59, currently lives in Chicago looking for Alan Skolnick, **CLINTON** '60, and Bruce Falcamata, **SCIENCE**. Also where are you Gary Bitter, Kenny Schniker, Mel Stanger and the others of our group?

MP 71 • Elaine Dunetz of the "Morris Ave. Group" looking to find Ned Truss who graduated **CLINTON** '56 and went onto Pratt.

MP 72 • Roberta McDonald (Torres) looking for anyone from Clarke Place. Concourse. "Our Crowd-Years 1958-61.

MP 73 • Looking for Marty Meadow. You and I lived in adjoining buildings on Popham Ave. and West 176th Street. I lived there during the years 1962-65. I would like to meet with you. Contact Maralee Sirota.

MP 74 • **TAFT** '63 Elaine (Hyman) Adler hopes to hear from Marsha Berkowitz, Steve Bussell, Gloria Krinsky, Regina Linder, Dale Maltz, Anita Obsgarten, Tina Perrin, Ronni Rothonberg, Sam Russo, Beverly Schnall, Paulene Schrager, Leslie Steigman and any other wonderful **TAFT** '63 classmates.

MP 75 • Margot (Wolf) Feldman – **TAFT** '53 and Sol Feldman – **TAFT** '50. Invite contact from old friends. Where are you Marilyn Yomtov – **TAFT** '53 and Debbie Wolf – **TAFT** '53? SAVONS? Grant Avenue Gang? We would love to hear from you.

MP 76 • Lou Zabbla – PS 36, JHS 125, **CLINTON** '57 looking for Bob Hills (Olmstead Ave. near Quimby). Denny Wandel (above Babes' Candy Store – Castle Hill and Watson). Anyone know whereabouts?

MP 77 • **CLINTON** '57 – NYU '62 – Matt Berliner would like to find: Mah Wallack, Bernie Belser, Mickey Cohen or Ed Peskin (NYU '62).

MP 78 • Lenore Mandelbaum Sattler **TAFT** '57, JHS 22 – Sheridan Ave & 169th St. – looking to find Harvey Ashe, Wade Mt. Eden Ave. Where are you and Hank of 170th St. & Grand Concourse.

MP 79 • Phyllis Wasserman (Mittler) Concourse and 170th St., class of **TAFT** '61, where are you? I've thought about you over the years. Remember Rockaway Phissyl? Please contact Janice Niederman Cohen, **TAFT** '60.

MP 80 • **TAFT** '60 Iris Kemier Burnham would like to contact Dianne Pardo.

MP 90 • **TAFT** '55. Myrna Garfinkel Petrello seeking whereabouts of Daniel Biegelman. Anyone having information on his whereabouts. Please contact me.

MP 91 • Would love to hear from Maija Bankhaus & Erika Wedikind of Macombs JHS '58 and others from JHS and TAFT '61.

Anyone in Brooklyn??!!! CONTACT Barbara Reiner.

MP 92 • Greetings to my neighborhood pals from Sedgwick House, 1956-1969. Remember the Community Center in building 1551 University Ave. at 174th St. Regards, Barry Bealick, **CLINTON** '69.

MP 93 • Joel Shapiro (**TAFT** '58) seeks his old Bx Y friends (Club BVDS) and any old Bronx "Blue Riilerss". Joel is still at Blue Rill after all these years.

MP 94 • Irving Kalet (**TAFT** '57) looking for Carole Steinholtz (PS 90, JHS 22) – I live in Israel, would like to meet any classmates who visit Israel. Also looking for Owen Goldwyn and Lloyd Arlind.

MP 95 • Becca Tussin Hoover, **TAFT** '62, now Los Angeles, CA, interested in finding out if any former **TAFT**ites, JHS '82 or Davidson Ave. acquaintances are in Southern California.

MP 96 • Alan Rosenberg looking for an old friend David Seifer (son of bookstore owner) **TAFT** '60. Where are you now?

MP 97 • Jackie Gisbert Nadal, **TAFT** '60 looking for Riva Lipton, Michele Furman, and Phyllis Wollman, all **TAFT** '60. Please contact me.

MP 98 • Myrna Leavitt, **ROOSEVELT** '62 looking to find Nancy Jeremiah of EBB and **ROOSEVELT** '62.

MP 99 • Joel Goldberg looking for Naomi Levy, **ROOSEVELT** '62, Eileen Koch, (Shorehaven), Carrie Siegel – **ROOSEVELT** '62 (lived on Phelan Pl.). Please contact.

MP 100 • Looking for members of Delkons Club from 167th St. YMYWHA. Call Elaine (Markowitz) Nachshen. **WALTON** HS graduates send in your names. We need our school represented.

MP 101 • Marion Elbert Goldberg **TAFT** '58 says hi to her old friends the Dominoes - she and Sandy Goldberg **TAFT** '55 have been married for 27 years.

MP 102 • Yonkel (All Schoolyard) Where are you? Also, others from JHS 44 area. Contact William Kent.

MP 103 • Anderson Avenue People – contact Richard Fuchs. We're looking for Alan Kordin, Joey Kost, Harold Epstein, Tom Lowe, Harvey Kash, Lenny Lipka, Sandy Cohen, Morty Zuckerman, Burt Resnick, Neil Rosenthal, Harold Schwartz, Malman Adelman, Billy Goodman, among others.

MP 104 • I am trying to find the whereabouts of a Murray (Moe) Golub who lived at 770 E. 178th St. graduated '57 or '58. Contact Morton Garfinkel.

MP 105 • UAWMF! **CLINTON** '69. Where's the old neighborhood? Barry Nelson, **CLINTON** '69.

MP 106 • Jackie Gisbert Nadal, **TAFT** '60 looking for Riva Lipton, Michele Furman, and Phyllis Wollman, all **TAFT** '60. Please contact me.

MP 107 • **CLINTON** '58, Jerry Vogel is looking for any old buddies or folks from

the old neighborhood, West Burnside Ave. and 179th St.

MP 108 • NOC-OUTS, where are you? JHS 22 **TAFT** and **WALTON** contact Arlyne Weiss Beck, **TAFT** '59.

MP 109 • **TAFT** '61 Barry Dratel, **TAFT** '63 Susan Sorokoff Dratel. We will be celebrating our 25th this year! Richie Glaser, **TAFT** '61, where are you?

MP 110 • 198th St. Gang – we're looking for guys and girls who lived there. We have had reunions for the past 13 years. We have been written up in the Daily News and on TV. Contact Joe Ricevuto.

MP 111 • **ROOSEVELT** '65 – Barbara Resnicoff Kramer and Alison Robbins Levine would love to find out whatever happened to Beverly Glushakoff and Natalie Ginsberg. Any other old friends of Barbara or Malcolm Kramer (**CLINTON** '65) or Alison out there? Foe needn't reply.

MP 112 • Missing persons – Any **TAFT** '55 grads living in Houston TX. Would love to exchange stories. Would also love to hear from Elaine Resnick, Claire Smilowitz, or Lenore Bloom. Contact Sheila Wolfe-Knipe.

MP 113 • Where are you guys and gals from Jesup Ave., Featherbed Lane, Macombs Rd., PS 104, JHS 82 from 40's and 50's. Contact Joel Adler.

MP 114 • Where are the girls from Capri Houseplan? (Hunter College). Roberta Goldman, Elena Lopez, Paula Kleinbaum, Hazel Saffer, Gail Podolsky, Marge Auletta, Joan Sandler, Harriet Kern, Elaine Samelson. Miss anyone? Contact Phyllis Meltzer Rothstein, Hunter '67.

MP 115 • Looking for anyone born or raised on Edward L. Grant Hwy. in the Bronx for a reunion. Please contact Ellen Howowitz.

MP 116 • Where are all the guys and girls from Grand Ave.? (Behind Loews Grand off Fordham Rd.). Doris Kornbluth, Carol and Ira Garber, Howie Melvin, Adrienne Friedman Teitelbaum living in Fla., Carol Gantwag (Valentine Ave.).

MP 117 • **CLINTON** '52 – "Toppers" Baseball Team Reunite! Manny, Marty, Julie, Larry, Bobby & Gerry, Leon, Allen & Stan. Let's hear from you all. Contact Len Mechner.

MP 118 • Judy Goldner – **TAFT** '67 – Last seen in Forest Hills. Please contact: Elly Garfinkel Mendelsohn.

MP 119 • Eileen Goldberg looking for Iris Baker and Howard Essenfeld – Tremont and University Avenues.

MP 120 • **TAFT** '50 grads – let's get together! Contact me, Zelda Prensky.

MP 121 • Frank Martocci, **CLINTON** '52, would like to contact Richard Sems of 194th St. & Marion Ave. – also Tony "44" Yaconetti of Marion Ave. Remember Orchard Beach Tony "444" Lifeguards – 1952-56. Get in touch, Frank.

MP 122 • **CLINTON** '65 Michael "Dirty Shoes" Bloom looking for members of

Scholarship School. Living in the wilds of Oregon and also looking for fellow **CLINTON**ite Oregonians.

MP 123 • Robert (Bobby) Johnson, **CLINTON** '53, PS 73 '49 would like to hear from any old classmates from PS 73. Jack Ross, Herb Rosen, Geo. Schueren, Harvey Kash, John Kokish, Carole Brenner, Etta Giattenberg, Doris Koran, Jane Trattner, & Adrienne Madoff, to name a few.

MP 124 • **TAFT** '58, Robert Woll is looking for old friends from the old neighborhood. Also PS 70, Wade and CCNY. I am upstate now and I haven't changed a bit!

MP 125 • Cheryl Gavard, **TAFT** '70 looking for Arlene Klein, Steven Bock, Stephanie Brown, Marilyn Serlin, or anyone who hung out on Macombs Rd. or Davidson Ave. or Fordham's Poe Park or even Kingsbridge!

MP 126 • Cheryl Bard, **TAFT** '65 looking for Carol Straczek from Shakespeare Ave. and Edie Fertig from Gerard Ave. Are you still out there? Let's get in touch!

MP 127 • Andy Kalmanson of 1405 Townsend Ave. is looking for Eden Weiss, Tommy Dodorian, and PS 64 classmates.

MP 128 • DWC Miss Razzari Italian Club – Scrafano, Patrici, Signorile Stein, Schwartz et al, where are you? Contact Ed Corvelli.

MP 129 • Who drove a Bungalow Bar truck with me in 1958,1959 or a Mister Softee truck out of the Bruckner Blvd. garage in 1959, 60, 61 (Fink?). Who was assaulted with me on Veteran's Day 1955 by the Fordham Baldies in Van Cortlandt Park? Contact Norman Mazza.

MP 130 • Judy Visconti Sumin would like to find her long-time best friend, Gina Russell Walters, '59.

MP 131 • Marty Faber looking for Gilbert Katz. Where are you?

MP 132 • Lichtenstein sisters, (**TAFT**) Carla and Rhoda looking for anyone who remembers the Sedgwick Projects or the Bronx "Y" late 50's early 60's.

MP 133 • I'm interested in finding Daniel Constantino (formerly of 198th St. in the Bronx). He's a 1970 graduate of **SCIENCE**. Also Jack Bulko, **CLINTON** '70. Contact Otie Ka Votie.

MP 134 • Shelby Landesberg would like to find Arlene Suckow (last known as Arlene Pressman) and the Landesberg Boys (Ronnie, Mitchell, Glen) from Andrews Ave. Any info?

MP 135 • Sam Verga, **CLINTON** '64. Where are you guys? Remember Mosholu Pkwy; the schoolyard of JHS 80; Knox and Gates Place; Bainbridge Gardens; Rochambeau Ave.? Let's reminisce.

MP 136 • Would like to hear from those who belonged to the teen group at the Hebrew Institute of University Hts. & E. Tremont Ave. '56-'58. Also, Irv Cordover & Jerry Silverman. Where are you? Contact Charles Ludwin.

MP 137 • Herb Schenk – **TAFT** '51 looking for fellow graduates from the "Fifties" living in south Florida. So far I've found

Marilyn Messenger and Stu Reich. I'd love to hear from others.

MP 138 • Betty Flaks is looking for Vickie Dresner who lived on Gerard Ave. and went to **TAFT**.

MP 139 • Looking for people who lived on Commonwealth Ave., Rosedale Ave., St. Lawrence Ave., and surrounding areas during the 50's and also attending PS 47 and Blessed Sacrament.

MP 140 • Steve Burns looking for Robert Silverberg, Gene Joseph, Michael Landis, Ira Gurin, Terry Dekoven or any of the "9-7 you are now 8-7" Class of '55, Wade JHS.

MP 141 • Looking for George Morris, Phil (Kingy) Badner, Jack and Gloria Frankel. I live in Cocoa Beach, FL and would love to hear from you. Anyone else remember Sid Blumenthal?

MP 142 • Looking for anyone who went to PS 42 (Washington Ave.) from 1942-1947; anyone who went to **BENJAMIN FRANKLIN** HS, JHS 55, from 1940-1950; graduated from **TAFT** HS in 1953. I now reside in Ft. Lauderdale, FL area.

MP 143 • I would like to know if anyone can remember the person who did a swan dive off the 30 ft. slide at Cascade Pool in the summer of 1949. Jerry Wertheimer.

MP 144 • **ROOSEVELT** '45 – Harold Benzer now living in Las Vegas & would like to hear from old East Bronx friends.

MP 145 • Martin Halpern, **CLINTON** '60 of Andrews Avenue, PS 26, and JHS 82, looking to renew old friendships. Peter Bloch and Fred Kramarow, where are you?

MP 146 • Allen Greenstein, PS 64, JHS 117, **EVANDER** '56 hopes to find old friends; classmates; particularly Gary Cutler, Fred Stern, Richard Cooper, Karen Kurtz, Ada Levy, Sara Kabakow, Diana Shapiro, Muriel Lederman, Sue Gendzel, Elsy Middleton, Marlene Newmark, Mona Citron.

MP 147 • '60 **CLINTON** grad looking for Yola Weiner '61 **WALTON** grad. Would appreciate any help!

MP 148 • Rhoda Press, **WALTON** '47. Ruth and Betsy looking for you.

MP 149 • Barbara Weinstein Goodman would love to find Johnie Risi or anyone else who hung out at Jahn's.

MP 151 • Elaine Weinstein of the "Morris Ave. Group" looking to find Ned Truss, who graduated **CLINTON** '56 and went on to Pratt.

MP 152 • Helen Wolfsohn Wilmers looking for Adele Toussaint Fisher of Andrews Ave., JHS 82, and F.I.T. '56. Where are you and how are you doing?

MP 153 • PS 86 and **CLINTON**, Kal Rosenberg is looking for Arty Greenberger, Adele Stern, any of the 198th St. Atoms or Kingsbridge Group, Louie's Pool Room, Pop's Bowling Alley or Solamoes Candy Store Losers.

MP 154 • Jewish Association for Counsel-

ing and Psychotherapy. Director: Dr. David Belgray, **CLINTON** '49, JHS '82, PS 104. Nelson Ave. near Edward L. Grant Hwy. (remember Boscobel Ave.?). Suffering from the demise of the old neighborhood or other disappointments. Call me.

MP 155 • Leo's Candy Store: what happened to the old gang that hung around for egg creams and pretzels? Best friend Linda Blumenfeld, where are you?

MP 156 • Looking forward to hearing from any of the grads of **EVANDER** '51-52 or any of the friends from Allerton Ave.

MP 157 • Richie Mann, Eddie Tavss, Dave Epstein Joey Maisei, how's it going? Remember van Cortland Park and Moshulu Pkwy.? Where are you? We have a 30 year gap to fill in. Judy Frechtman Rogers.

MP 158 • **TAFT** '56 – Does anyone out there ever wonder what happened to Rose Kessler of Gerard Ave. and 156? Well, she married Lenny Stein of Burnside Ave. and **CLINTON** '53 and both would love to hear from anyone from the past.

MP 159 • Arlene Schneider Radansky, **TAFT** '54, looking for graduates of Macombs JHS '82, Class of '51.

MP 160 • Ken Sussman (**TAFT** '46). Is anyone out there interested in a 45 year reunion? If not, how about 50 years in 1996?

MP 161 • Peter Deitchman, **TAFT** '54, now living in central Florida, would love to hear from members of same class, especially Stan Becker, Don Kabick, Ronny Mandelbrom, Brown Twins.

MP 162 • Harvey Applebaum, **CLINTON** '60, looking for Gary Hartman, **CLINTON** '60.I lived on Fieldstone Rd. in Riverdale and you lived on 263rd St. off Riverdale Ave.

MP 163 • Camp Hurley Reunion! Do you remember the red truck, the benches, the singing, the people? Contact Fran Stillman Landsberger (212) 535-3589 or Lucy Stepinoff Rosenblatt, (203) 236-9992.

MP 164 • Anyone remember College Rec. on 170th St.? Any 59 NYC Commerce Member of Vets Club in California, contact Arthur Finn, ex-Stallion.

MP 165 • Phyllis Miller Yenis says hello to her old friends from Moshulu Pkwy., JHS 80, and **EVANDER** Childs '55.

MP 166 • **TAFT** '57 – Suzanne (Schumer) Klein would love to find Estelle (Cookie) Benoze. Where are you? Let's talk about yesterday and today.

MP 167 • Would love to hear from anyone from Our Lady of Refuge Parish, years 1950-70, or gang from Briggs or Poe Park area. Like to reminisce about Fordham Rd., Kingsbridge Rd., Krums Candy Store or the "H" on Fordham Rd.

MP 168 • Where are you Phyllis Gold, Stuart Bolkin, Barbara Cornblatt, Steve Ceslowitz, Helen Berkowitz. Contact Sandra Joseph Filla.

MP 169 • **TAFT** '68, Wade JHS, PS 170 – if you remember me please contact Elaine

Welch.

MP 170 • TAFT '51, '52 graduates looking for nostalgia – Clarke Pl., Elliot Pl., 169th St., Walton Ave., 170th thru 161st. Please contact Suzanne Berne Kesten.

MP 171 • Barbara Brecker, Muriel Bergman, Marcia Waldman – would love to hear from you. Remember music class in JHS 22, Claremont Pk., 170th St.? Contact Sheila (Fox) Dimond.

MP 172 • Art Newman, Dave Hirsch, Jerry Tepper and Alan Krinsky are planning a Macombs Rd. reunion. Where are Forbes and Sandy Kapp, Fred Rosen, Lewis Limmer, Fred Richter, Carl and Roy Hermano, Steve Herman, Joel Sieger, Barbara Lewis?

MP 173 • JHS 22 SP's – TAFT '60. Where were you at the last reunion? Where are you now? Love to hear from any of you. Eileen, Paula, Jackie, Rita, are any of you out there? Contact Marcia Hyatt Gersh.

MP 174 • Joyce Sutton Levinson from Kingsbridge Terrace, in search of Shirley Barkan from Ward Ave. Charles J. Kaese, last known address, 103rd St. Have often wondered if you became the great attorney we used to talk about.

MP 175 • Gail (Dreier) Greenberg (PS 109, JHS 82, TAFT '63). Would love to hear from former classmates (especially PS 109). Couldn't attend reunion weekend. Looking for '82 SP-2 classmates like Kathy Keneally and Vickie Olson. Also TAFT '63 Jerry Ostroff.

MP 176 • TAFT '58 – Rochelle Cassell Weinberg would love to hear from old friends from PS 55,

MP 177 • Bernie Schwartz looking for Donny Novick.

MP 178 • It's about 28 years later! Steve Bayern and Ricky Molden would like to know where is Bonnie Green, Emily Cohen, Corrine Rubin, Laura Dierna, and anyone else. The Chow Chow cup might be gone on 170th St., but we're not.

MP 179 • Looking for the following TAFT graduates: Carol Judith, Carol Eisenstein, Lenore Freed, and Jeffrey Horowitz.

MP 180 • Wanted—1950 DeWitt CLINTON Yearbook—Larry Barton (nee Barshansky).

MP 181 • TAFT '59—Eileen Krain—looking for Isabel Mars and Benjamin Mindich. Haven't seen you since we graduated . Also Leah Duben .

MP 182 • Margaret O'Neill (SHM ' 73) and Hester (Mathews) O'Neill (SHM '40) are interested in hearing of any class reunions. Also old photos of the Academy of the Sacred Heart of Mary at Marmion Ave. and Park Terrace.

MP 183 • Leona Jacobs, where are you? You last said that you would serve me breakfast (1959). Well, I'm hungry. Pelham Parkway has changed. Chuck Gitlin.

MP 184 • Looking to contact Mimi with red hair who graduated TAFT HS in Jan. '60. Also all other members of Gamma Phi Omega. It would be fun to have a

reunion. Miriam Parton Sivak.

MP 185 • If you graduated from WALTON HS or EBB and now living in Southern California, call me: Gladys Chapman Layne, Marina Del Rey, CA (213) 305-1686 graduated WALTON '55.

MP 186 • CLINTON '58 – Jerry Vogel is looking for any old buddies from the old neighborhood W. Burnside & University Ave. 179th St.

MP 187 • Desperately seeking Henry Mooney, Judy Steiner, and Ida Henig (TAFT '65). Also need to know that Betty Berger (TAFT '62?) of Walton Ave. is alive and well.

MP 188 • EVANDER '56 – Leomi Waldinger Simkin looking for the following JHS 80 and EVANDER '56 girls – Barbara Yorburg (Knox Pl.), Phyllis Cashman (W. Gun Hill), Sandra Cohen (Gun Hill), Frances Oullette (E. 212 St. and Bainbridge). Has anyone info about these EVANDER '56 grads? Edith Lipman (Seymour Ave.), Jack Rothman (Seymour), Martin Block (E. Gun Hill).

MP 189 • 1951 graduate of PS 114, Class of Anne Reiter, is interested in hearing from classmates. Sylvia Neuwirth Wagner (301) 897-8099.

MP 190 • I am seeking the whereabouts of January 1953 TAFT graduates, especially George White, Elaine Fernbach, Connie Weinberg, Elaine Silverman. Contact Elaine Herzfeld Fast.

MP 191 • Gary Mortman lived on Walton Ave. and Mt. Eden Ave., now residing in Manalpan NJ. Would like to hear from old friends on the block: Melvin Seltzer, Alan Simon, Zack Trubita, Joel Abramson, Stuart Brill, David Epstein.

MP 192 • Andrews, University, Montgomery, Popham Ave.—174th to Tremont, looking for: Mel Moskowitz, Ronnie Sokoloff, David Shrone, Kenny Sloane, Jerome Lindauer, Marvin Megidow, Noel Grubin, Roger Gold, Paul Reiser, Bobby Bell, Frank Lasher, Norman Schienwald, Donald Seffinger, Diane Abrams, Irving Corendener, Ellen Hoffman, Roz Berger. Contact Jeffrey Lawson.

MP 193 • Mimi and Lanie want to know what happened to Sandy Turner and Nancy Fogelson, JHS 82 – 1952. Remember Ruschmeyers?

MP 194 • Artie Weinfeld – SCIENCE '57, also sells real estate in Briarcliff Manor. Old friends from Gun Hill Rd. please contact.

MP 195 • Joel Goldstein looking for lost friends from the 50's that lived on 208th St. Let's get together for a reunion. Also Peggy Hubler Medwin, EVANDER '62, last known address Suffern, NY 10901.

MP 196 • Marilyn Kasserman, Emily Gitnik – where are you? Carol Lieber Glickfeld.

MP 197 • TAFT '60 – Diane Pardo Abraham would like to contact Elsie Camni, Barbara Echtman, Barbara Feinstein, Edith Freter, Florence Kroop, Joan Lieberman, Anita Mandel, Barbara Oremland, Beverly

Perlman, Barbara Phillips, Mike Russo, Laura Schein, Janice Weisman, Madeline Varon, Leslie Stone.

MP 198 • Any members of SCIENCE, Class of '56, interested in a thirty-five year reunion, please contact Jerry Goldstein. Time is short but an event before the end of the year is still possible.

MP 199 • Diane Blagman, ROOSEVELT '70, would be interested to find any from ROOSEVELT '67-70 or those who hung out by Alexanders/Fordham Rd. or Poe Park. Where are you? Any residing in Washington DC?

MP 200 • Yo! I need some help looking for the boys who played hoops at the Echo Park playground during the early 60's. Anyone knowing where I can find Steve DeVito, Ron DeVito, Danny DeVito, Fred Veltri? I'm Nathan Oventhal CLINTON '62.

MP 201 • Art&Design '60 Harriet Katz Schaeffer is looking for old friends from PS 46, JHS, EBB or Art&Design. Neighborhood friends from the Bedford Park area.

MP 202 • Bainbridge Ave...looking for people who lived on Bainbridge between Fordham Rd. and 198th St. and/or pictures/memorabilia from the Avenue during the 1960's only. Did you go to or teach at PS 46 during the 60's? Contact Robert Blagman.

MP 203 • Ron Kaufman would like to locate the whereabouts of these people from Morris Avenue or TAFT: Ellen Markowitz, Gary Forcash '62; Roz Price, TAFT '64; Marsha Cohen, TAFT '65; Judy Kaplan, TAFT '67; Andrea Schneider, TAFT '66; Susan Snyder, TAFT '66; James Veres, EVANDER '66; Sherry Panzer, Music&Art '65.

MP 204 • WALTON '64 – Louis Meszler Wagman, where are you? Remember the Yankees and all the "guys" – Syd, Harry, and Jeanne would love to hear from you.

MP 205 • Looking for Lewis Greenbaum, Prospect Ave. – moved to Los Angeles in 1956 or 57. Contact Harriet Meltzer.

MP 206 • Allen Halpern, TAFT '55, would like to know the whereabouts of Carol Reider, TAFT '56.

MP 207 • 1948 Rams or Gremlins: Whitey, Milt, Wally, Howie, Al, Marko, Bert, Eugene, Lenny, Steve, Red, Cass, Joe – 174th St. Contact Irwin Schneider.

MP 208 • Richard Brooks would like to hear from John Evans, TAFT '62.

MP 209 • We are looking for the guys who hung out around Leo's window on College Ave. from 1950-53. Also looking for Morty Klein, Norman Appell, Irving Karp and the rest of that crowd. Contact Carol Speckler Fishbein and Marty Fishbein.

MP 210 • Seeking the whereabouts of Judy and Saul Broad, children of Dave. Last contact California 1937. Lived in East Bronx. Would be about 62 and 59 years old now. Cousins would like to reestablish contact.

MP 211 • Charlotte Eisner, Class of MORRIS '45, where are you? Remember Glenn

22

Miller, Cafe Rouge? Every Saturday – admission 25¢? Tony Mercorella, Marvin Kleinberg, or Solly Weiss. Contact Evelyn Blumenthal Yagoda.

MP 212 • TAFT '57 – Barbara Deutchman Collen would like to know the whereabouts of Laurel Fregenbaum. Michael Rogers.

MP 213 • Jimmy Bennings would like to hear from old friends from the Marble Hill Projects, 1958-1965.

MP 214 • Suzanne (Schumer) Klein would love to find Estelle (Cookie) Benoze – where are you? Let's talk about yesterday and today.

MP 215 • Joe Sabrin – CLINTON '60, founder of PC Etcetera, a North American PC & Mac Training company, wants to hear other success stories. Call him at 212-736-5870, 8-6PM EST.

MP 216 • Executive Search – Ron Sunshine CLINTON '58, specializing in engineering and manufacturing middle and upper management position – contact me.

MP 217 • Sheila Markin Klein, COLUMBUS '61 would like to hear from Janet Lehrer and Judy Rosenblatt, last seen during their first year at Boston U. Even longer since we shared a White Castle lunch at JHS 135!

MP 218 • Judi & Mervyn Fleisher, former Bronxites whose parents owned Hotel Fleisher, Parksville, NY would like to contact former guests and staff of hotel for reunion.

MP 219 • Larry Rosenberg, CLINTON '65 looking for old friends from Andrews Ave., All Star Bowl, Sedgwick Little League.

MP 220 • TAFT, Elliot Place. looking for Jules Madison, childhood friend of David Scher.

MP 221 • Robbie & Shelley Kaufman, Pat Paciello would love to hear from other punchball, stickball, and touch football greats who ruled PS 64 in the early 60's.

MP 222 • Dinny (Ross) Capin, SCIENCE '50 would love to hear from classmates and/or friends from Parkchester.

MP 223 • Fred Greenspan & Marty Flisser, MORRIS '61 looking for Barry Fisher (Southern Blvd.), Billy Reed Jr. from 145th St., Ronald Smith, Burt Shannes, and Bruce Gittleson.

MP 224 • Fred Eisgrub. ROOSEVELT '61 is seeking anyone who remembers him – hopefully, someone remembers me!

MP 225 • MONROE '60 – Johnny Cuomo. where are you? Last seen on Bryant Avenue Garden View. Where are you '62 TAFTites? "Cookie" Rubin, Paula Feigenbaum & Iris Rosensweig? Contact Sherrie Gross.

MP 226 • Walter S. Buckner – TAFT '53, Wade '50 – would like to hear from my former classmates in Southern California or anywhere.

MP 227 • Charlotte Eisner – Class of MORRIS '45, where are you? Remember

Glenn Miller, Cafe Rogue? Every Saturday – admission 25¢? Tony Mercorella, Marvin Kleinberg or Solly Weiss. Contact Evelyn Blumenthal.

MP 228 • From Perry & 20th; went to PS 56, JHS 80, CLINTON, Viet Vet. Hung out with the Oval Boys and partied with the Ducky Boys at French Charlies. Where are you? Help me find the Oval Boys. Contact Bob Wiemers.

MP 229 • Lila Smolen Hower – PS 94, 80, WALTON HS 1944-46. Still in contact with 6. Remember Miss Sicklick, Mr. Stantial, Mrs. Hefferman, Friday Night Community Center, The Oval, Red Letter Bay? Let's catch up on our lives.

MP 230 • WALTON '61, JHS 22 '58, Sandy Maduro, Lorraine Steiner, Paula Adler, Audrey Labor, Pat Lotocki, Kathy Debow. Where are you? Contact Judy Dugan if you think you know me.

MP 231 • Carl Markowitz would enjoy hearing from Mrs. Sween's class in PS 44 Mid?-late thirties: Jack, Betty, Bertha, Red, Sol, Annette, Bobby, Harold, Hippo, Leon, Phillip, Paul, for Sylvia Halpern. Where is Adele Lerman, Pearl Kaminsky, Mimi, Arlene Deutsh?

MP 232 • Beverly Soury, 171st & Walton Ave., looking for Jill Svigals, Lenore Solomitz, Shiela Kornsweet and anyone who remembers "Pasteles" and "Borekas" from 169th St., "Oriental Knishes" to talk about the good old times at TAFT, JHS 117 and PS 64.

MP 233 • Remember my father-in-law's deli, "Roxy", 161st., one of the Bronx's best? To discuss delis/otherwise reminisce, contact Myles Schulberg (PS 64, JHS 117, TAFT '67, Lehman '71)/Adrienne (Mirchin) Schulberg (PS 73, JHS 22, TAFT '69), Washington, DC area.

MP 234 • Where are the girls from Capri Houseplan? (Hunter College.) Roberta Goldman, Elena Lopez, Paula Kleinbaum, Hazel Saffer, Gail Podolsky, Marge Auletta, Joan Sandler, Harriet Kern, etc. Contact Phyllis Meltzer Rothstein, Hunter '67.

MP 235 • Grew up on 1655 Monroe Ave. w/Geller's and Barr's Candy Stores. I loved Claremont Park – we went there at night! Remember stickball, Marble Season, Ticket Season, PS 70, JH Wade JHS, handball. I loved Carol Ball – Teplin Story.

MP 236 • Paul Kandel desperately looking for Donna Mandel, Janet Mayer, Richard Singer – JHS 82.

MP 237 • Susan Engle looking for Phyllis Strassberg, Phyllis Schwartz, Marion Myers.

MP 238 • CLINTON '65 Michael "Dirty Shoes" Bloom would like to hear from the members of the Scholarship School. Also JHS 143 SP '62 classmates. Call me in Oregon at 503-638-1001. My ham radio call was WA2RAT, any Bronx radio friends?

MP 239 • Looking for Sandy Sara Shetes – Grand Concourse Bronx, TAFT 1964. She moved to Coop City in 1970 to live with friend Ann Santiago. I met her at Kimball Stationery/Bronx and Aston Cafeteria,

Manhattan; across from Macy's. She worked for Budget Dress, Manhattan.

MP 240 • Ira Stein and Floyd Lapp (JHS 82 '56). We stood up for Alan Freed and Rock'n'Roll. What's new? David Horowitz.

MP 241 • Has anyone seen Irwin Klepper, TAFT 1960? Reply – Ken Klein (TAFT 1960).

MP 242 • Anthony Vento looking for ROOSEVELTites '42-44 or graduates of Drake Prep Jan '44. Remember Lutz, CYO and St. Helena dances? Bronx Winter Garden, Chester Palace, Stardust Ballroom? Drop me a line. We can reminisce and locate old friends.

MP 243 • I would like to find a friend, Vincent Campbell, graduate of CLINTON June '56, joined Navy, have not heard or seen him since 1959. Joseph Norris, TAFT around 1960. He was a milkman for a while (remember those days). Alan Schultz, ROOSEVELT 1955, lived around Honeywell. Spoke to him last in 1980 when he visited me. Grace Young, ROOSEVELT 1956. She lived at Arthur Avenue.

MP 244 • Norman Pulafer, DeWitt CLINTON '57 – looking for the gang who played kick the can, punchball, etc. from Buchanan Place and Davidson Ave.

MP 245 • Joanne Treffert Kemp, WALTON '58 and William Kemp, CLINTON '58 celebrated our 31st wedding anniversary on 3/12/91!

MP 246 • Joel Upman, SCIENCE '61 and Sheila Lipman Obers, TAFT '56, would like to wax nostalgia with old friends from the Featherbed Lane/Shakespeare area.

MP 247 • Where is that old gang of mine? Remember Gil-Jacks? NESSA is longing to know whereabouts of Carol Volante, Annette Risl, Pat Colletti, Maureen Nooney, Claire, Grace Jody, Ralph "Cigar", Bobby Grillo, Muriel Henry, PS 113. I live in Boston now.

MP 248 • Carl Markowitz would enjoy hearing from Mrs. Sweeny's class in PS 44 mid/late 30's – Jack, Betty, Bertha, Red, Sol, Annette, Bobby, Harold, Hippo, Leon, Phillip, Paul, for Sylvia Halpern. Where is Adele Lerman, Pearl Kaminsky, Mimi, Arlene Deutsch.

MP 249 • Jr HS 82, 1948. Anyone from Perry's Pool Room, University Ave. or 82. Schoolyard football players especially.

MP 250 • Sid Kopperl, Undercliff Ave., looking for Larry Katz, CLINTON '65, Marla Riff SCIENCE '68 – anyone from the old neighborhood, or PS 109.

MP 251 • TAFT '59 – Nelson Ave. Ellen Horowitz. Like, desperately seeking Rona Newman.

MP 252 • Thea Asquith Greene, Bronx SCIENCE 1964, earned her ANA certification as a clinical nurse specialist in psychiatric nursing. She lives in L.I. with her husband and 2 teenage sons and works in an outpatient treatment center.

MP 253 • Terri Aber (now Adam), TAFT '52, looking for Lorraine Halpern (known as Lolly). Mother's name Rosenberg, first husband's name Monty. Want to renew friendship. Can anyone help reunite us?

MP 254 • PS 93 Thanksgiving Play 1941/2 – Albert Madigan, Seymour Rothenberg, Leatrice Feingold, David Sokol, Julius Margolis, Donald Deitch, Freddie Mooke, Rosalie Graf, and Renee. We honored the soldiers, sailors, and nurses of WW2. Call me!

MP 255 • Gun Hill Road – 215, PS 94, JHS 80, Bruce Freeman, Arthur Pornick, Howard Berger, Frank Dickson, Howard Weinfeld, David Switkin.

MP 256 • PS 26 – Barbara Jacobs from 1950 Andrews Ave. Would love to locate friends from the old neighborhood. I'm alive and well and living in California. A "1950" reunion would be fun!

MP 257 • Nancy Kravitz Zimmerman looking for anyone from the crowd at Jahn's and Creston JHS; Susan Edelman, Barbara Weinstein Goodman, Fran Podber and Marcia Silverberg Pulawitz.

MP 258 • Stuart Copans, Scottsdale, AZ – any CLINTON or Music&Art (1952) or CCNY (1957) grads living in Scottsdale, AZ area, please call.

MP 259 • Looking for my redheaded bridesmaids – Shirley Kopalz Sarris, Wanon 1955 & Joan Schwartz Shine, Far Rockaway HS 1955. We have much to catch up on. Miss you.

MP 260 • WALTON '58 – looking for classmates for 35th reunion. WALTONites, where are you?

MP 261 • TAFT '62 – Larry Mendelowitz would like to hear from old friends. Write or call.

MP 262 • Ken Cohen 171st St. and McCombs Rd. (PS 104, PS 82 CLINTON) is alive and, well, living with Barbara (Bernstein) Cohen and two boys in Yardley PA. OK, Tommy DeCallucia, Mike Klein, Peter Krakoff, Jay Stevelman and the rest of you Schoolyard Players get in touch. Stickball, Scully, Johnny On-The-Pony and Curbball are waiting to be played.

MP 263 • Looking for anyone who grew up south of 149th St. in the Willis/Alexander Avenue area. I'm doing "Oral History" interviews for a book about the South Bronx and would like to talk and reminisce with you.

MP 264 • Howard Arnheimer would like to hear from members of the Cavaliers and the Davidson Avenue crowd.

MP 265 • Steve Schnapp looking for Cromwell Avenue folks: "Juicy" Heisler, Cheryl Wolchan, David Singer, Barry and "Muggs" Latzer, Eugene Bruhin, Sol Goldberg, Tony Larmamora, Freddie Grunewald, Jason Berman, Mark Stoller, Lenny Erlich. Time for a game of Curb Ball.

MP 266 • Paul Pintel from Eastburn Avenue would like to hear from Panther Club members, stickball players, those who socialized with the club and went onto PS 70, JHS 117, CLINTON, TAFT, WALTON, SCIENCE.

MP 267 • Failed novelist, so-so feature editor, Taft Review 67- 68,now a happy Manhattanite. Do you remember me or my writing? Wilma Kuhn – I'd love hearing from you!

MP 268 • Missing – Rita Cavalik Hazelton, last known address Dunedin, Florida 1975. Barbara Berger Cooper and Edna Stein Cohen are looking for you. Rita, or anyone knowing her whereabouts, please get in touch.

MP 269 • Highbridge. Anyone live in Highbridge during the 40's and go to PS 73? Maybe we knew each other. Contact Jay Jacobson, CLINTON '51 .

MP 270 • Lynn Graff, 182nd St. and Davidson Ave. looking for Ira Karsh and others from neighborhood. Also, Richie Yessian and Frankie Morris from SCIENCE '57 and other friends from SCIENCE '59.

MP 271 • Where are you Rona Kaufman JHS 22 '58? Looking for Meet Chicks – Barbara Klugman and Lillian Heisler TAFT '61. Also Sandy Alekman, Estelle Balmuth and any other TAFT '61 people. Contact Lila Freilicher.

MP 272 • "Polycar" was my maiden name and I graduated in '64 from TAFT.

Looking for "old flames". Max Liebster, Sally Cohen, Barbara Wallerstein. Also old Scout Troop 234 BSA.

MP 276 • Looking for anybody who grew up in the Sedgwick and Burnside Avenue areas – especially the stretch from University Avenue down to Sedgwick Park. Any parishners from HOLY SPIRIT? Looking for Ben Jacalow who lived at 1955 Sedgwick Avenue – my boyhood buddy!

MP 277 • Club Metro 1947-1950: Jerry Rosmarin, Jerry Talcovitz, Herbie Lipman, Norman Klampert, Stanley Bowen, Dominick Calabrese, Jerry Goldstein, Joan Rose – where are the rest of you? 20 missing girls. Contact Norman Klampert.

MP 278 • WALTON '62 Audrey Ballan looking to find Sandy Rothman, WALTON '62 my maid of honor and best friend. Stephanie Ross, Myrna Krieger, Michelle Feiner, Susan Chapel. Class of '62, where are you?

MP 279 • Barbara Frankel Unger seeks Sally Haimowitz, Toby Cedar, Barbara Rosenthal, Joan Wesp, Al Ramrus, Rhoda Teller, Dolores Rand, Class of '50 people from EVANDER or former English students of Mrs. Unger from JHS117 or EVANDER, 1955-1959.

MP 280 • Nadine Scheiber (nee Gritz) looking for the old crowd from "The Coops" (Bronx Park East and Barker Avenue) and all "COLUMBUSites" who graduated 1945-47. Where are you "Mucky", "Wole", "Labie", Aaron, Lola, Rochelle, Bertha, etc???

MP 281 • Joey Santoiemma – PS32 ('64) – now in New Rochelle – I miss you all – "Nellie" Yomtov, Vinny Guiliano, Alan Shikowitz, Helen Ciemente, Christina Packer, Steven Rivetti, especially YOU, Erminia Marano! I'm in the book.

MP 282 • Stanley Weiner, TAFT '53 and Towson College, has just moved back

from Charleston, SC with Trudi Fisher Weiner, TAFT '53 and NYU '57. Stanley is Chief Operating Officer of Playtogs, Inc. in Middletown, NY. Trudi managed a boutique and Contemporary Sportswear in Charleston. They are happy to be back in the Big Apple.

MP 282 • Stanley Weiner, TAFT '53 and Towson College, has just moved back from Charleston, SC with Trudi Fisher Weiner, TAFT '53 and NYU '57. Stanley is Chief Operating Officer of Playtogs, Inc. in Middletown, NY. Trudi managed a boutique and Contemporary Sportswear in Charleston. They are happy to be back in the Big Apple.

MP 284 • Looking for first girl friend – Myrna Pflaster or second girlfriend – Janet Berkowitz or Tuba play.

MP 285 • Bobby and Valerie (Alessandro) Pavone are desperately seeking a copy of 1962 yearbook for John Philip Sousa, JHS142, Baychester Avenue, Bronx. Anyone having or knowing the whereabouts of one, please contact us.

MP 286 • Where are all the graduates of Theodore ROOSEVELT HS 1956, Pelham Parkway (Holland Avenue), 1950s PS105, PS83 grads. Contact Seymour Rush – love to hear from any of you out there.

MP 287 • Where are Howie Zwicker, Aviva Rosenbaum, Harriet Wittels, Mitzi Feldstein, Mitchell Berlin, Davida Karpel, Wilma Green, Sharon Letich, Dorothy Rebarber, Judy Taub?

MP 288 • ROOSEVELT '52, Selma Surenko looking to find Jerry (Jerome) Schwartz, TAFT '51 (Morris Avenue); and Phil Richman, CLINTON (Tiebout Avenue). Would like to hear from anyone who may know their whereabouts. Contact weekdays only 10-5.

MP 289 • Wendy Citron TAFT '67 would love to find Sheryl Berman, Heleine Haber, Judy Shack. Remember "hanging out" by the phone booths on Fordham Road? Please call.

MP290 • Frank Arce – ROOSEVELT '67. It's our 25th Anniversary! Is there anyone of us left for a possible reunion? Let's not wait another 25 years to get together. Looking for my pal Francisco Matos. Are you still alive? Get in touch!

MP291 • Shirley Stern Allen of 2350 Creston Avenue looking for WALTONites class of 1950. Gladys Hopkins Blum and Marilyn Swartz Kroop. Would love to hear from you!

MP 292 • Steve Glaizer, ROOSEVELT '63 seeking any old friends or schoolmates – members of Club Pendulum, Klapper '67. Please call or write.

MP 293 • Looking for Rhoda Teller, Dolores Rand, Candy Cashman, Toby Cedar, Marie Weston, Joan Wesp, Barbara Rosen. I am Barbara Frankel of 45 East Mosholu Parkway, PS80, EVANDER 1950. Welcome replies.

MP 294 • 1950s, JHS82, PS26, Grand Avenue, Tremont Avenue, Harrison Avenue – contact Jayne Magnus Frazelle.

Classifieds

MP 295 • 1960 Bronx **SCIENCE**. Physician, slim, short, looks 40, blue eyes, blonde hair, seeks younger, slim, non-smoking woman, 25-40. I am easy-going, down to earth, not materialistic, outgoing, excellent sense of humor, love animals and nature.

MP 296 • To the guys that played stickball in **TAFT**'s parking lot from mid-1950's to early '60s and hung out in Levine's Candy Store 172nd St. and Morris Avenue. Where are you? Also Bobby Cohen (Chigi). Please get in touch.

MP 297 • Looking for Mosholu Parkway participants, little or big Parkway 1957 through 1964. California Contingency Naomi Lipp, Lenore Greenwald, Janice Greider, Alan Bleiberg, Stanley Williams. Call or write.

MP 298 • Celia Baer, PS104, JHS82, **TAFT** '53. Now living in Washington state. Would like to be reminded of old times. Anyone remember? Left Bronx 37 years ago, from Andrews Avenue.

MP 299 • I would like to know if anyone could help me verify the fact that after **WALTON** HS seniors received their senior hat, they then wore them pinned to their shoulder. I would really love a picture.

MP 300 • Blue-eyed brunette, Bronx-Irish lovely seeks aging Bronx bad boy – definitely not a momma's boy – 44-45 for good time, good fun and rock'n'roll. Stop hanging out on the corner long enough to give me a call.

MP 301 • Does anyone remember me? Marion (Micki) Schweitzer, Featherbed Lane, Nappi's Pizza, **TAFT**, PS82, PS53. Sister Elaine, brother Charlie. Married David Gale Macomb's Road. Has anyone seen Marion (Elvis) Bornstein, Mom Ruth, Dad Frank? Please get in touch.

MP 302 • Bill Eberhart, **TAFT** Jan. 1944. Looking for Gil Yodowitz and Julian Hoffman both Jan. '44 graduates. Haven't seen Julian since Feb. 1945 in Holland – US Army. Gil last seen in 1974, NYC.

MP 303 • Looking for Mel Feldman from 2450 Fish Avenue and Mike Rabinowitz, **EVANDER** '61. Both attended LIU in 1961. Contact Doris (Weiss) Bass. Please reply.

MP 304 • Joyce (Grossman) Cinader – **TAFT** '63. Anyone who remembers please write all letters will be answered.

MP 305 • EBB '60, **ROOSEVELT** '63, 167th Street "4", remember them? I'd love to hear from you – Loni Kleinberg.

MP 306 • Looking for Edie Fertig of Gerard Avenue, Carol Streezek of Shakespeare Avenue and anyone from the crowd that hung out at the Sedgwick Projects. Are any of you out there? Please contact Cheryl Bard Benanti.

MP 307 • "Itchy" looking for old pals from Wallace Avenue; King Crawford, Demara, Rosenblaum...where are you?

MP 308 • Sylvia Cantor Weiss, **TAFT** '61, looking for Marion Bornstein, **TAFT** '61, Marcia Fishbein Goldey '62, Ellen Bell '61. I'm still married to Richie and living in Maryland. Write me...

MP 309 • WHERE'S CHARLIE? Allen Mandel, **CLINTON** '60, and the rest of the guys need to find Charlie Maley, Music and Art '60, for a 50th birthday reunion. I've been looking for him for years! Can anyone help? Sharpen up your memories.

MP 310 • Phyllis Meltzer Rothstein, **EVANDER** '63 and Richard Rothstein, **CLINTON** '60, celebrated their 25th anniversary by vacationing in Hawaii. They are the proud parents of Donna, a Ph.D. candidate at Cornell University, and Michele, a senior at Lehigh University.

MP 311 • Abe Roemisher, Harold Tayman, Ralph Stienman, Dominick Miteratondo, Howard Schneider, Joe Magrim, Helen Milano, Florence Brown, Irving Moscowitz, Aaron Goldberg, Albert Gonzola – 2765 Matthews Avenue – 826 Adee Avenue...where are you?

MP 312 • Remember the "Wall" by Pelham Pkwy, '69-'70? Chock Full 'O Nuts? The Huts? **COLUMBUS** HS, '69-'70? JHS135 '67-'68? Where'd you wind up? Bob Elber would like to know. Please make contact.

MP 313 • Brenda Bachman Wangel, **MONROE** '58, looking for my Gold Dust twin, Andrea Carco. Would also enjoy hearing from anyone else I grew up with on Vyse Avenue.

MP 314 • Several **TAFT** '53 graduates living in Tamarac, Florida: Susan Alouete Rich, Larry Milbauer, Wendy Lawner DeFortuna, Joseph DeFortuna. We're looking for more '52, '53 and/or '54 **TAFT** graduates residing in South Florida.

MP 315 • Chuck Schweitzer, **TAFT** '63, looking for friends in Mrs. Jacobson's official class. Roger Jelinek, where are you? Where are the kids from Featherbed Lane and Jesup Avenue? Although I did get a degree in Physics, I'm now a CPA with offices in North Atlanta and South Florida.

MP 316 • Does anybody know where they are – Joey McAuliffe, Mike Butler, Jimmy Barrett, Mary Farrell, Betty McWilliams, Billy Gorman, Bart Condon, Tommy McMahon, Phil Sasso, Frankie O'Brien, Diana Maldonado, Tito Pavon, Timmy Curtin?

MP 317 • Wanted: **WALTON** '61 grads – where are you? We are planning our 35th Reunion. Call Roberta.

MP 318 • Remember JHS22, classes 7-2, 8-2, 9-2, 1962-1965? Mrs. Mecray, math; Mr. Wagner, science; Mr. Tropp, social studies? So do I! If you want to reminisce, write me, Michael Janko. I was also **TAFT** '68.

MP 319 • Ita Adinoff of 205th and Webster Avenue, Susan Mandel Kaen would love to speak to you.

MP 320 • Parkside Projects, PS96, JHS135, **EVANDER** '64, CCNY Lasak '68 – do any of these ring a bell with you? They do for me – Steve Wagh. Let me hear from you, OK?

MP 321 • Paul Hogan, from Hughes Avenue and 182nd Street, looking for Louis Martucci, Joyce Russo of Adams Place, Danny Sica and others from 182nd Street/Belmont Avenue area. Where are you?

MP 322 • **TAFT** '62, Karen Plung Schneider wants to find Roni Epstein, Joyce Panzeroni and Maddy Krautheimer. Gale also wants to find friends from Elliot Place – Ellis Arnstein, Howard Pincus, Steven Tiger (PS64, JHS117).

MP 323 • Looking for people from "Wakefield Section" who were teens during the '60s. Also "1969" grads of Mother Butler Mem. Remember "Lowrys" Candy Store, 236th and White Plains Road?

MP 324 • Eddie my love, Eddie my first love! Where are you? Are you somewhere filling cavities like your Dad? We were a couple on and off from 1960–1963. Call Ellen.

MP 325 • My maiden name was Connie Honig, went to PS 26, PS 82 and **EVANDER**. Still in touch with Frank Ramundo, Zola Lieberman, Lillian Leverich, Herb Remer, Kitty Ramundo, and Betty Gottlieb (Leverich). Please call.

MP 326 • Barbara Ferrara looking for Eileen Isacman and Joel Aaronberg, **EVANDER CHILDS** class of '62. Would love to talk to them.

MP 327 • 1957 **TAFT** graduate looking for old friends and classmates, anywhere, news of class reunions, etc. Send replies to David Goodmacher, 12–4 Apple Ridge Road, Maynard, MA 01754, telephone 1-508-897-5163.

Goldfarb – *Vocational Rehabilitation Consultants.* Working compensation, spousal support, automobile liability, third party litigation, expert testimony

(CB 5, P 82) • **CLINTON** '50 – Bernard Geiman and his wife, Anne, under the stage name of "The Aldens," perform a highly acclaimed audience-participating ESP show.
For free brochure, call (718) 434-6050

(CB 6, P 83) •

SAMMY ROUMANIAN RESTAURANT
157 Chrystie St., New York, NY 10002

Picked as one of the 50 best restaurants in US; owned by Stanley Zimmerman **TAFT** '61 and Highbridge.

(CB 7, P 84) •

DIAMOND CLUB
47th St.
NYC.

If anyone is interested in purchasing diamonds at wholesale, I can be very helpful. Marilyn Asner.

(CB 8, P 85) • Get all your writhing needs met – brochures, newsletters, speeches, articles, press releases, (even resumes). Vicki Moss (718) 935-1310.

CB 1 • **TAFT** '61 - Judy Fixman Stine sells real estate in So. California's fastest growing area! Look me up if your relocating. (Judy Fixman Stine-23930 Via Rosa Linda, Valencia, CA 91335)

CB 2 • Harvey Brandwein **TAFT** '63 owner of

"The National Pastime"
Box 64H
Scarsdale, NY 10583,

promotes baseball card shows, baseball autographs and memorabilia.

CB 3 • To all members of the graduating class of 1966, 9-ESP-1, JHS 143, Alan Sloma says hello!

CB 4 • I'm Audrey Miller Rabinowitz, a freelance copywriter and direct marketing consultant. Lived on Grant Ave. and 164th St. and always felt like I was poor compared to the kids who lived on the Concourse (I was 3 blocks East). PS 35 was right across the street. Anyone around from Mrs. Streng's 6th grade class at PS 35? Fern Dorfman, Rochelle Lorber, Karen Kaminsky?

CB 5 • Stanley Weiner, **TAFT** '53 and Towson College, has just moved back from Charleston, SC with Trudi Fischer Weiner, **TAFT** '53 and NYU '57. Stanley is Chief Operating Officer of Playtogs, Inc., Middletown, NY. Trudi managed a boutique and bought contemporary sportswear in Charleston. They are happy to be back in the Big Apple.

CB 6 • I'm Louise Dichter Wilson, now married 33½ years (still) with two grown children-son a lawyer, daughter a banker. Husband owns a contracting business. I'm a sales and marketing director for a large new home developer and builder. One of three females of a forty member Board of Directors of Tri-County Builders Assoc.

CB 7 • The Jewish Service Center provides life sustaining/Jewish enrichment services for the Bronx Jewish poor/elderly. Individuals who wish to support this effort should contact:

Asher Moskowitz, Director
JEWISH SERVICE CENTER
2432 Grand Concourse
Room 502
Bronx, NY 10458
(212) 364-7900

CB 8 • Charles Seidner, **CLINTON** '60 and Roberta (Soloff) Seidner, **WALTON** '61 married 25 years (wow). Two children, David 24 and Marcia 21. Husband supervisor of kosher deli in the Bronx, Roberta an Executive Secretary at an Orthodox Synagogue.

Room 502
Bronx, NY 10458
(212) 364-7900

TEST YOUR MEMORY
answers

1. c		13. b
2. c	8. A=1,	14. d
3. b	B=2,	15. a
4. b	C=3	16. b
5. b	9. c	17. c
6. c	10. a	18. a
7. A=2,	11. c	19. a
B=1,	12. a	20. b

If you have a Bronx Test, samples for Mystery Bronxites or any sort of trivia, do not hesitate to send them in. Please make sure that you also supply the correct answer. Please use a blank sheet of paper following the format in this and past issues and enclose in the reader reply envelope.

To Reply to one of these ads, Call 914-592-1647. Please have the ad number (ex: MP 48) at hand when you call, and we will promptly direct you to the appropriate party.

Be a Part of our Next Issue

If you would like to meet new people, or find old friends, we are willing and able to help. Just turn to the back page and fill out the reader reply card. Use the envelope provided and send your information to us today. We'll get working on it right away. All submissions will be printed in our next issue on a first come first serve basis so please don't delay, Reply Today!
We'd love to hear from you!

Would you like to start or plan your own reunion? We can help!

We are gathering quite a large database of names of '50s and '60s Bronxites. Tap into this database and organize that reunion that you've thought about for years but never had time to follow through on. Let "Back in the BRONX" help with the networking needed to make that reunion a success. For more information, contact:

Steve Samtur at (914) 592-1647

READER REPLIES

It is vitally important that you fill out the information below. Your input will be essential to the success of this magazine, tailored and inspired by you, the former "Bronxite". We thank you for your participation.

Subscriber? ☐ Yes ☐ No

YOUR NAME _____

ADDRESS _____

CITY _____ STATE _____ ZIP _____ PHONE _____

HIGH SCHOOL ATTENDED _____ YEAR GRADUATED _____

TELL US A LITTLE ABOUT YOURSELF,
(Be sure to include your alma mater, old neighborhood, your best memories about your days in the Bronx, (or anything else you can tell us).

_____

_____

COULD WE SEND A FRIEND A FREE COPY OF BACK IN THE BRONX?
Do you know current or former Bronxites who would like to receive our magazine and reunion information?
If you do, we'll be happy to send them a **free** inaugural issue of **Back in THE BRONX**.
Write to Back in The Bronx, Box 141 H, Scarsdale, NY 10583 or call 1-800-7-BRONX 5

Last	First	Maiden
Address	City	State	Zip
Phone # ( )	School and year of Graduation

Last	First	Maiden
Address	City	State	Zip
Phone # ( )	School and year of Graduation

Last	First	Maiden
Address	City	State	Zip
Phone # ( )	School and year of Graduation

Last	First	Maiden
Address	City	State	Zip
Phone # ( )	School and year of Graduation

COME BLOW YOUR OWN HORN DEPARTMENT
Please tell us about yourself (include your name)—about your accomplishments, awards, titles or works in progress.
We're interested in hearing about them. List Below. _____

_____

_____

_____

_____

READER REPLIES

As a subscriber you are entitled to a FREE 40 Word Classified, Missing Persons, Blow Your Own Horn, or Personal Ad. Please write your ad below (if you are not subscribing to our magazine you can still place an ad in the next issue. The cost of an advertisement is 50¢ a word, there is no limit on paid ads).

_____

_____

_____

Is Your Mailing Label Correct?

In order to keep our database current, please correct any errors and place the label and or photocopy with corrections.

Account #	High School	Year Graduated
6817	Roosevelt	1958

SAMPLE
Mary R. Flowers
123 Anystreet Blvd.
Anywhere, USA 12345

Change of Address?

If you're planning a move please attach your label corrected with your new address and the date that you will begin receiving mail at that address. This will insure that you don't miss your next issue of **Back in THE BRONX**.

Ordering Information

YES, I'd like to order the following items:

QTY.

____ 1Yr. (4 ISSUES) Subscription(s) to Back in THE BRONX $19.95
____ 2Yr. (8 ISSUES) Subscription(s) to Back in THE BRONX* .. $29.95 } *FREE Jahn's Menu
____ 3Yr. (12 ISSUES) Subscription(s) to Back in THE BRONX* .. $39.95
____ 4Yr. (16 ISSUES) Subscription(s) to Back in THE BRONX* .. $49.95
____ The Beautiful Bronx............$25.00 (plus $3.95 S/H) $28.95
____ The Bronx: It Was Only Yesterday..$25.00 (plus $3.95 S/H) $28.95
____ Bronx High School Reunion Weekend Video $29.95
____ SAVE MONEY - BUY 4 FOR JUST $99.00!
____ THE BRONX Tracking Service $9.95
_____ I would like to receive all available back issues and have them applied towards my subscription (To date we have at least 12 back issues available - While They Last!)

TOTAL: $ _____

Please fill out completely and include $3.95 for shipping and handling for books only to: **Back in THE BRONX**, Box 141H, Scarsdale, NY 10583

A Great Gift Idea! In addition to your own subscription, a subscription to **Back in THE BRONX** makes a great and unique gift. Fill in the form below and we'll process the order in time for our next issue. So, order your subscription NOW, and order one for a friend!

Please Print Clearly   ☐ New Subscriber   ☐ Renewal

Name _____

Maiden Name _____

Address _____

City _____

State _____ Zip _____

Phone (___) _____

High School _____ Year Grad. ___

☐ Visa ☐ Mastercard ☐ Check ☐ Money Order

No. _____ Expiration Date ___

Signature _____

Back in THE BRONX

Box 141 H, Scarsdale, NY 10583
Phone 914-592-1647 • Fax 914-592-4893

ADDRESS CORRECTION REQUESTED

Volume I   Issue II

Back in THE BRONX

Celebrating the experience of growing up and living in the Bronx

Freedomland. . .

Courtesy of John McNamara, McNamara's Old Bronx

Freedomland is a name that can conjure memories for most any Bronxite over the age of 35 and no doubt many an album has photographs of the educational-amusement park that was to be the Disneyland of the East. In the 1950's, a vast marshy tract along the Hutchinson River in the northeast Bronx was eyed for development. Earlier plans had envisioned a race-track there and once it had been considered for an airport. But while these ambitious blueprints were gathering dust in some engineering office, William Zeckendorf of the real estate concern of Webb & Knapp promoted a venture that would entertain and educate the American Public on a scale that would outdo Disneyland. Two hundred and five acres of wetlands were filled in and Freedomland, in the shape of the United States, was built at an estimated $65 million.

The promoters predicted an annual attendance of five million people and in the spring of 1960, the extravaganza opened. Visitors rode horsecars and stagecoaches, paddlewheelers and replicas of San Francisco's cablecars. They saw reenactments of the Great Chicago Fire, the Pony Express, and other exhibits of American history but, as one reporter succinctly put it, "people don't go to amusement parks to be educated."

In it's first season, only 1,500,000 people came through the turnstiles and the following years were equally disappointing.

Apparently what was not taken into consideration was our northeastern climate which limited Freedomland to function only five months a year, whereas Disneyland, in California, never closed. Five summers after it opened, Freedomland—one of New York's most expensive misadventures, closed down. A year later, plans were under way to build Co-op City on the same site, and this time the story had a happy ending.

Games People Played

Lester A. Gerhardt

Living in upstate New York can, at times, complicate your life—particularly when it comes to leisure time. Faced with the decision of whether to go to the polo matches in Saratoga, sail on Lake George, or play tennis at the local club, the family had difficulty reaching a consensus. As the pros and cons were being hotly debated, I mentally faded back to another time, my childhood, when these decisions came a little easier.

When I became bored after eating and mistakenly asked what should I do to keep myself entertained, my grand-mother, who shared my parents apart-ment (there was no generation gap because we all grew up and old together) always offered the same solution if I remained inside—'Go bang your head in the wall,' I was too young to go to the

submarine races, and I didn't understand how you could tell who won anyhow. Consequently, I elected to go 'out.'

Out,' meant racing down four flights of worn marble stairs, usually two at a time, jumping down the last four (the big kids could jump six and even eight.) This last act always guaranteed the appearance of the first floor neighbor who had some unusual words of welcome for me.

Once 'out,' I passed between the two stone lions that guarded 'our' building (I never understood why we lived in one apartment if we owned the whole building, but I never had the courage to ask) and became exposed immediately to the fresh air. Apparently fresh air was also not allowed to enter the building.

Living in the Bronx in a neighborhood

Morris Avenue and 173rd Street just off the Grand Concourse, you had access to everything within walking distance, most of it just around the corner. We were self contained. Rosoff the druggist removed cinders from your eye without fear of a malpractice suit, the grocer never required payment but just wrote you up and was able to add faster than any soon to be invented computer, and Berger the barber never took orders from anyone except your mother as to style and length. And when you finished at Berger's, you stopped into the corner candy store to polish off an egg cream with a 'head' that was the last to go. We even had a hobby shop to browse. It hosted various model building contests and yo-yo competitions (Cherrio and Duncan) which was the event of the

Continued on page 3

From the Editors...

It is our hope that this second issue is as well received as our inaugural issue. We will still continue to send out the inaugural issue. Any friends, relatives, or neighbors wishing to receive it may write or call (for their complimentary issue).

Our database of Bronxites is growing extremely well. With this growth many people placing personal ads ARE finding friends and neighbors, many of whom they haven't seen in more than 25 years. On a personal note, I found a friend that I haven't seen since the late 50s and I received a note from a woman who my father dated 50 years ago!

We have been fortunate to get terrific media coverage for BACK IN THE BRONX. Stories have appeared in the Daily News, The New York Times, The Bronx Press Review, The Riverdale Press, the Voice of America, and 'Live With Regis and Kathie Lee', a syndicated television show.

We again turn to you, current and former Bronxites to contribute as you have been doing. BACK IN THE BRONX is for and about you. Send us stories, tests, trivia, memorabilia, pictures, 8 or 16 mm depicting the Bronx neighborhood. We will select the best, copy it, and promise to send it back in tact.

Thank you for your continued input...

Back in the BRONX
Celebrating the experience of growing up and living in the Bronx

Publishers and Editors   **Stephen M. Samtur**
Susan H. Samtur

Art Director   **Thomas R. Hamilton**
Herald Graphics Inc. Stratford Ct

A number of the photographs in Back in the Bronx are courtesy of
and available from the Bronx Historical Society

Live with Regis & Kathi Lee

The RIVERDALE PRESS

Vol. 41, No. 24   Thursday, August 16, 1990

DOES ANYONE out there remember Jahn's, *the* fifties place to take your date after a movie? The old-fashioned ice cream parlor on the corner of Kingsbridge and Fordham Roads is the subject of an affectionate recollection in a newsletter devoted to affectionate looks back at the Bronx. *Back in the Bronx* also includes a Bronx Trivia Test and pictures and stories of celebrities who hale from the ... of Parks and Universi-

ties. The product of a Scarsdale couple, Steven and Susan Samtur, who recently hosted a Bronx Block Party for 1100 Bronxites at the Concord Hotel, the 16-page newsletter is available free by calling 1-800-7Bronx5. The Samturs make the offer because they they hope you'll subscribe to receive future issues and they want your name and address in their Bronx database, which they use to publicize the reunions they sponsor.

Your Only Boro Paper!

Bronx Press-Review
THE ALL-BRONX NEWSPAPER — ONE OF AMERICA'S GREAT WEEKLIES   35¢ per copy

National Newsletter for Former Bronxites Launched

In commemoration of the 350th Birthday of the Bronx, Stephen and Susan Samtur have just published a 16 page ... The Bronx.

"Back In The Bronx" is a retrospective of The Bronx in the 50's and 60's, this quarterly newsletter will feature stories about Bronxites, (most likely former Bronxites), who want to share and reflect on their experiences and growing up in the Bronx. It includes a Bronx Trivia Test as well as pictures and stories of celebrity Bronxites.

Another feature of "Back In The Bronx" is a section devoted to finding "Missing Bronxites". It is the publisher's hope that the newsletter will help find lost high school buddies, sweethearts, etc. They are starting to gather a substantial computerized database of Bronxites and former Bronxites.

Bronxites are encouraged to send, fax, or call a toll-free number 1-800-7BRONX5. They will receive a complimentary issue of "Back In The Bronx" and we will be added to the database by Susan and Stephen ...

very successful in promoting this kind. They publish newsletter called Jackpot ... that currently has o 100,000 subscribers, and for t last 17 years have been p lishing "Refundle Bundle" which at one time had ov 400,000 monthly subscriber Susan has been a Contributi Editor for "Family Circle" an her book "Cashing in At The Checkout" sold over 400,00 copies.

It is their belief that as baby boomers grow older, they be come more reflective. Nostalgia takes on a more significant im portance. Just three months ago they captured this by having a Bronx Block Party at the Concord Hotel. Over 1100 Bronxites attended this weekend of fun and games. They participated in Bronx street games such as stally, potsie, stickball, jump rope, Johnny-On-The-... and of course bar stall. Many who at... from local high

The New York Times

SUNDAY, OCTOBER 14, 1990

Mr. Samtur, who grew up in the Bronx during the 50's and 60's, felt nostalgic about the people and places of his youth. So he started a 16-page newsletter, Back in the Bronx, filled with descriptions of the old neighborhoods, multiple-choice tests on the readers' knowledge of the Bronx, and personal ads to help people contact old friends.

He distributed 1,100 copies of the first newsletter at an April reunion of former Bronx residents at the Concord Resort in upstate New York. "The response was overwhelming," he said. "We now have 20,000 people on our mailing list and I'm aiming for 100,000. Over 500,000 students passed through Bronx high schools in the 50's and 60's and I intend to reach them."

Famous Names From the Bronx

The talk show host Regis Philbin, the comedian Robert Klein, and the members of Dion and the Belmonts have all been interviewed for Back in the Bronx. Now Mr. Samtur is writing about The Fordham Baldies and Dr. Jonas Salk, the inventor of a polio vaccine, for forthcoming issues.

VOA

USIA

DAILY NEWS

Bronx cheerleaders

For the last 25 years, Steve and Susan (a.k.a. the "Coupon Queen") Samtur, publishers of the Refundle Bundle, a supermarket coupon-clipping service, would get together once a year with friends from their old Bronx neighborhood.

The first questions would be, "Have you heard from Steve Taubman?" Everyone would answer, "No." Then someone would say: "But you wouldn't believe who else I heard from!"

Each passing year, the Samturs got more frustrated over losing touch with their old pals.

Steve decided "I was going to find our high school buddies who I haven't seen since the early '60s." So he started a newsletter, BACK IN THE BRONX, to help fellow Bronxites find "a buddy, high school sweetheart or neighbor whom you have lost contact with and would like to find."

By the way, through the newsletter, the Samturs did finally find Steve Taubman!

Games (cont'd)

neighborhood. A kosher candle was the best thing to use to wax the string so it would 'sleep' longer.

But I was 'out' and now had to decide what to do. Entertaining yourself usually cost nothing around the neighborhood and there were many options, provided you came 'out' with your Spauldeen, your pocketknife (which I wasn't supposed to have,) and your cigar box of marbles—real marbles, not your brains. We just called them immies.

If noon came along, I could play mumblypeg with my knife, a little known game developing a completely useless talent. You took your knife opened with the largest blade, and starting it point down on (not in) your head tried to flip (with one complete revolution) the blade into the ground. You then proceeded downward to your nose, chin, knee, toe etc. If you missed, you had to start over. This was a highly developed skill, but the toughest part were finding some dirt in which to play with all the concrete around, and explaining all those cuts to your mother.

By now someone always came along (a result of their mother or grandmother offering them similar options to my own.) We could then expand to higher levels of knife games-land and the ultimate game of chicken. Land was actually fairly decent as such games go. You drew a rectangle in the dirt and the first throw of the knife determined the partitioning into each other's territory (this was also the name of the game in other neighborhoods) and subdivide it into finer and finer parcels until the other guy (girls never played this) lost all his land and you won. It's a little like the suburban developer today who continues to subdivide and then sells off postage stamp sized lots. (In fact, now that I think about it, our developer always beat me at land when we were kids.)

Chicken (the only version we could play since we didn't drive—which was a good thing because we couldn't afford a car anyway) was a little more risky. You spread your feet as did your 'friend' and each took a turn at throwing the knife between the other's feet. Your 'friend' then was obliged to move his feet to the newly established mark. This continued till blood was drawn or one of you chickened out. This game usually left someone with one less friend for about a week. There were lots of other knife games, but I can't write about them—my kids might get the wrong idea about me. They already have found a black leather motorcycle jacket in the basement (I'm sorry—lower level, that's what we call it now in the suburbs) with a hand painted skull and crossbones which my wife is still trying to explain away.

The only reason I still need to work today is because my mother threw out all my baseball cards the day she opened her closet and the boxes of them I had collected fell on her head. The second cigar box full, I vividly remember, contained several Mickey Mantle cards, just a few of which could now pay off the entire mortgage on our house. Needless to say, I was big into baseball cards. Flipping them to match, tossing them to see who gets closer to a line in the sidewalk, getting a 'waller' playing against the curb, and trading them.

Marbles were another big source of entertainment and offered great opportunities for a potential entrepreneur. There were the traditional games of hit the penny (sometimes from across the street) where you tried to knock down a penny which was placed standing on edge against the curb (hitting wasn't good enough) and if you did you would get ten marbles from me—maybe more depending on distance; or rolling marbles into a cigar box which had different sized openings—the smaller the opening the more marbles you would get besides your own. The only time I recall that I was 'grounded' (today's term) by my father was when he discovered me playing hit the penny but with a wad of gum behind it. No, there was another time. He tried to get his marbles to roll into the holes in my cigar box and found that they were all too small. By the way, I still have my shooter and big puree.

But the little pink ball in my pocket, a Spauldeen, was the key to sports and happiness in the street. The city employees kindly laid concrete sidewalks with appropriately spaced lines to form boxes for us (maybe there was another reason, but I don't know what it was.) We accommodated and played baseball (only two people required), boxball, and hit the penny among others. The same city employees also installed curbs for us for stoopball and gutters with sewers for us to play stickball. I still remember the first time I hit two sewers; the time my grandmother came 'looking for me' because she thought I took her broom handle for a bat (she was right)—it was the same day the police came by and took our bat because we weren't supposed to play stickball in the gutter; and the creative use of a coat hanger bent to the right shape to recover the famous Spauldeen floating in the sewer on the corner where it rolled in after a grand slam. The greatest thank you goes to the people who put up the tall buildings expressly for us to play ball against. We played slug and Chinese handball against the smooth sided buildings. Two or three or many more could play depending on the size of your gang and the building, and the kid who could 'cut' the ball the best usually was the server in the first box. Periodically we had water thrown on us—either to cool us to stop and go someplace else. The people in the first floor apartment didn't understand this was the only building with smooth sides around.

The fire hydrants on each block were another gift given to us kids by the city. We jumped over them (most of the time; if not the Lebanon hospital was just around the corner—it was years later I found out this was the name of a country,) and used them for a safe haven for ring-aleveo. They were also magical. On super hot days they would (I guess) automatically open and spew out water to cool us off.

But the great value of the sidewalks and their carefully placed lines were lost to us when we put on our roller skates. Not ones with in line wheels or shoe skates—just plain roller skates with metal wheels and clamps which reliably ruined your shoes after one day. They made a racket on the rough sidewalk which quickly boxed the wheels. We were forced into the gutter and there the smoothness of the surface let us glide along for hours just skating. We also raced, played a type of hockey and just had a good time. The monied elite among us saved our allowance and once in a while splurged to go skating at the Fordham Road roller rink-indoors, on a wooden floor with shoe skates and wooden wheels. What a treat. Because it was crowded during a regular skate, I learned how to dance (everything was self taught) on skates. The obvious benefits were that the floor wasn't crowded, everyone was watching you, and you had to skate with a girl. I can't say much more—my wife doesn't dance on skates. But I did give her my skate key before my house plan pin. Ingenuity and creativity were everywhere even in skating.

3

Continued on page 14

Reminiscing

Miss Bronx, 1962

Sue Anne Laurie

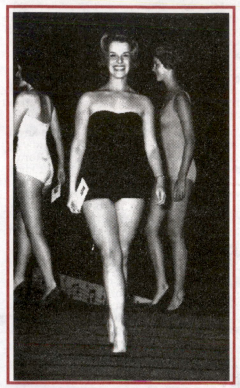

On Labor Day weekend, 1962, Sue Anne Laurie was crowned Miss Bronx 1962. The competition, sponsored by the Junior Chamber of Commerce of the Bronx, drew over 1000 entrants. On the memorable night of the coronation, at Freedomland, Sue Anne emerged the winner among twenty three finalists. Miss Laurie was awarded a $5000 cash prize and a "Key to the Bronx." She went on to graduate from Ithaca College, becoming a music teacher. Today, Sue Anne Book is a real estate agent, residing in California with her husband of 27 years, an attorney, and her two boys Corey, who has just taken the Bar exam and Todd, a Senior

Sue Anne Laurie, just before being crowned Miss Bronx at Freedomland, Labor Day, 1962

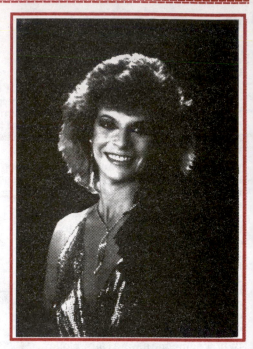

Sue Anne Book today.

at U.C. Berkeley. The photo at right shows that like many other former Bronxites, Sue Anne, nearing her 50th birthday is not getting older, she's getting better!

Someday I'm going to be...

These fine young Bronxites moved on to fame and fortune.
Can you guess the names of this talented trio of former Bronxites.
The answer is on page 21. (Don't turn right to the answer, that's cheating!)

Mystery Bronxite #1

Mystery Bronxite #2

Mystery Bronxite #3

Bronx Honor Roll
Bronxites who have achieved!

Bronx Science
Edggar Doctorow
Bobby Darren
Stokely Carmichael

Cardinal Hayes
George Carlin
Regis Philbin
Rocky Colovito
Kevin Loughery

DeWitt Clinton
James Baldwin
Paddy Cheyefsky
Daniel Shore
Neil Simon
Richard Rogers
Fats Waller
Don Adams
Martin Balsam
Judd Hirsch
Stubby Kaye
Robert Klein
Burt Lancaster
Jan Murray
Jimmie Walker
Nate Archibald
Dolph Shayes
James Caan

Evander Childs
Red Buttons
James Coco
Carl Reiner

Monroe
Hank Greenberg
Ed Kranepool
Jules Pfeiffer

Morris
Gabe Pressman
Angel Cordero

Roosevelt
June Allison

Taft
Eydie Gorme
Stanley Kubrick
Sanford Brown

Other notable folks with ties to the Bronx
Charles Osgood
Vic Damone
Bess Myerson
Dennis Day
Dion DiMucci
Jonas Salk
Roberta Peters
Jerry Vale
Jake LaMotta
Dianne Carroll
Ron Liebman
Gary Marshall
Al Pacino
Rob Reiner
Eli Wallach
Corazon Aquino
Edward Koch
Vin Skully
Joey Adams
Danny Aiello
Ellen Barkum
Alan Alda
Armand Hammer
Theodore Kheel
George Steinbrenner

Don Criqui
Lauren Bacall
Tony Curtis
Hal Linden
Sal Mineo
Charles Nelson Reilly
Isabel Sanford
Vanessa Williams
Herman Badillo
Ted Kennedy
George Burns
Avery Corman
Norman Cousins
Edgar Alan Poe
Geraldo Rivera
Pat Summerall
Herman Wouk
Teresa Brewer
Cab Calloway
Joey Bishop
Joe Franklin
Penny Marshall
Carroll O'Connor
Connie Selleca
Cardinal Cooke
E. Colin Powell
Robert Kennedy
Leon Cooper (Nobel Prize Winner)
Rosalyn Yallow (Nobel Prize Winner)
Anne Bancroft
Ralph Lauren

Thanks to Dr. William C. Wolfson and The Bronx Society of Science and Letters

Success Story!

Lenora "Lee" Rindner recently sent us this letter and a related article.
We're proud of you Lee!

There was a funny system back in the Bronx classrooms in the 50's and early 50's wherein, teachers would seat you alphabetically by the first initial of your last name. To me it seemed odd even then, I was under 5' 2" and an easily distracted individual. I could not see over the heads of the bigger kids who had an initial that preceded "Y", and that was almost everyone. Imagine knowing your friends would be your friends because you were alphabetically connected. Well, to compound things, some of the teachers also put the "bad kids" in the back of the room, as a punishment. That was an interesting message to the students, anyone who had the luck to have their last name initial S T U V W X Y Z were equated with "bad kids" in not only couldn't I see, I couldn't even hear. After a while I started acting just like them, —"the bad kids". My Homeroom teacher had an occasion to sit me up on her stool in the corner of the room—the dunce chair. I made it, I was "cool" and I was also humiliated. Lucky for me the "bad kids" were also the "cool kids". We were from another part of the Bronx unlike the "Grand Concourse" with the step down living rooms; it was the part of the Bronx where the struggling families lived. Our theater wasn't the Luxor or the Kent, it was the Fleetwood, or what we used to call "the Fleabag". It cost 15 cents to get in to see a feature and a cartoon or the "to be continued" Chapters like "Tarzan" and, of course, a cartoon. Sometimes for the same 15 cents we'd stay and see the whole set for a second or even third time. Now that we have Roger Rabbit, the theaters think they invented the novel idea of having a cartoon on the same billing with a feature film. In my Junior High School days we used to hang out at the corner candy store near JHS 22. The girls wore shiny pink satin short club jackets and different color scarves around our ponytails or around our neck when a hickey needed to be camouflaged. The guys wore leather jackets even in 80 degree weather. Back then "being cool" and "in" was more important than anything. Some of us weren't privileged enough to go right on to college after high school. I didn't go to college until 1981. I graduated last May '89 from SUNY New Paltz as class valedictorian and gave a speech to 6,000 people. Back in junior and senior high school if a teacher so much as called on me I would blush. I'm glad for having had the opportunity to experience a college education and more importantly a healthy life. I didn't make the "SPs" in P.S. 35 like Ira Flaumbaum but I obviously had potential. What I did learn is that what really matters—is the relationships and friends we make all along the way in life. It's nice to be able to remember the part of our lives that began and grew in the Bronx. Regards to my cool friend Matty Orlando, my high school sweetheart Marty Feldman, my friend Honey Nelson who danced with me in the aisle of the Apollo theater to such greats as Anthony and the Imperials, the Platters and Temptations.

Lenora "Yohay" Rindner
TAFT 1957

6

From Dunce Cap to Valedictorian

An article by Gary Pallassino, reprinted from the Rockland Journal-News

Lee Rindner of Monsey wasn't sure she should go back to school.

Rindner was 37 years old and had a good job in 1978, when she told a friend she was not satisfied with her life.

"I was really searching," she said. "I was looking for something to fulfill myself."

Her friend referred her to an educator, who in turn told her she should go to school. But Rindner worried that she might not fit into the college scene.

"I told him I wasn't like other students. I didn't know what they had that was different—only that they had something I didn't have. I was not comfortable seeing myself in that role," she said.

As it turned out, she fit in just fine.

Last month, she graduated as valedictorian of the Class of 1989 at SUNY/New Paltz. She compiled a 3.94 grade point average on a 4.0 scale, while holding down a full-time job at RCC as secretary to the dean of instructional services, and also raising a family.

Rindner credits her friend, Betty Jacobs, for finally persuading her to enroll in that first class at RCC more than ten years ago. Jacobs even came to the first three sessions of the class, Psychology 101, for moral support.

"Betty sat with me in those classes, raising her hand and answering questions," Rindner said. "By the time the third class came around, I wanted her to go home. I told her, 'That's enough; I want to be on my own.' And that was it."

That first class only made Rindner want more, although she said she was just as apprehensive when she enrolled in another course.

"Each time I went to a new class, I thought: 'This is the one that's going to show me that I don't have it'—whatever 'it' was," she said. "And each time, I was able to do well."

Rindner continued taking classes part time at RCC until she graduated in 1986 with an associate's degree in psychology.

She enjoyed counseling, and aptitude tests showed she was suited for social work. So, she decided to seek a bachelor's degree in health care management and community services at the state university

branch in New Paltz. The college offers some courses through a program at RCC, but for many classes, Rindner had to make the hour-long drive to the college's Ulster County campus.

"It was tough" she said. "But I have a husband who backed me up with all the physical work."

Rindner said her husband, Jerry, who manages the Kleen-Aid company in Spring Valley, "has a lot of nervous energy" to do house work, and described him as a caring father who got along well with their children.

Rindner said she hopes to pursue a master's degree in social work this fall at New York University, and will specialize in individual and group counseling. In the meantime, she will participate in a 12-week training course at Volunteer Counseling Service in New City.

She said she learned much about counseling during her field work at the Robert L. Yeager Health Center in Pomona, where she worked in the Young Adult Schizophrenic Program.

"You have to learn to listen more," she said. "That's the most important aspect of counseling."

Two members of the Rindner household will be attending college this fall. Rindner's 18-year-old daughter, Joyce, was one of five local high school students to receive a full, two-year scholarship in RCC's Mentor Talented Student program.

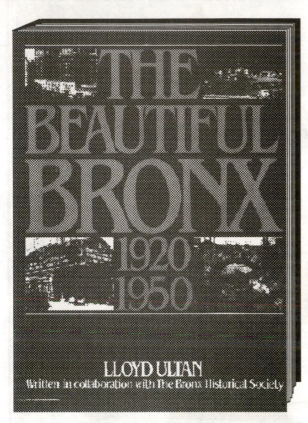
Bronx Style Fishing

By Maury Isaacs

As a youngster while living on the Grand Concourse, and 190th street, I would walk with a neighborhood friend down the Concourse and 161st Street. My friend and I would stop along the way and go "fishing, "Bronx Style".

We would stand over the subway grating and lower a fishing line down one of the grating spaces until it dropped one of the coins that people would inevitably lose down the hole!. We would attach to a pole and string a large wad of bubblegum chewed to just the right consistency for adherence properties. We then employed as delicate touch as the pole was lifted to the top of the grating, at which time the fisherman's assistant would insert his finger in the grate hole guiding the coin so carefully so as to not lose the coin when pulled through the grating.

This fishing exposition would require economic prudence and certain health practices. Each coin needed a new "bait" of course, chewing the gum once again to the desired consistency. The money was used to buy more bubble gum and to gain entrance into the bleachers at Yankee Stadium (fifty cents), and perhaps enough left over for a bus ride home (5 cents).

"ELSMERE CATERERS" - 170th

Rocky Marciano Dines at
Lido Riviera Restaurant

"THE ROCK"

ANOTHER ROCK!!

Reminiscing

Across the Bridge
by Merton M. Miller

I had my first taste of pizza at about age 14. A group of us walked across the "Little Washington Bridge" from University Ave., and W. 172nd St., Washington Heights, Manhattan. It was a warm summer evening and we were bored.

The five of us ranged in age from 14 to 17. I was the youngest.

As we walked along 181st St., we passed a lively Irish bar called Paddy's Pub or Blarney Stone or Emerald Bar, that had a "Pizza" sign out front.

It was 1953, before there were little pizza places on every main shopping street in the city selling slices through a window for 15 cents. Pizza still was a novelty for most of us. It wasn't readily available and even if it were, I doubt that my mother would have allowed me to buy it from a store where "you don't see what they put into it." My mother wouldn't think of allowing me to eat certain categories of foods, especially outside the house. I can't begin to estimate the number of hours of my childhood spent listening to my mother's rules and regulations about food.

* We don't eat frankfurters at the ballpark. Cousin Hymie works at Yankee Stadium and says they drop them on the greasy floor before they give them to you.

* We don't eat hamburgers at a restaurant; you never know what they grind up in them.

* We only buy Hellman's mayonnaise.

* We don't eat ices on a hot day; you'll get a sore throat.

So pizza was a bit of a gastronomical stretch for me.

Only Marvin, of course, was worldly enough to have eaten pizza previously. But then, Marvin had eaten everything previously. At 17, he was not only the oldest

in the "gang," but was also the largest, weighing in at about 260 pounds on his 5' 9" frame.

Marvin suggested we get a pizza and share it. The big question was would they even let us into the place; after all, it was a bar, and even if Marvin could pass for 18, there was no way the rest of us could.

But we were determined. We all put on our oldest-looking faces—tightly-lipped and squinty-eyed—and mustered our tough guy swaggers as we strode into the bar and pretended we did this every night of our lives.

There was no problem. The bar was the kind of place that would have served a double martini to the Lindbergh baby with no questions asked.

When the bartender delivered the pizza to our table, the reality of what I was about to do hit me. There in front of me was the most grotesque-looking thing I had ever seen on a table since my father squashed a roach with his slipper the year before.

But there was no turning back. I was about to eat a steaming, runny conglomeration of red and white lumps on a metal tray. I wondered how—and if—I would tell my mother about this.

You see, I was the kid who refused to eat sandwiches on white bread unless my mother first cut off the crust. I wouldn't eat cooked string beans because they were too

Continued on page 14

Now and Then . . .

That was then - 1959-64	This is now - 1989-90
Top Television Family	
"Father Knows Best" 29.7 rating; 43 share	"Roseanne" 23.4 rating, 35 share
It's a bird, it's a plane, it's Superwoman	
• 33.9% of women worked in 1964. In 1959, 18.7% of married women in the labor force had children under age 8.	• Women comprise 46.8% of the work force and 57.1% of married women have children under age 6.
A penny saved...	
• The minimum wage was $1 an hour; the average hourly wage was $2.02; the average weekly salary was $78.78; the annual median household income was $5417.	• The minimum wage is $3.80; the average hourly wage is $9.84; the average weekly salary is $335.20; the median annual income is $28,600.
Whiz kids	
• 4.5% of all persons had four years of college education; 3.9% of women and 5% of men had four years of college. 11% of men have four years of college.	• 10.1% of the population has four years of college; 9.3% of women and 11% of men have four years of college.
That's Amore	
• The marriage rate was 8.5% per 1,000 population; the divorce rate was 2.2 per 1,000 population.	• The marriage rate is 9.7 per 1,000 population; the divorce rate is 4.7 per 1,000 population.

Sources: Center for Health Statistics, Scientific Technical Information Branch; U.S. Department of Labor, Bureau of Labor Statistics, U.S. Bureau of the Census; Nielsen Media Research

Ritual of the Railing

by Judy (Frechtman) Rogers – Roosevelt–Bronx 1960

Growing up in the Bronx gives real meaning to "you hadda be there." In the 40's, who ever heard of a play date? Your mother said, "Go out and get some fresh air" and you went. The big preparation was changing from school clothes to play clothes–and, down the staircase you charged. No one called to make plans.

Phones were for emergencies and playing didn't qualify. The expectation was that no matter when you went out, there would be someone else there. Usually, to the dismay of the neighbors, there was a horde of kids.

Apartments weren't large enough to accommodate the antics of the young. So everyone "got fresh air." Nobody drove you to where you were going and nobody picked you up. Your exact whereabouts were a murky "somewhere on the block/playground/park" notion in the back of your mother's mind. You came home when you were hungry or when the crowd thinned–whichever came first.

As you grew up, and entered the nether world of the "big kids", the routine changed–but only a little. Now you were allowed out after dark. Everyone congregated on the park railings–weekends you went to see (or be seen) during daytime hours after school. Friday and Saturday you hit the big time.

After bolting down dinner and either washing or drying the dishes (if you couldn't make a deal with a sibling who couldn't go out or actually chose to remain home) you could join what my parents called "the rest of the pigeons on the railing."

Remember the railing? Railings were on the outside perimeter of the park facing the road. They lined Van Cortland Park and Mosholu Parkway. Hence, the teenagers also ended up "lining" the park areas. Up and down on railings were whole blocks of teens perched on railings.

If you arrived early you got a seat, otherwise you stood and faced the early arrivals. There was a strategy to arriving. No one wanted to be too early–that looked anxious. So, if you were early you "called for" someone. No phone calls–you went to their apartment and together went to rail-sit. This was a guarantee of having someone to "smooze with"–initially. Once the crowd came, you were on your own.

Status came with having a boyfriend. Then you were part of two cliques. No one needed be in love. If phone calls were a thing of the future, so were meaningful relationships. Just being linked as a couple was considered status enough. You walked hand in hand, dangled an oversized ring around your neck or wore a gargantuan team jacket (you should only be so lucky) to proclaim–Temporary private property.

Sometimes you broke out and went to another neighborhood rail. Then you were likely to be treated like a visiting dignitary. Then again, you had to play your cards right to retain this elevation in status. The understanding was this was a temporary arrangement–no extended incursions. You reported back to your home rail who broke up, who was going with who, when the next party was...and maintained your position on your home base. Too long a visit would mean a transfer of allegiance – God forbid!

We rail sat in summer, fall, spring and yes–even winter. Dreams of the NYC Park Department sending heat through the railing danced in our heads. It didn't occur to us to come in from the cold. Maybe that's why our ritual at the railing is our warmest memory.

13

Across the Bridge (cont'd)

squishy. And when my mother served me creamed corn the first time, I pushed it away saying, "I'm not eating that. It looks disgusting."

I only liked neat food.

I wasn't exactly prepared for pizza since my mother's idea of Italian cooking, I learned a little later in life, was slightly amiss. Her concept of veal parmegiana was ketchup with pepper. But beyond the question of what to eat was the point of where I was waiting. I was in a bar! And a bar was the kind of place my mother told me "we don't go into."

As a toddler walking with my mother, I remember her actually shielding me from the sight of the bar in our neighborhood. Bars were for "shickers," (a derogatory Yiddish expression meaning drinkers) she told me time and time again. So there I was about to break a multiplicity of sacred matriarchal commandments, excited by the prospect on the one hand, repulsed by the sight on the other hand, with my mother-dominated conscience thrown in for sheer confusion.

Is it any wonder I remember this event so vividly?

Of course I did the act, ate the pizza — AND LOVED IT!

When I walked into my house later that night, my mother began the requisite mother-son dialogue:

MOM: Where did you go tonight?

ME: We went for a walk across the bridge.

MOM: What did you do?

ME: I Went to an Irish bar and ate pizza.

Books for Gift Giving From

Games (cont'd)

When one skate broke, the other one was used to make a scooter from an orange crate. Two handles and a running board made from the same crate and the skate was all that was needed. A rock served as the hammer. We tried to make one last year here in the suburbs, but the corrugated cardboard they use today just didn't hold up for the kids.

If all else failed, the local school yard was the place to go to 'find a game.' Mine was PS 70 or Taft HS. You could always get up a game of basketball, handball or baseball if you wanted.

Winter was a special time. We could sled down the 173rd street hill, but needed a 'lookout' at the cross street below. We could ice-skate at Van Cortlandt Park lake with racing blades and really fly. If you got good enough, you might be able to enter the silver skates competition run by the Daily News each year. There were snowball fights, snow forts and a respect for time-outs when someone was called for lunch.

There were lots of other options for us. You could always go to Daitch's Dairy and get a cheesebox made of real wood to craft a gun which shot pieces of cardboard. All you needed was a rubberband. Please write for instructions. There was swimming at Cascades and Shorehaven (this seemed to be the preferred place to meet the opposite sex.) If you had a bike (I was 16 when I got one—a Rudge with three speed Sturdy Archer gears;

some friends got a Raleigh,) the rest of the Bronx was opened to you. I learned to ride in the gutter between the cars. It was an incentive to learn quickly. I still have my Rudge in the lower level ready to go. Give me a call. For $5 you could buy a city tennis permit for the year which allowed you to play on any of the city courts. We favored the ones behind Yankee Stadium. They were clay and keep very well, but the bonus was that we could get in to see the game after the seventh inning for free. I think I was in my twenties when I first paid admission to see a full game in person.

We had no specialists or experts in these sports. It seemed that everyone did everything, and most were self taught. A lot of self initiative paid off as did creativity. You had to get along with others because most of these games couldn't be played alone. Anyway they were nice friends, many of whom I still miss today.

I think you can look back at fond memories in the Bronx and to a less complicated time. When Lot looked back he turned to stone, but the only stone I remember are those two stone lions that guarded 'my' building that I had to pass through as I entered the fresh air and went 'out.'

It turns out it's raining at the lake, the polo matches have already started, and the courts are booked up at the club. I guess we'll just go 'out'...........to eat.

RED BUTTONS

by Aaron Rosloff

He was a handful of mercury, the kind of kid that teachers would appoint as a monitor to get him out of the class room. A red-headed kid, small of stature and build, but a bundle of energy. In the school yard, once he got his hands on a basketball it was an impossibility to get it away from him. He was quick, and he was clever.

His name was Aaron Schwatt. He lived just up the street from me, and we went to the same public school in the Bronx, (P.S. In class or out, he never stopped talking, and he made fun of everything).

Whether by design or accident, I don't know, but he turned his talent for comic gab into his livelihood, and went by the name of Red Buttons. At one time, he had his own television show, a comedy program, and one of his characters was a punchy prizefighter. This was back in the 1950's, when all programming was live. You had to be good or you were dead. He was good and his show was a success.

Red Buttons also made movies. He shared billing with Marlon Brando in "Sayonara", and received excellent reviews. He has played Las Vegas, Atlantic City, Miami, and others too numerous to count, but where I remember him best was in the New York State Catskill mountains in 1937.

That summer, I worked as a bus boy at the Woodlawn Villa. It was a lake side, middle of the price range resort, with small rooms and large dining room that served gargantuan meals. The other attraction was a casino, with nightly dancing and entertainment.

Music for the dancing was provided by four or five college students who played more or less in tune. The entertainment was provided by a Social Director, usually some third - rate unsuccessful Broadway performer, and his staff. The staff was likely to be a couple of high school kids who worked for room and board and "experience".

The "experience" would include making sets for the skits, taking part in the skits, and often times, trying out the beds in each others rooms. If their mothers only knew.

Through the good offices of my Uncle Andrew, who was the headwaiter at this resort, I worked at the Woodlawn

Villa during the summer of my sixteenth birthday. Evenings, after we had cleaned our tables and reset them for breakfast, we were permitted to mix with the guests in the casino, and to dance or watch the entertainment.

Lo and behold, who should turn out to be the star entertainer that summer, but Aaron Schwatt. Only now he called himself Red Buttons. At first, I was excited at the idea that someone I had gone to school with should be the feature performer. I was soon disillusioned. I couldn't get anywhere near him.

One night, as I was standing in the rear of the casino watching Red doing his rendition of "Sam, You Made the Pants Too Long". I caught the eye of another guest who also had known Aaron from P.S. 44, Rosalyn Schwartz. After that moment of recognition, when we realized we were acquainted, we both turned our eyes towards the stage and started to laugh, each knowing what the other was thinking.

"Red Buttons", the star of the Woodlawn Villa, was avoiding both of us like the plague for fear we would give away his secret. Schwatt was only 17 year old, but he was passing himself off as much older, in order to get the job as top banana. Never mind -- that summer, I learned all his songs and routines and used them to entertain my friends long after.

A year or two later, I ran into Aaron on a street in the Bronx, He was with two other men when I stopped to talk to him and chided him for avoiding me that summer in the mountains. He reacted in typical Red Buttons manner. He didn't try to excuse himself, he didn't even answer me. He proceeded to clown it up, by dancing and gesturing and making nonsense musical sounds. His friends laughed until the tears ran down their cheeks as they followed him up the street, still dancing and clowning. That was typical Red Buttons. He's still doing it, dancing all the way to the bank.

He should be 70 this year, and I wish him many more. We can always use another laugh.

Test Your Memory

OK Bronx movie buffs... heres a chance to test your memories. Can you name the location of these landmark theatres? You'll find the answers on page 21

A. RKO Franklin

B. Castlehill

C. Boulevard

D. Loews Fairmount

E. RKO Fordham

F. Loews Grand

Fordham Baldies
by Martin Schneider

A teachers remembrance of the late 50's was brought back recently after seeing the movie "Good Fellows." At various points in the movie references were made to "Idlewild Airport" (currently Kennedy) and the way certain items could be "obtained", and that conjured up memories of a certain group of students that I had taught.

In my first years of teaching at ROOSEVELT, I found it very easy and enjoyable to relate to my students in a friendly way. I was not much older than my students and was certainly young enough to remember what it was like to be their age, in their situation. I enjoyed my profession, and the kids responded well to my enthusiasm, and hopefully to my teaching.

Most of the kids that I taught were from the Fordham Road section, from Southern Boulevard to as far west a Sedgewick Avenue. As time went on, more of the students would confide in me about their personal and outside activities.

In the course of one of my conversations, I was asked if I "needed anything". This question came from some of my students who were obviously part of a "group" a gang if you will, called the Fordham Baldies. There was no doubt that these were tough kids. They were legendary for such acts as cutting girls pony tails off and generally being an intimidating lot. Almost any kid who wasn't a member was terrified of them. Well, in my naivety, I asked, what do you mean? Their response was, "things like T.V.s, radios, stuff like that." Still not getting the picture, I said "Sure, but what have you got to do with that type of stuff?" Their answer: "We can get you a good deal because stuff like that keeps falling off the trucks at Idlewild, and we like you so what do you say?" I must admit for a split second I still didn't get it, and then it hit me. "Thanks but no thanks" I said, and told them that it was wrong for them to get the stuff and would be equally or perhaps more inappropriate for me to take it. I did explain in some detail why it was wrong, but somehow they could not grasp that concept. For them, this sort of activity was a way of life.

We maintained a good relationship and I always thought that in some future stage in their lives they would change and maybe they did. It wasn't until some time later that I found out that many of the "Baldies" and other gang members were a younger version of a group that "had connections."

My hope as I look back, is that the movie did not mirror any of the later lives of my students from the Bronx.

Classifieds

Personals

P1 • A romantic, kind, considerate interesting male 40-65 who loves to travel, enjoys theatre, dine, and dancing and wants a loving romantic woman to enjoy all of the above.

P2 • Zany female, offbeat, youthful, adventurous woman with a social conscience. Loves rock music, dancing til I drop, camping, outdoors and best of all - PEOPLE! Seeking man w/similarities and strong love of humankind.

P3 • TAFT '48 You? Relative? Friend? Looking for a caring, fun-loving, healthy, marriage-minded male, 38-45, to introduce to a terrific, warm, romantic, family oriented, college grad sister.

P4 • ROOSEVELT '59-Italian, Catholic female, single, alive and well in NYC; wondering about you and how your life has developed since the threshold days of our youth. Interested in good conversation.

P5 • Vivacious, warm, sensitive, intelligent, New York lady who loves life, laughter and love wants to share her life with equal counterpart .

P6 • '57 Graduate (female) loves fishing, camping, boating and ballroom dancing. Petite 5'2" and a size 6. A non-smoker please.

P7 • TAFT '52 widowed Jewish female looking for well-educated, fun-loving, conversationalist. who also enjoys travel, theatre.

P8 • I graduated TAFT in '57 and am a fun-loving, honest, and sincere. Looking for a Queens or L.I. resident who is also fun-loving, honest, and sincere non-smoker.

P9 • Independent, caring, full-loving, great sense of humor, professional lady from Florida wants to meet tall, successful gentleman, ages 48-58. I 'm recently divorced and have a joi de vivae. Believe it! I've never lied to you before!

P10 • TAFT '54-Youthful, intelligent, independent, loving and witty divorced female seeking a fun-loving, sincere, secure and intelligent male. Single for 10 years, ready for a serious relationship.

P11 • TAFT ' 59-Very attractive interior designer, youthful, free spirited, loves to travel, enjoys photography, looking for intelligent spontaneous, multifaceted man who's happy with his life, enjoys people and loves to live.

P12 • Daughter of TAFT graduate '6O, attractive, professional, Jewish female 25, looking to meet a son (25-30) of a former TAFT graduate to quench my thirst for happiness.

P13 • EVANDER graduate single and living in Chicago, travels fairly frequently-and enjoys life to the fullest-If there is a super nice guy who has achieved and doesn't have facades-contact me.

P14 • TAFT '54-Well-Educated, down-to-earth, pretty, chatty widow with eclectic tastes, talents and experiences seeks interesting, hamish man who enjoys films, theatre, music, art or just hanging out.

P15 • TAFT '63 - Attractive, fun-loving, sincere, divorced female seeks warm, sincere, good humored N.Y. or N.J. male to enjoy conversation, dancing, quiet and happy times. Where are you?

P16 Walk this way: PS 104, JHS 82, TAFT HS, BRONX COMMUNITY, Macombs Rd., Featherbed Lane, Harrison Ave. Kingsbridge Rd.; this tall thin, athletic, divorced male seeks pony-tailable female for the right stoop, schoolyard, egg cream, pretzel, stickball game. Contact Kenny Fennessey.

Missing Persons

MP1 • ROOSEVELT GARDEN BOYS-WHERE ARE YOU? Helen Kaplan Bender wants you to know that Beverly Gold, Suzanne Goldman, Helen Kaplan, Diane Billis, Dave Friedman, Stuart Ostrowsky and Betty Zimmerman are still alive. Where are you Chucky Goodman, Leon Ruldolph, Jerry Sussman?

MP2 • "What's playing at the Roxy?" Where are you Ellen Resnick and the cast of Guys and Dolls? Anybody there from TMR Ranachqua Unit C1954-57?

MP3 • CLINTON '66-Friends & acquaintances of David Heller-keep in touch and help me find Joel Bernstock CLINTON ' 66 or Les Bernstock CLINTON ' 64 .

MP4 • ROOSEVELT '65, Barbara Kramer sure would love to know what happened to Beverly Glushakoff and Natalie Ginsburg. I'll pass your info onto Alison Robbins Levine; we're still friends after all these years.

MP5 • EVANDER '63 - Phyllis Meltzer Rothstein - Where are you, Diane Miller? Remember Fordham Rd. and Orchard Beach? Anybody from the Eastchester Projects?(Bouck & Burke Avenues)

MP6 • CLINTON '61 -Eddie Gootzait, where are you? Remember Clinton Pl. and Grand Ave. and Seymour's Candy Store. Contact Richard Rothstein .

MP7 • Where are you, Carol Medina Bonilla and gang? Remember P.S. 82 and the Hill Top Candy Store on Macombs Rd .

MP8 • Lou Zabbia-CLINTON ' 51 would like to find Bob Hills of Olmstead Ave. near Quimby, early to mid 50's . Your brother Al attended ALL HOLLOWS H . S . Would love to hear from anyone who may know your whereabouts .

MP9 • Ben Weissbach CLINTON '58 has been looking for twenty years to have a reunion with Jerry Kantor and Bruce Koyner . Can anybody help?

MP10 • CLINTON '65-Looking for old friends from the 50's and 60's from P.S. 48 and the Hunts Point section of the Bronx.

MP11 • CLINTON '58-Gene Gold is looking for Joyce Levay TAFT '59 from Burnside and Aqueduct Avenues, also, John Erickson CLINTON '58 from 209th St and Hull Ave.

MP12 • TAFT '61-Alice Neuman, Mike Stern, Music Class of J.L. Mott JHS '57-59. Where are you guys? Barbara Forman Iskowitz

MP13 • TAFT '58-May Forman looking for former TAFT grads, JHS 22, PS90 & 88, and people who lived on Marcy Pl.and Sheridan Ave.

MP14 • TAFT '62 -Regrets, I was unable to attend the Bronx HS Reunion at the Concord, but, would welcome contacts from old friends. Write me.

MP15 • CLINTON '62 - Joel Goldberg looking to find Steven Trauman CLINTON '62 from Mt. Eden Ave. with whom he studied with at CCNY Library..also CLINTON '62 Alan Lutrin with whom he played stickball & cut classes for lunch at Schwellers Deli....

MP16 • TAFT' 61 Jeff Weinstein trying to locate Michael Sandler- TAFT '62 from Andrews Ave. Remember playing football on Andrews and making fun of your mother's hamburgers (hockey pucks).

MP17 • Jeff Glatzer-TAFT '61- and JHS 82- Remember stickball on the Concourse-Where are you? Also, Steve Candell TAFT '61 contact Jeff Weinstein 'TAFT' '61 ASAP.

MP18 • David Laser-STUYVESANT '60-We were both in the All City Chorus-contact Myrna Leavitt Goldberg ROOSEVELT '62.

MP19 • Victor 'Chicki' DeVito-CLINTON '60-Myrna Leavitt Goldberg ROOSEVELT '62 would like to find him to talk about dancing to the American Bandstand when we were both in high school.

MP20 • Warren Tockerman CLINTON '60 is looking for Enid Klein Schoen who graduated WALTON in 1958. Please contact.

MP21 • TAFT '60-Janet Goldeberg Auerbach who lived near Tremont would love to get reacquainted with her good friend Joan Leiss TAFT '60.

MP22 • Sheldon Rambler CLINTON '62 wishes to find Stanley Rosen from Tiebout Ave. and CLINTON '62 and also wishes to find Susan Vassoff from Kingsbridge and Concourse and HUNTER '62.

MP23 • Gabe Gruber CLINTON '62 is searching for Alan Kipp CLINTON '62 and Davidson Ave. and Steven Haas (Burnside Ave.) and CLINTON '62

MP24 • Anyone that lived on Kingsbridge Terrace and went to P.S. 86 and EVANDER, please contact Carol Sutton Friedner. She would also like to find Frances Grecco last seen laughing with me in Mrs. Solomon's steno class

MP25 • Anita Kleinbaum TAFT '68 looking to find Wendy Sadovnick ROOSEVELT '68, Mark Holod TAFT '67 and Harriett Schwartz TAFT '68.

MP26 • Marjorie Levy Roberts P.S. 70 - '58, JHS 22 - '60, TAFT '63 and 167th St. & Concourse would love to find Lee Sanders, TAFT '65, last seen in 1970 in the Bronx. He may have moved to Yonkers and possibly to Virginia.

MP27 • Looking for Tommy Kelly TAFT '59, contact Matthew Wallis, owner and developer of Reborn Maternity, NYC, Huntington, Manhasset, Paramus, Livingston, NJ, Westport, CT and Los Angeles.

MP28 • Hal Levy TAFT '56 searching for Natalie Yagudnick last seen at Camp Emanuel summer of 1956.

MP29 • Susan Amerling-Stern (Susan Oppenheimer) of Highbridge, TAFT '59 who is a full professor at BMCC(/CUNY and a certified diver who got engaged 75 feet under the Carribean is looking to find Lenore Auerback of Woodycrest/Nelson Ave.

MP30 • Myrna Gertler TAFT '59-Michael Bruce Gold TAFT '59, where are the "heck" are you? Everyone wants to know how and where you are, especially me. Please appear before our 40th Reunion.

MP31 • Sarah Ball Cohen would like to find the following TAFT '62 friends: Ilene Shifrin, Sara Kaplan, Diane Grill, Sheryl Mazor, David Fenster, Barbara Ferrari, Marcia Levine, Karen Yanegida, Howard Shiller, Renee Turner, Phyllis Ustens, Millie Ross, Madeline Miller, and Diane Glassman.

MP32 • Brenda Ball Levy is looking for Carole Unger, Margie Lucas, Lai Fong Dong, Jackie Brown, and Andy Stern.

MP33 • Hi, remember Kathie Carr? If you do, I live in Ft. Lauderdale now and would love to hear from you.

MP34 • Susan Adler is looking for '59 WALTON, Grads, Gail Stein (Loring Place), Karen Sesky, Maxine Cohen; Music & Art and/or Hunter H.S Grads, Gloria Spilkowitz (Plimpton Ave) and Janice Gutter (Davidson Ave.)

MP35 • Gerald Sheindlin is looking for Patricia Myerson who lived on Sheridan Ave.

MP36 • ROOSEVELT '69-Ilana Zeev-where are you? Former teenage buddy, Barbara Kfefel Sylvester is wanting to make contact. Also, I would like to locate David Adler. Many years have passed since I wore the red pants outfit on prom night. All is very well; hope you are too, friend.

MP37 • TAFT '51 - Where are you Rita Webber

and Phyllis Goldberg? Remember the hours spent doubting if we would ever marry and leave the Bronx? Write Karel of Walton Ave.

MP38 • TAFT '62 Anne Soskil Greenspan, now South Bay, CA (Silicon Valley) interested in finding out if any former Taftites are in the area.

MP39 • WADE JR. H.S Hebrew class 53-55- also looking for Larry Levine, Stanley Orenstein, Marty Shifrin, Ceilia Weinstein, Linda Bale, Beth Levy, Esther Frank, and Rosemary Bardfeld-contact Carol Ball Teplin.

MP40 • TAFT '56 Joyce Amir Ben-Ezra looking to find Lola Schwartz, Carol Rosen, Mary Ellson TAFT '56. Where are you?

MP41 • David Saltzman, where are you? I remember all the laughs we had and the party in your house. Please contact Linda Nadler Dreishpon, TAFT '56.

MP42 • Judi Peskin, Macombs Rd looking to find Marilyn Visconti Guberman last seen in 1964. Known to have moved to Princeton, NJ area.

MP43 • CLINTON '56- Along with my brothers Alan and Dan, looking for Harrison Ave. stickballers from the 50's and early 60's. Remember P.S. 26, J.H.S. 82, Park Plaza theatre Contact Howard Silver.

MP44 • TAFT '57 - Where are you, Carol Feld, Wilma Mishkin, Dorothy Goldstein, Linda Wishnik, etc.? Remember great times at the 92nd St. Y'? Rita Levy lives! Let's talk! Let's laugh! Let's complain!

MP45 • I am seeking the whereabouts of Howard Negrin. He lived at 1411 Townsend Ave. and I believe went to SCIENCE in '52. Contact Joan Kaplan .

MP46 • Bobby Nahama, TAFT '62 or '63, last seen in Fort Lee, NJ. Interested party, Jeff Heller.

MP47 • Steven Kreiss is looking for the following: Steven Feldman TAFT '62 (basketball team), Harvey Castro TAFT '62 (went to CCNY), Ellen Jacobs TAFT '62 and Betty Ettman TAFT '64 or '65.

MP48 • TAFT '65-Roosevelt Garden Crowd-That was the place where we hung out. Looking for those who remember the great times. Contact Steve Bayern, Ricky Moldan.

MP49 • TAFT '60-Janet Goldenberg Auerbach looking for Joan Leiss. Lived near Tremont Ave. We were good friends. I would love to get reacquainted.

MP50 • Class of TAFT '61. Susan Ehrenreich - Where are you? We heard that you might be in Colorado, Anita Weiss 'TAFT '60.

MP51 • TAFT '53 - Where is Marvin Zeichner? East coast or West coast? Barbara Salant is looking for former "Taft Review" buddy, '63.

MP52 • ROOSEVELT & COLUMBUS HS and all my friends from Pelham Bay & White Plains Rd. contact Cindi Silverman Bayer.

MP53 • Looking for former Bronxites or Taftites who are now living in Colorado. I 'm near Denver. Also, I would like to find friends from TAFT '63 especially Michelle (Harris) Rosenthal, Helen (Waldman) Rummel, Gloria Krinsky, Francine Shuman. Contact Rosalie Paikin Richter

MP54 • Can anyone help me find Ivan Goldstein. Graduated CLINTON ' 57. Last seen living on Creston Ave. & Fordham Rd in 1962. Contact Goldie Rosner

MP55 • Anita Pomerantz Gore TAFT '60 looking for Marsha Fried TAFT '60 & Barbara Asch TAFT '59 .

MP56 • Susan Goldman Schwartz TAFT '62 hopes to hear from Karen Lieb TAFT '62

MP57 • Marcia Grossman Fox 'TAFT' looking for Rhoda Jaeger (Popham Ave), Sheila Wittenberg (Macombs Rd), Sandy Screiber (Davidson Ave & MUSIC & ART) and Julia Mitchell (Nelson Ave).

MP58 • TAFT ' 58-Rosalind (Roz) Katz would enjoys hearing from the gang she lost touch with .

MP59 • Steven Kreiss TAFT '62 is looking to find Neil Raphael (College & 171st), Betty Etman (170th & Concourse) Harvey Castro TAFT '62 last seen at CCNY.

MP60 • TAFT '60-Sheila Mencher has not seen Rita Fox from TAFT '62 and 167th off Concourse. Any help would be appreciated.

MP61 • Where are you'? Annette Weiss from Harrison Ave. TAFT '53, Audrey Engel, TAFT '53, Rhoda Silverstein, Annette, Evelyn Joseph from Morris Ave., Isaac Francis, originally from Grant Ave. Renee Weinberg Strauss wants to get in touch.

MP62 • Does anyone know where the following people are? Bette Flaks, Marty Zafman, Hal Welner, Normy Schatzoff

MP63 • Joel Goldberg Cinton '62 looking for Steve Taubman Taft' 62 from University Ave.

MP64 • Desperately seeking Phil Winkler, Bobby Mazur, Marty Conkiel, and Joel the Lizard (Hunter-Lehman)-Student Freak Committee gathering the tribe-Contact Buck Paradise, Joan (Luca) Leibowitz, Joan (Shirley Goodvibes) Lotz, & Arthur Kushner

MP65 • Myron Buchman would love to find Marble Hill survivors Ira Shapiro, Linda Wolf, Elaine Mandel, Paula Goldberg, Helene Kursman; How many guys still have their Mr. Shea box?

MP66 • Barbara Gurkin would love to hear from ang graduates of WADE JHS '62 or ROOSEVELT '65 who remember how great it was growing up in the Bronx and would love to relive some of those times.

MP67 • WALTON , Class of 1962. Remember our graduation at Carnegie Hall? Roberta Recht, Linda Roemer, Mildred Klein, and all my friends. Where are you now? Let's write and reminese after all these years. Contact Susan Stamm.

Classifieds

MP68 • 181st St. Grand Concourse, Valentine Ave. & 182nd St. Leo's Candy Store, Ryer Ave 181st St. Did you spend time in my apartment? Girls? Please contact Howie Simon

MP69 • Norm and Shelli Glaser looking for Simone & Buddy to say thanks for bringing them together 9/14/57.

MP70 • Phil Greenberg, CLINTON '59, currently lives in Chicago looking for Alan Skolnick, CLINTON '60, and Bruce Falcamata, SCIENCE. Also where are you Gary Bitter, Kenny Schnitzer, Mel Stanger and the others of our group?

MP71 • Elaine Dunetz of the "Morris Ave Group" looking to find Ned Truss who graduated CLINTON '56 and went onto Pratt.

MP72 • Roberta McDonald (Torres) looking for anyone from Clarke Place. Concourse. "Our Crowd-Years 1958-61"

MP73 • Looking for Marty Meadow. You and I lived in adjoining buildings on Popham Ave. and West 176th Street. I lived there during the years 1962-65. I would like to meet with you. Contact Maralee Sirota

MP74 • TAFT '63 Elaine (Hyman) Adler hopes to hear from Marsha Berkowitz, Steve Bussell, Gloria Krinsky, Regina Linder, Dale Maltz, Anita Obsgarten, Tina Perrin, Ronni Rothenberg, Sam Russo, Beverly Schnall, Paaulette Schrager, Leslie Steigman and any other wonderful TAFT '63 classmates.

MP75 • Margot (Wolf) Feldman - TAFT '53 and Sol Feldman-TAFT '50 invite contact from old friends. Where are you Marilyn Yomtov-TAFT '53 and Debbie Wolf-TAFT '53? SAVONS? Grant Avenue Gang? We would love to hear from you.

MP76 • Lou Zabbia-P.S. 36, JHS 125, CLINTON '57 looking for Bob Hills (Olmstead Ave near Quimby). Denny Wandel (above Babes' Candy Store-Castle Hill and Watson) Anyone know whereabouts?

MP77 • CLINTON '57-NYU '62-Matt Berliner would like to find: Mah Wallack, Bernie Beiser, Mickey Cohen or Ed Peskin (NYU '62)

MP78 • Lenore Mandelbaum Sattler TAFT '57, JHS 22-Sheridan Ave & 169th St.-looking to find Harvey Ashe, Wade Mt. Eden Ave. Where are you and Hank of 170th St. & Grand Concourse.

MP79 • Phyllis Wasserman (Mittler) Concourse and 170th St., class of TAFT '61, where are you? I've thought about you over the years. Remember Rockaway Phissyl? Please contact Janice Niederman Cohen, TAFT '60.

MP80 • TAFT '60 Iris Kemler Burnham would like to contact Dianne Pardo.

MP90 • TAFT '59, Myrna Garfinkel Petrello seeking whereabouts of Daniel Biegelman. Anyone having information on his whereabouts. Please contact me.

MP91 • Would love to hear from Maija Bankhaus & Erika Wedikind of Macombs JHS '58 and others from JHS and TAFT '61. Anyone in Brooklyn??!!! CONTACT Barbara Reiner

MP92 • Greetings to my neighborhood pals from Sedgwick House, 1956-1969. Remember the Community Center in building 1551 University Ave. at 174th St. Regards, Barry Bealick, CLINTON '69.

MP93 • Joel Shapiro (TAFT '58) seeks his old Bx Y friends (Club BVDS) and any old Bronx "Blue Rillerss". Joel is still at Blue Rill after all these years.

MP94 • Irving Kalet (TAFT '57) looking for Carole Steinholtz (PS 90, JHS 22)-I live in Israel, would like to meet any classmates who visit Israel. Also looking for Owen Goldwyn and Lloyd Arlind.

MP95 Becca Tussin Hoover, TAFT '62, now Los Angeles, CA, interested in finding out if any former Taftites, JHS '82 or Davidson Ave. acqaintances are in Southern California.

MP96 • Alan Rosenberg looking for an old friend David Seifer (son of bookstore owner) TAFT '60. Where are you now?

MP97 • Jackie Gisbert Nadal, TAFT '60 looking for Riva Lipton, Michele Furman, and Phyllis Wollman, all TAFT '60. Please contact me.

MP98 • Myrna Leavitt, ROOSEVELT '62 looking to find Nancy Jeremiah of EBB and Roosevelt '62.

MP99 • Joel Goldberg looking for Naomi Levy, Roosevelt '62, Eileen Koch, (Shorehaven), Carrie Siegel-Roosevelt '62 (lived on Phelan Pl.) Please contact.

MP100 • Looking for Members of DELKONS CLUB from 167th ST YMYWHA. Call Elaine (Markowitz)) Nachshen. WALTON HS graduates-send in your names. We need our school represented.

MP101 • Marion Elbert Goldberg TAFT '58 says hi to her old friends the Dominoes-She and Sandy Goldberg TAFT '55 have been married for 27 years.

MP102 • Yonkel (All Schoolyard) Where are you? Also, others from JHS 44 area. Contact William Kent.

MP103 • Anderson Avenue People-Contact Richard Fuchs. We're looking for Alan Kordin, Joey Kost, Harold Epstein, Tom Lowe, Harvey Kash, Lenny Lipka, Sandy Cohen, Morty Zuckerman, Burt Resnick, Neil Rosnthal, Harold Schwartz, Malman Adelman, Billy Goodman, among others.

MP104 • I am trying to find the whereabouts of a Murray (Moe) Golub who lived at 770 E. 178th St-graduated '57 or '58. Contact Morton Garfinkel.

MP105 • UAWMF! CLINTON '69. Where's the old neighborhood? Barry Nelson, CLINTON '69.

MP106 • Jackie Gisbert Nadal, TAFT '60 looking for Riva Lipton, Michele Furman, and Phyllis Wollman, all TAFT '60. Please contact me.

MP107 • CLINTON '58, Jerry Vogel is looking for any old buddies or from the old neighborhood, West Burnside Ave. and 179th St.

MP108 • NOC-OUTS, where are you? JHS 22 TAFT and WALTON contact Arlyne Weiss Beck, TAFT '59.

MP109 • TAFT '61 Barry Dratel, TAFT '63 Susan Sorokoff Dratel. We will be celebrating our 25th this year! Richie Glaser, TAFT '61, where are you?

MP110 • 198th St. Gang we're looking for guys and girls who lived there. We have had reunions for the past 13 years. We have been written up in the Daily News and on TV. Contact Joe Ricevuto.

MP111 • ROOSEVELT '65-Barbara Resnicoff Kramer and Alison Robbins Levine would love to find out whatever happened to Beverly Glushakoff and Natalie Ginsberg. Any other old friends of Barbara or Malcolm Kramer (CLINTON '65) or Alison out there? Foe needn't reply.

MP112 • Missing persons-Any TAFT '55 grads living in Houston TX. Would love to exchange stories. Would also love to hear from Elaine Resnick, Claire Smilowitz, or Lenore Bloom. Contact Sheila Wolfe- Knipe.

MP113 • Where are you guys and gals from Jesup Ave., Featherbed Lane, Macombs Rd., PS 104, JHS 82 from 40's and 50's. Contact Joel Adler.

MP114 • Where are the girls from Capri Houseplan? (Hunter College). Roberta Goldman, Elena Lopez, Paula Kleinbaum, Hazel Saffer, Gail Podolsky, Marge Auletta, Joan Sandler, Harriet Kern, Elaine Samelson. Miss anyone? Contact Phyllis Meltzer Rothstein, HUNTER '67

MP115 • Looking for anyone born or raised on Edward L. Grant Hwy. in the Bronx for a reunion in 1990. Please contact Ellen Howowitz.

MP116 • Where are all the guys and girls from Grand Ave.? (Behind Loews Grand off Fordham Rd.) Doris Kornbluth, Carol and Ira Garber, Howie Melvin, Adrienne Friedman Teitelbaum living in Fla., Carol Gantwag (Valentine Ave.).

MP117 • CLINTON '52-"Toppers" Baseball Team Reunite! Manny, Marty, Julie, Larry, Bobby & Gerry, Leon, Allen & Stan. Let's hear from you all. Contact Len Mechner.

MP118 • Judy Goldner-TAFT '67-Last seen in Forest Hills. Please contact: Elly Garfinkel Mendelsohn.

MP119 • Eileen Goldberg looking for Iris Baker and Howard Essenfeld- Tremont and University Avenues.

MP120 • TAFT '50 Grads-let's get together-contact me, Zelda Prensky.

MP121 • Frank Martocci, CLINTON '52, would like to contact Richard Sems of 194th St. & Marion Ave.-also Tony "44" Yaconetti of Marion Ave. Remember Orchard Beach Tony "444" Lifeguards-1952-56. Get in touch. Frank

MP122 • CLINTON '65 Michael "Dirty Shoes" Bloom looking for members of Scholarship School. Living in the wilds of Oregon and also looking for fellow Clintonite Oregonians.

MP123 • Robert (Bobby) Johnson, CLINTON '53, PS 73 '49 would like to hear from any old classmates from PS 73. Jack Ross, Herb Rosen, Geo. Schueren, Harvey Kash, John Kokish, Carole Brenner, Etta Giattenberg, Doris Koran, Jane Trattner, & Adrienne Madoff, to name a few.

MP124 • TAFT '58, Robert Woll is looking for old friends from the old neighborhood. Also PS 70, WADE and CCNY. I am upstate now and I haven't changed a bit!!

MP125 • Cheryl Gavard, TAFT '70 looking for Arlene Klein, Steven Bock, Stephanie Brown, Marilyn Serlin, or anyone who hung out on Macombs Rd. or Davidson Ave. or Fordham's Poe Park or even Kingsbridge!

MP126 • Cheryl Bard, TAFT '65 looking for Carol Straczek from Shakespeare Ave. and Edie Fertig from Gerard Ave. Are you still out there? Let's get in touch!

MP127 • Andy Kalmanson of 1405 Townsend Ave. is looking for Eden Weiss, Tommy Dodorian, and PS 64 classmates.

MP128 • DWC Miss Razzari Italian Club-Scrafano, Patrici, Signorile Stein, Schwartz et al, where are you? Contact Ed Corvelli.

MP129 • Who drove a Bungalow Bar truck with me in 1958, 1959 or a Mister Softee truck out of the Bruckner Blvd. garage in 1959, 60, 61 (Fink??) Who was assaulted with me on Veteran's Day 1955 by the Fordham Baldies in Van Cortlandt Park? Contact Norman Mazza

MP130 • Judy Visconti Sumin would like to find her long-time best friend, Gina Russell Walters, TAFT '59.

MP131 • Marty Faber looking for Gilbert Katz. Where are you?

MP132 • Lichtenstein sisters, (TAFT) Carla and Rhoda looking for anyone who remembers the Sedgwick Projects or the Bronx "Y" late 50's early 60's.

MP133 • I'm interested in finding Daniel Constantino (formerly of 198th St. in the Bronx). He's a 1970 graduate of SCIENCE. Also Jack Bulko, CLINTON '70. Contact Otie Ka Votie.

MP134 • Shelby Landesberg would like to find Arlene Suckow (last known as Arlene Pressman) and the Landesberg Boys (Ronnie, Mitchell, Glen) from Andrews Ave. Any info.?

MP135 • Sam Verga, CLINTON '64. Where are you guys? Remember Mosholu Pkwy; the schoolyard of JHS 80; Knox and Gates Place; Bainbridge Gardens; Rochambeau Ave? Let's reminisce.

MP136 • Would like to hear from those who belonged to the teen group at the Hebrew Institute of University Hts.-University & E. Tremont

Ave.-'56-'58. Also, Irv Cordover & Jerry Silverman. Where are you? Contact Charles Ludwin.

MP137 • Herb Schenk-TAFT '51 looking for fellow graduates from the "Fifties" living in south Florida. So far I've found Marilyn Messinger and Stu Reich. I'd love to hear from others.

MP138 • Betty Flaks is looking for Vickie Dresner who lived on Gerard Ave. and went to TAFT.

MP139 • Looking for people who lived on Commonwealth Ave., Rosedale Ave., St. Lawrence Ave., and surrounding areas during the 50's and also attending P.S. 47 and Blessed Sacrament.

To Reply to one of these ads, Call 914-592-1647. Please have the ad number (ex:MP48) at hand when you call, and we will promptly direct you to the appropriate party.

Be a Part of our Next Issue

If you would like to meet new people, or find old friends, we are willing and able to help. Just turn to the back page and fill out the reader reply card. Use the envelope provided and send your information to us today. We'll get working on it right away. All submissions will be printed in our next issue on a first come first serve basis so please don't delay, Reply today! We'd love to hear from you!

Test Your Memory

A. 161st St.

B. Castle Hill Rd.

C. Southern Boulevard near Westchester Ave.

D. Tremont Ave.

E. Fordham Rd. & Valentine Ave.

F. Fordham Rd. & Jerome Ave.

This issue's Mystery Bronxites

1. Eydie Gorme

2. Judd Hirsch

3. Penny Marshall

What a Weekend!

The Bronx High Schools Reunion Weekend

Two Hours of Memories $29.95!

Nostalgia reigned on the weekend of March 23 thru 25th as the Bronx of the 50's and 60's came to life at the beautiful Concord Hotel. A thousand Bronx high school alumni gathered at the Concord Hotel for a weekend of excitement, meeting new friends and reaquainting themselves with old friends. It was the first annual Bronx High Schools Reunion Weekend and now you can capture all the fun and excitement of this unique weekend. Those who did not attend will have the opportunity to find long lost friends, and perhaps learn why the next reunion will be an event that should not be missed. You'll see stickball and basketball games, a sock hop, a unique version of the newlywed game, a video tour of all the Bronx high schools as they appear today, and much more!

Sweatshirts and T's from your Alma Mater

Bronx High School Sweatshirt (Size L only.)

ONLY **$16.00**

Bronx High School T-Shirt (Size XL only.)

ONLY **$10.00**

We will special order any sweats or T's for the other Bronx High Schools. A minimum order of 10 shirts is required.

Order your video and T-shirts on Page 16

READER REPLIES
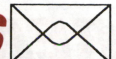

It is vitally important that you fill out the information below. Your input will be essential to the success of this magazine, tailored and inspired by you, the former "Bronxite". We thank you for your participation.

Subscriber? ☐ Yes   ☐ No

YOUR NAME _____

ADDRESS _____

CITY _____ STATE _____ ZIP _____ PHONE _____

HIGH SCHOOL ATTENDED _____ YEAR GRADUATED _____

TELL US A LITTLE ABOUT YOURSELF,
(Be sure to include your alma mater, old neighborhood, your best memories about your days in the Bronx, (or anything else you can tell us).

_____

_____

COULD WE SEND A FRIEND A FREE COPY OF BACK IN THE BRONX?

Do you know current or former Bronxites who would like to receive our magazine and reunion information?
If you do, we'll be happy to send them a **free** inaugural issue of **Back in THE BRONX**.
Write to Back in The Bronx, Box 141 H, Scarsdale, NY 10583 or call 1-800-7-BRONX 5

Last	First	Maiden
Address	City	State	Zip
Phone # ( )	School and year of Graduation		

Last	First	Maiden
Address	City	State	Zip
Phone # ( )	School and year of Graduation		

Last	First	Maiden
Address	City	State	Zip
Phone # ( )	School and year of Graduation		

Last	First	Maiden
Address	City	State	Zip
Phone # ( )	School and year of Graduation		

COME BLOW YOUR OWN HORN DEPARTMENT

Please tell us about yourself (include your name)—about your accomplishments, awards, titles or works in progress. We're interested in hearing about them. List Below. _____

_____

_____

_____

READER REPLIES

As a subscriber you are entitled to a FREE 40 Word Classified, Missing Persons, Blow Your Own Horn, or Personal Ad. Please write your ad below (if you are not subscribing to our magazine you can still place an ad in the next issue. The cost of an advertisement is 50¢ a word, there is no limit on paid ads).

_____

_____

_____

Is Your Mailing Label Correct?

In order to keep our database current, please correct any errors and place the label and or photocopy with corrections.

Account #	High School	Year Graduated

6817   Roosevelt   1958
SAMPLE
Mary R. Flowers
123 Anystreet Blvd.
Anywhere, USA 12345

Change of Address?

If you're planning a move please attach your label corrected with your new address and the date that you will begin receiving mail at that address. This will insure that you don't miss your next issue of **Back in THE BRONX.**

Ordering Information

A Great Gift Idea! In addition to your own subscription, a subscription to **Back in THE BRONX** makes a great and unique gift. Fill in the form below and we'll process the order in time for our next issue. So, order your subscription NOW, and order one for a friend!

YES, I'd like to order the following items:

QTY.

____ 1Yr. (4 ISSUES) Subscription(s) to **Back in THE BRONX** $19.95
____ 2Yr. (8 ISSUES) Subscription(s) to **Back in THE BRONX*** .. $29.95
____ 3Yr. (12 ISSUES) Subscription(s) to **Back in THE BRONX*** } *FREE Jahn's Menu* .. $39.95
____ 4Yr. (16 ISSUES) Subscription(s) to **Back in THE BRONX*** .. $49.95
____ The Beautiful Bronx...........$25.00 (plus $3.95 S/H) $28.95
____ The Bronx: It Was Only Yesterday..$25.00 (plus $3.95 S/H) $28.95
____ Bronx High School Reunion Weekend Video $29.95
____ SAVE MONEY - BUY 4 FOR JUST $99.00!
____ THE BRONX Tracking Service $9.95
____ I would like to receive all available back issues and have them applied towards my subscription *(To date we have at least 12 back issues available - While They Last!)*

TOTAL: $ _____

Please fill out completely and include $3.95 for shipping and handling for books only to: **Back in THE BRONX**, Box 141H, Scarsdale, NY 10583

Please Print Clearly ❑ New Subscriber ❑ Renewal

Name _____

Maiden Name _____

Address _____

City _____

State _____ Zip _____

Phone (   ) _____

High School _____ Year Grad. ____

❑ Visa ❑ Mastercard ❑ Check ❑ Money Order

No. _____ Expiration Date ____

Signature _____

Back in THE BRONX

Box 141 H, Scarsdale, NY 10583
Phone 914-592-1647 • Fax 914-592-4893

ADDRESS CORRECTION REQUESTED

Volume I   Issue III

Back in THE BRONX

Celebrating the experience of growing up and living in the Bronx

Making Out — A Bronx Tradition

by Merrill Lamb, Taft H.S. '58

Let's face it. The single greatest... most unforgettable, most enjoyable activity we did as kids growing up in the Bronx was "making out". What was better than "making out" for an hour and a-half to two hours? When was the last time you made out with your husband or wife for two hours?

Think back to a cold, overcast Bronx day in the winter of 1958. It's about 4 o'clock in the afternoon and it's you and her alone in her apartment. She's dressed in a tight sweater, a lot of perfume, make-up and teased hair. She puts a record on, the turntable drops down and then you hear that music. It's Johnny Mathis, and he's singing;

"It's heavenly, heavenly.

That's how it feels when you're with me."

Your heart is pounding and you pray that nobody rings the doorbell for at least an hour.

I always thought that Bronx girls really made out great. I once went to a place called Forest Hills and the girls didn't quite have "it". (Maybe they had too much money.) I don't know about Brooklyn girls because who ever went to Brooklyn. At that time I thought Brooklyn was near South Carolina. When I got out of High School I was surprised to find out

Brooklyn was so close to New York.

The most looked-up-to guys in school were the high scorers of the basketball team and the guys who "made out" with all the girls. It was debatable as to which guy worked harder at his trade. The "make out" guys were always dressed nice, were good dancers and were always on the lookout for their "prey". Their biggest thrill was to come back to the pool room after their session and have somebody ask them: "How was Linda?" "Linda, I *made out* with her." Bingo, end of conversation, he "made out" with her. Another one bites the dust. What a cool guy. His reputation as a make-out artist intact.

So here I am having already pushed 50, being happily married to a fantastic lady for 27 years but, hey, if Irene Schiff, Harriet Meltzer, Judy Schiffman or Lena Tenuzzi (whom I never made out with but wished I did) read this and want to give me a call, I got maybe 5 to 10 good minutes left in me. We could put a little Johnny Mathis on and hear:

"I can only give you love that lasts forever and the promise to be near each time you call and the only heart I own, is for you and you alone,

THAT'S ALL, THAT'S ALL...

From the Editors...

Welcome to the third issue of Back in the Bronx!

We would like to thank our readers for the wonderful response to our requests for interesting stories and anecdotes about the good times they remember from their days in the Bronx. We have received many great stories and we will try to use them all, in whole or in part in this and upcoming issues. Your continued participation in this unique newsletter assures that we can all continue to share the happy memories of growing up in the best place on earth, the Bronx of the forties, fifties and sixties.

In addition to the stories we are in need of photos, news clippings of the era, and other visual memorabilia. We assure you that if you send it to us we will return it promptly and intact.

We would like to thank all those who attended the Concord reunion weekend, and to those who didn't, you missed a great time! We are planning several other events and hope that you won't miss out on the fun!. Among the possibilities are a Yankee Game, a cruise, and more. We encourage you to sign up for these events when plans are finalized. The old saying is true, "The more...the merrier"!

We hope you enjoy this issue of Back to the Bronx, and when your finished reading it, share it with a friend! That is how our database has grown and con-tinues to grow. The more subscribers we have, the more we can do for you!

Susan J. Samtur

Stephen M. Samtur

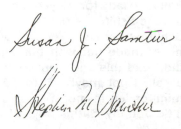

Back in the BRONX

Publishers and Editors	**Stephen M. Samtur**
	Susan H. Samtur
Art Director	**Thomas R. Hamilton**
	Herald Graphics Inc, Stratford Ct

A number of the photographs in Back in the Bronx are courtesy of and available from the Bronx Historical Society

Take Beverly Hills—*PLEASE*

While you are more likely to be winged by a stray bullet on the Grand Concourse than on Rodeo Drive, people in the South Bronx have a higher moral standard than residents of Beverly Hills, according to a recently published book.

Statistics in a chapter of "The Day America Told The Truth" that compares the two communities show:

People in Beverly Hills are twice as likely to use illegal drugs (38 percent) as are the residents of the South Bronx (17 percent).

People in Beverly Hills are much more likely to have an extramarital affair than are people living in the Bronx.

Child abuse is just as common in Beverly Hills as in the South Bronx.

The average resident of Beverly Hills is four times as likely to own a gun as the average resident of the South Bronx.

Twice as many people in Beverly Hills as in the South Bronx reported that they had actually shot somebody.

The 46 percent of people in the South Bronx who give to charity contribute more of their income than the 70 percent of Beverly Hills residents who give to charity.

People in Beverly Hills are much more willing to impose the death penalty on criminals; 43 percent said they would execute an insane person; 27 percent have no objection to executing the mentally retarded; and 23 percent would execute a 10-year-old criminal.

Neither the book nor James Patterson, one of its authors, specified exactly how many people were interviewed in each community for the survey. But the book put the figure in the "hundreds". Patterson said the survey for this chapter, unlike other surveys for the rest of the book, was conducted by phone.

"I think what it shows is that stereotypes of wealth and lack of wealth...(are) not a direct comparison of somebody's morals," said Clint Roswell, a spokesman for Bronx Borough President Fernando Ferrer. "In other words, it doesn't translate. Whether you're rich or you're poor is not what makes you a good person or not."

(From a Newsday Editorial)

In our last issue we heard a somewhat negative view of Freedomland. As with most things there are two sides to every story and in this issue we hear from someone with fonder memories of the big park.

Standing Up for Freedomland

by Bob Mangels

One of the Bronx's major accomplishments for too long has been criticized unfairly, inaccurately written about and in general given a bad reputation by some misinformed authors. As a former resident of the Bronx, and a long time amusement park fan, let me very easily state: Freedomland USA was one of the best theme parks ever built. I'm not alone in these thoughts either, having talked to many folks with nothing but the best of memories of this park that was bigger than Disneyland, and featured many similar attractions, and even surpassed Disneyland with others.

I would point out that the Freedomland of 1960 (shaped like the United States), is better than many parks of 1991! Keep in mind that Freedomland was open for five years and added attractions each year to increase it's appeal.

Some who have pointed out that Freedomland was too educational, that people didn't go to amusement parks for that reason, should think about EPCOT in Orlando.

Freedomland was such a great park that let you explore little old New York with its stores; ride the New York harbor tug boats; visit the Schaeffer Brewery; ride the horse-drawn street cars; in old Chicago, fight the Chicago fire every twenty minutes; ride the two river boats, the American and Canadian in the Great Lakes; ride the Sante Fe train (authentic trains with enclosed coaches), or in the Fort Cavalry catch a stage coach; nearby visit Elsie the cow at the farm with Elsie and her calves in lavish settings that included a bed! Freedomland also was one of the first parks to feature the bucket sky ride called Ore Buckets. Freedomland was the only place and still is to this day the first to have two ore buckets traveling in each direction. In San Francisco, complete with Chinatown and Fisherman's Wharf, was the Earthquake ride. One of the best boat rides anywhere was the Northwest Furtrappers boat, complete with falling bridges, Indians, a skeleton city and more. Add to this a burro train, a mine cavern ride, gunfights, Western stores, a Casa Loca house that defied gravity—and you're still not done. In New Orleans, experience the Civil War in an outdoor ride: see the Blue and Grey battle it out with explosions all around you. The Buccaneer ride, a great pre-Disney Pirates of the Caribbean adventure, was great and very similar in nature. Danny the Dragon gave a tour of children's stories. The Tornado ride, an indoor ride that offered you the experience of being caught in a twister in the Louisiana area.

Satellite City featured: a flying saucer that seated 250 to experience a trip over the Western hemisphere through simulation (now popular at Disney World and other parks) and the Satellite City Turnpike, where you could drive cars or visit the buildings of space exhibits. The Moon Bowl featured many big name performers and one of the largest outdoor dance floors made of wood: a span over 15,000 square feet. All this was a part of Satellite City. Yet another Freedomland attraction was the nightly 15 minute fireworks show. This is only a sampling of what the world's largest outdoor entertainment center offered.

When Freedomland closed after the 1964 season and the announcement came that Co-op City would be built, I was, to say the least, very upset, and I continue to be so to this day—for many reasons.

First of all, the park still could have existed with Co-op being built! The majority of Co-op City was built on Freedomland's parking lot! In fact, after 23 years, construction started for a mall and industrial park on what was Freedomland. Furthermore, when that infamous announcement was made that Co-op City was to be built it was also reported that the operators of Freedomland had planned to keep the park open by reducing the size of the park to 30 acres. This never happened as we all know, but there are some odd situations concerning the clos-ing of the park.

As far as Co-op City is concerned, it has had its problems as a replacement for Freedomland. The company in charge went bankrupt and state taxpayers have had to come to the rescue. When water gave out a few years ago it was discovered that Co-op City had been using Freedomland's intricate water system.

I'm sure after reading this you can see that this is one Bronxite who will tell anyone, whenever the topic arises, that the Bronx had one of the best amusement parks ever built, Freedomland U.S.A.

FREEDOM LAND U.S.A.

FUN!

Note: The author is a morning personality on 99.3 FM K-LITE Radio in Ellenville, NY and also an amusement park fan, who has located where some of Freedomland's attractions are now featured. The author is interested in hearing from fellow Freedomland fans (914) 647-5678.

Reminiscing

The Concourse
by Betty Bruges

My son, who knows how nostalgic I am, recently sent me a subscription to Back in the Bronx. Although I'm a James Monroe graduate (June '32), I know the best Bronx area near Taft very well. When I was married, in 1940, we lived on Grand Ave. near 174th St. Then in 1943 we moved to Sheridan Ave. near 165th St., where we lived until 1967, after my husband died. So all my memories center about the Concourse, the Joyce Kilmer Park, 161st St., etc. My husband and I took evening courses in the Adult Education Center at Taft for several years.

The enclosed snapshot was taken on the Concourse, somewhere near 165th St.—I think probably outside the senior citizen residence (we called it an Old Age Home then) between 165th St. and McClellan St.

...from Another View
by Ira Schwartz, MD

Your notice about the 2nd reunion at the Concord just arrived— as my first indication about *Back in the Bronx*.

The memories are fine, but I wouldn't want to go back now! I grew up near Pelham Parkway (early) and the Tremont/Concourse area (later); attended PS 28, JHS 117 and Science High (1950). The list I'm providing are former Bronxites whom are relatives and friends.

The old photo, circa 1950, is from the rooftop of 1900 Grand Concourse facing northwest. It was clean and uncrowded in those halcyon days!

Someday I'm going to be...

These fine young Bronxites moved on to fame and fortune.
Can you guess the names of this talented trio of former Bronxites?
The answer is on page 19. (Don't turn right to the answer, that's cheating!)

Mystery Bronxite #1 **Mystery Bronxite #2** **Mystery Bronxite #3**

Bronx Honor Roll

Bronxites who have achieved!

Bronx Science
Edggar Doctorow
Bobby Darren
Stokely Carmichael

Cardinal Hayes
George Carlin
Regis Philbin
Rocky Colovito
Kevin Loughery

DeWitt Clinton
James Baldwin
Paddy Cheyefsky
Daniel Shore
Neil Simon
Richard Rogers
Fats Waller
Don Adams
Martin Balsam
Judd Hirsch
Stubby Kaye
Robert Klein
Burt Lancaster
Jan Murray
Jimmie Walker
Nate Archibald
Dolph Shayes
James Caan

Evander Childs
Red Buttons
James Coco
Carl Reiner

Monroe
Hank Greenberg
Ed Kranepool
Jules Pfeiffer

Morris
Gabe Pressman
Angel Cordero

Roosevelt
June Allison

Taft
Eydie Gorme
Stanley Kubrick
Sanford Brown

Other notable folks with ties to the Bronx

Charles Osgood
Vic Damone
Bess Myerson
Dennis Day
Dion DiMucci
Jonas Salk
Roberta Peters
Jerry Vale
Jake LaMotta
Dianne Carroll
Ron Liebman
Gary Marshall
Al Pacino
Rob Reiner
Eli Wallach
Corazon Aquino
Edward Koch
Vin Skully
Joey Adams
Danny Aiello
Ellen Barkum
Alan Alda
Armand Hammer
Theodore Kheel
George Steinbrenner

Don Criqui
Lauren Bacall
Tony Curtis
Hal Linden
Sal Mineo
Charles Nelson Reilly
Isabel Sanford
Vanessa Williams
Herman Badillo
Ted Kennedy
George Burns
Avery Corman
Norman Cousins
Edgar Alan Poe
Geraldo Rivera
Pat Summerall
Herman Wouk
Teresa Brewer
Cab Calloway
Joey Bishop
Joe Franklin
Penny Marshall
Carroll O'Connor
Connie Selleca
Cardinal Cooke
E. Colin Powell
Robert Kennedy
Leon Cooper (Nobel Prize Winner)
Rosalyn Yallow (Nobel Prize Winner)
Anne Bancroft
Ralph Lauren

Thanks to Dr. William C. Wolfson and The Bronx Society of Science and Letters

Spartans AC

Jerry Young writes us to set things straight—there *were* other gangs besides the Fordham Baldies!

Dear Susan and Stephen,

Hoping that you don't mind my using your first names, I would love to comment on the last issue, Volume I, Issue II. By way of introduction, my name is Jerry Young and I am still a member of the Spartan's AC from the Sherman Ave. PS 90 area of the Bronx.

1. The article about the Fordham Baldies and another bunch of thugs you didn't mention, the "Guinea Duke" should not overshadow some of the true AC clubs that existed in our hometown, the Bronx.

The members of this AC were joined by other clubs, i.e. the Ravens, Skulls, All Stars, Yips and Tigers, just to mention a few that participated in the Mirror Park Department football, basketball and baseball tournaments held at Macombs Dam Park behind Yankee Stadium and also at Mullaly Park on Jerome Avenue. What wars they were.

Every corner had their favorite candy store which served a multipurpose. Just around PS 90 we had four famous candy stores that harbored literally dozens of young men and women. When some of the older guys went to World War II and Korea, their names would be painted on a sidewalk block with hopes that they would return unhurt.

2. To play softball in PS 90 you would have to be signed up by 6:30 AM in the morning both Saturday and Sunday to make the first twenty that played; four outfielders were used.

Basketball, full or half-court, sometimes went on simultaneously. Such former greats as Ed Roman, the Kaplowitzes, (one time Knick) Sid Dawhrot and Howie Stein could be seen playing the afternoon prior to a CCNY game at the Old Garden (need I say more).

Most neighborhoods enjoyed the same sports outlets. PS 90 was open in the evening for HS students who wanted to participate in everything from knock hockey to making out on the steps.

Right before the Korean conflict, the Spartans rented a basement room for all types of events. The room was opened with a big party with the center of attraction being a fluorescent bar that had at least sixty apartments 5 foot bulbs flashing on and off. What a scene!

Team jackets were the dress code and of course if you were going steady the jacket was worn by that special gal.

3. When the Spartans AC first came into existence it was called the Warhawks—bad name, especially if your largest member was 6 feet even as just weighed 160 lbs. We just celebrated our 50th year of being together with a weekend outing in Atlantic City with our friend and one of the Bronx' best known entrepreneurs Budd Friedman, the owner and creator of the Improvisation.

The other point that most of us seem to forget is that most apartment buildings had sixty-five with at least one child per apartment. What a built-in playground.

There are twelve of us that have kept in touch for the past fifty years and here are the names: Morty Zerner, Arty Sandler, Jerry Wertheimer, Joel Silverman of Montgomery, Alabama; Leo Richman, Shelly Klein, Milty Negrin, Budd Friedman of Hollywood, CA; Bryant Berkowitz, Jerry Rosenblatt and myself Jerry (Benny) Young.

We have been looking for Ted Kalichstiem Kole, John Gentilla, Shelly Rutkin and Stan Sacks.

I hope I haven't bored you but there are many more things to remember than the Fordham Baldies.

Jerry Young
Woodmere, NY
(516) 295-1549

Gathering of the Spartans. Standing Left to Right: Mr. and Mrs. Mal Tarkin, Morty Zerner, Joan Hasdara, the author, Milt Hegrin and Mrs. Budd Friedman. Seated: Budd's daughter Zoe, Mr. and Mrs. Jerry Wertheimer.

Mr. and Mrs. Budd Friedman. Budd is wearing his forty-five year old Spartan sweater. Talking about loyalty!

Memories of the Bronx

by Marylin Weber Newman, Walton HS

When I look back now on my growing up in the Bronx, I realize how innocent life was. During the 50's and early 60's, the Bronx was a haven from the rest of the world. There was the cold war with Russia but when my friends and I hide under our desks at PS 86 it seemed very remote.

My early years were on Kingsbridge Road and Sedgwick Avenue. My building was on Sedgwick and 195th Street. I used to wait with my friends for the No. 20 bus in front of the Bronx VA hospital to go to Alexander's on Fordham Road.

Before the supermarket on Kingsbridge and Jerome, there was the Kingsbridge theater where I saw *The Greatest Show on Earth* and *A Star Is Born*. Who can forget the matron who was always nearby to supervise the children's section.

I'll always remember the Kingsbridge Armory where at the age of three, I would run up the steps to the top and pretend it was a stage and sing aloud for all to hear.

When I was in my early and mid-teens, my friends and I "hung out" on the corner of Claflin Avenue and 197th Street. Our summer days were spent at Orchard Beach, but at night there would be a group of about 10 to 20 kids who would talk and sing until it was late and time to go home. Neither we, nor our parents, ever were concerned that something might happen walking home the couple of blocks. Neighborhoods were safe!

As a matter of fact, probably around 1957, a group of us wanted to go see Alan Freed's Rock and Roll show at the Brooklyn Paramount. We walked to the "D" train at the Grand Concourse and Kingsbridge Road and rode the subway to "another country", Brooklyn. After the show we took the train back and walked the route from the Concourse to Sedgwick Avenue on Kingsbridge Road. No one was afraid.

"My early years were on Kingsbridge Road and Sedgewick Avenue."

When I was seventeen we moved to a brand new building on Morris Avenue and 190th Street. It was a 1/2 block from St. James Park and one block from Alexander's. This was where I lived during my senior year at Walton High School.

Many years have passed, but I will always carry those wonderful memories of my growing up years in the Bronx.

P.S.: The girl who became my best friend in my junior year in High School is still my best friend after 31 years, Gloria Kaplan Silverman.

Memories of the Block

by Barrie Brett

What was it like growing up on the BLOCK? The memory of it is wonderful. It was warm, friendly, loving and fun. It was home.

The BLOCK had a center...a connection...that united all who lived in the surrounding six story apartment buildings. Ours was called JOE'S. JOE'S CANDY STORE was the answer to the world around us. It held the secrets of the adult world...who worked where, who had a birthday coming up, who was sick, who was on vacation, who had a fight with their husband or wife and most important...who won the Yankee or Giant game that day!

JOE'S had school notebooks, comic books, red stools and booths. This eating establishment held the BLOCK together. Old and young gathered just to talk, to catch up and to be connected at JOE'S CANDY STORE.

The heart beat of the block was evidenced by the intense feeling of loyalty and FAMILY. Everyone who lived on that BLOCK was united by a common bond of sharing the grey surroundings of 198th street. For everyone heard the elevated train zoom by at early morning and late evening hours. Most everyone on the block had children who attended the same schools, shopped at the same food store, used Loy Wang for laundry and dry cleaning, had Dr. Kay care for their teeth and watched as Larry from 3 East, Loy Wang Jr. from the corner store and cousin Gary get hit by fast moving cars. Not all at the same time, but the screeching of the carbrakes and parents yelling in anguish can still be heard ringing in my ears.

As the ambulance pulled up to take each boy away, it was the embrace of the BLOCK that became family...everyone reaching out for each other, calling from windows with information that each boy would be all right, getting blankets to keep them warm and most important...showing that they cared. When Larry was hit by the car, his mother came down with a warm blanket, not knowing that it was her son who lay stretched silently on the street below.

The BLOCK also had fat Bertha. As she sat by her window, she loomed from her 3rd story apartment as a presence always there ready to swoop. And it was comforting to know that she was there...to see that children crossed the street safely...there to watch out for any strangers who might enter onto our BLOCK and there to leave her window vantage point...knitting bag in hand...sit herself down at 5:00 PM on the dot in her canvas back director's chair placed in the proper street position...to save her

Continued on page 10

7

Theodore Roosevelt High School

500 East Fordham Road, Bronx 58, N.Y.

MISS MARY CLARE CALLAN
Principal

Published monthly by the Department of Publications. Subscription by membership in Theodore Roosevelt Organization.

Friday, June 15, 1962

Vol. LVIII   No. 8

ALAN WITROCK .... Editor-in-Chief
HERBERT FOX .... General News
BEVERLY WINKELMAN .... Features
AVRIL FIEULLETEAU .... Clubs and Departments
PETER REICH .... Boys' Sports
MARILYN SHAWULSKY .... Girls' Sports
ALAN MANDEL, SHERMAN REISCH .... Photographers
TOM CHIFFRILLER .... Business Manager
VINCENT FUSELLI .... Publicity

NEWS STAFF

Dave Bicofsky, Carol Borstein, Phyllis Cohen, Dalio Ehrlich, Harold Ferber, Vincent Fuselli, Judy Geller, Lorraine Gidali, Judy Goldber, Judy Geller, Caryn Jastrow, Jerry Katz, Susan Lent, Harold Lloye, Susan Morin, Eileen Morris, Jane Murphy, Georgia Racano, Leslie Reicher, Ward Riley, Joan Rauchwerg, Barbara Schwartz, Mary Slayton, Merrie Weiss, Judi Zeitlin.

NATALIE SHEIDLOWER, *Literary Adviser* MARIE MINUTO, *Literary Adviser*
GERTRUDE PETERSEN, *Art*   LOUIS LAZARUS, *Business*

75

Produced by ROBIN HOOD PRESS, INC., *New York City*

Buy Hit Records At TRO Store

THE SQUARE DEAL
THEODORE ROOSEVELT HIGH SCHOOL

Vol. LXIII

FRIDAY, APRIL 28, 1967

Boat Ride
Poster Contest
See Page 2

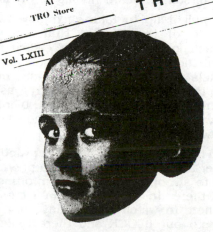

who is more sophisticated?

8

Scrapbook

Free Elvis Presley Photos To Be Given

Free autographed photographs of Elvis Presley in uniform will be available at all Loew's theaters on Saturday. They are being distributed to promote his newest film, "King Creole," currently showing in Loew's State Theater.

Cousin Brucie Accents Youth

COUSIN BRUCIE with SQUARE DEAL's own Celia Schechter and Elizabeth Oliveras.

Diamondmen Beaten In Playoff End Season With An 8-3 Record

9

I *may be living in Las Vegas, but who says my heart is not in the Bronx?*

My personalized Nevada plate depicting my roots.

—Charles Medwin
1065 E. Flamingo Rd. #601
Las Vegas, Nevada
89119
(702) 732-9387
Graduated Clinton June, 1961

A Study of Science
by Joseph Greif, Science '61

I attended Bronx Science, Class of '61, part of the first group into the new building, mural and all (but no swimming pool for the championship swimming team!). As some of you may personally recall, Clinton guys were fond of hanging out after school on the ramp at the north entrance to Science, gawking at the girls and chanting "Science girls wear undershirts." Of course, the guys said that because everyone at Clinton wore undershirts so they assumed everyone at Science did too, including the girls. Well, bad news folks, I must report to you (better late than never) that the Science girls most definitely did not wear undershirts. Sorry, fella...

My home was a half block off Fordham Road, and about two blocks from the Bronx campus of NYU. I had a long walk to the Jerome Avenue subway to get to school, plus of course the walk from the subway to the school. By today's standards in the suburbs, my daily walking would probably qualify me as some kind of athletic eccentric. Then, it was the norm. I would never have had the nerve to ask my parents to actually *drive me* to the subway! They would not have taken me seriously, had I asked! Now, kids who have to walk from their front door further than the mailbox at the curb think nothing of asking for a ride from

The Block (cont.)

son Jerome a parking place for the night. As she knit, It seemed that Madame DeFarge's secrets were being passed on through her colors of yarn, and that fat Bertha was recording the block's happenings in each of her knitted sweaters.

The BLOCK had something else...the foundation for all our childhood games...our sidewalk. Though it was only concrete that formed the sidewalk surrounding our BLOCK, to us, it seemed like much more. To us, it seemed to be a carnival. A mixture of boxes and lines used for playing our ball games, *Hit the Penny, Johnny on the Pony*, potzie, jump rope, roller skating and skooter races, the sidewalk was our playground. These concrete boxes were decorated with both white and colored chalk, and as far as I can remember the BLOCK'S concrete sidewalk witnessed our very first *Simon Says* game, the planting of one tree and the gleeful arrival once a year of the portable amusement ride *"The Whip"*.

Even though this wondrous park bruised many a knee, we never held it responsible and couldn't wait to get outside each day to play and feel that concrete under our feet. It may not have been a fancy jungle gym set with rubber tires to climb on and swing in, but it was a carousel to us...filled with gold rings and shiny multi-colored horses circling our BLOCK.

Our sidewalk had a personality that changed with each

mom or dad. WE were tough!

What are some of my favorite memories? First and foremost, are my high school friends, most of whom I am still in touch with. Science had some great kids, who have long since become great "grown-ups". Unfortunately, none of them had the good sense to settle in the Washington area, so I do not get to see them as much as I would like.

Second, of course, are those special places — the Paradise (especially the star-lit balcony), Shorehaven (the girls didn't wear undershirts there, either), my high school fraternity's (Mu Sigma) basement apartment (more like a dungeon)

Who were those girls who didn't wear undershirts?

in an apartment house near Taft, Jahn's (two of my friends could each individually finish a "Kitchen Sink"; how, I never could figure out), and Yankee Stadium (the only survivor of the decades).

Talk about survivors, our generation can remember when there were no self-service gas stations, cruise control, interval windshield wipers, Concordes, Super Bowls, Walkmans, Watchmans, cassettes, CDs, computers, and even electric typewriters. How did we ever survive without them? And guys did not wear pony-tails (well, maybe at Clinton, but not at Science)!

passing season. As we walked the six blocks to PS 86, the colored autumn leaves covered this concrete carnival making it so much fun for us to jump and crunch the fallen leaves. In the winter, the snow piled high on the edge of the street gutter made a wonderful sliding mountain. And in the spring, these sidewalks led to the high school flower garden four blocks away where we snipped white and yellow carnations to bring back to *Grandma*.

The BLOCK had a center...a connection...that united all...

Yes, the people who lived on our BLOCK were family, not blood relations, but by sharing the building we called home. Those on our BLOCK who lived in building 10 East were one family, 1 East, where our friends Enid, Iris and Madeline lived were another family and 5 East yet another. Though these buildings physically touched each other, each building was separate and was its own family.

Living in 10 East, our family, of course, was the closest and the best. There was a blend of young and old, from newborns to grandparents. There were six floors with eight families on each floor and the superintendents's family living in the basement. The biological family in each apartment had its own life, yet we all shared the building family life of 10 East.

Continued on page 15

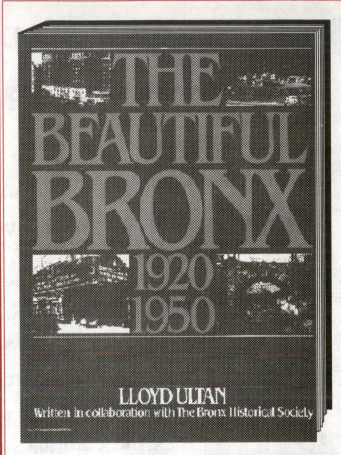

198th St. Dictionary

Proverbs & Sayings

§

Hindoo: (a do-over while playing ball)

Roly Poly: you roll the ball after you catch it and try to hit the stick ball stick on the ground

The New Fields: The Bronx baseball fields

Sidewalk Hockey: wearing out your shoes

Penny in a Loafer Shoe: The 1940's macho look

A Federal: lunch at Clinton High School—Ugh!

Ring-A Leevio: Oh! to run like that again

Kick the Can: not your rear end—a soda can

3 Steps to Germany: Glad 198th St. wasn't so wide

Skelly: game played on sidewalk with bottlecaps

A Nuggie: a shot in the head with your knuckles

Play Knucks: card game—bleed—blood—ouch!

Lido Theatre: where Sambo was King Usher

King & Queen: hitting ball against wall

Off the Point: hitting ball off point; baseball

Egg Cream: only Sarah, George and the Bronx can do it

A Lariet: a strip of long paper on a string and you swing it around

13

The Bronx Time Capsule

Better Than Manhattan...
by Len Daykin, PS 70, JHS 117, Taft '58

I just looked at my wife's copy of "Back in the Bronx," and immediately called to order a subscription. It is one of the most warm, real, comforting things I've ever read.

We all want to be "Back in the Bronx," at least in our minds.

The Bronx was the best place in the world to grow up. Better than Brooklyn. Better than Manhattan. Certainly better than Queens. And now, hearing my own Long Island-born-and-raised kids continue to tell me how empty and sterile life in the suburbs turned out to be...The Bronx was light years away from growing up in places like Huntington, Woodmere, Morris Plains, Briarcliff—you name it.

What was it about the Bronx? For one thing, it was smaller, more manageable. You could know almost all of it, first-hand. Then, the Bronx had hills. Great for biking, sledding, roller skating. What other place had such great hills? Forest Hills had *hills*? Nah!

So there were hills. And more local parks. Claremont Park...Crotona Park...Macombs Dam Park...St. Mary's Park. And, as soon as you were big enough, the independence to go by subway, by bus to the world that was the Bronx. The libraries, Orchard Beach, Woodlawn Road, and from there on foot into the exotic frontier land of Yonkers and Tibbetts Brook park. Who knew from carpools?

But most of all, it was the teeming, nosey people — kids and parents alike—that made the Bronx one big extended family. You were never alone. Even friendless, you could have thousands of kids. Scores of surrogate moms and dads. Limitless options.

Oh, yeah: You could be afraid in the Bronx. You could be afraid of the super's huge, vicious German Shepherd, lurking in some alley. You could be afraid of getting pounced on by a gang—The Fordham Baldies, the Boca Chicas, the Cobras. You could be (and rightfully so), morbidly afraid of being called on in class. We could all be afraid then, in the Bronx. But never *Afraid*. It all seemed so permanent. So immutable.

We didn't know how good it was while we had it...and we didn't understand—how fragile it all was.

So we cherish and preserve our memories like Time Capsules. Here are a few of mine:

• The never-ending parade of vehicles, and vendors. The knife sharpening truck. The jelly apple and jelly marshmallow man. Angelo and his horse-drawn produce wagon. The "I cash clothes" man. The Whip ride truck. The Bungalow Bar truck (was there ever a Häagen Dazs, Ben & Jerry's, Steve's or Baskin-Robbins that could compare to a Bungalow All-Chocolate Pop...or Toasted Almond Bar?)

• Movie theaters, like the Mt. Eden, Surrey or Luxor, where on a Saturday, for 14¢, you got: A newsreel, several cartoons, a serial like Dick Tracy or Mysterious Island, two full-length movies, never mind which they were, coming attractions. Better yet, one kid could pay and hold the exit doors open for a half-dozen friends to sneak in, right under the nose of the white-uniformed, feared and hated Matrons!

• The sewer-cleaning truck that, twice a year, brought forth from the stench of the earth, a bounty of previously owned Spaldeens.

• Sidewalk and schoolyard games: boxball, stoop ball, hit the penny, flies up, slug (Queens & Kings), many varieties of stickball, and punchball (played only in cold weather, in T-shirt, in junior high schoolyard).

• Paper-thin hamburgers, better than any Whopper, at luncheonettes like Cappy & Joe's, across the street from Wade Junior High School.

• Dancing lessons at the YWCA??? on Kingsbridge Road.

• Greasy, fat, unbelievably wonderful french fries in a paper bag, drenched in ketchup (can you feel the pimples erupting on your face?).

• Pink shirts with black collars, turned up. Garrison belts. Dungarees. Engineer boots. The uniform.

• Belly whopping down a decent hill on a day when there was no school...on and on, into the night. There was no snowstorm like a Bronx snowstorm.

King of the Bronx
by Beverly

These photos of White Castle were taken in May of 1971.

The location of the White Castle is Allerton Avenue and Boston Post Road. The old White Castle had a large parking lot and car hop service.

One photo is the old White Castle. The other photo is both side

The original White Castle site.

• The familiar, reassuring, omnipresent sound of The El. Drop a Bronxite 30 years removed onto Jerome Avenue, and the tremendous rush of noise would probably not cause the bat of an eyelash. That sound was always there—like the sound of the heartbeat in the womb.

• Hanging out at "Pop's" Candy Store on Morris Ave. and 174th.

• The smell of the PS 70 lunchroom: A melange of oranges, peanut butter, milk and tomato soup.

• Giant goldfish in the lobby, and clouds scudding across the starlit ceiling of the Loew's Paradise. Was ever a movie palace more aptly named?

• Parades up the Concourse on "Decoration Day". Tanks, an American Legion truck resembling a locomotive, horses, marching cops and firemen, and the greatest marching band of all time—Cardinal Hayes.

• Once-in-a-blue-moon eating out occasions. At Tom's Inn on the Concourse, South China Restaurant on Mt. Eden, the Mos-Kov Deli on Mt. Eden.

• The wonderful smell of running through freshly hung wash in someone's backyard.

• Spin-the-bottle parties, and afternoon "dates". Putting on Old Spice.

• Summer evenings, with the whole neighborhood out in the street. TV sets dragged outside so a whole bunch could watch a ballgame. Women playing Mah Jongg or Canasta. Pitching pennies. Flirting with the girls. The sky still light, it seemed, at 9:30 pm.

We could all keep this up, until all the memories are brought out, looked at, and loved all over again. Meanwhile, I think I hear my ma calling me for dinner. I'll call for you later!

Len Daykin (Sudakin, back then)
PS 70, Wade JHS 117, Taft '58
61 Clifford Pl., Bronx 53, NY
LU 3-7004

by side. They did not break down the old until the new one was fully constructed and ready for operation.

They were located across the street from Gino's Italian Restaurant—wonderful food, a good hangout and down the street from A&P (a big deal supermarket in that era).

Enjoy!

Beverly
(201) 536-0179

The original and redesigned White Castles side by side.

The Block (cont.)

Dr. Kay was our dentist and his office was on the first floor. Everyone in the building went to him, as did everyone on the BLOCK. So, if you didn't see everyone in JOE'S CANDY STORE or on the corner, you certainly saw them in Dr. Kay's office.

We lived on the 4th floor. My brother and I grew up in apartment 4G. Joan, Alvi and Richie were in 4H, Carol and Michael in 4C and Peter and John in 4D. Marilyn and Joel lived on the fifth floor along with Robin and George and Linda and Cheryl. New families, it seemed, moved onto the sixth floor.

We loved our super and his family...all 10 of them. Since the children on each floor seemed to share everything, including measles, mumps and chicken pox, it was the super's wife who babysat for all of us.

The elevator was also the place where one practiced gymnastics. For this confined space had a bar rail three feet off the floor that was perfect for wall somersaults. And every once in a while you did "get stuck" in the elevator. To the children, this was an adventure and just fun. To the adults, it was an inconvenience. Yet I don't ever remember anyone getting really upset or concerned.

There was one other bond in the building...security. Since everyone knew everyone, any stranger coming in stood out. And you never went in the elevator with someone you didn't know. As a matter of fact, if a stranger appeared, miraculously so did the adults who were home...ready to protect the children and the building.

Looking back, the memory of growing up on the BLOCK is warm. It was friendly, loving and safe. It was HOME. It has been said that "You can never go back home." But after all these troubled years, it sure would be wonderful to try.

Now and Then . . .

General Colin L. Powell —
The Hero Comes Home to the Bronx

by Marlene C. Piturro

He had not been back in 37 years, not since graduation from Morris High School in 1954. In the intervening years he had risen from humble beginnings as a son of immigrants who worked in Manhattan's garment district, to his appointment as the twelfth Chairman of the Joint Chiefs of Staff.

With a raft of medals across his broad chest, including the Distinguished Service Medal, the Legion of Merit, and the Purple Heart, the general revisited his old neighborhood on April 18th in the South Bronx and said softly: "I remember." There was much for General Powell to remember as he toured his old neighborhood — Kelly Street (where he grew up), Morris High School (ROTC, top of his class), Yankee Stadium, the Bronx County Courthouse, and an impromptu visit to his aunt, Beryl DeLeon, who lives on Union Ave.

As tens of thousands of Bronxites wearing yellow ribbons and waving American flags looked on, Powell told about going to school in the Bronx — PS 20, PS 39, PS 52, and Morris High. At PS 52, students gave him a set of Desert Storm trading cards. At Morris High, where he was the treasurer of the school service league, he got a brass doorknob, Bulldog cap and sweatshirt and some laughs, when he said that as a teenager he hated the Yankees and spent his time at the Polo Grounds, rooting for the Giants. He spoke of his dread at winding up in the principal's office, and his odyssey every morning getting through the mean streets of the South Bronx on the way to school. Running down three flights of steps, up Kelly Street, down Westchester Avenue, over the hill on Intervale, crossing Prospect, then Longwood, and up 166th Street to Morris High — he made it!

Today, the Hunts Point section of the Bronx where General Powell grew up is a burned out, drug-infested shell of its former self. The apartment house where he grew up is long gone. In the 40's and 50's, though, Hunts Point was a mostly middle class Jewish neighborhood of hard-working people. Powell and his good friend, Gene Norman, now the President of the Harlem International Trade Center, spent hours at each other's apartments and on the ballfield. Another chum, Bernie Schwartz, now president of the Loral Corporation, a defense contractor in the South Bronx which built the guidance systems in the Tomahawk and Maverick missiles instrumental in the Persian Gulf war, established a Colin Powell scholarship fund at City College, to help other Bronx kids succeed as their famous predecessor did.

General Powell capped his day at a Grand Hyatt dinner, hosted by the South Bronx Overall Economic Development Corporation (SOBRO), to commemorate its 20th Anniversary. His cousin, Bruce Llewellyn, chairman and CEO of Philadelphia Coca Cola Bottling, presented him with the "Bronx Legend" award, and the general joshed about his elder cousin keeping him on the straight and narrow during his youth. He said: "As I drove through the Bronx I asked myself, "What if we used in our schools, the same general approach to our children that we use in the armed forces. I know schools can't be run like an infantry platoon, but, it seems to me, it was like one when I went to school." Wherever he went, he advised kids to "...stay off drugs and get your high school diploma. I'm the general — and that's an order!"

Sixth grader Satie Singleton of PS 52, summed up General Powell's impact on the throngs that greeted him throughout the Bronx: "You have proven you don't have to come from an upper class neighborhood to be a success." The principal of Morris High, Irene Fitzgerald said, "He's our own personal hero." But the general put everything in perspective when he said, "This is a day of homecoming, a day of remembrance, a day of nostalgia, a day of hope, a day I will never forget."

SOBRO'S 20TH ANNIVERSARY
From Left to Right: Fernando Ferrer, Bronx Borough President; John Patterson, President of SOBRO; General Colin Powell, Chairman of the Joint Chiefs of Staff and recipient of the "Bronx Legend" award; Bruce Llewellyn, Chairman and CEO of Philadelphia Coca/Cola Bottling Co.; and Francesco Galesi, Chairman of the Galesi Group and recipient of the "Bronx Means Business" award.
Allen Morgan Photo Service

The General Powell Trivia Quiz

1. His favorite game was:
    a. mumbleypeg
    b. Johnny-on-the-pony
    c. hopscotch
    d. stickball

2. He went to College at:
    a. West Point
    b. City College
    c. Florida A&M
    d. C.U.N.Y.

3. His parents are natives of:
    a. Trinidad
    b. Grenada
    c. Jamaica
    d. Haiti

4. He grew up on:
    a. Fox Street
    b. Kelly Street
    c. Intervale Avenue
    d. Union Avenue

5. In Morris High School, he was on this team:
    a. baseball
    b. basketball
    c. track
    d. football

6. His favorite spot for a snack was:
    a. The White Castle
    b. the local hot dog stand
    c. Banana Kelly's restaurant
    d. Prospect Avenue diner

7. His favorite food was:
    a. pizza
    b. hot dogs
    c. ice cream
    d. hamburgers

8. On his visit to Yankee Stadium, he threw the first pitch out against:
    a. Boston Red Sox
    b. Detroit Tigers
    c. Chicago White Sox
    d. Oakland A's

9. He visited a Bronx defense contractor called:
    a. Grumman
    b. Loral
    c. Sperry Rand
    d. McDonnell-Douglas

10. In college, he majored in:
    a. history
    b. English
    c. mathematics
    d. geology

Answers on Page 19

17

Classifieds

MP177 • Bernie Schwartz looking for Donny Novick.

MP178 • It's about 28 years later! Steve Bayern and Ricky Molden would like to know where is Bonnie Green, Emily Cohen, Corrine Rubin, Laura Dierna, and anyone else. The Chow Chow cup might be gone on 170th St., but we're not.

MP179 • Looking for the following **Taft** graduates: Carol Judith, Carol Eisenstein, Lenore Freed, and Jeffrey Horowitz.

MP180 • Wanted—1950 DeWitt **Clinton** Yearbook—Larry Barton (nee Barshansky).

MP181 • **Taft** '59—Eileen Krain—looking for Isabel Mars and Benjamin Mindich. Haven't seen you since we graduated. Also Leah Duben.

MP182 • Margaret O'Neill (**SHM** '73) and Hester (Mathews) O'Neill (**SHM** '40) are interested in hearing of any class reunions. Also old photos of the Academy of the **Sacred Heart of Mary** at Marmion Ave. and Park Terrace.

MP183 • Leona Jacobs, where are you? You last said that you would serve me breakfast (1959). Well, I'm hungry. Pelham Parkway has changed. Chuck Gitlin.

MP184 • Looking to contact Mimi with red hair who graduated **Taft** HS in Jan. '60. Also all other members of Gamma Phi Omega. It would be fun to have a reunion. Miriam Parton Sivak.

MP185 • If you graduated from **Walton** HS or **E.B.B.** and now living in Southern California, call me: Gladys Chapman Layne, Marina Del Rey, CA (213) 305-1686—graduated **Walton** '55.

MP186 • **Clinton** '58—Jerry Vogel is looking for any old buddies from the old neighborhood W. Burnside & University Ave. 179th St.

MP187 • Desperately seeking Henry Mooney, Judy Steiner, and Ida Henig (**Taft** '65). Also need to know that Betty Berger (**Taft** '62?) of **Walton** Ave. is alive and well.

MP188 • **Evander** '56—Leomi Waldinger Simkin looking for the following JHS 80 and **Evander** '56 girls—Barbara Yorburg (Knox Pl.), Phyllis Cashman (W. Gun Hill), Sandra Cohen (Gun Hill), Frances Oullette (E. 212 St. and Bainbridge). Has anyone info about these **Evander** '56 grads? Edith Lipman (Seymour Ave.), Jack Rothman (Seymour), Martin Block (E. Gun Hill).

MP189 • 1951 graduate of PS 114, Class of Anne Reiter, is interested in hearing from classmates. Sylvia Neuwirth Wagner (301) 897-8099.

MP190 • I am seeking the whereabouts of January 1953 **Taft** graduates, especially George White, Elaine Fernbach, Connie Weinberg, Elaine Silverman. Contact Elaine Herzfeld Fast.

MP191 • Gary Mortman lived on **Walton** Ave. and Mt. Eden Ave., now residing in Manalpan NJ. Would like to hear from old friends on the block, Melvin Seltzer, Alan Simon, Zack Trubita, Joel Abramson, Stuart Brill, David Epstein.

MP192 • Andrews, University, Montgomery, Popham Ave.—174th to Tremont, looking for: Mel Moskowitz, Ronnie Sokoloff, David Shrone, Kenny Sloane, Jerome Lindauer, Marvin Megidow, Noel Grubin, Roger Gold, Paul Reiser, Bobby Bell, Frank Lasher, Norman Schienwald, Donald Seffinger, Diane Abrams, Irving Corendener, Ellen Hoffman, Roz Berger. Contact Jeffrey Lawson.

MP193 • Mimi and Lanie want to know what happened to Sandy Turner and Nancy Fogelson, JHS 82-1952. Remember Rusch-meyers?

MP194 • Artie Weinfeld—**Science** '57, also sells real estate in Briarcliff Manor. Old friends from Gun Hill Rd. please contact.

MP195 • Joel Goldstein looking for lost friends from the 50's that lived on 208th St. Let's get together for a reunion. Also Peggy Hubler Medwin, **Evander** '62, last known address Suffern, NY 10901.

MP196 • Marilyn Kasserman, Emily Gitnik—where are you? Carol Lieber Glickfeld.

MP197 • **Taft** '60—Diane Pardo Abraham would like to contact Elsie Camni, Barbara Echtman, Barbara Feinstein, Edith Freter, Florence Kroop, Joan Lieberman, Anita Mandel, Barbara Oremland, Beverly Perlman, Barbara Phillips, Mike Russo, Laura Schein, Janice Weisman, Madeline Varon, Leslie Stone.

MP198 • Any members of **Science**, Class of '56, interested in a thirty-five year reunion, please contact Jerry Goldstein. Time is short but an event before the end of the year is still possible.

MP199 • Diane Blagman, **Roosevelt** '70, would be interested to find any from **Roosevelt** '67-70 or those who hung out by Alexanders/Fordham Rd. or Poe Park. Where are you? Any residing in Washington D.C.?

MP200 • Yo! I need some help—looking for the boys who played hoops at the Echo Park playground during the early 60's. Anyone knowing where I can find Steve DeVito, Ron DeVito, Danny DeVito, Fred Veltri? I'm Nathan Oventhal—**Clinton** '62.

MP201 • Art & Design '63—Harriet Katz Schaeffer is looking for old friends from PS 46, JHS, **E.B.B.** or Art & Design. Neighborhood friends from the Bedford Park area.

MP202 • Bainbridge Ave....looking for people who lived on Bainbridge between Fordham Rd. and 198th St. and/or pictures/memorabilia from the Avenue during the 1960's only. Did you go to or teach at PS 46 during the '60's? Contact Robert Blagman.

MP203 • Ron Kaufman would like to locate the whereabouts of these people from **Morris** Avenue or **Taft**: Ellen Markowitz, Gary Forcash '62; Roz Price, **Taft** '64; Marsha Cohen, **Taft** '65; Judy Kaplan, **Taft** '67; Andrea Schneider, **Taft** '66; Susan Snyder, **Taft** '66; James Veres, **Evander** '66; Sherry Panzer, Music & Art '65.

MP204 • **Walton** '64—Louis Meszler Wagman, where are you? Remember the Yankees and all the "guys"—Syd, Harry, and Jeanne would love to hear from you.

MP205 • Looking for "Lewis Greenbaum", Prospect Ave.—moved to Los Angeles in 1956 or 57. Contact Harriet Meltzer.

MP206 • Allen Halpern, **Taft** '55, would like to know the whereabouts of Carol Reider, **Taft** '56.

MP207 • 1948 Rams or Gremlins: Whitey, Milt, Wally, Howie, Al, Marko, Bert, Eugene, Lenny, Steve, Red, Cass, Joe—174th St. Contact Irwin Schneider.

MP208 • Richard Brooks would like to hear from John Evans, **Taft** '62.

MP209 • We are looking for the guys and gals who hung out around Leo's window on College Ave. from 1950-53. Also looking for Morty Klein, Norman Appell, Irving Karp and the rest of that crowd. Contact Carol Speckler Fishbein and Marty Fishbein.

MP210 • Seeking the whereabouts of Judy and Saul Broad, children of Dave. Last contact California 1937. Lived in East Bronx. Would be about 62 and 59 years old now. Cousins would like to reestablish contact.

MP211 • Charlotte Eisner, Class of **Morris** '45, where are you? Remember Glenn Miller, Café Rouge? Every Saturday—admission 25¢? Tony Mercorella, Marvin Kleinberg, or Solly Weiss. Contact Evelyn Blumenthal Yagoda.

MP212 • **Taft** '57—Barbara Deutchman Collen would like to know the whereabouts of Laurel Fregenbaum, Michael Rogers.

MP213 • Jimmy Bennings would like to hear from old friends from the Marble Hill Projects, 1958-1965.

MP214 • Suzanne (Schumer) Klein would love to find Estelle (Cookie) Benoze—where are you? Let's talk about yesterday and today.

MP215 • Joe Sabrin—**Clinton** '60 Founder of PC Etcetera, a North American PC & Mac Training company wants to hear other success stories. Call him at 212-736-5870 8-6PM E.S.T.

MP216 • Executive Search—Ron Sunshine **Clinton** '58 Specializing in engineering and manufacturing middle and upper management position—contact me.

MP217 • Sheila Markin Klein, **Columbus** '61 would like to hear from Janet Lehrer and Judy Rosenblatt, last seen during their first year at Boston U. Even longer since we shared a White Castle lunch at JHS 135!

MP218 • Judi & Mervyn Fleisher, former Bronxites and whose parents owned Hotel Fleisher, Parksville, NY would like to contact former guests and staff of Hotel for reunion.

MP219 • Larry Rosenberg, **Clinton** '65 looking for old friends from Andrews Ave., All Star Bowl, Sedgwick Little League.

Continued on page 20

This issue's Mystery Bronxites

1. Anne Bancroft
2. Bobby Darin
3. Gen. Colin Powell

If you have a test or questions for a test, do not hesitate to send them in. Please make sure that you also supply the correct answer. Please use a blank sheet of paper following the format above and enclose in the reader reply envelope.

Classifieds

Come Blow Your Horn

Spaldeen Harvest
by Sam Ezraty, Taft '54

For those of us who remember the good old days, we also remember that there was no money to speak of. We were all comparatively poor kids, but we didn't really know it or care.

There was always Orchard Beach in the summer and that was only about an hour and two bus rides away. The winters were spent playing Monopoly and going to lots and lots of movies. There were lots to pick from too. From the Luxor, the Loews 167th Street, the Kent, the Zenith and the good old Paradise, there was always something to see.

I guess most of all there were sports. Sports of all types. This is not to confuse you with things like the marble season, and the ticket season (I wonder how much they're worth today?) No, this was the real thing. I'm talking about games like "two hand touch", "off the point", "box ball", "stick ball", "hardball", and "softball". Some of the "ball" games were played in the street (naturally) and some were played in Tafts field. We used to call it the "dust bowl" or the "rock garden", depending on whether you got sand in your eyes or hit in the face from a ground ball that bounced off a rock.

The problem with most of the "ball" games was that most of the times we just didn't have any ball to play with and that my friends is where the great sport of "fishing" came in. Now I'm sure that most of you know from where I come, but for those of you who might be showing this to your kids let me explain.

Fishing was the art of getting balls to play with for free. All it took was a little ingenuity and about three or four guys. The process was simple. We all went from sewer to sewer. Since I was the chunkiest, I was the sewer top lifter. All you did was simply pry the sewer top up by sticking a stickball stick (broom handle) under the small cut on all sewer tops and pry it up about three inches. The sewer top lifter then grabbed the sewer top with both hands and lifted and moved the top away from the opening. Then came the good part. We would either take a wire hanger fashioned into a hoop and attached to the stick ball stick and fish the balls out or sometimes we'd lower the skinniest kid head first into the sewer and he would scoop up as many balls as he could. We would repeat the process if necessary.

This provided us with balls to play with for at least a month. There were all kinds of balls too. Spaldeens hardballs, softballs and even hand balls.

We divided the ball among all of us by "choosing" up to see who would pick first, second and so on. Then we would take all the balls home and wash them with soap and water, because after all, "cleanliness was next to godliness."

That was fishing in the Bronx. Your kids are probably saying "how gross" but to do it was an adventure, as was every day in the Bronx. When I think of fishing in the Bronx, I always think fondly of my fishing companions of those days. Here's to all of you...Charlie May, Donny Sheer, Ray London, Marvin Brown, Murray Solomon, Dave Rose, Perry Golod, Bob List, Abie Bottner, Howie Aster, Jack Jamgochian, Badgie, Howie Horowitz, and Charlie Blitz. If I missed anyone, please forgive me. After all, it was only about forty years ago.

To commemorate W.H. Taft High School's
50th Anniversary,
"Back in the Bronx"
is offering this
1950's-60's
Woolen Replica Jacket
in the
traditional **TAFT**
Blue and Gold!

Only $99

This coat is quality constructed using a full 24 ounce reprocessed wool for the body and sleeves to give long service and then they line it with a full quilt lining. The fabric and workmanship are exceptional. The result is a statement of beauty and durability. The really classic features include a heavyweight mixed rib collar, cuffs and waistband, contrasting snaps, and leather trimmed insert pockets. You'll wear this jacket with pride for as many years to come.

Reminiscing

My Memories
by Annette Jeremia

I can't believe that yesterday I was 18, and today I am 48. Thirty years of my life passed by so quickly, to leave me with such good memories of the Bronx where I was brought up. I lived on lived on 182nd Street between Third Avenue and Bathigate. Up the corner from my house was the Third Avenue El. Across the street was St. Barnabas Home for the Incurable. Which it is now St. Barnabas Hospital. I went to PS 59 which was right around the corner from my house. We lived in an apartment building that had five families on each floor. Everyone knew each other, doors were left unlocked and opened to all. It was like one big happy family.

We would go to church dances, Our Saviours was on Washington Avenue and 183rd Street. I will never forget there was an old, old house on the corner we would call the haunted house. It had gas lights in the windows and a broken fence and gate. If only I could have seen the inside of that house; it had a lot of character. We would hang out in the candy store on 183rd Street. It was Joe's candy store. Around the corner on Third Avenue was Peppers Ice Cream Parlor. It was a great place. They had booths, and a seven foot counter with wrought iron chairs and of course a jukebox. We would have an ice cream soda and talk about the future and if we would get married. As I write this I see my life all over again, the happy memories as a teenager growing up.

On Saturday morning I would go shopping with my mom to Arthur Avenue. We would stop and have lunch at Cantania's Pizza store. They had the greatest pizza. Of course, you couldn't go home without buying an outfit from Valley's Sportswear. I just loved that store.

My grandmother lived in a house on Arthur Avenue, we were there as much as we were home. I had friends on both sides, 182nd Street and Arthur Avenue. I went to PS 59, JHS 118, and Theodore Roosevelt High School. When I graduated in 1961 we moved into my grandmother's house on Arthur Avenue. I lost contact with my friends once everyone went different ways. In 1970 we moved to Queens, but we were back in the house every weekend. After ten years we moved backed to the same house where I spent most of my life.

My daughters are the fifth generation in this house. My dad and his dad and granddad spent all of their happy lives here. I am proud to be an American in the Bronx. I tell my girls many stories of this house, because the roots are so deep. Now when people ask me where I live, I say "Arthur Avenue". They say "the famous Arthur Avenue." I am in contact with friends I haven't seen in thirty years. You never forget them, they are just hidden away for awhile. I hope my daughters will never forget they are Bronxites. By the way, my house is 100 years old, and I work in one of the greatest places in the Bronx. The Bronx Zoo. I have met so many of my old friends and made so many new ones just working here for ten years. I have seen so many changes within the Zoo and recall all my younger days here in the 1950's.

Thank you for this great paper, I enjoyed reading the different articles. I hope you can print my article; this would make my day. Thanks again. I have been in contact with friends that I haven't seen in thirty years. Keep up the good work.

AJ
Annette Jeremia (Melillo)
2487 Arthur Avenue
Bronx, New York 10458
Work Number—(212) 220-5188

Reunited!
by Karel Cooperman, Taft '48

My ad number was MP37—Taft '51. It read, "Where are you Rita Webber and Phillis Goldberg? Remember the hours spent doubting if we would ever marry and leave the Bronx? Write Karel of Walton Avenue."

My phone rang two weeks after the ad ran. It was a husky, strangely familiar sound. "Hello, Karel? This a voice from the past. Your past!" I couldn't answer. For a brief moment I was swept back into time. I was standing in my foyer at 1475 Walton Avenue, phone in hand, talking to my best friend...Phyllis Goldberg! "Yes, it's me. A friend saw your ad and phoned me. I got your number from the Samturs, and here I am."

Needless to say, we had a lot to talk over. We wanted to catch up on 35 years of living. Phyllis is living in New York, I live in Maryland. However, geographic disparity did not bother us—we were determined to meet.

The next problem was finding Rita Webber, another friend whom we grew up with. Phyllis' son was a private detective, lo and behold, found Rita's address. She now lived in Queens. A few more phone calls and we found Rita living and working in New York. We all talked on the phone to arrange our meeting.

Phyllis and Rita drove down to Maryland and met me October 12, 1990. After 35 years, three friends who had gone through elementary school, (PS 64, JHS 117) Taft High School, renewed old friendships.

Our concerns about what we would look like, could we communicate, could we revive old friendships, faded away. We giggled, laughed and learned to love each other as if we were school girls again.

Three old friends reunited by *Back in the Bronx*.

Karel Cooperman, Taft '48
10116 New London Drive
Potomac, Maryland 20854

READER REPLIES

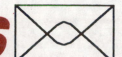

It is vitally important that you fill out the information below. Your input will be essential to the success of this magazine, tailored and inspired by you, the former "Bronxite". We thank you for your participation.

Subscriber? ☐ Yes ☐ No

YOUR NAME _____

ADDRESS _____

CITY _____ STATE _____ ZIP _____ PHONE _____

HIGH SCHOOL ATTENDED _____ YEAR GRADUATED _____

TELL US A LITTLE ABOUT YOURSELF,
(Be sure to include your alma mater, old neighborhood, your best memories about your days in the Bronx, (or anything else you can tell us).

_____

_____

- -

COULD WE SEND A FRIEND A FREE COPY OF BACK IN THE BRONX?
Do you know current or former Bronxites who would like to receive our magazine and reunion information? If you do, we'll be happy to send them a **free** inaugural issue of **Back in THE BRONX**.
Write to Back in The Bronx, Box 141 H, Scarsdale, NY 10583 or call 1-800-7-BRONX 5

Last	First	Maiden	
Address	City	State	Zip
Phone # ( )	School and year of Graduation		

Last	First	Maiden	
Address	City	State	Zip
Phone # ( )	School and year of Graduation		

Last	First	Maiden	
Address	City	State	Zip
Phone # ( )	School and year of Graduation		

Last	First	Maiden	
Address	City	State	Zip
Phone # ( )	School and year of Graduation		

COME BLOW YOUR OWN HORN DEPARTMENT
Please tell us about yourself (include your name)—about your accomplishments, awards, titles or works in progress. We're interested in hearing about them. List Below. _____

_____

_____

_____

READER REPLIES

As a subscriber you are entitled to a FREE 40 Word Classified, Missing Persons, Blow Your Own Horn, or Personal Ad. Please write your ad below (if you are not subscribing to our magazine you can still place an ad in the next issue. The cost of an advertisement is 50¢ a word, there is no limit on paid ads).

_____

_____

_____

Is Your Mailing Label Correct?

In order to keep our database current, please correct any errors and place the label and or photocopy with corrections.

Account #	High School	Year Graduated
6817	Roosevelt	1958

SAMPLE
Mary R. Flowers
123 Anystreet Blvd.
Anywhere, USA 12345

Change of Address?

If you're planning a move please attach your label corrected with your new address and the date that you will begin receiving mail at that address. This will insure that you don't miss your next issue of **Back in THE BRONX.**

Ordering Information

A Great Gift Idea! In addition to your own subscription, a subscription to **Back in THE BRONX** makes a great and unique gift. Fill in the form below and we'll process the order in time for our next issue. So, order your subscription NOW, and order one for a friend!

YES, I'd like to order the following items:
QTY.

____ 1Yr. (4 ISSUES) Subscription(s) to **Back in THE BRONX** $19.95
____ 2Yr. (8 ISSUES) Subscription(s) to **Back in THE BRONX*** ⎫ *FREE .. $29.95
____ 3Yr. (12 ISSUES) Subscription(s) to **Back in THE BRONX*** ⎬ Jahn's .. $39.95
____ 4Yr. (16 ISSUES) Subscription(s) to **Back in THE BRONX*** ⎭ Menu .. $49.95
____ **The Beautiful Bronx**..........$25.00 (plus $3.95 S/H) $28.95
____ **The Bronx: It Was Only Yesterday**..$25.00 (plus $3.95 S/H) $28.95
____ **Bronx High School Reunion Weekend Video** $29.95
      SAVE MONEY - BUY 4 FOR JUST $99.00!
____ **THE BRONX Tracking Service** $9.95

____ **I would like to receive all available back issues and have them applied towards my subscription** (To date we have at least 12 back issues available - While They Last!)

TOTAL: $ _____

Please fill out completely and include $3.95 for shipping and handling for books only to: **Back in THE BRONX**, Box 141H, Scarsdale, NY 10583

Please Print Clearly ☐ New Subscriber ☐ Renewal

Name _____

Maiden Name _____

Address _____

City _____

State _____ Zip _____

Phone (_____) _____

High School _____ Year Grad. _____

☐ Visa ☐ Mastercard ☐ Check ☐ Money Order

No. _____ Expiration Date _____

Signature _____

Back in THE BRONX

Box 141 H, Scarsdale, NY 10583
Phone 914-592-1647 • Fax 914-592-4893

ADDRESS CORRECTION REQUESTED

Volume I   Issue IV

Back in THE BRONX

Celebrating the experience of growing up and living in the Bronx

HURRICANE ELVIS HITS THE BRONX

by Gerald Rosen

Although we didn't have "blasters" or "Walkmen" or CDs or cassettes, or even stereo, somehow, in the Bronx in the 50's music seemed to be everywhere, accompanying our lives.

There was Frankie Laine ("Jezebel" and "Rose, Rose, I Love You"), Teresa Brewer ("Music, Music, Music", to which we would do "The Lindy"), Patti Page ("Tennessee Waltz" and "Doggie in the Window"), Johnny Ray ("Cry"), along with Kay Starr, Doris Day, Georgia Gibbs, Vaughn Monroe, The Four Aces, Dinah Shore, and a host of others.

The music was largely romantic, white, harmless, and idealistic. Remember Perry Como's "It is better to light just one little candle, than to stumbling the dark..."? And if you were Jewish, you might have sung Jewish versions of the hits, such as "Throw Mama from the Train, a knish, a knish," or Johnny Ray's "The Little White Cloud That Cried," which became, "The Little White Knish That Fried."

Music in the 50's was the medium in which boys and girls floated as we strove to get to know each other, an excuse to touch and even hold each other as we danced to big, heavy, very breakable, 78 RPM records on the jukeboxes.

Our gang's jukebox, in Highbridge, was at the YM-WHA on the Concourse at 165th Street, just north of the Concourse Plaza Hotel. After playing basketball

The Eye of Your Storm?

in the gym, we guys would join the girls in the lounge to dance to the 50's music that was available–slow dances to Joni James' "Have you Heard?" and Don Cornell's "I'll Walk Alone", or Eddie Fisher's "Wish You Were Here", and cha chas to "Cherry Pink and Apple Blossom White."

I even got my friend Albie Zelnik to go with me all the way up to Fordham Road to take cha cha, mambo, and meringue lessons at a dance studio across from the Loew's Paradise. I thought this would make me more popular with the girls, but it didn't.

Yet, at this same time a revolution in popular music was beginning to simmer on the back burner of the American psyche. The kids in Harlem and the South Bronx were beginning to make up their own kind of music–rhythm and blues. At DeWitt Clinton we heard about this early, since our school included kids from these two areas.

Clinton had seven major bathrooms, and each one became the home of an R&B group who would practice there daily, beneath a fog of smoke, between (and sometimes during) classes. Now the songs we began to hear were, "Why Do Fools Fall in Love?" by Frankie Lyman and the Teenagers (Lyman went to school just across the river from The Bronx, at George

Continued on page 10

From the Editors...

Welcome to the fourth issue of Back in the Bronx!

Some you seasoned Bronxites have inquired why we seem to address only the decades of the 50's and 60's. Well, as the beer commercial goes, "This *Bronx* Is For You!" Take the ECHO ASSOCIATES for example. These Bronxites have been meeting for close to fifty years!

We are not directing the magazine to particular decades; many of the stories and pictures come from you, our subscribers. We often read these stories several times and often find ourselves tearfully enjoying them. *These stories are written from the heart.* You can imagine all the memories they bring back for us, too!

Keep contributing to our little time capsule. Would anyone be interested in helping us out in a big way? Are you a budding editor, artist, historian, writer or storyteller? We know there's plenty of home-grown talent who want to share personal experiences of their lives in the Bronx.

Keep the memory alive!

Stephen M. Samtur
Clinton '61

Susan J. Samtur
Taft '62

Back in the BRONX
Celebrating the experience of growing up and living in the Bronx

Publishers and Editors	**Stephen M. Samtur**
	Susan H. Samtur
Art Director	**Thomas R. Hamilton**
Art, Gridlock	**Mac Parsons**
	Herald Graphics Inc, Stratford Ct

A number of the photographs in Back in the Bronx are courtesy of and available from the Bronx Historical Society

Graffiti

Dear Steve,

Your newsletter found its way to Kansas City! I can't tell you how much I enjoyed the article by Susan Thayler. It was very moving. I xeroxed parts of your newsletter and sent them to ex-Bronxites in Connecticut, California, and Norway. My mother still lives in the old neighborhood near the reservoir and DeWitt Clinton, and although it is physically relatively intact, socially it has changed quite a bit.

Maybe some of us are on the same wavelength–because in the last couple of years I have tried to locate my high school friends with only partial success. I think I am more nostalgic than some ex-Bronxites because I live in a part of the country that is so removed from the place that I grew up. Speaking of nostalgia, are you familiar with the book *Growing Up Bronx,* by Gerald Rosen, published in 1984? To quote the flyleaf: "a powerful, bittersweet portrait of the twilight of a society." It is set in Highbridge in the 1940's and 1950's.

Coincidentally, a couple of weeks before I received your newsletter, a new deli opened here called "d'Bronx". I am hoping to make contact with other Bronxers through it.

Ray Lynn (Weinstein) Govert
Evander '60

Dear Steve and Susan,

When I placed a missing persons ad in the third issue of *Back in the Bronx* for a very dear friend who I had lost contact with fourteen years ago, I never really expected anything much to come of it. But to my surprise, when I picked up the phone one night and heard her voice, we were like two kids again and living in the Bronx!

Since that phone call we promised each other that we would never lose contact again, even though she lives in Las Vegas and I in New York.

So, we would like to thank you, and most of all, thanks to *Back in the Bronx.*

Toby Goldstein

ECHO ASSOCIATES
Remember that famous radio show, "Can you top this"?
Well, Echo Associates tops them all!

Our association's name stems from our block, Echo Place, which is still located one block North of Tremont Avenue, running East/West from the Concourse, two blocks long to Echo Park. Some of the members went to Kindergarten together at P.S. 28 (corner of Tremont and Anthony) back in 1933! As teenagers the group (approx. 22) formed an athletic club called the "SAINTS", and you name them, the Fordham Baldies, the Guineau Dukes, the Spartans, the 178th St. Club, the Saints beat them all.

Echo Place was our stadium and the sports mecca of the Bronx. Teams and individuals came from far and near for every "season", which somehow started and stopped with miraculous regularity year after year. Stickball, Roller Hockey, Touch Football, Mushball, Triangle Captain, BATW, Immies, Baseball and Indian Cards, and also Basketball (using the bottom rung on the fire escape ladder as the basket), were the activities that filled each "season", and I know I've left some out. The "SAINTS" took on all challenges.

We also had our candy store, Mrs. Burns' on Tremont Avenue, where almost every evening you would find some of the group gathered on a sidewalk inch deep with pumpkin seed shells. Petes' Poolroom and the Cuckoo's Nest filled in the balance of our active sports related youth. We knew nothing of female diversions and suffered a lot from headaches and cramps.

With the advent of WWII, practically everyone enlisted after graduating H.S., some never to return. In 1947, we put our old uniforms on one last time for the memorable photo taken on the steps of DeWitt Clinton H.S. and at that time the Echo Associates was formed to keep us in touch as life went on.

And to this day some 13 original members, wives, kids and grandchildren, still gather together twice a year. The latest photo of the group was taken in August 1991, at our summer pool party, everyone in it was also in the 1947 shot (photo) with just a little more hair!

1st Row - Mendy Weiss, Marvin Millstein, Sol Maskin, Richie Markoe, Marvin Greenbaum, Stan Finkelstein, Bernie Novick, Irwin Deitz
2nd Row - Stan Queller, Len Kantor, Fred Rothman, Norman Beier, Emerich Rudolph, Dave Pollack **3rd Row -** Don Moss, Ernie Stark, Dave Cooperman, Jerry Schwartz, Sonny Applebaum, Marvin Adler, Howie Walode

If any of your readers would like to communicate with the Echo's, get in touch with Richie Markoe, 42 Homer St., Norwalk, CT 06851, (203) 847-1226.

Reminiscing

Barbara Smolin Forman gives us her unique view on growing up in the Bronx

Growing Up In the Shadow of Yankee Stadium . . .

You could go up to most of the roofs on Gerard Avenue and watch the Yankees play and if you were boy crazy, there were a good place to be.

On the corner of 157th Street and Gerard Avenue, there was a deli, Semrycks. This corner served as a hangout for "the older" boys. If you were halfway attractive, you could expect whistles and bravado-type comments as you walked by. You just got used to this "attention" and never thought of it as harassment. Any attention was better than being ignored!

The apartment building between 153rd Street and 157th Street had huge lobbies and entrances to both Walton and Gerard Avenues. Walton Avenue had park benches that were used by older people and young mothers with babies. It was very sedate and boring. If you had a date that you were proud of, you would parade past the boys' hangout on Gerard Avenue. If it was a blind date that was a disaster, you would exit the building on Walton Avenue. The day after a date, the big questions would be, "did you walk on Walton or Gerard?"

In the late 40's very few boys and no girls had cars. We used the subways, which were totally safe at any time of the day or night. The subway was our lifeline to Fordham Road, high schools like Taft and Bronx Science and any place more than a mile away. Otherwise, we walked.

I can remember when I was in P.S. 73, how we used to pray for snow so that the school bus would get stuck at the foot of steep Anderson Avenue. This happened often and meant some good snowball fights and a day off from school.

I can also remember the after-school activities we girls did like jump rope, hopscotch, territory (you needed a knife to play this) bike riding and yo-yo contests.

The three blocks between 153rd and 161st streets were our neighborhood. We walked those blocks every day. On Saturdays, we went to the Earl Theater, where the "matron" made sure we were reasonably quiet. It cost 15¢ for admission, sometimes obtained by returning soda bottles for deposit. Those double features plus the many "selected short subjects" were a great bargain and took up the entire afternoon. In those days you went tot he movies at any time you wanted, even in the middle of a movie. And you could sit there for as long as you wanted; it was called continuous performances. You could see the same movies three times for the same money, if you could sit that long. The standard format for a birthday party was lunch at Semryck's and a movie at the Earl.

Another memorable feature of our neighborhood was the local drugstore, Entenberg's Pharmacy. Entenberg's was the place to go when you got something in your eye. Mr. Entenberg was always able to remove it right there on the spot. He must have removed "foreign" objects from hundreds of kids' eyes with never a second thought about liability of malpractice.

Easter Sundays were also a big deal. For a Jewish neighborhood, we celebrated Easter with a vengeance. We dressed up in brand new suits and patent leather shoes to parade up and down Walton and Gerard Avenues. It was the Bronx answer to the 5th Avenue Easter Parade. For weeks before Easter, the hottest topic of conversation was about what we would wear on Easter Sunday.

Courtesy of The Bronx Historical Society, taken from "The Beautiful Bronx" ©Bronx Historical Society.

Although Addie Vallins on 161st Street was a popular place to go for "adult" ice cream, it never became a kids handout like the local candy store on 157th Street. There you could have an egg cream and keep getting it freshened up with more seltzer or more syrup as you munched your pretzel stick. Egg creams have never tasted quite as good.

I remember Curland's Butcher on 157th Street, where I would be sent with a shopping list that invariable included a "fresh" piece of chuck steak to be chopped before your eyes. Of course, on the way home, several large handfuls of the delicious raw meat mysteriously disappeared.

All of the local storekeepers were "kept honest" by the third degree type of questions thrown at them by the local housewives. Are you sure it's fresh? Are you sure the weight is right? When did it come in? Can you trim it better? If it's not good, I'm bringing it back. And they did.

The most bittersweet fact about growing up in the Bronx is that there is no way I can share what it was like with my children. The neighborhood no longer exists today. We never thought it would change and certainly didn't think to preserve any tangible memories. Now we can't go home again, even to visit.

... while Dale Thomas grows up in the company of one of the Bronx' many social clubs, the Clovers

Club Sweatshirts – How Much More BRONX Can You Be?

I read Edwin Doctrow's *World Fair* ad was so overcome with nostalgia that I had to write him a zippy letter. "Hi", I started, "I'm that quiet brown haired girl that lived on the corner of Weeks and 175th Street", but alas, he never answered.

What struck me was, how amazing that here was a person, Edwin Doctrow, who had literally shared all my childhood experiences and minutely remembered and recorded every single detail. Most of those I had long since forgotten, until your Bronx newsletter again stirred my now aging memory.

The most outstanding item that I recall from that time is my green and white club sweater. We were the Clovers Social Club (SC), to clearly distinguish from the AC (Athletic Club) sweaters or jackets that the fellows had. The main aim of our S.C. was to make contact with 'you guys' in those A.C. jackets.

I remember how we got our sweaters: We printed and sold raffle books, ten cents a chance, grand prize FIVE DOLLARS! A cherished event in my memory is the evening that I disposed of five raffle books to my father's pinochle cronies. To top it off, I won the five dollar prize!

Anyway, on the right front appeared a large white clover, our name was on the left front and the letters CLOVERS' SC were in white on the backs of our beautiful green sweaters.

Some of the fellows, especially in the East Bronx, where there were more private homes, had enough money to rent their very OWN CLUB ROOM. All we girls had were one another's living rooms to meet in, a whole wide Grand Concourse to march up and down on, and en masse to show off our sweaters.

I have, in later life, been accused of being a 'clothes-aholic'. Guess that must have been true, because I seem to remember clothing most of all. When it was too cold to wear our sweaters as outer garments, we turned to our genuine Navy surplus pea coats, with white kerchiefs, white socks and penny loafers. These were later upgraded to contain dimes when the Concourse bus raised its fares to ten cents.

What about Fridays at Taft High School when we were Seniors! We could wear our Senior's Hat to class. The idea was to collect as many school buttons from other schools as one could pin those on the Hat. For us girls the caps also served wonderfully to hide our hair rollers (in hopes to look beautiful for the weekend festivities). It was great!

I did go on to Hunter College and got married after that. Most of the surplus junk, including my precious Clover sweater, was left with my mother. One day Mom Called: She had taken it upon herself to throw away the old sweater since the moths had feasted on it. This took place just as I was preparing to leave the Bronx as a resident and take my rightful place in the 'burbs. The old sweater must have known about my treachery.

But hey! I'm lucky: I don't have to advertise for all the missing Clovers because most of us are still friends and see each other regularly. We attended each other's weddings, then came children's bat- and bar mitzvahs followed by their weddings and just recently I mailed a gift to the grandchild of a former Clover.

How much more BRONX can *YOU* be? Anyone out there still have their old Club sweaters or jackets? How about wearing them to the reunion?

Reminiscing

The Bronx is many things and has many scenes – *even people!*

So one of our readers, Judy Issacs, takes us back to scenes of yesteryear, the Fifties, and shows us how to pass the time – Bronx style.

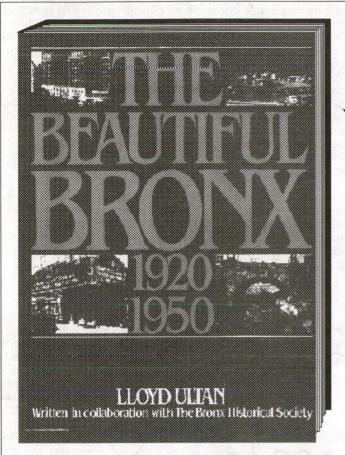

But don't dare skip school (or work) to indulge in these favorite Bronx pastimes–Ms. Issacs and her siblings all became teachers! With the exception of the "Roof Diva" who became–what else? A secretary!

Above, a soulful strut through the Bronx Zoo reveals a pretty young lady rolling up...

...meanwhile *below,* a young family sightseeing is captured by the camera.

The Metropolitan Oval in Parkchester, circa 1942. At its center was one of the most spectacular fountains the Bronx ever had.

6

Telling My Kids About *the Bronx*

Sid H. Kopperl, Clinton '65

I remember the Bronx. Being a Baby Boomer, I was a child in the Bronx in the 50's and a teenager in the 60's. I grew up in the West Bronx, watched the Major Deegan being built, and went to Yankee Stadium to watch the Mick play. I remember the cobble stones near the old Chase Bank near Featherbed Lane. I wonder if that story about George Washington, and the Feather Beds was true after all.

We played stick ball in the streets and our biggest fear was the police would come and take our bat. Ah, the Good Old Days. Of course I remember dating in the Bronx. First dates, or girls you really didn't like, you took to the Park Plaza or the Jerome Theaters. Big dates you took to the Paradise and watched those twinkling stars on the ceiling. Afterwards, if the budget allowed, it was off to Krums or maybe even Jahns. I remember those Kitchen Sinks. In those days, it was so much fun going to Fordham Road, usually we would walk. I remember the opening and the closing of Vic Tanny's. I knew I was at the heart of civilization when I passed Alexanders. Then there was that mens' clothing store next to the RKO Fordham where I got my first Banlon

Continued on page 21

Below left, a sunbather basks at Orchard Beach in 1954. *Below right:* a real Bronx rooftop would be incomplete if not for the splendour of curvacious contours complimenting the angles of modern architecture, whilst young male eyes against binoculars bask. Tar Beach, *indeed.*

Courtesy of the Bronx Historical Society, from the book The Beautiful Bronx.

Courtesy of The Bronx Historical Society, taken from "The Beautiful Bronx" ©Bronx Historical Society.

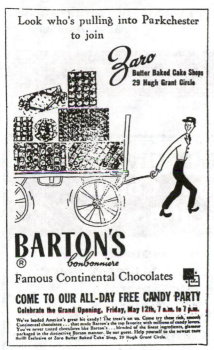

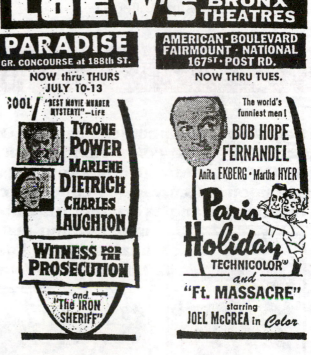
"Although I really grew up in the Bronx of the '30's, 40's and early '50's, I am still interested in all Bronx affairs. As you can see, I still live in the Bronx. I also belong to the Bronx Historical Society.

I was born on Stebbins Avenue near East 169th Street and attended PS 54 and JHS 40, which probably no longer exist. I attended Christopher Columbus HS, Class of June 1946 and Hunter College–first class back on the Bronx campus."

Ms. Dolores H. Lessner

This snapshot was taken with the reader and her friends in the Pelham Parkway area on Lydig Avenue, West of White Plains Road.

Dolores H. Lessner

How many here for a healthy game of bicycle dodge ball? This kid looks like he's asking for it. Kids in my neighborhood would race home after school, grab their bikes and anything throwable, and attempt a dare through the gauntlet. Frisbees, basketballs, Spaldeens, footballs, hardballs and rocks– the bigger the better–were employed to cause the best wipeout. Steel pipes of a rather large diameter were rolled in the direction of oncoming tires, even those not privy to the "game". When we got a little older and had more expendable cash, the game increased in sophistocation. Bottle rockets and other low flying engines were launched from hand-held pipes to augment the assault. Air Force, eat your heart out!

Circa 1964, in the Marble Hill Projects.

HURRICANE ELVIS, *continued from page 1*

Washington H.S.) and, "They Often Call Me Speedo, But My Real Name Is Earl."

Suddenly, I, a "good boy," straight, clean living, awkward, shy, began to tune in Alan Freed's *The Moondog Show* on 1010 WINS in my bedroom at night on my old Emerson Radio and listen to the Moon-glows, the Harptones, the Nutmegs, Laverne Baker, and "The Late and Great Johnny Ace."

I felt so cool. I might have been a flop with girls in the short term, spending most of my time day dreaming about them or playing basketball, or studying to get into "an out-of-town college," but someday, when R&B came into style, then they would see who was really hip.

But for the present, none of the Taft girls who hung out on the corner at the Noonan Plaza at Nelson Avenue and 168th Street or at the Y paid much attention to me. I couldn't really blame them. Nonetheless, I had a crush on a Taft girl named Heather who hung out with a different crowd at the Y, and one day, in a fit of madness, I asked her for a date in two weeks. Somehow, she accepted.

Why would Heather, who was blonde, pretty, a great dancer, popular, and lived in a better building that I did, go out with me? I didn't understand it! (I still don't.)

But she had accepted. For the next two weeks I heard music all around me. Some of it was literally me singing. The Philtons, my SAC, held football practice in Jerome Park , right across from where Heather lived. We would try to play on the grass there, until mysterious little men in green uniforms known as "Parkies" would come and kick us out. (Did they live in the park in some kind of barracks?) Each day, on the way to practice, I would walk by her house, enthralled, singing quietly to myself (seriously!) "On the Street Where You Live," from *My Fair Lady*, hoping that Heather, my blonde

fairy princess, would miraculously come down from her tower and see me in my shoulder pads.

I was mad. Moonstruck. I didn't even like *My Fair lady*. Damn it. But I kept singing that song like an idiot.

Finally the big day arrived. I lived at Nelson Avenue and Boscobel, now called Edward L. Grant Highway. (I think it was named after the first baseball player killed in WWI.) I walked to Heather's house, past the Snowball Luncheonette, past Sacred Heart School, past the huge, prestigious, Noonan Plaza (which, incredibly, had a live swan in the courtyard in a little cement pond,) past the Highbridge Library on Woodycrest, down the long hill at the end of Shakespeare Avenue, past P.S. 114, and alongside the Park.

Heather lived on the part of Jerome Avenue that was not under the el, just north of Yankee Stadium where the el continued on River Avenue and Jerome turned off to run alongside Jerome Park. She lived at the bottom of the long stairs which ran up the cliff to P.S. 76, in a big apartment house across from Mullaly Gym, where we Philtons, Benny Nadelberg, Ronny Powel, Sid Ritkes, Bobby Weinstein (N.Y. Giants Batboy) from Clinton; Barry Klansky, Harvey Goldenberg from Taft: and Joel Buxbaum and Scotty Wiles (the only Protestant we knew) from Science High, had won the Bronx Championship of the Mirror-Parks basketball tournament.

But this was more than basketball. This was a date! With Heather! Heather Finkel! The very name was like music to me.

Fortunately her mother answered the door: I was great with mothers. They could understand why I was studying to go to an out-of-town college. They didn't know I had a secret life in which I listened to Alan Freed.

They had a Baby Grand piano in their sunken living room.

When Heather appeared, her mother had her play a little piece (Perry Como's "If") for me. This was getting more unbelievable by the minute. Heather was not only beautiful and charming and wealthy and popular, but she played the piano! And she looked so pretty that night. It had rained that afternoon, and she was wearing a yellow rain slicker and a round, yellow "fisherman's" rain hat over her soft, blond hair, but it all looked golden to me.

There were movie theaters all over in our neighborhood, many of them named after high places in society or the world: The Earl, Crest, Zenith, Mt. Eden, the Heights (across the bridge in Manhattan.) There was also the Loew's 167th Street, where one Saturday afternoon I had seen the matrons lose control of a full house of kids who, deliriously high on a Martin and Lewis movie, had run onto the stage and torn the curtains down. There were also the Ogden, Park Plaza, Kent, Surrey, and Luxor. But Heather had class. She was obviously a Loews Paradise or RKO Fordham kind of date. But, no, she had missed a movie that was playing at the Earl. Was that OK?

Was that OK? If she had said, "How about catching the late show at the R.K.O. Calcutta?" it would have been okay. I would have merely called a taxi and instructed

him to take us to India. I was absolutely ecstatic.

We walked along Jerome Avenue, my feet hardly touching the ground. We walked under the shuttle tracks, which carried the two car train which ran from 167th Street in the Bronx over the rickety Harlem River Walking Bridge, to the Polo Grounds. We strolled past Babe Ruth Field, the best sandlot field in the Bronx, past Yankee Stadium and Nedicks; to Addie Vallins where we had malteds with real malt. Then across to the Earl Theater.

Apparently it rained some more during the movie, for when I walked her home the streets shone as if the pavement was embedded with jewels.

The next week when I went to the Y, Heather was back with the popular girls and I understood she had put me on hold. She was always busy when I asked her out, and I was sure this was true. Yet she was still friendly and we'd often dance together, so I still had my hopes. Perhaps things would change and in some amazing way people like me would become fashionable and we could resume our magic together.

But one evening, when I entered the lounge, I saw immediately that something powerful and strange was going on. The girls

Continued on page 21

Someday I'm going to be...

These fine young Bronxites moved on to fame and fortune.
Can you guess the names of this talented trio of former Bronxites?
The answers are on page 19. (This will be an irregular feature from now on.)

Mystery Bronxite #1

Mystery Bronxite #2

Mystery Bronxite #3

Bronx Honor Roll

Bronxites who have achieved!

Bronx Science

Edggar Doctorow
Bobby Darren
Stokely Carmichael

Cardinal Hayes

George Carlin
Regis Philbin
Rocky Colovito
Kevin Loughery

DeWitt Clinton

James Baldwin
Paddy Cheyefsky
Daniel Shore
Neil Simon
Richard Rogers
Fats Waller
Don Adams
Martin Balsam
Judd Hirsch
Stubby Kaye
Robert Klein
Burt Lancaster
Jan Murray
Jimmie Walker
Nate Archibald
Dolph Shayes
James Caan
A.M. Rosenthal

Evander Childs

Red Buttons
James Coco
Carl Reiner

Monroe

Hank Greenberg
Ed Kranepool
Jules Pfeiffer

Morris

Gabe Pressman
Angel Cordero

Roosevelt

June Allison

Taft

Eydie Gorme
Stanley Kubrick
Sanford Brown

Other notable folks with ties to the Bronx

Charles Osgood
Vic Damone
Bess Myerson
Dennis Day
Dion DiMucci
Jonas Salk
Roberta Peters
Jerry Vale
Jake LaMotta
Dianne Carroll
Ron Liebman
Gary Marshall
Al Pacino
Rob Reiner
Eli Wallach
Corazon Aquino
Edward Koch
Vin Skully
Joey Adams
Danny Aiello
Ellen Barkum
Alan Alda
Armand Hammer
Theodore Kheel
George Steinbrenner
Don Criqui

Lauren Bacall
Tony Curtis
Hal Linden
Sal Mineo
Charles Nelson Reilly
Isabel Sanford
Vanessa Williams
Herman Badillo
Ted Kennedy
George Burns
Avery Corman
Norman Cousins
Edgar Alan Poe
Geraldo Rivera
Pat Summerall
Herman Wouk
Teresa Brewer
Cab Calloway
Joey Bishop
Joe Franklin
Penny Marshall
Carroll O'Connor
Connie Selleca
Cardinal Cooke
E. Colin Powell
Robert Kennedy
Leon Cooper (Nobel Prize Winner)
Rosalyn Yallow (Nobel Prize Winner)
Anne Bancroft
Ralph Lauren
Eddie Pinckney
Mario Merola
Robert Abrams
Bobby Bonilla
George Cukor
Avery Fisher
Gertrude Elio (Nobel Prize Winner)
Robert Hofstadter (Nobel Prize Winner)
Herman J. Muller (Nobel Prize Winner)
Melvin Schwartz (Nobel Prize Winner)
Steven Weinberg (Nobel Prize Winner)
Gerald Edelman (Nobel Prize Winner)

Now and Then . . .

The Other Side of the Counter

by Ed Eisenberg Eames, Science '48

Last week my wife, Toni, and I had dinner with a friend at a New York-style fifties diner in our adopted hometown of Fresno, California. Sharing memories of growing up in the Bronx with our friends, we made the mistake of ordering an egg cream. When I described the process of making this "exotic" drink to our waitress, she said it would be easy. After the fourth ill-fated attempt to recreate this bit of nostalgic gastronomy, I gave up and ordered a diet Pepsi! However, the incident set off a chain of memories of the hundreds of egg creams I have consumed and created.

In 1939, when I was nine, my family bought a candy store-luncheonette a few blocks from where we lived in the Hunts Point section of the East Bronx. My father was an unemployed house painter, my brother Sid didn't have a steady job, my other brother Irv was in college and my mother was the typical Jewish balabust housewife. The store would give all of us an opportunity to work and help support the family. We sold the store when my brothers entered the army in 1942. Our store was located on the corner of Faile Street and Spofford Avenue. We were diagonally across from P.S. 48 and our local playground was on one of the other corners. The store opened for business every day at 7 A.M. and closed at 11 P.M., except on Saturdays, when we closed after midnight.

Being the son of the owners of a candy store had its bad as well as good points. Well, before I ever took a course in sociology at City College and learned about the role of the man-in-the-middle, I lived it. My folks expected me to take care of the candy counter during lunch and after school. Every kid I knew expected to get extra tootsie rolls, malted milk balls and pretzels. On the other hand, my family kept pretty good inventory records of all candy items. Under these conditions, friendships came and went! Another problem I had was with my teachers who came in for lunch. My mother was always asking them about how I was doing and I hated it.

For me, the positives far outweighed the negatives. I got to read every comic book as soon as it arrived. Each night I got the opportunity to make myself a sundae with any kind of topping I wanted. Running the candy counter, despite its problems, did give me a sense of power over the other kids.

We were one of the few stores in the neighborhood selling Breyers ice cream, then considered one of the finest ice creams in the city. My mother used to get aggravated when people who shopped at other candy stores came to our store only to buy ice cream. She would usually mutter when she saw these "Breyers only" customers coming into the store. When they stood in front of her while she was ladling the ice cream from the large vats into the pint and half-gallon containers urging her to pack the ice cream in harder, she would usually explode and tell them to get their ice cream where they got their other purchases. One of her favorite expressions was: "If you don't like it here, go to Shub.'s (our neighborhood competitor)."

One of our functions was to serve as the local telephone answering service. Many of our customers did not have their own telephones and we took calls for them. My job was calling them to the phone while the caller held on. Usually, my errand earned a tip for me. I particularly liked relaying a message to Mr. Cantor, the post office worker who lived in the building in which the store was located. Instead of schlepping up the four flights of stairs, we had a signal,

"My family bought a candy store-luncheonette a few blocks from where we lived in the Hunts Point section of the East Bronx."

three rings of the bell in the hallway and he hustled down while I ran back to the phone and told the caller to hold on. He always rewarded me with a nickel tip.

It seemed as if there were constant crises: newspapers didn't get delivered on time, a strike would hold up the delivery of syrup, a store window was broken or the juke box wasn't working. None of these everyday crises could match the anxiety we all felt one night when my brother, Sid, called home from the store to say he had been arrested. In today's world where legalized gambling in Las Vegas, Reno and Atlantic City, as well as state lotteries are part of contemporary life, it may seem ludicrous, but Sid was arrested for paying off pin ball machine winners. The winners turned out to be two plain clothes detectives who had played our machines and won a couple of bucks. My mother couldn't believe he had paid off strangers since

she had always warned us never to pay cash unless we knew the person playing the machines. Big Brother, Inc., the company that placed the machines in the store, bailed Sid out after a couple of hours but he was still upset when he got home.

In our store, two pin ball machines paid our monthly rent plus bringing in additional income. Initially, we had one and that was so successful we got a second one. Big Brother, Inc. brought the machines to us and changed them every few weeks. We shared the proceeds and they supplied us with plenty of nickel slugs which I used at night to play the machines when no one was around. In 1940, Mayor LaGuardia targeted the pin ball machine industry as one dominated by the mob when he went on his anti-crime crusade. I still remember pictures of him using an axe to destroy huge piles of confiscated pin ball machines. Anyway, he never got ours! We had connections with the police, who could always count on a free lunch and coffee at our store. One of our police friends warned us of the pin ball machine raids and we got our machines into the basement until Big Brother picked them up. We never again could replace this easy source of paying the rent.

Like all good Bronx candy stores, we prided ourselves on our egg creams. It seems simple to describe making one but try as I could with step-by-step directions, the end result is never the same. Shpritz some chocolate syrup into a glass, pour in some milk, turn on the seltzer spigot until the seltzer reaches the point where the glass widens, insert a long spoon and stir, push the seltzer spigot into the opposite direction to aerate the mixture and fill to the top with seltzer. Seems simple, but they can't do it in Fresno. I wonder if they can still do it in the Bronx.

Ed Eisenberg Eames graduated from Bronx Science in 1948, City College in 1951 and obtained a Ph.D. from Cornell in 1965. He recently retired as a professor of anthropology from Baruch College.

Toni Steele Gardiner Eames graduated from Taft in 1961, from Adelphi University in 1966 and received her M.S. from Hunter College in 1970. She retired from her job as rehabilitation counselor at Kings Park Psychiatric Center.

Ed and Toni currently reside in Fresno, California with their three cats and two guide dogs. They team teach courses on disability issues and write a monthly column on assistance dogs for Dog World magazine. Their greatest regret in leaving New York was giving up their culinary heritage. They recently solved this problem in part by importing authentic New York bagels from Bagelicious, 1-800-55-BAGEL.

"We were one of the few stores selling Breyers ice cream . . . people who stopped at other candy stores came to our store only to buy ice cream."

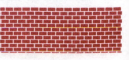

Growing Up on Fordham

by Charles Medwin

I was privileged to grow up in the best decade of the century, 1955-1965. Good times were prevalent by all, being after the Korean War, and before the Viet Nam conflict.

Those happy memories begin for me on Creston Avenue, and 188th Street, just around the corner from the beautiful atmospheric Loew's Paradise. From the beginning of my teen years, I was a movie fanatic. When I was 15 years old, and a junior in DeWitt Clinton High School, I was already working at the ASCOT Theatre, then known as an "art house" specializing in the finest of foreign films. The Bronx was abundant of movie theatres and from the time I was twelve or thirteen, I would be at the theatre doorstep week-ly with my closest and dearest friend, even today, Roy Pautz. Roy lived on Tiebout Avenue, several blocks east of my home, but we were inseparable. Even today, with me living in Las Vegas, Nevada, Roy is my closest friend, and has made the trek out west several times to visit. As teenagers, we both would have a plan: we would bowl in the "Paradise Lanes" then located on the top floor of the Poe Building, located just opposite the Loew's Paradise Theatre. We would usually meet by 10am, and after several lines on the scoresheet, (at 35¢ a line then), we would be ready for our magical venture to a double feature. Where would we go? Loew's Paradise? The RKO Fordham, the bargain Lido Theatre? (The only theatre to my knowledge that was "air cooled", not cooled by refrigeration.) The Valentine? Loew's Grand? For a second and third run house? Who knew? But where ever we did go, it was a double feature, with newsreel, usually a short and/or cartoon, and of course the trailers of up and coming attractions...

Growing up in the Fordham section of the Bronx afforded me the convenience of the great Fordham Public Library, located on Bainbridge Avenue. I think back today at the many class reports and projects I undertook there, trying to be smart and "copying portions" of texts from their encyclopedias, only to find out

Fordham and Kingsbridge Roads in the late 40's was heavily traveled. Note Fordham University in the background center.

Courtesy of The Bronx Historical Society, taken from "The Beautiful Bronx" ©Bronx Historical Society.

"I was caught up in this sudden wave of nostalgia by accident, but your newsletter, and the articles contained herein, have transported me back. Back to a time of more innocent living and good clean fun. I present here my memories of growing up in the Fordham Road section of the Bronx..."

some other "slick" classmate of mine had the same idea, and we often had identical passages in our reports.

Shopping was so convenient and abundant with Alexander's Department Store just a block from my home, not to mention the entire mile and a half from Jerome Avenue, east to Webster Avenue, culminat-

ing at the great Sear's Department Store. Being an avid record collector, (even today), I and my friends always would drop in to "Cousin's Records", near Webster Avenue, for until as late as the mid–sixties, you could still "audition" the records you considered purchasing in little booths in the rear of the store.

After receiving my first English Racer bicycle around 1956, my world expanded even more with bike trips, (sometimes alone) to Van Cortlandt Park, and to what would eventually be my high school, DeWitt Clinton, and Harris Field to watch and sometimes partake in softball and other sports.

The evenings

Fordham Road and Morris Avenue were punctuated by Grant's five-and-dime and the local bakery in the late 40's. Note the abundance of Art Deco details.

Courtesy of The Bronx Historical Society, taken from "The Beautiful Bronx" ©Bronx Historical Society.

when there was no school and I was allowed to stay out in the evening, our crowd would always wind up at Krums for their delicious and (in those days) reasonable ice cream sodas and sundaes. For a quick pick me up, ten cents would buy an egg cream and a nickel would buy a Coke, Pepsi, or small flavored drink from our candy store.

There is so much I can remember of those innocent, clean, pure days, but to list them all would take an entire issue. Again, thank you all for the wonderful articles, especially the one's about Freedomland, certainly one of my steady haunts until they closed.

But that's another story.

These photos (right and opposite) were taken of me about 1942 or '43. This is looking notheast across West Fordham Road between Davidson and Jerome Avenues. The theatre is the Loews Grand and the marquee shows the double feature then,

Norman Medwin

Norman Medwin

Pardon My Past and *Tars and Spars.* I used to live on Creston Avenue, between East 188th Street–just behind the Loews paradise. The huge wall was our playground: stickball, handball, baseball–anything against the wall–and occasionally sneak in.

17

Classifieds

Freddie Mooke, Rosalie Graf, and Renee. We honored the soldiers, sailors, and nurses of WW2. Call me!

MP255 • Gun Hill Road–215, PS 94, JHS 80, Bruce Freeman, Arthur Pornick, Howard Berger, Frank Dickson, Howard Weinfeld, David Switkin.

MP256 • PS 26–Barbara Jacobs from 1950 Andrews Ave. Would love to locate friends from the old neighborhood. I'm alive and well and living in California. A "1950" reunion would be fun!

MP257 • Nancy Kravitz Zimmerman looking for anyone from the crowd at Jahn's and Creston JHS; Susan Edelman, Barbara Weinstein Goodman, Fran Podber and Marcia Silverberg Pulawitz.

MP258 • Stuart Copans, Scottsdale, AZ–Any Clinton or Music and Art (1952) or CCNY (1957) grads living in Scottsdale, AZ area, please call.

MP259 • Looking for my redheaded bridesmaids–Shirley Kopatz Sarris, Walton 1955 & Joan Schwartz Shine, Far Rockaway HS 1955. We have much to catch up on. Miss you.

MP260 • Walton '58–looking for classmates for 35th reunion. Waltonites, where are you?

MP261 • Taft '62–Larry Mendelowitz would like to hear from old friends. Write or call.

MP262 • Ken Cohen 171st St. and McCombs Rd. (PS 104, PS 82 Clinton) is alive and well–living with Barbara (Bernstein) Cohen and two boys in Yardley PA. OK, Tommy DeCallucia, Mike Klein, Peter Krakoff, Jay Stevelman and the rest of you Schoolyard Players get in touch. Stickball, Scully, Johnny-On-The-Pony and Curb Ball are waiting to be played.

MP263 • Looking for anyone who grew up south of 149th St. in the Willis–Alexander Avenue area. I'm doing "Oral History" interviews for a book about the South Bronx and would like to talk with and reminisce with you.

MP264 • Howard Arnheimer would like to hear from members of the Cavaliers and the Davidson Avenue crowd.

MP265 • Steve Schnapp looking for Cromwell Avenue folks: "Juicy" Heisler, Cheryl Wolchan, David Singer, Barry and "Muggs" Latzer, Eugene Bruhin, Sol Goldberg, Tony Larmamora, Freddie Grunewald, Jason Berman, Mark Stoller, Lenny Erlich. Time for a game of Curb Ball.

MP266 • Paul Pintel from Eastburn Avenue would like to hear from Panther Club members, stickball players, those who socialized with the club and went on to PS 70, JHS 117, Clinton, Taft, Walton, Science.

MP267 • Failed novelist, so-so feature editor, Taft Review '67-'68, now a happy Manhattanite. Do you remember me or my writing? Wilma Kuhn–I'd love hearing from you!

MP268 • Missing–Rita Cavalik Hazelton, last known address Dunedin, Florida 1975. Barbara Berger Cooper and Edna Stein Cohen are looking for you. Rita, or anyone knowing her whereabouts, please get in touch.

MP269 • Highbridge. Anyone live in Highbridge during the 40's and go to PS 73? Maybe we knew each other. Contact Jay Jacobson, Clinton '51.

MP270 • Lynn Graff, 182nd St. and Davidson Ave. looking for Ira Karsh and others from neighborhood. Also, Richie Yessian and Frankie Morris from Science '57 and other friends from Science '59.

MP271 • Where are you Rona Kaufman JHS 22 '58? Looking for Meet Chicks–Barbara Klugman and Lillian Heisler Taft '61. Also Sandy Alekman, Estelle Balmuth and any other Taft '61 people. Contact Lila Freilicher.

MP272 • "Polycar" was my maiden name and I graduated in '64 from Taft.

Come Blow Your Horn

CB3 • To all members of the graduating class of 1966, 9-ESP-1, JHS 143, Alan Sloma says hello!

CB4 • I'm Audrey Miller Rabinowitz, a freelance copywriter and direct marketing consultant. Lived on Grant Ave. and 164th St. and always felt like I was poor compared to the kids who lived on the Concourse (I was 3 blocks East). PS 35 was right across the street. Anyone around from Mrs. Streng's 6th grade class at PS 35? Fern Dorfman, Rochelle Lorber, Karen Kaminsky?

CB5 • Stanley Weiner, Taft '53 and Towson College, has just moved back from Charleston, SC with Trudi Fischer Weiner, Taft '53 and NYU '57. Stanley is Chief Operating Officer of Playtogs, Inc., Middletown, NY. Trudi managed a boutique and bought contemporary sportswear in Charleston. They are happy to be back in the Big Apple.

CB6 • I'm Louise Dichter Wilson, now married 33 1/2 years (still) with two grown children–son a lawyer, daughter a banker. Husband owns a contracting business. I'm a sales and marketing director for a large new home developer and builder. One of three females of a forty member Board of Directors of Tri-County Builders Assoc.

CB7 • The Jewish Service Center provides life sustaining/Jewish enrichment services for the Bronx Jewish poor/elderly. Individuals who wish to support this effort should contact:

Asher Moskowitz, Director
Jewish Service Center
2432 Grand Concourse
Room 502
Bronx, NY 10458
(212) 364-7900

This issue's Mystery Bronxites

Bess Myerson
Carl Reiner
Neil Simon

If you have a Bronx Test, samples for Mystery Bronxites or any sort of trivia, do not hesitate to send them in. Please make sure that you also supply the correct answer. Please use a blank sheet of paper following the format in this and past issues and enclose in the reader reply envelope.

The Egg Cream Mystique

by Kal Rosenberg

Egg cream. The very name evokes mystery and fascination, for the product contains neither eggs nor cream, and the white-aproned aficionados who prepare them intensify the mystery, insisting certain rites be performed without deviation, like casting a spell. Unfortunately for these witch doctors, different white aprons insist on different steps, which casts some doubt upon their magical properties.

The mysterious egg cream's secrets unravel through little more than keen observation. It is simply a chocolate soda with a little milk in it, stirred to produce a foamy head. That's it. Period. It doesn't matter if you put the syrup in first or last, it doesn't matter what kind of glass you use, it doesn't matter if you pipe the seltzer right down the middle or deflect it with a spoon so it hits the side of the glass. As long as it's chocolate syrup, milk, and seltzer, you should get an egg cream.

Science has limits. It can dissect the egg cream into it's components, but try walking into a Bronx candy store and ordering a chocolate soda with a little milk in it. They would throw you out, or if they didn't it would stick in your throat. So we are back to magic again, where the whole is more than the sum of its parts.

The eight-cent delight that I remember came with a repertoire of rituals, without which its appeal would soon have faded. True, the order of introduction of the elements was irrelevant; it seemed indispensable that they accompany a characteristic style, the signature of its maker.

Tony, at Joe's College Luncheonette on Jerome Avenue and 198th Street, always needed a shave. He might serve other drinks in a paper cup, but never an egg cream, the making of which he approached as a religious rite. Using only large Coca-Cola glasses, stirred and foam-flicked only by a long handled spoon, this became a serious business. And anything other than Fox's U-Bet syrup would have dishonored the profession. Still, each white apron held fast to his own formula. Like French chefs, soda jerks Bronxwide measured correctly, stirred correctly, wiped their hands off on their aprons correctly, all in accordance with ancient wisdom–even waiting that split second for the foam to settle before lifting that concoction from the fountain, delivering it with a flair to its recipient.

A few years ago I returned to Kingsbridge Road for a visit. Stopping at the candy store on Creston Avenue, I said to the boy, "Give me an egg cream. You know, I used to work here."

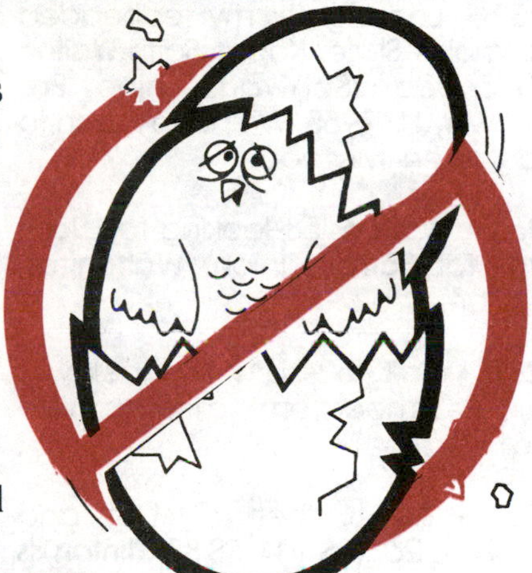

"You did? When?"

"In 1950."

"Are you serious? In 1950? I wasn't born."

I watched this second generation genie serve me up an egg cream. Not exactly the way I used to believe it had to be done. He used his own singular magic. But it was still magic.

The Bronx *Genuine Authentic* Egg Cream *Recipe*

In a large glass (perferrably an old Coca-Cola soda glass), pour a desirable amount of Fox's U-Bet Chocolate Syrup followed by a couple of ounces of milk. Stir with a long handled spoon. Mix with a few ounces of seltzer water until a foamy head is produced . . . ***Definitely NO EGGS!***

The 20's: Good Times, Bad Times

by Phyllis Stang

As the saying goes, "The Best of Times" and "The Worst of Times" could describe my life in the Bronx. I was born on the lower East Side of Manhattan in 1920 and moved to the Bronx when I was 3. The Bronx for me was always having lots of family around and good neighbors. People were good to each other. We always wanted to help people around us and became part of their lives. I watched and helped with all the babies in the neighborhood, enjoyed it and would never accept payment for it.

I always had friends who were sincere and accepting of me as I was and I felt that way about them. We could get together with groups on the "stoop" and have a ball, just laughing about anything. You did not need a skating rink, the streets did just fine. We played Pottsie, jumped rope or did what is now known as "crafts", (i.e. embroidery, sewing clothing for cupie dolls or making raffia baskets).

We lived through good times, depression, wars and always felt like part of a very large group, who had the same feelings we did. We accepted foreigners as our own and taught them the language so they could join our games and understand us. We accepted retarded people and tried to help them. I thoroughly enjoyed my youth in the Bronx.

Although I live in California, I still exchange visits with some of my school chums. The last twenty some odd years in the Bronx, my husband and I had a Mama & Papa business on Gunhill Road. Life, Thank God, has been good to me. My husband and I have two wonderful daughters, who have married wonderful men and given us wonderful grandchildren, God Bless them. I could go on and on but I don't think that's what you want. God Bless you and help you give us more information about other people in and from the Bronx.

"I grew up in the West Bronx, watched the Major Deegan being built..."
The Major Deegan, under construction way back when. Remember the land the way it was before?

HURRICANE ELVIS, continued from page 11

kept playing the same song over and over again on the jukebox. And all the girls, including Heather, were screaming wildly and crying, and they were tearing their hair and saying, "Oh, my God," and dancing in a new way, shaking their hips. There was even a new, racy look in their eyes.

The song was "Heartbreak Hotel." *Hurricane Elvis* had hit The Bronx. My ship was floundering in its wake. People did begin to listen to the sweet, harmonious R&B songs I loved more often now, but these were clearly minor compared to the big storm of Tennessee. Elvis the Pelvis! Exactly the opposite of a shy, awkward, self-conscious guy like me, who was studying like mad to Ace his Regents.

Elvis wouldn't give a damn about his Regents. Anyone could see that. I was finished. I had bet on the wrong horse again. And The Bronx would never be the same.

I, of course, tried to hide my disappointment and loneliness by affecting a "cool" attitude to all these events. This "white music" was nothing like the real music, the rhythm and blues I had been listening to for years on Alan Freed. I protested. Although I came to like rock and roll too, of course. I even dragged my pal Albie Zelnik up to Forhdam Road with me again, this time to the Loew's Paradise to see Jerry Lee Lewis live, bashing out "Great Ball of Fire" on his piano.

 But I never got to go out with Heather Finkel again. The last time I saw her she was dancing the fish with a guy from the East Bronx whom she was going steady with, a guy with a D.A. haircut and big arms, who carried a pack of cigarettes on this shoulder, rolled up in the sleeve of his tight white tee-shirt.

Gerald Rosen's fifth book, *Growing Up Bronx*, ("A humorous, touching novel" – N.Y. Times) is available from North Atlantic Books, 2800 Woolsey, Berkeley, CA 94705 for $10.00 (postage and tax included).

TELLING YOUR KIDS, continued from page 7

shirt. After a quick stop at Sears, I was off to Cousin Records Shop. Lunch was usually 5 to 10 White Castles. Those were the Good Old days. I remember the opening of that new Frances Marion Library on University Avenue, an egg cream at the neighborhood candy store, or a slice of pizza for 15 cents.

I haven't been back to the Bronx for over ten years. It's easier just to sit back, and tell my kids "I remember the Bronx."

22

READER REPLIES

It is vitally important that you fill out the information below. Your input will be essential to the success of this magazine, tailored and inspired by you, the former "Bronxite". We thank you for your participation.

Subscriber? ❑ Yes   ❑ No

YOUR NAME _____

ADDRESS _____

CITY _____ STATE _____ ZIP _____ PHONE _____

HIGH SCHOOL ATTENDED _____ YEAR GRADUATED _____

TELL US A LITTLE ABOUT YOURSELF,

(Be sure to include your alma mater, old neighborhood, your best memories about your days in the Bronx, (or anything else you can tell us).

_____

_____

COULD WE SEND A FRIEND A FREE COPY OF BACK IN THE BRONX?

Do you know current or former Bronxites who would like to receive our magazine and reunion information?
If you do, we'll be happy to send them a **free** inaugural issue of **Back in THE BRONX.**
Write to Back in The Bronx, Box 141 H, Scarsdale, NY 10583 or call 1-800-7-BRONX 5

Last _____ First _____ Maiden _____

Address _____ City _____ State _____ Zip _____

Phone # ( ) _____ School and year of Graduation _____

Last _____ First _____ Maiden _____

Address _____ City _____ State _____ Zip _____

Phone # ( ) _____ School and year of Graduation _____

Last _____ First _____ Maiden _____

Address _____ City _____ State _____ Zip _____

Phone # ( ) _____ School and year of Graduation _____

Last _____ First _____ Maiden _____

Address _____ City _____ State _____ Zip _____

Phone # ( ) _____ School and year of Graduation _____

COME BLOW YOUR OWN HORN DEPARTMENT

Please tell us about yourself (include your name)—about your accomplishments, awards, titles or works in progress. We're interested in hearing about them. List Below. _____

_____

_____

_____

_____

READER REPLIES

As a subscriber you are entitled to a FREE 40 Word Classified, Missing Persons, Blow Your Own Horn, or Personal Ad. Please write your ad below (if you are not subscribing to our magazine you can still place an ad in the next issue. The cost of an advertisement is 50¢ a word, there is no limit on paid ads).

_____

_____

_____

Is Your Mailing Label Correct?

In order to keep our database current, please correct any errors and place the label and or photocopy with corrections.

Account #	High School	Year Graduated

```
6817        Roosevelt       1958
S A M P L E
    Mary R. Flowers
    123 Anystreet Blvd.
    Anywhere, USA  12345
```

Change of Address?

If you're planning a move please attach your label corrected with your new address and the date that you will begin receiving mail at that address. This will insure that you don't miss your next issue of **Back in THE BRONX**.

Ordering Information

YES, I'd like to order the following items:

QTY.

____ 1Yr. (4 ISSUES) Subscription(s) to Back in THE BRONX $19.95
____ 2Yr. (8 ISSUES) Subscription(s) to Back in THE BRONX* .. $29.95 } *FREE John's Menu
____ 3Yr. (12 ISSUES) Subscription(s) to Back in THE BRONX* .. $39.95
____ 4Yr. (16 ISSUES) Subscription(s) to Back in THE BRONX* .. $49.95
____ The Beautiful Bronx...........$25.00 (plus $3.95 S/H) $28.95
____ The Bronx: It Was Only Yesterday..$25.00 (plus $3.95 S/H) $28.95
____ Bronx High School Reunion Weekend Video $29.95
____ SAVE MONEY - BUY 4 FOR JUST $99.00!
____ THE BRONX Tracking Service $9.95
_____ I would like to receive all available back issues and have them applied towards my subscription *(To date we have at least 12 back issues available - While They Last!)*

TOTAL: $ _____

Please fill out completely and include $3.95 for shipping and handling for books only to: **Back in THE BRONX**, Box 141H, Scarsdale, NY 10583

A Great Gift Idea! In addition to your own subscription, a subscription to **Back in THE BRONX** makes a great and unique gift. Fill in the form below and we'll process the order in time for our next issue. So, order your subscription NOW, and order one for a friend!

Please Print Clearly ☐ New Subscriber   ☐ Renewal

Name _____

Maiden Name _____

Address _____

City _____

State _____ Zip _____

Phone (_____) _____

High School _____ Year Grad. _____

☐ Visa ☐ Mastercard ☐ Check ☐ Money Order

No. _____ Expiration Date _____

Signature _____

Back in THE BRONX

Box 141 H, Scarsdale, NY 10583
Phone 914-592-1647 • Fax 914-592-4893

ADDRESS CORRECTION REQUESTED

Volume II   Issue V

Back in THE BRONX

Celebrating the experience of growing up and living in the Bronx

CASTLE HILL POOL:
Memories of the Bronx Riviera

by Martin A. Jackson, Science '58

It was at the far end of Castle Hill Avenue, where the buildings stopped and were replaced by open fields of cattails and weeds. The Whitestone Bridge soared above the Pool's acres which were carved out of marshlands and meandering brooks where little houses on stilts still survived into the 1950's, homes for fisherman or (so I was told) hunters who peddled muskrat pelts. Outside the high fences of the Pool itself, was a wilderness, where parents warned their children never to venture, even after a softball or windblown hat. Once a band of wild dogs actually killed a child who dared beyond the boundaries, and I can tell you from personal observation that very large rats held sway in the mud and bull rushed along the creeks.

The fences were a fitting symbol of Castle Hill Pool, for it was a self-contained world in the 40's and 50's. Actually, the official title was Castle Hill Beach Club, but everybody called it "the Pool", as in "are you going to the

Pool today?", or, "I'll see you at the Pool around eleven o'clock." As a private beach club, Castle Hill wasn't obligated to admit the public nor anyone else who didn't quite "fit in". But the several generations of mostly Bronx dwellers who made Castle Hill a summer oasis considered it a family. Mostly Jewish, yes, but with a substantial number of Italian and Irish members who (so far as I remember) got along just fine. Once inside the forest green doors, everybody looked the same in bathing suits and shorts and there was a deep feeling of a big family picnic underway, especially on the weekends and holidays.

Getting into the pool wasn't simple, mind you. You had to have a pass. The pass was the portable symbol of mem-

bership, and consisted of a (usually) terrible picture of yourself stapled onto a card with the year in big letters and slipped into an imitation leather holder with a clear plastic front. Every year, when you or your father paid the membership dues (about $35 during the 50's), you were notified to come up to the pool and take your annual picture. This was done usually in the early spring, so that taking the picture for your pass was an early sign of the summer ahead, a wonderful reminder to the kids in school that, yes, it would someday end and you could come back to Castle Hill again. The picture itself was generated in a mysterious wooden booth that sat near the entrance gate, something like the Coney Island fifty cent picture booths, complete with a sliding wooden chair and curtains. A few weeks after the event, which often was the occasion for meeting old friends and going out to eat, the treasured pass itself was ready and you picked it up at the desk on the first day of the season. Losing your pass was a serious
See CASTLE HILL, p. 9

From the Editors...

For many of you, this fifth issue of **Back in the BRONX** (including our inaugural release) will be your final issue. It is our hope that the **Back in the BRONX** issues that you received have lived up to your expectations and have given you some moments to reflect on your childhood and adolescence.

If you wish to continue to receive **Back in the BRONX** please take a few minutes to renew your subscription (see pages 23 and 24) which will be your passport to travel back in time, back to the old neighborhood and back to good times with great people–fellow Bronxites like yourselves. For those renewing for two years (eight issues), we are giving out a *free* laminated **Jahn's** menu (circa 1950). If the names of the items don't bring back the twenty or forty more years, the prices certainly will!

Do you have friends, neighbors, or relatives who might be interested in a free inaugural issue? Please give us their names and addresses and we will be happy to send it to them. If they wish they may call our toll free number 1-800-7 **BRONX** 5 and we will see to it that they receive an issue.

Are you a budding editor, artist, historian, writer, or storyteller? We know that there's plenty of home-grown talent who want to share their personal experiences. To date their effort has truly made publishing **Back in the BRONX** a labor of love.

Thank you for your previous patronage and we hope that we can count on you again for your continued support.

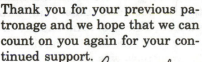

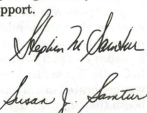
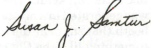

Publishers and Editors	**Stephen M. Samtur**
	Susan H. Samtur
Art Director	**Thomas R. Hamilton**
	Herald Graphics Inc. Stratford CT

A number of the photographs in **Back in the BRONX** are courtesy of and available from the Bronx Historical Society.

Graffiti

Dear Stephen,

I have enclosed my thoughts on the PS 64 Bronx 1949 reunion on Sunday, June 7, 1992 at the LaGuardia Marriot. I attended with a fellow classmate.

I informed my radio audience about the reunion on a recent show featuring reunions, that they could find out about Bronx reunions by reading **Back in the BRONX**, so I hope you receive inquiries for the newspaper.

I have expressed my thanks to Richard Cohen and David Horowitz for making this reunion possible. It was a job well done.

Sincerely,

Roberta (Bobbe) Rosenberg Firtell
(originally from 40 Elliot Place, Apt. K
Bronx

Dear Sirs:

As I sit here at O'Hare airport awaiting my return flight to Los Angeles, I have just completed reading volume one number three of **Back in the BRONX**. I cannot believe the memories which have come flooding back during these past few hours...Cappies Candy Store on the corner of Walton Avenue and 176th Street (across the street from Wade Junior High School's schoolyard, the Grand Concourse, Freedomland, and much, much more).

I agree with Bob Mangels about the glories of Freedomland. My first date with my now wife took place at Freedomland, only because I lost several dollars to her playing blackjack and "had to" take her out. Freedomland was great.

I received the newsletter from a dentist in Philadelphia who was in the audience yesterday as I spoke at the Liberty Dental Conference on emergency medicine. As always, I preface my talks with background information, including the fact that I went to PS 70, JHS 117, and the High School of Music and Art (M&A 1961). I am amazed at how often persons in all parts of our country come to me and mention that they too are from New York City, and on rarer occasions, that they are from the Bronx.

How many places are there in the world that have "the" as part of its name? The Hague in the Netherlands and the Bronx! What other part of New York City is attached to the U.S. mainland? Not Brooklyn, not Queens, not Manhattan, nor Staten Island. Only the Bronx.

See GRAFFITI, p. 5

The BRONX, After All These Years

by Roberta Graff

I didn't move from the Bronx; I escaped. That was almost 30 years ago when the only acceptable manner of getaway was matrimony. My marriage license became my passport when I said "yes" to the handsome Ivy Leaguer who elicited signs of approval from the neighbors who governed my life and judged my every move.

They congregated on camp chairs in front of my apartment building on warm summer evenings, patiently watching as my boyfriend circled the block several dozen times looking for a parking space. They nodded to each other as if to say, we knew you'd never find a spot as he double parked. Taking the steps to the lobby two at a time he dashed into the elevator and pressed the button for four.

I was always ready and it was only a matter of minutes before we walked past our audience on the way back to the car.

"See, I told you he was for 4B," Mrs. Waxman whispered.

"So again you're right," her husband answered.

How I resented their comments and stares, which inevitably led to a heated discussion with my mother the next day. "Why are they so damn nosey?" I would ask impatiently. "Can't they mind their own business?"

"They don't mind their own business because they have no business worth minding." My mother answered in her most condescending tone. "They are interested in you because you are something special. They were always

interested in you. You were the most beautiful baby on the Grand Concourse. You had a white coach carriage. When I wheeled that carriage by Poe Park every head turned. Believe me, they are still talking about that white carriage!"

Though I found it highly questionable that my baby carriage could only be on anyone's mind for more than 20 years, no matter how uneventful their own lives had been, I wisely chose not to challenge my mother's statements. Instead I would change the subject to my upcoming marriage, my new apartment, my new life.

"Are you going to move, Mother?" I would ask.

"Because you are moving away that means I should too," my mother would answer, giving me just that little stab of guilt she obviously found necessary to keep me in line.

The author, 1937.

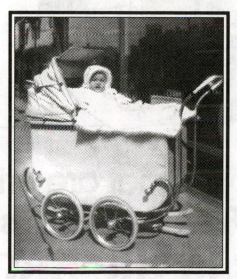

"Why should I give up such an apartment — facing the Concourse, southeast exposure, tile kitchen, sunken living room, always a breeze?" she continued like a real estate agent with an unsure prospect. And I would think of the sweltering July nights when you could barely breathe, the limited closets, and keep my mouth closed. "No dear," she would conclude, "apartments like this you simply do not give up."

True to her word, she never gave up the apartment, even when her winters in Florida ran into spring and then summer. "Why should I come home?" she would ask me on the telephone from Miami on the Fourth of July. "It's not even hot here." However, to her newly made Floridian friends, she would boast, "I have a beautiful home up north, you know, and I'll probably go for a visit next month."

But next month never came and the apartment became a store house for possessions and memories that my mother would never give up.

Now I have returned to the Bronx, considerably more mellow and minus the hostilities I carried with me when I left. The job of giving up the apartment is now mine. The furniture dealer has been contacted, the charitable organizations, always happy for contributions, have been called, and the landlord has been notified...after five decades, 4B is now for rent.

I drive around the block at least six times looking for a place to park. I am luckier than my former boyfriend; someone pulls an old Chevrolet out of a spot not far from my mother's

building. I walk down the street where I once roller-skated and notice the neighborhood is only vaguely familiar; the kosher deli is now a bodega, the candy store where I'd quench my thirst on egg creams is a bar.

I pass two little black girls jumping rope as I enter the apartment house and look around the once elegantly furnished lobby. There is an old stained sofa pushed off in a corner. It's stuffing is falling out. I walk into the mail room where I once played hide-and-seek. My mother's mailbox is crammed full of junk mail addressed to Occupant and Tenant. One envelope is addressed to Our Friendly Neighbor. I laugh. My mother was hardly a friendly neighbor. The names on the letter boxes have changed. Levy and Goldberg have been replaced by Gomez and Hernandez. I open the elevator door. The walls are covered with obscenities I didn't know until I was too old to derive any satisfaction from using. I feel for the keys in my pocket. There

are four, one for each lock on the door of my mother's apartment.

The elevator stops at one. A very old lady eyes me suspiciously, hesitates and slowly walks in. She looks vaguely familiar. "Mrs. Waxman?" I ask uncertainly.

"Yes, who is it?" she asks me nervously as though I had rung her doorbell in the middle of the night.

"I'm sure you don't remember, but I used to live here." Moving a little closer, she looks up at me and a faint smile crosses her wrinkled face.

"Of course, 4B, what a big beautiful girl you've become," she says appraising all 5 feet, 2 inches of me.

"I can't believe you remember me, after all these years," I reply.

"Why, who could forget that white carriage?"

ABOUT THE AUTHOR:

Roberta Nussbaum Graff is the travel, art and features editor of the South Shore Record, an award winning Long Island weekly. In addition, she freelances to a variety of national and international magazines and newspapers. Her work has been published by the *New York Times*, *Newsday*, *Country Accents*, *Victorian Accents*, *Bride's*, *American Baby*, *Good Housekeeping* and *Travel/Holiday*. She is presently working on a novel.

The first twenty two years of her life were lived in the Bronx at 2675 Creston Avenue. She attended P.S. 86 and then spent the next four years on the D train commuting to the High School of Performing Arts.

Graffiti, continued

Reading through the articles submitted by readers, and especially the classifieds, made the two hour flight from Philadelphia to Chicago feel like but a minute.

It's been a year since I talked about Spaldeen's, Jahn's (where the waiters never wrote any order down, and *never* made a mistake!) Alexander's, Krum's and the Paradise Theater (before it became a multiplex).

Keep up the good work. I hope that our landsmen who have spread throughout the world hear about *Back in the Bronx* and start to write in and subscribe. The opportunity is too good to miss.

Sincerely,
Stanley Malamed
Scarsdale

Anatomy of a Reunion

by Allen Mandel

In the summer of 1990 seven former Bronxites descended upon the grounds of Kutcher's Country Club and discovered old friendships. It was as if we had just parted the week before. Oh, there were the obligatory hugs and handshakes, but we soon settled into some serious reminiscing. We learned about each other's lives, each other's families, children, jobs. But the most important thing we discovered during that weekend, was that we had all left our egos back home. No one dragged out the "brag-books" and foisted those terrible baby pictures on the others. No one found it necessary to "one up" the others with their successes. No one passed out their raised-letter business cards, soliciting business. We were just a bunch of old friends getting together, reliving our youth, retelling old lies, and in general, enjoying each other's company.

Over the years, I've been in regular contact with one of the guys I grew up with, Joel Draper (Clinton '60). We decided a long time ago, that he would call me on his birthday, and I would call him on mine. As it happens, he was occasionally in touch with another of the guys, Joel Feerst (Music and Art '60), and he had a little contact with Marc Meyer (Clinton '60). Beyond that, the other guys had sort of disappeared: Sid Friedland (Stuyvesant '60), Ed Schulman (Clinton '60), and Charlie Maley (Music & Art '60). The three of us decided it was time to find the others, and after some research, we found all but Charlie. (We still haven't found him!) After a frenzied round of "phone-tag" we spoke to each other, and decided to get together the following year. The last time many of us spoke, much less met face-to-face, was at my wedding twenty-seven years ago!

Joel D. and I remembered when we first met in the fourth grade at P.S. 56, and we decided that we were not perfect angels, even back then. Our desks were alongside the coat closet, and between the doors were the ever-present bulletin boards. Our desks were next to the current events board and we remembered spending a good deal of time throwing "darts" at the board. Actually, the darts were made of sewing needles we stuck into the eraser ends of our pencils. Emblazoned over the board were clippings of newly-captured bank robber Willie Sutton, and by the time we were finished, the board was no longer useful. There were more holes than board. We remembered Mrs. Bolger becoming so upset that she went to her desk to sit down, missed her chair and landed in the waste paper basket! Yes, we did get in a little trouble for that. Although Joel didn't remember it quite that way, it made for a good story.

We also remembered the spirited "punchball" games in the '56 schoolyard during lunch, and how Jerry Fisher (another name from the past), and I were always captains, choosing sides, because we were the only ones at the time able to punch the old Spaldeen

Reunion, 1949 Style

I recently attended my public school reunion, from PS 64 in the Bronx. When I told friends that I was going to a sixth grade reunion, they wondered, why? I would not recognize anyone from so long ago, having last seen them when they were eleven. I thought about that. After all, it involved a plane trip, staying at a friend's home, and going back to a time that could no longer be.

In the end, I chose to go, to try to recapture when I was eleven years old. After all, who else could I speak with that would remember 170th Street, the Grand Concourse, the Luxor and Zenith movies, the Jerome Avenue El, Taft High School, and the place where most people went on their first date big date, the Paradise Movie Theatre. Remember the stars in the ceiling that looked like a sky?

I attended the PS 64 1949 reunion on Sunday, June 7, 1992. I went with Irene Abdel Santini, a fellow classmate. Immediately upon entering, we saw Lenny Luner and Leslie Kallenberg, both of whom looked the same as we remembered them. I reminded Susan Epstein Ross that she was the first person I knew to own a ballpoint pen.

Among my classmates was David Horowitz, consumer advocate and host of "Fight Back with David Horowitz," a TV show for the last eighteen years. There were TV cameras, newspaper reporters and radio commentators at the reunion with us. It was very exciting. There was the atmosphere of a *happening*.

That night we watched the six o'clock and eleven o'clock news and videotaped them, especially since David Horowitz, Irene Leona Schuman and I were featured. Then, to open the papers the next day and see the reunion featured in both papers, even quoting Irene, was a blast.

The Bronx Borough President was very angry at us for having the reunion in Queens instead of the Bronx. The newspapers called it "The Reunion of Fear," because we were afraid to go to the Bronx.

There was a ripple effect after this

onto the roof of the gym and get it back.

Our reminiscing took us on to JHS 80 (Class of '57), and the time we were invited to dance on T.V. on Ted Steele's Dance Party. I wonder what my date, Arlene Schreiber is doing now? We remembered hanging out on the fence and the grass on the "parkway", outside '80, and the name "Lefty" Drillick came up. Lefty was the sometimes nonviolent "leader" of the parkway. I seemed to remember reading an article, years ago, that Gary Marshall loosely patterned "the Fonz" after Lefty, but I couldn't recall the source. You

have to remember, this was the late 50's, and without realizing it, we were living "Happy Days" in the Bronx.

Those of us that went to Clinton remembered Irving Packer, a math teacher who lived in the neighborhood, and during bad weather, always allowed us to hitch a ride with him. I don't think our suddenly appearing at his car fooled him. He knew what we were after, and he accommodated. Nice man. I understand he's now Chairman of the Math Department, and the boys congratulate him.

As we strolled around Kutcher's lake, we were suddenly taken back to the "Oval" off Bainbridge Avenue, and up the street from '80. We were into all the sports then, football, baseball, and even a little tennis. Speaking of football, there was one more guest with us, John (Gene) Klein, and we just had to re-live some of the better football games we played, both as opponents and together. John began his football career with the Semanon's (which backward spelled "no names"), and my career started with the Webbs. Looking back, some of those games were memorable, and some of the pain still exists.

Someone recalled our first experiments with tobacco, our first taste of alcohol, and our experiences with "the opposite sex". We remembered the girls of our past: Susan Garber, Sheila Ober, Judy Colodne, Helene Lessinger. (Anyone out there still in contact with them? Contact the writer via *Back in the Bronx* office. The guys would like to say hello.)

by Roberta (Bobbe) Rosenberg Firtell

reunion. The ripples from the original splash that extend out and touch other areas, and other people, never cease to amaze me. For example, I went to my sixth grade reunion expecting only to see some familiar faces and wax nostalgic; too simplistic!

One of the ripples from the reunion was having David, a person experienced in broadcasting, call me from California after forty years, and suggest that I do a show on reunions. How far do the ripples extend? Saying the name "Lenny Luner" for the first time in decades and corresponding with him as if only a few days had passed since sixth grade. Staying at Irene Abdel's home and going dancing with her and her husband, which I never expected to do, and now my husband Dave and I are taking dancing lessons, because I discovered another world that I didn't know existed.

Another ripple: David Horowitz returned to the Bronx to give the commencement speech at the PS 64 graduation, held at Taft High School. He also dedicated the library in the school in the name of the 1949 graduating class and raised $3,000 from the reunion for

the library. He told me that many parents came up to him and thanked him for remembering and for helping their children.

Isn't it interesting to see what became of someone? I last saw them as eleven year olds. Now David is a TV personality , Stuey Altman is Past President of Brandeis University, Lenny Luner is President of a Fortune 500 company, the nice quiet boy, Leslie Kallenberg, retired at a young age, becoming very successful with an X-rated greeting card company. It reminded me of the movie "Annie Hall," where Woody Allen had the kids in elementary school stand up and say who they were and what they had become years later. I don't think that anyone could have predicted the futures of these kids from PS 64.

Just think, if I has not gone to New York, the reunion would not have existed in just the same way, and I would have rationalized that I was right in deciding not to go. I had a wonderful time and I'm looking forward to the next reunion. Perhaps, next time we will be able to have it *Back in the Bronx.*

During the weekend, the fellows sometimes asked about my parent's candy store on the corner of 205th street and Webster Avenue. They've long sold it and retired, but contrary to other reminiscing, there was no hanging out in this store, even for my friends. When I was working, they were allowed a "brief" visit, and for all others, it was make-your-purchase-pay-your-bill-and-leave. (Just to add to the "Great Egg Cream Controversy", I always thought I made the best egg creams. My father believed his were great, but my mother says she *knows* hers were outstanding. The controversy continues!)

Throughout our reminiscing, many of the stories were "challenged". As time had passed and we went our separate ways, apparently so did our memories. Events known to us to be true, were

See REUNION, on p. 13

It's a teaspoon of gas away from anywhere in the Bronx.
It costs less than a weekend in the Catskills.

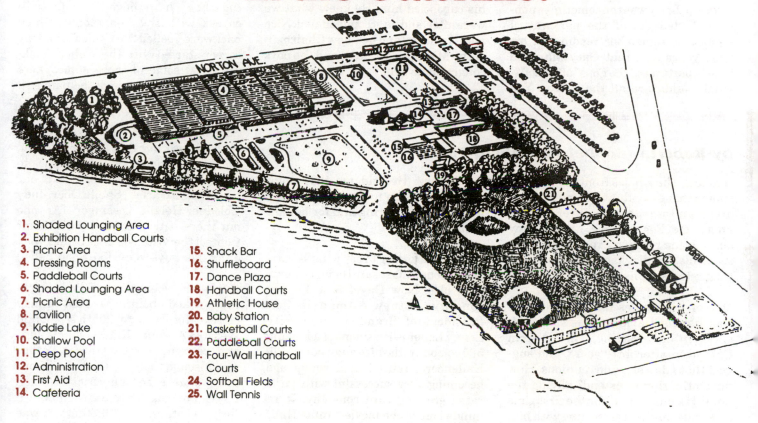

1. Shaded Lounging Area
2. Exhibition Handball Courts
3. Picnic Area
4. Dressing Rooms
5. Paddleball Courts
6. Shaded Lounging Area
7. Picnic Area
8. Pavilion
9. Kiddie Lake
10. Shallow Pool
11. Deep Pool
12. Administration
13. First Aid
14. Cafeteria
15. Snack Bar
16. Shuffleboard
17. Dance Plaza
18. Handball Courts
19. Athletic House
20. Baby Station
21. Basketball Courts
22. Paddleball Courts
23. Four-Wall Handball Courts
24. Softball Fields
25. Wall Tennis

Castle Hill,
continued from p. 1

offense in the early 50's, because it was necessary for everything: admittance to the Club, use of facilities and proof of identity. To get into the pool, for example, you had to go through a gate and show your pass to one of the guards whose job was to bar non-members. Really small kids, of course, would be on their parent's pass, but around twelve or so, one was considered old

enough to carry one's own pass and it was a great thrill, a symbol of maturity, to show your pass to the guard at the gate. An even bigger achievement, though, was to get one of your neighborhood friends in with your pass: providing he or she looked vaguely like the picture, it was possible to wait for a crowded moment at the gate, hold the pass with your thumb over the picture or at arm's length, and rush through. That accomplished, you ran down the long hallway to the wire fence alongside the locker rooms and handed the pass back to its rightful owner, who

then sauntered through with a sly smile—another successful caper.

Once inside, the first sight was the trophy and photo hall. On both sides of the walls leading to the locker rooms and pools were dozens of pictures taken in the 30's and even late 20's. Every year another few pictures went up: the winning softball team, the handball champions and, most vital, the year's swimming award winners. I used to wonder how they could keep putting up pictures forever but somehow there was always room—and forever turned

out to be not so far away. Continuing past the photos, one quickly entered the outdoors, where the sharp smell of chlorine and the sound of kids yelling announced that the pools were filled and ready for business. There were two pools (three really, if you counted the kiddy wading pond): one was shallow and known as "the four foot pool" and the other, for serious swimmers, divers and suntanners, the "eight foot pool". Up to the age twelve or thereabouts (around the time you began to notice girls, or boys) the four foot pool was homebase. In this friendly and generally tepid body of water, you could learn to swim, play games and cool off with the older folks. I discovered a financial windfall around the age of ten: adults who went swimming in the four foot pool sometimes dropped money out of their swim trunks. If I swam around underwater long enough, say until my eyes were red and my skin textured like prunes, I could on a good day find seventy or eighty cents laying on the pool's bottom. One year my father bought me underwater goggles and I multiplied my earnings considerably. But for reasons still unknown to me, the management posted a rule against masks and fins, and I had to return to more primitive methods. Still, I often made enough from this sudden treasure to buy myself mashed potatoes and creamed corn in the cafeteria, or Bazooka bubblegum at the candy stand.

Before swimming, of course, there were the locker rooms. The lockers were really the heart of Castle Hill Pool and while I can only talk about the men's lockers, I suspect the same is true of the women's area. In the lockers, outdoor wooden dressing rooms about the size of coffins standing on end, the men kept their sports equipment, chairs, shaving stuff and street clothes. It was a matter of considerable importance, status-wise, as to locker location for the year ahead. Long time members would have their lockers for decades, staking out virtual residences where they would become figures of stability in a changing world. Some of these lockers would be elaborately improved, at least as elaborately as a three by seven box could be improved, with mirrors, seats and carpeting. For modesty, the lockers would be equipped with a dutch door, so that the owner could be nude but still carry on a civilized conversation with the world outside. Not that nudity was banned: I think, in fact, it was a mark of masculinity to walk from the outdoor showers (wonderful on a hot night) to the locker in bold nakedness without even a towel to keep the social conventions.

The lockers stretched in long rows, numbered as in A-10 or G-220, and there were showers placed strategically around, with numerous entrances from the outside playing fields and sitting areas. Adjoining the men's lockers were, of course, the womens' and it took only a feeble imagination plus adolescent hormones to make the connection between a hole in the wooden partition and a look at a real naked woman. If a hole wasn't available, you could make one, which is what Melvin and I did one summer, only to be caught by one of the guards and reported to the authorities: our parents.

Once changed into leisure attire, there was a choice of many sports and activities at the pool. Swimming, of course, was taken for granted but there was handball, softball, basketball and tennis (against a wall, not real nets), plus shuffle board and ping pong. For little kids there was a sand box adjoining a kind of nursery where bottles could be heated for infants and a shallow wading pool. Castle Hill was a sports-minded club, where the annual softball tournament was playing with intensity that matched the Giant/Dodger pennant races. The winningest team of my era was the Indians, led by a short dark pitcher whose windmill delivery always drew whistles of admiration from the viewing stands.

Continued on p. 12

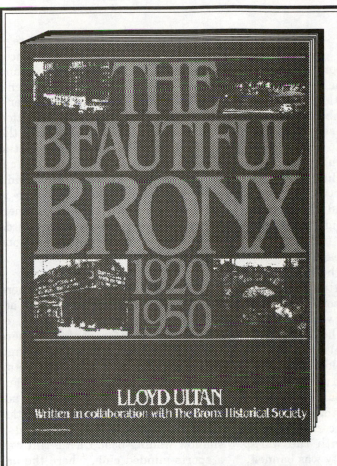

West Bronx

by Michael P. Hyman

The West Bronx was our world. The west border was NYU on University Avenue and its Hall of Fame. Dad would take us there on weekends, where you can climb the cannons and artillery around the lawn or stare at busts of famous Americans high above the Harlem River, upper Manhattan in the distance. Those sculptures held me in awe, and to them I attribute a large part of the yearning to learn an accomplish that led me to becoming a successful pathologist.

There was the night that my folks went out and my older brother Pete was babysitting but needed worms for fishing and dragged me in PJ's in the middle of the night where he dug for worms. Did he ever catch it from Dad the next day when I tattled . . .

The Aqueduct Park was for countless walks and gatherings. Nearby was PS 91. On the east end was the Grand Concourse (we lived at 181st Street and Grand Ave). Do you remember Memorial Day with the fabulous parades that filled the Concourse with color and music? High school graduation was at the Paradise movie theatre, with its glittering chandeliers and velvet curtains. For special times we dreamed of Jahn's ice cream. Dark Jerome Ave. lay in between us and the Concourse and the "el" overhead rattled our windows.

At the north end, a vague boundary was fabled Alexander's on Fordham where we bought shoes that never fir, or Van Courtlandt Park, scene of determined attempts at ice skating, or the Poe house, which caught my imagination (he must have been very short – it was so low!). To the south were Burnside and Tremont Avenues, with other movies, and napoleons, bialys, marble cake and all the serious shopping.

At the corner of 181st Street and Grand were four apartment buildings, about five stories each (no elevators!). On the ground floor was Minnie Mermelstein's candy store, with egg creams, comics, and yo-yos; Ann's grocery store where you got these miniature fruit pies, or cupcakes for school desert; Jimmy's barber shop; and Mr. Ohlman's fruit market. He had a shaved head like a honeydew.

Most summer evenings were spent outdoors on the stoop, socializing. We had one window fan in the living room, one bathroom for four and Pete and I shared a bedroom. It was comfortable. We didn't expect more. When we got the first T.V. on the block (a huge Dumont) the place was filled watching Ed Sullivan or Milton Berle.

When we moved first to Whitestone, then Rego Park, we spent summer days at Shorehaven, the highest density of people ever stuffed into one giant swimming pool. With constant handball games, sultry evening dance contest, and ubiquitous barbecues, there was never a break in the din. Claustrophobia was a way of life.

It was decided (nobody really asked me) that I should try for Bronx Science, which I barely made. It took four buses (from Whitestone via West Farms) or 1 1/2 hours by bus and train (via Flushing) each way to go to high school each day in the Bronx. The subway was after-school life and I was never afraid. At Science there was fearsome competition (in those days not reviled quality) but also a genuine love of learning that I never saw equalled in college, medical school, or anywhere!

Now I live in a pleasant part of a pleasant city (Denver) and when people speak favorably of Washington Park as a "real" neighborhood, I just smile. Once there was such a thing, in the West Bronx.

Hall of Fame at NYU, circa 1950's

Aqueduct Park, circa 1950's

NYU campus, circa 1950's

Castle Hill,
continued from p. 9

The handball competition was just as deadly, both in one wall and four wall varieties. There was a professional-looking four-wall handball structure, stuck way out in left field behind the softball diamonds and it was always exciting to trek back there to watch both men and women sweating after that little black ball. More conventional one-wall courts were scattered in various spots, the most coveted being those next to the cafeteria. Handballers were a breed apart, and I seem to remember many husband and wife teams who did nothing but slap the ball around, summer after summer regardless of heat or age.

Of course there were the card players, whose favored spot was next to the first aid station. There, in the pitiless sun, marathon gin rummy games would roll on from early morning until the lights went out at night. My favorite player was a midget, a little person, whom everyone called with careless 1950's innocence, "Inches". These card players would grow darker and darker from the sun, until by Labor Day they would appear to be groups of swarthy Arabs sitting around, kibbetzing in Yiddish and yelling about "shnides".

The women had their equivalent in mah-jongg, of which my mother was a devotee along with a couple of hundred others from that day. By ten or eleven on any given day the mah-jongg tiles would be clacking all over Castle Hill Pool and would stop only for hurried meals, or unavoidable interruptions from children who needed ice cream money. Such needs as ice cream, candy and soda would be satisfied by two refreshment stands, one opposite the cafeteria and another sited next to the kiddy pool (where I worked one summer during college). There was a fascinating system of tickets in use at these stands: one first paid for tickets at a special booth, and then took the necessary amount in tickets, never cash, to the ice cream or candy lines.

In the cafeteria, however, the usual cash transactions took place. I remember the cafeteria as a dark, cool respite from the sun, where the food was classic American diner style and very good too. I especially liked fried fish and tuna fish sandwiches; later on I discovered that the coffee was first rate too. There were big steam tables with half a dozen main dishes, the familiar tubs of vegetables potatoes and gravy, and lots of interesting desserts. The whole cafeteria was done in a 20's rustic style, the walls made of big rocks and there was a massive fireplace (never lit) on one side. The rustic theme was repeated outside, the whole cafeteria building being surrounded by a low stone wall, where, after showering, families would gather for the trip home. Attached to the cafeteria, and often spoken of with disapproval, was a modest beer hall. I never saw much drinking at Castle Hill but those for whom a beer was part of the vacation could find their fill inside the bar, which, by the way, served only beer. This was, however, not a heavy drinking crowd and I don't imagine the bar room was a big money maker.

It was an eating crowd, however. Most people dragged hampers and coolers with sandwiches and soft drinks, and there were shaded picnic tables provided alongside the kiddy pool. Others preferred to eat where they were, on their beach chair or under one of the many shade trees throughout the grounds. If all of that didn't satisfy, there was always the glorious greasy fast food just across the street from the Pool. This was a favorite; of the kids, notably the teenagers, who could get away from the searching parental eye for a bit; and it meant leaving the Club. Directly across from the main entrance, adjacent to a bus stop that took us home, was a motley cafe/frank stand that sold questionable franks but unsurpassed french fries. The fries were made in oil that must have dated from the First New Deal and which were served in little conical soda cups—

twenty five cents, as I recall. Sometimes my mother would spring for an order or two of fries as we waited for the bus and when I was older and worked at the Pool, my after job treat was a cup of fries. They haven't been matched yet in my experience. Alongside this cafe, incidentally, was a dangerous and incongruous night club, where nobody from the pool ever went and which was widely suspected of being Mob headquarters.

All this existed for most of the 60's, and I even took my first child to swim there in the four foot pool. It was destined not to last, of course, and the last time I drove there, the Pool was in the process of demolition, shuttered and empty. I suppose its gone by now; replaced by something useful like a McDonald's drive-in or another housing project. Too bad. It gave pleasant memories to a couple of generations, who either grew up or grew old at Castle Hill Pool.

Martin A. Jackson lived on Andrews Avenue.

Reunion,
Continued from p. 7

to say the least, embellished over the years. Our current versions had a degree of interest and amusement, but as it turns out, lacked some degree of factuality. As friends, we corrected the narration, and while the stories then lacked the same flair, they nevertheless brought back wonderful memories. I suppose when we returned to our own lives and retold them again, we went back to our old recollections and disjointed memories. After all, who's to know?

Anyone planning a reunion take heed. The ego question, the correcting of stories, and the bragging may all have their place, but if the intent of the reunion is to renew old friendships, then enjoy each other's company. Relish the fact, privately, that your shape is better than theirs, bask in the nostalgic remembrances, take the addresses and phone numbers, but don't abuse the contacts. We all have new lives and

new businesses to attend to. Arrange another meeting if it's convenient to all. Keep in touch with letters, pictures, cards and calls, but don't overdo it.

Finally, savor those renewed friendships. Savor all you went through, growing up in the best borough in the city – DA BRONX!

13

Back in the BRONX

Dear Fellow Bronxite,

Some time ago, you subscribed to a publication designed to rekindle a very unique brand of happy memories. It's been over a year since we published our inaugural issue and as a subscriber to **Back in the BRONX,** you've received three issues packed with fond memories and memorabilia. The stories in **Back in the BRONX** are for the most part written not by professional authors, but by people like yourself who want to share their experiences with fellow Bronxites. We've received snapshots, stories, news-clippings and other memorabilia from former Bronxites from coast to coast and beyond. We have found lost friends, and created new friendships. We have brought back memories of hot August nights at Freedomland and reported on summer dances under the stars at Poe Park. More than anything else, we want to continue to be able to bring you **Back in the BRONX**.

Continuing to do the magazine depends on two important things. One is the continued contributions of our subscribers to write stories, send photos, and provide us names to add to our Bronxite Database. But, most importantly, we need you. **Renew your subscription now** and continue to be one of the thousands of Bronxites who are currently subscribers. For only **$19.95** (four issues, or **$29.95** for a two-year subscription of eight issues), you can renew your passport to travel back in time, back to the old neighborhood and back to good times with great people – fellow Bronxites like yourselves.

We here at **Back in the BRONX** will do our best to see that the stories remain fresh and fascinating. **Renew today and continue to share in the fun!**

Sincerely,

Stephen M. Samtur

Stephen Samtur
Publisher – **Back in the BRONX**
Clinton '62

Subscribe or Renew Now!

Order your subscription (and maybe even one for a friend). We welcome your personal check, *VISA* or MasterCard.

Please fill-out the form below to subscribe or renew your subscription to **Back in the BRONX**. Remember, **Back in the BRONX** is a great gift for a fellow Bronxite. It's a unique and imaginative way to put a smile on the face of a relative or friend .

Please sign me up for a _____ One year subscription(s) to **Back in the BRONX** @ $19.95 ea.

or

_____ Two year subscription(s) to **Back in the BRONX** @ $29.95 ea.

TOTAL DUE $_____

Special Bonus!

Subscribe or renew for *two years* and receive with our compliments a FREE laminated replica of a vintage JAHN'S Menu!

Super Bonus! Complete the following Bronx Trivia "Commercial Jingle" correctly and receive an extra issue!

MELROSE 5- _ _ _ _ was the number of _____ store.

Please fill out the information below and send with payment to:

Back in the BRONX, Box 141H, Scarsdale NY 10583

Name_____ Maiden _____ Address_____

City _____ State _____ ZIP _____ Phone _____

High school attended and year attended _____

Method of payment: __ Check   ___ Visa   __ MasterCard   Total Amt. Enclosed $_____

Card No. _____ Expiration Date _____

Use these lines to list the names and addresses of your gift subscriptions

Name_____Maiden _____   Name_____Maiden _____
Address_____   Address_____
City _____State _____ZIP_____   City _____State _____ZIP_____
High school attended and yr. graduated_____ High school attended and yr. graduated_____
Phone # _____   Phone # _____

The BRONX Marquees

by Michael R. Miller

The Bronx, lying in the shadow of its important neighbor Manhattan to the south, has always been the victim of neglect. The few recent studies of movie theaters have taken a fleeting glance at the Loew's Paradise, and then moved briskly on to the brighter lights of Broadway downtown. Certainly a more lingering look is in order.

Crossing the Harlem River, we find a city-within-a-city; the home of over 1¾ million people. As such, the borough has as varied a cultural history as any of the country's biggest metropolises.

The early past of the theater in the Bronx is clouded and obscure. Certainly there were small music halls before 1890, at least in the more populous areas in the southern sections. Among the earliest recorded openings was that of the EMPIRE, which opened its doors on October 28, 1894. This was on Westchester Avenue, in what would in fifteen years be one of the two great centers of amusement in the borough. Other smaller houses followed in the next few years; it was not until after the turn of the century that the first great playhouse was born.

In 1904, William Seitz, a pioneer local builder, opened the METROPOLIS on Third Avenue and East 142nd Street, just south of the borough's "Hub" at 149th Street. The theater, being in a class by itself, immediately became the gathering place of the socially-

Concluded on opposite page

Concluded on opposite page

A List Of Bronx Theatres

As Compiled By Michael R. Miller

The following is as complete a list as can be obtained from present records. The following order is used: Name, Address(Seats), Chain(approx. years of operation), (Architect), present status.

Key to abbreviations: Chains A(RCA), B(Brandt), C(Consolidated), F(Fox), L(Loews), R(RKO-Keith), S(Skouras).

ACE: See CONGRESS

ALLERTON, 774 Allerton Ave. (1226) (1927-present)

AMERICA: See KEITH'S BRONX

AMERICAN, 1450 East Ave. (1998) L (12-40 – 4-72, being remodeled) (Eberson)

APOLLO, 747 E. 180th St. (433) (c1912-late 30's)

ARCADIA, SW corner Westchester & Prospect Aves. (1929-?)

ART, 1C77 Southern Blvd. (600) (c1928-present)

ART (a.k.a. YIDDISH ART): see RITZ

ART: See JEROME

ASCOT, 2313 Grand Concourse (?) B (1935-pres.)

The Loew's Grand Theatre on the corner of Fordham Rd. and Jerome Avenue in the late '20s.

AVALON, Burnside & Anthony Aves. (1200) C (1928-early1950's) Razed; gas station

BAINBRIDGE: See MOSHULU

BANDBOX, 37 W. Fordham Rd. (600) (1920's-30's)

BARNES, Allerton & Barnes Aves. (1300) A (early 1930's)

B-B, 3837 White Plains Rd. (599) (1927-30's?) Razed

BEACH, 1810 Randall Ave. (?) (?-1970) Church

BEDFORD, 3119 Webster Ave. (600) F (1925-1941)

BEDFORD, 2841 Webster Ave. (?) (c1912-20's)

BELMONT, Tremont & Belmont Aves. (1458) F (1920-33, then DELUXE to pres.)

BENENSON, 1546 Washington Ave. (1312) (1921-32, then FENWAY to 1970) Razed 1972

BLENHEIM, 466 E. 169th St. (1847) F (1920's-40's?) Razed; housing project

BORINQUEN: See COLEMAN'S

BORO, 752 Melrose Ave. (559) (1911?-43. Had other name prior to 1932.)

BOSTON ROAD, 1472 Boston Rd. (1500) L (1925-40's) Warehouse & lounge

BOULEVARD, Southern Blvd. near Westchester Ave. (?) (2187) L (1912-pres.)

BROADWAY OPEN AIR, Bdwy & W 231 St. (1500) (1935)

The Loew's Grand Theatre lobby in the late '20s.

select. Besides the theater proper, the building also housed a rathskeller in the basement and roof garden. It would prosper until 1913, when Sam Harris (partner of George Cohan) and several other Broadway notables opened the BRONX OPERA HOUSE several blocks to the north, in the center of the business district. The owners of the new theater naturally sent the best of their Broadway attractions to the OPERA HOUSE, and business at the METROPOLIS suffered accordingly. To save the latter, the owners installed a dramatic stock company headed by Cecil Spooner, an extremely popular actress of the day. Miss Spooner was able to bring the crowds back to the theater, but her success doomed the METROPOLIS to failure. Within several months, she was popular enough to open her own theater, the SPOONER, a mile to the east, on Southern Boulevard near East 163rd Street. Upon her departure, the theater tried dramatic stock, vaudeville, motion pictures, and Italian shows. None caught on. By 1925, the METROPOLIS was considered too far "downtown" by Bronxites. In 1926, a burlesque troupe made one last fling, but it was closed by the police for indecency. The METROPOLIS remained shuttered for three years, and then was sold to Loew's for use as a "scenic studio". Part of the original building stands today; the auditorium was razed years ago.

The Bronx OPERA HOUSE, successor to the METROPOLIS, would remain the major legitimate house for only a dozen years. Before the Twenties were out, it was already on a grind policy. As such it remains to this day.

Back in the BRONX wishes to thank Mr. Miller and the Bronx Historical Society for the use of this article.

'Some Like It Hot' Stars Marilyn at the Paradise

'Some Like It Hot'

Tony Curtis, Marilyn Monroe and Jack Lemmon are co-starred in "Some Like It Hot," on the screen of Loew's Paradise Theater.

'Sleeping Beauty'

The Sleeping Beauty, Aurora, (above) is seen in the Walt Disney cartoon feature presentation of the fairy tale classic in the RKO Chester and Castle Hill Theaters.

Disney Cartoon In Loew Houses

The Loew's Grand Theatre stage in the late '20s.

BRONX OPERA HOUSE, 436 E. 149th St. (1920) (1913-28, then BRONX to pres.) (Geo. Keister)

BRONX PARK OVAL (?) (1910's)

BRONX PLAYHOUSE: See ROYAL PHOTOPLAYS

BRONX WINTER GARDEN, 1874 Washington Ave. (?) (1920's)

BRONXDALE OPEN AIR, White Plains Rd. & Lydig Ave. (1500) A (1935)

BURKE, 3210 White Plains Rd. (1078) (4-9-27 – 1962) Factory & warehouse

BURLAND, 985 Prospect Ave. (1896, 283 open air) L (1916-71) Vacant

BURNSIDE, Burnside & Walton Aves. (2219) L (1926-50's) Supermarket

CARVER: See CRESCENT

CASINO: See WILLIS

CASTLE HILL, 1320 Castle Hill Ave. (1450) R (1927-69) Bingo & assembly hall

CENTRAL: See KEITH'S BRONX

CENTURY, Prospect Ave. nr E. 167th St. (?)

CHESTER, Boston Rd. & Tremont Ave. (2743) R (12-26-27 – 1968) Geo. Keister) Truck depot

CIRCLE, 82 Hugh Grant Cir. (?) (1939-pres.)

CITY CINEMA, Bartow Ave. Co-Op City (?) B ('72)

CITY ISLAND, 385 City Island Ave. (?) (?-1971)

CLAREMONT, E. 174th St. nr 3rd Ave. (?) (1900's-?)

COLEMAN'S, 745 Westchester Ave. (1919?-40's, a.k.a. LOUIS (1930's), JACKSON (35-42), and BORINQUEN (42-closing) Razed

COLUMBUS, 247-9 E. 151st St. (?) (1910's-20's)

COMET, 1015 Boston Rd. (?) (c1911-?) Church

COMMUNITY, 3911 White Plains Rd. (1200) (1934-6)

CONCOURSE, 209 E. Fordham Rd. (577) (1930-late 40's) Store

CONGRESS, 554 Southern Blvd. (1800) (1926-40, then ACE to late 40's) Offices

CRAFT, 4420 White Plains Rd. (?) A (c1938-40's)_

CRESCENT, 1165 Boston Rd. (1693, + open air) (1914-35, then TOWER to late 40's, CARVER to 50's) Church

CREST, 1145 Ogden Ave. (?) (1936-early 1960's) Razed

CROTONA, 435 E. Tremont Ave. (2210) F, S (1910's-

© 1992 The Bronx Historical Society

18

60) Warehouse & stores

DALE, 189 W. 231st St. (?) 1930's-pres.)

DALY, 892 E. Tremont Ave. (1460) (1928-35, then VOGUE to 50's) Stores

DAVID MARCUS: See TUXEDO

DECATUR: See UNITED STATES

DELUXE: See BELMONT

DEVON: See TREND

DOVER, 1723 Boston Rd. (?) (1930's-pres.)

EARL, E. 161st St. & River Ave. (?) C, B (1936-pres.)

EL DORADO, 1297 Wilkins Ave. (?) (1912?-20's)

ELSEMERE, 1926 Crotona Pkwy., (1552, later 1721) L (1914-c1950) (Shampan & Shampan) Community Center

EMPIRE, Westchester Ave. & E. 161st St. (1660) R (10-28-1894 – late 40's) Church

FAIRMONT, E. Tremont Ave. & Clinton Pl. (2518) L (9-12-28-69) Museum & offices

FENWAY: See BENENSON

FLEETWOOD, Norris Ave. & E. 165th St. (1650) C (1925-40's) Supermarket

FOLLIES: See KEITH'S BRONX

FORDHAM, 2508 Webster Ave. (?) (1910's)

FORDHAM, Fordham Rd. nr Grand Concourse (2446) R (1920-pres.) (Wm. H. McElfatrick)

FORUM, 490 E. 138th St. (2447) C (1921-40's, then PUERTO RICO to pres.)

FRANKLIN, Prospect Ave. & E. 161st St. (2855) R (1920-50's) Supermarket

FREEMAN, Southern Blvd. & Freeman St. (1604) (1921-72) Vacant

GARDEN, 2755 Webster Ave. (?) (c1914-?)

GLOBE, 640 Pelham Pkwy. S. (?) (1938-pres.)

GOLDEN RULE, 3749 3rd Ave. (?) (1920's)

GRAND, 5 W. Fordham Rd. (2430) L (2-17-27 – c1960) (Eugene DeRosa) Dept. store

GRANT, Tremont & Webster Aves. (planned 3500 seats in 1920, E. DeRosa; probably never built)

HAVEN, See PEERLESS

HIPPODROME, 1313 Prospect Ave. (?) (1910's)

In 'South Pacific'

Mitzi Gaynor (above) is starred in "South Pacific," on the screens of the RKO Chester and Castle Hill Theaters.

RKOs Present 'South Pacific'

The film version of "South Pacific," by Rodgers and Hammerstein, Pulitzer Prize-winning musical, is presented on the screens of the RKO Chester and Castle Hill Theaters. For the run, a policy of continuous performances is followed, and admission for children at all times is set at 50 cents.

The color presentation of the smash hit which played on the Broadway stage for five years has Mitzi Gaynor starred in the role created by Mary Martin.

Others in the cast are Rossano Brazzi, John Kerr, France Nuyen, Ray Walston and Juanita Hall, the "Bloody Mary" of the original stage cast.

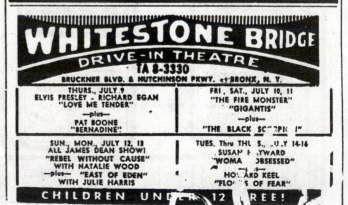

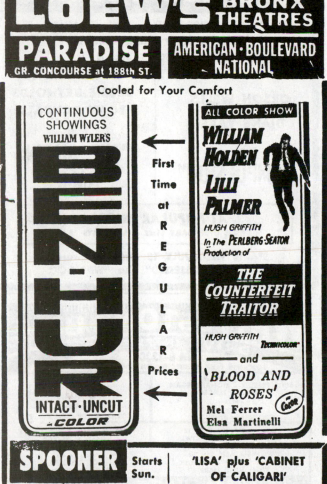
HOUSE OF FUN, Prospect Ave. nr Westchester Ave. (?) (?-c1912)

HUB, 440 Westchester Ave. (550) (1931?-38, then REX to 40's)

IDEAL, 772 Westchester Ave. (?) (c1910-20's?)

INTERBORO (orig. INTERBOROUGH), 3462 E. Tremont Ave. (1550) F, S (1925-pres.)

INTIMATE, 2133 Boston Rd. (2840) (1920's-?)

JACKSON: See COLEMAN'S

JEROME, 1 W. Tremont Ave. (1660) (1926-50's, then ART to pres.)

KAMEO: See NEW LYRIC

KEITH'S BRONX, 581 Melrose Ave. (1220) (1909-18; B.F. KAHN'S FOLLIES 1918-c1920; MINER'S BRONX c1920-28; AMERICA 1928-31; CENTRAL 1931-40's) Razed

KENT, 190 E. 167th St. (?), C, B (1920's-pres.)

KING: See McKINLEY SQ.

KING, 4048 3rd. Ave. (?) (1920's-?) Razed

KINGSBRIDGE, 15 E. Kingsbridge Rd. (1125) F, C (1921-early 50's) Supermarket

KNICKERBOCKER, 879 Prospect Ave. (?) (1910's)

LACONIA, White Plains Rd. & E. 224th St. (1160) (1926-pres.)

LIDO, 15 E. Fordham Rd. (600) C (1913-pres.) (+ Letters above marquee say "UNIVERSITY," though no record of this name in this location. There was a UNIVERSITY two blocks to west on Fordham Rd.)

LONGWOOD, 866 Longwood Ave. (?) (1910s-?)

LOUIS: See COLEMAN'S

LUXOR, 120 E. 170th St. (1452) C, B (1923-pres.)

MARBLE HILL, 5625 Bdwy (1638) R (1927-69) Bingo hall

MELBA, 3428 Boston Rd. (?) (c1938-pres.)

MELROSE, Melrose Ave. & E. 155th St. (400) (1910's)

MELROSE, 417 E. 161st St. (1129, roof 1092) (1916-40's) Ballroom

METRO, 2269 Webster Ave. (1500) (1926-50's) Razed 1968

METROPOLIS, 2634 3rd Ave. (?) (1904-26) "Loews Scenic Studios 1929-?) 1/2 razed, 1/2 vacant

MINERS IN THE BRONX: See VICTORY and KEITH'S

BRONX

MIRACLE, Melrose Ave. & E. 156th St. (?) (1930's)

MONROE, 1513 Westchester Ave. (482) (1930's?)

MOSHOLU, 268 E. 204th St. (911, roof) F (1925-40's, BAINBRIDGE to pres.)

MT. EDEN, W. Mt. Eden & Inwood Aves. (1745) C (1928-mid50's) Razed

McKINLEY SQ., 1319 Boston Rd. (1800) (c1916-40's, the KING to ?) Church

NATIONAL, 500 Bergen Ave. (2397) L (9-1-10 – pres.)

NEW LYRIC, 4367 3rd. Ave. (550) (c1930-winter '31, then NEW KAMEO to c1936)

NEW ROYAL: See ROYAL PHOTOPLAYS

NEWSREEL, Grand Concourse nr 188 St.? (?) (1930's)

NICOLAND, 3220 3rd Ave. (?) (early 1910's-20's?)

OGDEN, 1431 Ogden Ave. (1370) C, S (1922-c60) Stores

167th STREET, E. 167 St. & River Ave. (2321) L, B (1-20-28 – 69) Stores

OSCEOLA, 258 St. Anns Ave. (556) (c1935-late '40s)

OXFORD, 2264 Jerome Ave. (1950) C (1928-40's) Bronx Community College

PARADISE, Grand Concourse & E. 187th St. (3884, later 4100) L (9-7-29 – pres.) (Eberson)

PALACE, 1601 Unionport Rd. (?) (1948?-pres.)

PANTHEON, 71 W. Burnside Ave. (?) (1927-40's) School annex

PARK, 451 E. 169th St. (437) (1930's)

PARK, 1471 Wilkins Ave. (?) (1910's) Razed

PARK, 819 E. 180th St. (?) (1910's)

PARK: See YORKE

PARK PLAZA, 1746 University Ave. (2000) F, S (1926-64) School annex

PARKWAY, 3952 3rd. Ave. (2000) F (1926-40's?) Factory

PEERLESS, 310 E. 138th St. (?) (1920's-32, then HAVEN to c1945)

PELHAM, White Plains Rd. & Maran Pl. (1300) R, S (c1928-65) Razed; bank

PICTORIUM, 937 E. 180th St. (?) (c1913-30's?)

PILGRIM, Westchester & Edison Aves. (1060) S (1934-

Curtain Call . . .

thoughts by James Montesarchio

Just a few lines to let you know about the Windsor Theatre. It was on Kingsbridge Road, just down from Jahn's Ice Cream Parlor about two blocks on the opposite side of the street. When I was a kid I'd come up from the south Bronx to run errands for the actors who worked on stage at the theatre and just make tips. Here is a list of some of the entertainers that I remember being there at the time.

Phil Regan (Irish tenor), James Barton ("Tobacco Road"), Henry Anetta (movie star), Johnny Downs (movies), Johnny Coy (dancer), Buddy Ebsen (actor), John Boles (actor), Dixie Dunbar (dancer), Sally Rand (fan dancer), Jimmy Durante

Concluded on opposite page

50's) Stores

PLAZA, 2408 Washington Ave. (1044, roof 625) (c1912-30's?)

POST ROAD, Boston Rd. & Fenton Ave. (1170) L, B (10-21-37 – 64) (Thomas Lamb) Bingo hall

POWER, 1178 Boston Rd. (1693) (1930's)

PRESIDENT: See STRAND

PRESIDENTE: See STRAND

PROSPECT, 851 Prospect Ave. (1600) L (c1910-pres.)

PUERTO RICO: See FORUM

QUEENS, E. 169th St. nr Park Ave. (?) (1920's) Razed

REX, 579 Prospect Ave. (?) (1910's)

REX: See HUB

RITZ, 1014 E. 180th St. (787) (c1927?, later ART, YIDDISH ART to ?) Razed

RIVERDALE CINEMA, 258 Riverdale Ave. (?) (c1960-pres.)

ROSEDALE, 1741 Westchester Ave. (1285) (1926-40's?) Storage

ROYAL, 423 Westchester Ave. (2070) R (9-7-13 – 62) (Thomas Lamb, Buchanan & Fox) Razed

ROYAL PHOTOPLAYS, 1350 Southern Blvd. (600) (c1917-20's, then BRONX PLAYHOUSE; NEW ROYAL c1930-5; RADIO 1935-c40)

SAVOY, 2341 Hughes Ave. (1141) (1923-70) Vacant

SPOONER, Southern Blvd. nr E. 163rd St. (1910) L (c1913-70) Store

SQUARE, 58 Westchester Sq. (?) (c1935-pres.) S

STAR, 3877 3rd. Ave. (?) (c1914-?) Stores

STAR, 960 Southern Blvd. (600 + open air) (c1913-pres.)

STRAND, 827 Westchester Ave. (1184) (c1917-30's, then PRESIDENT, PRESIDENTE to pres.)

SUPERIOR, 930 E. 172nd St. (?) (1910's)

SURREY, 66 Mt. Eden Ave. E. (?) C, B, (1935-pres.)

TIFFANY, 1007 Tiffany St. (601, roof 582) (c1913-40's) Supermarket

TIME, 786 Cortland Ave. (?) (1910's)

TOWER: See CRESCENT

TREMONT, 1942 Webster Ave. (987) (c1910-40's; a.k.a.

TREMONT YIDDISH & CINEMA TREMONT: Warehouse

TREND, 241 E. Tremont Ave. (600) (1-21-30, then DEVON c1940-pres.)

TUXEDO, 3464 Jerome Ave. (1716) F, S (1927-40's, then DAVID MARCUS to 1972) Off-track betting parlor

UNITED STATES, 2715 Webster Ave. (1627) F (1916-41, then DECATUR to c1946) Warehouse

UNIVERSITY, 33 W. Fordham Rd. (600) (c1920-40's) See also: LIDO

VALENTINE, 237 E. Fordham Rd. (1252, roof 482) F, S (1920-pres.)

VICTOR, Intervale Ave. & Dawson St. (?) (1910's)

VICTORIA, 594 E. 134th St. (?) (1910's)

VICTORY, 3rd Ave. E. 156th St. (1750) L (1910 as MINERS IN THE BRONX, VICTORY c1920-50's) Lobby razed; warehouse

VOGUE, See DALY

WAKEFIELD, 4212 White Plains Rd. (1330) (1926-pres.)

WALTON, ? (?) (1920's-?)

WARD, 1545 Westchester Ave. (1862 S (1927-pres.)

WEBSTER, 400 E. 167th St. (1189) (c1910-?)

WILLIS, 250 Willis Ave. (2166) C (1923-5, then CASINO to 50's) Assembly hall

WINDSOR, 315 E. Fordham Rd. (1600) B (c1920-early 50's)

YORKE, 764 Morris Park Ave. (1360) (c1928-40's, then PARK to ?)

ZENITH, 14 W. 170th St. (?) (1937-early 50's)

Special thanks to the Bronx Historical Society for allowing this article to be reprinted.

© The Bronx Historical Society

(comedian), the Dead End Kids (movies), the Three Stooges (movies), Shep Fields (band leader), Russ Morgan (band leader), Ina Ray Hutton (all girl orchestra), Rosco Ates (comedian), Ted Lewis (orchestra leader), Cab Calloway (singer), Bob Crosby (band leader), Ella Logan (Broadway star in "Finnias Rainbow"), Erik Rhodes (actor), Ray MacDonald (dancer and brother of Marie MacDonald (actress), Nicholas Bros. (dance team), Tip, Top and Toe (dance team), Peg Leg Bates (one legged dancer).

There were many more that I will remember later on. The Windsor Theatre was a great show, just like the old Loew's Paradise but the Windsor was strictly stage shows. I really cried when they closed that place down.

The Bronx was really a great place, as was Brooklyn. The Bronx has always been my kind of place.

Classifieds

Missing Persons

MP273 • WALTON '61 – Valentine Avenue. Dancing at Gail Friedman's house the "Lindy". My best friend is still Marylin Weber for 32 years. My goals are to make sure my four children are happy. My work is to help find homes for the homeless, and pass the word on to help one needy person.

MP274 • As a "child of the '30s and '40s" in the neighborhood of Tremont Avenue to 182nd Street and from Southern Blvd. to Third Avenue – I would love to hear from anyone who could share those fond memories with me.

MP275 • TAFT June '46 Esther Berzofsky and Alvin Lowenberg married 41 years are in touch with old gang of **TAFT**ites and PS90 classmates. Looking for "old flames". Max Liebster, Sally Cohen, Barbara Wallerstein. Also old Scout Troop 234 BSA.

MP276 • Looking for anybody who grew up in the Sedgwick and Burnside Avenue areas – especially the stretch from University Avenue down to Sedgwick Park. Any parishners from **HOLY SPIRIT**? Looking for Ben Jacalow who lived at 1955 Sedgwick Avenue – my boyhood buddy!

MP277 • Club Metro 1947-1950: Jerry Rosmarin, Jerry Talcovitz, Herbie Lipman, Norman Klampert, Stanley Bowen, Dominick Calabrese, Jerry Goldstein, Joan Rose – where are the rest of you? 20 missing girls. Contact Norman Klampert.

MP278 • WALTON '62 Audrey Ballan looking to find Sandy Rothman, **WALTON** '62 my maid of honor and best friend. Stephanie Ross, Myrna Krieger, Michelle Feiner, Susan Chapel. Class of '62, where are you?

MP279 • Barbara Frankel Unger seeks Sally Haimowitz, Toby Cedar, Barbara Rosenthal, Joan Wesp, Al Ramrus, Rhoda Teller, Dolores Rand, Class of '50 people from **EVANDER** or former English students of Mrs. Unger from JHS117 or **EVANDER**, 1955-1959.

MP280 • Nadine Scheiber (nee Gritz) looking for the old crowd from "The Coops" (Bronx Park East and Barker Avenue) and all "**COLUMBUS**ites" who graduated 1945-47. Where are you "Mucky", "Wole", "Labie", Aaron, Lola, Rochelle, Bertha, etc???

MP281 • Joey Santoiemma – PS32 ('64) – now in New Rochelle – I miss you all – "Nellie" Yomtov, Vinny Guiliano, Alan Shikowitz, Helen Clemente, Christina Packer, Steven Rivetti, especially YOU, Erminia Marano! I'm in the book.

MP282 • Stanley Weiner, **TAFT** '53 and Towson College, has just moved back from Charleston, SC with Trudi Fisher Weiner, **TAFT** '53 and NYU '57. Stanley is Chief Operating Officer of Playtogs, Inc. in Middletown, NY. Trudi managed a boutique and Contemporary Sportswear in Charleston. They are happy to be back in the Big Apple.

MP282 • Stanley Weiner, **TAFT** '53 and Towson College, has just moved back from Charleston, SC with Trudi Fisher Weiner, **TAFT** '53 and NYU '57. Stanley is Chief Operating Officer of Playtogs, Inc. in Middletown, NY. Trudi managed a boutique and Contemporary Sportswear in Charleston. They are happy to be back in the Big Apple.

MP284 • Looking for first girl friend – Myrna Pflaster or second girlfriend – Janet Berkowitz or Tuba play.

MP285 • Bobby and Valerie (Alessandro) Pavone are desperately seeking a copy of 1962 yearbook for John Philip Sousa, JHS142, Baychester Avenue, Bronx. Anyone having or knowing the whereabouts of one, please contact us.

MP286 • Where are all the graduates of Theodore **ROOSEVELT** HS 1956, Pelham Parkway (Holland Avenue), 1950s PS105, PS83 grads. Contact Seymour Rush – love to hear from any of you out there.

MP287 • Where are Howie Zwicker, Aviva Rosenbaum, Harriet Wittels, Mitzi Feldstein, Mitchell Berlin, Davida Karpel, Wilma Green, Sharon Letich, Dorothy Rebarber, Judy Taub?

MP288 • ROOSEVELT '52, Selma Surenko looking to find Jerry (Jerome) Schwartz, **TAFT** '51 (Morris Avenue); and Phil Richman, **CLINTON** (Tiebout Avenue). Would like to hear from anyone who may know their whereabouts. Contact weekdays only 10-5.

MP289 • Wendy Citron **TAFT** '67 would love to find Sheryl Berman, Heleine Haber, Judy Shack. Remember "hanging out" by the phone booths on Fordham Road? Please call.

MP290 • Frank Arce – **ROOSEVELT** '67. It's our 25th Anniversary! Is there anyone of us left for a possible reunion? Let's not wait another 25 years to get together. Looking for my pal Francisco Matos. Are you still alive? Get in touch!

MP291 • Shirley Stern Allen of 2350 Creston Avenue looking for **WALTON**ites class of 1950. Gladys Hopkins Blum and Marilyn Swartz Kroop. Would love to hear from you!

MP292 • Steve Glaizer, **ROOSEVELT** '63 seeking any old friends or schoolmates – members of Club Pendulum, Klapper '67. Please call or write.

MP293 • Looking for Rhoda Teller, Dolores Rand, Candy Cashman, Toby Cedar, Marie Weston, Joan Wesp, Barbara Rosen. I am Barbara Frankel of 45 East Mosholu Parkway, PS80, **EVANDER** 1950. Welcome replies.

MP294 • 1950s, JHS82, PS26, Grand Avenue, Tremont Avenue, Harrison Avenue – contact Jayne Magnus Frazelle.

MP295 • 1960 Bronx **SCIENCE**. Physician, slim, short, looks 40, blue eyes, blonde hair, seeks younger, slim, non-smoking woman, 25-40. I am easy-going, down to earth, not materialistic, outgoing, excellent sense of humor, love animals and nature.

MP296 • To the guys that played stickball in **TAFT**'s parking lot from mid-1950's to early '60s and hung out in Levine's Candy Store 172nd St. and Morris Avenue. Where are you? Also Bobby Cohen (Chigi). Please get in touch.

MP297 • Looking for Mosholu Parkway participants, little or big Parkway 1957 through 1964. California Contingency Naomi Lipp, Lenore Greenwald, Janice Greider, Alan Bleiberg, Stanley Williams. Call or write.

MP298 • Celia Baer, PS104, JHS82, **TAFT** '53. Now living in Washington state. Would like to be reminded of old times. Anyone remember? Left Bronx 37 years ago, from Andrews Avenue.

MP299 • I would like to know if anyone could help me verify the fact that after **WALTON** HS seniors received their senior

hat, they then wore them pinned to their shoulder. I would really love a picture.

MP300 • Blue-eyed brunette, Bronx-Irish lovely seeks aging Bronx bad boy – definitely not a momma's boy – 44-45 for good time, good fun and rock'n'roll. Stop hanging out on the corner long enough to give me a call.

MP301 • Does anyone remember me? Marion (Micki) Schweitzer, Featherbed Lane, Nappi's Pizza, **TAFT**, PS82, PS53. Sister Elaine, brother Charlie, Married David Gale Macomb's Road. Has anyone seen Marion (Elvis) Bornstein, Mom Ruth, Dad Frank? Please get in touch.

MP302 • Bill Eberhart, **TAFT** Jan. 1944. Looking for Gil Yodowitz and Julian Hoffman both Jan. '44 graduates. Haven't seen Julian since Feb. 1945 in Holland – US Army. Gil last seen in 1974, NYC.

MP303 • Looking for Mel Feldman from 2450 Fish Avenue and Mike Rabinowitz, **EVANDER** '61. Both attended LIU in 1961. Contact Doris (Weiss) Bass. Please reply.

MP304 • Joyce (Grossman) Cinader – **TAFT** '63. Anyone who remembers please write all letters will be answered.

MP305 • EBB '60, **ROOSEVELT** '63, 167th Street "4", remember them? I'd love to hear from you – Loni Kleinberg.

MP306 • Looking for Edie Fertig of Gerard Avenue, Carol Streezek of Shakespeare Avenue and anyone from the crowd that hung out at the Sedgwick Projects. Are any of you out there? Please contact Cheryl Bard Benanti.

MP307 • "Itchy" looking for old pals from Wallace Avenue; King Crawford, Demara, Rosenblaum...where are you?

MP308 • Sylvia Cantor Weiss, **TAFT** '61, looking for Marion Bornstein, **TAFT** '61, Marcia Fishbein Goldey '62, Ellen Bell '61. I'm still married to Richie and living in Maryland. Write me...

MP309 • WHERE'S CHARLIE? Allen Mandel, **CLINTON** '60, and the rest of the guys need to find Charlie Maley, Music and Art '60, for a 50th birthday reunion. I've been looking for him for years! Can anyone help? Sharpen up your memories.

MP310 • Phyllis Meltzer Rothstein, **EVANDER** '63 and Richard Rothstein, **CLINTON** '60, celebrated their 25th anniversary by vacationing in Hawaii. They are the proud parents of Donna, a Ph.D. candidate at Cornell University, and Michele, a senior at Lehigh University.

MP311 • Abe Roemisher, Harold Tayman, Ralph Stienman, Dominick Miteratondo, Howard Schneider, Joe Magrim, Helen Milano, Florence Brown, Irving Moscowitz, Aaron Goldberg, Albert Gonzola – 2765 Matthews Avenue – 826 Adee Avenue...where are you?

MP312 • Remember the "Wall" by Pelham Pkwy, '69-'70? Chock Full 'O Nuts? The Huts? **COLUMBUS** HS, '69-'70? JHS135 '67-'68? Where'd you wind up? Bob Elber would like to know. Please make contact.

MP313 • Brenda Bachman Wangel, **MONROE** '58, looking for my Gold Dust twin, Andrea Carco. Would also enjoy hearing from anyone else I grew up with on Vyse Avenue.

MP314 • Several **TAFT** '53 graduates living in Tamarac, Florida: Susan Alouete Rich, Larry Milbauer, Wendy Lawner DeFortuna, Joseph DeFortuna. We're looking for more '52, '53 and/or '54 **TAFT** graduates residing in South Florida.

MP315 • Chuck Schweitzer, **TAFT** '63, looking for friends in Mrs. Jacobson's official class. Roger Jelinek, where are you? Where are the kids from Featherbed Lane and Jesup Avenue? Although I did get a degree in Physics, I'm now a CPA with offices in North Atlanta and South Florida.

MP316 • Does anybody know where they are – Joey McAuliffe, Mike Butler, Jimmy Barrett, Mary Farrell, Betty McWilliams, Billy Gorman, Bart Condon, Tommy McMahon, Phil Sasso, Frankie O'Brien, Diana Maldonado, Tito Pavon, Timmy Curtin?

MP317 • Wanted: **WALTON** '61 grads – where are you? We are planning our 35th Reunion. Call Roberta.

MP318 • Remember JHS22, classes 7-2, 8-2, 9-2, 1962-1965? Mrs. Mecray, math; Mr. Wagner, science; Mr. Tropp, social studies? So do I! If you want to reminisce, write me, Michael Janko. I was also **TAFT** '68.

MP319 • Ita Adinoff of 205th and Webster Avenue, Susan Mandel Kaen would love

to speak to you.

MP320 • Parkside Projects, PS96, JHS135, **EVANDER** '64, CCNY Lasak '68 – do any of these ring a bell with you? They do for me – Steve Wagh. Let me hear from you, OK?

MP321 • Paul Hogan, from Hughes Avenue and 182nd Street, looking for Louis Martucci, Joyce Russo of Adams Place, Danny Sica and others from 182nd Street/Belmont Avenue area. Where are you?

MP322 • **TAFT** '62, Karen Plung Schneider wants to find Roni Epstein, Joyce Panzeroni and Maddy Krautheimer. Gale also wants to find friends from Elliot Place – Ellis Arnstein, Howard Pincus, Steven Tiger (PS64, JHS117).

MP323 • Looking for people from "Wakefield Section" who were teens during the '60s. Also "1969" grads of Mother Butler Mem. Remember "Lowrys" Candy Store, 236th and White Plains Road?

MP324 • Eddie my love, Eddie my first love! Where are you? Are you somewhere filling cavities like your Dad? We were a couple on and off from 1960–1963. Call Ellen.

MP325 • My maiden name was Connie Honig, went to PS 26, PS 82 and **EVANDER**. Still in touch with Frank Ramundo, Zola Lieberman, Lillian Leverich, Herb Remer, Kitty Ramundo, and Betty Gottlieb (Leverich). Please call.

MP326 • Barbara Ferrara looking for Eileen Isacman and Joel Aaronberg, **EVANDER CHILDS** class of '62 . Would love to talk to them.

MP327 • 1957 **TAFT** graduate looking for old friends and classmates, anywhere, news of class reunions, etc. Send replies to David Goodmacher, 12–4 Apple Ridge Road, Maynard, MA 01754, telephone 1-508-897-5163.

Come Blow Your Horn

CB8 • Charles Seidner, Clinton '60 and Roberta (Soloff) Seidner, **WALTON** '61 married 25 years (wow). Two children, David 24 and Marcia 21. Husband supervisor of a kosher deli in the Bronx, Roberta an Executive Secretary at an Orthodox Synagogue.

Bronx Honor Roll
Bronxites who have achieved!

Bronx Science
Edgar Doctorow
Bobby Darren
Stokely Carmichael

Cardinal Hayes
George Carlin
Regis Philbin
Rocky Colovito
Kevin Loughery

DeWitt Clinton
James Baldwin
Paddy Chayefsky
Daniel Shore
Neil Simon
Richard Rodgers
Fats Waller
Don Adams
Martin Balsam
Judd Hirsch
Stubby Kaye
Robert Klein
Burt Lancaster
Avery Corman
Ed Lopat
Jan Murray
Jimmie Walker
Nate Archibald
Dolph Shayes
James Caan
A.M. Rosenthal

Evander Childs
Red Buttons
James Coco
Carl Reiner

Monroe
Hank Greenberg
Ed Kranepool
Jules Pfeiffer

Morris
Gabe Pressman
Angel Cordero

Roosevelt
June Allison

Taft
Eydie Gorme
Stanley Kubrick
Sanford Brown
Mal Z. Lawrence

Other notable folks with ties to the Bronx
Charles Osgood
Vic Damone
Bess Myerson
Dennis Day
Dion DiMucci
Jonas Salk
Roberta Peters
Jerry Vale
Jake LaMotta
Dianne Carroll
Ron Liebman
Gary Marshall
Al Pacino
Rob Reiner
Eli Wallach
Corazon Aquino
Edward Koch
Vin Scully
Joey Adams
Danny Aiello
Ellen Barkan
Alan Alda
Armand Hammer
Theodore Kheel
George Steinbrenner
Don Criqui
Lauren Bacall

Tony Curtis
Hal Linden
Sal Mineo
Charles Nelson Reilly
Isabel Sanford
Vanessa Williams
Herman Badillo
Ted Kennedy
George Burns
Norman Cousins
Edgar Alan Poe
Geraldo Rivera
Pat Summerall
Herman Wouk
Teresa Brewer
Cab Calloway
Joey Bishop
Joe Franklin
Penny Marshall
Carroll O'Connor
Connie Selleca
Cardinal Cooke
E. Colin Powell
Robert Kennedy
Anne Bancroft
Ralph Lauren
Eddie Pinckney
Mario Merola
Robert Abrams
Calvin Klein
Bobby Bonilla
George Cukor
Avery Fisher
Leon Cooper
Rosalyn Yallow

...Nobel Prize Winners
Gertrude Elio
Robert Hofstadter
Herman J. Muller
Melvin Schwartz
Steven Weinberg
Gerald Edelman

READER REPLIES

It is vitally important that you fill out the information below. Your input will be essential to the success of this magazine, tailored and inspired by you, the former "Bronxite". We thank you for your participation.

Subscriber? ☐ Yes   ☐ No

YOUR NAME _____

ADDRESS _____

CITY _____ STATE _____ ZIP _____ PHONE _____

HIGH SCHOOL ATTENDED _____ YEAR GRADUATED _____

TELL US A LITTLE ABOUT YOURSELF,
(Be sure to include your alma mater, old neighborhood, your best memories about your days in the Bronx, (or anything else you can tell us).

_____

_____

COULD WE SEND A FRIEND A FREE COPY OF BACK IN THE BRONX?

Do you know current or former Bronxites who would like to receive our magazine and reunion information? If you do, we'll be happy to send them **a free** inaugural issue of **Back in THE BRONX.**
Write to Back in The Bronx, Box 141 H, Scarsdale, NY 10583 or call 1-800-7-BRONX 5

Last	First	Maiden	
Address	City	State	Zip
Phone # ( )	School and year of Graduation		

Last	First	Maiden	
Address	City	State	Zip
Phone # ( )	School and year of Graduation		

Last	First	Maiden	
Address	City	State	Zip
Phone # ( )	School and year of Graduation		

Last	First	Maiden	
Address	City	State	Zip
Phone # ( )	School and year of Graduation		

COME BLOW YOUR OWN HORN DEPARTMENT

Please tell us about yourself (include your name)—about your accomplishments, awards, titles or works in progress. We're interested in hearing about them. List Below. _____

_____

_____

_____

READER REPLIES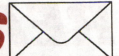

As a subscriber you are entitled to a FREE 40 Word Classified, Missing Persons, Blow Your Own Horn, or Personal Ad. Please write your ad below (if you are not subscribing to our magazine you can still place an ad in the next issue. The cost of an advertisement is 50¢ a word, there is no limit on paid ads).

_____

_____

_____

Is Your Mailing Label Correct?

In order to keep our database current, please correct any errors and place the label and or photocopy with corrections.

Account #	High School	Year Graduated
6817	Roosevelt	1958

SAMPLE
Mary R. Flowers
123 Anystreet Blvd.
Anywhere, USA 12345

Change of Address?

If you're planning a move please attach your label corrected with your new address and the date that you will begin receiving mail at that address. This will insure that you don't miss your next issue of **Back in THE BRONX.**

Ordering Information

A Great Gift Idea! In addition to your own subscription, a subscription to **Back in THE BRONX** makes a great and unique gift. Fill in the form below and we'll process the order in time for our next issue. So, order your subscription NOW, and order one for a friend!

YES, I'd like to order the following items:

QTY.

____ 1 Yr. (4 ISSUES) Subscription(s) to Back in THE BRONX $19.95
____ 2 Yr. (8 ISSUES) Subscription(s) to Back in THE BRONX* .. $29.95 ⎫ 'FREE
____ 3 Yr. (12 ISSUES) Subscription(s) to Back in THE BRONX* .. $39.95 ⎬ Jahn's
____ 4 Yr. (16 ISSUES) Subscription(s) to Back in THE BRONX* .. $49.95 ⎭ Menu

____ The Beautiful Bronx............$25.00 (plus $3.95 S/H) $28.95
____ The Bronx: It Was Only Yesterday..$25.00 (plus $3.95 S/H) $28.95
____ Bronx High School Reunion Weekend Video $29.95
____ SAVE MONEY - BUY 4 FOR JUST $99.00!
____ THE BRONX Tracking Service $9.95
____ I would like to receive all available back issues and have them applied towards my subscription *(To date we have at least 12 back issues available - While They Last!)*

TOTAL: $ _____

Please fill out completely and include $3.95 for shipping and handling for books only to: **Back in THE BRONX**, Box 141H, Scarsdale, NY 10583

Please Print Clearly ☐ New Subscriber ☐ Renewal

Name _____

Maiden Name _____

Address _____

City _____

State _____ Zip _____

Phone (_____) _____

High School _____ Year Grad. _____

☐ Visa ☐ Mastercard ☐ Check ☐ Money Order

No. _____ Expiration Date ____

Signature _____

Back in THE BRONX

Box 141 H, Scarsdale, NY 10583
Phone 914-592-1647 • Fax 914-592-4893

ADDRESS CORRECTION REQUESTED

Volume II Issue VI

Back in THE BRONX

CELEBRATING THE EXPERIENCE OF GROWING UP AND LIVING IN THE BRONX

The El

by Ray O Brien

Between the Bronx Borough "hub" at 149th Street and the rail yards along the Harlem River, the old Third Avenue El actually veered away from Third Avenue and sliced the blocks from 144th to 132nd Streets down the middle. I grew up in one such block that was sliced by the El—at 355 East 142nd Street between Willis and Alexander Avenues. Here, I grew up with the El.

It's not that I rode the El trains all that often. When I did, it was usually with my parents for the ride to Fordham Road, to the station by the gates to Fordham University. We would walk east on Fordham, past the pet shop where I bought my first dog, and past Theodore Roosevelt High (my mother's alma mater) to the White Castle, two blocks from my grandparents apartment. The El opened up what was to me the far reaches of the North Bronx.

What I remember of riding the El trains was mostly this: the blue and white station signs above the splintery platform boards, the tattered cane seats that would stick to your legs, especially if you wore short pants. The cane weaving created a pattern of dimples on my knees when I knelt to look out the train windows. From the rails above the Third

Continued on page 4

Faith of a Bronx Dreamer

by David A. Horowitz

Thirty-five years and three thousand miles from the Bronx, I dream of it as if it still was my home.

One night I awoke from sleep to realize that a nocturnal fantasy had taken me to the sixth floor of the now-demolished building on Popham Avenue, midway down the block between West 174th and 175th Streets. My family had lived on the second and then third floors, facing west with a view of the Harlem River, Washington Heights, and the rotating beacon of the George Washington Bridge.

My dream now placed me above the trees of the back lots so far up that I even thought I saw the mountains of Oregon rising behind distant New Jersey. "Do you think it'll be hot on the top floor?" I asked Gloria, a Bronx instinct momentarily cutting at my euphoria. "No," she answered, "there'll be a nice breeze up here."

1495, the "Townsend Arms," was the classiest apartment house on the block. The product of 1920's expansion to the hills west of University Avenue, it once provided a doorman and jitney service to the Jerome Avenue elevated train. The entry featured a walkway divided by a shrubbery garden with a quaint, wrought-iron fence. Above the double-paneled front door lay a decorative, sloping roof. Its rustic lines continued across the entire top of the building, offering an English distinctiveness that matched its fancy name.

Like its Bronx counterparts, the building was a self-contained community. The kids knew everyone, from old Mrs. Lieberman who roamed the midnight halls shrieking for a lost son, to the comely librarian said to be a war widow, to the family of German Jews who had fled the Holocaust, to the congenial father out of work for two years. There was Morris, the gruff, cigar-chomping refrigerator repairman who helped everyone, the short and

Continued on page 2

From the Editors...

Sorry for the delay in getting out this issue. We changed our printer and typesetter at the same time, and unfortunately, unforeseen problems occurred with each of these changes. However, we will make an attempt to send your next issue sooner so that we may catchup and stay on schedule.

We are in the process of writing a book, as tour of Bronx life and experiences done with a tongue in cheek attitude, but with unmistakable affection. It is our aim to recapture the mood and texture of Bronx life in the years after World War II by means of interviews, pictures and connecting text to set the material in perspective. We want to look back with fond nostalgia on those years when the Bronx was a lively and comfortable place to live, and perhaps speculate on the reasons for its success.

Are you a budding editor, artist, historian, writer or storyteller? We know that you are out there and would love to hear from you. If you have so much to say and so little time, you may send us a cassette tape and we will consider using it for the book and/or the magazine. We want to make it as easy as possible for you to contribute. To date, we have received many stories from our subscribers, and we urge you to continue to contribute to the magazine and the forthcoming book.

Finally, do you have friends, neighbors, or relatives, who might be interested in a free inaugural issue of Back in the Bronx? Please give us their names and addresses and we will be happy to send it to them...

If they wish they may call our toll free number:

1-800-7 BRONX 5.

Back in the BRONX

A number of the photographs in **Back in the Bronx** are courtesy of and are available from the Bronx Historical Society.

Publishers and Editors:
Steven M. Samtur   CLINTON '61
Susan H. Samtur   TAFT '62

Contributing Editors:
Barbara Fasciani
Martin Jackson   SCIENCE '58

Art & Production: Ellen Grodjesk

Printed By: Bronx Age Press

Reminiscing

Bronx Dreamer
continued from page 1

serious man on the fourth floor who played violin in a concert orchestra, and Ida and Benny, whose first-floor apartment provided our collective exposure to television and Howdy-Doody.

We kids spent time by "riding the trails" in the back lots, excavating boulders, engaging in occasional rock fights, and (once) setting fire to the thick underbrush. (When the engines came, Lenny's mother terrified us by threatening to "turn us in.") When the snow was deep in winter, we used the ash heap from the coal burner of a neighboring building for sledding.

On the street, we played ball, floated sticks down the curb when the "super" washed the pavement, fiercely scampered at frantic ring-a-levio games on the triangular street island we called "the square", and waited for the ice cream truck.

In our world, ice cream affiliation connected to baseball identity and social class. Good Humor's fifteen cent offerings were for Yankee fans and rich kids. Howard Johnson's twelve cent bars only sold to strangers who didn't know any better. In contrast, Bungalow Bar's ten cent specialties like pistachio and toasted almond were consumed by regular people and New York Giant fans like ourselves.

The Giants taught me a life-long lesson on an October day in 1951. In my initial year as a fan, the miracle-makers from Coogan's Bluff came from thirteen-and-a-half games behind the Brooklyn Dodgers to force a three-game playoff for the pennant. But as the ninth inning of the rubber match approached, Brooklyn stormed ahead four to one.

Hoping to spare me further pain, my mother pleaded with me to abandon the television set and go to Hebrew School. In a state of depression, I agreed. The next thing I knew, someone was barging into the classroom screaming "Davey, the Giants won, the Giants won, they won!" It was my mother, my brother in tow, not the least phased by the rabbinical surroundings nor the one-mile run along University Avenue. There on the top floor of that Bronx synagogue, Bobby Thomson's bottom-of-the-ninth, pennant-winning home run "heard 'round the world" gave me a lasting lesson on the importance of faith.

Having missed my team's greatest victory, I vowed not to miss out on rock'n'roll when Tommy Schumacher invited Lenny Diamond and I to a 1955 New Year's Eve party at which I first drank beer and heard Allen Freed. In two quick hours, I became a fanatic follower of the murky beat of rhythm and blues with its intriguing hints of sexuality.

Weeks later, only three of us were willing to defend rock'n'roll against charges of immorality in an eighth grade English class at JHS 82. Diane, Floyd, and myself all had bad cases of acne, but we were proud to stand behind Allen and Jackie. Although we could not compete with the coolness of the hell-studded "rocks" and toughs who roamed the neighborhoods of the mid-1950s West Bronx, We were prophets in a time of need.

I still keep the faith.
When I dream of home, I'm back in the Bronx.

Bronx Honor Roll
Bronxites who have achived!

BRONX SCIENCE
Edggar Doctorow
Bobby Darren
Stokely Carmichael

CARDINAL HAYES
George Carlin
Regis Philbin
Rocky Colovito
Kevin Loughery

DEWITT CLINTON
James Baldwin
Paddy Cheyefsky
Daniel Shore
Neil Simon
Richard Rogers
Fats Waller
Don Adams
Martin Balsam
Judd Hirsch
Stubby Kaye
Robert Klein
Burt LAncaster
Jan Murray
Jimmie Walker
Nate Archibald
Dolph Shayes
James Cann

EVANDER CHILDS
Red Buttons
James Coco
Carl Reiner

MONROE
Hank Greenberg
Ed Kranepool

Jules Pheiffer

MORRIS
Gabe Pressman
Angel Cordero

ROOSEVELT
June Allison

TAFT
Edie Gorme
Stanley Kubrick
Sanford Brown

OTHER NOTABLE FOLKS WITH TIES TO THE BRONX
Charles Osgood
Vic Damone
Bess Myerson
Dennis Day
Dion DiMucci
Jonas Salk
Roberta Peters
Jerry Vale
Jake LaMotta
Dianne Carroll
Ron Liebman
Gary Marshall
Al Pacino
Rob Reiner
Eli Wallach
Corazon Aquino
Edward Koch
Vin Skully
Joey Adams
Danny Aiello
Ellen Barkum

Alan Alda
Armand Hammer
Theodore Kheel
George Steinbrenner
Don Criqui
Laren Bacall
Tony Curtis
Hal Linden
Sal Mineo
Charles Nelson Reilly
Isabel Sanford
Vanessa Williams
Herman Badillo
Ted Kennedy
George Burns
Avery Corman
Norman Cousins
Edgar Alan Poe
Geraldo Rivera
Par Summerall
Herman Woulk
Teresa Brewer
Cab Calloway
Joey Bishop
Joe Franklin
Peny Marshall
Carroll O'Connor
Connie Selleca
Cardinal Cooke
E. Colin Powell
Robert Kennedy
Leon Cooper (Nobel Prize Winner)
Rosalyn Yallow (Nobel Prize Winner)
Anne Bancroft
Ralph Lauren

Thanks to Dr. William C. Wolfson and the Bronx Society of Science and Letters

Reminiscing

The El

Continued from page 1

Avenue the apartment windows seemed almost within arm's reach and the forest of store signs (Hearns, Nedicks, Devaga's. Vim's, and Alexanders) pressed close against the El. And I particularly liked the look of the Bronx Borough Hall sitting atop the hill at Tremont.

Yet my memories of the El come more from having lived in an apartment literally in its shadow. Everyday things were conditioned by the El. We got used to the squealing metal wheels and the vibrations that came every twelve minutes or so and we paid no heed to the fact that the clothesline displayed our wash for all the passing world to see. In summer, stickball was always played up the block towards the Loew's scenic warehouse on the corner of Alexander Avenue so as not to lose precious pink hi-bouncing "spaldings" on the El tracks or in the back of the El fence. And when I built a tent made of blankets on the fire escape, the fire escape itself would shake alarmingly with the rattle of the trains. My bedroom window faced directly onto the El platform between 142nd and 143rd streets. It couldn't have been more than a hundred feet from the apartment, across the narrow alley green with Sumac and across the backyard of the neighboring wood frame house where the widow Graves sometimes tended a vegetable garden. After so many years I must confess to this: from my bed and from behind my curtains, I would slide the window screen and, being very careful not to be seen, would pepper the advertising signs on the El platform with my pea shooter...as well as the windows of the passing trains! I don't think I ever hit anyone (on purpose), nor did I really intend to—it was just the "pinging" sound made by the peas striking metal and glass was addictive. And besides, my "spud guns" wouldn't reach quite that far. This pastime came to an abrupt end on the day I spied a man in uniform on the El platform who caught a glimpse of me as the summer breeze blew aside my curtain. No more pea shooter, at least for me, that summer.

As a grade school pupil at St. Pious who had lunch at home, I had to walk down to and across Willis Avenue. This took me beneath the El four times each day. The few seconds it took to walk beneath the El were always filled with foreboding, since my parents, like most parents in the block, issued daily warnings to stay away from "under the El". Only as a last resort would anyone park thier car under the El for fear of sparks or other falling debris. The phase "under the El," and what it suggested might lie in the gloom beneath the tracks or in among the shadows of the arched brick support pillars behind the 8-foot high fence, came to signify a place of definite danger. "Under the EL" evoked the negative in the same way that "up on the roof" exalted the positive—tar beach, family photo sessions, being tossed high into the air wrapped in my father's army blanket. All these warnings would one day hit home...

But meanwhile, life alongside the El was simply taken for granted. Though no one in my family ever thought to photograph the El because it was the El, this dark superstructure of steel beams and wood was always there, usually just out of range of the old Kodak box camera or in the back of grandparents and cousins, communions and confirmations on the 8mm home movie reels. And sometimes, as on a summer day in 1951, its image appeared alongside of me...reflected in the shiny black fender and chrome bumper of my father's old Plymouth...the car my father wrapped around an El pillar at 149th Street on Christmas Eve with a carload of presents in the days before reflectors were put on the El pillars.

Though taken for granted, the El would soon be gone. It had outlived its usefulness, they said. And so I watched as the flag-draped trains ran down to Manhattan and into history. For years the neighborhood was left with the abandoned and deteriorating platform, and fences where a kid was killed with a "zip" gun...this, around the time the police began raiding backyard "zip gun factories" in the South Bronx. At that age I was terrified of and unfamiliar with death; indeed, my only knowledge of death had been gained by peeking through the sidewalk-level windows into the embalming cellar of Walter B. Cook's funeral Home. So, on the day of the "zip-gun" shooting I hid in my room rather than see the boy's body carried out fro under the El. But I remembered for a very long time what could, and did happen to people, "under the El."

It took a few more years before all the girders and beams were finally torn down and hauled away (to be sold to Japan as scrap, rumors said; to be used as girders in the third tube of the Lincoln Tunnel, the New York Times said.) What the neighborhood was left with then was a wide and airy open space in the middle of the block that the neighborhood kids quickly cleared of the remaining rubble and ruins, of the glass and other trash that had accumulated for decades under the platform (along with, no doubt, unaccountable number of little peas!) Soon we had a lot for playing baseball, but only for a short while...

The demolition of the El was a prelude to the demolition of the whole neighborhood. By the late 1950's city planners became convinced of the worth of "slum clearance" and so began to clear away the "slums" between 140th and 144th Streets to make way for Mott Haven housing project. It was sad when the El and then the apartment house were torn down, but sadder still when the entire block was obliterated. As with so much of the South Bronx, now the only way back home is through what Civil War film-maker Ken Burns calls "emotional archaeology"—using memories and photos to reconstruct a place no longer a part of the real world. At least there will always be this Bronx of memory....bits and pieces of memory called up from dreams of summer days and the passing El.

4

LOST & FOUND

Reminiscing

Explaining the Bronx to Your Children

by Mike Gumpel

I have not lived in the Bronx since 1969. Lately, I have been feeling extremely nostalgic and have reminisced with my children. It did not take a genius to quickly realize, however, that my kids could not relate. That though I was out of my mind or had grown up in a different universe. What in the world was tis place called the "Bronx" that I was always talking about?

Of course, you have to understand that my son lived his first seven years in the Republic of Korea and his last 12 in Southern California. My daughter is 10, and has only lived in California. They are true suburban-California kids, who just happen to possess a strange (to them) father: a displaced Bronxite.

They are great kids with a father who has a weird need to explain his background to them. At times this results in inexplicable (to them) statements or actions from me. But I have two standard excuses which explain away my strangeness.

First, my mother told me that there was a tremendous blizzard before New Years Day, 1947, and she slipped on some ice in Times Square during the final months of her pregnancy. Perhaps I suffered brain damage,.

Second, I attended Creston Junior High and DeWitt Clinton High School. In those days that ment six years in all boys schools—which I consider to be a true example of deprivation!

My children are deprived too, but in other ways. For example, there's the matter of distances. They cannot conceive having 50 kids near your age in a one - or two block area around your home. While my kids have had times they were bored, this was something unheard of in my youth on the streets of the Bronx. There was too much going on all around. On the other hand, most of my children's friends live within driving distance.

What in the world is a "spaldeen" anyway?

Driving to visit a friend in the Bronx? Unheard of!

Then there are my stories. If I tell them about walking a dozen blocks to P.S. 28 in a snowstorm, they figure it is just the kind of story that Dad makes up when he wants to tell you how good you have it. Pure fiction.

Or what about sewer fishing? Who would fish a spaldeen out of a sewer and what in the world is a spaldeen, anyway?

I've tried to explain to them how the concrete streets became our playgrounds by playing games such as stickball, curb ball, off the point, king and queen, and how this spaldeen was so necessary for these.

But it seems to escape them. They laugh at playing basketball with the bottom rung of a fire escape as the basket. (At least they know what a fire escape is, they have seen them in the movies.) Then I tell them that fire escapes were Bronx patios. We could all sit out on them, especially on hot summer evenings, and also keep a few plants there. They nod and look bored.

This is not to say that there is no communication at all. My son, who sails and surfs, has asked me about the beaches in the Bronx. I told him about Orchard Beach when I was a teenager and he could easily identify with it. But he was more interested in the real waves and, for those, you had to go to the south shore of Long Island. The most commonly used beach in the Bronx was, of course Tar Beach— completely foreign to him.

Since my kids have never lived in an apartment building or in a house with a flat roof, they thought sunning yourself and hanging out on the roof was different, but nevertheless, understandable.

But when I mentioned our local candy store, these kids envisioned something like Fannie Farmer or Barton's, not a store that sells newspapers, magazines, sandwiches, school supplies and is equipped with a fountain. To tell you the truth, they are not even sure what a soda fountain is! My son did not like the egg cream I made for him, even after I swore there was no egg or cream in it.

Perhaps they are just not supposed to understand my background. These kids have never ridden a bus, and the train does not really exist here. Yet, in Dad's old high school yearbook there is a picture of him climbing into a side window of a bus. They have no conception of how badly I would have missed that quarter fare.

They also find it unbelievable that I attended a high school with over 5,000 students. Add to this, the fact that it was an all boys school and they really believe that a court must have ordered me to go there. They may have a point.

Even so, there are some similarities. Just on our block in

the Bronx, among my friends were kids of Irish, Jewish, Italian, Afro-American, Puerto Rican, Cuban, Dominican, Armenian and Greek decent. Here in southern California, there are just as many ethnic backgrounds, though the kids do not mix together as much as we did in my day. Perhaps that is because there were more people living in the three apartment buildings on my block then reside within the three-square- mile area which makes up our current housing tract.

I must admit that there is some hope. A few years ago, as I arrived home from work, there was a wondrous sight in front of our home. My son, James, had chalked a strike zone on the garage door and a friend of his was pitching to him with a tennis ball. James had a short stick, and they were obviously playing their version of stick ball.

I quickly got him a broom stick, but the tennis ball had to stay for lack of a proper replacement. At that point I new that my surfer, catamaran-sailing son was not completely with out redemption.

My daughter, who is an actress (for real—she has appeared in national TV commercials), has a great talent for mimicry. She does a fantastic Brooklyn accent but has not mastered the subtle differences in order to speak proper Bronxese.

Being a real daddy's girl, she has been working on me about going back to visit the Bronx this summer. We have no family there any more, but she wants to see the sights and hear the sounds of the strange place her dad came from.

Even though there is no family in the Bronx and no contact with my old friends in more than twenty years, we will make the trip. Perhaps we could see a movie at the Paradise, have a ice cream at Krumbs—ARE these places still there?—Then walk up to Fordham Road. There, I could show here our equivalent of hanging out at the mall: the phone booths at Fordham and the Concourse and, of course, Poe Park. Even in freezing weather, we would be there and, if we needed climate control. we simply shut the phone booth door. A game at Yankee Stadium and a visit to the Bronx Zoo also would be nice, but I doubt they could give her any insight into her dad's childhood. However, I might find out how much things have changed.

The media has not been too kind to the Bronx, but I know there is rebuilding going on. We could see if the kids still play the same games. Are the goals of most people still to move to a better apartment building or neighborhood— someday even to Jersey or Westchester and buy a house?

I have this fear that I am a displaced person coming from a place that does not exist anymore except in my own mind. Many of my friends in California come from places that are essentially the same today as they were years ago. They visit and return with stories about their old friends. I do envy them.

Does my Bronx still exist? Certainly the place is still there. The faces may be different, but wouldn't it be great to find out that the plans and dreams of the people are still the same? Perhaps some omnipotent force has made the Bronx just tough enough to encourage a good portion of her population to work hard and then get out. Maybe it is a cosmic pattern: each wave followed by successive groups doing the same thing. Unfortunately for the Bronx, while it gives her a great list of alumni, it causes her to struggle eternally.

We will make our pilgrimage, and maybe my daughter will gain insight into both her father and the place from which he came. If so, then there will be sequel to this story: my Bronx and, just maybe, her Bronx too.

Reminiscing

THE AVENUE
By Marvin Rosen

Bainbridge Avenue was a string of stores and markets serving a mixed group of Jewish, Irish, and Italian families in the West Bronx. While the groups maintained their ethnic integrity according to rigidly maintained geographic lines, they rubbed elbows at Daitch's Dairy and Hanscom's Bakery. The Avenue lured housewives from a twenty block radius. They came pushing their shopping carts and baby strollers from vegetable market to appetizing store, from the dry cleaner's to the kosher butcher shop.

Few women owned or drove cars so shopping entailed a morning or afternoon excursion on foot. It represented a social occasion as well as a functional activity. Even the old "bubas" living with their married children participated, often their only outing for the day. Children accompanied their mothers, holding onto carriage handles if they were old enough to walk, and dwadling at the candy store until they were obliged with a Mary Jane bar or a set of baseball cards (the bubble gum was discarded) or penny wooden glider. By age ten we were allowed to travel alone for a six cent egg cream of chocolate syrup, soda and milk or the latest ten cent issue of Superman, Captain Marvel or Plastic Man.

The Avenue originated to the north at the imposing Montefiore Hospital in a residential neighborhood and extended south past Reservoir Oval at 208th Street and deadended eight or ten blocks later under the "El" at Webster Avenue. At 205th Street, the northernmost stop of the Independent Subway System provided a convenient link with the downtown business districts of Manhattan. Crosstown busses also stopped at the corner, proving a free transfer to the subway system. Rain or shine, there was always a bus dispatcher on the corner. A double amputee in a wheelchair operated a news stand a few feet from the bus stop. Large grated openings above the subway tunnels brought the subterranean sounds to the surface. It was common to see older boys inserting long bamboo sticks with chewing gum at the tip through the grating, fishing for shiney pennies or nickels that had been dropped from above. Five cents purchased a subway ride to Chambers Street and the financial district at the tip of Manhattan Island. By the time I left the Bronx, the same D train went all the way

to Coney Island but the price of the ride had increased.

Two blocks to the south was the Mosholu Movie Theater. We called it "The Mosh" A double feature was a quarter for adults and eighteen cents for kids. The Saturday matinee included cartoons and a continuing serial. Audiences were lured by lottery drawings for a set of dishes.

Crimi, the Italian barber, often stood at the door of his shop greeting the passersby. The shop was exclusively for men but the mothers were allowed to scrutinize their son's haircuts, giving Crimi precise instructions about the styling. He gave me my first haircut at age three, shearing off my curls to solidify my masculine identification.

The fruit and vegetable market was as much outside the store as within. Produce was displayed in rough wooden crates that we used to make skateboard scooters. Green peas could be purchased fresh each day for shelling and sometimes when a pea was found to have sprouted the beginnings of a white root, it was placed in water and later planted in an earth-filled Breakstone's cream cheese box.

The appetizing store had a succulent array of smoked fishes, belly lox, herring, saurkraut and sour pickles stored in a deep wooden barrel. My father delighted in selecting the fattest he could locate and in filling a jar with the vinegary pickle "yucht" which he later drank from a glass.

Woolworth's, with its intriguing conglomeration of affordable toys and games, was known only as the "Five and Ten." To some of my friends it was a perpetual shop-lifting challenge. Although I never risked a theft, the impulse was always there to "hook" a model airplane or yo-yo that "slept." During the war, the most valuable metal trucks and guns were replaced by cheap plastic or wooden models and the lure of Woolworth's faded.

The Avenue assumed a different character with each season. The concrete sidewalks radiated heat in the summer. It was bedecked in festive green at Christmas time with vendors hawking trees at every corner. Winter snows made rubber galoshes a necessity for negotiating the icy sidewalks while pushing a two-wheeled shopping cart. Our area of the West Bronx was a prestige location, rich in parks, playgrounds, schoolyards and recreational areas. Yet it was the Avenue that provided the daily rhythm to our lives — the punctuation, pauses and accents of living found at the "Mosh," the candy store and the "A&P".

A BRONXITES SUMMERS

By Judith Miller nee Greif

The first seventeen years of my life were spent living on Webb Avenue and the corner of 195th Street in a five story, walk-up apartment building. My parents were from Poland and though we were not in any way wealthy, my parents considered it important for the health of myself and my brother to get away from the sweltering city for the summer months and reap the benefits of grass, trees and fresh air. It should also be remembered that these were the days before Jonas Salk, and polio was a very real threat during many summers.

My father was a postman so for us, summers in the Catskills were a real luxury. They were in fact paid for by the Christmas tips that my father made from his route. I can still remember evenings when he sat at the kitchen table counting the day's tips which were largely a single dollar from each family. Somehow, you could always count on a few dollars more from the businesses he delivered to and naturally the convent on Burke Avenue. I don't believe that the total of these tips ever exceeded $250, but that was enough to purchase a summer in the "Country" for us.

In May, through newspaper ads, my father would take the Short Line bus to a designated are; sometimes Monticello, sometimes Accord, once Woodburn, and check out several bungalow colonies in that area. After one or two trips and some haggling on price a deposit was given and my brother and I waited with great expectation for the getaway day, generally the day after school ended.

As these bungalows were equipped with nothing more than bare bones and rickety furniture, my mother literally packed up half of our household possessions: linens, dishes, pots and pans and finally clothes. A "Hackie" was engaged for the trek and though we had enough of our own possessions to fill the entire limo, these vehicles served many individuals much as todays airport shuttles do. You could expect to find your fellow passengers to be individuals or couples heading for a couple of weeks at a hotel and always one or two families like us, laden with almost everything we own. Suitcases and cartons were tied on the back as the trunk never closed and the roof was laden with the overflow, tied tightly down.

At that time, the route to the "Mountains" was route 17, and the trip took approximately 4 hours. The midway point was the Red Apple Rest, a giant cafeteria. I can't remember any food being purchased but it was the designated "Pit stop" for every Hackie. My main recollection of the Red Apple Rest, was a din of voices not unlike the tape played when you visit Elis Island's Great Hall today.

Once in the Catskills, passengers disembarked according to thier destination, which often entailed unloading very nearly the entire trunk and roof each time someone departed.

Upon reaching our destination, my father paid the balance due. We carried and dragged our possessions to our bungalow. Our accommodations always consisted of a kitchen, a bedroom, a screened porch and a bathroom, sometimes shared. It would take my mother days to scour everything and put our possessions away and in truth, my mother never seemed to have any more leisure time in the "Mountains" than she had in the city.

Because we had bare bones accommodations, we generally did not have a pool and considered ourselves lucky to have a icy cold stream which, with luck, had a deep spot. One summer we lucked out with the use of a distressed hotel's pool and one summer when we actually had a pool the algae was so thick, it looked like pea soup, and was drained by mid July.

We were expected to amuse ourselves as we could not afford the more affluent colonies which had a casino which afforded, bingo, a juke box, a soda counter and perhaps minimal and very poor entertainment as well as a sixth rate movie which generally had the film break a half a dozen times during a showing. Being the poor vacationers, we would often successfully sneak into the movies or were permitted to pay a small sum for admission.

It always seemed that other families in our bungalow colony did not have children my age and sex. Somehow, my brother lucked out most of the time, and I was left to my own devices or spent my time with my brother's friends. (My husband of 26 years is the brother of one of my brother's friends, but that is another story). One of my fondest memories of a summer activity is berry picking. I'd take a glass milk bottle and go out for blueberries or black berries. I remember that I would bring home quarts of these and to this day, not only love berries far above other fruit but it seems the cultivated product are never as good as those I picked.

As we were generally located a considerable distance from town, the proprietor of the colony generally took his residence into town once a week to shop. Milk, bread, ice cream, vegetables, etc. arrived by truck on a set schedule, and the arrival of these truck was a major event of the day.

Generally, on Friday or Saturday night we would take a flashlight and go walking down the main road toward town. While this was an enjoyable evening pastime on the weekends, you hoped to meet your father suitcase in hand trudging up the road from the Short Line Depot for his well earned 2 days with his family.

For the most part, the bungalow colonies, including the large fancy ones, are long gone, as are the majority of the Catskill Hotels. However, like my memories of Webb Avenue/195th Street, these memories of summer fun, of a time and way of life that is no more, linger fondly.

Reminiscing

Mosholu Parkway

By Marvin Rosen

In the days before television and instant vacations to London, Jamacia or Touramalinas, people sought simple ways to ease the tensions of work or home. The local park was such a diversion. What better way to pass a few peaceful hours than by sitting on a shady bench, rocking the baby carriage, letting the kids run free and watching the Fords and Chevys go by.

Two short blocks from 3280 the greenery of Mosholu Parkway offered an endless expanse for strolling, playing or just plain sitting. No small city park, enclosed by tall buildings and department stores, Mosholu Parkway stretched for miles from Bronx Park to the south to Van Cortlandt Park to the north. It was possible to walk along the Parkway to the Bronx Zoo or New York Botanical Gardens. A geological museum offered an afternoon's diversion. Van Cortlandt Park offered hills and trails for exploring, an artificial lake for boating in summer and ice skating in winter. An attractive golf course brought enthusiasts from all over the city; Uncle Eli caddied there as a teen ager.

Mosholu Parkway symbolizes the era between two world wars. To a generation born during the Great Depression, the park offered a calm stability. We didn't realize it then but we were advantaged beyond the dreams of our parents whose memories of the East side tenements and pushcarts was still too fresh. Mosholu Parkway represented the slow and easy freedom that was later lost somewhere between Hiroshima and Korea.

Freedom was roaming from one end of the park to the other, racing a stretch of the center island until we dropped from exhaustion, skipping flat stones across the lake or sailing our miniature boats on long white lines, crawling through large drain pipes beneath the golf course, crunching along crisp fall leaves searching for snakes, belly flopping our sleds down dead man's hill, vaulting the park rail gracefully with one hand, loitering among crowds of boys and girls, smoking and trying to appear tough, listening to Mel Allen describe on WINS radio, another win by the New York Yankees buying a Good Humor bar from the white uniformed vendors pushing their antiseptic wagons, encountering Iris Tannenbaum or Arlene Schlesinger or Rita Feinberg or some other nymphet ... doing all these things, or none of them as we desired.

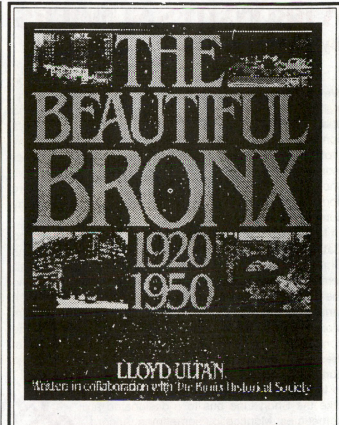

THE OTHER BRONX
By Steve Winkler

Although they may not have thought about it at the time, the kids who came from the section of the Bronx near the Grand Concourse, etc. were to us the "rich" kids! They had it all— elevator buildings that stretched to the sky, parks (like Poe Park) to hang out in, Jahn's to walk to, Yankee Stadium, and the "end all" of movie theaters—the Loew's Paradise (were watching the stars twinkle and the clouds move across the ceiling "sky" made it very difficult to watch a film— but oh, the magic of it all!).

Years later I made a special trip to show my new wife (a girl from—oh God— Brooklyn) the most wondrous of movie theaters. But, I digress. Our folks were always talking of moving to the "Concourse"—were the rich people lived. (The Concourse people talked of moving to Queens...).

We lived on the fourth floor of a five floor walk up apartment building—no elevator. Coupled with the style of very thick heavy shoes we were forced to wear (because they lasted longer and thus monies could be saved) climbing all those stairs really made us into athletic types, long before the onset of exercise machines. We lived, the four of us, in a small one bedroom apartment. Very few families in our building had two bedroom apartments. Our Bronx was such that we even locked our apartment doors. Almost no one owned a car. Our block stretched from 174th to 176th streets on the East side of Boston Road and Southern Blvd. (Near "West Farms") and consisted of a dozen walk-up apartment buildings. The "neighborhood" was comprised of about four of these blocks. On our corner were a half dozen stores including Shapiro's candy store were according to the full page article in the New York Post one Sunday, "THE VERY BEST EGG-CREAMS IN NEW YORK" were made! (This should finally lay to rest all those other imposter's claims to fame!) Another of those stores was Julie's Grocery, were one paid once a month or so (did Julie invent the credit card?) and marveled at Julie adding up the totals on the brown bag faster than today's cash registers ever could.

Then there was the Playground—a two-level concrete

place run by the weird, frightening N.Y.C. Parks department employee—the Parkie. It was here that punchball reined supreme—we played from the first light to dusk whenever school wasn't in session. We almost always stayed close to home because venturing out into someone else's neighborhood could mean getting our butts kicked by one or the other of the gangs that ruled our side of the Bronx. Sometimes we did go forth, like the time the three of us dared to go to the Bronx Zoo (at the tender age of 13) where the police found us unconscious after being attacked by about 15 of those guys they called the "Baldies". It seems they didn't like the bell bottoms we were wearing!

Some things were the same in all parts of the Bronx: playing ball, streetgames, and of course, there were girls to love in our Bronx also. Speaking of playing ball we played as the only independent (sponsored by a bar on Daly Ave.) baseball team in the N.Y.C. Leagues of very highly organized teams. We won the P.A.L. City Championship and then for the next two years won the City Championship over such teams as the "Billikens" and the "Redwings". I was now about 15. High school was coming to an end for most of us. But—unlike that other Bronx almost none of my "crowd" of thirty guys and fifteen girls desired to go to college and few even wanted to work! There parents were worn down by the oppression of being poor and it was transferred to them to accept their place in society as that of the lower class. Some got arrested. Some died violently. And some, like myself, whose parents were always striving for more out of life, went on to college and eventually "made it". I feel fortunate to have gone through "hard times" though because now it helps me to cope with whatever situations might arise.

Grandma

By Marvin Rosen

The crowd was hushed as the Rabbi asked the mourners to recite the traditional kaddish service for the dead. "Y'is gedal ve y'is gedash ... Mechanically I rose with my aunts and uncles to chant the sacred Hebrew words. Gently my uncle pushed me down again to my seat. "Only the children," he reminded me. "She was like a mother to me," I murmured.

Grandma lived with us in our five room apartment in the Bronx. My parents occupied the large master bedroom. My sister and I were down the hall. With my aunt, grandma shared the back room, facing south toward 206th Street. From their window I often watched the Borden horse struggling to pull the milk wagon on the hill on icy winter days.

A proud, attractive woman in her younger years, Grandma bore herself with grace and straight backed dignity even in her declining years. In old photographs, dating back before the turn of the century, she stands tall, highbreasted and tightly corsetted, a practice she followed all her life. No one was to see her in her coffin, she instructed my mother and this wish was fulfilled.

Grandma was a "kuchlefel," a mixing spoon who liked to stir things up. She would take no guff from anyone. She fought with her sisters, letting no insult, real or imagined, go unnoticed or unanswered. She had names for all the neighbors and could spot hypocrisy with great accuracy. She did not hesitate to criticize my mother or feud with my father. She had a strong, stubborn streak that has been passed on for three generations.

Never fiercely religious, grandma respected tradition. She kept a kosher home for us and God help the one who mixed the "milechdiche" (dairy) with the "fleischedicher" (meat) silverware. Every Friday at sun down she lit the Sabbath candles, intoning a prayer that only she and God could hear. Yet she seldom set foot inside a synagogue except for weddings and bar mitzvahs.

I was the favorite of her grandchildren. She knew I loved her and she fussed over me. When I was very young she read to me about "Watermellon Pete" and "Little Black Sambo" who was chased by a tiger who ran around the tree so fast that he turned into pancakes with butter on them. She promised to buy me a pushcart so that I could sell apples on the corner.

An ancient Victor console radio stood in our living room. Grandma spent many hours listening to H. V. Kaltenborn or Gabriel Heater interpret the war news, while she crocheted little doilies that went under her crystal heirlooms on the foyer buffet or on the cushions of intricately carved high-backed chairs. She had a way with plants and kept large potted varieties of snake plant

and bromeliad healthy year after year without the use of chemical fertilizers. Grandma could make anything grow.

She loved to shop on Bainbridge Avenue and found excuses to make the daily pilgrimage to replenish her pantry with some staple or other. She enjoyed the "movies" at the Mosholu or Tuxedo and went once each week or more. She would have loved TV but it came too late for her.

Grandma savored her cup of coffee and sipped it European style through a lump of sugar held fast between her teeth. She loved to cook for the holidays. I helped her roll the dough for three cornered "Hamentasheu" at Purim. She made wonderful blintzes from Saltine crackers and cottage cheese. She liked the dry farmer cheese from Daitches Appetizing store near Webster Avenue, spreading it thick on soda crackers and absent-mindedly rolling the cheese in balls.

She nursed us through our illness and fevers; she patched the wounds and healed the hurts. So what if her remedies were Old World. They worked. She set up the steam tent with a large Turkish towel and a kettle of boiling water when we had the "Croupe". She annointed our chests with cod liver oil and flannel to loosen the phlegm. She fed me castor oil and administered the enemas. She could detect a fever by kissing the forehead and forced us to sip hot tea and honey for a cold. Before the days of penicillin, when the "grippe" meant ten days home from school, she watched us like a hawk to be sure we followed the doctor's orders.

She, herself, was a regular patient of Dr. Raginsky, the family practioner. She had chronic stomach problems and was constantly trying new remedies. The druggist joked behind her back that she was addicted to the alcoholic content of her prescriptions. In the end, the doctor missed the diagnosis of an obstructed colon. She suffered several weeks, then died on the ambulance. She could have lived a few more years.

And yet, perhaps she willed her death. We were leaving the apartment. My aunt, still unmarried, was moving to Long Island to be nearer her friends. My parents had purchased their home in Yonkers. I was off to college. She didn't know which way to go, which daughter to follow. She could not live alone. Her death resolved the issue.

The Streets Where I Lived
By Arthur Buffman

From the 1940's through the 1960's, my parents and I lived in a five-story, thirty-six tenant apartment building on Morris Avenue, near Burnside Avenue. Electric trolley cars in the 40's could be seen moving on the tracks along Burnside Avenue headed for Webster Avenue and beyond. At times, the overhead wires to which the trolleys were connected expelled large bright sparks, lighting the early evening sky. Along Burnside Avenue were stores such as Smilen Brothers, for fruits and vegetables; John's Bargain Stores, sundry household goods; Loew's Burnside, movie theater; Garden and Bloom's bakeries having delicious bread, cakes, cookies; Peckerman's, Hy's and Blaines, drug stores; Spievack's, Zion and Hebrew National, delicatessens; Silver's, grocery; Irving's, radio store; Kalishman's, lamps, tables, knick knacks; Pressler's, dry goods; and numerous other retail establishments.

One store that I particularly liked, as a little boy, was Silver's. There I would watch the owners cut slices of butter from a giant mound to sell customers. Most of all, I would anxiously await getting empty wooden cheese boxes for planting seeds to grow beautiful flowers such as zinnias. Who needed to buy window boxes!

Everyone Knew His Neighbor

When the weather was favorable, tenants on Morris Avenue would carry bridge chairs from their apartments to sit in front of the building. Many would wait for Bungelo Bar, Mr. Softee or the Eskimo Pie truck to bring their favorite ice cream. Who ever heard of ice cream being sold in supermarkets! While relaxing and talking, many a friendship developed. In fact in my building, one lonely spinster, whom everyone thought would never marry, found true love with a man only three floors below her. He had recently lost his wife and eagerly desired this lady. What a marriage that made. Not only was the wedding the "talk of the town" but everything was accomplished without video dating or matchmakers!

Naturally, every building had a "busy body" who would know everyone's business. My house had one also. This lady, who never married, would sit near her ground-floor apartment window and observe every passerby. She could tell you who was dating whom, who was pregnant, what the

baby's sex would likely be, and which stores had the best bargains.

To save money, she would bring her own cooked chicken to eat at the Brighton Cafeteria on Jerome Avenue near Burnside. For 5¢, she would be a "sport," order a whole cup of coffee, and spend hours delving into the latest gossip at the tables. If the cafeteria had many customers like her, it wouldn't have lasted as long as it did! However, despite her shortcomings, this lady really wanted love and attention.

Pleasant Memories of Doctors and Pharmacists

Another interesting aspect of my neighborhood were the doctors and pharmacists. From anywhere between $2.00 and $5.00 one could visit Dr. George Sheinberg on Walton Avenue, near Burnside Avenue, or perhaps Dr. Bacher on Morris Avenue near Burnside or Dr. Samuel Lieberman on Morris Avenue. Dr. Sheinberg would offer my dad a little alcoholic beverage to relax and patiently listen to his health problems. He was kind, understanding and a well-liked physician. Dr. Bacher was also highly regarded. However, Another doctor was most famous for being a Romeo or "ladies man." Many a young mother said that he gave an examination, including a thorough physical of the erogenous zones, which went beyond the call of duty. However, the ladies continued to use the good doctor either because of health benefits or perhaps he had a better technique than their husbands! All these wonderful general practitioners are not living today but fond memories of a bygone era remain.

Some additional mention should be made of the pharma-

Reminiscing

cies like Hy's or Peckerman's. If anyone got a cinder in their eye, they went right to the drug store and it was removed without charge. Today, if this happens and we visit an opthalmologist, the charge could be $100.00

My Apartment Building

Growing up on Morris Avenue was quite different from today. My kitchen had a combination sink, part for dishes and part for washing clothes. A metal washboard was placed in the sink and clothes were hand scrubbed with Octogon, a brown hard soap. After completion, the finished items were placed on a bathroom clothes line which was hoisted to the ceiling. The water dripped on the floor or in the toilet. Washers and dryers were not the rage yet! Garbage disposal was on a dumbwaiter. A bell would ring in our apartment late afternoon, signaling that this contraption had arrived. My parents and I would place our brown paper garbage bags on the dumbwaiter which was then hoisted down to the next apartment. Who knew of incinerators!

The various landlords of our building always instructed the super to give heat sparingly. On cold winter days, I would knock on the radiator to signal the super that we needed steam heat. Sometimes the radiators would get hot, other times not. Who knew if the super heard the knocking or cared. However, I survived and hoped for warmer days.

One day television was introduced in the early 1950's. The Bushman family, who lived in my building, was one of the first to get a black and white Pilot television. Neighbors took turns, every Tuesday at 8 P.M., going to their apartment to see the Milton Berle show. Every seat in the living room was taken. Who could forget the comedian Sid Stone, on his show, when he clapped his hands and said, "So you want more for your money, here's what I gonnz do ..."

TV wasn't the only form of new entertainment. My friend, Lester Krasnogor, practiced many hours with his clarinet and saxaphone, allowing the neighbors to hear a free concert. When he became proficient during the mid-1950's, Lester and his band played music at Kaufman's Garden House Hotel and Country Club in Hurleyville, New York. Today my friend is a successful pulmonary specialist. What a career switch!

Scrapbook

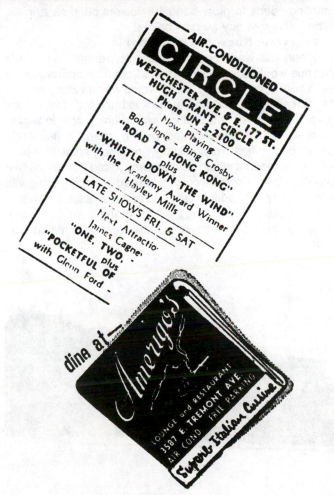

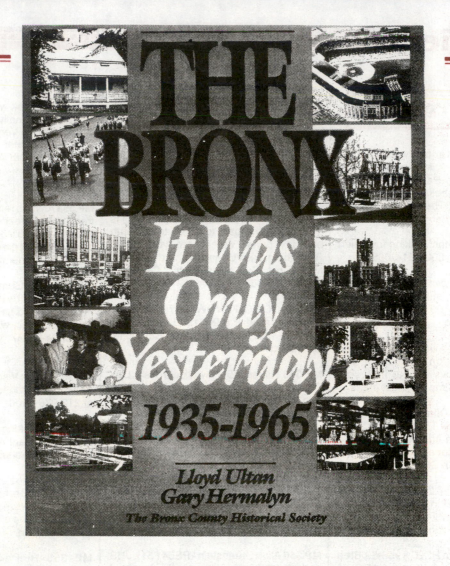

The period from the middle of the 1930's to the middle of the 1960's
was a dynamic one in the history of the country.
The depths of the Great Depression brought the New Deal
to combat the economic disaster, and this was followed quickly
by the ferment of the Second World War.
Peacetime brought great changes in our society,
including the movement from the cities to the suburbs
and a vast influx of different ethnic groups into the cities.
No area was more affected by these changes than The Bronx.
Yet, in the midst of this upheaval, The Bronx was also marked
by islands of stability and by its continuity with the past.
Now, that story is told in

The Bronx It Was only Yesterday, 1935-1965.

ONLY

$25.⁰⁰

plus $3.95 for shipping and handling

Classifieds

Missing Persons

MP 328 Marvin Kantorowitz of 544 Claremont Parkway is looking for Lenny Douglas, family also Pauline Cehall and family, Carmella Matrella and family and Louis Breen (Louie), The Martini family of Tremont

MP 329 Herb Lowenthal looking for Helen Den-**Taft** '53 - Call 1-800-881-0665

MP 330 Let's get together - write to me: Sedgwick Projects Area; **Taft** 65-67, **Clinton** 65, JH82, PS109.Carla Lichtenstein and Larry Rosenberg

MP 331 Linda Dillon wants to say Hi to everyone from Marion Avenue. If you remember me, I'd love to hear from you, especially Joe Zinzi, my first best friend

MP 332 Bob Baram, **Clinton** '63 would like to hear from Harvey T, John King, Ron Halbreich of Creston and Morris Ave. We all hung out at Joe Robert's candy store at Creston Ave. & 184th St.

MP 333 Looking for the Longfellow Avenue crowd - 30s - 40s - Hangers on at Moishe Ginsberg's candy store - Longfellow & Jennings St. What happened to you all?

MP 334 Anyboy from PS26 1958-63 Brett Sadovrick, Martin Salinsky, Morton Rubenstein, Harvey Glick, Norman John, Neii - Anyone hit on the head during class by Rabbi Walder? Remember his hole in the wall Hebrew School? Where's Skippy's now? Sedgwick Ave. looks better now - Mark Garber

MP 335 '69 **Taft** Phyllis Shandler living in California for 22 years and still wondering what happened to Fred Schiller, Music & Art, CCNY Sheridan Ave. Anyone knowing the whereabouts, please get in touch

MP 336 I'm interested in hearing from any one from Plimpton Ave. from the 50's/60's

MP 337 Herb Marks and Barbara Rosensluth Marks are looking for former Highbridge people: Merriam Ave., 170th St., Ogden Ave., etc. Graduated from High School: 1948-1952. South Floridians especially

MP 338 Whatever happened to Marty Seanlon, Larry Fagan, Mel Klein etc. of the Scorpions from the Freeman St. on So. Boulevard around 1950-54 - How about Mel Elkin - Irwin Brown of Stebbins Ave. Call Larry Meshibosh 301-292-4818

MP 339 St. Simon Stock Parish 182nd & Valentine Ave. Slattery Park and Mama's from 40's to 54. Give me a ring 201-768-0640. Jack McTigue

MP 340 Butch Brody - **Taft** 56. Where are you guys Billy Palace, Jerry Gabbamonte, Enrie Gulko and Bob Stark!! How about a game of poker? Contact me 516-433-5234

MP 341 Howard Rosenkrantz (**Taft** '61) is trying to locate pals to come to his 50th birthday party. Where are you David Rosenberg, Larry Levine, Richard Mellman, Max Varon, Burt Messer, etc.? Call Judy (203) 255-4988

MP 342 DO YOU KNOW ME? I'm Harvey (Whitey) Yalkut, P.S.90 - 1949, **Taft** - 1953, N.Y.U. - 1957. P.O. Box 5451, San Jose, CA 95150

MP 343 Hayes '45, Ray Olceere is a Law Professor - St. Thomas Law 16400 NW 3rd Ave., and a visiting Professor at Fordham Law. Call 305-623-2371

MP 344 Roy Kanofsky PS26, 82, **Clinton** '58, CCNY, and Davidson and Tremont would love to find anybody! How about this 167 St. 4 ? Reply

MP 345 Heda and Ed Goldberg looking for - Arnie Sanchez, Stuart Hutt, Phil Rothchild all from Grand Ave.

MP 346 Allen Greenstein - PS64 ('51), JHS 117 ('53), **Evander** ('56) would be delighted to hear from any of his old friends. A previous ad in this space has already reaquainted me with one delightful lost friend

MP 347 JHS82, PS26 - It is very important for me to find Donna Mandel and Janet Mayer. 1950-58. Contact Paul Kandel, please. 914-232-7121

MP 348 Harvey Felix, P.S.114, P.S.90, **Taft** Jan., '53 Lived at 1265 Walton Avenue, then in projects at University Avenue and Featherbed Lane; currently retired in Las Vegas, Nevada. Would enjoy hearing from old friends and classmates

MP 349 PS94. Anyone interested in helping to plan a reunion of 1955-1960, PS94 graduates please contact Alan Gordon (sister Karen Gordon Marrinon) c/o Back-In-The Bronx or call 800-356-3754

MP 350 **Walton** '37. Here's an oldie but goodie. Remember my mom, Shirley Trolman?

MP 351 Mary Ellen (Cookie) Schaefer,. if you are out there please write and let me know where

MP 352 It took years but Ron Barnett **Clinton** '56 finally met Marvelin Garcia **Evander** (?) in Vero Beach Fl and married her 4 months later. Can't beat those Bronx girls. Remember us? Contact us at 407-778-3111

MP 353 Anyone remember Miriam Brandes from 167th Street? PS'53 - JHS22 (1949-1951) - **Taft** (51-53) (I should have been class of '54 but graduated early). I'd love to hear from former classmates

MP 354 Mike Gumpel, **Clinton** 64 looking to make contact with old friends from school, Fordham Road & Poe Park, 180th St., and Sedgwick Ave. - write or call 2674 E. Main St., Suite C-187, Ventura, CA 93003, Tel 805-389-1106

MP 355 Martin Visconti, Gic Mason, Martin Brownstein, time for a reunion, contact me at 212-979-6000

MP 356 Looking for old friend, Ralph Bornstein, Grant Avenue, Fort Dix buddy, contact Don Scheer

MP 357 Missing Persons - Melvin Weinberg, et.al. from Grand Ave. & 181 Street. Remember Seymour's candy store? Love to hear from the old crowd. Please contact Rich Rothstein

MP 358 Hi Pelham P'kway people! Remember Bronx House Milton's, Jessels, Hennies, Pelham and Globe Theatres? How about the "Love-in" in Bronx Park? Remember Miss Kaiser, the typing teacher (J.H.S. 135) - Remember the Park Restaurant? Let's hear from all the **Columbus** Grads! From Ronii Witkin-Schwartz - Columbus '67

MP 359 Anyone from Ol Mercy, Creston & 192nd, St. James Park, Poe Park, 193rd & Marion, etc., out there? Tom McConnell (TRHS '68) would like to hear from you! Where are Abby Jacobs, Mike Solomon, Joe Borelli?

MP 360 Jerry Isaccs (**Taft** '54) looking for Bobby Eisenstein, Harry Falber, Donald Mazur, Ronald Feldman, Arthur Cohen, Bob Sober, Roberta Bengis, Lois Keit, Ellie Wygod. College Ave. crowd, where are you? Please get in touch

MP 361 Bob Zimmerman, **Taft** '62. Where is everybody from Andrews, Montgomery & Popham Avenues, PS 109 & JHS 82? Contact me for a reunion. Remember two hand touch football, off the WLB, pitchin' in & Tony's Pool Room?

MP 362 Where are the '64 **Clinton**ites (expecially the scholarship class?) If you are out there, give me a holler

MP 363 Bronx Science - 1954. Living in L.A. Anyone else here? Rudy Pearl (213) 687- 0740

MP 364 Still searching for Betty Berger (**Taft** '62), Judy Steiner and Henry Mooney (both **Taft** '65). Also hoping for a P.S. 114 reunion. What d'ya think?

MP 365 "If you live in California and went to **Columbus** High School or lived in Pelham Parkway please send your name and address to Paul Katzeff 43876 Rd 409, Mendocino, California 95460. I have a list of 241 people and will be sending out a directory to everyone on the list."

MP 366 Judith Greif Miller, Webb Avenue/ 195th St, Walton 1961 married to Stephen B. Miller for 26 years, Bryant Avenue/160th St., James Monroe 1954. Happily residing at 3920 Harlequin Terace, Fremont, CA for 7 years. Would like to meet and reminisce with Bay Area Bronxites

MP 367 Miriam Benitez, **Roosevelt** '69, seeking people of all ages who enjoy singing to join the Parckchester Chorus - the oldest chorus in the Bronx - going into its 53rd year. Contact me if interested

MP 368 Taft '57 looking for old friends and classmates, and information about class reunions. Please write to: David Goodmacher, 12-4 Apple Ridge Road, Maynard, MA 01754. Also seeking information as to the whereabouts of Frank Cavalluzzi, P.S. 44 and 92, **Stuyersant** '57. Reply to address above

MP 369 John Hurley, living in Florida, love to find Ann Marie Koller. Lived on Briggs Ave. and 194th St. 1960's - 70's. Had a older sister Diane. Worked at GVMT Printing Office, Manhattan

MP 370 Johnny Fasio, looking for Alan A. Nathans teacher at **Christopher Columbus** H.S. 57 also Morris Park Ave. P.S. 83 1954. Would like to hear from you

MP 371 Where are the people who grew up on Andrews Ave near 175th & 176th St. in the early 50's? Robert Bell, Alan Abrams, Ronald Sockoloff, Joyce Sydner, Susan Schuman, and many others from the same neighborhood

MP 372 Phyllis Sonenschein Greene, **Evander** '57 - looking for any old friends and grads from Gun Hill Rd., Allerton Ave., Eastchester Rd., Hillside Homes. Where are you all? Goloen Guiners (phone 914 359-6041) Barettas & Eastchester Girls too

MP 373 Artie Buckingham, last known whereabouts Yipsilanti, Michigan and working for Kent Cigarettes, please contact Len Rinaldi &/or Harry Melnichuk

MP 374 Where is Lucille Levinson, who I last saw at my "leaving party" in June 1959. She went to **Monroe** High. I went to **Columbus**. We shared many happy years and memories. Anne Kass Newman

MP 375 Columbus '63 Ken Goldstein looking for people in the Chicago area - former P.S. 105 regulars, etc.

MP 376 Ginger Dorlini Foster is trying to find Rosemarie (Terry) Bruno Gortych. Originally from Decatur Ave., last know address orangeburg. Graduated **Music & Art** 62, attended **Pratt or FIT**. Any info appreciated

MP 377 Where are the Nyads? From **Christopher Columbus**: Iris, Diana, Eugenia, Slema, Sheila, Roberta and Marilyn. Get in touch with Fran at 412-367-1369

MP 378 Joel Katz, **Columbus** '53 would like to find Jerry Gersch of Union Port Rd., **Evander Child** '54 and Morty Rosenberg, **Columbus** '53. Let's try to get together and remember the good old days

MP 379 If there is anybody reading this from Pelham Parkway who was born in the 1930s or 1940s who does not know the periodic Pelham Parkway Reunions, contact Howard "Bubbles" Cohen, 303 Eighth St. E. Northport NY 11731 - 516-266-2342

MP 380 Bernard "Bo" Criscuolo, **Monroe** '48 seeking old friends from Longfellow, Home st. and Weeks Ave., i.e. Herbie Dauber, Robert Techo, Tony Cuna, Jessie Smith, Andy Soann, Wanda ReRubies, Joyce Marin, Leonard Rothenberg et. al.

MP 381 I'd like to contact Isabel Baruch (maiden name) who lived on Cromwell Ave. Former playmate & school chum Leatrice Joy (Mayer) Richardson

MP 382 Herb Hitzig living in S.W. Florida looking for friends from **Clinton** 1957 - East Gunhill Rd., P.S. 80, J.H.S. 80. Eddie Berger, Howard Berger, Allan Salat, Bruce Klein, Stuart Korn. Phone 813-697-5966

MP 383 Sherman Avenue - Mel Turner would like to hear from all guys/gals from **Taft** school yard and Levine's candy store. Ronnie Cohen, Bobby Miller, etc., Where are you?

MP 384 I would like to locate: Irma Gottlieb Kopstein, Natalie Shapiro '61, and Selma Weingarten, Ca 1943

MP 385 "Most Wanted" Anyone who remembers us, and wants to reminisce about the "Good Old Days" - avid ice cream fans who loved Addie Vallins and Jahn's now own a Bresler's in Maryland. Sybil (Goldmano Moskowitz - **Taft** and Jerry Moskowitz - **Science**)

MP 386 Looking for June 1957 graduates from Thorpe Secretarial School. I'd specially like to hear from Margaret (Albrecht) Buone, Catherine Raymond and Catherine Burke. Please call Marily Zampino Taibi

MP 387 Simone Gold Brandt looking to find Sheila Klein, Carolynn Hanft, Lorriane Huft

MP 388 Craig Rose from Shakespeare Ave. looking for William Birken or any other 40-something from west of Jerome around 167th St.

MP 389 Columbus, P.S. 105, Bronx Park East are in mid 60's please write to Marilyn Goodman in North Miami Beach, Florida. Let's get reaquainted. Lillian Prince, Harriet Rosenblatt, Florence Shore, June Brown and whomesoever

MP 390 Looking for connections with or information about Abe Schechterson (brothers Jack & Ben), Sheldon Farber (Sister Zelda and her husband Bernard Ginter), Harold Siegel (sisters Arelene & June), Herbie Hertzel (brother "Bucky"), Irene Rindner (brother Jerome) or anyone from 2100-2110 Bronx Park East and vicinity. Norman Erlichman, RD1 Box 57B, Walton, NY 13856 - 607-865-7908

MP 391 UAWMF! I'm back in circulation. **Clinton** '69. Barry, 518-456-7288

Classifieds

MP 392 Michael Zwick - P.S. 86, Creston **Clinton** - 61 (Age 48) misses old friends - Call me - 212-496-9572. Lived at 95 W. 195th Street, 3215 Arlington Ave., - Riverdale

MP 393 Where are you Pearl Mendelsohn? Shakespeare Ave., wasn't the same after your mother's early death and your move away. Would love to hear from you. Rose Lavissiere Greenfield

MP 394 Richard Chaleff - **Columbus** '60 - looking for Mariano Diaz, **Columbus** '60 from Fenton Avenue and Guy Zummo, **Columbus** '60 from Rhinelander Avenue. Remember our parties at Rosemary's house on Muliner Avenue?

MP 395 Where are the "Sirens" - JHS 80, class of '52 - Helen, Rohda, Nedra, Lenore, Audrey, Rozzy, Doris, Sandy - Loretta Hitzig Weinzimer would like to have a reunion

WP 396 Elaine Holtz Wagman, P.S. 92, (1950-1956) - looking for Marilyn Ringel (bridesmaid at my wedding on June 19, 1965); also looking for Gail Horowitz and Dorothy Schwartz. Would love to see you! Please contact me!

MP 397 Would like to hear from anyone from Mosholu Parkway, Rochambeau Ave., PS 80, **Dewitt Clinton**, Daves candy store, (corner of 206 St. & Bainbridge Ave.) 1940's-1950's-1060's

MP 398 Mariyln Goodman looking for classmates **Columbus** '43 & '44, P.S. 105ers and Bronx Park Easters. Lillian (Prince) Loomas, Harriet Rosenblatt, Florence (Shore) Nadell where are you? I'm now in North Miami Beach. Love to hear or talk to you old timers!

MP 399 Pat Hayward **Walton** '55 Grad would like to hear from you also anyone from LaFontaine Ave. across from Crotona Park. John Angelilleo haven't called me in years - Carol Gevaerts, Storey Chatsworth, CA 818-341-2151

MP 400 Looking for anyone from the 50's hanging around 183rd and Washington Ave. Attended Our Saviors Church dances. Played stickball on Washington and 184th, hung around Barney's candy store on 183rd and shopped at Joe Baker's or Irving's - contact Danny Cirilli

MP 401 Norma Weber is alive on L.I. **Evander** '53, P.S. 80. Searching for old friends - especially Sandy Goldberg, Lois Heit. (Do you remember the "Jades")? If you lived on/near 45 E. Mosholu Parkway (Sonny Bratter where are you?) Let's reminisce

MP 402 Mr. Joseph Bell, former science teacher at JHS 123X and **Columbus** H.S.: retired principal of Olinville (JHS 113X) welcome hearing from former students - P.O. Box 574, Teaneck, N.J. 07666

MP 403 I remember many old friends fondly: Raymond Feldman, Marlene Brody, Martha Bienstock, Suzanne Rubin, Missi Cooper, Ronnie Gordon...Contact Barry Kramer, **Taft** '61, 170th St. & Grand Concourse, 770 Bryant Ave.

MP 404 *Rosalyn (Steinberg) Pulfer - **Monroe** 1961, Marvneo 30 years - Norman - SR. PROXY Specialist - U.S. Trust Co. Rosalyn - former medical secretary (Monrovian's please answer)

MP 405 Matty & Bobby Wellington (Drexler) **Taft & Columbus** Pelham Pky. Alive & well, living in Westchester, Arch & Red where are you? Any Spartans out there?

MP 406 Arlene Goldberg, JHS 80 '63, **Evander** '66, from Mosholu Parkway, would love to hear from old friends & classmates. Please write, I will answer. I have been living in South Florida since 1976

MP 407 I'm Jerry Freedman. My father owned "Sams Appetizing" on Gunhill Road. P.S. 94 ('52) **Clinton** ('58). Taught at JHS 82 in '62 & Flushing HS 1963-78. Would love to hear from people i knew back then

MP 408 Barry Eisenberg, **Taft** '65, SCCC '67, Southern, Ill., Univ. '67, living in Yonkers. Would like to hear from classmates, old friends from Sedgwick Projects and little league and old Nelson Avenue crowd. Also remember PS 104 & JHS 82?

MP 409 Allen Nemeth - Brenda Hirsch Nemeth - **Columbus** 55. Just Phones, Ontario, Ca. 714-984-4473. LaCellular, Pactel Service for So. Ca. Inland Empire

MP 410 Where are the guys from the Club Pendulum/Klapper '67? What ever became of the girls from 181st and Daly Ave. - Leslie, Goldie, Margarie, Linda and Judy? Contact Richard "Zang" Gerstenzang - 424 Raven Way, Naples, FL 33942

MP 411 Frank Cavalluzo, where are you? Jerry Gross would like to hear from you

MP 412 Looking for residents of 1741 Clay Avenue between 1941 and 1955. Please write Judy Jellinger Speiller to plan a reunion. Judith Jellinger Speiler, 2811 Waterford Dr., Cinnaminson, NJ 08077

MP 413 THEODORE ROOSEVELT HIGH SCHOOL THE BRONX '58 GRADUATES - If you or someone you know graduated from **Roosevelt** High School in 1958 we want to talk to you! We are working on our "35 year reunion" and need your help in locating as many alumni as possible. Please contact the person closest to your location for further information

MP 414 We are planning another renunion for people who hung around University and Burnside Avenues 1958-1964. If interested contact Ellen Strickler Norrholm (married Leif) at 301-977-6613

MP 415 Murray Glick, **Roosevelt** 52, JH, PS92, PS42, lost contact with all, would like to renew old friedships & create new ones. Class reunion. **Clinton** & 180, Mohegan, Belmont & Treamont, Hughes & 179, Beltree Club

MP416 Public School #6 The Bronx, East Treamont Avenue. Reunion planned for May/Oct. 1994. Did you or anyone you know graduate at the R.K.O Chester in June 1949? Seeking P.S. 6 graduates from the years 1947, 1948, 1949! Contact Laura C. Hogopa Wunderman

MP417 Interested in hearing from **Clinton** Newsers 1946-1949 era as well as other Clintonites who might recall Mitch Badler, **Clinton** '48

MP418 Joel Bengait, **Taft** 1962 would like to hear from old friends. Write: Joel Bengait 3170 Onyx Street, Eugene, OR 97405

MP419 Wolfson, Herb & Pat (Goodman) Macombs Jr. H.S., PS 82 Class of 1951, 1952. **Clinton** 1954, **Taft** 195. also shield of David Home looking for any residents of home. Would love to hear from anyone from the past.

MP420 Andrews Avenue, between Burnside and Tremont. nybody who sat Skippy's, later Dave's, candy store in the mid-50's or played handball in courtyard. Lenny, Samuels, Sussman, G.Burnes... contact Marty Jackson.

Come Blow Your Horn

CB • Bernard H. Mendix is Chairman of the Mendix Company and has been an owner and developer of office, commercial and residential properties since 1957.

READER REPLIES

It is vitally important that you fill out the information below. Your input will be essential to the success of this magazine, tailored and inspired by you, the former "Bronxite". We thank you for your participation.

Subscriber? ☐ Yes ☐ No

YOUR NAME _____

ADDRESS _____

CITY _____ STATE _____ ZIP _____ PHONE _____

HIGH SCHOOL ATTENDED _____ YEAR GRADUATED _____

TELL US A LITTLE ABOUT YOURSELF,
(Be sure to include your alma mater, old neighborhood, your best memories about your days in the Bronx, (or anything else you can tell us).

_____

_____

_____

- -

COULD WE SEND A FRIEND A FREE COPY OF BACK IN THE BRONX?

Do you know current or former Bronxites who would like to receive our magazine and reunion information? If you do, we'll be happy to send them a **free** inaugural issue of **Back in THE BRONX**. **Write to Back in The Bronx, Box 141 H, Scarsdale, NY 10583 or call 1-800-7-BRONX 5**

Last	First	Maiden
Address	City	State	Zip
Phone # ( )	School and year of Graduation

Last	First	Maiden
Address	City	State	Zip
Phone # ( )	School and year of Graduation

Last	First	Maiden
Address	City	State	Zip
Phone # ( )	School and year of Graduation

Last	First	Maiden
Address	City	State	Zip
Phone # ( )	School and year of Graduation

COME BLOW YOUR OWN HORN DEPARTMENT

Please tell us about yourself (include your name)—about your accomplishments, awards, titles or works in progress. We're interested in hearing about them. List Below. _____

_____

_____

_____

_____

READER REPLIES

As a subscriber you are entitled to a **FREE 40 Word Classified, Missing Persons, Blow Your Own Horn, or Personal Ad.** Please write your ad below (if you are not subscribing to our magazine you can still place an ad in the next issue. The cost of an advertisement is 50¢ a word, there is no limit on paid ads).

_____

_____

_____

Is Your Mailing Label Correct?

In order to keep our database current, please correct any errors and place the label and or photocopy with corrections.

Account #	High School	Year Graduated
6817	Roosevelt	1958

SAMPLE

Mary R. Flowers
123 Anystreet Blvd.
Anywhere, USA 12345

Change of Address?

If you're planning a move please attach your label corrected with your new address and the date that you will begin receiving mail at that address. This will insure that you don't miss your next issue of **Back in THE BRONX**.

Ordering Information

A Great Gift Idea! In addition to your own subscription, a subscription to **Back in THE BRONX** makes a great and unique gift. Fill in the form below and we'll process the order in time for our next issue. So, order your subscription NOW, and order one for a friend!

YES, I'd like to order the following items:

QTY.

____ 1Yr. (4 ISSUES) Subscription(s) to Back in THE BRONX $19.95
____ 2Yr. (8 ISSUES) Subscription(s) to Back in THE BRONX* .. $29.95
____ 3Yr. (12 ISSUES) Subscription(s) to Back in THE BRONX* } *FREE John's Menu .. $39.95
____ 4Yr. (16 ISSUES) Subscription(s) to Back in THE BRONX* .. $49.95

____ The Beautiful Bronx............$25.00 (plus $3.95 S/H) $28.95
____ The Bronx: It Was Only Yesterday..$25.00 (plus $3.95 S/H) $28.95
____ Bronx High School Reunion Weekend Video $29.95
____ SAVE MONEY - BUY 4 FOR JUST $99.00!
____ THE BRONX Tracking Service $9.95
____ I would like to receive all available back issues and have them applied towards my subscription (To date we have at least 12 back issues available - While They Last!)

TOTAL: $ _____

Please fill out completely and include $3.95 for shipping and handling for books only to: **Back in THE BRONX**, Box 141H, Scarsdale, NY 10583

Please Print Clearly   ☐ New Subscriber   ☐ Renewal

Name _____

Maiden Name _____

Address _____

City _____

State _____ Zip _____

Phone (_____) _____

High School _____ Year Grad. ____

☐ Visa ☐ Mastercard ☐ Check ☐ Money Order

No. _____ Expiration Date _____

Signature _____

Back in THE BRONX

Box 141 H, Scarsdale, NY 10583
Phone 914-592-1647 • Fax 914-592-4893

ADDRESS CORRECTION REQUESTED

Volume II Issue VII

Back in THE BRONX

CELEBRATING THE EXPERIENCE OF GROWING UP AND LIVING IN THE BRONX

ORCHARD BEACH OUR DAY IN THE SUN

by Arlene (Schneider) Radansky

Orchard Beach circa 1950

Photo Credit: Van Cortland, Pelham Bay Park Dept. of Parks and Rec.

It was 7:00 A.M. on a weekday morning in July and I was asleep. Suddenly I was awakened by my mother saying in a singsong lilt, "Rise and shine - it's a beautiful day. Let's go to the beach." To a ten year old, the sound was wonderful.

Mom, being mom, had been up for hours. Dad had already left for work. The hard boiled eggs were already made, the towels, a pillow case and the blanket were rolled up, the fruit washed and put in a "poultry" bag, and our bathing suits were staring at us, waiting to be put on under our clothes. Mom's idea of going to Orchard Beach was "get there at the break of dawn and go home before the noon day sun."

It really was a beautiful day. My brother and I got dressed quickly and, carrying the blanket roll, along with the bag of sandwiches, hard boiled eggs and fruit, we headed off on our excursion. Since we lived on the corner of Nelson Avenue and 172nd Street (across the street from P.S. 104), we first walked several blocks to University Avenue to take the bus to Fordham Road. At that time, the bus ride cost five cents, and you were able to get a free transfer. At Fordham Road we would wait in line for another bus (and what a line - adults, kids, beach chairs, "portable" radios that weighed a ton), everyone with the same destination in mind - a day at Orchard Beach.

Even before the bus parked at the beach, we could smell the marvelous salt air. To this day I can still close my

Continued on page 4

SATURDAY

by Bert Neufeld

Like EST and Silvermind and Primal Scream, we had our weekend intensives. It started at 10AM every Saturday and didn't let out until about four in the afternoon. We, too, screamed and cried, got angry and frightened, stood up and yelled. It was so intense that one hardly ever came home without a headache. You did not have to sign up or register, you just showed up. The cost was not $500 but one thin dime.

It was called the movies.

Today, if you've got five dollars, you can see one movie. If you want a double feature you go downtown and pay less. But when we went to the movies it was like a seven-course meal. There was a double feature, a cowboy picture, two or three cartoons and selected shorts, a newsreel, the races that gave away prizes and the highlight of all—the one single attraction that drew us there week after week called the Chapter. People today, refer to them as cliffhangers. Someone got

Continued on page 6

From the Editors...

As promised, this issue has been printed much sooner allowing us to once again get back on regular schedule. Thank you for your patience.

Our book that will capture the special feel of the Bronx in the 40's, 50's, and 60's is moving closer and closer to completion but we need the help of current and former Bronxites to make it a success. Specifically, we'd like your memories, stories, anecdotes, legends and personal histories to flesh out the structure of our book.

We invite, therefore, the readership of *Back In the Bronx* to contribute in whatever way seems comfortable. Some of you may want to write out your memories, others may want to volunteer for interviews. We are especially interested in pictures, home movies, memorabilia and paper records of your time in the Bronx. It may be that we will organize some discussion groups of interested people who can get together for a few hours to reminisce about their Bronx days.

So, whatever neighborhood you came from, whatever your experience in school or sports, whatever your ethnic background, we invite you to contact us. With your unique aid, this book may be the one you've been waiting for.

Finally, do you have friends, neighbors, or relatives who might be interested in a free inaugural issue of *Back in the Bronx?* Please give us their names and addresses and we will be happy to send it to them...If they wish they may call our toll free number: **1-800-7BRONX-5.**

Back in the BRONX

A number of the photographs in **Back in the Bronx** are courtesy of and are available from the Bronx Historical Society.

Publishers and Editors:
Stephen M. Samtur   CLINTON '61
Susan H. Samtur   TAFT '62

Contributing Editors:
Barbara Fasciani
Martin Jackson   SCIENCE '58

Art & Production: Ellen Grodjesk
Printed By: Bronx Age Press

Reminiscing

SABATELLI'S CANDY STORE

By Rita Sabatelli Perota

Is there anyone out there who remembers Sabatelli's Candy Store located at 396 East 154 Street near Melrose Avenue?

It was during the years 1940 to 1946 that my parents known to the neighborhood kids as "Mr. Sabatelli and Mrs. Sabatelli", ran a Mom and Pops candy store. It was also during the war years. I often express that this particular time of my life was the worst and yet the best of times.

My father would open the store at 6:00 A.M. and my mother would take over at 10:00 A.M. until 10:00 P.M. My father would take a nap and go to work at two thirty in the afternoon. They did this to save because after the war was over they would buy a house. Unfortunately, their dreams never materialized. My mother passed away in 1947.

The candy store was the hub of the neighborhood. It was here that the boys and girls would congregate every day. It was here that post cards from neighborhood boys that were in the service would be posted so that everyone could see. It was here that the newspaper drive started. Also the metal drive—we would collect metal and rubber for the war use. It was also in front of the store that we celebrated the end of World War II and had the block party. My mother and father donated the soda and the kids went door to door to collect money for a block party.

During this time many people did not have their own telephones. It was my job to ring their door bells and yell "telephone". They would run to the store to receive their call. Many times it was their sons calling long distance from army bases.

Across the street was the Bricklayers Union house. It was made out of wood and looked as if a strong wind blew, it would cave in. We always said that if each bricklayer would place one brick, it would look better. These same bricklayers would have a union meeting and come to the store for cigarettes, cigars, playing cards, etc. They would smell the food my parents were cooking in the backroom and ask if my mother and father would open the empty store next door and make food for them.

I always say that every child should be raised in a candy store - not for the ice cream, candy, soda (although when I look back it wasn't a bad idea), but for learning how to talk to people, how to work hard for something you believe in, and how to keep a beautiful memory alive.

I dedicate this story to the gang at Sabatelli's candy store - Virginia, Florence, Sis, Al, the Marinaccio brothers, Pat in our age group, and Grace, Zina, Yolanda, Ann, Joan, Whitey, Johnny of the age group above us.

Bronx Honor Roll
Bronxites Who Have Achieved!

BRONX SCIENCE
Stokely Carmichael
Bobby Darin
Edggar Doctorow
William Saffire

CARDINAL HAYES
George Carlin
Rocky Colavito
Kevin Loughery
Regis Philbin

CHRISTOPHER COLUMBUS
Robert Abrams
Anne Bancroft
George Jorgenson

DEWITT CLINTON
Don Adams
Nate Archibald
Richard Avedon
James Baldwin
Martin Balsam
David Begelman
James Cann
Paddy Cheyefsky
George Cukor
Avery Fisher
Arthur Gelb
Judd Hirsch
Stubby Kaye
Theodore Kheel
Robert Klein
William Kunstler
Burt Lancaster
Jan Murray
Charles Rangel
Richard Rogers
A.M. Rosenthal
Daniel Schorri
Dolph Schayes
Neil Simon
Larry Storch
Jimmie Walker
Fats Waller
William Zeckendorf

EVANDER CHILDS
Red Buttons
James Coco
Carl Reiner

MONROE
Jules Feiffer
John Garfield
Alan Lansburg
Hank Greenberg
Ed Kranepool

MORRIS
Angel Cordero
Gabe Pressman

ROOSEVELT
June Allison

TAFT
Sanford Brown
Eydie Gorme
Stanley Kubrick

OTHER NOTABLE FOLKS WITH TIES TO THE BRONX
Joey Adams
Danny Aiello
Alan Alda
Robert Alda
Mel Allen
Corazon Aquino
Herman Badillo
Lauren Bacall
Anne Bancroft
Ellen Barkin
Mario Biaggi
Joey Bishop
Teresa Brewer
Ralph Bunche
George Burns
Cab Calloway
Diahann Carroll
Samuel Clemens
Cardinal Cooke
Leon Cooper (Nobel Prize Winner)
Avery Corman
Norman Cousins
Don Criqui
Tony Curtis
Vic Damone
Dennis Day
Dion DiMucci
John Foster Dulles
Geraldine Ferraro
F. Scott Fitzgerald
Joe Franklin
Arlene Francis
Connie Francis
Edward J. Flynn
Rudolph Giuliani
Samuel Gompers
Armand Hammer
George Jessel
Robert Kennedy
Ted Kennedy
Theodore Kheel
Calvin Klein

Edward Koch
Fiorello LaGuardici
Jake LaMotta
Louise Lasser
Ralph Lauren
Ron Leibman
Lee Leonard
Hal Linden
Nita Lowey, Representative
Vince Lombardi
Gary Marshall
Penny Marshall
Glen Miller
Sal Mineo
Gary Morton
Bess Myerson
Gil Noble
Carroll O'Connor
Charles Osgood
Al Pacino
Floyd Patterson
Joseph Papp
Joe Pesci
Roberta Peters
Edgar Alan Poe
E. Colin Powell
Vincent Price
Charles Nelson Reilly
Rob Reiner
Geraldo Rivera
Billy Rose
Jonas Salk
Isabel Sanford
Connie Selleca
Carly Simon
Stanley Simon
Vince Skully
Curtis Sliwa
Wesley Snipes, Jr.
George Steinbrenner
Pat Summerall
Mother Teresa
Arturo Toscanini
Leon Trotsky
Lloyd Ultan
Jerry Vale
Eli Wallach
Vanessa Williams
Herman Woulk
Rosalyn Yallow (Nobel Prize Winner)

Thanks to Dr. William C. Wolfson and the Bronx Society of Science and Letters

Reminiscing

Orchard Beach

Continued from page 1

eyes and smell it, even though I haven't been to a beach in years.

We walked across the sand, which wasn't too hot yet (remember, we left the house very early) toward the water and placed our blanket just before the tide line. We always stayed by a rope, so that we could later find the blanket. Not that we went far into the water - going past the knees was something I did very seldom, and only with an older person with me. We didn't know how to swim, and I was always intimidated by the waves, so there was no problem of my disobeying the rules - I stayed in shallow water.

At that time, the bus ride cost five cents, and you were able to get a free transfer.

Around 11:00, we were all starved. We sat on our blanket, watching the friendly clouds, picking out shapes in them, and happily eating our lunch. This was a two-fold project; not only did we satisfy our appetites, but our bathing suits had a chance to dry. The towels also had a two-fold purpose.

Mom would take a towel and wrap it around one of us at a time, and inside our cocoons we would take off our bathing suits and put on an outfit to wear home. As the sun rose straight overhead, it was time for us to leave. Mom felt that the hot, direct sun was unsafe for our skin. She was right, although she was way ahead of her time.

We were now ready to go home. A rinsed out ice cream cup held some tiny fish that we caught with the pillow case (the fish never lived past the journey home) or some sea shells that we would keep forever (but lost interest in after getting home). Carrying towels wrapped in the blanket, and the "poultry bag" which now held our sandy bathing suits, we got on line for the bus. Actually there were two lines - one for sitting and one for standing. The sitting line was always much

Photo Credit: Van Cortland, Pelham Bay Park Dept. of Parks and Rec.

Waiting for the bus at Orchard Beach, 1945

longer, so we got on the standing line. As people got off the bus, we were able to get seats, so it wasn't bad. We later sat on the University Avenue bus, and this relaxed us enough for the walk in the summer heat to our house.

We never felt we missed anything by leaving the beach at mid-day. We had our fill of the marvelous ocean smell, the sand, the water, and the sky. We were content, rejuvenated, and happy to have had our day in the sun. ∎

DEPARTMENT OF PARKS REGULATIONS GOVERNING USE OF BATHING AREAS & BOARDWALK

NO
PEDDLING, ADVERTISING, LITTERING, DOGS OR FIRES.
ACROBATICS, BALL PLAYING, THROWING OF MISSILE OR SAND.
BICYCLING, ROLLER SKATING, VEHICLES OTHER THAN -
BABY CARRIAGES AND WHEEL CHAIRS FOR INVALIDS.
NEWSPAPERS OTHER THAN FOR READING.
SITTING ON RAILING OR STEPS.
BATHING RINGS, RAFTS, INFLATED OR BUOYANT DEVICES.
PERSONS ON BEACH FROM MIDNIGHT TO DAWN.
DRESSING OR UNDRESSING.
TENTS OR SHELTERS OTHER THAN BEACH UMBRELLAS.
CHAIRS OR PICNICKING ON BOARDWALK.
ARTICLES HUNG ON SIGNS, BENCHES, BASKETS, RAILINGS.
FENCES, ROPES OR UMBRELLAS.
BOATS LAUNCHED OR BEACHED.
FISHING EXCEPT IN DESIGNATED AREAS.
FLYING OF KITES, FLAGS OR PENNANTS
DIGGING OF HOLES, CREATING HAZARDS OR COMMITTING -
PUBLIC NUISANCES.
BATHING NEAR JETTIES (BATHE WITHIN LIFELINES)

A sight familiar to most Bronx residents of the 50's and 60's—the famous "Orchard Beach NO" sign.

Submitted by: Abraham Assa, which, oddly enough, he came across in a book French high school students learn English by!

ONE SATURDAY

Continued from page 1

smart and built them into a multi-billon dollar industry that is now known as the soap opera or serial.

Now I don't know if there are still places where a kid still has to collar an adult just before he reaches the box office and in his cutest, littlest kid's voice ask the adult if he could be the kid's parent and buy his ticket. He would then give the adult the money, which would allow the kid to enter and thus beat the sign that read, NO MINOR IS ALLOWED IN WITHOUT BEING ACCOMPANIED BY A PARENT OR GUARDIAN. Once in, however, the fleeting family tie would be severed with the adult and the kid parting company.

But at that time we had no problem since Saturday was devoted solely to the masses of screaming kids of all ages. And to keep those masses of screaming kids of all ages from the few brave or crazy adults who had hopes of enjoying themselves, the children were sectioned off and guarded by one big, beefy, powerful schtarker called the Matron. I believe these Matrons were in every moviehouse in the Bronx, from The Blenheim to The Earl, from The Rex to The Zenith, The Luxor to The Ward, were all built the same, yelled the same and ejected kids in the same way; with a firm grip about the ear. These Matrons, I do believe, eventually became the prototype for the SS manual.

You'd obey these ladies in the white coats quicker than your parents because punishment was instant. There was no, "You're grounded for a week." or, "wait until your father gets home." It was instant fresh air by way of the side exit. Just imagine the embarrassment of having to walk bent-over like a spastic in front of all your friends, hobbling with your left ear pulling this meaty, red nail-polished hand... terrible. So you behaved.

Now you would think that standing up and screaming, yipping and booing would be grounds for instant fresh air. But since kids scream, yip and boo

Screaming, yipping and booing became part of the sound track of the Saturday Theatre.

and since hundreds of kids screamed, yipped and booed all at the same time, how could the Matron eject the entire audience?

No, screaming, yipping and booing became part of the sound track of the Saturday theatre. The only real offence a kid could commit that would warrant the hot ear, the hunchback hobble and the iron doors was getting caught eating his lunch.

In those days there was no food sold, let alone a candy counter. So the only thing left for a kid to do was pack a couple of tunas or sardines and onions on pumpernickel or rye, two pieces of fruit, some

Photo Credit: Courtesy of the Bronx Historical Society

raisins along with those hard candies with the jelly inside, which everybody left on the floor. After all, if one goes to a seven-course movie, one must seven-course brown-bag it.

We learned what kind of women were the ideal; blonde, blue-eyed and gorgeous.

These hefty repasts soon created major problems. One, being the oil from the tuna and sardine sandwiches leaking through the bags onto the upholstered seats, which led to a second and greater problem... roaches. This was brought about by the weekly carpeting of half-eaten sandwiches, orange and banana peels, apple cores, tuna and sardine oil and lots of hard candies with the jelly inside.

The management, needless to say, had something to say about this. And since the roaches couldn't get up the price of admission, they had to go, together with the audience's lunch hour.

Now you would think that this edict would halt or, at least, curtail the weekend consumption of tuna fish and sardines. Yet there remained, still, a few diehards who, through ingenuity and the fear of pain from a growling stomach, sought devious countermeasures. The bigger knit hat to hide the smaller lunch. The casual coat-over-the-arm carry or the evenly distributed items-under-the-clothes carry.

But my way was as good as the rest and better than most because I used, what was then, the most natural bulge of the times. You see, long pants, in that day, was reserved either for the wealthy or the eighth graders. The standard mode of attire for the young boy was the economical, wear-like-iron and winter-warm corduroy knickers. Plenty of room for the lunch and it couldn't fall out. I never got caught nor missed a meal.

The pictures we saw were the originals. Not the re-runs or the Bogart, Marx Brothers, Fred Astair Festivals. And we didn't laugh at the corny dialogue. We believed it, every word. We didn't look for imperfections of factuality or credibility. We didn't look for visual effects because most of the stuff was in the story. An awful lot of messages about how a guy should act or a girl. They called them inspirational and we did learn a few corny things like honor and respect and manners.

To us kids it was the biggest thing in the world. It taught us our morals, our values, how to act and what to say. We learned what kind of women were the ideal; blonde, blue-eyed and gorgeous. Definitely not dark, heavy, ugly or even natural looking. And men had to be men. Big, strong, tough and, preferably, Irish. It sure gave a little Jewish guy like me a complex. I was doomed right from the start.

The movies gave us our dreams and goals. It soothed and squelched the drabness of life. It carried us away, calmed us down, screwed us up, turned us around and brought us out of. It was our little world where Mamma couldn't reach us, gangs couldn't pummel us, teachers couldn't embarrass us and sisters and brothers couldn't tease us.

It was the day of the week that was truly ours. ∎

Reminiscing

PARKCHESTER

By James B. Fay

I grew up in Parkchester in the 1950's. While the majority of Bronxites grew up in neighborhoods that had streets that ran East and West and avenues that ran North and South, Parkchester was different in that it had two main streets that criss-crossed each other and smaller private side streets that were basically parking areas for the residents. This, along with its park-like theme, made Parkchester appear to be, not only different, but somewhat unique.

However, it really wasn't. The people, the problems, and the memories didn't make Parkchesterites any different.

But one thing was different from other areas at that time. Parkchester had its own security force. Something most communities did not have, nor needed.

Not that Parkchester was crime ridden, but The Metropolitan Life Insurance Company that built and managed the development thought it was a good idea to have a group of men to look after the small things that would otherwise go unnoticed and that the NYC Police would not or could not get involved in.

One of those infractions that caused the "Parkchester Cops," as we called them, to take "immediate action" was the most violated "walking on the grass" infraction. Simply entering the chained-off grass areas to, lets say, retrieve a errant ball or toy airplane was, if observed by the always vigilant "cops," admonished with a wave of the hand and a "go play in the playground" order from the uniformed officer. The degree of the offense, however, increased if one was observed running on the grass to make a quick dash to the other side of the grass area. This

would sometimes result in the Parkchester cop "taking your name," which would be kept on record in the Parkchester Management Officer. Several of these "name taking" episodes (maybe three or four) would result in a formal letter being sent to

Metropolitan Oval, Parkchester 1942

your parents, who would be warned that activities such as entering the grass areas "by your son, James," will not be tolerated in the future! This would also happen for incidents such as hanging out in the halls of the buildings on a cold day.

Greater offenses would result in

Rumor had it that three of these "LETTERS" would result in an eviction process against the family.

---

greater responses by the officers. If you and a group of friends had a lapse of comprehension of right and wrong and decided to actually play a game on the grass, such as playing "soldier" or "tag" or, God forbid, an organized game

of football, this resulted in the rounding up of the usual suspects, even if it meant pursuing you during your flight from the area! If this was not accomplished, apprehension the next day or the day after that would suffice. This would also result in a "taking into custody," so to speak, where the security officer would take you to the Office" for name verification and notification immediately to your parents! Needless to say, the embarrassment of being led by a "Parkchester cop", paraded like felon, passed the people of the community and other nine- and ten-year-olds (some of who were as "guilty" as you were made out to be), would be deterrence enough from doing it again. But this one type of incident would result in the receipt of the greatly-feared "LETTER" signed by "Douglas Lowe, Resident Manager," who was the on-site administrator of the development and "chief" of the security force (sadly for them, the security their upper-level supervisors would tremble in his presence almost as much as the children did).

Rumor had it that three of these "LETTERS" would result in an eviction process against the family. I never knew anyone that left Parkchester because "he got too many letters," but looking back at the strictness of the place, I'm sure there were some. Once, my father got a "LETTER" reporting that on a certain date "...your son, James..." had his "name taken" for climbing a tree. My parents were taken aback by this accusation, which was perceived to be an indictment, until my mother remembered that I was at home sick on the day in question! Not wanting this unjustified "LETTER" in our file, my mother immediately put a coat on and reported to the office with a prescription bottle with the exact date on it! Obviously, someone used my

easily spelled name in order to avoid getting himself into trouble, This will be taken into consideration, Mrs. Fay, she was told, and a subsequent letter was received negating the first. We all breathed a sigh of relief. No one wanted too many letters!

Like many things during the 50's, ceremony was an accepted part of life. Even to the Parkchester Security Force. One ceremony that took place daily (except when it rained or snowed)

One ceremony that took place daily was the lowering of the flag.

was the lowering of the American Flag that waved from the flag poles that were located in each of the four "quadrants." The flag poles were located centrally within each quadrant, and mounted on a concrete pedestal. This pedestal also proved to be a convenient sitting place, but this, too, was a "wave and admonish" offense when the colors were being displayed. At a certain evening hour everyday the flag was up, two Security Officers would exit their locker room and approach the front of the flag pole. Standing at attention next to each other, both would look upward towards the flag and give a sharp salute. People walking towards the flag pole, usually heading home with their heads filled with their own thoughts of the day, would stop in their-tracks to watch this very simple but very respectful ceremony. Both officers would then approach the pedestal as if it were a priest approaching the altar. The flag was lowered and folded and the officers returned to their room with the flag for storage for the night.

Parkchester was not different from the rest of the Bronx, it only looked different. Admonishment for doing wrong and appropriate punishment; open signs of respect to those people and things we respected. We look back at these beliefs now as if it was on some different planet.

Parkchester wasn't different— we, all of us, *became* different. ∎

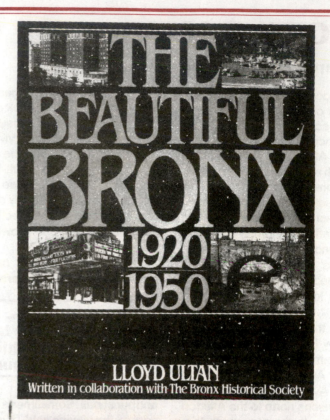

BRONX GAMES

By George Rosen

My boyhood coincides with the '30s. At the start of the decade, I was old enough to acquire a measure of the independence which comes with starting school. At the end of the decade, I was in high school and old enough to be considered an adolescent. This was the decade of the Depression. While I do not remember being aware of it, it did affect my family's attitude toward spending, and this percolated down to me. I have told my children that they had deprived childhoods - they never knew what it was to be poor.

I spent those years in an area bounded by Bronx Park East on the west, Pelham Parkway on the north, Matthews Ave. on the east, and Bronxdale Ave. on the south. There were excursions north to the Allerton Theater, west to the zoo, south to a library sub-branch on Unionport Rd., and I attended Paul Hoffman Jr. High near Fordham Univ. But most of the time was spent within those limits.

Several differences between those times and now stand out. Foremost was the lack

of organized activities. Organized, that is, by adults. Looking back on it, I am amazed at the lack of supervision which we were able to survive. Someone wrote a book with the Q/A title, "Where Did You Go? Out. What Did You Do? Nothing." Those answers would have been perfectly clear, perfectly honest, and perfectly understandable to anyone growing up in that time and place.

Depending upon the number of boys available, there were stickball

---

Looking back, I am amazed at the lack of supervision which we were able to survive.

---

and punchball. Sometimes a car would park on the playing field. "Hey, mister. Please don't park there. That's first base." The driver would almost always oblige.

Several games depended upon the separation lines in the cement of the sidewalks. There was boxball in the center of the sidewalk and slugball against a wall. There might be as many as eight boys lined up in a game of slugball.

One of the buildings included a playground with some grass plots. This was mainly used by girls and by parents with young children. The grass, of course, was gone and this provided the opportunity for a game of Land or Territory. Most boys carried pocket knives, usually "Boy Scout" knives. A rectangle was marked off into approximately equal areas, one for each player, with a knife. The object was to acquire your opponents' territories by cutting off pieces into which he could not fit his heel. This was done by throwing the knife into it point first. If it landed with-

out the handle touching the ground, a line drawn extending in both directions from the knifepoint in the direction of the width of the blade divided his territory into two parts. He kept one. The knife wielder got the other. If he could not fit his heel into either, he was out.

I remember once being challenged by two older boys, whom I beat handily. They consoled each other by saying that I won because I was closer to the ground.

Those were good weather activities. In winter, there was bellywhopping down snow-covered Brady Ave. next to P.S. 105. There always were guards posted at the cross streets to warn of oncoming cars.

Then there were the seasons. I don't mean spring, summer, fall, and winter. There was top season, Yo-Yo season, marble season and Hi-Li season. I recall seeing twenty or more boys lined up on Bronxdale Ave. next to the wall of the Bronxdale Pool, each one batting his Hi-Li paddle and ball and counting the number of consecutive hits, each one going for a record. I don't ever remember one boy's count being doubted by another.

"Hey, Mister. Please don't park there— That's first base!"

Then there was the rubber band gun season. To make a rubber band gun, take the end of a fruit crate and separate the square support frame. From this, cut an "L" shaped piece and tack a rubber band to the bottom of the long side near the end. From the corner, remove the outer plies in triangular shapes to leave exposed the inner, untouched ply. To cock the gun, pull the rubber band over the top of the long edge and anchor it on the remaining corner. Ammunition is cardboard cut into about two inch squares. Slip a piece of cardboard over one and under the other length of stretched rubber band near the anchor point. To fire, slip the rubber band off the anchor

point with your thumb. All that was needed to start a season was for one boy to make one.

One day, for reasons I will never know, I once bought a water pistol. Within the week, there were water gun wars around the neighborhood.

A feature of the neighborhood which probably no longer exists was the empty lot. This provided an arena for various activities. During the day, there were explorations, ball games if the lot was level enough, follow the leader, and other group diversions. At night, there could be a mickey roast, (mickeys are potatoes, the name, now that I think about it, probably being derived

from the slang for the Irish), a campfire with ghost stories, or whatever a young imagination could devise.

The strangest happening that took place on that empty lot was a rock

---

There was top season, Yo-Yo season, marble season, and Hi-Li season.

---

fight. This was not a fight between two gangs. It was an afternoon's activity in the lives of active, independent boys.

I would now guess that about twenty youngsters were engaged in the friendly activity of throwing rocks at

about twenty other youngsters. I do not recall anyone being hurt. I cannot now imagine how anyone in his right mind could initiate this piece of potential mayhem, But I do know that the whole affair was innocent of any malicious intent.

Looking at the advantages our children have - much adult oversight, full pockets, video games, television, single family homes where they have to be transported to their playmates, I wonder whether they really are better off now than we were then. I will leave it to a psychologist to analyze. Looking back, it was fun. ■

Scrapbook

YENTING - A WAY OF LIFE

By Susan Thaler

If, as some say, one's first memory determines one's way of viewing the world, then mine has to do with loss and redemption.

I am not yet two years old, I wake up from a nap in my carriage, which is parked against the wall of my building, 1818 Davidson Avenue. I reach out to touch the warm, rough brown bricks. Then, realizing that my mother is nowhere in sight, I begin to cry. Suddenly I hear a soothing voice: "Don't cry, darling. Your mommy went upstairs to get your bottle. She'll be right down." The voice belongs to Mrs. Dolberg, whom I will later come to know as one of the chief "yentas" in our building—one of a cadre of women who spend their days gossiping about everyone and everything. Mrs. Dolberg is sitting a few yards away, on an orange metal folding chair which she has pulled into a shady corner of the courtyard that separates the two sides of my building. She smiles at me. I stop crying. In another moment, my mother appears, milk bottle in hand. Once again, all is right with my world.

This incident typifies for me the essence of living in the Bronx in the forties, fifties and early sixties—community. No one ever was—could ever be—alone. My mother knew she could trust this elderly lady, a grandma (my own grandma lived far away, in Connecticut), to watch over me for the brief time it took to go upstairs, heat my bottle (our mothers warmed our milk until we were practically teenagers in those days) and return.

Our building housed sixty families, and every year brought a new crop of babies. Toddlers, preschoolers (pre-Kindergarteners, that is, who knew from nursery school or, heaven forbid, daycare back then?) and older·kids filled every inch of space in our courtyard and the sidewalk in front of our building, day after day, year after year. Most of the time, mothers were on

hand to care for their children, but on the rare occasion they were called away (a quick trip upstairs to the bathroom, around the corner to Finkelstein's grocery for a container of milk) there was always someone around to fill in. I am not talking baby-sitter here, no one was ever paid to keep an eye on someone's child—that would be an insult. Although the phrase hadn't yet been invented, we lived in what could reasonably be described as an extended family, and blood ties were irrelevent.

The older generation and the youngest shared an uneasy coexistance. The noise level was often too much for the older yentas.

The older generation and the youngest shared an uneasy coexistence. The noise level was often too much for the older yentas—especially in the spring, when roller skates came out and baseballs began to fly.

"Go skate somewhere else!" Mrs. Natoff would yell in heavily-accented English. "You're giving me a headache!"

If, God forbid, a baseball should find its way within their grasp, the hapless boy (it was always the boys) would never see it again. In spring and summer, Mrs. Becker, who lived in the

corner ground floor apartment, would actually sit by the window and wait for the balls to come sailing through her bedroom. When they inevitably did, that would be the end of that particular game. ("No, you're not getting it back! Dont'cha know you could hoit someone with the ball?!") I have often wondered how many balls Mrs. Becker eventually accumulated over the years—the number would have to be in the thousands.

Yenting, or gossiping, was integral to our lives back then. I don't remember exactly when I began to find the adult's conversations more intriguing than playing with kids my own age, but I do remember my mother urging me to "Go jump rope with Arlene" or being informed that "Rosalie wants you to play potsy." I was no dummy. I knew she and the other women were planning to discuss something extremely interesting, something not meant for a child's ears. I would go, reluctantly, but never too far, and I would always try to catch a few words here and there.

Whenever a certain Mrs. W., a very attractive woman who lived on the sixth floor, emerged from the building to go across the street to where a certain dentist had his office, the yentas would lean close and begin whispering. Phrases like 'She's going to have her cavity filled" and "I wonder if he's drilling her yet" were bandied about. Years later, I learned that this lady and the dentist across the street were indeed carrying on a torrid love affair, the dentist's wife left him for a while, came back, and the dentist moved away.

When gentle, timid Betty developed

cancer, the yentas shook their heads and blamed her husband, a tall, thin man with slicked-back hair, because

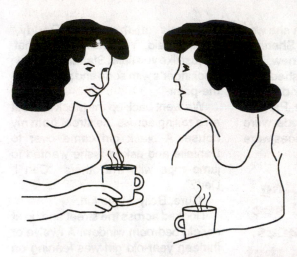

he had a "roving eye." The implication that his womanizing had somehow caused his wife to become fatally ill was unmistakeable. After she died, leaving three young children, Betty's mother, Mrs. Gorton, would come to our apartment and cry while my mother did everything possible to console her. I listened, from another room, to Mrs.

Early on I realized there is no such thing as "ordinary" when it came to people

Gorton describe how much Betty's children missed their mother, how they couldn't understand why she would not come home. It moved me in ways I could not articulate then, but the pain of Mrs. Gorton and her motherless grandchildren stayed with me for a long time to come.

There is no doubt in my mind that the stories I heard while I was growing up in the Bronx—stories about "ordinary" people leading uneventful lives—fueled my desire to become a writer. Early on I realized that there is no such thing as "ordinary" when it came to people, and even the most humdrum existence is often fraught with drama, pain and triumph.

My mother was largely responsible for this realizion. Over the years she gradually became a sort of "oracle" to the troubled who lived in our building. People were always knocking at our door, asking for advice or just seeking a chance to be heard. They knew they would find a sympathetic ear in my mother, that their secrets would go no further than the kitchen where they sat drinking coffee and "schmoozing." As I got older, I, too, became privy to these tete-a-tetes:

There was Lena, the frail, half-blind seventyish lady whose daughter-in-law hated her and made her life miserable; there was beautiful Helen, whose husband hadn't worked a day in over ten years, and who had to become the breadwinner for the family; there was the **other** Helen, married to the macho phys-ed teacher, who couldn't have children and didn't know what to do about it.

Sickness, death, rebirth, the entire life cycle seemed to be playing itself out in our tiny kitchen—a room so small one couldn't turn around without bumping into the refrigerator, the table, whatever.

Room size was unimportant, of course; only compassion mattered. Compassion, and the knowledge that they were never alone in their suffering, that there was always someone to listen, to care.

To this day I carry their stories with me; voices mix with visions of morning light shining on brick, chalked squares drawn on cement, balls arcing through air. Children's voices shout, older voices warn; broomsticks echo on pavement. "Don't cry, darling, your mommy will be right down..."

Community.
The Bronx, the way it used to be.

GOING HOME

By Bob Grand

After years of hearing my stories about growing up in the Bronx one of my kids, I think it was Anna, convinced me to take them up to see my old neighborhood. All five of them piled into the car with me and I drove there.

I parked in front of a fenced-in vacant lot that was littered with broken red bricks and trash. There had once been a building on that lot 201 Marcy Place. My friend Mimi used to live there.

The rest of the buildings on the block were still standing, but abandoned and desolate. Windows were broken, doorways boarded up or bricked over, staircases had collapsed. There was rubble and filth all over the street. A couple of drunks huddled in the doorway of my friend Josh's old building. A drug deal was going down in the middle of the street.

The kids started to get out of the car. I stopped them. "Let's go home," I said.

Old Timers' Day 1991

Danielle was ten. She'd never been to a ball park to see a game. I took her to Yankee Stadium. Before the regular league game began there was a two inning game for the stars of my era. Some of them played, some were just introduced. Dimag was there, and the Scooter, Phil Rizzuto. Ol' Reliable Tommy Henrich, and Charlie "King Kong" Keller and Yogi and Mickey and Whitey Ford. Mel Allen announced from the field. It was a great day for me. It was a terrific day for Danielle, too. The regular game was an extra inning slugfest that the Yanks won something like 13-11. She didn't know anything about baseball except what I taught her that day, but she went hoarse yelling "Go Yankees."

After the game I drove up to my old block, less than a mile away. Danielle didn't want to go. She still remembered how it had been when she was six. But when I turned onto Sheridan what we saw was fresh and new. The buildings had been refurbished and sandblasted. It was a sunny day and people were out in the street. Parents sat on beach chairs and kids were playing all around us. The faces were

> "Thought of going back, but all I'd see are strangers' faces, and all the scars that love erases. But as my mind walks through those places, I'm wonderin' what's come of them? Does some other young boy come home to my room? Does he dream what I did as I stood by my window and looked out on those Brooklyn Roads.
>
> From "Brooklyn Roads" Neil Diamond

black and Hispanic now, but the life force of the block was a lot like it had been when I lived there.

There was a bodega on the corner where Beckinger's grocery had been. We went in and got a couple of sodas. Some teenagers were playing off-the-point against the wall next to the bodega.

"That's off-the-point, Daddy," Danielle said. "You told me about that. It's just like you said. Standing outside Beckinger's with soda and playing off-the-point."

We went back up the block and sat on a railing across the street from my house. A black girl came over to Danielle and asked if she wanted to jump rope with the others. "Can I, Dad?"

"Sure, Belly. Have fun."

I looked across the street and up at my old bedroom window. A twelve or thirteen year-old girl was leaning on the sill looking out onto the street. I waved at her. She drew back from the window and went into my room.

A couple of people came over to talk to me. I told them that I'd lived on the street until about thirty years ago. They wanted to know what it was like back then. I wanted to know what it was like now. They were happy to be living in the neighborhood. The Bronx was coming back, they said, and this block was a great place to live.

Two hours passed quickly. I told Danielle it was time to go. We got into the car. The little girl who'd asked Danielle to play came over. "You gonna come up again, Danielle?"

"Sure. My father will bring me. Won't you, Daddy?"

"You bet, Belly." The girl smiled and waved, and walked away.

"I had a great time, Daddy. That was Mattie. She's ten. She goes to your old school, 88. She's in the fourth grade. Now I know why you loved growing up here. I could live here."

I was about to drive away when a black kid of four or five walked up to the curb between my car and the one in front of it. He unzipped his fly and began to urinate into the gutter.

I did that at his age. Probably on that very same spot. "How about that," I thought.

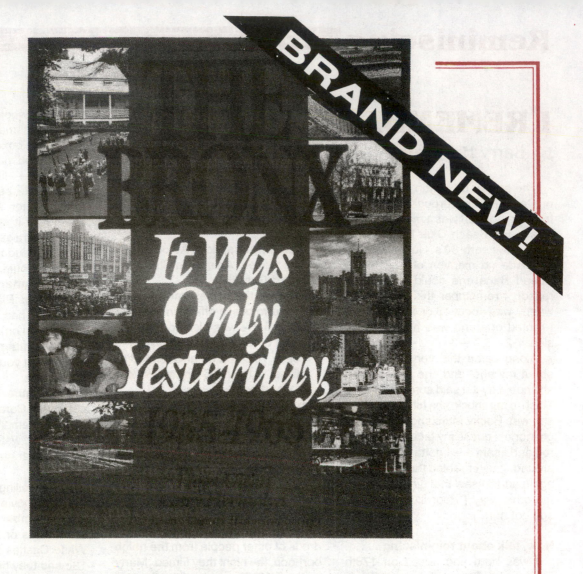

I REMEMBER...

By Barry H. Horney

The article, by Martin A. Jackson, on Castle Hill Pool brought back many fond memories. I was a member of the Castle Hill Beach Club for two seasons in the early 50's. However, Martin made no mention of the Boxing Speed Bags one could "rent." The reason I remember this is because when I was about 13 or 14 years old, I rented one and was hitting it very slow 1-2—3, 1—2—3, 1—2—3.

Along came this very pretty girl, about my age, and she asked me if she could try it. I said sure, go ahead. Much to my shock, she hit that bag like she was Rocky Marciano. When she got done, I guess my face was kind of red and I said a— I gotta go, see you around. I never rented the speed bag again and if I saw that girl, I would go the other way ("Poor little baby, his ego got hurt.")

Now, talk about reminiscing . . .

I was born and raised on 178th Street and Bryant Avenue. Some people called it the South Bronx, some people called it the East Bronx. I lived four blocks from the Bronx Zoo. I went to P.S. 6, J.H.S. 98 and James Monroe High School. I attended J.H.S. 98 with "Sonny" Pacino (You probably know him better by his first name Alfred or Al Pacino). He lived on Hoe Avenue. He was a grade ahead of me, but I played ball with him. He was a tough, funny, chunky little kid and a good ball player. He was in dramatics and appeared in several plays in school.

At James Monroe High School we had an annual "Red Letter Day." On this day, they would invite famous people, who had gone to James Monroe High School, back to the school to be inducted into the school's "Hall of Fame." Every year, two or three people came back and would be inducted into the Hall of Fame. They would give a little speech and tell us what it was like

when they attended school there. Some of the people I remember in the school's Hall of Fame are:

Robert Strauss, Movie Actor
He played "Animal" in Stalog 17.
Sanford Garalik
He was the highest ranking uniform police officer in the NYPD. He was elected President of the City Council in the early 70's and he also served as Chief of the NYC Transit Police Department.
Paul A. Fino, Congressman
Paul Scravine,
Sanitation Commissioner

I remember trolley cars having to switch tracks at West Farms Road. Some went up Tremont Avenue, some up Boston Road and some up 180th Street. I was present, along with hundreds of other people from the neighborhood, the night they filmed "Marty" by the RKO Chester and the Stardust Ballroom. I used to cross the Cross Bronx Expressway on my way to high school before it was opened to traffic.

I remember Starlight Park, the jelly apple man, the sweet potato man, the good humor man on a bike and Mr. Softy trucks. My favorite ice cream was a pistachio pop from the Bungalow Bar man whose truck looked like a little house.

I remember the organ grinder man (he didn't have a monkey) and the violin man who played in the courts and alleys and people would throw down money wrapped in paper or napkins. As children, we would pick it up and give it to them.

I remember the knife sharpener man, the umbrella man, the seltzer man and the man who came around and took your picture and developed it on the spot (this was before polaroids). We made scooters from orange box crates and roller skates. We made go-

carts from wood and wheels and axles from baby carriages. We planted things in "cheese boxes" or your father kept screws and nails in them. We had "seasons" — like water gun season, pea shooter season, sling shot season, scooter season, etc. Nobody knew how it started, but something would be in a season for a week or two and then suddenly end and a "new season" would start!

I remember Charlotte Ruses and Mello Rolls. Plastic bubbles and tattoos (you had to lick your arm and press them on).

I remember wax lips and moustaches that you could chew and 2 for 1¢ candies.

I remember playing cowboys with cap guns. Carnival and bazaars setting up on empty lots. Eating corn-on-the-cob or watermelon in the street after supper during the summer.

movie posters in store windows telling what was playing in the local movie theater.

I remember when there were no McDonalds or Burger Kings — only White Castles and hamburgers cost 12¢ and they had carhops!

I remember having a savings account in the "Dollar Savings Bank" and bringing money in a "bank envelope" to school every Wednesday to make deposits.

I remember my high school song "Beyond The Cities Noise and Clamor . . ." and my junior high school "98 Our Best and Brightest, Thoughts About Thee Cling..."

I remember water trucks cleaning the streets in the summertime. Buses were red/white. Police cars were white/green/black and cabs had little jump seats in the back.

I remember getting working papers and registering for the draft on Arthur Avenue. I even got my marriage license there.

I can remember much more and I love to reminiscence, but enough already, let's hear from someone else.

Missing Persons

MP 421 Linda Silverberg Cohen - P.S. 64-'65, JHS 82-'67, **Taft**-'70, looking for Martha Grodd, Sharon Greenberg, Barbara Silver, Elsie Ramos, Robin Reiff, Frances Singer or any former friends who would like to reminisce

MP 423 David Neumann now residing in Boca Raton, Florida and grew up in the shades of Yankee stadium wants to touch base with anyone who remembers the Hanks and Eagle jackets

MP 424 Taft '62 - Barbara Moskowitz Assa and "Abo" Assa living in Marblehead, MA would love to hear from other Bronxites in North Shore/Boston area, especially those from around Walton and 167th-170th St.

MP 425 To any **Clinton**ite looking for fellow **Clinton**ites living in Southern Calif., contact Herb Kriegstein. I am co-ordinator for De Witt **Clinton**, Southern Calif. Alumni, and have a membership listing of over 600 members. Reawaken friendships and old ties

MP 426 Barbara Owaroff Fischler (**Taft** '63) and Nick Fischler (**Clinton** '58) are interested in hearing from classmates or neighborhood friends. We are living in Florida, where are you? Care to swap stories about the good old days? Let us know!

MP 427 Living in So. Calif. Would love to bring back such good memories of the graduating class - summer 1950. Let's go down memory lane. My dear friend Ruthanne Dennison, in New Jersey also wants to hear

MP 428 Evander Childs H.S., class of '44, where are you? Kitty Graziano, Norma Macillo, Adam Reisz, Vinny Frisora, -contact Ronnie and Joe Witkin - 5187 Deerhurst Crescent Circce, Boca Raton, FL. 33486 407-392-6212

MP 429 PS 114, J.H. 22 (Jordan L. Mott) **Taft** 60. Lived at 1240 Walton Ave., (across from Morrisania Hosp.) Lenny Berner, Myron Oleans, Arnold Jaeger, Jeff Roth, Roy Block, etc. Contact Hy Weinstein 305-722-2344

MP 433 Looking for old friend from Eastchester Road area, PS 97, Olinville J.H.S. '50, De Witt **Clinton** '53, **Baruch** College '57, Bob Bolnchick

MP 434 Where is the gang tht hung out at Sabatelli's candy store at 396 East 154 Street? Would love to hear from you - Rita Sabatelli Perota

MP 435 In search for graduates from "**Herman Ritter** JHS 98" and **James Monroe** HS years 1947 - 1958. Where are you? We all remember Sonny (Al) Pacino - in "Handcuffs for Two" what an actor, what a show - Marvin and Janet Gross Ritter (407) 479-3886

MP 437 Where is that Dekalb Ave. crowd, Paul Abramsky, Charlie Christ, John Carlsen, Ron Zec, George Rolita, et Al.

MP 438 Where are the members of Lambda Alpha Sigma - **Taft, Evander, Columbus** '59 and '60? Sharon Bernstein seeking Marlene Shore Silver, and Phyllis Bilder, Rose Katz, Barbara Sorapo

MP 439 Lucille Tamor Adler '50 hopes to hear from Marilyn Aarenson Friedman and Phyllis Kopelman - It's been a long time!

MP 440 Taft H.S. - Louie Bernstein - where are you? Richie Steinberg's in Atlanta and cousin Phyllis Glass (Silverstein) is in Florida. Would like to hear from Grant Avenue friends too!! From 167th St. to 170th St. - Luxor and Kent Theaters - remember??

MP 441 Toby P. Nash of Grad. class '56 married Gerald Posner Grad. class '54 in 1959 - still married and we would both like to hear from old friends

MP 442 Susan Schlachter Thaler (**Taft** '56) would like to hear from Barbara Braunspiegel Weil, Carol Shefrin, Marilyn Mishkin. (Remember Mr. Stoopak and his Tom Lehrer records?) Where are you guys?!

MP 443 P.S. 76 and **Evander** '53, '54 Guys and Gals from the Mayfair and Mayflower, Arnow Ave., Barnes Ave., etc. Let me hear from you

MP 444 Where are the guys and girls of P.S. 47? Lois and Joel who lived at 1328 Commonwealth Ave., Also Linda and Pauline who lived up the block. Roberta who lived on street moved a few blocks away

MP 447 Bill Sperling, **Taft** '59 looking for Bob Pocsik, **Taft** '59, Sheldon Zalkin, '59

MP 448 Taft-1951 - looking for Renee Willensky - Davidson Ave., 170-1711-1726 - etc. P.S. 82-104 - **Taft**. Contact Roz Russman Gersten

MP 450 Anyone finishing or went to PS63 - '30. Finished Prospect Jr. High in '33, from there I went to **Central School** of B & A

MP 451 PS 94, JHS 80, '57, **Clinton** grad. Dekalb Ave., Gunn Hill Raod, Mosholu Parkway. Where are you? Now living in Texas, but lonely for the old days. Robert Miller 817-292-9565

MP 452 "Evelyn Krieger, June 1943 - **Taft** High School. P.S. 28 and HS 117. Would love to hear from old classmates and friends"

MP 455 Anyone looking for Marilyn Rogers (55) of Sheridan Ave., and 170th St.? I'm now living in Las Vegas. Please contact me.

MP 456 Arlene Dumas seeks Sydelle Trushin, Fran Barnett, Barbara Schleicher, Roberta Lefkowitz. Please call or write - 464 Duncan St., S.F., CA 94131, 415/647-0733

MP457 Marjorie McCullough Modlin, **Roosevelt** '52, JHS 118 '49, P.S. 59 '47, Bathgate Ave. & 181st St., Tremont Church- Is anyone else around with fond memories of growing up there?

MP458 Naomi (Nikki) Bererstein Mayo- P.S. 104, JHS83, **Taft** HS '53, Hunter College '56. Looking for the Duchesses. Also anyone from Andrews Ave Area. Remeber the Park Plaza Movie? The "Y" on University Ave and also the benches. If you remember please call, it will be alot of fun!

MP459 Jay Bloomberg & Wife Deena, **Taft** '53, after 30 years in North & South Carolina are alive and well in Vineland, New Jersey. As a result of last issue I have found great friend Stanley Weiner—40 years later.

MP460 Horowitz sisters (Sharon, Arlene, & Bonnie) **Columbus** H.S., Wallace Avenue- want to hear from our friends from Pelham Parkway. We're all in New Jersey.

MP461 Anybody from E.B.B. J.H.S.115— Phyllis Gold—Pat Bertsford—where is Stuart Bolkin—Steve Field—Authur Schwartz—Vic Hoffman—Helen Berkowitz. Contact Sandra "Joseph" Filla.

MP462 1965 on: Zimmermans Playground, Pel-Park Lanes, the Wall, 6 Brothers, Bronx Park, the Projects, **Columbus**, P.S. 96 yard. Is there anyone out there who remembers? Was it a figment of our imagination? Wendy S.

Classifieds

MP463 Jackie (Sperling) Reckseit lives in St. Thomas, U.S. Virgin Islands, with husband Ronnie. We own and operate ABC Auto Rentals. (ABC Jeeps were featured in "Week-end at Bernies II", filmed in St. Thomas). We're here Nov-May, (809) 776-1ABC. Most of June-Oct we live in Scarsdale, NY (914) 472-3590. Would love to here from old friends.

MP464 Larry Klein, **Monroe '59**. Retired stockbroker living in Florida for past 8 years- would like to hear from old fiends.

MP 465 Looking for persons from club Maxim's on Jerome Ave & Burnside Year 1957-1964, From Fred Waltmen & Larry Kline—**Clinton** 1953, also Monroe Grad 1959, Delroy Beach, FL.

Personals

MP 430 Taft '52 (P.S. 90) Divorced, teaching H.S. and living in Queens, non-smoker still hoping 718-353-4489

PR 432 Author, Writer of story for July 1993 issue of Back in the Bronx would like to meet a pretty, never married, kind, feminine, Orthodox Jewish female about mid-30's who may live in Manhattan, Queens or Brooklyn. Please call Steven M. Samtur, publisher 914-592-1647 who will contact Arthur

PR 445 Taft '54. Widowed attractive, looking for male to share a movie, cup of coffee and good conversation about yesterday, today and tomorrow

PR 454 Exhausted female entrepeneur, thin, petite blond, borderline recluse, **Taft** '59 grad, is looking for a single male to laugh, dance and be silly sometimes. Must be DRUG FREE. I live in Manhattan and am interested in the present. If you are a loner, slightly eccentric, reasonably sane, let's get together

Classified

MP422 Harriet Rosen Smith, Owner, Unlimited Care Inc., Home Health Services N.Y., N.J., Mass., and Calif. - 18 offices. Graduated **Taft** June 1954. We provide professional and non-professional nurses to homes, hospitals and all types of facilities - Corp Office - White Plains

MP431 Christopher Columbus High School class of 1969 will celebrate its 25 year reunion on May 14, 1994 at the Holiday Inn, Suffern, NY. For information or to update your address, please call 1-800-677-7800. (Christine Hackl)

MP449 Anyone interested in having a reunion of **PS 11** graduates - all years call Ken Katz (1941) at 516-678-5245 to see if we can get one started

Come Blow Your Horn

MP446 Lived in Dallas since 1969 - graduated **Columbia** College 1959, State University of New York Downstate Medical Center Cum Laude 1963. Eudacrine fellowship Mass General Hospital 1967-69

MP 453 Linda Comac, **Taft** '65, is co-author of Sharks Don't Get Cancer (Avery Publishing, 1992) and an outside agent is sister Tema Comac Goetzel's (**Hunter** H.S., '59) travel agency, Hi-Lo Travel, Morganville, NJ

Are you trying to find someone from your past or maybe, someone to start a future *with...*

If so, why not try an ad in our Classified Section.

Our **Missing Persons** can —
Connect you with long lost friends and relatives.

Our **Personal Ads** can —
Help you meet that special someone.

Our **Classifieds** are —
A great place to announce any current Get-togethers, Reunions or any other Special Events

&

Come Blow your Horn is —
Just a great way to let others out there know what you've been up to all these years!

TO PLACE AN AD simply fill out the form that appears on the back of each issue. Please print *clearly* and *legibly- Thank you!*

Remember- if you are a subscriber, the 40 word ad is **FREE!!!**

ADDRESS YOUR RESPONSE TO:

Back in THE BRONX, Stephen M. Samtur
Box 141 H, Scarsdale, NY 10583

*Be sure to include the number that appears before the ad. (**MP 1089** for ex.) and a long, **stamped** envelope so we can mail your letter to the person placing the ad.

READER REPLIES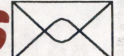

It is vitally important that you fill out the information below. Your input will be essential to the success of this magazine, tailored and inspired by you, the former "Bronxite". We thank you for your participation.

Subscriber? ❑ Yes ❑ No

YOUR NAME _____

ADDRESS _____

CITY _____ STATE _____ ZIP _____ PHONE _____

HIGH SCHOOL ATTENDED _____ YEAR GRADUATED _____

TELL US A LITTLE ABOUT YOURSELF,
(Be sure to include your alma mater, old neighborhood, your best memories about your days in the Bronx, (or anything else you can tell us).

_____

_____

COULD WE SEND A FRIEND A FREE COPY OF BACK IN THE BRONX?

Do you know current or former Bronxites who would like to receive our magazine and reunion information?
If you do, we'll be happy to send them a **free** inaugural issue of **Back in THE BRONX**.
Write to Back in The Bronx, Box 141 H, Scarsdale, NY 10583 or call 1-800-7-BRONX 5

Last _____ First _____ Maiden _____
Address _____ City _____ State _____ Zip _____
Phone # (____) _____ School and year of Graduation _____

Last _____ First _____ Maiden _____
Address _____ City _____ State _____ Zip _____
Phone # (____) _____ School and year of Graduation _____

Last _____ First _____ Maiden _____
Address _____ City _____ State _____ Zip _____
Phone # (____) _____ School and year of Graduation _____

Last _____ First _____ Maiden _____
Address _____ City _____ State _____ Zip _____
Phone # (____) _____ School and year of Graduation _____

COME BLOW YOUR OWN HORN DEPARTMENT

Please tell us about yourself (include your name)—about your accomplishments, awards, titles or works in progress.
We're interested in hearing about them. List Below. _____

_____

_____

_____

19

READER REPLIES

As a subscriber you are entitled to a FREE 40 Word Classified, Missing Persons, Blow Your Own Horn, or Personal Ad. Please write your ad below (if you are not subscribing to our magazine you can still place an ad in the next issue. The cost of an advertisement is 50¢ a word, there is no limit on paid ads).

_____

_____

_____

Is Your Mailing Label Correct?

In order to keep our database current, please correct any errors and place the label and or photocopy with corrections.

Account #	High School	Year Graduated

```
6817        Roosevelt      1958
SAMPLE
    Mary R. Flowers
    123 Anystreet Blvd
    Anywhere, USA  12345
```

Change of Address?

If you're planning a move please attach your label corrected with your new address and the date that you will begin receiving mail at that address. This will insure that you don't miss your next issue of **Back in THE BRONX.**

Ordering Information

A Great Gift Idea! In addition to your own subscription, a subscription to **Back in THE BRONX** makes a great and unique gift. Fill in the form below and we'll process the order in time for our next issue. So, order your subscription NOW, and order one for a friend!

YES, I'd like to order the following items:

QTY.

____ 1Yr. (4 ISSUES) Subscription(s) to Back in THE BRONX $19.95
____ 2Yr. (8 ISSUES) Subscription(s) to Back in THE BRONX* .... $29.95   *FREE John's Menu
____ 3Yr. (12 ISSUES) Subscription(s) to Back in THE BRONX* $39.95
____ 4Yr. (16 ISSUES) Subscription(s) to Back in THE BRONX* $49.95

____ The Beautiful Bronx...........$25.00 (plus $3.95 S/H) $28.95
____ The Bronx: It Was Only Yesterday..$25.00 (plus $3.95 S/H) $28.95
____ Bronx High School Reunion Weekend Video $29.95
____ SAVE MONEY - BUY 4 FOR JUST $99.00!
____ THE BRONX Tracking Service $9.95
_____ I would like to receive all available back issues and have them applied towards my subscription (To date we have at least 12 back issues available - While They Last!)

TOTAL: $ _____

Please fill out completely and include $3.95 for shipping and handling for books only to: **Back in THE BRONX**, Box 141H, Scarsdale, NY 10583

Please Print Clearly ☐ New Subscriber ☐ Renewal

Name _____

Maiden Name _____

Address _____

City _____

State _____ Zip _____

Phone (_____) _____

High School _____ Year Grad. _____

☐ Visa ☐ Mastercard ☐ Check ☐ Money Order

No. _____ Expiration Date _____

Signature _____

Back in THE BRONX

Box 141 H, Scarsdale, NY 10583
Phone 914-592-1647 • Fax 914-592-4893

ADDRESS CORRECTION REQUESTED

Volume II Issue VIII

Back in THE BRONX

CELEBRATING THE EXPERIENCE OF GROWING UP AND LIVING IN THE BRONX

Memories From My Mother's Kitchen

by Roberta Graff

The road back in time is frequently bumpy; strewn with obstacles that impede the memory and dull the senses. But sometimes a sound, a taste sensation, or a smell evokes a series of memories that come rushing back with the speed of a movie reel on re-wind.

And memories can make a person's mouth water. For, like many of my generation and middle-class Bronx pedigree some of my earliest and fondest recollections are of food.

All it takes is one whiff of frying onions and I recall those heavy, hearty, robust meals of my youth, each one copious enough to make even the gourmand among us shake his head and sigh, "I can't eat another thing."

There were days my mother must have raced the sun up, when the smells that held the promise of dinner greeted me at breakfast.

She shopped daily, pushing a little metal cart in and out of the stores on Kingsbridge Road. There were stops at Moe's fruit stand, Lanoff's fish store, the A&P (her only concession to "big business") and the Burnside Meat Market. Here, displaying the critical eye of a jeweler selecting a gem for an empress, she would choose a nice fat pullet, (it was never lifted out

of the display case, but came instead from "the back" where it was being held expressly for her). From this chicken of all chickens she would make a soup that could cure not only present ailments but was guaranteed to ward off whatever germs were foolish enough to plan an attack.

The soup was unpredictable in that we never knew what would be in it.

Sometimes little white matzoh balls floated on top of the golden broth; other times meat-filled dumplings (kreplach) bobbed up and down. But to our delight there were always bright yellow, unborn chicken eggs, which the butcher, with whom my mother had more than ordinary influence, saved especially for her.

Tears rolled down my mother's cheeks as she sliced huge white onions which she fried to a golden brown in yellow chicken fat. She would add livers, cook it all together, then chop it in a wooden bowl with three hard boiled eggs. Little bits of chicken fat that had not melted would stick to the

Continued on page 4

Letters From Lewisberg

by Michael Glazer

Dear Home Boys,
I am sending you a story that I have been keeping pretty much in my head for a bunch of years. It is a tale of long ago, when English as a second language referred to your grandparents speaking Yiddish or Italian.
Things have changed. I Graduated from Christopher Columbus High School in 1969. Now I live smack dab in the middle of Pennsylvania, with cows. No crime! But, a hell of a lot of cows.
Your magazine was given to me by a friend back home (that means NY) it's great. I write for the local paper here and recently had a radio show. Yup, a Jewish kid from the Bronx playing country music to truckers all night on the radio. It's great out here. But, they don't know egg creams.
Hope you like the story.

1951 was a good year for me.
I was born.
What was even better, I got to grow up in the Bronx.

My childhood, at least until was eleven years old, was spent in a fourth floor walk-up, one bedroom apartment shared by my mom, dad, older brother and me.

We lived in the Hunts Point section - at 636 Barretto Street, between Spofford and Randall Avenues.

I remember the day Mayor Wagner came to the neighborhood to dedicate the Spofford Boy's Home (I believe it is now called a detention center) right at the corner of my block and across from Jimmy's Candy Store on Spofford Avenue.

But, this is not a story of the old neighborhood in a reminiscent sense.

Continued on page 6

Bronx I.Q. Test - Pg. 7 • Missing Person - Pg. 8 • Witkin's Famous Deli - Pg. 12

From the Editors...

WE NEED YOUR HELP!!!

We're asking for your help in the writing of our book about the Bronx in the 40's, 50's and 60'. We think that you, our **Back In The Bronx** readers, are a priceless historical source, and we are eager to enlist your help in this important project. **Specifically, we are looking for pictures, 8mm film, menus, school photos and yearbooks, report cards and other artifacts from the Bronx of the post-World War II era.** We'd like to see those old black and white pictures of the neighborhood, the corner candy store, the baseball teams or the clubs...and even those shots of the family in the new car. Anything you've got will be carefully handled and returned, and if we use it in the book, we promise to give you full credit.

Also, we'd be happy to listen to your ideas for subject matter. Are there some special events, people or places you think should be included in the book about the Bronx? Let us hear from you.

Finally, do you have friends, neighbors, or relatives who might be interested in a free inaugural issue of **Back in the Bronx**? Please give us their names and addresses and we will be happy to send it to them...

If they wish, they may call our toll free number:

1-800-7 BRONX 5

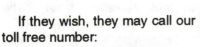

Back in the BRONX

A number of the photographs in **Back in the Bronx** are courtesy of and are available from the Bronx Historical Society.

Publishers and Editors:
Stephen M. Samtur — CLINTON '61
Susan H. Samtur — TAFT '62

Contributing Editors:
Barbara Fasciani
Martin Jackson — SCIENCE '58

Art & Production: Ellen Grodjesk

Printed By: Bronx Age Press

Reminiscing
"FOR THE LOVE OF 2-WITH"

by Stewart & Paula Lester

For the past 16 years, my wife, family (son and daughter) have made our home here in Houston, Texas. Our lives are here, our children grew and matured here, our success, to whatever measure you use as a standard of success developed here, but our hearts, our minds, our attitudes toward others, our self-esteem, our very consciousness, is the Bronx, for this is our home in our hearts and mind. That is to say we are "Bronxites" and rightly proud of it....

At least once a year my wife and I travel to New York to visit family and friends. We have developed a routine to our visits. First of course we arrive in N.Y. pick up a car at the airport, and our odyssey begins.

Even before we make our first visit, we drive to our old neighborhood (Westchester Ave.) park the rented car, go to our old "deli" sit down and wait. Soon the tired old waiter shuffles over to our table, the same hand towel draped across his arm and says in a bored tone a voice "so where you been". That alone brought tears to our eyes.

Our selections are always the same, we order two with, a knish, and two sodas. One coke and for me a creme soda (what else?). Nothing else need be said. He shuffles off, yells in our order, and the rest is like we are back home and never left. Often we eat our hot dog mixed with a little salty tear. We wouldn't have it any other way.

We often walk from the Soundview station, where my wife, Paula, grew up (172nd st. and Manor Ave.) down past the Ward Theater to the Elder Avenue Station, where I grew up (Wheeler Ave.) I don't care how the old neighborhood has changed or how it seems to have deteriorated, it's our "home" and we see what we saw all those years ago. Our hearts remember, our thoughts are kept to ourselves, we walk and just remember.

That crazy little odyssey keeps us for at least another year, or until we can return and be allowed to remember again.

Our children cannot share these feelings with us. These personal memories we cannot pass on to our children, you just have had to live it, and we are thankful we have.

REVISED

Bronx Honor Roll
Bronxites Who Have Achieved!

BRONX SCIENCE

Stokely Carmichael
Bobby Darin
Edggar Doctorow
William Saffire

CARDINAL HAYES

George Carlin
Rocky Colavito
Kevin Loughery
Regis Philbin

CHRISTOPHER COLUMBUS

Robert Abrams
Anne Bancroft
George Jorgenson

DEWITT CLINTON

Don Adams
Nate Archibald
Richard Avedon
James Baldwin
Martin Balsam
David Begelman
James Cann
Paddy Cheyefsky
George Cukor
Avery Fisher
Arthur Gelb
Judd Hirsch
Stubby Kaye
Theodore Kheel
Robert Klein
William Kunstler
Burt Lancaster
Jan Murray
Charles Rangel
Richard Rogers
A.M. Rosenthal
Daniel Schorri
Dolph Schayes
Neil Simon
Larry Storch
Jimmie Walker
Fats Waller
William Zeckendorf

EVANDER CHILDS

Red Buttons
James Coco
Carl Reiner

MONROE

Jules Feiffer
John Garfield
Alan Lansburg
Hank Greenberg
Ed Kranepool

Leon Lederman (Nobel Physicist)
Regina Resnick

MORRIS

Angel Cordero
Gabe Pressman
E. Colin Powell

ROOSEVELT

June Alyson

TAFT

Sanford Brown
Eydie Gorme
Stanley Kubrick

OTHER NOTABLE FOLKS WITH TIES TO THE BRONX

Joey Adams
Danny Aiello
Alan Alda
Robert Alda
Mel Allen
Corazon Aquino
Herman Badillo
Lauren Bacall
Ellen Barkin
Mario Biaggi
Joey Bishop
Teresa Brewer
Ralph Bunche
George Burns
Cab Calloway
Diahann Carroll
Samuel Clemens
Cardinal Cooke
Leon Cooper (Nobel Prize Winner)
Avery Corman
Norman Cousins
Don Criqui
Tony Curtis
Vic Damone
Dennis Day
Dion DiMucci
John Foster Dulles
Geraldine Ferraro
F. Scott Fitzgerald
Joe Franklin
Arlene Francis
Connie Francis
Edward J. Flynn
Rudolph Giuliani
Samuel Gompers
Armand Hammer
Babe Herman
Davis Horowitz
George Jessel

Robert Kennedy
Ted Kennedy
Theodore Kheel
Calvin Klein
Edward Koch
Fiorello LaGuardici
Jake LaMotta
Louise Lasser
Ralph Lauren
Ron Leibman
Benny Leonard
Lee Leonard
Hal Linden
Nita Lowey, Representative
Vince Lombardi
Gary Marshall
Penny Marshall
Glen Miller
Sal Mineo
Gary Morton
Bess Myerson
Gil Noble
Carroll O'Connor
Charles Osgood
Al Pacino
Jack Palance
Floyd Patterson
Joseph Papp
Joe Pesci
Roberta Peters
Edgar Alan Poe
E. Colin Powell
Vincent Price
Charles Nelson Reilly
Rob Reiner
Billy Rose
Jonas Salk
Isabel Sanford
Connie Selleca
Carly Simon
Stanley Simon
Vince Skully
Curtis Sliwa
Wesley Snipes, Jr.
George Steinbrenner
Pat Summerall
Mother Teresa
Arturo Toscanini
Leon Trotsky
Lloyd Ultan
Jerry Vale
Vanessa Williams
Herman Woulk
Rosalyn Yallow (Nobel Prize Winner)

Thanks to Dr. William C. Wolfson and the Bronx Society of Science and Letters

Reminiscing

My Mother's Kitchen

Continued from page 1

pan, she would scrape it off and let it cool and harden on the side of the stove. It was called "gribben" and we would eat it like popcorn.

Could anything this side of heaven taste like Hungarian stuffed cabbage? Holishkes, we called them; little rolls of chopped meat tenderly tucked inside a leaf of cabbage that was slowly simmered with raisins, tomatoes, and ginger snaps. This dish was matched only by the gefilte fish which was prepared on Thursday and served on Friday. It was accompanied by the forerunner of the nasal spray, homemade horseradish.

She hurried along in pursuit of the perfect Challah.

Imagine a brisket of beef, lovingly simmered for three hours, a crisp coating of course salt and paprika on the outside, insulating a fork-tender interior. A volcano of mashed potatoes by its side, the crater oozing lava-like gravy. A crusty seeded rye bread from Flakowitz helped with the mop-up, unless of course it was Friday.

On Fridays my mother would walk down the Concourse to Sutters. She would nod to her friends sunning themselves on the benches in Poe Park as she hurried along in pursuit of the perfect Challah. She made her choice from among the golden loaves and never left without buying one charlotte russe. It greeted me when I came home from school that afternoon.

On holidays there were flowers from Kanganis. The florist was on the corner of Jerome Avenue which was only steps passed the liquor store where my mother purchased the sugar sweet wine we all loved. Zenophiles would say it dulled the appetite; but on those special occasions we always managed to eat more.

In no time we devoured the results of hours spent in the kitchen; mammoth broiled rib steaks, crunchy noodle kugel, tzimmes, a mixture of stewed prunes and carrots, and of course, crisp thin potato latkes, no bigger than a half-dollar. As we ate the grinning teapots on the wallpaper smiled down on us, obviously satisfied with our incredible appetites.

I still don't think the dessert has been invented that matches warm, baked apples bursting through their skins dripping with honey, or lumpy rice pudding, studded with raisins and dusted with cinnamon. There was frequently a strudel or a fresh fruit pie hardly an afterthought, considering the hours of rolling and kneading required to make the dough thin enough to satisfy my mother.

Such meals were always washed down with cups of steaming tea. When the leaves settled at the bottom of the cup, my mother would tell our fortunes. The lifetime of excitement promised by the scattered tea leaves left me fantasizing for days.

But I was a little girl a long time ago. And as I grew up and away from my Bronx kitchen, my culinary horizons broadened. Though I dearly missed the wonderful meals of my youth, I discovered a world of exotic cooking, using spices and products never found in my mother's pantry. I began to buy soy sauces from Japan, pastas from Italy, vinegars and oils laced with fruit and herbs, coffee hinting of amaretto and chocolate. I purchased Oriental, French and Italian cookbooks, and filled my kitchen with a food processor, a wok, imported cutlery, and every new gadget necessary for the serious cook.

The autumn before my mother moved to Florida, I planned a dinner in her honor. Using many of the beautiful platters and dishes she had handed down I prepared a gourmet menu choosing recipes I had gathered from around the world; a country pate, little round blinis; dim-sum, and my favorite spinach turban in phylo. I arranged everything on the buffet which gave my guests an opportunity to help themselves and be dazzle by my efforts at the same time.

My mother was beaming as she survey my handiwork. "Chopped liver, latkes, kreplach, strudel. I see you still use my recipes."

"You bet," I replied laughing, as my family began sampling my delicacies.

"Like mother, like daughter," Uncle Sol commented. And everyone nodded in agreement.

LOST

&FOUND

Track down your old friends, neighbors and lost relatives with
THE BRONX TRACKING SERVICE

Did you ever wonder what some of your high school buddies are doing? Where do they live now?

Well, **Back in THE BRONX TRACKING SERVICE** may be able to help you find them and maybe even discover long lost relatives you never know you had. Find the phone numbers and addresses from a database of 70 to 100 million people from all across the U.S. You can find that special old friend who you haven't heard from in years (decades). If you are like most people, as you get older you wonder more about those special friends you've lost touch with over the years. Wouldn't it be great to give them a call to swap stories and reminisce? If you are interested in tracing your genealogy, looking for lost parents, or children, we can help.

Mail the completed form and $9.95 for each person you want tracked to: Back In THE BRONX, Box 141H, Scarsdale, NY 10583

THE BRONX TRACKING SERVICE
APPLICATION
Name (Print or Type)

Last   First   Middle

Maiden Name

Address (Last know address or general location)

City   State   Zip

Approximate date living at above address

High School   Year graduated

Age

Requested By:

Address:

City   State   Zip

Phone:

THE BRONX TRACKING SERVICE
APPLICATION
Name (Print or Type)

Last   First   Middle

Maiden Name

Address (Last know address or general location)

City   State   Zip

Approximate date living at above address

High School   Year graduated

Age

Requested By:

Address:

City   State   Zip

Phone:

I understand that I will receive a list of name and addresses and phone numbers for each person from a database of over 80 million names throughout the United States. I further understand that I will have to search through theses names and determine the approximate name that matches the one(s) I am trying to trace.

Reminiscing

Letters From Lewisberg

Continued from page 1

This is a story about something that happened to me almost 40 years ago. An occurrence that I simply have to close my eyes to live again, as if it were now.

Barretto Street in the 1950's was like many other streets in the Bronx. It was a mixture of all people living comfortably together. The shock troops of fear,

---

1951 was a good year for me. I was born.

---

hate and decay may have been on the move, but their artillery could not yet be heard on the 600 block of Barretto Street, at least not for a few more years.

The building that I grew up in, was your typical 30 or 40 year old tenement. There was an occasional mouse problem - rats still hadn't moved into the neighborhood either - and a constant cockroach problem. As I have said, we all lived comfortably together.

Fresh summer afternoons were especially nice. We had a southern exposure from our fourth floor kitchen window. It overlooked low factory buildings all the way to the East River and Rikers Island, about a mile or two to the south, and to La Guardia Airport beyond. The living room and bedroom each had western exposures where you could see the Manhattan skyline, the towers of the George Washington Bridge and the glowing sky above Yankee Stadium during night games.

I'm sure none of this description is alien to anyone who grew up in the Bronx in the 1950's and 60's. At least not in the East Bronx where there was still some open space, here and there, known as a vacant lot. Three such lots existed on my block. These were virgin vacant lots, not the rubble-strewn, caved in skeletons of old memories that pass for vacant lots today.

I look back at all of this as paradise. So when I tell my story, even its vivid memory only adds to the mystique and enjoyment of growing up in a place that someday may be thought of as heaven.

My mom told me a story about an old man who lived in our building at the time she and my father had just gotten married and moved in. This was in the early 1940's.

"Pop" McElroy was a retired policemen. He had served on the force starting in the early 1900's. His beat was exclusively the Bronx.

My mom said McElroy would sit on the stoop of our building and tell all who would listen about what the Bronx was like in the early part of the century. He was a nice man who was well liked.

"Pop" McElroy lived with his son, who was also a policeman.

McElroy's son was not feeling well for a time, and finally was persuaded to see a doctor. The younger McElroy was found to have cancer, but he had waited too long to seek help and shortly thereafter he passed away.

His father became depressed and despondent over his loss.

According to my mother's story, one night "Pop" walked the three blocks to Faile Avenue, which runs bordering the East River, and then two blocks over to the Tiffany Street pier and jumped into the cold water.

Years after this incident, I was born and, as things happen, some five or six years later I was five or six years old.

I was sitting on the end of the living room couch. I was leaning against its high, padded arms stretching my arms out to the dark wooden side table, which held on it a rough-textured, grey, ceramic lamp. I always remember that lamp because it had thin vertical of shinny black glaze around. The glaze reminded me of how Bosco would drip down the side of its bottle.

I was playing with cowboys and Indians around the lamp. The cowboys and Indians were the kind of rubber figures that you could snap apart at the waist. You could have a red top half of a cowboy on a green bottom half of an indian. I guess that's instant equality.

It was a beautiful afternoon. A breeze was blowing the living room curtains and sun was streaming onto the wooden floor and area rug. My mother was down the hall visiting with our neighbor Jean. Our front door was propped open and so was Jean's, about 20 feet away. Leaving doors open was not unusual in those days, it was a way of getting cross ventilation, still, according to my mother, better than air conditioning.

While I was playing, I just happen to turn around and looked toward the living room doorway. Any door that might have ever existed in that doorway had been removed long before anyone remembered. There in the doorway, leaning against the left side of the jamb, was an old man.

The old man had a placid smile on his face, he didn't move. I could look right through him and see the wall and the jamb behind him. He was one color from head to foot. Kind of a hazy-fog white.

My reaction was to turn away and scream "Mommy." So I did!

As these, maybe 10 seconds were transpiring, my mother was, coinciden-

---

Leaving doors open was not unusual in those days, it was a way of getting cross ventilation, still, according to my mother, better than air conditioning

---

tally, walking across the hall back to our apartment. She ran in, when she heard my yell, passing nobody who happened to be transparent along the way.

My mother searched the apartment, three rooms dosen't take long, and, of course, found nothing.

This had to have occurred 37 years ago. My mother dosen't remember the incident ever happening. She never has. Of course having a 6 year old scream "Mommy" isn't an experience to remember.

In my mind, did it or didn't it happen isn't the question. The question is, if it wasn't "Pop" McElroy, who was that ghost?

Who Am I?

Can you name these two mystery Bronx high schools alumni?

To find out who they are turn to page 15.

Mystery Bronxite #1

Mystery Bronxite #2

BRONX I.Q. TEST
By Harvey Felix

1. Name the Bronx High School named after the 27th president of the United States?

2. Define the term "Spaldeen"

3. What is the subtle difference between a "Chocolate Soda" and an "Egg Cream"?

4. Name three Bronx telephone prefixes prior to the establishment of three digit numerals.

5. Define the term "Zip Gun".

6. What was always done with the "broomstick" used in stickball when a police car visited the neighborhood?

7. Where was the clothesline inside a Bronx apartment located?

8. How was garbage collected in a Bronx apartment?

9. Name three "Super Hero Comic Book" characters read by Bronxites in their local candy stores.

10. Name three popular radio shows heard during the forties and fifties on Sunday over Bronx radios.

11. Define: "He can hit three sewers".

12. Define: a."Poodle Skirt"
b."Knickers"
c."The Projects"

13. Define: a."G.O."
b."Regents"
c."Arista"

14. Define: a."Crinoline"
b."Waterman"
c."The Super"

15. What is the common denominator in the following terms: "The Zenith", "The Luxor", " The Kent"

Answers on page 9

A MISSING PERSON OR NOT — THAT IS THE QUESTION

by Harriette Schwartz

I must admit that when my sister phoned to tell me that I was among the missing it was quite a shock. After all, I have known all along (more or less) who and where I was. Actually, what she said was that her lifelong friend Janet had sent her some page copies from a magazine called, **Back in the Bronx.** In them were some "MP" ads (MP meaning, missing person of course.) Apparently a women by the name of Anita Kleinbaum had listed three people along with their high school and year of graduation— Harriette Schwartz, Taft '68, Wendy Sadovnick, Taft '68, and Mark Holod, Taft '66. Though Kleinbaum and Sadovnick did not initially ring any bells for me, I am Harriette Schwartz, Taft '68 and Mark Holod set off an old alarm.

Mark Holod was this "older" guy I dated during the summer of 1965 (my Concourse Cabanna Club Summer).

I lived in Sedgwick Projects—1551 University Avenue, Apartment 13G. This was the building with the public library and the Community Center. So what brought me to Macomb's Road and Mark Holod? One of my pals from JHS 82— Anita. Anita Bernstein back then but obviously Anita Kleinbaum now. Eureka!

I asked my sister what I needed to do. Well, this issue as it turns out was already a year old, however, I merely had to call the magazine and reference the ad. The conversation I had with the women who answered the phone was so pleasant and interesting. I mean, here was a whole magazine dedicated to the resurrection of what was good about the Bronx, unlike all the trash the general public is used to imagining when they think about my old "hometown". Immediately and without hesitation I signed up for a two year subscription.

Armed with Anita Bernstein-

Kleinbaum's address and phone, I prepared to contact my teenage girl-friend. I dialed her New Jersey home phone number and got the answering machine and I immediately hung up. How do you leave a casual and "brief" message after an almost 30 year lapse of communication? Finally, I could not wait until an evening to call and so I took the message plunge. Within an hour, she called me back—"is it really you?" "Yup, it's me—"Is this really Anita Bernstein?" We filled each other in, as best as old friends suddenly reunited can in one short phone call from work. Somehow, I can't imagine Anita married for 23 years with 3 children, the oldest 2 in college and the youngest in middle or junior high school (where she and I first met!!)

The Anita I remember was tall and thin and that same summer of 1965 we worked clearing tables in her father's Italian restaurant on Jerome Avenue. The place was know as BARNITAS. Barnitas was named after Anita and her younger sister Barbara. Actually, Anita and I spent more quarters from the bar on the juke box than we could possible have earned and ate more pizza than that as well. However, it was alot of fun and in truth this was the easiest job I have ever had. We promised to write and keep in touch. Anita also told me she keeps in touch with some of our other friends, since they have settled in neighboring New Jersey townships. She agreed to let them know that I was alive and well.

As soon as we got off the phone, I called Kenny. Kenny Rudin and I have known each other since 1963. He was my first boyfriend and we have remained good friends throughout the years. Ken is a political reporter for a national public radio in Washington, D.C. and lives in Maryland with his wife and little boy. Ken is also a, "Taft '68" person. When I told him about all

Have You Seen Me?

Name:
Height:
Weight:
Hair Color:
Age:
Last Seen: In "The Bronx."

of this and about Anita his response was, "tomorrow you will get a call from Gail Fox and Denise Bumgartner." (Two of our other JHS classmates.) Yeah- sure Ken!

The next day at work I get a call. It is a woman who says she is a voice from my past. She then proceeded to relate to me an incident from my past— "Do you remember when you were walking home from JHS 82 one afternoon and a girl named Linda and you got into a fight and she ripped your blouse off in the street? Well, I was with you that day!" Frankly, the fight is only a vague memory and if someone was with me I am clueless as to whom it was . Here I was at work and this calls comes out of the blue. My only response was, "who is this!!???" To which the women replied, "Denise Baumgartner." Somebody tell me what are the odds???

I am glad to have been found, re-discovered if you will (though as I stated at the outset- I've never been lost) Knowing that I am no longer considered by some a MIA is somehow a source of comfort. More importantly finding that there is still a healthy and alive connection to the Bronx of my youth which I thought was long gone is even more comforting.

TEST ANSWERS

1. William Howard Taft High School. (3 Points)
2. A pink ball used in stickball. (3 Points)
3. A chocolate soda contained no milk. (3 Points)
4. JErome, SEdgwick, TRemont, et al (1Point Each)
5. A homemade pistol. (3 Points)
6. It was thrown under a parked car or otherwise removed.(3 Points)
7. Over the bathtub, it came up and down as needed. (3 Points)
8. The "Dumb Waiter" (3 Points)
9. Superman, Captain Marvel, Plastic Man, Wonder Woman, Batman and Robin, et al (1 Point Each)
10. "The Shadow, Inner Sanctum, Mr. Keen, Tracer of Lost Persons", (1Point Each)
11. A stickball batter that could hit a "spaldeen" about 120 feet; sewers were 40 feet apart. (3 Points)
12. a. A felt skirt with a Poodle as a design. (1Point)
    b. A pair of boys pants reaching just below the knee, worn with high socks. (1Point)
    c. A City housing development. (1Point)
13. a. A High School Organization and Store (1 Point)
    b. A required Statewide Examination required for graduation. (1Point)
    c. An Honor Society (1Point)
14. a. A wide slip fitting under a dress to project a "full effect" (1Point)
    b. A fountain pen of the period (1Point)
    c. The superintendent of an apartment building (1Point)
15. All three are Bronx movie theaters. (1 Point)

EVALUATION

39 TO 45 A true Bronxite (Congrats)

27 TO 38 Some Bronx smarts still there (Not Bad)

15 TO 26 Fading memories of a bygone era (Shame on you)

O TO 14 Relocate to Brooklyn (Do not pass go)

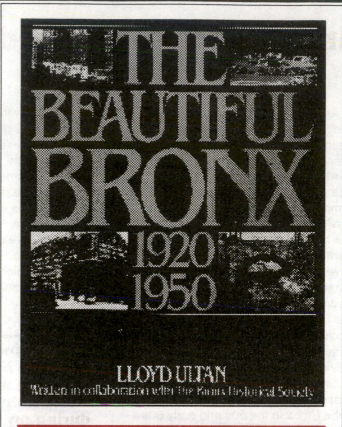

Indispensible Spaldeen

By Lee Stroh

As I made my way into adulthood and the New York middle class, I discovered that not all children spent their entire summers in the neighborhood as I did. For many children, there was summer sleep-away and day camps as well as the time honored family vacation to take you away from the humid, unairconditioned apartments and streets. My parents did not drive, so family vacations consisted of two weeks at my cousin's house in the "country," Levittown, Long Island. The rest of the summer was spent on the block, Morris Avenue between 181st Street and Burnside.

I realize now that what played a big part in saving me from intolerable boredom during my summers growing up in the Bronx in the 50s and early 60s was the "spladeen", a little pink rubber ball manufactured by Spalding. While tracing the origin of this pronunciation may be difficult, buying a spaldeen was not.

I would take my quarter (a nominal amount, even then) around the corner to Al Tare's candy store across from Creston Junior High and sample his entire inventory. The larger ones were desirable because they were usually harder, move lively and easier to grip. For those kids with inferiority complexes carrying a spaldeen in your pocket was assurance that you wouldn't be "chucked" from the team if the play ball happened to be yours.

The spaldeen for me opened an array of street games that children in other parts of the country could never imagine.

Stickball

As anyone knows who has seen the newsreel of Willie Mays playing stickball in the neighborhood near the Polo Grounds, the conventional form of stickball is played in the city streets. It is played with a broom handle, a rubber ball and without the benefit of pitching, i.e. hitting the ball fungo. A player's proclivity (and machismo) is measured by how many sewers he can hit. The game hardly ever involves running bases.

Broom handles were usually "borrowed" from mom. In later childhood, stickball bats were actually manufactured. They were shorter and fatter than broom handles, and had a short strip of electrical tape wrapped around the end.

> I realize now that what played a big part in saving me from intolerable boredom during my summers growning up in the bronx in the 50s and early 60s was the "Spaldeen"

My block was on a hill (as is most of the West Bronx), so stickball played on the street was not practical because of the incline, but we managed to play at times. When I think of street stickball, the picture that comes to mind was one of quickly tossing the sticks under parked cars when a patrol car from the 46th precinct was spotted creeping up the block. Because cops had to field an array of complaints from residents who felt they were being deprived of a quite, child-free neighborhood (certainly not because the street is a dangerous place to play!), cops tended to confiscate sticks. Isn't stickball guaranteed in the Constitution?

The more memorable games were played in the Creston J.H.S. schoolyard. There was the ever present group of older and stronger guys who could constantly hit the ball on the roof of the apartment building over the outfield fence, a distance of about 250 feet and six stories up. My friends and I hardly ever played that type of game, however. One that included pitching was more competitive.

With pitching, you could play on a smaller field and needed only one or two players per team. Fastballs, curves and knuckleballs (actually digging your knuckles into the ball) were all possible with a spaldeen. You could retire an opponent by strikeout (balls and strikes were determined by a box drawn on the wall directly behind the batter, by fielding a ground ball cleanly, or by catching a ball off the adjacent apartment building wall.

I understand that in the suburbs, stickball was played with a tennis ball. But a tennis ball is not as lively as a spaldeen, and besides, tennis was not popular in most areas of the Bronx where there were few tennis courts.

Stoop Ball

Stoops come in various shapes and sizes. Apartment building steps, curbs and other abutments are all stoops. We played a form of stoop ball called, "off the point," which made use of the exposed edges of bricks or cement at the bases of some walls, common features in pre-war buildings.

Like stickball, off the point could be played with one or two per team, and parked cars and other obstructions were part of the field. The "batter" stood near the building wall and aimed the ball at the point. The batter was automatically out if the ball missed the point and the infielder (the only fielder, if there was one player per team) who stood in the street next to the car parked across the street fielded the ground ball cleanly. If the infielder misplayed the ball, the batter was given one base on the error.

A ball that hit the point tended to project sharply off the wall and was a potential hit so long as it struck the ground before it was caught. The batter was given as many bases as the amount of times the ball bounced on the ground. If a fielder caught the ball

before it bounced (either directly off the point, off a car, or off the apartment building wall across the street) it was out. If the ball reached the apartment building wall on a fly and then hit the ground, it was a home run.

Since there were no strikes or balls, the games progressed rather quickly, an advantage on a 90° August afternoon. You could play a nine inning game in twenty minutes!

Punchball

Punchball was played in elementary school, sometimes during gym class or recess. In many cases, it was a child's first exposure to playing a form of baseball. Sometimes even baseball gloves were worn, totally unnecessary when fielding a soft rubber ball, but it must have looked cool to a ten-year old.

A good hitter could drive a ball a great distance by "serving" the ball over his head (like a tennis serve) prior to punching it. A poor hitter like myself needed to measure his punch by swinging his arm and fist parallel to the ground and thereby placing the ball.

At an age when you hadn't yet developed good hand-to-eye coordination, it was nevertheless less easy to place a ball by punching it (hitting it "where the ain't"). The absence of pitching made for a lot of running and scoring, a feature attractive to grade schoolers.

Slug

As most of us know, for many street games, the evenly spaced square grooves in the cement sidewalks form "natural" boundaries and served to define a player's territory. Such was the case with box ball, box baseball, hit-the-penny and slug.

In other boroughs and even other neighborhoods within the Bronx, slug was also known as "ace-king-queen." This game is sort of an inverse form of handball in that rather than slapping the ball directly against the wall, it is slapped on one bounce (slug was

sometimes referred to as the nowadays politically incorrect, "Chinese handball".) A player may continuously slap the ball against the wall within his/her box and then, without warning,

slap it into another player's box. If the next player failed to continue the sequence, he/she was "out" and had to go to the end of the line.

The game came replete with "hindus," "stringbeans" and other "babies." A hindu was when the ball hit a crack or other obstruction and usually resulted in a "do-over." Stringbeans and babies were hit so close to the wall and sidewalk as to make them virtually unplayable by the player to whom the ball was served. Long apartment building walls enabled as many as six or seven children to play at a

time, and, unlike many of the other games in which spaldeens were used, slug was as likely to be played by girls as by boys.

A game that was played almost exclusively by girls was the one that required continuously bouncing the ball on the ground under your leg reciting things like. "'A,' my name is Alice and my husband's name is Arthur, we come from Alabama and we make asphalt."

I haven't ever forgotten some of the names. Remember the game where you throw the ball in the air and call someone's name and that person has to catch the ball before it bounces, and if he does, he may throw the ball in the air and call someone else's name; but if he doesn't, he has to retrieve the ball and attempt to hit someone else with it? What fun!

As an adult, I have done some pretty foolish things with my money, but the 25¢ cost of a spaldeen was probably the best investment I have made to date.

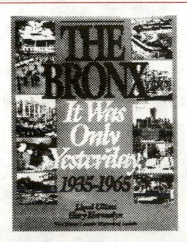

WITKIN'S FAMOUS DELI-RESTAURANT

By Joe Witkin

We lived at 2131 Vyse Avenue and 181st Street, on the second floor, which was the third window up from the ground level...I always had a problem understanding this. There was probably one telephone in the building housing about forty plus families, and the telephone, lucky for us, was on our floor! I remember almost all the tenants being friendly and helpful—and not anyone being anything but simply nice! I must have had a "thousand" friends, well maybe a little less, and maybe some were just acquaintances, but to me they were all "friends!" I believe that because my dad owned and ran the neighborhood delicatessen restaurant, and I helped him run it since I was 10 years old, that I had gotten to know more folks than most, for maybe ten blocks square! Dad's deli was called WITKIN'S FAMOUS DELICATESSEN, and it *was* famous!

My dad, Louis Witkin, and his younger brother, Meyer, had begun business in 1929, lasting 40 years until 1969! It's the year 1993 as I write this, and I cannot tell you how many people I meet, almost on a weekly basis that remind me of the great deli

we used to have! We must have sent a thousand salami's to the boys who were serving in the armed forces overseas during WWII. I'll remember alot of things said, all good about Witkin's Deli, but one stands out in my mind. An article in the then called "Bronx Home News" had a reporter asking some of the boys in Europe, on the front line, during WWII, what they would wish they could have at that point of time, and one of the boys stated, as it was printed: "A hot pastrami sandwich on a club roll, with mustard and cole slaw, an order of french fries, and a Dr. Brown's Cel-Ray soda at Witkin's Deli."

I worked at Witkin's Deli when I was ten years old, and left to become a stockbroker, when I was forty years old!

We had only one block to walk to work, and on Saturdays and Sundays we were so busy, the customers would literally line up for almost a whole block to wait their turn!!

I worked like a "dog" - it was very hard work, and very long hours, and I hated it then, but, looking back and having all those wonderful memories, all those wonderful customers, friends and relatives—it was very much worth it!

Joe Witkin, 1948

EAST OF WITKIN'S DELI

- Messings Commission Bakery
- Lobels Butcher Shop
- Nat Klein's Hosiery
- Leff's Appetising
- Rosenblum's Candy Store
- Mendy's Florist
- Gishkin's Dry Cleaners
- Blum's Barber Shop
- Hand Rolled Cigars
- Civil War Cemetary
- Ritz Bar & Grill
- Boston Rd. Lumber Yard
- Boston Rd. & 181: Last Stop for Subway Trains

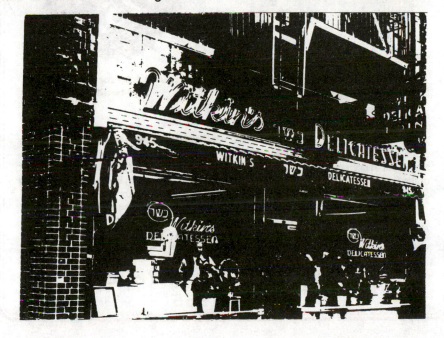

Reminiscing

THE SIGHTS, SOUNDS & SMELLS OF THE BRONX

By Arlene Radansky

Sights

- The sight of the table set for Passover dinner-there was always enough room for "one more" person.

- Walking up 170th Street, past the stores, window shopping.

- The two piece sweater sets - in light pastel colors. Oh, how I wanted them. The store on 170th Street would have them monogrammed for you. And the neckerchief to go with them what a choice to make!

- Cinch belts - how can I describe them - they were about three inches wide, make of some kind of elastic, and hooked in the front. Make for <u>thin</u> girls. I never wore one. Always wished I was thin enough. Girls would wear them with flare skirts with crinolines under the skirts (also only for thin girls - I never wore them). Skirts sometimes had poodles of felt sewn on them near the bottom toward one side. Skirts were down to their white bobby socks.

- Saddle shoes - black and white, or brown and white. You had to step on them and get them dirty as soon as you bought them - that was the style.

- Middy blouses (this was before your time). Once a week, while in elementary school, girls wore middy blouses and skirts and boys wore white shirts, ties, and pants. The girls wore sailor ties, tied in square knots, with the middy blouses.

Sounds

- The trolley on Edward L. Grant Highway (but known in trolley time as Boscobel Avenue). For five cents you could ride the trolley, get a transfer to the train, and then ride another trolley at the other end. ALL FOR THE SAME NICKEL.

- The sound of the two party line telephone. We didn't get a telephone until I was 13 - we were on a waiting list for years - and then it was a two party phone. The other people were always on the phone. It was awful. You also never had privacy, since you didn't know if they were listening in.

- The sound of the "I Cash Clothes" man pushing his cart up the block.

- The sound of the knife grinder as the man sharpened your knife blades.

- The sound of the shoe repair shop when their motors were going 'round.

- The sounds from the P.S. 104 school yard in the afternoons and during the summer, when boys played there until the bell rang, informing that the school gates were about to be closed for the night.

- The sound of kids yelling up to their mothers from the courtyards to drop down money for ice cream.

- The sound of radios heard through open windows playing soap operas.

- The movies on a Saturday afternoon.

Smells

- The smell one summer of the hot tar on the roof when I was around eight and had the measles - mom took me up on the roof for a picnic. We found space between the clothes lines and spread the blanket cover. The tar was gummy, but it was more comfortable than the hot apartment.

- The clean smell of our apartment hallway every week after the superintendent washed the halls. This was not an elevator building. We had to walk up the stairs (I was on the third floor - I always felt lucky I wasn't on the fifth). And heaven help you if you walked on them when they were still wet - I don't know which was worse, the fear of the super or the fear of our mothers after he told them what a crime we performed.

- The smell and excitement of new textbooks the first day of school. I always loved the first day - hated the rest of the term.

- The smell of Orchard Beach as the bus nears it - what a wonderful smell.

- The smell of Shorehaven Beach Club when the tide came in what an awful smell - luckily it only happened once a day

- The smell of ammonia when you walked up the beginning of 170th Street on the way to Taft - there was an ice plant and we would run past the open doors. We never knew how anyone worked in there.

THE AGE OF INNOCENCE IN THE BRONX

by Marion Sternberg Pollack

I grew up in Parkchester, which I thought was the most beautiful spot on earth. I didn't know that people lived in single family dwellings until I went to college. Parkchester was a place where a "Parkie" was a cop who carried only a flash light, where a "quad" was a quadrant which divided Parkchester into four sections, and the "Oval" was a lovely wooded park with a pool of goldfish and art deco fountains spouting water.

As children, we delighted in playing for hours with our pink "Spaldings" including games from "A My Name" to punch ball with the boys. When our Spalding wore out we would walk to the candy store next to the shoemaker, with our friends, for a new one.

Bike riding, potsy, jump rope, mostly "Connie One on Time", and roller skating, (skate key around the neck) were my favorites. In the winter, the snow plows came and created a magical mountain in the parking lot which we slid down and played on all day, until we froze and went upstairs for a break.

At twelve years old we were allowed to take the bus to Pelham Parkway, transfer to the Bronx Zoo bus, and spend the whole day at the zoo with our friends. Later, we took the same bus to Fordham Roller Rink where our skirts had to be "finger tip length" and our skate boxes were bold colored metal.

We branched out to subway travel at fourteen. The subway at 177th Street was elevated. Each day I walked by Zaro's bakery to the train which took me to James Monroe High School.

By age sixteen we had boyfriends and were sophisticated enough to go to Wolman Memorial Ice Skating Rink, the Museum of Modern Art, and 42nd Street. On Saturday night we would dress up in spiked heels, a straight skirt, sweater with a neckerchief and topped it with a "topper". We would board the train to Manhattan. All the couples hung on straps, or leaned on the pole and joked around. Sometimes we would walk from car to car to find the best one. This was no mean feat, as you stepped gingerly with our "spikes" over the windy gap between cars.

The biggest thrill was going to Birdland and Basin Street East where we saw every jazz musician and singer from Louis Armstrong to Count Basie, to Ella Fitzgerald, Thelonius Monk, Duke Ellington, and Dizzie Gelespie. We sat at great, close up tables for a small cover charge and the price of a few drinks. At sixteen, we ordered Canadian Club and gingerale, no questions asked, smoked cigarettes and had a ball.

The subway trip home was truly a joy ride. Late at night the train was empty, we were all "tipsy" and giggly and laughed all the way. We would clear our heads by walking the long stretch from the station. Sometimes we took off our spikes and ran the last few blocks in stockinged feet. We ended up at home on the couch, "necking" We felt very free and grown up.

When I got to James Monroe High School, I discovered a new and scary phenomenon, "Club Rooms". These were basement rooms of two and three family houses rented out to groups of guys who formed clubs. They had names like, Copaca-basement, Club Apollo, and Club 36. Here young men felt powerful, grown up and in charge; unencumbered by parental rules. They were furnished creatively with family discards and occasionally furniture stolen from local apartment building lobbies. The walls were hung with 78 records and there was a bar. The clubrooms were used to hang out in, to drink, and to have sex. Sex, mostly took the form of dancing the "Fish" and the "Grind" to the sound of recordings by black rock and roll singers. It also included necking and petting, couples all sitting together in a darkened room giggling and groping Some couples may have gone "all the way", but I certainly wasn't one of them.

It was all very thrilling, but we never felt unsafe, Even my mother had no qualms about my staying out until one or two a.m. She, of course, did not know everything I did.

When I went off to college "out of town", I left the wonderful, exciting world of the Bronx behind. But it all remains emblazoned in my heart and memory forever. It was the greatest!

ANSWERS TO "WHO AM I?"

Mystery Bronxite #1 is Stanley Kubrick Taft '46

Mystery Bronxite #2 is Gabe Pressman Morris '40

THE "SCHOOLYARD"

By P. Kalman

Growing up in "the Bronx", there were often places in your life that had special significance; places where your life "centered around" One such place was known as the "SchoolYard", such as "see ya at the schoolyard; meet at the schoolyard; goin' to the schoolyard?", etc.

For me, that wonderous place was the school yard of P.S. 86. It was tucked neatly in between Walton H.S. and the Kingsbridge Armory, on Reservoir Avenue (its official address). In addition to being the location of my daily attendance (the school that is), it provided the playground when not "hangin' out" on "the block" or at Joe's Candy Store. But it was much more than just the scene of "great athletic feats" or a place where legends were made. It became the social gathering place for kids who attended or had attended P.S. 86.

I remember well reaching that magical age where I could walk along Jerome Avenue, crossing the "big

street" by myself, to go to the schoolyard. Of course, having reached the schoolyard, one was confronted with a bewildering choice of activities in which to participate. There was always a punchball game going on in the inner courtyard. And if the punchball players where not currently "usin' the field", the stickball players where at it. We had modified the great game of stickball to conform to our particular set of circumstances. What a wonderful game we had devised; we drew boxes on one wall of the U-shaped inner yard; that was the pitching target (home plate as it were); the batter stood in front of it with his bat (the handle of someones mother's broom). The pitcher stood several steps in front of the opposite wall (chalklined pitchers rubber-at many times a simple rock served to draw the line). The fielder positioned himself somewhere in between the two walls, off to either the right or the left of the pitcher, depended upon the batters handedness. Mind you now that both walls of the inner yard where lined by classroom windows. The batter swung at the now famous spaldeen, rocketing the ball off one and or possibly two walls. Of course catching the ball on the fly was an out! The height of the wall the ball contacted determined whether it was a single, double, or triple. Over the roof of the five story structure was a homer. It also ended the game, since the spaldeen was lost. Likewise hammering the ball through a classroom window, an event that invariable drew the ire of all the players, since it usually signalled the arrival of one of the resident school custodial staff in a very unfriendly— mood. The catches made for wonderful acrobatic athleticism that Willie Mays would have marvelled at. It was no small feat catching a speeding, spinning spaldeen off the wall on the fly.

I must admit that I can barely remember anyone powering the ball off one wall with enough velocity to reach the second wall which was probably 60 to

70 feet away. Of course there were the other wonders of that school yard. There was the handball wall, which stood at the end of the concrete softball diamond. There was also a basketball court, which was always in use. Trying to catch a fly ball to the outfield during a softball game inevitably required shouts of "heads up" and the muttering and curses of the basketball players. Then there was the "short" right field fence, (Yankee Stadium had one too) a fence which closed in a dirt field used as a hard-ball field. Lefties were only allowed a double for hitting the ball over the right field fence. And retrieving the ball meant squeezing through a hole cut in the fence for just that purpose.

Of course later in the evening, "the girls" would make their appearance. This led to even greater "feats of athleticism".

This wonderful school yard was truly our Garden of Eden. There was even a small "garden" enclosed by fencing in the right center field outfield. I will never forget the day a somber little "Lighnin' Lou Shapiro (the only kid who could run faster than me) marched into the schoolyard, walked back to the "garden" carrying a little box, climbed the fence (the gate was locked at all times you see) and proceeded to bury his pet parakeet. So again the schoolyard took on another dimension in our lives. This center of our universe lasted from grade one through high school. The regulars came from Reservoir, and Claflin Avenues, from University, Webb and

Continued on page 17

The "Schoolyard"

Continued from page 16

Sedgwick Avenues on the westside; from Jerome Avenue (underneath the El), and Morris Avenue on the eastside.

There were of course the "street rivalries" (the Morris Avenue guys against the Webb or Claflin or Sedgwick Avenue guys); there were the class rivalries as well - the class 6-1 vs 6-7 games.

Even the breakup for Junior High couldn't dim the brilliance and the lure of the schoolyard. The eastside boys went to Creston JSH; the girls to EBB; the westside crowd went the JHS 143, the "new school" that was coed. After a long day at Junior High, which for us eastsiders involved a subway ride (2 stops) or a bus ride along the "Grand Concourse" down to 183rd St. it was always great to meet at the "Schoolyard" and renew old friendships and rivalries; a place to recount the days events. And of course now that we

were "big men", there was the novelty of the girls! They were a constant presence, and slowly but surely that all male macho thing began to slowly be whittled away by their sweet wonderfulness.

Even the "night center" (the gyms were open in the evenings during the winter and thats where we all went to play basketball, ping pong, (for the less athletic), and other indoor games, kept P.S. 86 in the forefront of our lives. And of course there were "dances" Friday nights, which was heavily attended by the girls.

Through high school, the school yard was still a major gathering place. A place where one could demonstrate his new and better athletic skills; a place where one could talk about the "prospects for the weekend"; a place to just "hang out" and hope, and dream, and wonder what the future would be like.

I live in Connecticut now. My sons will never know the joys of hangin' around the school yard, a place they can walk to; a place to prove one's

athletic ability; a place where you can "meet girls"; a place to just be a kid, with only the pressures of the 50's and 60's; a place to talk guy talk; a place to just start a "pick-up game"; they'll never understand about boxball, and spaldeens.

The center of their universe now is the car! Their world is soccer tournaments and organized PAL basketball, and organized baseball, and being driven everywhere.

In one of life's truly ironic twists, I still maintain a small degree of contact with P.S. 86. My sister-in-law is a bi-lingual teacher in the Bronx, at of all places, Public School 86! The yard is a parking lot for the teachers now. No longer do great future Willie Mays' or Michael Jordans or Frank Giffords and Kyle Rotes train there. But somehow I know the "ghosts" of "Brother", and Jimmy, and Stuie, and Marty, and Kenny, Artie, Harlan, Lenny, Bobby, Mickey, Alan, brothers David and Barry, Chester, Lance, Loren, and "Lightnin'" Lou still roam the "Schoolyard".

Scrapbook

"BUTTER!" The days of shortages. Kingsbridge Road, February 16th, 1946
Photo Cortesy of Lawrence J. Parish, M.D.

VIEW FROM THE STOOP

By Arlyne M. Diamond, PH.D.

My mom worked. At the time I thought that fact qualified me for the Cinderella of the Year award, primarily because I had to take care of my sister, and was responsible for doing the laundry, shopping, and cooking. Looking back, I now realize how liberating it was to be without a parent looking over your shoulder all the time.

Because my mom worked (and also because she was clever and trusted me), I had almost unlimited freedom.

The stoop was my family room.

I say "almost" because I couldn't wear lipstick as early as my other friends and because I had one of the earliest curfews in the neighborhood. Other than that, I could come and go as I pleased. I could wander in and out of other neighborhoods. I could entertain any friends I chose - on the stoop - not in the house unless my parents were home. I could get lost in my books, wander over to the Cloisters, spend a day in the Highbridge library, or visit interesting people such as the Monsignor of the Catholic Church (we were Jewish).

The stoop was my family room. It belonged exclusively to me and I could control it. My stoop was a wonderful place, in the middle of Walton Avenue, between Clarke Place and 169th Street. It was mine because only two apartments shared the entrance - and Irene, our next door neighbor, had no children.

When I was younger, the "older boys" sat on our stoop. That was thrilling. I remember so clearly the first time I wore high heels and wanted to make a good impression. I walked out of my apartment, down the very small corridor, and tripped and fell as I started to walk down the stoop steps. So much for being grown up and making a good impression.

When we came into our teens, the stoop was our meeting place. We solved most of the world's problems from the stoop. Our discussions often would start on Friday and end on Sunday. Often one or more of their parents would call my house to remind them to stop at home for a meal and change of clothes.

I remember the years when the bagels and bialys were delivered in our hallway late Saturday night, early Sunday morning around 3:00 A.M. (instead of at the front door of the grocery store across the street). We'd take out a bunch and leave a note with our IOU and continue to sit on the stoop, in the hallway - or later, in my kitchen, munching on the hot fresh breads, talking and talking and talking. I'm not sure which is more wonderful, the smell and taste of those noshes or our camaraderie and conversation. They're entwined in my memory.

We solved most of the world's problems from the stoop.

My best friend - and worst enemy - growing up was Joy. She too lived in a basement apartment. Her private entrance was also on Walton Avenue, but on the other side of Clarke Place. Joy was the Debbie Reynolds of the neighborhood. She was blonde, blue-eyed, very pretty, had a knockout body (which means she developed before the rest of us) and had a sweetness to her that made everyone like her....I liked her...and hated her. I was jealous.

I wanted so badly to be a femme fatale - but it wasn't my fate. I was the pal and confidante of all the boys in the neighborhood. It was to me they came with their problems about dating. I'd listen, and learn a lot about the issues confronting boys growing up. But, I never learned the secret to having bunches of men fall head over heels in love with me.

The Bronx was a place filled with choices. Within easy walking distance from my stoop were four movie theatres: Luxor, Zenith, Loew's 167th St, and one other, whose name I no longer remember.

We had bowling alleys, miniature golf, ice-skating, swimming (standing up because the pool was so crowded) and other forms of entertainment within walking distance. We could even take the subway downtown to museums, art galleries and theatre.

We had Chinese Restaurants and delicatessens everywhere. Otto's Bar & Grill, ostensibly off limits to juveniles, made the best hamburgers in the world. It also was the place in which I learned how awful it is to drink too much.

There was the 167th St. Cafeteria where crowds of kids went to have knishes, coffee and conversation. And, then there was the luncheonette.

Of course, there were many other luncheonettes, including the one on 170th St. and Walton Ave., and the one I worked in, owned by my "cousin" Eddie Rubin, on the corner of Jerome Avenue and Marcy Place. Eddie taught

Continued on page 19

18

VIEW FROM THE STOOP

Continued from page 18

me to make the best egg creams in the neighborhood. But, none hold the memories the one on Elliott Place holds - because that's where I met Sonny.

Before my mom owned her own yarn Shop (Bess' Yarn Shop) on Clarke Place, she worked for Carl's on Elliott Place and Jerome Avenue, just across from the luncheonette. She lunched at the luncheonette and became friendly with the boy who worked in the hardware store part time. That was Sonny. She insisted I meet him. I, of course, refused. How could anyone's mother ever fix them up with anyone interesting....But, one day, I was having lunch with my mother when this tall, handsome boy walked in and I fell in love. Imagine my surprise when I learned he was the guy my mother was trying to have me meet.

Sonny and I became friends. We went to parties in crowds. He came over to my house with his best buddies. We even necked while babysitting. But - we never actually really dated. I loved him madly. I never knew how he felt 'bout me.

Sonny wandered in and out of my life for years.

While I dreamed of Sonny, I hung out with the guys on the stoop. Friday nights we'd all go over to the bowling alley, or go to the movies. When something special played, we'd walk up to the Loew's Paradise .

Then there was another Sonny. Sonny Palladino. He worked in the fish store on Elliott Place and was the best public relations the store could possibly have had. Sonny Palladino was gorgeous. He was one of the best looking boys in the world and Sharon, Gloria, Myrna and I (along with millions of other girls in the Bronx) would find excuses to walk down Elliott Place past the fish store, hoping to catch a glimpse of him. He liked girls. He treated us all well. We each had him escort us to important parties. I don't know if he liked any one of us more than any other - if so, he hid it from us.

But, he was fun and a good dancer and slightly older than the rest of us. We started eating fish regularly in those days. The sacrifices we made for boys.

We lived for boys. They were all that mattered. Of course we filled our time with other things - but only because the "right boy" wasn't around. The boys weren't quite as obsessed about girls as we were about them. It was only later that some of us learned we could enjoy activities - and even our own company - without boys being around.

We roamed the Bronx looking for boys. Favorite places were the Bronx Zoo and Palisades Amusement Park.

The Yankee Stadium was another favorite haunt of ours, especially when we were younger. My friend Sonia (another Sonny) and I would go early on Saturday home games and reserve a bunch of seats in the bleachers by spreading out and playing five hundred rummy. Later, my mother, sister, and a bunch of friends would join us. During those afternoons, while waiting for the games to start the players would be practicing and would often come over to chat with us. Sometimes, when publicity pictures were needed, I'd be selected to stand beside one of the handsome Yankees, to receive a kiss and have my picture taken. Occasionally they'd invite us to have a drink with them after the game. We were young and clean-cut. They were always gentlemen with us. I've remained a loyal Yankee fan through the years, even when they left the Bronx and lost their fame.

The Bronx was a wonderful world of kids in the neighborhood. Scores of us of all sizes and ages played together every day in the streets with a few mothers around supervising the crowd. The choices were unlimited.

For example, when I was in Junior High School (Wade J.H.S.), I ran with three different crowds. I fantasized that, like Herb Philbrick, I led Three Lives. There was the neighborhood crowd clean cut and bright. There was

the gang at Mullaly Park -exciting and slightly bad and there was B'nai Brith Girls - where we polished our halos regularly. I could be part of the activities of each of these groups and yet not belong to any.

There was only one place we could go for privacy. It was a sanctuary. I don't remember anyone ever getting hurt on the roof. It was to the roof we'd go for solitude or very secret conversations.

The Bronx was a mixture of rich and poor, Catholic and Jew, black and white. Because we lived in high rise apartment buildings we were all together. The richer folk just lived in bigger apartments. The diversity of people allowed for a range of ideas and experiences that stimulated and enriched us in ways few other areas in the world have allowed.

We, the kids on the streets of the Bronx, were worldly. We learned to negotiate with each other, to accept our differences, and to respect the opinions of those from vastly different heritages. We also were tuned into the world around us. We talked religion, philosophy, interpersonal relationships and politics endlessly. We talked. We didn't cruise. We rarely drank. We didn't get into trouble. We talked, or, we read plays and poems aloud.

It was a time for exploration of ideas. No subject was taboo. We were a bunch of bright and curious young people who came together to share companionship and our thinking process. Although there was liquor and drugs around us, we didn't indulge. We were heady enough with our fun and intellectual power. We thought we had everything and that the future was ours to mold.

The Bronx, unlike any other place I've ever known, or ever been told about, was a place for diversity of people and ideas. It was a melting pot and a starting place for many people who went on to make something special of their lives.

Classifieds

Missing Persons

MP 466 Where are you: ALAN HELFAND: Lived on Ward Ave. Graduated: James **Monroe** - 1952. Whenever old friends get together your name comes up. All is well, hope you are to. Contact an old friend - Phyllis Fried Hollander, 1 Fountain Lane, Scarsdale, NY 10583. 914-472-3910

MP 467 Irwin Werbausky **Taft** '59 looking old friends - also 161 Street Walton Ave group Bob - Dick - Mel - Stu - David - Joan - Charlie, etc.

MP 468 The President of EJM Entertainment is the son of former Bronx-ites (Cynthia & Don Mirabel - Tiffany Street and Bruckner Boulevard and Fox Street areas) "For the party of your life," call EJM, "The life of the party," at 1-800-EJM-is4u

MP 469 I would like to hear from any members of the graduating class of 1941 **Monroe** HS. To exchange reminisceses of the Bronx of the 30's and 40's. (PS20 graduates, too!)

MP 470 Bernie and Judy (Schlessel) Kamidt **Monroe** '65, living in FL past 24 years - looking for old friends from **Monroe** or Parkchester. During the day Bernie is reachable at 800-227-0986

MP 471 Looking for Danny Smith - **Taft** '55 - Mt. Hope Place - Musician - and Richard Newman - Pittsburgh to Bronx J.H.S. 22 - to Mr. Greenhaus Electric Shop - Please contact Shelly Hechtman

MP 472 Greta Finklestein on Westchester Ave. Married Lenny. I still think of you! Remember me? Thelma Rosen from Hoe Ave. Married Billy at that time. Please let me hear from you. Still have your wedding picture

MP 473 Wileen Schneiderman - Toperosky is looking for old friends from the neighborhood - **Monroe** '64 and JHS 123. Susan Leiterman, Adrienne Miller - where are you?

MP 474 I'd like to hear from - or about - Louis Cohen, **Monroe** 1940

MP 475 Elaine Nemeroff where are you? - Eunice

MP 476 Renée Geller (Levine) **Taft** class June '52 waiting to hear from any of that old gang of mine (and yours!) Please get in touch. I live in the Ft. Lauderdale, FL area

MP 477 Remember the days in Poe Park with the babies (1965 on). If you were one of the group that sat together (sometimes we went to St. James Park). It would be great hearing from you. Pat Kelly

MP 478 Manny Backenroth PS 64 class of '66 and 1455 Townsend Ave till '67 looking for Michael Benghiat his brother Larry or just anyone from the old neighborhood who has time to drop a line and reminisce

MP 479 Eugene Weinstein, PS 66, Herman Ridder and Olinville JHS, **Monroe** HS lived on Longfellow Ave., between Freeman and Jennings. Contact me for old times

MP 481 Sharon Bernstein 1960 looking for Sorority Sisters of **Lambda Alpha Sigma** (LAS), especially Rose Katz. Sharon Bernstein, 399 E. 72nd St. Apt 4K, New York, NY 10021

MP 482 Larry Semegram is looking for Steve Berger, of Parkchester **Columbus** HS year of 1962

MP 483 Looking for former **Monrovians** classes '60 thru '63 or kids that grew up in the neighborhood of JHS 123 or PS 77. Contact Diana Pickover Ditzian 1135 Boynton Ave. - Apt. 2A - Bronx, NY 10472

MP 484 Anybody from **Phi Sigma Chi** 1957 - 1960 **Taft** HS contact Judy Smith Cohen - 516-981-6348

MP 485 Suzanne Engel is interested in locating the following former classmates: Simon Gottlieb and/or Marty Leighold. Or anyone who knows of where they are

MP 486 I am looking for anyone (male or female) that use to live on Weeks Ave between Mt. Eden Ave and 176th Street and went to PS 70 and Wade JHS 117. Am looking for Herman Roth, parents had a walk-in store on Monroe Ave and Mt. Eden Ave.

MP 487 Lou Leveen class of '47. James **Monroe** looking for Stella Brill - **Monroe** '48. Where are you? Write 10649 Riverside Dr. Toluca Lake, CA 91602

MP 488 Monroe - 1947 Louis Leveen is search of Stella Brill (maiden name), class of 1948. Telephone 518-762-1137

MP 489 Steve Goldstein, I grew up in Highbridge 170th St. and played ball all over the Bronx. Enjoyed the friendship of those in many different neighborhoods, whom I would like to hear from. I graduated in 1959

MP 490 Joel Levy - **Clinton** '56 PS 46 '52 - where are the Guys and Gals from Briggs and Valentine Aves. (194th - 196th St) - who went to Schiff Center, 167th St. Hung around Poe Park - (Remember the Hornets) and partied Friday and Saturday nights

MP 491 Lynda Goldstein Rubin Alexanders, **Monroe** '58 Parkchester now residing on LI - coordinator for "Newsdays" Student Briefing page would like to hear from fellow classmates

MP 492 Hello out there. Is there anyone from James **Monroe** High School class of '39? Have we enough for a reunion. Miriam Hammer Willinger wants to know. Write to me at 85 South Salem St., Dover, N.J. 07801

MP 493 Joyce Park - Across from the courthouse - 1965-1970 on Kilmer. Is anyone alive that hung out there? Contact Steve Billig **Taft** '69. Sunning himself in Southern California

MP 494 Lived in the Bronx 28 years, went to PS 4 (Third Ave.) **Roosevelt** '55 - so many happy youthful memories. Love reading your newsletter

MP 495 Mel Citrin, **Columbus** '59, looking for anyone from Pelham Pkwy, PS 105. Remember RKO Pelham, Globe, Smitty's, 15¢ pizza on Lydig Ave., original Bronx Housers, Town & Campus. Love to hear from you: Box 323, West Nyack, NY 10994

MP 496 Taft '59 interested to hear if there has been or will be a reunion - (also JHS 22). Where are you now? Contact Edith Cicchetti-Cardaci

MP 497 Looking for Raymond Berger and Aaron (Arthur) Penier we live on Bryant & Vyse Avenues. Attended James **Monroe**. Were good friends who drifted apart contact Seymour Teitelbaum 914-941-4890

MP 498 Looking for Gus Gross - 1929 **Monroe**

MP 499 Evelyn Krieger, June 1943 - **Taft** High School PS 28 and JHS 117. Would love to hear from old classmates and friends

MP 500 Taft 1950 - Lucille Adlea (Tampa) hoping to find Ed Epstein - (Clinton) after 40 yrs. - Jules is no longer here. Just moved to N. Ft. Myers, FL. Any Taftities in SW FL?

MP 501 Stuart Klipper, **Monroe** '58, was at the South Pole and missed the Big Reunion, 3rd Order Encounters with PS 106, JHS 125, **Monroe** HS, Parkchester, Troop 74, TMR and Washington Sq. tolknik friends would be eagerly welcomed. In Minneapolis at 612-922-1553

MP 502 Mel Citrin looking for Sy Galland, Jack Waxler, Nadine Hurwitz - remember Sunrise Bungalows?

MP 503 Monroe '39 - Looking for Harry Futornik, Harris Feldman, Bob Slavin, Felix Lorio and other members of "Viva L'octet". Also other glee club people for a "singing" reunion.

MP 504 Where are you Myrna Landau of Eastburn Avenue? Last seen in California. Bob would sure like to hear from you. Remember we belong together by Robert & Johnny - Call Bob

MP 505 Desperately seeking Sandra Levinson?? Daughter of Irving & Leah Levinson - mother's maiden name - Cohen. Father died about 50 years ago and that was the last time I saw you - cousin Howard Levinson would love to contact you! 310-205-0257

MP 506 Al Chale would like to hear from old friends from JHS 82 '51, De Witt **Clinton** '54. Lived at 1971 Grand Ave. Call me (516) 484-2502

MP 507 All you guys & gals from our Friday night gatherings on Wheeler Ave. Would love to hear from you. Anyone from PS 93 still around?

MP 508 I graduated **Monroe** in 1955. Anyone in my class, let me hear from you. My name is Joan Scheiwiller Zuk - 7658 Villa Maria, North Syracuse, New York 13212

MP 509 University Ave., Brandt Pl., Nelson Ave. Where are you, Norinne Siegel, Sondra Levy, Sue Feferblum, Marilyn Weinstein and others from the old neighborhood? Shirley Greenberg Kamp - **Taft** HS Jan. '53

MP 510 Muriel Kramer - **Taft** '60, looking for Lynn Levy, **Taft** '60. Still needs help in French. Lew Weinerman - **Monroe** '58. Would like to hear from the "Mop Society" George Auerbach & Danny Katz

MP 511 Did you hang out on Mosholu Parkway near JHS 80 from 1958 to 1962? I am looking for David Reiter, Ira Tepper, Marty Nadler, Marilyn Katz, Barry Roberts or any other members of the Mosholu crowd. Contact Marty Lott

MP 512 Monroe '54 - Bob Demas, Mike Silber, Lenny Cohen, Jim Barski, Billy Herrschaft, Lenny Bader, Mickey Drucker & all others from PS 47 or **Monroe** HS

MP 513 Marilyn Goodman, **Columbus** '44 looking for classmates and Bronx Park Easters - William Prince & Harriet Rosenblatt. Where are you PS 105ers? I'm in Florida 305-947-8405

MP 514 Would like a call from Peter Deitchman MP 161. Call us toll free at: 1-800-722-3122

MP 515 Attention graduates of the Jan 1945 class from Our Lady of Refuge Grammar School for a reunion - if interested, call Joe Ricevuto 718-335-6669 or George Gilmore at 516-737-6212

MP 516 Lyne looking for Sonny- (ArLyne - Red) (Schwartz) Diamond would love to talk with Alexander (Sonny) Waterman. If you know him, please pass this information on, and/or contact ArLyne Diamond, Ph.D., Diamond Associates, 85 Saratoga Ave. #130, Santa Clara, CA 95051. Phone: 408-554-0110 Fax: 408-554-0113

MP 517 Vivian nee Mentz from Far Rockaway & Bob Karow from 164 St & Gerard Ave. - looking for old friend, Jackie, a red head from Finlay Ave. We first met at Laurels Country Club

MP 518 Bob Karow from 164 St. & Gerard Ave. - looking for long time friend Ronnee Deutschman from Walton Ave. Please contact me. Bob Karow, 57-43 NW 24 Ave., Boca Raton, FL 33496

MP 519 Looking for **Taft** 1952 graduates and friends from Nelson Ave. Where are Mona Merems, Dora from across the street Phyllis Hertz (who taught me knitting and mah jongg). Where is Flo Schoenfeld - remember our fuschia and black club jackets? Contact Laura Lustig

MP 520 Class of 1970 for **Taft** HS (graduates from **Forest Hills** High School in 1970) 164 West 174th Street Sedgwick Projects - looking for anyone who hung out in buildings #6 or 7. Great times, great fun, great music! Also former grads from PS 109 or JHS 82. Please contact - share the memories!

MP 533 I'm Lila Freiliche, a free lance copywriter and direct marketing consultant. I lived on Grant Ave. and 164th St. and always felt like I was poor compared to the kids who lived on the Concourse (Iwas 3 blocks East). PS 35 was right across the street. Anyone around from Mrs. Streng's 6th grade class at PS 35? Fern Dorfman, Rochelle Lorber, Karen Kaminsky.

MP 535 Looking for 1947 graduates of **Samuel Gompers Voc. H.S.**, especially those from the Electrical group i.e., Vincent Bertolini, Charles Bauer, Leon Meyerson, Stanley Straus, Robert Schwartzman, Walter Weems and many others. Let's get together and have a reunion!

MP537 Looking for Donald Schwartz and Fred Sussman, June '44. How about those Friday night gatherings at Dolly Stein's. Anyone interested in getting back in touch?

MP 538 El Greco, Monroe 1944, its 50 years-where are you?!

MP 539 Fred Goldberg, Monroe, Jan. '45. Would like to hear from old friends on swimming team. Would like to hear about 50th anniversary party

MP 540 Sheila (Fox) Dimond, would love to hear from Muriel Bergman, Barbara Brecker and Marcia Waldman - where are you? anyone from 1330 Morris Ave?

MP541 Maxine Herzberg Weiner, H. Ritter J.H.S '48, **Roosevelt** '51, looking for Bobbie Bologh, Gladys Brettschneider, Enrico Rivera, Ronnie Pantelo, Harold Salem, Phil Pollack, Norma Pollack or any of the "gang" from Leff's candy store or Crotona Park East.

MP542 Looking for Mel Feldman, graduate of **Columbus** HS. Lived on Fish Ave. (Bx) attended Long Island University 1961. Please contact Doris Weiss Bass: 914-638-3730

MP 543 Looking for Judy (Goldman) Rubin, **Taft** HS, Hunter College, JH 22 and Myrna Kornreich. Please contact Joyce (Grunwald) (Goldstein) Kazan at area code 609-452-7273. I still see Barbara (Bernstein) Wandner.

MP 544 Looking for people from PS 94 (Class '59) & JHS 80 (Class '62) who hung out around Gun Hill Road/DeKalb Avenu & Mosholu Parkway to renew old friendships. Mel Gadd, from 3530 DeKalb, living in Massachusetts. 1-617-492-4557

MP 480 Allan Wolk, Ph.D., J.D. - Attorney and Iris Wolk (Fleischman), CSW - Social Worker, **Monroe** 1954 and 1958, respectively, does DIVORCE MEDIATION to help couples negotiate their separation agreements amicably and inexpensively. Allan also does PROBATE. (914) 639-6700 or (718) 295-4100

Classifieds

MP 521 Monroe Novell is married to Joan Rosenthal Novell; **Monroe** '52, two grown children; daughter in medical school; son a computer programmer. We're looking for a good game of dipple dapple or Ringalevio or corner tag. Living in Washington, DC area

MP 522 I was a physical education teacher at JHS 101, and JHS 123 Bx, June 1956. Graduated NYU 1961. Currently Professor of Physical Ed. - part-time at Rockland Community College

MP 523 Judith Levine Rosen is married to the former Mayor of Miami Beach - I am a licensed Real Estate Broker with an office at 1430 Ocean Drive in the heart of the Art Deco District

MP 524 Sol Schechter - married Anna Peffsen (**Roosevelt** alumni 1949). 43 years, had three sons. Currently credit manager for Pajamas & Robe Co.

MP 525 Joe Prezioso - as you know after teaching & coaching at Dewitt **Clinton** for 38 years retired in 199, I now do volunteer work in the Dewitt "C" Alumni office on Weds. If you are in the neighborhood - come in say hello & you can buy me a cup of coffee. (of course bring oatmeal cookies)

MP 526 Bernie Kamiat - Vice President, Meridian Capital markets. Two great children, David (11) and Jenna (8)

MP 527 Charles Rein, married to Marsha Miller for almost 31 years, 3 children. All 3 children graduated college & working. 2 children married, 2 grandchildren and 1 due in July 94. Postal employee 33 years. Been postmaster - Montgomery, NY (Orange County) since 1979. Been in management since 1970

MP 528 Joseph Green is Director of Internal Audits for Storer Communications Inc. - a TV/Cable company. Corporate headquarters in Miami, FL. Graduated NYU - BS in Accounting 1956, MBA in 1962. Two years in the Army 1952-1954

MP 529 Bernie Berkeley (Berkowitz) **Taft** '51, Principal in an Atlanta Career Management company. Fulfilled a life-long dream of caring for animals by purchasing a Veterinary practice as a graduation gift for his daughter Allison, a recent University of Georgia graduate. Bernie and his wife Jessie will be active in the boarding end of the business. Bernie intends to be a Vet Tech later on

MP 530 Iris Burnham (Kemler) 1960 is the owner-director of a private school in El Paso, Texas and was recently named to the El Paso Woman's Hall of Fame

MP 531 Stuart Kipper, 5044 XerXes Ave., So., Minneapolis, Minn., 55410; Phone: (617)922-1553. **Monroe** '58. Additional data: I am an artist-photographer with a reasonable degree of prominence in my field, eg. I am in the collections of most of the country's major museums, etc.; I have had one-person exhibitions at the Jewish Museum, and the Museum of Modern Art (hometown museums), etc.; I have been the recipient two Guggenheim Foundation Fellowships, etc. I often travel abroad to do my work, usually to polar regions and across oceans and high latitude seas under sail

MP 532 Claire Samuelson Meadow, ESQ. Mrs. Meadow is in the private practice of law, specializing in real property transactions. She is the editor of Title Alert, a newsletter distributed to lawyers in the real estate practice. She is listed in Who's Who in America Women and Who's Who in American Law. She is a 1989 recipient of a Westchester County Woman of Achievement Award and a Certificate of Special Congressional Recognition from Congresswoman Nita M. Lowey for "outstanding" and invaluable service to the community"

MP 545 Maxine Herzberg Weiner, lived in California from 1959 to present. Briefly lived 3 years in Milford Mass. and now back in Calf. B.A. Degree, Deans List, Leadership Awards, 2 children and 2 grandchildren. Would love to hear from former classmates. (805) 495-7295

MP 46? Muriel Bernsein, **Monroe** '46 Semi-Retired as VP of Fosroc-Preco, Chemical Co. on Precast Concrete Industry. Know as "First Lady of Precast". Gave speeches to architechs and Engineers all over the world on Precast Concrete. Violinist-played with Hicksville Symphony and Doctor's Orchestra in NYC. Am "Fellow" of American Concrete Onst. Widow, 2 children: Lawyer and an Artist.

MP 547 Ira Goldberg, Principal, Elizabeth Barrett Browning Middle School 115 (E.B.B) Attended P.S. 46, JHS'79, Dewitt **Clinton**, Hunter College-Bronx, (Lehman College) Pace University.

MP 548 Alan Laskin attended PS 33 and 79 in 1952 where he had Ms. Stella and Mrs. Maxwell for Kindergarten teachers. Just as his mother Mildred had almost 25 years earlier. Alan went on to the University of Rochester and Harvard Business School and now lives in Washington DC.

MP 534 E.B.B Alumni (Elizabeth Barrett Browning) Support you old school, all donations appreciated to support student activities. Ira Goldberg, Principal.
EBB Middle School, 115 Bronx 120 East 184th Street, Bronx, NY 10468 (New location since 1974)

MP 536 Rich Schmeizer. I was in the family business for about 18 years. I moved to California in '88 and started my own sales company which has been very successful. Of course, I never forget the Bronx. I'll never forget the "Crowd" and the corners we hung out on and the places we hung out on Ward Avenue-Rich's Deli or Sid's Candy Store and of course our clubhouse.

MP 549 Mal Eiselman-1961 **Taft** grad , Internist. Cardiologist in Hollywood Florida; Married to Fern Dorfman (1961 **Taft** also) since 1965, 4 children: girls- 24, 21, 16 & 1 boy 13; Ham Radio Operator NC4L

READER REPLIES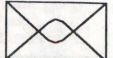

It is vitally important that you fill out the information below. Your input will be essential to the success of this magazine, tailored and inspired by you, the former "Bronxite". We thank you for your participation.

Subscriber? ☐ Yes ☐ No

YOUR NAME _____

ADDRESS _____

CITY _____ STATE _____ ZIP _____ PHONE _____

HIGH SCHOOL ATTENDED _____ YEAR GRADUATED _____

TELL US A LITTLE ABOUT YOURSELF,

(Be sure to include your alma mater, old neighborhood, your best memories about your days in the Bronx, (or anything else you can tell us).

_____
_____
_____

COULD WE SEND A FRIEND A FREE COPY OF BACK IN THE BRONX?

Do you know current or former Bronxites who would like to receive our magazine and reunion information? If you do, we'll be happy to send them a **free** inaugural issue of **Back in THE BRONX**. **Write to Back in The Bronx, Box 141 H, Scarsdale, NY 10583 or call 1-800-7-BRONX 5**

Last	First	Maiden	
Address	City	State	Zip
Phone # ( )	School and year of Graduation		

Last	First	Maiden	
Address	City	State	Zip
Phone # ( )	School and year of Graduation		

Last	First	Maiden	
Address	City	State	Zip
Phone # ( )	School and year of Graduation		

Last	First	Maiden	
Address	City	State	Zip
Phone # ( )	School and year of Graduation		

COME BLOW YOUR OWN HORN DEPARTMENT

Please tell us about yourself (include your name)—about your accomplishments, awards, titles or works in progress. We're interested in hearing about them. List Below.

_____
_____
_____
_____

READER REPLIES

As a subscriber you are entitled to a FREE 40 Word Classified, Missing Persons, Blow Your Own Horn, or Personal Ad. Please write your ad below (if you are not subscribing to our magazine you can still place an ad in the next issue. The cost of an advertisement is 50¢ a word, there is no limit on paid ads).

_____

_____

_____

Is Your Mailing Label Correct?

In order to keep our database current, please correct any errors and place the label and or photocopy with corrections.

Account #	High School	Year Graduated
6817	Roosevelt	1958

SAMPLE
Mary R. Flowers
123 Anystreet Blvd.
Anywhere, USA 12345

Change of Address?

If you're planning a move please attach your label corrected with your new address and the date that you will begin receiving mail at that address. This will insure that you don't miss your next issue of **Back in THE BRONX.**

Ordering Information

A Great Gift Idea! In addition to your own subscription, a subscription to **Back in THE BRONX** makes a great and unique gift. Fill in the form below and we'll process the order in time for our next issue. So, order your subscription NOW, and order one for a friend!

YES, I'd like to order the following items:

QTY.

____ 1Yr. (4 ISSUES) Subscription(s) to Back in THE BRONX $19.95

____ 2Yr. (8 ISSUES) Subscription(s) to Back in THE BRONX* .. $29.95

____ 3Yr. (12 ISSUES) Subscription(s) to Back in THE BRONX* .. $39.95   } *FREE John's Menu

____ 4Yr. (16 ISSUES) Subscription(s) to Back in THE BRONX* .. $49.95

____ The Beautiful Bronx............$25.00 (plus $3.95 S/H) $28.95

____ The Bronx: It Was Only Yesterday..$25.00 (plus $3.95 S/H) $28.95

____ Bronx High School Reunion Weekend Video $29.95

____ SAVE MONEY - BUY 4 FOR JUST $99.00!

____ THE BRONX Tracking Service $9.95

_____ I would like to receive all available back issues and have them applied towards my subscription (To date we have at least 12 back issues available - While They Last!)

TOTAL: $ _____

Please fill out completely and include $3.95 for shipping and handling for books only to: Back in THE BRONX, Box 141H, Scarsdale, NY 10583

Please Print Clearly ☐ New Subscriber ☐ Renewal

Name _____

Malden Name _____

Address _____

City _____

State _____ Zip _____

Phone ( ) _____

High School _____ Year Grad. _____

☐ Visa ☐ Mastercard ☐ Check ☐ Money Order

No. _____ Expiration Date _____

Signature _____

Back in THE BRONX

Box 141 H, Scarsdale, NY 10583
Phone 914-592-1647 • Fax 914-592-4893

ADDRESS CORRECTION REQUESTED

Volume III   Issue IX

Back in THE BRONX

CELEBRATING THE EXPERIENCE OF GROWING UP AND LIVING IN THE BRONX

The Bronx County Historical Society Research Library

Love Bronx Style

By Richard Stetsky

Dating in the 50's for a Jewish guy was akin to picking your way through a mine field. For a while I dated a college mate named Sylvia Patavino who lived near Bruckner Boulevard. Sylvia was smarter than I was, certainly better looking than I had a right to expect, and, needless to say, was not of the Jewish persuasion. I was so afraid to tell my mother that Sylvia was Catholic that I made up a Jewish last name for her and was careful never to allow Sylvia to come close to my neighborhood. I didn't tell my mother (the East Coast distributor of guilt) that I had dated a "shiksa" until I was thirty-five, and then only by telephone. Alas, love was fickle and Sylvia dumped me for a nice Catholic boy, and, in retrospect, did both of us a favor.

To soothe my bruised ego I started dating another. This time the ultimate heresy - she lived in Brooklyn. I don't remember her name or what she looked like, but I do remember my father giving me the business about putting eighty miles on the car every Saturday night. Fearing my driving privileges would be revoked I decided to straighten up and do what all the other guys did - date a Bronx girl.

Joyce lived in the same neighborhood (Hillside), on the same street (Corsa Avenue), and, as a matter of fact, in the next building (3459). She was literally the girl next door. Her only problem was that she lived three floors up. I made it a practice not to date anyone who lived higher than the second floor. Since she was in a four story building, she was only one floor down. I would go "over the roof."

The start of our relationship can be described in one word - crazy. I was racing to catch the bus (the 15A) to get to school. There she was. Keep in mind, we lived in the same neighborhood for years and I'd seen her "around" but I'd never spoken to her. She was two years younger than I was then, (she's much younger than that now) and in a different crowd - and you just DIDN'T. But I was a college man now and I could break the rules with impunity. So we talked during the twenty minute ride to the D

Continued on page 4

The Center of Bronx Social Life

by Charles M. Greenburg, Taft

In the mind of a Bronxite, can there ever be any question as to which institution served as the "epicenter" of social life in the Bronx?

Take a look at how our "home town" was divided. The first geographical division of the Bronx was my "neighborhood". Each of us lived in specific neighborhoods or communities like Highbridge, The Concourse, Mosholu, Kingsbridge, Pelham Parkway, etc.

And then, our neighborhoods were further defined and divided by the core of our social scene -"The Candy Store". Each candy store sold a wide range of products including sodas, ice cream, tobacco products, newspapers and magazines, etc.. But, no matter what else might have been sold, to us it was always, The Candy Store.

To be a Bronx candy Store, it was mandatory there be a front window that opened to the sidewalk. One of life's pleasures was to stand at this window and enjoy an egg cream. Customers would stand to the side of the window and sip or gulp their drink-gulping was most appropriate after a long, hot game of stickball or after an evening's round of "Hit The Penny". (Author's note: If you don't know what

Continued on page 4

Wanna Dance - Pg. 2 • **Poverbs & Sayings** - Pg. 10 • **Yankees of Old** - Pg. 15

From the Editors...

Believe it or not, we are starting our third year of publishing **Back in THE BRONX**. We thank you all for subscribing and encouraging many of your friends to subscribe. Think of all those magazines— Hunting, Fishing, Time, New Yorker, Newsweek, or LA. Thousands devoted to today—the NOW. But only one publication actually celebrates and recounts the things that molded us into what we are today. **Back in THE BRONX**. It's your magazine. Don't lose touch with your second family. So if you're subscription has expired or is about to expire, RENEW today, and while your at it, subscribe for a friend or two. What a great gift for all.

We're happy to tell you that our book about the Bronx in the 40's, 50's and 60's is moving right along. To date, we have interviewed the following celebrities: Dion, Jan Murray, Connie Selleca, David Horowitz, Jerry Vale, and N.Y. State's current Attorney General, G. Oliver Koppell. Just as importantly, we are looking for other Bronxites (not celebrities) who are eager and willing to be interviewed and can contribute in some small way. If you have a story to tell, we want to hear about it. Does, Arthur Avenue, Botanical Gardens, Bathgate Avenue, the Paradise Theatre, Parkchester, Orchard Beach, Wave Hill, or the Grand Concourse conjure memories? Won't you share them with us?

Finally, do you have friends, neighbors, or relatives who might be interested in a free inaugural issue of **Back in THE BRONX**? Please give us their names and addresses and we will be happy to send it to them. If they wish, they may call our toll free number: **1-800-7 BRONX 5.**

Back in the BRONX

A number of the photographs in **Back in the Bronx** are courtesy of and are available from the Bronx Historical Society.

Publishers and Editors:
Stephen M. Samtur   CLINTON '61
Susan H. Samtur   TAFT '62

Contributing Editors:
Barbara Fasciani
Martin Jackson   SCIENCE '58

Art & Production: Ellen Grodjesk
Printed By: Bronx Age Press

Reminiscing
Wanna Dance?

by Marion Sternberg Pollack

Dancing was everything to me in high school. From the raucus dances at the James Monroe gym, to dressing up for sweet sixteen parties, to the synagogue, to house parties, to dimly lit club rooms, the words, "wanna dance?" evoked excitement.

I remember the first actual ballroom dancing lessons I took at Arthur Murray's. I, along with hordes of gawky twelve year-olds were swept around the floor in an upstairs loft on Tremont Avenue by the tall, gorgeous dance instructor. I was lost forever. All I wanted to do was dance.

We danced them all; the foxtrot, cha cha, merengue, samba, mambo, lindy, stroll, even the peabody, polka, charleston, and hora.

In the fifties, when sex was taboo, dancing took its place. Slow dancing was the all time sexiest pass time, while fast dancing left us spent!

I will never forget the night of the Halloween dance at the Young Israel Synagogue.

The air in the steaming gym was electrified. The music pulsed loudly, the hormones racing. All the girls hung on the side, waiting for the bewitching words, "wanna dance?"

The fear, of course, was that the short chubby, sweaty palmed young man, who was already plagued with pattern baldness, would ask us to dance. Naturally, I was his first pick.

After an eternity, blessed relief came as the tune ended. A tall red-haired stranger appeared before me, swooping down out of nowhere repeating the famous words, "wanna dance?". That was it! We danced on into the night.

Every spin, dip, turn, slide between the legs, kick, and throw from the hip was perfect. This was absolute heaven. The hours flew by to Dim, Dim, the Lights, Go Have Your Fun, Earth Angle, White Port and Lemon Juice, and Rock Around the Clock.

Abruptly, the strains of Good Night Sweetheart, and Goodnight Irene blared and everyone grabbed their last dance partner. Singing loudly in unison, we ended with "Don't Forget Whose Taking You Home".

It was sheer magic.

Perhaps we all tend to enhance and glorify the experiences of youth. Maybe they seemed so wonderful because it was all so new. But dancing in the fifties stands out as an all time peak experience to me.

Bronx Honor Roll
Bronxites Who Have Achieved!

BRONX SCIENCE
Stokely Carmichael
Leon Cooper
Bobby Darin
Edggar Doctorow
Sheldon Glashow (Nobel Prize Winner)
Russell Hulse (Nobel Prize Winner)
William Saffire
Melvin Schwartz (Nobel Prize Winner)
Steven Weinberg (Nobel Prize Winner)

CARDINAL HAYS
George Carlin
Rocky Colavito
Kevin Loughery
Regis Philbin

CHRISTOPHER COLUMBUS
Robert Abrams
Anne Bancroft
Geoge Jorgenson

DEWITT CLINTON
Don Adams
nate Archibald
Richard Acedon
James Baldwin
Martin Balsam
David Begelman
James Cann
Paddy Cheyefsky
George Cukor
Acery Fisher
Arthur Gleb
Judd Hirsh
Stubby Kaye
Theodore Kheel
Robert Klein
William Kunstler
Burt Lancaster
Jan Murray
Charles Rangel
Richard Rogers
A.M. Rosenthal
Daniel Schorri
Dolph Schayes
Neil Simon
Larry Storch
Jimmie Walker
Fats Waller
William Zechendorf

EVANDER CHILDS
Red Buttons
James Coco
Carl Reiner

MONROE
Jules Feiffer
John Garfield
Alan Lansburg
Hank Greenburg
Ed Kranepool
Leon Lederman (Nobel Physicist)
Regina Resnick

MORRIS
Angel Cordero
Gabe Pressman
E. Colin Powell

ROOSEVELT
June Allison

TAFT
Sanford Brown
Eydie Gorme
Stanley Kubrick

OTHER NOTABLE FOLKS WITH TIES TO THE BRONX
Joey Adams
Danny Aiello
Alan Alda
Robert Alda Corazon Aquino
Herman Badillo
Lauren Bacall
Ellen Barkin
Mario Biaggi
Joey Bishop
Teresa Brewer
Ralph Bunche
George Burns
Cab Calloway
Diahann Carroll
Samuel Clemens
Cardinal Cooke
Leon Cooper (Nobel Prize Winner)
Avery Corman
Norman Cousins
Don Criqui
Tony Curtis
Vic Damone
Dennis Day
Dion DiMucci
John Foster Dulles
Geraldine Ferraro
F. Scott Fitzgerald
Joe Franklin
Arlene Francis
Connie Francis
Edward J. Flynn
Ruldolph Giuliani
Samuel Gompers

Armand Hammer
Davis Horowitz
George Jessel
Robert Kennedy
Ted Kennedy
Theodore Kheel
Calvin Klein
Edward Koch
Fiorello LaGuardici
Jake LaMotta
Louise Lasser
Ralph Lauren
Rob Leibman
Lee Leonard
Hal Linden
Nita Lowey, Representative
Vince Lombardi
Gary Marshall
Penny Marshall
Glen Miller
Sal Mineo
Gary Morton
Bess Myerson
Gil Noble
Carroll O'Connor
Charles Osgood
Al Pacino
Jack Palance
Flyod Patterson
Joseph Papp
Joe Pesci
Roberta Peters
Edgar Allan Poe
Vincent Price
Charles Nelson Reilly
Rob Reiner
Billy Rose
Jonas Salk
Isabel Sanford
Connie Selleca
Carly Simon
Stanley Simon
Vince Skully
Curtis Sliwa
Wesley Snipes, Jr.
George Steinbrenner
Pat Summerall
Mother Teresa
Arturo Toscanini
Leon Trotsky
Lloyd Ultan
Jerry Vale
Vanessa Williams
Herman Woulk
Rosalyn Yallow (Nobel Prize Winner)

Thanks to Dr. William C. Wallace and the Bronx Society of Science and Letters

Reminiscing

Love, Bronx Style
Continued from page 1

train and then parted. I heard my confident voice say, "I'll call you". There was only one problem. I didn't know her name. Later she told me she didn't know my name either (how was that possible?) and told her family that if some strange guy called with a name they didn't recognize, it was me. Shortly thereafter, I saw her with a guy I knew and I asked him for her name and phone number. He told me and never saw her again.

She was going to Hunter College (scorn) while I was attending C.C.N.Y. (Adspice, Respice, Prospice) but I decided not to hold that against her. She was smarter than I was and better looking than I had a right to expect but she decided not to hold that against me. There are definite advantages in dating a neighborhood girl: she knows all the right candy stores, her parents are not quite as suspicious of you and your gasoline bills are a lot lower. One time she went home from my house and decided to go "over the roof". When she was up on "tar beach" she discovered what I hadn't bothered to tell her; the heavy metal door to her building had no knob and she couldn't get the door open. By the way, the roof was still "tar beach" even though it was covered with two feet of snow and the temperature was ten degrees. She'd always called me when she got home, and when she didn't, I went to investigate. Naturally, I went over the roof. There she was, up to her knees in snow trying to get that stupid door open. Before I had a chance to show her how smart I was she reached down, grabbed the door vent and swung the door open, thus depriving me of my one chance to look brilliant. We've been together for thirty-seven years and I haven't had another chance since.

After all this time we still mention things about the old neighborhood and smile. That's something our kids can't understand. They never had a neighborhood.

We didn't know that we were living the end of an era. It was a great time, it was the Yankees winning every year, it was love, Bronx style. ♥

Continued from page 1

"Hit The Penny" is, or how it is played, this entire article, obviously, is not for you. I advise you to immediately go to the kitchen and make a corned beef sandwich on white with mayo.)

On the other hand, the candy store window was far more than a convenient way to dispense thirst quenchers. It was a neighborhood town hall and social center. The "sippers" were those who tended to linger. They were the ones with the time to catch up on the latest neighborhood gossip.

Pretzels, were one of the mainstays of the candy store. They were traditionally sold in two formats: rod and twist. For some reason, beverages like an

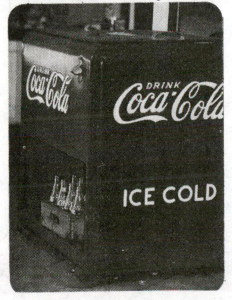

egg cream, were best accompanied by a pretzel rod which was taken, by the customer, from a glass container strategically positioned on the countertop.

Another fixture inside most candy stores was the magazine rack. A large portion of the magazine rack was taken up entirely by comic books, Those were simpler times, and if there was a category of publication which was off limits to the youngsters, it was the horror comics. In any case, most of the comics were quite innocent with superheros helping protect America from the bad guys - both foreign and domestic.

The candy store owner often had a concern with customers reading magazines and comics and not buying them. As a result of this concern there was likely to be a small, hand lettered sign which appropriately reminded readers: "This Is Not a Library".

There were brands of soda which may or may not still exist on the East Coast but which are certainly not known here in California. In those days we enjoyed Cott's (It's Cott to be Good), Hoffman's, Kirsch's, No-Cal, and others.

Many candy stores charged more for a cold soda than a warm one given the fact, I guess, that the owner had to recover the costs of refrigeration,. And using the word "refrigeration" is a bit of a stretch since many stores had a Coca-Cola cooler that chilled water and it was into this murky cold water

Continued on page 6

4

LOST
&FOUND

Reminiscing

Bronx Social Life
Continued from page 4

that the soda bottles were placed. While it did the job most of the time, there were some bottles of soda whose labels slid off into the dark icy waters of the cooler, thus creating the mystery game "name that drink".

Ours was an innocent time. The candy store owner, who more often than not was either named Irv or Izzy or Sol, didn't mess around with drugs, booze or even Playboy. He might have had a fondness for the ponies but his real joy was likely to be a pastrami on rye. He and his spouse kept an eye on the neighborhood and while it may seem ludicrous, her served as the "town sheriff" keeping an eye on comings and goings, good and bad, helping us to grow up.

Our children don't know about "The Candy Store". And they're poorer for it. It was a rich thread that helped to weave the tapestry that we knew long ago, the tapestry that we fondly remember, the tapestry that was our home - the Bronx.

PS 80
by Marvin Rosen

MOSHOLU PARKWAY J. H. S.

New York City schools, numbered, not named.
Brick boxes behind chain link,
Backboards and baselines.

Yet 80 was the Queen.
Columned facade on tree-lined boulevard.
Funneling from ghettos like ink
Into wells on wooden desks.
Cursive letters over slate,
Father George above the flag.

Through fifth story windows I watched
A thousand stickball games until
Snow purified the coarse concrete.
I heard the whistles as classes filed
Through graffiti doors.

Inside tyrants and crones banged heads
While more gentle souls gave stars
As we traced arcs in Penmanship.

Fridays we sat assembled,
White shirts on blue knit ties,
Singing of "Our school upon the parkway
In voices full of glee."

But not of Donald who cursed a teacher
and made her cry.
or Mr. Reich who threw a chisel,
Or crazy Shu who
Prepared my tooth for root canal.
And no one left Miss Martin's class.

I could not skip in kindergarten,
But I skipped 1b
And never caught up socially,
And couldn't do cordwork.

Boys went to shop and girls did cooking,
And we learned Amaryllis and Country Gardens,
And planted a tree on Arbor Day
And sang "Holy, holy, holy,
But I was a "listener."

In eighth I worshipped Arlene
From across the room,
Took her to the prom and gave tea roses
And never dared to speak with her again.

Graduation and my friend Robert signed my album
"May your face never turn the color of this page,"
And I said goodby to our school upon the parkway.

Who Am I?
Can you name this mystery Bronx High School Alumni?

To find out who it is turn to page 14.

Mystery Bronxite

Hey Masse— Whats "The Number"?

by Avery Bruce

Every evening at 5:15 everyone in our house had to be quiet, because dad was "taking THE NUMBERS". Sitting in front of the radio, we all would hear the unmistakable call of the bugle announcing that the horse racing was about to begin. My dad's job was to write down all the win, place, and show amounts of each race—up to the ninth race. Then he would do a particular formula, by adding all the amounts and manipulating other numbers to come up with that evening's NUMBER.

Sometimes, my mother and we three daughters could not stay quiet—like when we heard the name of some of the horses. Like maybe Nellie's Girdle came in third, and Tired and came in last. One by one we would get the giggles....gradually increasing the noise level of our laughter. But then my father would start laughing himself and at the same time yelling at us....because now he "missed THE NUMBER".

Laughter and talking were not the only restrictions when dad took THE NUMBER. If anyone turned on the bathroom's florescent light, the radio would static and you could not hear the announcer, and of course dad would have a fit. So every one tried to make sure not to use the bathroom at that forbidden time.

If dad did "miss THE NUMBER", he would have to get a morning paper for the race results, or maybe call someone else to see if they heard "what came out". When he called to find out what number came out, he would ask the person on the listening end, "How much was the meat? blouse? suit? He was disguising the phrase "What came out?" just in case someone was listening on the phone line. When he found

out THE NUMBER, he would tell my mother. Now there were usually several standard responses to this information:

1. @!#$$%^)*($%^^$#)* (In English)
2. $%%$#@#^$&*(*^&%$$#% (In Italian)
3. That's a lousy NUMBER or That's a Stiff.
4. I used to play that.
5. Joe down the block plays that NUMBER.
6. Didn't you used to play that NUMBER.
7. Sophie dreamt of that NUMBER last week.
8. WE HIT!!!!!!!!!!! For how much????

During the 1940 and 50's you could play THE NUMBER for as little as ten cents or go as high as ten dollars. My dad used to take THE NUMBERS in apartments, stores, and bars, in and around Morris Avenue. Sometimes one or more of us girls got to go with my father on his rounds of collecting.

Once we got out of his car, it seemed as though everybody knew my father. "Hey Masse, how ya doing," I would hear and everyone was happy to see him. Somehow that made me feel important—I felt proud to be with him. Then we would start collecting THE NUMBERS and money from people in the apartment buildings. As soon as we walked through the halls, you could smell delicious aromas, like red peppers being grilled on the gas stoves.

He would knock on the door or on warm days, the door might even be open. Neighbors might be talking in hall. But they were all waiting for Masse to tell them what came out the day before, and you would hear those

same standard responses in different voices. Some people collected money if they hit THE NUMBER. Of course, the money varied according to whether you played straight, or combination. Then they would play THE NUMBER for that day. Sometimes THE NUMBER would be written on a piece of paper with the money wrapped-up inside.

But we couldn't stay long at each place because we had a bunch of collecting to do. It seemed as though my dad knew every male, female and animal in a few blocks of the Bronx. Although playing THE NUMBERS was illegal it seemed pretty innocent and gave these small investors pretty good returns if they hit. Even dad's mother played THE NUMBERS. And of course my father could tell the best stories about judges and priests (the highest of beings) playing THE NUMBERS, so how bad could it be?

THE NUMBER was played on every day except Sundays and possibly Christmas. So my father did a lot of walking and a lot of stair climbing all year round in all kinds of weather. He took very few days off. I cannot recall my dad ever taking a vacation. But he truly loved what he was doing. He enjoyed making people happy and in turn that was what made him happy.

When my dad got older and illness got him down, sometimes one, two or three of us went collecting. We were treated with the utmost respect because we were Masse's daughters.

Now reflecting back, I realized that my father never got past the 6th grade in school. But he was smart enough to make enough money in his lifetime to support his family well and live life abundantly. In their retirement, my parents enjoyed shows, eating out and most of all Atlantic City.

You can now play a number for a dollar—legally in most states, but it just isn't the same anymore. It was much more fun to hear, "Hey Masse, what came out?"

7

Born in the Bronx

By Richard Stetsky

You can take the kid out of the Bronx, but you can't take the Bronx out of the kid. With the exception of sometime in college and the Air Force, I spent the first twenty-eight years of my life in the Bronx. Most of that time was spent figuring a way to get out. I wasn't sure what I wanted in life, but I knew what I didn't want. I didn't want to spend the rest of my life living in a second floor walk-up surrounded by concrete with the next door neighbor so close you could hear him snoring on a quiet summer night when the windows were all wide open.

I was born in the Bronx. My first memories include the night we were huddled in the basement with the rest of the tenants during an air raid drill. The pay washing machines were also in the basement and I remember thinking that if we were bombed, at least we'd all go clean. I remember the day F.D.R. died and I remember VE Day. "The war is over", I was told, "and the world has survived. Everything will be like it used to be." We didn't yet know about Auschwitz or that Harry Truman, with Tojo's help, was about to bring

us into a new age.

I remember P.S. 78 on Needham Avenue and how we had to wear a white shirt and red tie on Fridays for Assembly.

Who remembers what books we had to read in school, but there was the day that some girl slipped me a copy of

> **I spent the first twenty-eight years of my life in the Bronx. Most of that time was spent figuring a way to get out.**

"The Amboy Dukes". That was the book of choice of the guys whose hormones were just beginning to stir. I read every titillating word and wondered how such filth could be printed (although I was very happy it was). If that book were around today it would probably be rated PG and be required reading for every ten year old.

I remember that at that time I was always known as Sally's son. My mother was the piano teacher who taught only classical music and was well known in the neighborhood. I didn't need a name - nobody used it anyway. I was Sally's son and that's all there was to it. So when I entered P.S. 78 I was sure that even Wonder Woman's reputation couldn't follow me there. (If you think Linda Carter was Wonder Woman, you're wrong. Sally Stetsky was.) With head held high and chest stuck way out, I told some old girl student (she must have been at least twelve and probably nearing the end of her useful life) that I was Richard Stetsky. "Oh", she said, "you're Laura's brother". Coises, foiled again. I didn't realize that it would be years before I'd be known by my real name - Joyce's husband and the

father of the twins.

I loved music. Growing up in a house that only listened to music by composers who were dead at least two hundred years presented a problem. I was almost fifteen before I realized that WQXR wasn't the only station on the radio. My sister had long since discovered WNEW with William B., and WHN with Ted Brown and the Redhead, and WMCA and WINS long before they went to an all news format. But I was a late bloomer. My mother had been a concert pianist in Canada before she moved to New York and married my dad. She was bound and determined that I would follow in her footsteps. But when, after several years of piano lessons I was barely able to pick out Chopsticks, she began to get the picture. So the kicking and screaming about leaving the punchball game (I could hit the ball almost three sewers) to come upstairs and practice stopped. I discovered Vic Damone and Eddie Fisher and Perry Como (rock & roll hadn't moved into the white community yet) and things became a bit testy. When I bought my first Elvis record, everything hit the fan. I was ordered to shut the door and keep the volume LOW.

We had a swimming pool in Hillside at the back end of the playground. That one was for the older kids. My mother would never let me go in either pool because she was sure I'd get polio. The Sabin vaccine wasn't around yet. The Salk vaccine hadn't been discovered yet. I complained bitterly that the other mothers let their kids use the pools, but that cut no ice with Wonder Woman.

I remember the National League playoff games in 1951. The Giants had come from thirteen and a half games out of first place at the All Star break to finish the season in a dead heat with the Dodgers. It was a three game playoff and the Giants easily won the first game. In game #2 the Dodgers clobbered the Giants to set up the third and final game. I was a Yankee fan and the Yanks had long since won the American League pennant and were resting up, just

Continued on page 9

8

Born in the Bronx

Continued from page 8

waiting like a lion in the tall grass watching a herd of Impala. I didn't much care who won the playoffs. However, most of my friends were Giant fans, and since I wasn't much of a fighter and couldn't run all that fast, I assured them I was on their side against the hated Dodgers. That is, until I found myself talking to Dodger fans. These guys were crazy. Whatever they said I agreed with. Discretion is the better part of valor. Walking home from school, the grapevine told me the Dodgers were leading in the third game. I reasoned this was better because during the World Series I didn't want to be separated from my friends like Israel from the Gaza Strip. Dissension is dangerous. I walked into the house just as Bobby Thomson was coming to bat and the Dodgers brought in a new pitcher. The first pitch was a strike and I reasoned the Giants were dead. I reasoned wrong. Bobby Thomson sent the second pitch into the left field stands and Ralph Branca into oblivion. I was amazed that an adult like Russ Hodges was screaming like a lunatic, "The Giants win the pennant, the Giants win the pennant". Big deal, the Yankees won the pennant every year and you'd never hear Mel Allen go ballistic. Then again he was a Southerner and much more laid back. You might hear him say, "How about that - the Yankees do it again, and again, and..." The World Series was a foregone conclusion. The Yankees murdered Giants four games to one and I gloated - inwardly.

Then came High School (Evander) and things began to change. My friend's father had a great year in the dress business and they bought a house in New Rochelle. His telephone number had a Scarsdale 3 exchange and he told everyone he lived in Scarsdale. Scarsdale was THE PLACE and he badly needed to live in THE PLACE. I would have gladly settled for New Rochelle. His bedroom was bigger than our entire apartment. I'd drive up to visit him from time to time in my dad's 1950 Buick with the floor under the driver's feet rusted out (so you could drag your feet in case the brakes failed). I wondered how his friends could afford Cadillacs and convertibles. My friends never could. When I got back home to the Bronx my mind had been made up. THIS WAS THE PLACE OUT OF WHICH I MUST GET. Some years later Joyce and I did just that. It was partly due to the strong work ethic, partly due to the driving force of Joyce's personality, but mostly due to a wealthy aunt who loaned us the down payment on a house in Yorktown Heights, in the poor man's part of Westchester County. Then a strange thing happened. Having fought like tigers most of our lives to get out of the Bronx, whenever we were asked where we were from, the answer was invariably, "the Bronx". We've been to most parts of this country and we've met people from all over the world but our answer is always the same. Sometimes we meet people who claim to be from Riverdale or Woodlawn. That usually evokes a smile and I say, "You're from the Bronx, and don't ever forget it."

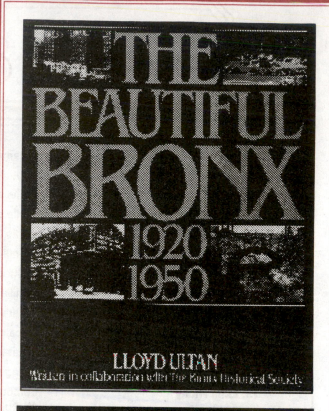

Proverbs & Sayings

1. **Chinese Checkers** — A game played on a board shaped like a star with marbles

2. **Immies** — Another name for marbles

3. **Saddle Shoes** — White and black shoes; worn by both boys and girls

4. **Saddle Stitch** — White stitching down the side of boys pants

5. **Peg Pants** — Pants tapered at the cuffs

6. **Bells/ Bell bottoms** — Pants wide at the bottom

7. **A Black & White Soda** — A Chocolate ice cream soda w/Vanilla ice cream

8. **Creamsicle** — Vanilla ice cream inside orange ice on a stick

9. **Frappe'** — What we called an ice cream sundae in the Bronx

10. **Cockamamy** — Decals of fruit on refrigerators or kitchen cabinets

11. **Oil Cloth** — What we used to call linoleum (Floor covering)

12. **Parlor** — Living Room

13. **Lime Ricky** — Lemon & Lime soda w/a cherry in it served in a tall slim glass

14. **Charlotte Ruses** — Sponge cake in a cylindrical body of cardboard with a lot of whipped cream and as you eat it, you push it up from the bottom

15. **Mello Roll** — Ice cream wrapped in a cylindrical shape that you peeled off the wrapper and pushed in a special mello roll cone

16. **Pitching Pennies** — Throw pennies against the wall; the furthest one thrown wins

17. **Cats Cradle** — A game played with string (Mostly by girls)

18. **Flipping Cards** — 1st person flips 3 or 4 baseball cards; If 2nd person matches his flips, he wins

19. **Slug or Chinese Handball** — Ball must hit ground than wall: King, Queen, Jack were positions

20. **Knock Hockey** — Played on a table in after-school centers

21. **Curb Ball** — Hit the ball off the curb, the four corners were the bases

22. **Iron Tag** — One person was "it", you had to run and touch something metal before you got tagged or you would be" it"

23. **Land** — Draw a square in the dirt, then throw a penknife in the dirt and carve up the land

24. **Statues** — Someone would count and then say freeze and you would make a pose like a statue

25. **Haggies or No Haggies** — When someone bought a box of candy, you would yell haggies and he would have to share with you unless that person had shouted no haggies first

"I Remember", A Daughter's Interview

By Lauren Meiner about her father Howard Meiner

My daughter, Lauren, recently had a creative writing class at the University of Wisconsin. It was a reminiscence, based upon an interview of a parent (me), from my childhood. "I Remember" is the result, in freeform poetry. I would love to share it with our readers, the guys & girls I grew up with during those special times, "Back In THE BRONX."

—Howard Meiner, Taft '57
P.S.   Lauren got an A+!

I Remember

I remember the seasons from my childhood,
Not the one's you may think,
Spring, Summer, Winter, or Fall,
But, the seasons of street games.

No problems with traffic back then,
Especially on Townsend Avenue,
Cars weren't allowed to pass through our street,
When we were playing the games.

I remember *marble* season,
marbles burst out,
The immee, special pretty one, afraid to lose,
Roll our marbles against the curb, into the cigar box,
Done only when you rolled all your marbles.

Day in, day out,
We'd be outside and play,
After school in sunlight,
Until dark at the end of the day.

I remember stickball and punchball seasons,
I was sewerman because I hit 3 sewers on a fly.
Sometimes you'd lose a ball on a fire escape,
To get it, you feared a lady will yell about a broken window.

Spauldeen, were the balls we used to use,
They don't make them like they did before,
Stoopball, or off the point,
Hit the penny when it got too dark.

I remember *slapball* and *baseball* seasons,
Players on each street corner,
Sometimes the ball would go in the sewer,
We fished it out with string and a wire.

Wearing "dungarees,"
black high top sneakers, and Keds,
Tom McCanns or Converse,
Bungalow bars from the Bungy truck,

Mom sent down a dime in a tissue from the window.

Basketball was always a season,
We didn't need equipment, just the schoolyard,
Out until dark, Mom and Dad mad,
Came and drag us home by the ears.

I remember a special season, in colder weather,
We'd go to the movies, double feature,
First to the deli for two hot dogs, French fries and soda,
35 cents to drive the waiter crazy and forget a tip.

In the warmer months, a fun season. If you didn't go to Rockaway or Coney Island,
You'd play *knock hockey* all day,
Or go to Cascades pool on Jerome Ave. and 167th Street.

I remember sleighriding and snowball fight seasons,
Then, there were fewer cars and plows,
Snow stayed for days, lots of fun fights,
Belly whopped to see how many could go *down* on one sled.

One of the most popular games was at school,
Johnny on the Pony,
We played all the time when we were older,
The fattest guy by the tree, we called the "pillow."

I remember Yankee Stadium,
Getting in for 50 cents or less,
Baseball card flipping,
Stupid —then we didn't know what they'd be worth.

My favorite season,
Since it was good for me,
The *yo-yo* season,
I was a Duncan and Cheerio yo-yo champion.

I remember running bases,
Fathers would be the catchers,
Everybody would cheat,
an easy way of tiring them out,
Or you'd do something bad to make them chase you.

These are all special seasons to me,
Like Fall and Spring, Winter, and Summer,
My seasons of street games
I'll always remember.

THE BRONX IN ITS HEYDAY

By Barry Horney

I remember VJ Day. The whole building had a party in our court and flags were flying and everyone was blowing horns.

I remember my fifth birthday (1946). You couldn't get new bicycles or they were very expensive because of the war. My father got me a second hand chain bike, a three wheeler from a bicycle store on Boston Post Road. It was an Olsen and it was fire-engine red. I don't know if the company is still in business and I don't think three wheeler chain bikes are even made anymore.

I remember the Kosher butcher store and the old Jewish lady in the back who would pluck the feathers from the chickens and then burn off the rest and what an awful smell it made.

I remember my mother sending me to the grocery store to buy something and then telling the grocer "my mother said to put it in the book".

I remember going to the grocery store for my mother and the grocer would add up the purchases on the side of a brown bag with a pencil that he kept behind his ear. It always amazed me when I went to the fruit store with my mother that the "uneducated" fruit store guy could figure out the right price so fast when it came to fractions. For example, apples were 29¢ per pound. My mother would buy four apples. The fruit store man would put them on the scale and it would weigh 1 pound and 3/16. He would mark the price right on the bag, where I would have to write down the calculations-he did them right in his head!

I remember delivering orders for the butcher, fruit store, grocery store or the laundry mat and people gave you empty bottles to take to the store and the deposit was your tip.

I remember my mother buying things in bulk, like tub butter or sour pickles from the barrel.

I remember Izzy, the pickle man on Jennings Street.

I remember when buses replaced trolley cars and then they took down the poles and wires and paved over the cobblestone streets. This was in the 1950s.

I remember when there were some public schools in the Bronx, like PS 6, that went from kindergarten to the 8th grade and when you graduated, you went right into High School without going to Junior High School. This changed in 1952.

I remember "take-cover" drills in schools when you had to hide under you desk facing away from the windows with your hands covering your head.

I remember "air-raid" drills when everyone had to get off the streets. This was well into the 1950's.

I remember mother going to Vouge Movie Theater on Tremont Avenue every Wednesday evening to get a free dish. As much as she went, she never got a full set.

I remember Fordham Hospital, especially the emergency room, where as a youngster I got many stitches and broken bones set and still have the scars to prove it.

I remember the Adventurer's Inn just over the borderline of the Bronx in Yonkers. My father would take the family for hot dogs and french fries on Sunday and they also had rides for kids. When I got a little older, there was Rye Beach and of course, the Bronx got its Freedomland.

I remember that every summer after the last day of school, all the boys would get a GI or crew cuts and you didn't get another haircut until just before school started in September.

I remember that there was a radio and phonograph store on Tremont Avenue between Boston Post Road and Bryant Avenue. They also sold GE light bulbs. Whenever my mother sent me to buy a bulb, they would test it in the socket first before they sold it to you. We had a reflector or pole lamp in our living room; it took a 3-way bulb. When you had company, you'd put it

on and it really lit up the room. I remember when I was sick, my mother would take any empty milk bottle to the candy store and bring me back a malted with a raw egg in it (I didn't know about the raw egg until many years later!)

I remember when everyone didn't have a telephone and there was a public telephone on the 3rd floor of our apartment building.

I remember that when I was a kid in the 40s and 50s, Jewish delis were as popular as pizza places today.

I remember hot dogs selling for 12¢ a piece and the delis used to give you mustard in "wax paper cones" that you squeezed out.

I remember that in the 40s grocery stores and supermarkets didn't sell

The Bronx County Historical Society Research Library

ice cream, and candy stores sold only chocolate coated vanilla pops, dixie cups or loose vanilla ice cream. However, Bungalow Bar and Good Humor would come around in the summertime and you could get chocolate malt, maple walnut, pistachio, black raspberry, toasted almond or coconut pops. In the early 50s, Mr. Softee trucks started coming around. They were brightly lighted, had musical chimes, served soft ice cream and made sundaes and shakes.

Continued on Page 14

13

BRONX: IN ITS HEYDAY

Continued from page 13

I remember that in the Fall the jelly apple man came around. He had a push cart, painted orange, with a big copper kettle. There was a fire under the kettle to heat the jelly. He had apples on a stick, marshmallows on a stick and prunes on a stick. He would dip them into the hot jelly. The apples were 5¢ and the marshmallows or prunes were 3¢. He also sold pieces of coconut for 2¢.

I remember the fruit store man had a sheet metal cart with drawers. He would put sweet potatoes in the drawers and make a fire on the bottom with wood from orange crates. A sweet potato was a nickle and he would give it to you in the tissue paper the pears came wrapped in.

I remember that on Halloween we would go trick-or treating in the

The Bronx County Historical Society Research Library

evening, but, after school, the boys would buy "indian chalk" and mark up the girls coats. Sometimes, we would crush the chalk in a nylon stocking until it was like powder and then hit the girls with the stocking. It was as if you hit them with a powder puff.

I remember playing baseball in the PAL (Police Athletic League) and the PAL supplied the bats and balls,

I remember that when my brother, sister and I were younger, my mother would take us to Macy's in Parkchester to get our shoes and back-to-school clothes. They would x-ray your feet to make sure the shoes fit right.

I remember that my mother used to take me to the dairy restaurant

(Knish Store) on Tremont Avenue and Southern Boulevard. I would eat a potato knish and my mother would play the numbers with her bookie Motel (pronounced like Motel the Taylor in Fiddler on the Roof) who hung out there.

I remember getting the Daily News at night (about 7:30 pm) on West Farms Square. It was called the Night Owl Edition and the front pages were pink.

I remember playing stick ball in the street and the cops would take our sticks and ball bats away. If we saw the cops in enough time, someone would yell "Chickie, the cops," and we would throw the bats under a car and stand around pretending we were doing nothing. The cops knew we were playing stickball, but they would just ride by and not bother us. After they had passed, we would retrieve the sticks and start playing again. If we didn't have a stick, we would look in the cellars of buildings and take the Super's broom. We would cut the sticks down by turning them in a sewer. Sometimes we would tape them. If our balls went down the sewer, we would get a wire, make a loop, lay down on our stomachs and fish it up. If we lost the ball or if it split in two, we would chip in and get a new one. But, first, we would have to test them. There was a box of Spaldeens in a glass case in the candy store. We would go behind the counter, take two balls out of the box, hold one in each hand and let them bounce. We did this with all of the balls in the box (about 1 dozen). We would then buy the one that bounced the highest. The candy store guy never seemed to mind, it was just that this is the way one bought a spaldeen. If you wanted to make the ball bounce higher, you'd put it under hot water, but as soon as it cooled down (about 1 minute), it would bounce the same as before.

I remember people used to sit outside in front of their buildings on wooden folding chairs.

I remember that most people who lived in the Bronx and who were not members of beach clubs went to Orchard Beach in the summertime. However, from my neighborhood, one could take a train and then a bus (about 1/2 hour ride) to Tibbetts Brook in Yonkers. You had to pay to get in, but it was clean and there were picnic grounds and you felt like you were in the country. In the late 1950s or early 1960, you had to be a resident of Westchester or they wouldn't let you in. When I was in my late teens, I used to go to Bronx Beach and Pool in Throgs Neck.

I remember that if you really liked a girl and you were thinking of taking her to the movies, the Loews Paradise on 188th Street and Grand Concourse was the place to go. It had stars shining in the ceiling and goldfish in the fountain in the lobby when you came in. It was one of the most beautiful theaters I can remember.

Last, but not least, I remember young women with baby carriages and senior citizens sitting on benches along Southern Boulevard and Bronx Park South without a fear in the world. There was no crime, nobody bothered you... **It was when the Bronx was in its heyday.**

THE YANKEES OF OLD

An important phase of my Bronx experience of some 30 odd years was baseball.

As a Bronxite, I've always lived within walking distance of the Yankee Stadium and as a result I spent many a steamy but exciting Sunday afternoons in the sun drenched bleachers cheering loudly for the Bronx Bombers.

When I arrived at the ballpark, usually a little past noon, with enough money for soda and ice cream and carrying my lunch, the crowd in the stands was sparse but long lines of fans were already filing through the turnstiles.

However, by 2PM, when the first strains of the Star Spangled Banner echoed throughout the park, the stands were pretty well filled with a large crowd.

As the final notes of the National Anthem slowly faded away there was a resounding cheer from the assembled crowd and everyone sat down prepared to enjoy an exciting afternoon of thrilling baseball. By the time the game would be over the sun would be slowly sinking in the west behind the stadium.

As the first batter stepped up to the plate a roar went up from tens of thousands of throats and if the pitcher threw an opening strike the noise was deafening. The park literally shook.

The crowd had come out to watch and enjoy the play of one of baseball's great teams. Many fans and sports writers considered the club as bordering on the invincible. There were many cries throughout the baseball world demanding the break-up of the Yankees. Fortunately, this did not happen. Today no club even comes close to deserving such treatment.

During the era of the murderous Yanks-primarily the thirties and the forties - televised games were still something with a future date, night games were far-off on the distant horizon, the million dollar salary was just a figment of a player's imagination, the designated hitter was unheard of, complete games was something expected from pitchers and baseball was more of a sport than the big business it is today.

In addition to their fantastic ability to win ball games, the Yankee power house included one of the most colorful characters ever to wear a New York uniform. His name was Vernon "Lefty" Gomez, a tall, lanky, left handed pitcher. Every time he appeared on the mound the fans would roar with laughter. Whenever he pitched a game he would stop to watch any airplane that flew over the ball park. His ready wit and pranks made him a great crowd pleaser.

Another great favorite with the fans was first baseman Lou Gehrig. His heart was as great as his batting average. He always found time to stop and sign a fan's autograph book.

The team had an assortment of great ball players capable of the slide, the steal, the bunt, the extra-base hit, the gigantic homerun and the practical joke.

Between 1934 and 1964 the bombers won 22 pennants and 17 world series. It was primarily done under the leadership of Joe McCarthy and Casey Stengel. During that 30 year span, the club gave the fans some of the greatest thrills in baseball and they couldn't ask for anything more.

by Jesse Levine

The Bronx County Historical Society Research Library

Reminiscing

Neighborhood Nostalgia

by Marian O'Neill

Reading your **Back in THE BRONX** magazine brought back my memories of growing up in the Bronx with a torrent of nostalgia and bittersweet memories. My neighborhood was White Plains Road with Parkchester as our backyard - literally. For us kids, tormenting the Parkchester police was part of our daily existence. They had such patience with us as we stood on the concrete line considered White Plains Road - not their domain- na, na,

The Bronx County Historical Society

na, na! On many of our vigilante attacks on the then sterile, prestigious Parkchester, we would attempt to pluck the beautiful tulips so exquisitely maintained for our teachers or mothers; we waded with the goldfish at the Oval after skating at St. Helena's church; rang doorbells; played hide and seek in the network of underground tunnels connecting the complex; rode the elevators; etc. Recently at a funeral I met an old playmate, now well into his forties, who admited to swimming in the watertanks on top of the building. This was even too much for this mini terror to comprehend!

My apartment building was supported by a "lovely" candy story known as Dave's and Mrs. Dave. This is where we slid in on our roller skates and enjoyed our egg creams and rested. He would even let us read comic books in the back until we made the decision which one is the one we wanted to buy. Sometimes after reading all of them,

we decided we didn't like them well enough to purchase. He was such a lovely man, with a sour expression! (resembling Laurel of Laurel and Hardy) always with a derby hat on his head summer or winter! He had two pay phones in his store, and part of his service was to ring the door bells for anyone in the building who had a call. Some service. I also later found out from two fellows in their forties that one would call the other phone and ask for so and so. Mr. Dave would leave the store to summon the person asked for and these "children" would help themselves to cigarettes! Oh, our wicked youth. Seems tame by today's standards, but still shocked me!

Also supporting my "home" was a Chinese laundry. This laundry afforded all the adults the luxury of wooden boxes to sit on in front of the house. First come, first serve. My mother would send us down to reserve her seat in front of the house. We didn't have a stoop, just a courtyard, so these boxes were a luxury. Naturally, we had to make sure there were no "roaches" hiding in this natural habitat. Oh, the perils of a Chinese laundry in the Bronx. We also used the laundry as a good place to hide when playing Hide-go-seek. George, the owner, was very cooperative. George was GEORGE just like DAVE!

My mom and dad transported my sister and I when we were about four and five years of age from our apartment on Longwood Avenue back in 1942. My mother felt all the way back then that the neighborhood was going downhill. What a forecast- since this area is now the burnt out South Bronx. When she found our apartment at 1383 White Plains Road, we thought we were in mini heaven - what with lovely Parkchester and its lovely Macy's, Lerners, and the then prestigious Cornells for children, 5&10, Loews American, the Circle Theater, all within a five to ten minute walk. Even with all this development,

my block afforded us kids three empty "lots" to play in, cops and robbers, cowboys and Indians, sleigh riding in the winter and victory gardens in the summer. I have yet to see suburban kids want their own garden. We worked so hard clearing the "dump" areas just to see a few radishes or flowers come up through the hardened city dirt. What pride we took if the weather and "the block bully" allowed our vegetation to grow.

Needless to say the surrounding territory with its combination of urban and suburban amenities was everything a kid could ask for, but let me not forget to mention the hallway itself. Hallways were marvelous places for social interaction plus refuge for a little kid. A place for the bicycles to be placed under the stairwell, where while in the process of locking up your bike you can see if you had a new admirer by the chalky scrawls on the wall - ET Loves MN... WOW! How embarrassing, but nice! Oh, well, probably next week it would change. I could hardly wait! It was the place you would go to dry out you soaking wet gloves from a snowball fight on the radiator - a way to delay your mom from thawing out the rest of you and end the fun. It was a place to sit on a rainy day waiting for an equally lonely friend for a game of "knuckles" or "Old Maid", while inhaling the ethnic aromas emanating from each apartment. And, let us not forget the "roof", otherwise know as "Tar Beach". Back then we baked till we were deep red and blistered for that desired tanned look. It was a place to picnic, to watch the spectacle of a 4th of July, gaze at the stars with your beau, and a place for mom to hang here laundry - very flexible.

It was an era gone by never to return. Who would have a landlord giving all the kids candy and pennies when he arrived once a month for rent, and who would have a beloved Dave or George - only in the Bronx on White Plains Road.

You Know You're Getting Old... When You Can Remember...

Cracker Jacks came in a red, white and Blue wax box

Stoves had legs

Movie Theaters showed the news (Movie Tone)

Man who came around and took picture on pony and developed right away

Washboards

Lamp Posts were brown

Remember Vaudeville

Bus stop signs were round

Double decker buses on 5th Avenue in N.Y.C.

Movie theaters had ushers and matrons

The Evening Edition of the N.Y. Daily News was pink

Tydol Flying "A" Gasoline

Man came around sharpened knives

Man came around fixed umbrellas

Knickers

Exxon was called Esso

Taxis' had fold up seats

Staten Island Ferry was a nickel

Movie Theaters gave dishes on Wednesday

Ebbetts Field

Dumbwaiters

Milk bottles with wire around them

Milk deliveries by horse & wagon

Wooden cheeseboxes (Breakstone)

Pay toilets

Police cars were black, green and white

Telephone Co. trucks were all olive green

Radios were large pieces of furniture

The Bronx County Historical Society Research Library

Reminiscing

X-ray for shoes

Radio and T.V. had tubes

Made toast on stove, electric toaster didn't pop

Mother gave child Castor Oil to stay healthy

Cars had flat one piece windshields and then two piece windshields

The first cars with automatic transmissions were called Hydromatic

Magnifying glass in front of T.V. set

The Pledge of Allegiance didn't have the words "Under God" in it

There were only 48 states and 48 stars on the flag

Tolls on the TBTA crossings were 25¢

N.Y.C. had newspapers such as:
World Telegraph Sun., Daily Mirror, Herald Tribune, Journal American, Brooklyn Eagle

Mellow Rolls

You could buy hot jelly apples or sweet potatoes from street vendors

Pay phones had individual slots for Nickels, Dimes, Quarter

Telephone had separate mouth piece and ear piece

Take Cover drills in school

Telephone only came in black

Washing machine with wringer on top

Mustard in tubes from the Jewish Deli

Horn and Hardart Automats

Miss Reingold Contest

People kept doors' open and slept on the fire escapes in the summertime

Big white wall tires

Bungalow Bar Ice cream and truck Seltzer man

Subway trains had wicker seats

Dugan's cakes

Silver Cup, Bond and Tip Top White Bread

Crawford and Howard Clothes

Ebbinger and Cushman Bakeries

There were no subway tokens

Savings bank deposits made in school

Called Linoleum "oil cloth"

Pinboys in bowling alleys

Newspapers were tied with wire

Old Gold cigarettes in yellow package

Lucky Strike cigarettes in green package

John's Bargain Store

Lucky Strike cigarettes in green packages

China teapots in Chinese restaurants

Toilets with tank on top with pull chain

Tube testers in drug stores for testing t.v. and radio tubes

George Washington Bridge only had one level

Shefield and Bordon Milk

Painters only used brushes

Pinboys in bowling alleys

Advertisement- Guy kicking sand in skinny guy's face

Football helmets had no face gaurds

Football players used stickem

Penny Gum and Spanish peanut machine in subway

Penny scale with fortune

Elevated train platforms made of wood

3D movies and comic books with glasses

Advertised movies in store windows

Double winged airplane

Taylor Tots Wicker Stroller

Products didn't have "Proof of Purchase" seals

Look Magazine

Popular Mechanics Magazine was small

The National Enquirer was the only "rag" newspaper

Men only got cuts in barber shops

Man who cut your hair was called a barber not a "hair stylist"

One could get a shine in the barber shop

Dancing Old Gold cigarette packs

Classifieds

MP 550 Ruth Gottlieb Fox, **Roosevelt** '55, seeking Madeline Mestman, Ellen Milchin, Carol Hacker, Eugene Sheinfeld, Edward Grossman, Ronald Kovacs, Miriam Sirota, or anyone who remembers me.

MP 551 Hi! Grew up at 1475 Boston Road, Bronx. Went to Herman Ridder, **Morris** HS & PS61. Gee its a shame that "our" area is "gone."

MP 552 Stanley "Sandy" "Zeke" Bergman - would like to hear from old friends - of Highbridge - **DeWitt Clinton** High School - 102nd Engr (C) Battalion - 42nd Div. - N.Y.N.G.

MP 553 Judy Dugon - **Walton** 1961 - JHS22, 1958 would like to find Paula Adler, Lorraine Steiner, Kathy DeBow, Pat Gotocki, Audrey LuBor, Mickey Bentrup, Adele Tribuzio, Sandy Madaro, Iris Goldtaden. Call 718-543-2756.

MP 554 PS104, JHS82, **Taft** '67. Karen Sanders is alive, well, and yearning to hear other Bronx accents and reminisce. I'll respond to all. Andrea Eligs, Judy Hirsh, and all the other guys/gals. Please get in touch with me.

MP 555 Where are you David Kutler of Marcy Place and Lennie Aronowitz of Sheridan Ave.? Your old "Eagles" teammate Harvey Glassman of the Grand Concourse, now of Chicago, is curious. Did you see Mal Z. Lawrence on Broadway?

MP 556 Eugene Berman - **Clinton** '45 - Norma Berman (nee Nelson) - **Walton** H.S. Petes Pool Room, the fountain, Paradise Bowling Alley, Sals Candy Store, Mrs. Kothberg's, Creston Jr. High, EBB, Poe Park. Living Marina DelRay, CA. Call/write us - please.

MP 557 Noonan Plaza, The Crest, The Ogden, The Earl! Anyone out there who use to go to the "CAF", the 167th St. Cafeteria after a Saturday night date? Bernholz's candy store next to the Luxor? Write me, Stuart Reich.

MP 558 Searching for old friend - Burton Forman - PS28, Wade J.H. '67. You last visited me in '69. We shared a lot but never connected. Call or write - Brenda.

MP 559 Rosalie Fish Grumet looking for old friends. Graduated 1952 - **Taft**.

MP 560 Any **Clinton** golfers who played on '52 team around? We played at Van Cortlandt Park Golf course. Mike Meadow was captain, Dave Tobey was coach. Please call Mike (914) 834-6472.

MP 561 I'm Beverly Weinreb - grew up on Buhre Ave. and went to **St. Helenas** and Our Lady of Solace dances. I'm a purchasing agent in the aerospace industry with 3 grown children. Divorced and would welcome hearing from old pals - Zerega Ave. & Buhre Ave. "Golden Guineas" people especially - **Columbus** 1959.

MP 562 Pearl Hershkowitz, 6th grade teacher, P.S.93, 1949-50. One of your students wants to say "thank you."

MP 563 Ronald Singer Grad. **Samuel Gompers** 1949 looking for "Assorted Nuts" members from Grand Ave. & 181st & North St.

MP 564 **Taft** '59 - Rhoda Berk Beame - where are you! Roberta Kosberg - Carol Shapiro - Roy Reingold - Marvin Pomerance. I'm in Miami, Florida.

MP 565 Hoping to find 1971 **Taft** graduates who remember Marcel Rein. Married Sam Birnbaum graduate of **Clinton** 1969. Heard last reunion cancelled due to lack of people. Donna Lax (green & brown jumper), where are you?

MP 566 Hi! Went to PS61 - **Herman Ridder** & **Morris** H.S. Lived on Boston Rd. and Wilins Avenue. Remember the Dover, RKO Chester & Freeman Movie?

MP 567 Popham, Montgomery Andrews, University Avenues, 8 Duchesses looking for 9 more. Where are you - Elaine Riello, Pat Elkin, Renee Epstein, Dotty Altschul, Fran Stein, Elaine Gentile, Rhoda Weisbrot, Sandy etc. Remember the benches, Percy's Poolroom? Please contact Leonore (Kleinberg) Schlissel.

MP 568 Dead End Kids! Davidson?174th, looking for old pals Bobby Horowtiz, Marv Fields, Allen Nadel, etc. Also P.S.104-82 classmates, softballers, ringoleevioers. I'm here in So. Cal. "Chuck" Rapoports.

MP 569 Jerry Oppenberg - **Taft** '59 looking for Mark Wurzel - **Stuyvesant** '60 or '61 co-member of Royaltones Band - also where's stickball guys from Townsend and Mt. Eden Aves.? Call at (201) 227-0264.

MP 570 Len Chasen, **Columbus** '63, Lydig Ave, Pelham Pkwy. Brothers Al and Mike, sister-in-laws Joan (Barish), Barbara (Levine). Len living in St. Croix, VI, 24 years. Anyone out there? Let's hear from you.

MP 571 Allen R. Hirsch, 71 Carolina Dr., New City, NY 10956. (914) 634-1945 - looking for Paul F. Kagan - **Taft** '54.

MP 572 LEHMAN COLLEGE ALUMNI - WHERE ARE YOU? If you're not receiving mail from the College drop by the Alumni Office or call in your correct address. Don't miss the fun! 718-960-8046.

MP 573 Leslie Kaufman looking for Joan Roldan, 1961. Call 516-331-1406.

MP 574 Dr. Richard S. Klein - Psychologist, practicing in N.J. is interested in hearing from anyone from Carroll Place, 1100 Grand Concourse, Sherman Ave., P.S. 90, '50, **Taft** '53, '54, '55.

MP 575 Looking for College Ave. & **Taft** friends: Jerry Ostroff, Barry Rabinowtiz, Mark Wexier, Vinny Rush, Frank Harjo, Jeffrey Miller, Regina Cohen, Norman Cohen, Bruce Weiss, Simon Gerson & anyone else from '50s. Contact Ronald Paul at **Taft** (I'm still there, working.)

MP 576 Frank Schwarz is looking for old friends Tony LoCicero and Sal (Solly) Marchese. Would also like to hear from classmates at PS61, class 6BiA, Jan. 1940. Teacher Mr. Siegel.

MP 577 Wolfson, Ted - Andrews Ave. & 176th St. - Macombs J.H. 1948. **Taft** 1951 - Harriet (Greenbaum) Wolfson - Valentine Ave. & 187th E.B.B. 1952 **Roosevelt** 1955. Now living in California and would like to hear from past friends.

MP 578 Joan Scheiwiller Zuk looking for anyone from Ellis Ave. in the Bronx who lived there in the 40's & 50's. Went to P.S.119 - graduated in 1949, went to P.S. 36 - graduated in 1951, went to **James Monroe** - graduated in 1955. Please contact me (315) 452-0921. Would like to renew old friends.

MP 579 **Columbus** '59 graduates or anyone who remembers the late Susan (Berger) Schack, please contact her sister Judy (Berger) Goldberg, **Columbus** '64. I am writing a book about her and would welcome any reminisces or stories about her. Also, Sarah Weinberg, Ellen Jacobowitz Boxer, Bonnie Hodus, Janice Eder: where are you?

MP 580 **Taft** '57 Barbara Goldman Goichman. Looking for old friends Judy Halpern, Judy Bloom, Golda Liebawitz, Loretta Gutmen and Rennee Lesser. I lived on 175th & Davidson Ave. Remember Fetherbed Lane J.H.S 82, P.S. 104, Park Plaza, Jr. 69'rs Gang, Fordham Road, RollerRink. I was Tuptim in H.S. Play.

MP 581 Stu Mehlworm, **Clinton** '65. Would like to hear from crowd from Gerard Ave. between 165th and 167th street.

MP 582 Mel Kalechstein P.S.48 (1948) Hunt's Point, **Monroe** '52. Currently living in Woodland Hills, CA (818) 347-1463

MP583 Interested in hearing from 1940's & early 1950's "Brady Ave Gang" (Pelham Terrace Apts) & '47 to '51 graduates.

MP 584 PS 93 class of 6/41 Where are you cast of Snow White and 7 Dwarfs (I was Sneezy)?

MP 585 Saul Stolzberg, **Taft**, '53, 167th Street & Walton Ave., Hess Bros. Poolroom, Wade J.H.S. 117. Currently in Private Practice as Marriage, Family and Child Counselor in Southern California. Would love to hear from old friends. 25152 Whitespring, Mission Viejo, CA 92692. 714/457-1141

MP 586 Where are the guys from Hull Ave? Looking for Dennis Tave, Kenny Silverman, Alan King and the rest of the baseball team the Warriors. Call Bernie 212-525-5130

MP 587 Clara Kerpen and Janet (Levy) Hoskowitz are looking for friends from Phelan Place and **Walton** '49 particularly Helene (Bookbinder) Scherer, Beverly (Bubbles) Kaufman, Ruby Wilt, Arlene Saviet, Rose Levitt, Rhoda Schecter. We plan a second reunion in Sept. 1994

MP 588 Dead End Kids! Davidson/174th, looking for old pals-Bobby Horowitz, Marv Fields, Allen Nadel, etc. Also P.S. 104-82 classmates, Soft Ballers, Ringoleevioers. I'm here in So. CA—Chuck Rapoport

MP 589 Donald Rich of 181st and the Grand Concourse would like to contact his old friends: Ronald Rosen, Elliott Rubin and Stanley Ipp, all from Creston Ave. I sincerely hope all is well!

MP 590 Creston JHS '43: Stan Hirsch, Paul Silberman, Theo, Reich, Maurise Nobelman, hope you're all hale & hearty. Call or write: Bob Rothstein, 13 Rutgers Ct., Rancho Mirafe, CA 92270 (619) 324-9888

MP 591 Mark Adler living in Pittsburg PA. Looking for old friend Ira Litzenblatt (**Science** '67) Ira is probably a doctor, last know address was in Manhatten. If he reads this, call Mark Adler at 412-833-6001

MP 592 If you grew up on Walton Ave. between Cameron Place and 182nd St. in the 40's & 50's - PS 79 - **Clinton** '60, contact Jerrey Lebowitz

MP 594 Jesse/Highbridge/Satanic Dukes/ Back of PS 73/Anderson Ave. Carole still with me. So is Alex, Dusty, Wassy, Paul Joseph, Mike Levine. Where are the rest of the Dukes, Jr. Ikes, Lords, even Napoli Boys?

MP 595 Graduates '51, St. Joseph Parochial School on Bathgate Ave. or the crowd from La Fontaine and Tremont, across from Crotona Park, I am living in S.F. Valley, CA. Please call Carol (Gevaerts) Storey (818) 341-2151

MP596 Anyone remember the "Elsmere Tims" from Elsmere Place and Southern Blvd. Contact "Charlie Boy" Weinblad 1954-57

MP 597 Looking for any Bozacudas from University Ave. and Kingsbridge Rd. - Late '40s. Len Reifberg, **Clinton** '49

MP 598 Looking for Julius Altman, **Monroe** H.S., **Fordham** University '57. Contact Nernard Grubstein (504) 443-1378

MP 599 Mu Sigma, where are you? Joe Greif, Science '61, looking for **Science & Taft** grads active in Mu Sigma '59 - '61. Remember the Dungeon! I now practice law in Washington (202) 686-7000

MP 600 Looking for the kids from 815 Hunt's Point Ave. and around. Tessie & Anna Reda, Harvey & Robert Kessler. Gertrude Frankel, Stanley & Carl Gelband, Sheila Fine, Natalie Newman and others. Contact Beryl Levy Shapiro 718-843-4857 or Dorothy Gentry Murray 201-697-4500

MP 601 Mare Minick would like to hear from the 80 Crowd and the Pelham Pkwy Wall Crowd. PS80 '62, JHS 80 '65, **Evander** '68

MP 602 Anyone remember us? Judy Lieberwitz (**Theodore Roosevelt** 6/67) Married 25 years to Robert (Bub) Eisenberg (**Gomphers** '67) Desperately seeking copy of 6/67 T.R. yearbook!

MP 603 Frank Schwarz is looking for: Tony LoCicero, Sal Marchese from Minford Place-Jennings St. Also students from 6B1A P.S. 61. Mr Siegal, Teacher

MP 604 Mark Rosenberg and Steve Rivetti working together in California. **DeWitt Clinton** '70. Looking for football team, ex. Spedalino, Peck, Foster, Kaufman. Also members of **Lehman** Dirty Dozen wrestling team: Billy Davis, Sonny McCarthy.

MP 605 Bob Edelman who lived on 165 St. & University Ave. Went to P.S. 73 & **Clinton** '49. Now lives in Los Angeles. Looking for old friends and neighbors.

MP 606 Stephen Hecht MSW, and Mark Haimain (Colonel, USMC, Retired) would like to hear from the 106 - 125 **Monroe** '58 & Parkchester gang.

MP 607 Muriel (Mitzi) Bernstein-anxious to hear from or about Sidney Schnitzer. Lived on Linford Place, sister Millie. Was Anti Aircraft WWII. Moved to Philadelphia. Still pining after all these years! Call 212-679-1632 (Manhattan)

MP 608 I lived at 1649 Washington Ave. 1936 - 41. I also lived at 1986 Grand Ave. 1942-44. Anybody from those areas and era, please contact especially Albert Rothstein A.K.A. Sonny! **Taft** '44

MP 609 Looking for Alan Lewis, **Monroe** '62, formerly of 1114 Stratford Ave. Where are you now? Please contact Diana Pickover Ditzian, 1135 Boynton Ave., Apt 2A, Bronx, NY 10472. Any other **Monroe** '62 grads out there?

MP 610 Childhood friends who went to P.S. 85 '50, E.B.B., '53. **Walton** '56 with Deana Becker or neighborhood friends from 2392 Valentine Ave. Love to hear how you are. Deana Becker Petty, 2301, West 95th St., Leawood, KS 66206

MP 611 Taft '53: Eve Markman Sputz, Carol A. Sanders, Susan Daffner, Betty A. Cohen Schwartz, Bette Feingold Cohen & others who remember Bobby Kaden, call 708-808-8812(I'll call you back) 37 years later I married Mel Rumstein , my first love and prom date.

MP 612 Violet Fettman Liptscher, **Monroe** '37, went to P.S. 93 Hung around and lived on Wheeler Ave. Looking for Charlotte Groden. Present Address: 6969 Collins Ave., Miami Beach, Fla. 33141

MP 613 Gerry Gafka would like to hear from anyone from Vyse Ave. and 180th St., P.S. 6 graduates '52. Now in North Carolina but would like to hear from old friends.

MP 614 Remember those days in Poe Park with the babies (1956 on). If you were on one the group that sat together (sometimes we went to St. James Park) It would be great hearing from you. Pat Kelly

MP615 I, Madeline Levy Broitman, am looking for Janet Morse my dancer friend from **James Monroe** class of '58. Please contact "Madel" at 516-491-1923

21

Classifieds

MP616 Richard (Richie) Horowitz, **Clinton** '64: Calling all "Bush Street & Creston Ave. Gang" together for a game of punchball. Sandy, Mark, George, Ronnie, Sheldon, David, Martin, Babara B., Barbara W., Inez, Eva & anyone else who remembers those days. Call 713-495-2255

MP617 Wanted PS98 **"Ridder"** grads 1951 (+-) Charlotte St., Seabury Pl., Crotona Pl., Minford Pl. - Also graduated of Minford Pl. Synogoge - Witkins Ave. Synogoge - Kl Synogoge. Lets get together for dinner.

MP618 Martin Greenwald, **DeWitt Clinton**, Jan. 1940 - Looking for Alfred Davis, same school and class.

MP619 I did not go to high school in the Bronx, I attended **PS77** for 8 years (1943-1952) Where is everyone? Irving Morrow, Burt Katz, Arlene Hoodkin, Eda Hymes, Marilyn Toroka, Joan Umberg. Even Philip Kantor. I am Carol Abbe Grimald. Call me, I now own Patsy's Pizzeria in Bklyn: 718-858-4300

MP620 Joan Scheiwiller Zuk looking for anyone from Ellis Ave. who lived there in the 40's & 50's, went to **PS119**, graduated in 1949, went to **PS36**, graduated in '51, went to **James Monroe** '55. Please contact me, I would kile to renew old friendships (315) 452-0921

Come Blow Your Horn

Myron J. Meadow, **DeWitt Clinton** H.S. 1953, Claire S. Meadow, William H. **Taft** H.S. - 1955. Claire and I are practicing lawyers married 32 years, 3 children, (2 girls, 1 boy), I'm on board of Bronx House Jewish Community Center. Mike Meadow.

Graduate **Hunter** College - class of '52. Lived on Hering Ave. - sister of Marilyn ('52) & Bea ('44). Recent Nat'l Board Member of the Union of American Hebrew Congregations - one of the 1st women to be president of a synagogue. Retired bus. women, now a professional volunteer, mother of 3 children & 3 stepchildren & grandma to 4.

The Schlifkin Twins turned 50! Rita & Barbara celebrated their 50th at La Costa Resort, California. They look as beautiful today as they did when you knew them, as does Renee Berson and Bonnie Silverstein, who celebrated with them. Congratulations!

Bernie Gubstein, Licensed Pharmacist in NY, Louisiana and Nicaragua C.A. - Importer of Pharmaceuticals in Nicaragua (Import from Ireland, Italy & Mexico) 4 boys and a girl.

Edward Kippel - **Stuyvestant** HS '59 is a program leader for Consumer Reports Magazine. He is married with 2 children, Diana 5 and Glen 1. His wife is the former Ellen Landau, **Walton** '63.

Roger Ashley, retired Tele-Communications Engineer. Playing "Lotsa" Golf in the Palm Springs area. Have survived L.A. Riots, Fires. Earthquakes & my kids! Yearn for my carefree, poverty ridden youthful friends and days. Life was simpler & tough times make meaningful memories.

The Schlifkin Twins turned 50! Rita & Babara celebrated their 50th at La Costa Resort, California. They look as beautiful today as they did when you knew them, as does Renee Berson and Bonnie Silverstein, who celebrated with them. Congratulations.

READER REPLIES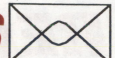

It is vitally important that you fill out the information below. Your input will be essential to the success of this magazine, tailored and inspired by you, the former "Bronxite". We thank you for your participation.

Subscriber? ☐ Yes ☐ No

YOUR NAME _____

ADDRESS _____

CITY _____ STAT E _____ ZIP _____ PHONE _____

HIGH SCHOOL ATTENDED _____ YEAR GRADUATED _____

TELL US A LITTLE ABOUT YOURSELF,
(Be sure to include your alma mater, old neighborhood, your best memories about your days in the Bronx, (or anything else you can tell us).

_____

_____

_____

COULD WE SEND A FRIEND A FREE COPY OF BACK IN THE BRONX?

Do you know current or former Bronxites who would like to receive our magazine and reunion information?
If you do, we'll be happy to send them a **free** inaugural issue of **Back in THE BRONX.**
Write to Back in The Bronx, Box 141 H, Scarsdale, NY 10583 or call 1-800-7-BRONX 5

Last	First	Maiden	
Address	City	State	Zip
Phone # ( )	School and year of Graduation		

Last	First	Maiden	
Address	City	State	Zip
Phone # ( )	School and year of Graduation		

Last	First	Maiden	
Address	City	State	Zip
Phone # ( )	School and year of Graduation		

Last	First	Maiden	
Address	City	State	Zip
Phone # ( )	School and year of Graduation		

COME BLOW YOUR OWN HORN DEPARTMENT

Please tell us about yourself (include your name)—about your accomplishments, awards, titles or works in progress.
We're interested in hearing about them. List Below: _____

_____

_____

_____

_____

READER REPLIES

As a subscriber you are entitled to a **FREE 40 Word Classified, Missing Persons, Blow Your Own Horn, or Personal Ad.** Please write your ad below (if you are not subscribing to our magazine you can still place an ad in the next issue. The cost of an advertisement is 50¢ a word, there is no limit on paid ads).

_____

_____

_____

Is Your Mailing Label Correct?

In order to keep our database current, please correct any errors and place the label and or photocopy with corrections.

Account #	High School	Year Graduated
6817	Roosevelt	1958

Mary R. Flowers
141 Anystreet Blvd.
Anywhere, USA 12345

SAMPLE

Change of Address?

If you're planning a move please attach your label corrected with your new address and the date that you will begin receiving mail at that address. This will insure that you don't miss your next issue of **Back in THE BRONX.**

Ordering Information

YES, I'd like to order the following items:

QTY.

	Item		Price
____	1Yr. (4 ISSUES) Subscription(s) to Back in THE BRONX		$19.95
____	2Yr. (8 ISSUES) Subscription(s) to Back in THE BRONX*	*FREE John's Menu	$29.95
____	3Yr. (12 ISSUES) Subscription(s) to Back in THE BRONX*		$39.95
____	4Yr. (16 ISSUES) Subscription(s) to Back in THE BRONX*		$49.95
____	The Beautiful Bronx...........$25.00 (plus $3.95 S/H)		$28.95
____	The Bronx: It Was Only Yesterday...$25.00 (plus $3.95 S/H)		$28.95
____	Bronx High School Reunion Weekend Video		$29.95
____	SAVE MONEY - BUY 4 FOR JUST $99.00!		
____	THE BRONX Tracking Service		$9.95
____	I would like to receive all available back issues and have them applied towards my subscription *(To date we have at least 12 back issues available - While They Last!)*		

TOTAL: $ _____

Please fill out completely and include $3.95 for shipping and handling for books only to: Back in THE BRONX, Box 141H, Scarsdale, NY 10583

A Great Idea! In addition to your own subscription, a subscription to Back in THE BRONX makes a great and unique gift. Fill in the form below and we'll process the order in time for our next issue. So, order your subscription NOW, and order one for a friend!

Please Print Clearly ☐ New Subscriber ☐ Renewal

Name _____

Maiden Name _____

Address _____

City _____

State _____ Zip _____

Phone (_____) _____

High School _____ Year Grad. _____

☐ Visa ☐ Mastercard ☐ Check ☐ Money Order

No. _____ Expiration Date ____

Signature _____

Back in THE BRONX

Box 141 H, Scarsdale, NY 10583
Phone 914-592-1647 • Fax 914-592-4893

ADDRESS CORRECTION REQUESTED

Volume III   Issue X

Back in THE BRONX

CELEBRATING THE EXPERIENCE OF GROWING UP AND LIVING IN THE BRONX

ALEXANDER'S: Goodbye & Thank You

by Marilyn Greenbaum

Dear Back in THE BRONX,

How wonderful of you to pass on our heritage and remembrance of the greatest of times to Bronxites old and new. I wish you well and hope your efforts of taking us back to the Bronx are fruitful.

Reading an issue of your paper inspired me to write a letter to my mother's old friend, Ruth Farkas, the owner of Alexander's Department Store. She in turn sent my letter to Alexander Farkas who sent a postcard from Australia thanking me for my kindness. He said it made him feel very proud for someone to have such wonderful feelings about their efforts over the years.

My letter was kept in the computer at the Daily News and was to be printed when the store closed, but at the last minute I decided that it was personal and I preferred to send it to the Farkas family instead of having them read it in the newspapers. The store had closed it's doors, the Farkas family has read the letter and my mother, Rose Greenbaum, has passed away. Although, I still feel that my writing is personal, I can think of no one else I would rather share it with than you and your readers.

Yours Truly,

Marilyn Greenbaum

Closing the doors of Alexander's was to me as closing a chamber of my heart.

In 1941, when I was five, I remember my mother paying a nickel for the trolly car ride along University Avenue to Fordham Road, the exclusive Grand Concourse and the dream store where one could buy a variety of needs under one roof, Alexander's. Shopping there was a reward to ladies of any age, as ice cream is to good children. Alexander's was the pride of the Bronx,

second only to the Yankees.

My mother put together wonderful design ideas from the fine selection of clothing and accessories you offered. Rose is 75 now and is always admired for her fine taste in clothing. When she steps out of your store with a new outfit, she looks as though she shopped on Madison Avenue. Her loyalty is one of the reasons you stayed in business all the years.

My whole family were outfitted by your fine store. My Brooklyn aunts were

corseted from your girdle department. Your blankets kept us warm in winter. Your pillows softly raised our heads as we slept. Your soft, irregular sheets smelled so clean, besides, more chose the ones that were nearly perfect. Your towels dried us as we stepped out of our bath and your toys and games brought delight and amused us as we grew up.

When I danced for the soldiers on a make-shift stage of tables at NYU in

Continued on page 4

1

From the Editors...

TAFT '62

CLINTON '61

Magazine editors are always mindful of how readers view their publication. They listen to readers comments and evaluate the quality (and quantity) of stories that are submitted and count the number of referrals and 'gift subscriptions' given. In addition, and from a practical standpoint, they also want to know how well their readers respond to renewal requests.

For many, the previous issue that you received was to be your last. We asked you to make a critical choice regarding a subscription renewal. We were anxious to know how you would respond. Well, the votes are in and counted, and we are happy to report that our renewal effort has been a *tremendous* success. The renewals are still pouring in!

Thank you so much for your vote of confidence. We pledge to continue to make *your* magazine as interesting and enjoyable as it can be. With your steady contribution and with our ever-increasing number of subscribers, the magazine will continue to improve. You have all contributed to its success!

Finally, do you have friends, neighbors, or relatives who might be interested in a free inaugural issue of **Back in THE BRONX?** Please give us their names and addresses and we will be happy to send one to them. If they wish, they may call our toll free number: **1-800-7 BRONX 5.**

Back in THE BRONX

A number of the photographs in **Back in THE BRONX** are courtesy of and are available from the Bronx Historical Society.

Publishers and Editors:
Stephen M. Samtur   CLINTON '61
Susan H. Samtur   TAFT '62

Contributing Editors:
Barbara Fasciani
Martin Jackson   SCIENCE '58

Art & Production: Ellen Grodjesk

Printed By: Bronx Age Press

Reminiscing

Mr. Richard Stetsky
c/o Back in THE BRONX

Dear Richard;

I just read your article in Back in THE Bronx, Love Bronx Style. In a word fantastic! Let me describe my years in the Bronx and you will know why your article really touched me.

Lived at 3218 Corsa Ave. (1/2 Block from Given Ave.) Graduate of P.S. 78 in 1955 First love was a nice Jewish girl named Barbara who I added the vowel "i" to her last name when discussing her with my mother (Francis the other East Coast distributor of guilt).

Since guilt from Frances always worked I started to date "one of your own". A very pretty little girl who looked very American. I first met this American looking girl at the Friday night dances at Holy Rosary Church on Eastchester Road and Gunhill Road. The reason I classified her as American, if you recall, if you couldn't tell if a girl was Italian, Jewish, Irish, or any thing else she was "American Looking". I walked the American home after the dance, notice walked, not eighteen yet and no license to drive. When she told me her phone number, Ollinville 2 ????, I was excited that she wanted to see me again. Then when she told me her last name was DellaPenna, I knew that mom's prayers were, and still to this day, always heard.

Well Linda DellaPenna from Pelham Bay was my girl. She wore my DeWitt Clinton HS senior ring. We went to the senior prom together, limo, Copa Cabana, Staten Island ferry, Orchard Beach the next day. I graduated DWC in 1959 and off to college in Rochester New York in September. What could be better then the summer of 59. Got my license in May. Took dad's car when he didn't take it to work, Linda in the front seat sitting up close, who on God's earth had it better then me.

The parallels continue between you and I Richard. Linda the American looking girl and I were married in 63. We were blessed with two great kids. We lived in Westchester County for ten years, before moving to Massachusetts. The move to Westchester was, as you recall, the move "UP". As you wrote in your article little did we know it was the end of what I now realize was a wonderful place "The Neighborhood".

Remember; Red's Candy Store on the corner of Corsa and Boston Post. My first job at the Loew's Post Road movie, .55¢ an hour. The Melba Theater and Melba Bakery. The synagogue Violet Parks? off of Boston Rd.

So by now you are wondering what in God's name is a Bronx boy doing living in a place called Duxbury Mass. The move started as a business relocation, I then went into my own printing business and the rest as they say is history. This is a great area to raise a family and we have my daughter living close by with her family, which include two wonderful grand daughters. My son as it turns out after traveling the country after college has settled in New York City living on West 72nd street. He lives in a "Neighborhood".

I can't tell you how much I enjoyed "Love Bronx Style". Your words made it possible for Linda and I to relive our Love Bronx Style.

Ed Corvelli Jr.
31 Seabury Point Road
Duxbury Ma. 02332

Bronx Honor Roll
Bronxites Who Have Achieved!

BRONX SCIENCE
Stokely Carmichael
Leon Cooper (Nobel Prize Winner)
Bobby Darren
Edggar Doctorow
Sheldon Glashow (Nobel Prize Winner)
Russell Hulse (Nobel Prize Winner)
William Saffire
Melvin Schwartz (Nobel Prize Winner)
Steven Weinberg (Nobel Prize Winner)
Nita Lowey, Representative

CARDINAL HAYES
George Carlin
Rocky Colavito
Kevin Loughery
Regis Philbin

CHRISTOPHER COLUMBUS
Robert Abrams
Anne Bancroft
Geoge Jorgenson
Alan Landsburg

DEWITT CLINTON
Don Adams
Nate Archibald
Richard Avedon
James Baldwin
David Begelman
James Cann
Paddy Cheyefsky
George Cukor
Avery Fisher
Arthur Gelb
Judd Hirsch
Stubby Kaye
Theodore Kheel
Robert Klein
William Kunstler
Burt Lancaster
Jan Murray
Charles Rangel
Richard Rogers
A.M. Rosenthal
Daniel Shorr
Dolph Schayes
Neil Simon
Larry Storch
Jimmie Walker
Fats Waller
William Zechendorf

EVANDER CHILDS
Red Buttons
James Coco
Carl Reiner

MONROE
Jules Feiffer
John Garfield
Hank Greenburg
Ed Kranepool
Leon Lederman (Nobel Physicist)

MORRIS
Angel Cordero
Gabe Pressman
E. Colin Powell

ROOSEVELT
June Allison

TAFT
Sanford Brown
Eydie Gorme
Stanley Kubrick

OTHER NOTABLE FOLKS WITH TIES TO THE BRONX
Joey Adams
Danny Aiello
Alan Alda
Robert Alda Corazon Aquino
Herman Badillo
Lauren Bacall
Ellen Barkin
Mario Biaggi
Joey Bishop
Bobby Bonilla
Teresa Brewer
Ralph Bunche
George Burns
Cab Calloway
Diahann Carroll
Samuel Clemens
Cardinal Cooke
Avery Corman
Norman Cousins
Don Criqui
Tony Curtis
Vic Damone
Dennis Day
Dion DiMucci
John Foster Dulles
Geraldine Ferraro
F. Scott Fitzgerald
Joe Franklin
Arlene Francis
Connie Francis
Edward J. Flynn
Rudolph Giuliani
Samuel Gompers
Armand Hammer
David Horowitz

George Jessel
Robert Kennedy
Ted Kennedy
Theodore Kheel
Calvin Klein
Edward Koch
Fiorello LaGuardia
Jake LaMotta
Louise Lasser
Ralph Lauren
Ron Leibman
Lee Leonard
Hal Linden
Vince Lombardi
Gary Marshall
Penny Marshall
Willie Mays
Glen Miller
Sal Mineo
Gary Morton
Bess Myerson
Gil Noble
Carroll O'Connor
Charles Osgood
Al Pacino
Jack Palance
Floyd Patterson
Joseph Papp
Joe Pesci
Roberta Peters
Edgar Allan Poe
Vincent Price
Charles Nelson Reilly
Rob Reiner
Billy Rose
Jonas Salk
Isabel Sanford
Connie Selleca
Carly Simon
Stanley Simon
Vince Skully
Curtis Sliwa
Wesley Snipes, Jr.
George Steinbrenner
Pat Summerall
Mother Teresa
Arturo Toscanini
Leon Trotsky
Lloyd Ultan
Jerry Vale
Vanessa Williams
Herman Woulk
Rosalyn Yallow (Nobel Prize Winner)

Reminiscing

Alexander's
Continued from page 1

1944, you provided the white blouse I needed. I'll always remember the black skirt with the 4" thick elastic waistband that seemed to be waiting, in your basement, just for me. It was exactly what I needed for the school play.

Your slippers and shoes helped keep me warm and comfortable, except on the day the girl scouts took me on the 20-mile hike to Alpine, New Jersey. I wore holes right through the new, brown penny-loafers. Can anyone ever forget your refund department? The hours we spent there! You almost always took the merchandise back. You agreed with my mother that the loafers shouldn't have worn out within a week, no matter how much walking one child did.

In the summer of 1950, my family moved clear across the Bronx. I cried for 20 days and nights. My father assured me that at fourteen, I was old enough to take two buses and go back to visit my best friend Tina. I was frightened the first time until I passed your familiar landmark. I suppose that was when I began taking you for granted. I could get off the bus to call home, shop or use your bathroom and I did all of the above many times over the years.

I was invited to the De Witt Clinton Prom in 1952. I wore the lavender, strapless evening dress. On New Year's Eve, he took your black velvet evening coat from my shoulders before giving me my first taste of Moet Chandon. You gave me my first bra, first stockings, first black dress, the one with all the buttons down the front, protection from eager young hands. You gave me the grey dress with the purple and black velvet collar, which I wore that fateful night he came back from the army. I never blamed you that he broke-up with me instead of giving me the engagement ring he'd promised.

My mother recognized you rummaging through a counter at the front of your store one Saturday. We stopped to talk to you and asked what you were doing amongst us ordinary folks. You replied you wanted to know if the customers were happy with the merchandise.

There were tears in your eyes the day you told us you had to put a guard at the door because there had been so many robberies and people weren't the same anymore.

I spent so many hours of my life going through your racks, counters and drawers and your store remained a good source for meeting old friends. The last time I saw Tina was in your basement. I had gained weight and hoped she hadn't seen me as I foolishly hid behind a pole. I wish now I had spoken to her. I'll probably never see her again.

Sandy and I used to meet inside your front door each cold, Friday even-

ing on our way to the Jerome Avenue Ice Rink. She used to joke and say "I leaned on the counter while I was waiting for you and someone bought me for $1.99." She wasn't kidding, the women were rough. Clothing were thrown three feet into the air. You provided us with great entertainment. We laughed and watched the women pushing, shoving and screaming to get their hands on the bargains.

In 1957, I became engaged and wore the pink polka dot with the satin sash. Everyone thought I looked beautiful. I'm sorry I didn't thank you before. I never gave you a second thought.

In 1958, I married and wore your nightgown on my honeymoon. We found statues of Michelangelo and the Three Graces in your gift department. My mother's are still at her home in Florida. We once asked you who chose the beautiful gift items?

You said your mother-in-law travelled all over the world, searching for unusual and inexpensive gifts. Sometimes selling them for less than she paid. She liked to shop, loved the customers and knew that many of them couldn't afford to travel.

We were poor and choice became necessity for shopping at the big A. In 1961 we selected our son's layette from your third floor. By 1970, my five year old daughter was hiding under your racks and having long conversations with the mannequins, calling them by names she made up just as I had thirty years earlier.

In bad times too you were there for us. My dad died in 1968. You found us the appropriate black. When my son's accident didn't afford free time or money, I came to you for comfort, sometimes just to buy a treat, as I did when my husband and I were divorced.

I met my new husband and bought our wedding clothes in your store in 1975. We worked and saved and bought a home in New Jersey.

The surroundings were unfamiliar and crossing the George Washington Bridge was much like the feeling I had moving to the new neighborhood when I was young. Then Knapps beautiful tile mural led me to you and I was at home again.

Each year, when my mother went back to Florida I worried about her and on the way home from the airport I'd spend some time with you. Last year, I met an old friend in the blouse department.

We sat and talked over a cup of coffee for more than two hours at your snack bar. My mother was safely home in Florida before I was.

My dear friend, what will I do with my time when you're gone. I will feel abandoned as the people of Brooklyn did by the Dodgers. Life will never be the same again without you, my surrogate parent. One of my doors closed too. Would it have helped if I had written and thanked you all these years? Perhaps if Rose had been able to shop last year. Should I feel guilty because I shopped at other stores? I do.

4

LOST &FOUND

Track down your old friends, neighbors and lost relatives with
THE BRONX TRACKING SERVICE

Did you ever wonder what some of your high school buddies are doing? Where do they live now?

Well, **Back in THE BRONX TRACKING SERVICE** may be able to help you find them and maybe even discover long lost relatives you never know you had. Find the phone numbers and addresses of 70 to 100 million people from all across the U.S. You can find that special old friend who you haven't heard from in years (decades). If you are like most people, as you get older you wonder more about those special friends you've lost touch with over the years. Wouldn't it be great to give them a call to swap stories and reminisce? If you are interested in tracing your genealogy, looking for lost parents, or children, we can help.

Simply complete the application below—
We do the rest.

THE BRONX TRACKING SERVICE
APPLICATION

Name (Print or Type)

Last   First   Middle

Maiden Name

Address (Last know address or general location)

City   State   Zip

Approximate date living at above address

High School   Year graduated

Age

Requested By:

Address:

City   State   Zip

Phone:

THE BRONX TRACKING SERVICE
APPLICATION

Name (Print or Type)

Last   First   Middle

Maiden Name

Address (Last know address or general location)

City   State   Zip

Approximate date living at above address

High School   Year graduated

Age

Requested By:

Address:

City   State   Zip

Phone:

I have enclosed a payment of $9.95 for each person that I am looking to trace. I understand that I will receive a list of name and addresses and phone numbers for each person from a database of over 70 million names throughout the United States. I further understand that I will have to search through theses names and determine the approximate name that matches the one(s) you are trying to trace.

5

The Sedgwick Projects

By Harriette J. Schwartz

In 1955 when I was five and my sister Deena was three, my parents decided that Simpson Street near Southern Boulevard was indeed "changing" and it was time for us to move. No more Brody's Candystore (a place I can now just barely remember.) Gone would be the fire escape sitting and the coffee klatching on the stoop with all the old ladies. Yes, we were leaving the South Bronx behind. I couldn't truly say I would miss it because being at that young age in that era, awareness was not yet an asset for me.

My parents chose to take a big step-way over to the West Bronx!!! Oh yes, they had tenement style living over there, but we were headed for something new - a middle income housing project. In those days, project living was an avant garde experience. The buildings were erected to almost skyscraper heights - 14 stories tall! My parents selected the Sedgwick Housing Project but in the years we lived there (1955 through 1969) everyone simply referred to it as living in "The Projects".

It was built on hilly land at 174th Street and University Avenue, just where University met Featherbed Lane (which supposedly got it's name because one night during the Revolutionary War, women put down their featherbeds so that cannons and weaponry of the time could be rolled more silently over the cobblestone grounds to surprise and win a battle with the English). We also had the Old George Washington bridge on our South side, across which my girlfriends and I would take walks to shop and eat lunch in the Highbridge sections of Manhattan when I got older.

I am told that the site was formerly the home of a convent, some of the old stone walls from which were left standing and still partially bordered our rather large enclave. Each building unit was a large, pink brick rectangle with casement-style windows and no fire escapes (so very modern!) To my astonishment our apartment had no dumbwaiter inside but each floor had an incinerator instead. In those days, superstition still had not gotten the better of the Bronx borough and we actually lived on the thirteenth floor (apt. 13G).

What was really great was that you could look out of your bedroom window and see who was out in the playground. Even better was that I could see into my best friend's apartment on the 6th floor of the opposite building and find out if she was home. Many times, we would just talk (more like yell) from window to window and friend to friend. You could be making plans and then meeting in the playground to jump some double-dutch rope, roller skate or whatever games we chose to spend our time playing. Mothers could keep tabs on their kids, simply by watching them through the window. If dinner was ready, they'd call them to come upstairs and eat. In our case, when Esta, my youngest sister, got a little older my mother would have me and Deena keep her out in the playground in her stroller, while she watched all three of us from upstairs.

There were some super summer nights as a teenager, hanging out in the playground with all the project kids and some from surrounding areas, listening to WABC-AM and Cousin Brucie. Maybe I'd take a quick walk down to the corner of University Avenue for either chocolate Italian ices, or a slice and a coke at Tony's Pizza (for a quarter total) with Arlene, my

Sedgwick then...

...and now

Continued on next page

Sedgwick
Continued from page 6

best girlfriend. I can also vividly remember my total embarrassment at
my mom or dad calling down from the
window at 10pm that it was time to
come upstairs!!

My building address was 1551 University Avenue. This particular
Sedgwick unit had another very special couple of items in it—a public
library and a community center in the
basement. I never really appreciated
the convenience of the library while
we lived there, except as a place to go
and attempt homework but mostly
using it as a hangout with the girls. I
can honestly say that I was never late
returning books! Now that I have an 8
year old, I dearly wish we still had such
library access, especially when she
has a book report due! The community center had every board game
under the sun, as well as bumper pool
tables (my favorite), ping-pong, knock
hockey, et al. It also offered arts and
crafts classes, laniards (box and barrell

stitches in all colors) ceramics and
the like. Everyday after school, one of
us would bring our records (45's of
course) and dance our hearts out for
a couple of hours to the phonograph
the center had.

Sedgwick Projects was a neighborhood unto itself, almost alive with
the pulse of it's people all of whom
cared for (and knew practically everything about) each other for those few

years in time.

I can still hear the laughter and
even smell those punks burning on the
Fourth of July, or in my mind see my
friends and me hanging out in the
playground with our transistor radios
at night. I can do so because they are
a part of the fabric of my soul which
despite the changes to the terrain on
which they occurred will forever remain the same.

BRONX Film Trivia

1. What movie did this academy award actor play in?
2. When did he win the academy award?
3. What was his occupation in the movie?

For answers
see page 17

The Grand Concourse Remembered

By Marla Daru

> *The following pertains mainly to the area of 149th Street to 167th Street from about 3rd Avenue to Jerome Avenue.*

The Concourse Plaza Hotel.

The Jerome Cafeteria on 161st St. & Jerome Ave across from the Yankee Stadium.

Nedicks on the corner of 161st Street & Jerome Ave.

The little cigar store on the corner of 161st St. & Jerome Ave surrounded by the Jerome Cafeteria.

The Earl Dress Shop on 161st St.

The Earl Movie Theatre on 161st St.

Bartons Candy Store on 161st St.

G&R Bake Shop on 161st St. (The best hard rolls.)

Bohacks Supermarket on 161st St.

The Fruit and Vegetable Stand on 161st St.

The Newspaper and Stationary store on 161st St.

The Hebrew National Deli on the corner of 161st St. & Walton Ave. across from the Court House.

The Shoemaker shop on 161st St. between Walton & Gerard Aves.

The Roxy/Lori Bakery on the corner of 161st & Gerard.

Addie Vailins Ice Cream Shop on 161st.

The Grand Union on Gerard Avenue off 161st St.

Grand Union gave Triple S Blue Stamps

Monday Night Bingo at the Concourse Plaza Hotel.

Sam's Beauty Parlor on 161st St.

Walking down to Morris Ave. off 161st St. to rent bicycles for 25¢ an hour.

Going to the Italian grocery on Morris Ave. off 161st St. & buying a combination hero for 25¢

The A&P on Morris Ave. & 163rd St.

PS 35 on 163rd & Morris.

St. Angeles Parochial School on 163rd & Morris.

The Shoemaker on 163rd & Sheridan Avenue.

The Fleetwood Theatre on Morris Ave.

Hearns Department Store on 149th & Third.

Alexander's on 152nd & Third Ave.

The Bridal Shop on Third Avenue near 149th St.

The Post office on 149th & Grand Concourse

Going down to the Bronx Terminal Market to buy a live Christmas Tree every year.

Sleigh riding at Franz Sigel Park by the ball field in the winter.

All the ladies dressed up on the Jewish Holidays and sitting in Joyce Kilmer Park on the Concourse.

The YWHA on 166th St. & Grand Concourse.

The Convent on the Concourse at 165th St.

JHS 22 (Jordan L. Mott) on 167th St. & Morris Ave.

The Loews 167th St. Theatre on 167th St.

The 167th St. Cafeteria.

Stadium Lanes (on 158th & Jerome Ave.

Yankee Lanes on Jerome Ave. off 161st.

The Fordham Skating Palace

The Kent Theatre on 167th Street.

Grand Concourse

Continued from page 8

Poe Park

Alexander's on the Concourse at Fordham Road.

Krums Candy Kitchen on the Concourse.

Sachs Quality Furniture Store. (Jingle: Melrose 5-5-3 hundred)

Robert Hall on the Concourse.

Jahn's Ice Cream Parlor

Stella D'Oro Restaurant on 232nd & Broadway.

Feldman's Drug Store on 156th & the Concourse.

The Kosher butcher shop next to the Drug Store.

The Deli next to the Butcher Shop on 156th St.

The Taxi stand in back of my building on Sheridan Ave between 156th & 158th Sts.

The Train Yard on Sheridan to Morris between 149th & 161Sts., before the butchers union built a coop there.

Fleischman Labs on the corner of 158th & the Concourse before it was torn down and 800 Grand Concourse apartment building was built.

840 Grand Concourse - *the apartment building took up the whole block.*

Saturday night dances at Immaculate Conception

The Dutch Reformed Church at 162nd St.

Graduation at the 167th St from JHS 22. June 1958.

Graduation from Walton H.S. at Carnegie Hall, June 1961.

The Bronx before the Cross Bronx Expressway was opened.

Before the Throggs Neck Bridge was opened.

Taking the Ogden Avenue bus to the GW Bridge to go to Palisades Amusement Park.

Ogden Lanes Bowling Alley on Ogden Avenue.

Cardinal Hayes High School at 152nd St.

The $1.00 Car Wash on the Concourse at 152nd St.

Fleet Hollow Swim and Tennis Club on Gerard Ave. at about 153rd St. *($1 per day to swim)*

Swimming at McCombs Dam Swing Park in the Summer (162nd or 163rd at Jerome Ave.) *It was more a wading pool.*

Taking sun baths on "Tar Beach"

Hanging the laundry out to dry on the roof

Cedars of Lebanon Hospital on the Concourse at Mt. Eden Avenue.

H&H Photographers on the Concourse about 184th St.

Tardi's Caterers *(Opened in 1964)* on the New England Thruway in the Bronx.

The Third Avenue EL.

Freedomland in the Bronx.

When telephone exchanges had names instead of numbers *(Ex. Tremont, Melrose, Motthaven etc.)*

1326 Grand Concourse

Standing in line at elementary school waiting to go into the school.

Day Camp at PS 90 in the Bronx. Mr. Louis Schwartz was the principal.

Being in the Music Class in JHS 22.

Annual (or semi-annual) Bazaars at the Concourse Plaza Hotel. *(They had everything.)*

No Snow Days

"Senior Red Letter Day" at Walton H.S. All the seniors wore red costumes to school on this day.

When it cost 25¢ for children to see a double feature movie.

When bowling costs 50¢ a game.

Playing jump rope and "Potsie."

The A&P that was built on Sheridan Avenue between 156th & 153rd St.

You had really "arrived" when you dated a guy who had a car.

PARKCHESTER
The Grand Old Neighborhood

By Hank de Cillia, St. Raymond's Grammar School '57

North Ballfield before it was paved (circa 1950)

I'll never forget picking up the Sunday New York Times in 1980 and reading an article in the real estate section about Parkchester. My wife Pat and I, both born and raised there, had been living in Massachusetts since the late sixties and lost contact with the place. The Times article began "Located on 110 acres in the southeast Bronx, Parkchester is..." I couldn't believe my eyes! Only 110 acres? In 1972, together with two other couples (also from Parkchester) we almost purchased a 135 acre parcel of land in western Massachusetts to build homes on 'collectively' (You remember those days, don't you?) It immediately dawned on me that just 3 families might have lived on a piece of property in Massachusetts that was 25 acres larger than 12,500 families lived on in the Bronx! Parkchester

Yes, that's right. When it was completed in 1941 by the Metropolitan Life Insurance Company, Parkchester had *12,000* apartments, making it the largest housing 'project' in the world at the time! Just as amazingly, over *52,000* people lived in those apartments, during its peak population period from the late Forties to the mid sixties.

I lived in Parkchester from birth in 1944 (actually, Pat and I didn't get there until we were a week old, since we were born two days apart in nearby Westchester Square Hospital) until 1966 when she and I got married in St. Raymond's Church and immediately moved to Westcheser County (that other 'chester up north...no relation or similarity).

My parents, Kay and Harry, moved into Parkchester in 1941 from Isham Street in northern Manhattan. My mother was then a clerk at Met Life, which apparently helped them get in. I'm told it was very difficult to get 'accepted' for Parkchester...you had to fill out long applications and even provide photos! (Unfortunately, this latter requirement enabled them to keep people of color out..a common housing practice at the time, and the only blemish on Parkchester's record that I can remember.)

Kay and Harry were overjoyed to get into Parkchester, but very anxious about their standing in the new community. For example, after my father died, my mother told me this story. At the time they moved in, Harry was working in the South Bronx as a steel fabricator... not a white or even a blue collar job. To get to work, he would walk from our apartment over to Hugh Grant Circle and take the subway. He was so concerned about 'fitting in' that he bought two suits and a briefcase just to wear to work. Every day, he would put on his suit, put his lunch in his briefcase and set out for the subway station with the other 'executives' heading for work. Upon arriving at the shop, he would change into his real work clothes. Mom told me he did this for over a year, until he realized they wouldn't get thrown out for dressing inappropriately.

Parkchester
was literally a
"town within a city"

Parkchester was so large it took almost four years to complete. It was literally a "town within a city", as described in a New York Times Magazine feature article in 1941. In describing the place back then, the author John Stanton noted, "Parkchester has a staff of 500 employees. The staff includes gardeners to take care of the parks and recreation directors to coach teams that flourish on its playfields...

Continued next page

10

Parkchester

Continued from page 12

Parkchester has its own police department and a large staff of 'servicemen' to keep everything working.

Every Parkchester playground had a 'Rec Office' in the nearest apartment building on the ground floor, where 'Rec Teachers' supervised all activities. Most parents would let their kids go down to the playground after school or for the whole day on weekends and in the summer, coming home only for lunch and dinner. We also had our own movie theatre, the Loew's American, inside Parkchester and three others on the perimeter...the Palace on Unionport Road, the Circle on Hugh Grant Circle and the RKO Castle Hill. There was so much to do that most kids don't remember ever leaving Parkchester until they went to High School!

Parkchester had its own stores of all types...drug stores, deli's, newspaper stores, supermarkets and even three bars: the Manor House, the Park House and the Chester House. The biggest store was Macy's, where my mother worked in Toys, Records and Sporting Goods for 15 years after she left Met Life. My collection of 45's was the envy of all my friends, and whenever I wanted some game or sporting item, my mother would have it "put in the window" and then buy it at a marked down price as a display item the next

day. Talk about spoiled.

Here's a unique Parkchester Christmas story. On the Nothern boundary of the project, along East Tremont Avenue, ran the train tracks. It was some kind of depot area and there must have been eight sets of tracks running side by side. Every year, in early December, an entire train with 40-50 railroad cars would pull up to the tracks closest to East Tremont Avenue, completely filled with Christmas trees! I'm told over 8,000 trees were on board. They would open the car doors and sell trees right on the tracks for the next three weeks to all the Parkchester families who would walk them home to their apartments. It was a major production for everyone in the family to be involved in picking out their tree. After Christmas, the trees would be placed in huge piles on the island along the center of Metropolitan Avenue, to be picked up by garbage men. We sure had a great time building tree forts before they arrived.

Parkchester consisted exclusively of 7 story buildings with one elevator and 12 story buildings with two. The apartments had one, two or three bedrooms, but just one bathroom regardless of size.

In grammar school, all my friends lived in my building (building buddies) and we played right outside on the stoop, or in the East playground. On rainy days, the elevator and staircases in our building were perfect for hide and seek. We learned how to stop the elevator between floors during our games, which really endeared us to the grown-ups on their

way home from work. The staircases were also ideal for playing cards later as teenagers... in our case, however, we played bridge for money because poker was too boring.

Parkchester was a monumental social experiment...and it worked. Virtually all of the lower middle class families moved there between 1940 and 1965 bettered themselves, as a result of living in that unique place. Although I have lost contact, I've heard it continues to work for families living there today, ironically now mostly people of color.

As a member of the first generation of children born and raised in Parkchester, I cannot conceive of a more ideal environment to grow up in. Having said this, I can't explain why all of us desperately wanted to move out the moment we got a job, got married or both. I'd like to think it's because living there gave us a glimpse of how much more we could achieve, but I'm not sure. Later, Pat and I raised our daughter Amy in a nice private home in a small Massachusetts town with

The Bronx County Historical Society Research Library

a great school system, but we often wish she had the same experience as we did growing up in a wonderful place like Parkchester.

They say you can't go back, but we certainly took something enormously valuable from that life experience worth revisiting.

"Coast to Coast They Remember Hoe Avenue"

FROM CALIFORNIA
Life On Hoe Avenue

By Thelma Rosen Kimble

1545 Hoe Avenue

Frieda Wasserman Glassman & Thelma Rosen Kimble on Hoe Ave. near 173rd Str. (1947)

Looking back, I realize what a wonderful time of life it was. Here are some of the things I remember:

Going to PS 50 in the summertime and getting under the tall showers they put out in the school yard during the summer months to give us kids relief from the heat.

Mothers with jars of milk waiting outside of PS 50 for their kids to come out.

Shooting bottle caps filled with several layers of corks held down with a thumb tack and then shoot them into chalked out numbered spaces on the sidewalk.

Playing stoop ball all over, but when we did that on the steps of the little synagogue diagonally across from 1525, we would be chased away. But on the holiday, they gave the most delicious sponge cake and apples.

"Cut Outs" which are now called "paper dolls". I still collect today! Oh, to go back to Woolworth's on Wilkins Ave. to buy some more!

Sledding down the hill on 172nd St. out to Southern Blvd., always afraid that we would land in front of a trolly car. Snow fights, building snowforts and then warming our gloves on the building radiators.

Going to Crotona Parks and renting a bike for 50¢ an hour and riding around their bike rink. The park benches were filled with men and women eating pumpkin and sunflower seeds sold by very old men who would give you a shot glass full from a bag for 2¢.

The Dover and Freeman Theatre and dish night, the same dishes I now find myself putting together from flea markets and antique shops.

Joining a club called "jivettes" and desperately wanting to get club jackets.

Thelma in front of Goldfarb's drugstore.

Statman's Grocery Store on Hoe, Goldfarb's drug store, Sweisky's with its delicious egg creams and mello-rolls and shoe leather candy; the 1¢ chocolates that were cream filled, and if you had a pink center you got a 5¢ candy bar.

The Sunday papers which we went for on Saturday night, the jelly apple man with red hot jelly, and Bungalow Bar Ice Cream trucks that were sparkling and immaculate

Those parties on Friday and Saturday nights for the young people called "Gatherings". How important it was to meet with your friends and find out who was having a "Gathering" and who was going! Or worse, who was not going!

Yes, that was life in The Bronx fifty years ago.

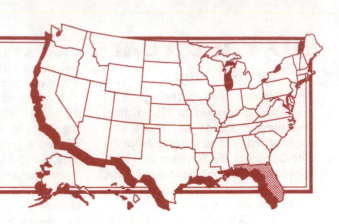
"Coast to Coast They Remember Hoe Avenue"

FROM FLORIDA

Hoe Heights alias Hoe Ave.

By Janet Gross Ritter

Who says growing up in the South/East Bronx wasn't fun. Hoe Avenue was a predominantly low to low middle income area....even when television first came out, that didn't keep us in.

Going down memory lane between Hunts Point to West Farms Road and Southern Blvd, Boston Rd to Boone Ave

Remember:

The Hot Jelly Apple/Prunes, Apricots and Marshmallows

The Good Old Carnival on Hoe Ave between 174th and 175th Streets

Buying school supplies at Spunds.

Going down Danger Hill at 172nd St between Bryant and Longfellow when it snowed.

The Freeman Street YMYWHA

The Ice Cream Parlor on Southern Blvd and Freeman St.

Seeing Jake the Pickle Man

Calucci Italian Restaurant on Freeman and Southern Blvd.

The Iceman, Organ Grinder, Scissor Sharpener Man

The Ragman "RAGS-OLD IRON"

The Fiddler in the yard.

Pops Pool Room - George Bennett

Nat's Restaurant

The Stardust Ballroom

Hunts Point Palace

The Fish store on 174th St between Bryant and Vyse

Gauch's and Stubby's Candy Stores

I hope some of these memories strike a responsive chord and bring back good memories.

You may contact me at:
9203-C Boca Gardens Circle South
Boca Raton, FL 33496

2104 Vyse Avenue

50 Fast Years

By Norman Vale

In January 1944, at the age of 14 and looking forward to high school and maybe college (for those who could afford it or had the grades for the City Colleges), life 50 years later after elementary school graduation was remote. It wasn't even a concept we could grasp at the time.

During the height of World War II, we were more in tune with identifying aircraft, uniforms/medals, Allied progress on several wartime fronts as well as average adolescents think of and do. None of us could have anticipated how long and how far we might travel in the face of a world engaged in conflict.

Yet, some of us graduates of the PS 80 (Mosholu Parkway) Class of January 1944 managed to bridge 50 years. We assembled this past spring for an evening of the celebration of life and a great deal of progress, family reports, achievements, loss of classmates and a tremendous amount of nostalgia. It was an evening devoted to reminiscing about our classes, about people in other classes, about the 'Parkway' and about the Bronx.

If we consider the small sample of 22 guests who came to the reunion, the Class of January '44 has accomplished a great deal. Doctors, lawyers, teachers, business' executives, internationalists and others but no Indian Chiefs. Clearly, PS 80 had established the educational base and the interest to pursue knowledge; we continued to build on that.

Time has been kind to us. Except for some graying, additional weight, loss of hair and a few other indicators, we had no difficulty recognizing one another. We didn't need prompts from old photos which are generally the key to class reunions. It's hard to believe that for some of us, perhaps, 40 to 50 years later we had a renewal of contacts. Time and absence slip by so quickly.

Incredibly, one of our teachers made it, too. Ben Weinstein was just a recent college graduate when he began his teaching career at PS 80 not many years older than his students. He was still full of grace, humor and intelligence. He had the 'floor" for a few minutes of spontaneous remarks, and we marveled at his recall. Perhaps he couldn't tell us about breakfast the day before but no one raised that question. Yet his response was complete in all respects, and we cherished the time with him.

In closing, someone recommended that we meet 10 years from the date ... similar to the 40th anniversary pledge made at our last class reunion but good judgment, sound minds and pragmatism prevailed. We unanimously agreed that five years was long enough.

PS 80 still stands as a testimony to our group and we plan to stand for the 55th reunion. Who knows, maybe we'll meet in the Bronx for old times' sake? But it's certainly something to which we look forward and not to soon to plan for an even larger group.

"Of our school upon the Parkway, we all delight to sing: in its praises and its reason for meeting again.

Parkchester: What It Meant To Me

By Henry de Cillia

Watching the retired men play shuffleboard near Purdy Street playground...

Rollerskating down Machine Gun and Suicide Hills...

Playing punchball in Maple Drive with Spaldeens...

Shooting marbles at the East flagpole...

Buying baseball cards with gum from Mrs. Tyler at Parkchester News...

Watching the girls dance at the Indian Pageant...

Buying 7¢ ices and 10¢ humorettes

Riding the "Twenty" bus down East Tremont Avenue, over to the Prop...

Going out to Pelham Bay Park on our bikes to pick chestnuts...

Walking to Lambiase's for Italian ices...

Bowling at the Playdrome on Saturday mornings...

Having chocolate eggcreams at Bunny's on Starling Avenue...

Buying cherry lime rickeys in a wing ding cup at Oval Drug Store... to go ...

Buying 25¢ worth of potato salad at Arfstein's Deli

Going down Purdy Street to the "climbing signs" at Starling & Castle...

Going to Rye Beach, and riding the Cyclone

Buying Hardy Boys books and Duncan Yo-Yo's at Wormwarths...

Eating eggs at the Castle Hill Diner after spending all night at the Rats...

14

Thoughts From Dixie—South of the Borough

By Bernie Berkeley

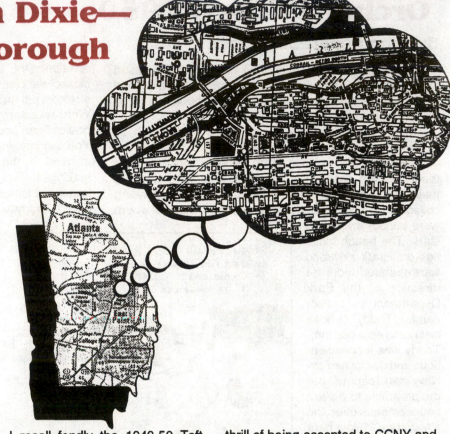

If any of my buddies from Anderson Avenue would have told me some forty years ago, that this Ol' Bronx boy would be living in Atlanta, Georgia one day, I would have questioned their sanity. Yet, here I am practically a native after fourteen years. I have prospered, and together with my wife Jessie, have raised two wonderful, successful children. The South has been good to the Berkeley family.

I would, however, be less than honest if I did not admit that fond memories of the old neighborhood still linger in the caverns of my mind.

The "block", Anderson Avenue from 167th street to 164th street was the world to so many of us. You didn't have to stray any further in order to enjoy the social activities of a young and vibrant society. It was within those boundaries that love affairs were spawned and mega sporting events took place. The competitive three sewer stick bell games, cause of many a broken window, the stoop ball contests, often interrupted by the superintendent of building number 1080, the gathering on hot summer nights under the nearest street light, of the boys and girls to share the excitement of individual happenings of the day. These are phenomena which my children never would experience as they grew up in Atlanta.

I recall how proud I was to exhibit the colorful maroon and gold "club" jacket of the RODS which was almost immediately, the target of every organized gang in the Bronx. I was the first in my group to have his jacket worn by his sweetheart, Sandy. (I hope my wife doesn't read this)

I recall walking to Taft High with some buddies to save the bus and train fare and calling food orders through the street grating of the diner on 170th street under the "EL".

I recall fondly the 1949-50 Taft Soccer team, of which I was a member, and the many practices the coach would miss because we had to pass through a barroom to get to the Sterling Oval practice field.

I played football as a member of the Highbridge Chiefs and the ego pump of performing before all the cute girls who lived at the Noonan Towers at 168th street and Nelson Avenue.

Walking across the Harlem River Bridge to the Polo Grounds to watch my beloved Football Giants win the big one against the hated Redskins or the Bears. Or racing down the Anderson Avenue "hills" to get to Yankee Stadium in time to buy one of the coveted 60¢ Bleacher seats. Eating a rarely cooked hot dog at Joe Garber's little store under the Jerome Avenue "EL" across from the Stadium.

"Hanging out" with the SIRENS, a female social club, whose members lived near 161st street and the Grand Concourse. This was a "bonus" for being a member of the RODS! The thrill of being accepted to CCNY and the disappointment of the concrete campus.

The workouts with the freshman boxing team with the strict training regimen as dictated by coach Yustin Sirutis, one of the best instructors I have ever known in my brief, and, far from illustrious, boxing career.

Attending the Tuesday night Amateur fights with my Dad at Jerome Stadium which was owned by Joey LaMotta, brother of champ Jake LaMotta.

Coming home from a date with my best girl, now my wife, Jessie. Getting off the "EL" at 167th street and racing up the 102 stairs from River Avenue to Anderson Avenue taking them two at a time. Of course, that was 30 pounds ago!

Unfortunately, most of us do not appreciate these moments as they occur, but only recognize their significance when they become "MEMORIES"

15

Orchard Beach-1950

By John Robert Schweizen

Rummaging through memorabilia after my wife passed away a year ago, I found an Orchard Beach scene that I had sketched one summer morning in 1950; the last of three years that I worked as a NYC lifeguard.

There were over fifty guards assigned to the beach, all of whom had to pass a rigorous Park Department training course with a final exam in which the instuctors darn near tried to drown each of us. We were a group comprised mainly of military service returnees (who were attending college on the GI Bill) and high school lads, many of whom were school swimming stars. The beach facilities and park environs were operated under the direction of the Park Department supervisor named "Toddy" (whose last name escapes me). Toddy was a conscientious and disciplined ex-Navy man. I can still hear the preamble to his announcements over the PA system - "Now here this!! Now here this!!"

Over a million people visited Orchard Beach each season and yet amazingly there were few drowning victims. One year however, I remember that we had an unfortunate drowning early in the season. Everyone became more wary and alert, especially the beach director Toddy, who had to answer to a publicly sensitive "downtown" Park Department hierarchy. After about a week of stepped-up beach surveillance and numerous PA system directions by Toddy, the guards decided that something had to be done to ease the tension.

To resolve our problem we came up with a radical solution. One evening at twilight, after the beach had closed, we placed two lifeguards, covered with parkas, on stretchers in an unused area of the outdoor locker pavilion. Word was sent to Toddy that we had just fished out two bodies from opposite ends of the beach-beach 1 and 17. You can imagine it didn't take him long to arrive, flashlight in hand. In the dusk, with a dozen lifeguards somberly looking on, Toddy stepped between the stretchers, lifted a parka and aimed the flashlight into the "victim's" face. With a yelp, Toddy took off, tripped over a stretcher, and crawled another half dozen yards. As the laughter subsided and Tod realized he had been taken, he also started laughing and said, "I never expected a drowned man to look back at me and blink."

From then on, Toddy eased up on us and naturally treated the incident lightly. It also helped that we didn't suffer any more drownings on our watch that season —thank goodness.

Since season's end in 1950 I have never been back to Orchard Beach. I went on to graduate from Manhattan College in the Bronx, move to New Jersey, married a Jersey girl and raised a brood of great kids. However, I fondly remember those days and my hardy and happy-go-lucky fellow lifeguards including Carl Feinaun, Tom Collins, Bill Ambrosini, Lou Benson, Bob Davson and a host of others. I hope that they all have fared well since those best of times-back in the Bronx.

ORCHARD BEACH AUG 2, 1950
AS SEEN FROM TOWER 9
"SLOW DAY"
J.R.SCHWEIZER

Illustration by Jogn Robert Schweizen, 1950

Stadium Hardware

By Robert Karow

I lived in the shadow of the Yankee Stadium, 1006 Gerard. When I couldn't afford a ticket to the game, a few of us would go to the roof of 831 Gerard and look right into home plate from just behind the right field stands...several times a day after a game a few of us would stand outside the press gate to see some of our heros...if we were lucky we could shove a pen and paper in front of them for an autograph, most of them signed—it was the best of times.

My father had a hardware store on the corner of 161st and Gerard. "Stadium Hardware". It is still there today—third generation in operation. Has the neighborhood changed? You might say that is the case...the stores are still there, all under different owners. Stadium Hardware is the last original store of the late 1920's to survive the same ownership. I started in that store in 1954, after I was discharged from the service. It was only supposed to be a temporary hold for me—it lasted 38 years. I saw all the changes that took place over the years. The fire that eliminated "Goldman's Restaurant" (now the site of McDonalds). "Addie Vallins" is now a medical center. The "Roxy Deli" is now a donut luncheonette. The "Earle Theatre" is now a Twin Restaurant. "The Cafeteria" is now Nedicks.

As the years passed I found myself saying the same things my father used to say to some of the customers, "I knew your mother when she was your age".

The area is somewhat stable. The courthouse is still there. The park between Walton and the Concourse, between 161 and 164, is not as pretty as it once was. The apartment buildings have changed their appearance. Iron gates now adorn the fronts of most buildings, drugs and violence have taken over. This leads to the worst of times.

Friendships that were started and bonded in the early years lasted through the test of time. As it is the case, people move about, change addresses, change cities, etc. One old friend (Dick Dakin), after 42 years decided to try to find me. He called my last place that he remembered (Stadium Hardware), hoping the new owners would possibly know of my whereabouts. As it turned out, my son now runs the business and was surprised to hear someone asking for me. Needless to say, we got together and have been having reunions once a year with other friends from the past...Larry Barton nee (Barshansky), Larry Meyers, and Marty Winkler.

I now live in Florida for 9 months of the year and come up to a summer home in Putnam Valley for three months. I have camp in both places. From the small world area...I have met several people in Florida that lived just a stones throw from where I lived in the Bronx...David Newman and his wife Susan nee (Bregman). David lived on Gerard Ave. just south of 161st...Susan lived on Jerome Ave. From just a chance conversation I was able to meet David Curland of Gerard Ave., just south of 161st. Of course we all went to school together and we were able to have a mini

reunion and talk over all the old memories. I guess, the most famous memory was the store on Gerard Ave., just north of 161st. It was a combination ice cream and pennant store, owned by Charlie Worton. At gametime in the stadium ice cream vendors would roam throughout the area with the ice cream chant and the pennant vendors would set up their board and sell pennants and souvenirs just before game time and after the game. Stanley Worton, Charlie's son, is a famous doctor living somewhere in Florida.

Memories of the good old days and good friends, that is the best of times...

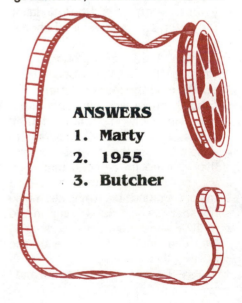

ANSWERS
1. Marty
2. 1955
3. Butcher

My Turf Revisited: The East Bronx

By Charlotte Krepismann

Charlotte Krepismann

"Sam, Momma asked you to give me 10 cents 'n greens," I'd say, never really understanding that I was buying very important ingredients for Momma's "if it's Friday, it's soup" schedule. Sam always knew exactly what I needed. Sam is gone now; Momma is gone too, and I don't make chicken soup very often. But the past is alive in my memory and exists comfortably with my present.

It isn't true that you can't go home again. I do it all the time — in my mind. The Bronx is my home because the years I spent there laid the foundation for the dreams and values I cherish today.

It isn't the entire borough of the Bronx that I revisit. Young people grew up in neighborhoods where the schools, shops and atmosphere became indelibly imprinted on their minds. Say "Grand Concourse" to someone from the West Bronx, and they conjure up a broad boulevard with solid brick apartment houses, a major shopping hub, a majestic movie house with a star-studded ceiling and many trolleys, buses and cars vying with one another for space on the bustling thoroughfare.

Say "Tremont Avenue" to me and I am on my own turf. It's the main street of our "small town," the East Bronx, a less affluent neighborhood where most of the brick buildings take on the patina of old age, where the 5 and 10 cent store means just what it says, and where theaters often show "B" movies that are quickly forgotten. But it's also where the aromas coming from the stores are enough to pull in the faithful, eager to devour pickles, kosher hot dogs and greasy knishes.

To shop on Tremont Avenue was an all-day adventure since the large supermarkets had not as yet invaded the neighborhood. Mothers worked their way from the small grocery, where milk still came in bottles with the cream on top; to vegetable stores where the ubiquitous "Sam" or Sidney" selected "for you, Mrs." only the best tomatoes and the perfectly ripened melons.

If Momma was lucky, both stores offered delivery service, saving time for a trip to the chicken market to sniff out the freshest chickens before the plucker started his ritual dance of pluck and singe, pluck and singe. How I hated the stench. The only smell quite like it is the old-fashioned dental drills that grind their way into your teeth sending out the same odor of burning flesh.

A stop at the butcher was another colorful experience — the main color being bright red, which the butcher managed to smear in a Rorschach pattern all over his white apron. "Momma says to cut her a nice piece of brisket, not too much fat," I'd chant, ever the dutiful daughter.

"Sure, darling. I have a beautiful slice just for you." I'd hurry out to avoid getting my cheeks pinched by fingers that were almost as red as his apron.

The visits to those food emporiums were vital to our mother's daily existence, but for the young, the candy store was the magnet after a weary day at school or before the constant warfare on the subways. Actually our warfare was not synonymous with graffiti-covered walls and young muggers. Instead we fought over too few seats for too many riders. The candy stores offered up the energy stored in penny candies and the salivating smoothness of cold malts mixed professionally behind the marble-topped counter. My friends and I would argue endlessly about the relative merits of chocolate halvah compared to a meltingly chewy Hershey bar with almonds.

Outside the candy stores were the daily newspapers, there for the taking for those with the correct change, left strewn over the top paper by harried people rushing off to work. Also outside were the ever-shifting groups of boys and girls.

For Tremont Avenue was also the social target for teenagers with time on their hands, a sort of cheap Champs Elysee. We window-shopped, poked around in Woolworth and stopped for a Charlotte Russe. The real business on hand, however, was to attract the attention of the opposite sex. How innocent it all was; how safe we felt wherever we wandered. Our greatest concern was to meet our parents' curfew but we knew exactly how far we could stroll and still make it home on time.

Our apartment houses existed to fulfill familiar rules and basic needs, but our real lives were played out on the stoops and on the streets. Throwing jacks, gossiping, reading and flirting kept us busy on the stoops, while stick ball and marble games played with cheese boxes made life difficult for vendors and others who drove.

"Watch out for old lady Goldberg" went the cry when our raucous shouts brought the red-haired dragon to her window armed with a large pot of water. Most of the time she missed, but when she succeeded in soaking some of us, she'd shake her fist and utter incoherent warnings of the next time!

Another kind of world was played

Continued on next page

East Bronx

Continued from page 18

out in the cement backyards where clothes lines criss-crossed the space and alley cats slunk around, eternally searching for something to eat. I detested both the cats and the clotheslines. Apartments facing the street went for higher rentals and were one more way to separate the poor from the not-so-poor. I dreamed away hours staring out of my bedroom window, careful to hide from the voyeurs who openly gawked at young girls across the court.

Children's plea for "a nickel, please Ma, throw down a nickel" and the walking advertisements of the man who sang out, "I cash clothes" were background noises that rarely interrupted my dreaming.

We lived on Vyse Avenue, one short block from the neighborhood artery of Tremont Avenue and part of the circuit travelled by our Romeo of the violin. He surely fiddled on other blocks as well, but we claimed him as our own. A nondescript man of uncertain age, he flattered every woman who passed with his rendition of some syrupy song, like "Dark Eyes," which he sang as he wielded the bow with a melodramatic flourish. He, and the long-suffering Fuller Brush man, were the objects of our derision and delight, coloring our days with their plaintive needs. Our parents taught us compassion, but it was easy to forget when faced with such colossal failures.

Part of me has never left 2000 Vyse Avenue. The music I stored under my bed, the black and red beaded dress that I borrowed from my mother to look grown-up, and the "True Romance" magazines hidden from adult eyes are still there. Where else would they be?

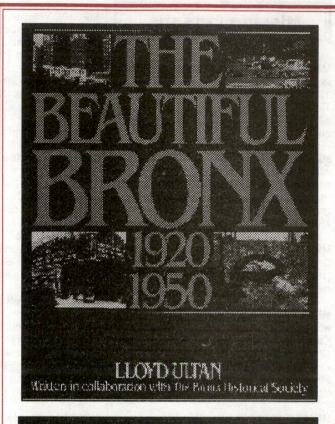

- **Over 200 photos**
- **Almost every neighborhood represented**
- **A treasure chest of memories**

Take a trip back in time to the glory days and the golden years of the Bronx. Author Lloyd Ultan, a native Bronxite, takes us back to those wonderful years to witness a way of life long passed. 200 rare and beautiful photos take us back to the familiar brick apartment houses, children playing stickball and Potzie, and many other scenes of everyday life that all of us remember fondley. See the long-gone buildings and landmarks, the beautiful Loews Theaters with their magnificent lobbies, the old Yankee Stadium & many other familiar sights.

If you're from the Bronx, you'll find this book to be a treasure chest of memories, and a nostalgic look into your past. Order a copy today! To order, simply turn to the back page of this issue and fill out the order form.

Classifieds

MP621 Judy Schubowsky, **Taft 1967**, wants to hear from old friends who hung out on 170th St., Fordham Rd., Van Cortland Park. Tina Sperling — How do I reach you? I'm alive and well in Miami. Let me know what's going on!

MP622 Would love to hear from the guys who played stickball on Vyse Ave. (Freeman and Home Streets) 1947 - 1952 and went to St. John Chrysostom School. Also, 1953 grads from **Monroe**. Call Bill Doherty 516-732-8408.

MP623 Looking for old time friends from Crotona Park North, P.S. 44 and P.S. 92 (1942-1947) especially Laura Balter. Write me. Ronnie.

MP624 What happened to Bernie Kaplan who lived on Longfellow Ave. Whitey Kalinsky's parents owned a bakery on E. 174th Street between Bryant & Vyse Avenue. Joey Marcus lived on East 173rd Street and Vyse Avenue next to candy store across from P.S. 50.

MP625 Shelly (Wagner) Wright has been living in South California for 17 years. Originally from Hunts Point section of the Bronx, P.S. 48, J.H.S. 60 and **Morris High 1953**. Looking for friends from that time and place.

MP626 Margot (Wolf) and Sol Feldman, **Taft 1953 and 1950**, have just celebrated the arrival of their first grandchild and would love to hear from old friends (Grant Avenue, etc.). Call 815-756-4305.

MP627 Looking for Jerry Heppenheimer, Steve Paskie, and Murray Denmark from Davidson Avenue and 174th Street. Graduated from P.S. 104, P.S. 82, and **DeWitt Clinton in 1951**. Also, in reply to MP588, chuck Rappaport, I think I knew your brother, Melvin. Joey Bach, New City, NY.

MP628 Anyone 182nd Street and Tiebout Avenue. Phyllis Gold, Steve Field, Stuart Bolkin, Janet Shavin, Barbara Cornblatt (Russo), Pat Beresford (Balolas), and Helen Berkowitz. Call Sandra Joseph Filla, Florida, 305-741-4649. Stuart Reich contact Richard Filla (Bernholz candy store).

MP629 If anyone remembers me from **Taft, Jan. 1945** and feels nostalgic, write Richard Loebman, 3 Granary Drive, Baltimore, MD 21208. I'll blow the dust off my yearbook and let memories of happy days recur.

MP630 Where are you all from Jesup Avenue, Featherbed Lane, Nelson Avenue, McCombs Road from the 1940's and 1950's. Contact Joel Adler.

MP631 Ira Jacobson, **Taft 1956**, looking for Eddie Heller, Steve Morris, Mel and Donnie Mitzner. Call me 516-928-4211.

MP632 Gerry DePoalo, **Manhattan Prep, 1953**. Looking to locate former alumni, Parkchester and Sedgwick Avenue friends.

MP633 Would like to have **1960 Walton H.S.** yearbook. Housefire destroyed mine. Will arrange for collect postage.

MP634 Hey, Leo Stadt, Jerry Nadler, Barry Spegler, and anyone else from the parkway. Where are you? Stan Newman is looking for you or anyone else who remembers us.

MP635 Roosevelt 1958. WE NEED YOU! Planning reunion. If you graduated or would have graduated in 1958, send your name (maiden), address, telephone number and some information on other classmates known. **'58 Roosevelt** Reunion, 56 South Parker Drive, Monsey, NY 10952-1514.

MP636 Looking to locate anyone who was a student or knows of the whereabouts of anyone who was at Hawthorne Ceder Knolls School, Hawthorne, NY from 1952 to 1955. Please call Jack Tare at 407-622-2211.

MP637 Bob Rabinowitz, **Roosevelt 1951**, wants to contact Ruth Klang, Roosevelt 1951. Also Angel Masi, Cathy Devane, Prospect/Garden/182nd Street. Also Myra Kirschenbaum, 770 Garden. Nice surprise for you. From Montgomery Avenue, West Bronx, Arlene Gross, Louise Kaplan, Circa 1956.

MP638 Phil Luboff, **Taft 1965**, is looking for old friends, especially Michael Cohan, Neil Goldstein, Max Needleman, Elliot Rubenstein, Ann Jacobs, Gloria Siegel, Jeff Spivak, Bill Martin, Joseph DiMaria, etc., etc. P.S. I live in France now.

MP639 Howard Leshaw, **Music and Art, 1961**. I am a musician and have recently recorded a cassette of Jewish and Klesmer music. I would love to hear from old friends.

MP640 Barbara Bergman Dick, **Taft 1957**. Seeking information on whereabouts of Carol Herstick of Parkchester, Nursing Major, Hunter College, graduated 1962-1963, Peace Corps. Nurse. Lost contact with Maid of Honor at my wedding. Any information, please contact.

MP641 Relocated **1962 Taft** now lives in the Chicago area. Would love to hear from classmates, especially Ellen Forman, Harriet Nachtigal, Janet Neumeistec and Joan Kroll. Thelma Frankel Krause is looking for you.

MP642 Remember Marilyn Dorfman? P.S. 92, J.H.S. 44 (Co-President), **Roosevelt H.S. 1953**. Boyfriend Irving Picker (where are you?). Gloria Beckman, Gloria Tinkelman, Judy Deckelbaum, Betty Golden.

MP643 Where are you Barbara Zaret and Toni Elnick? It's been since 1963! from "An Angel".

MP644 Andrews, Popham, Montgomery, and University Avenues. 8 Duchesses looking for 9 more. Where are you Elaine Riello, Pat Elkin, Renee Epstein, Dotti Altschul, Fran Stein, Elaine Gentile, Rhoda Weisbrot, Sandi, etc. Remember Percy's Poolroom, the Benches? Please contact Lenore (Kleinberg) Schlissel, 10 Swallow Avenue, Spring Valley, NY 10977.

MP645 Linda Gerhung Pevar, **Taft 1960**, Echo Place and the Grand Concourse, is in Ft. Lauderdale, FL. Where are all the fellows from **Taft 1959** and girls from **Taft 1960**?? Call or write 2068 Windward Circle, Ft. Lauderdale, FL 33326, 305-384-4344.

MP646 Anyone from Simpson Street Reunion held in 1984. Joan Massella would love to know if you plan on holding another one. Would love to hear from Catherine Stavredes.

MP647 Ina Haimowitz and Sondra Winner are looking for Lenny Hecht, Marcia Golden, Rhoda Karp, and anyone else from neighborhood, **Monroe H.S. 1956**. Ina Haimowitz Cronin, 58 Primrose Lane, Bricktown, NJ 08723, 908-458-4660.

MP648 Joan Altman Schulson, **Walton 1961**, would like to find Darrel Pines, Maureen Litter, Charlene Nasshorn, Gail Keating, Toby Stutman, etc.; and also Bronx Community College friends, 1963. Call 718-231-3114.

MP649 Barbara Miller Stone, P.S. 11 1951; Walton H.S. 1955. Looking for Stephen Weisberg. Lived in Noonan Plaza, graduated **Bronx H.S. of Science**. Had a dream of riding a bike to Palisades Amusement Park with you. 407-274-3445.

MP650 Taft 1955, Diane Honig (Robbins) of Selwyn Avenue is looking for Gloria Appelbaum of College Avenue. Also, where is Phyllis Strassberg, Bernice Holland, Laura Penken, Elayne Schloss? Contact me at 516-889-3332. Marcia Levine is also interested in Evelyn Kabchefsky.

Classifieds

MP651 Proud of upcoming 100th anniversary of DeWitt Clinton H.S. in 1997. Alumni Association has branches in Los Angeles, Atlanta, Miami, Washington, D.C., plus one for former football players and one of members of the Clinton News alumni. (Monroe Benton, Alumni Association, Board Member, June 1941).

MP652 The Comets of Boston Road and Vyse Avenue are alive and well in Westchester and New Jersey. Ted Shuster, Jerry Tolkov, Jerry Schwartz, Dave Schwartz, Al Schuman, etc. **Ridder 1949, Monroe 1953.** We welcome all renewals of old friendships. 908-566-8065.

MP653 Allyn Herz Kanowsky and Neil Kanowsky are looking for former summer residents of Cold Spring Village from the 1950's and early 1960's for a possible reunion in 1995. If you attended Cold Spring Village in Monticello, please call or write to Neil and Allyn Kanowsky, 1713 Coral Avenue, North Lauderdale, FL 33068, 305-726-0903.

MP654 Harriette J. Schwartz, P.S. 104, J.H.S. 82, and finally **Taft 1968.** Remembers Sedgwick projects and lived in 1551 University (with Library and Community Center). Call if you remember me and let's reminisce. 818-347-4676.

MP655 Ellen Kippel, **Monroe 1963,** is looking for Sandra DiRoma Albala. Sandy, I tried find you when I moved to South California in 1975 and would like to see you again. Call 714-893-7621.

MP666 Robert Zimmerman, **Taft 1962,** is looking for ball players from Andrews, Montgomery and Popham Avenues for a reunion.

MP667 Anyone out there from **Monroe 1946 or Hunter 1950** (Tau Sigma Phi)? I was Marilyn Walters (Klein-Lemberg), now Rotella! (Oi) Still teaching at Hillcrest School, New City, NY 10956 (Rockland County). Drop a note.

MP668 **Taft 1967.** Do you remember Victor Tadelis, Howard Rosenblum, Ronnie Tobias. Get in touch.

MP669 Looking for any of my old friends from Creston, **Clinton 1964** or Harrison Avenue. Contact Michael Schwartz, 201-984-9405.

MP670 Gene Zelazny (Frenchy) asks: "Where are you Mrs. Mildred Engelberg, Alan Rosenoff, Seymour Cooperman, P.S. 98, 1947-1949?"

MP671 **Columbus**, Pelham Parkway, 1960. We are the Horowitz Sisters (Sharon, Arlene and Bonnie) who lived on Wallace Avenue. Want to hear from our friends.

MP672 I would enjoy hearing from anyone who knew Carolyn Lebowitz (Cooperman). Remember Jahn's, Krum's, Luhr's? From one who thought the stars were real atop the Loew's Paradise. P.S. 70, E.B.B., **Walton 1965**, Queens College 1969. From 182nd Street and Walton Avenue. Trekked to University Avenue (IDYC Group).

MP673 Thelma Rosen from 1525 Hoe Avenue is looking for June **1949 Monroe** grads. Also Greta Finklestein, Shirley Rudolf, Linda Weiss, Marilyn Horowitz, Arlene Hershkowitz, Esther Wechsler, Hilda Kessler, Marilyn Henig, and Rita Millstein. Somebody's got to be out there!!! Call 714-548-1736.

MP674 If there is anybody reading this from Pelham Parkway who was born in the 1930's or 1940's who does not know about the periodic Pelham Parkway reunions, contact Howard Cohen, 303 Eighth Street, East Northport, NY 11731, 516-368-2118.

MP675 Hey, Shakespeare Avenue and 172nd Street? P.S. 104 schoolyard in the 1940's. Al Polon and "Brother" Arty . . . . Carl, Saul, Jerry and Arty M. last heard working for Morris Agency. Too many years ago. Where is anybody? Stan Newman.

MP676 Dr. Emanuel Barouch, DeWitt **Clinton 1941.** From Clafin Avenue by Circle Park overlooking the Reservoir. City College graduate. NYU College of Dentistry 1948. Married Irma Lambert, Walton 1941. Living in Greenwich Village. Remember the Aciremas?

MP677 Barbara Asher, maiden name Roseman, lived as a young child 175th Street in the Bronx. Attended **Evander Childs H.S. in 1950's.**

MP678 Irving Kalet, **Taft 1957,** is looking for Carole Steinholtz (P.S. 90, J.H.S. 22) and Rochelle Nitzberg.

MP679 Graduated **Monroe 1955.** Looking for Joan Finkelberg, Myrna Robins, and Elaine Krause. Also anyone from Bryant Avenue, 176th Street, Garden View, and Natie's Candy Store, etc. Contact Sheila Kleppner McMullen, 13610 SW 75 Street, Miami, FL 33183.

MP680 Howard Kessner, **Science 1963,** is living in Dallas, TX. Married with three children, 22, 19, and 16. Practicing general dentistry.

MP681 I lived at 1640 Washington Avenue, 1936-1941. I also lived at 1986 Grand Avenue, 1942-1944. Anybody from these areas and era, please contact me, especially Albert Rothstein a.k.a. Sonny! Joseph Van Grover, 8939 Windtree Street, Boca Raton, FL 33496.

MP682 Jean Churchill Kienzle, **Monroe January 1947.** Retired in Lancaster, PA. Would love to hear from Dolores Govendy, Doris Lipshitz or any other classmates. Still have yearbook. Also graduated from all girl J.H.S. 60. Lived on Elder Avenue until 12/51.

MP683 Bob Karow is looking for Ronnie Deutchman from 911 Walton Avenue. Call 407-997-5226.

MP684 Vivian (Mintz) Karow and Bob Karow are looking for Jackie Friedman from Findlay Avenue in the Bronx. Way back to 1957. Call 407-997-5226.

MP685 I lived at 1121 Elder Avenue. I left the Bronx when I was twenty and moved to Queens; got married at 21 and moved to Long Island. In 1983, I moved to NJ. I have three children and own an electronic company.

MP686 Jolene Sayles Venetianer, **Evander '53,** seeking Arlene Price. Jerry Vetetianer, **Evander '51,** seeking Ronnie Blatman - or anyone seeking us call 914-238-3677

MP687 Maddy Pearl (Nee Goldman) looking for Edie (Chickie) Cicchetti from Sheridan Ave., **Taft HS - class of '59.** We have 35 years of catching up to do.

MP688 Rapaport, Sylvia, **1950 Taft,** lived 1664 Weeks Ave. Pres. of a Packaged Parties, Woodland Hills, CA. Love to hear from friends. Home: 805-371-9931 Office: 818-710-1222.

MP689 Lenny Green looking for old friends: Alan Silverman, who played the trumpet and lived on Tremont Ave- across from PS 6 and David Seinfeld who lived on Vyse Ave around 1958-his parents owned an egg store on Tremont.

MP690 Bill King, **Clinton 44-45,** lived on Davidson Ave, between 150 & 181st 1942-50. Would like to hear from anyone living there. Played basketball with the Amerks and Dolph Schayes-loved the Giants (Football & Baseball) Please call or write

MP691 Looking for Marty Tannenbaum or Stella or Herbie Klinick or Lee Barar or anyone who hung out at Lep's Deli at 167th and Morris Ave. 1937-1941. Call Dan Schwartz (619) 324-8538

21

Classifieds

MP692 Phil Frank, PS90 under Principal Gewertz, **Taft 1942-46**. Sheridan and McClellan (2 candy stores and 4 corners) near the Fish House on the Concourse. The Heights '46-'49 The trolleycars. Great basketball team. Anybody remember? Let me hear from you.

MP693 Anyone from Hennessy Place in the 40's. I lived at 1923 (two family house)

MP694 Milton Goldstein, 1937. Sid, Grant & Murray Weill., would like to hear from you. We are the only taurians left and we can remember the good times we had.

MP695 Hey, any of you Hoe Ave kids (or other streets around) still have any of your Mother's "Wednesday night dish night" dishes from the Freeman Theatre? I'd love to hear from you. Even a picture of them would be great! Thelma Rosen Kimble, 656 Beach Street, Costa Mesa, CA 92627 (714) 548-1736

MP696 Looking for PS70 friends who graduated **1951-1952 from Monroe** Ave-Weeks Ave-173rd St-174th st area and want to get together. Call Claire (Davidowitz) Bergling (914) 357-9244

MP697 Dianne (Pardo) Abraham **1960 Taft**. Looking for Lois Barham, Elsi Camhi, Barbara Echtman, Barbara Feinstein, Edith Freter, Ben Hauben, Florence Kroop, Joan Lieberman, Anita Mandel

MP698 Would love to hear from anyone. I attended **Roosevelt** and graduated with me in **Jan '47 or June '47**.

MP699 Lana Cohen, 181st and Grand Avenue, **Walton '61**. Moving to FL, would like to hear from anyone there or anyone that remebers me. Researching for future book on "Growing Up in the Bronx" Contact me at: 240 Captains Walk, Delray Beach, FL 33483

MP700 Does anybody remember me? Norman Carabet, **Taft '50**, PS64. Looking for old friends. Write 7730 Greystone Dr., Canoga Pk, CA 91304

MP701 Searching for friends from featherbed Lane, Jesuo Ave, Macombs Rd, University Ave and **Taft 60-62** for reunion. Next one needs to include you. Contact Marcia Fishbein Donath.

MP702 Irwin Kirshbaum, **Bx Science '51**. Also PS86 '47. It would be great to communicate. Please write or phone. 8130972-1770, Tampa, FL

MP703 David Korn '32, hoping to hear from anyone that hung around Clay Ave and 174st, attended PS70 circa 1927-1930 or from members of stars a.c. football team- Residence: 9110, NW 72st, Tamarac FL 33321 (305) 722-7647

MP704 Bob Workman, **Monroe '60**, looking for old friends in old neighborhood, Boyton and Watson Ave's.

Come Blow Your Horn

Warren Lipkin **(Monroe 1961)** and Sheila Kotofsky Lipkin **(Monroe 1962)** are living in Central Florida and enjoying it. Warren is Controller/General Manager of major swimming pool contractor, and Sheila is Controller of the Jewish Community Center of Central Florida.

Arthur Levine, **Science 1966**, Creston and 180th Street, was recently named President of Teachers College at Columbia University. Before coming back to NY, Arthur served as a "fellow" at the Carnegie Foundation, President of Bradford College and a professor at Harvard.

Shelly Wagner Wright, **Morris 1953**. I've been working behind the scenes at the Grammy Awards for the past 17 years. I'm married for 38 years, have 3 children and 2 grandchildren. I've never stopped missing New York.

William Kling, **Clinton '44**. Commissioner, FL Dept. of Veteran Affairs (appointed by Governor Chiles). President Plantation Democratic Club (700 members) Member, Management Committee, Deputy Sheriff-Brown County, FL-17 yrs, Broward Democratic Exec Committee, 20th Congressional Dist. Director-AARP/Vote and many others.

Arthur Dougherty played saxophone, served in the Navy 1945-46, went to NYU, taught high school in Westbury, Long ISland and New Canaan, Conn before moving to California in 1962. Played with bands and orchestras in NY, Reno and San Francisco. Continued to teach in Danocille, CA and part-time at college level. Retired from school district administration in 1986 but I continue to 'blow my horn" as part time musicain.

READER REPLIES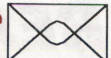

It is vitally important that you fill out the information below. Your input will be essential to the success of this magazine, tailored and inspired by you, the former "Bronxite". We thank you for your participation.

Subscriber? ☐ Yes ☐ No

YOUR NAME _____

ADDRESS _____

CITY _____ STATE _____ ZIP _____ PHONE _____

HIGH SCHOOL ATTENDED _____ YEAR GRADUATED _____

TELL US A LITTLE ABOUT YOURSELF.

(Be sure to include your alma mater, old neighborhood, your best memories about your days in the Bronx, (or anything else you can tell us).

_____

_____

_____

COULD WE SEND A FRIEND A FREE COPY OF BACK IN THE BRONX?

Do you know current or former Bronxites who would like to receive our magazine and reunion information? If you do, we'll be happy to send them a **free** inaugural issue of **Back in THE BRONX**.
Write to Back in The Bronx, Box 141 H, Scarsdale, NY 10583 or call 1-800-7-BRONX 5

Last	First	Maiden	
Address	City	State	Zip
Phone # ( )	School and year of Graduation		

Last	First	Maiden	
Address	City	State	Zip
Phone # ( )	School and year of Graduation		

Last	First	Maiden	
Address	City	State	Zip
Phone # ( )	School and year of Graduation		

Last	First	Maiden	
Address	City	State	Zip
Phone # ( )	School and year of Graduation		

COME BLOW YOUR OWN HORN DEPARTMENT

Please tell us about yourself (include your name)—about your accomplishments, awards, titles or works in progress. We're interested in hearing about them. List Below. _____

_____

_____

_____

_____

READER REPLIES

As a subscriber you are entitled to a FREE 40 Word Classified, Missing Persons, Blow Your Own Horn, or Personal Ad. Please write your ad below (if you are not subscribing to our magazine you can still place an ad in the next issue. The cost of an advertisement is 50¢ a word, there is no limit on paid ads).

_____

_____

_____

Is Your Mailing Label Correct?

In order to keep our database current, please correct any errors and place the label and or photocopy with corrections.

Account #	High School	Year Graduated
6817	Roosevelt	1958

SAMPLE
Mary R. Flowers
13 Anystreet Blvd.
Anywhere, USA 12345

Change of Address?

If you're planning a move please attach your label corrected with your new address and the date that you will begin receiving mail at that address. This will insure that you don't miss your next issue of **Back in THE BRONX**.

Ordering Information

A Great Gift Idea! In addition to your own subscription, a subscription to Back in THE BRONX makes a great and unique gift. Fill in the form below and we'll process the order in time for our next issue. So, order your subscription NOW, and order one for a friend!

YES, I'd like to order the following items:

QTY.

____ 1Yr. (4 ISSUES) Subscription(s) to Back in THE BRONX $19.95
____ 2Yr. (8 ISSUES) Subscription(s) to Back in THE BRONX* ... $29.95
____ 3Yr. (12 ISSUES) Subscription(s) to Back in THE BRONX* ... $39.95 } *FREE John's Menu
____ 4Yr. (16 ISSUES) Subscription(s) to Back in THE BRONX* ... $49.95
____ The Beautiful Bronx...........$25.00 (plus $3.95 S/H) $28.95
____ The Bronx: It Was Only Yesterday..$25.00 (plus $3.95 S/H) $28.95
____ Bronx High School Reunion Weekend Video $29.95
____ SAVE MONEY - BUY 4 FOR JUST $99.00!
____ THE BRONX Tracking Service $9.95
____ I would like to receive all available back issues and have them applied towards my subscription *(To date we have at least 12 back issues available - While They Last!)*

TOTAL: $ _____

Please fill out completely and include $3.95 for shipping and handling for books only to: Back in THE BRONX, Box 141H, Scarsdale, NY 10583

Please Print Clearly ☐ New Subscriber ☐ Renewal

Name _____

Maiden Name _____

Address _____

City _____

State _____ Zip _____

Phone ( ) _____

High School _____ Year Grad. _____

☐ Visa ☐ Mastercard ☐ Check ☐ Money Order

No. _____ Expiration Date _____

Signature _____

Back in THE BRONX

Box 141 H, Scarsdale, NY 10583
Phone 914-592-1647 • Fax 914-592-4693

ADDRESS CORRECTION REQUESTED

Volume III   Issue XI

Back in THE BRONX

CELEBRATING THE EXPERIENCE OF GROWING UP AND LIVING IN THE BRONX

Summer in the Rockaways— A Bronxite's Escape

By Bert Neufeld

Even before air conditioning was a gleam in General Electric's eye, people would go to their windows, throw them open, jam a folding chair against the open door of their apartments to create the wireless current of cross-ventilation and thus, begin the season of summer.

To the majority of city dwellers the options were either the stoop, the fire escape or tar beach. For the ones with somewhere in the vicinity of seventy-five to one hundred dollars, there was Rockaway.

Rockaway was the Monte Carlo of the matzo breakers, the Mecca of mothers whose dreams were for their jet-haired Marlenes to meet their red-haired (preferably professional) Myrons upon the love arena of the boardwalk or beach blanket. It was Araby for teenagers, and a great sandbox for toddlers. However for husbands it was either a terrible daily commute or a four-day-a-week vacation alone in the city, depending upon how great their wives' cooking was.

The Jewish section stretched from Edgemere, in the twenties and thirties, all the way up to the sixties and seventies of Arverne. Like a ribbon, its narrow width was beaded together with the brocade of hundreds of red, green, black and brown shingled rooftops of small white stucco buildings called bungalows. There was just enough space between them to allow

a fat lady, such as Sloppy Sadie, complete with shopping bag, to access comfortably on her way to the ministrations of her many tenants. Every second or third row had a wider lane to accommodate things a little larger than Sadie Karnovsky, perhaps carts or the small trucks of Dugan the Baker

George's fruits and vegetables. And since the kids outnumbered the mothers, the most important item of all was ice cream. For this, you had two institutions vying for the kids' patronage: Good Humor and, of course, Bungalow Bar. Continued on page 4

57th Street in the Arverne Section of Rockaway in the mid 50's.

Lessons I Learned On Grant Avenue

By Lila Freilicher, Taft '61

To an eight year old, Grant Avenue, at 164th Street in The Bronx, was the center of the universe. During the early 1950s there was more than enough to learn about life right there—in the courtyard and hallways—of our walk-up apartment building.

977 Grant Avenue and the surrounding blocks between 161st and Jerome Avenue (on the South and West) and 170th Street and Morris Avenue (on the North and East) nurtured me from birth until I was 16 when we moved to Continued on page 15

From the Editors...

TAFT '62

CLINTON '61

Many subscribers tell us how much they look forward to receiving **Back In THE BRONX** and reliving bits and pieces of their Bronx experiences. However, if subscribers had their choice they would choose to read stories *only* about *their* neighborhood. We enjoy **Back In THE BRONX** but "How come I never get to read about my neighborhood?"

When you consider that the borough of the Bronx consists of approximately 840 miles of streets and that we have only been publishing **Back In THE BRONX** since 1992, it would be physically impossible to publish stories for *all* Bronx neighborhoods in such a relatively short period of time. Eventually, you should find a story about your neighborhood. Since stories come from you, our subscribers, we can only publish what you submit.

Therefore, if you want to read stories about *your* neighborhood, the best way is to send us *your* Bronx neighborhood story. Once your story is published it becomes a motivator for others to do the same. Soon you will start reading about old friends and neighbors.

If writing is not your bag (do they still use this word?) consider an interview with us. How about neighborhood pictures, posters, transfers, tokens, or old Bronx restaurant menus? Or, have you recently had a chance meeting with some old friends whom you haven't seen in many years? We want to hear about it because everyone has experienced something similar in their lifetime.

Finally, do you have friends, neighbors, or relatives who might be interested in a free inaugural issue of **Back In THE BRONX**? Please give us their names and addresses and we will be happy to send it to them. If you wish, they may call our toll free number: **1-800-7BRONX 5.**

Back in THE BRONX

A number of the photographs in **Back in THE BRONX** are courtesy of and are available from the Bronx Historical Society.

Publishers & Editors:	Stephen M. Samtur	Clinton '61
	Susan H. Samtur	Taft '62
Contributing Editors:	Barbara Fasciani	Roosevelt '65
	Martin Jackson	Science '58
	Sandra Zuckerman	Jefferson '57
	Al Zuckerman	New Utrecht '50
Art & Production:	Ellen Grodjesk	
Printed By:	LNJ Printing, Bridgeport, CT	

Reminiscing

Summer Nights

By Sheila (Fox) Dimond

Before air conditioning, we had the street. Summer nights found all the kids of our neighborhood — 170th and Morris Avenue — out in the streets. We usually came down after dinner (we called it supper) eating corn on the cob or a piece of cantaloupe. About an hour later, our parents (chairs in hand) would come down and sit in front of the building. It was very hot in those apartments and sometimes you might catch a gentle breeze in the streets.

What was it about those Bronx nights? Why do they haunt me with their siren songs? Often a breeze will blow gently with a scent that transports me back. I am nine or ten or eleven. I can see Arline, Leona and Renee as they were then. In my mind, they are waiting for me on the steps; we'll play "Russian Ten," jump rope or maybe have a game of telephone.

We may walk to the corner of Morris and 170th and go right up to College Avenue where the luncheonette — which we called Larry's for some unknown reason — provided us with pretzels, malteds, mello-rolls and anything else that could delight the heart of a child.

Those days were free of cares, fears and troubles. We knew nobody would ever try to harm us in those streets of ours. The storekeepers knew us and they knew our parents.

Once in a while, we'd walk along the Grand Concourse all the way up to Fordham Road. I had my first taste of pizza at Dave and Charlie's Pizza Stand across the street from Alexander's. I still have the 45 rpm records I bought in the record shops on Fordham Road. Remember the shoe stores... Simco, A.S. Beck, National?

We were so young and so innocent. Those streets were our playgrounds and they held no danger for us. Those summer evenings in the Bronx were sweet and gentle. We were a lucky generation... we who grew up in the late 40's and early 50's. Those wondrous days are gone and those delicious streets are lost to us forever.

Ah, but the memories...

1305 Morris Avenue

Bronx Honor Roll
Bronxites Who Have Achieved!

BRONX SCIENCE
Stokely Carmichael
Leon Cooper (Nobel Prize Winner))
Bobby Darin
Edggar Doctorow
Sheldon Glashow (Nobel Prize Winner)
Russell Hulse (Nobel Prize Winner)
Nita Lowey, Representative
William Safire
Melvin Schwartz (Nobel Prize Winner)
Steven Weinberg (Nobel Prize Winner)

CARDINAL HAYES
George Carlin
Rocky Colavito
Kevin Loughery
Regis Philbin

CHRISTOPHER COLUMBUS
Robert Abrams
Anne Bancroft
Christine Jorgenson
Alan Landsburg

DEWITT CLINTON
Don Adams
Nate Archibald
Richard Avedon
James A. Baldwin
David Begelman
James Caan
Paddy Cheyefsky
George Cukor
Avery Fisher
Arthur Gelb
Judd Hirsch
Stubby Kaye
Theodore Kheel
Robert Klein
William Kunstler
Burt Lancaster
Jan Murray
Charles Rangel
Richard Rogers
A.M. Rosenthal
Daniel Schorr
Dolph Schayes
Neil Simon
Larry Storch
Jimmie Walker
Fats Waller
William Zeckendorf

EVANDER CHILDS
Red Buttons
James Coco
Carl Reiner

MONROE
Jules Feiffer
John Garfield
Hank Greenberg
Ed Kranepool
Leon Lederman (Nobel Physicist)

MORRIS
Angel Cordero
Gabe Pressman
E. Colin Powell

ROOSEVELT
June Alyson
Chaz Palmatieri

TAFT
Sanford Brown
Eydie Gorme
Stanley Kubrick

WALTON
Bella Abzug

OTHER NOTABLES
Joey Adams
Danny Aiello
Alan Alda
Robert Alda
Corazon Aquino
Herman Badillo
Lauren Bacall
Ellen Barkin
Mario Biaggi
Joey Bishop
Bobby Bonilla
Teresa Brewer
Ralph Bunche
George Burns
Cab Calloway
Diahann Carroll
Samuel Clemens
Cardinal Cooke
Avery Corman
Norman Cousins
Don Criqui
Tony Curtis
Vic Damone
Dennis Day
Dion DiMucci
John Foster Dulles
Fernando Ferrar
Geraldine Ferraro
F. Scott Fitzgerald
Joe Franklin
Arlene Francis
Connie Francis
Edward J. Flynn
Rudolph Giuliani
Samuel Gompers
Armand Hammer

David Horowitz
George Jessel
Robert Kennedy
Ted Kennedy
Theodore Kheel
Calvin Klein
Edward Koch
Fiorello LaGuardia
Jake LaMotta
Louise Lasser
Ralph Lauren
Ron Leibman
Lee Leonard
Shari Lewis
Hal Linden
Vince Lombardi
Gary Marshall
Penny Marshall
Willie Mays
Glenn Miller
Sal Mineo
Gary Morton
Bess Myerson
Gil Noble
Carroll O'Connor
Charles Osgood
Al Pacino
Jack Palance
Floyd Patterson
Joseph Papp
Joe Pesci
Roberta Peters
Edgar Allan Poe
Vincent Price
Charles Nelson Reilly
Rob Reiner
Billy Rose
Jonas Salk
Isabel Sanford
Marvin Scott
Connie Selleca
Carly Simon
Stanley Simon
Vince Scully
Curtis Sliwa
Wesley Snipes, Jr.
George Steinbrenner
Pat Summerall
Mother Teresa
Arturo Toscanini
Leon Trotsky
Lloyd Ultan
Jerry Vale
Fran Warren
Vanessa Williams
Herman Wouk
Rosalyn Yallow (Nobel Prize Winner)

Thanks to Dr. William C. Wolfson and the Bonx Society of Science and Letters

3

Reminiscing

Rockaway

Continued from page 1

For what else can you call a small ice cream truck complete with jingling bells and a brown shingled roof that wound its way through these endless corridors?

In this crowded community, privacy was not the standard dress code because of the proximity of these tiny dwellings and because of the decibel level of conversation. Jewish people tended to talk very loudly, even when they weren't arguing. In fact, even today, many Jewish

Rockaways' Playland

people, when in the company of a WASP, have experienced the terrifying feeling of going deaf.

While the wealthy could afford the two hundred dollars a season for the bungalows, other modest means were provided for the masses who weren't satisfied with the open window and the wedged bridge chair. The cheaper alternative was even less privacy called hotels. Now although we called them hotels they were a far cry from your Hilton - more like a Milton. Actually, they were large rooming houses or kuchelens (pronounced coochelane), which means to cook yourself or cooking privileges.

My parents, with all the other parents, would go out there before the season to shop. And despite the, 'Better grab this one,' or 'I already got a party interested in this one,' or 'For you, darlink, I would only do this,' the mothers would take their time going through every room in the building poking the beds, examining the ice boxes, measuring the closets, checking the view and flushing the toilets.

Once the matter of the room and price were agreed upon, then came the heavy "hondling." 'I need a bigger ice box.' 'Not enough drawer space.'

'New oilcloth for the floor.' 'Who's gonna scrape all that paint off the windows?' And 'Where are my screens?' But in spite of all the shopping and hondling, my mother would get the same type of room season after season... the cheapest, the one with no bathroom.

"Why pay for something you don't live in?" was her prelude to each season. And for less money we'd end up getting two bathrooms. Of course they were down the hall. And to make things even cheaper, she'd get the smallest room.

"Why pay for all that room when we're hardly going to be in it?" These little rooms got to be called 'Elsie's room.' They name wings in hospitals and halls in colleges and rooms in clubs, but only my mother gets one in Rockaway named after her.

I want you to know that these rooming houses had some very fancy names like The Frontenac, The Lorraine, The Jefferson, The Edgemere and one hotel even had two names of wide diversity.

Above its portals, lettered in gold, was The Palace, but since it was owned by the widow Karnovsky, it was called Sloppy Sadie's.

In the evening the huge porches and the entire lobby bustled with the clack of tiles, the clank of coins and the snap of cards. The conversation around the tables were N-32 B-15, call and raise a penny, six-no-trump, one crack two bam, knock with three and little pinnocle. The heartier souls

took their brisk constitution along the boardwalk, round-tripping it from Edgemere to Arverne.

On Saturday nights a band made the trip from the city and there was dancing. Since my curfew was 9PM, I found myself wishing I were older, instead of a prisoner in my own bed. I could hear the one instrument that dominated the trio, the saxophone. It lulled me with the strains of "Skylark", "Where Or When", "Moon Over Miami", "Fools Rush In", "Red Sails In The Sunset." Their crooning melodies gave me inklings of romance and pangs of bittersweetness.

However, that time my nine year old mind was interested only in lust of another kind. Since a nickel a day could only get me one Milky Way, I craved the whole pot of gold. At about every ten blocks of the beach there stood a small wooden shack. It wasn't for first aid and it wasn't the rest room. On three sides of this shack were three wooden slabs that were locked for the night. But during the day these slabs were raised upward and outward like awnings revealing the most wonderful array of confectionery a wide-eyed kid ever laid his wide eyes upon: Hershey bars, Tootsie Rolls, Baby Ruths, Milky Ways, Butterfingers, Jujubes, Mounds Bars, Juicy Fruit Gum, boxes of Chicklets, bubble gum and bottles and bottles of soda. There were kites and kite cord, all the things money (which I had none of) could buy.

I would pass there four, five, eight times a day watching people paying and taking away more than one Milky Way. And each day I got crazier and crazier. I was nearing rabid when one

Continued on page 9

What's in a NAME?

Have you ever wondered how some streets got their name?

Featherbed Lane

Featherbed Lane

On an 1868 map, it is written Feather Bed Lane, and the lower end was formerly Belmont Street until 1889.

There are three well-known versions of the origin of this name. During the Revolution, residents padded the road with their feather beds to muffle the passage of the patriots. Another story is that the spongy mud gave riders the effect of a feather bed. Still another tale is that the farmers found the road so rough, they would use feather beds on their wagon-seats to cushion themselves.

There is a fourth supposition advanced by a native of Highbridgeville that Featherbed Lane was a sly allusion to ladies of easy virtue who lived there. In short, it was the red light district during the 1840's when work on the nearby Croton Aqueduct was going on. Unsuspecting real estate developers of a later time liked its quaint name and retained it.

Bathgate Avenue

This Avenue is a remainder of the extensive Bathgate farm from which Crotona Park and portions of Tremont were carved. The first Bathgate was an overseer of the Morris Manorlands. The farm was conveyed to his three sons in 1847 by Gouverneur Morris II. At one time, this once-fashionable tree-lined street was known as Cross Street and also as Madison Avenue. Another early name was Elizabeth Avenue.
Both William and James Bathgate were on the membership rolls of the Westchester Agricultural Society in 1820.

Bathgate Avenue

Arthur Avenue

Arthur Avenue

Catherine Lorillard Wolfe and her uncle, Jacob Lorillard, owned this tract in Belmont in the 1880's. She was an admirer of President Chester A. Arthur and donated a statue of him to the City and it stands in Madison Square Park. Originally the street was called Broad Street in Treamont (correct original spelling), and Central Avenue in Belmont. There is a local story that an Arthur Hoffman was a City surveyor, and had this avenue and nearby Hoffman Street named after him, but there is no record of any such surveyor.

Excerpts taken from book, *History In Asphalt,* by John McNamara

I Never Played Carnegie Hall

by Bob Grand

When I was ten, Aunt Esther took me to Carnegie Hall to hear the popular pianist, Jan August. That was the day I decided to become a concert pianist. There wasn't any room for a piano in the family budget, so for a while I kept my mouth shut.

Then I read a biography of George Gershwin. I thought I was reading about myself. He'd grown up in a New York apartment overlooking a noisy street. Me, too. He was the youngest of two brothers. Me, too. He was from a Jewish family. Me, too. He had a funny-shaped nose. Me, too. Okay, so he was from Brooklyn and I was from the Bronx, but hadn't my parents lived in Brooklyn before I was born? Gershwin died in 1937. I was born in September of 1938. There was no question about it. I was the reincarnation of George Gershwin.

One of the photographs in the book showed him as a twelve year-old, seated at his piano bench while his friends were playing outside on the street. He was sacrificing stick ball, marbles and skelly for his music. These were sacrifices I too, would make if I had a piano.

I decided to talk to my parents. But first I wanted to enlist Aunt Esther's moral support. She was the most devoted music lover in the world. She went to concerts, Broadway musicals and musical films, and brought the music home to the Bronx with her. She hummed to us and to herself. She hummed incessantly in the house, on the streets, in New York's subways, at work and while relaxing. No one ever knew what she was humming. Aunt Esther couldn't carry a tune. But she never let that stop her. She continued to hum away, and took great pleasure in doing so.

Aunt Esther sat in on my conversation with Mom and Dad. As it turned out, I didn't need her support. My folks' enthusiasm surprised me.

"No one in the family ever had any musical talent," my mother said. "Maybe you'll be the first."

My father told me not to worry about

the money. "We'll find a way."

"But you have to promise to stay with it for at least three years," my mother said.

I promised.

Henrietta Lackides taught piano in her apartment on the top floor of my building. She was in her middle or late forties, tall and slim, with a thin, elongated face. Her long black hair was curled into ringlets and was amply flecked with gray. She wore wire rim glasses and had rings on every finger except her thumbs.

Her husband George was chubby and about three inches shorter than she. He was a soft-spoken man with a Greek accent. He was a charming, friendly man who laughed readily and seemed to get a lot from life. Everyone I knew liked him.

Mrs. Lackides she said she'd be delighted to tutor me. She charged two dollars an hour, and could fit me in on Tuesday afternoons at four o'clock. She volunteered to go to 149th Street with us the following Saturday to help pick out a used piano.

The days passed too slowly, but when Saturday morning came I was more excited than I'd ever been. At ten o'clock my mother, Mrs. Lackides, Aunt Esther and I got on the southbound Concourse bus. We transferred at 149th Street for the bus to Third Avenue. The trip took about forty-five minutes. I was bouncing up and down the aisle. Mom kept asking me to sit down and be still.

149th Street was the major shopping hub in the south Bronx. There were giant department stores like Hearn's and Alexander's, and large old discount warehouses that had the best bargains in the city. The streets were crowded with browsers and shoppers and pickpockets. Sidewalk hawkers displayed their wares on pushcarts.

Traffic moved at a snail's pace. Irritated drivers leaned on their horns to vent their frustration.

The Third Avenue El loomed high above the scene, casting its giant lattice-work shadow. Hordes of people bumped and elbowed each other as they scrambled up and down the staircase between the street and the elevated platform. The roar of the trains thundering into the station drowned out everything else, even the mayhem on 149th Street.

In the midst of this hubbub was Horowitz's Piano and Organ Exchange, an ancient four-story building jammed with bulky instruments. On the first three levels were pianos. The fourth level had one section filled with pianos while another, occupying about half the floor, was crowded with organs. A precariously narrow wooden staircase without a railing led from one floor to the next. On each level, the walls were lined with uprights and spinets. In the center of each floor were grand pianos and baby grands through which one had to weave in order to walk around the floor. There were pianos as far as the eye could see, every one of them neatly polished and gleaming.

We each had a different agenda when

Carnegie Hall

Continued from page 6

it came to choosing the piano that would sit in the living room. Aunt Esther wanted one she could hum to. Mom wanted one that would match the decor of the living room, sort of early anarchy. Mrs. Lackides was concerned with the practical aspects of sound and durability. I wanted a piano that would allow me to play and compose music like George Gershwin.

Mom saw what she wanted in a corner of the second floor, a dark mahogany Baldwin upright. Mrs. Lackides put it to the test. She sat down on the matching bench and started to play. She played popular tunes and sonatinas. She tested all the keys and the three pedals at the base of the piano. A small crowd gathered to listen. I felt proud that Mrs. Lackides was going to be my piano teacher.

When she finished playing the crowd dispersed. Mrs. Lackides looked up at my mother. "This is a fine piano. The sound is excellent, and it's sturdy. It will last for years."

A salesman accompanied us to the cashier's office, where Mom paid and made delivery arrangements. The piano was $125. It would be delivered the following Saturday morning.

The next week was one of glorious anticipation. I told everyone about the piano. Most of the kids said "so what?" The adults, especially my relatives, at least feigned interest. But nothing dulled my excitement and enthusiasm, and the whole family eagerly awaited the arrival of my piano.

At seven-thirty on Saturday morning we began to move the furniture out of and around the living room. The piano was going to be placed against the wall the breakfront had occupied. We moved the breakfront, a family heirloom, to a less honored place. At eleven o'clock we saw Horowitz's truck pull up in front of my building. Three men got out and came up to our apartment. The supervisor, a short, swarthy, powerfully built middle-aged man, looked around the living room and clucked his disapproval.

"This is going to be a tough one," he said.

He left one of the men in our apartment to remove a living room window from its frame while he and the other man went back down to the street.

By now the neighborhood was awake. A crowd of thirty or forty people had assembled across the street. They watched the delivery men throw blankets over the piano and tie ropes around it. The two men came back up to my apartment and set up a hoisting mechanism near the open window frame, letting its ropes drop to the street. They attached the ropes to others that had been tied around the piano. One of the men went back down to the street to balance the piano. The other two remained in the living room to work the hoist.

The crowd across the street had doubled. The piano began its slow ascent. My family was on the fire escape outside the other living room window. We watched the blanketed hulk being raised slowly toward our second floor apartment. The hoist creaked and squeaked, and the piano seemed to move only inches at a time until, finally, it was dangling directly in front of the open window frame. The three workers were sweating profusely. The muscles in their arms and backs strained as they labored to maneuver the piano through the window frame and into the living room. The people across the street, who had until then been gesturing, pointing, and murmuring comments to one another, heaved a collective sigh of relief and applauded. The delivery men, following instructions from their new supervisor, my mother, moved the piano against the wall, replaced the window and left. After my family got the living room back in order, it hit me. I have a piano! I sat down, lifted back the keyboard cover,

149th Street beneath Third Avenue El station.

The Bronx County Historical Society Research Library

and began to play. What I played sounded like Aunt Esther's humming, but I didn't let that stop me. I had a piano!

The next Tuesday I had my first lesson. In the weeks that followed I practiced at least two hours a day. For the first month I didn't play with my friends. Not once. Mrs. Lackides said I was making great progress.

When school let out for the summer I practiced while my friends played outside. The sounds of their merriment came through the open windows and I longed to be with them. But I had promised my parents three years. So I kept practicing. Every day it became more of a chore. It stopped being fun that first summer, but I was determined to keep my word.

A few months into the third year something unpredictable happened. Mrs. Lackides, by then nearing fifty, became pregnant. It was a difficult pregnancy. She was unable to teach for the last four months. It gave me the excuse I needed to break away and be with my friends. Practices became few and far between.

Mrs. Lackides gave birth to a son, Nicky. Two months later she began to teach again. I halfheartedly continued lessons and practicing for a month or so, then stopped, three years to the day after I'd begun. I'd kept my promise. And that was enough.

Besides, I was George Gershwin. I felt it in my bones. In my previous lifetime I had worked my ass off and died young. In my present lifetime I would have fun and live to a ripe old age.

"Immies Uber Alles"

by Henry Meyerson

There was a phenomenon which reliably occurred on my block at least once a year, sometimes twice, (but this was unreliable), which could only be attributed to a cosmic consciousness. Without prior discussion or reason, marble season began.

Usually in spring, as if drawn by some unfathomable, primordial urge, we emerged from our apartments onto the street, in various combinations, sometimes singly, moving toward the curb across the street from my house, toward a space cleared by the fire hydrant, pockets stuffed with marbles, marbles of all sizes and colors and called, for some inexplicable reason known now only to runic masters, "immies."

Marble season was comparable to the brief, but highly effective, period known to insects as the appropriate time to "swarm." By some apparent biological determinant, out we came, blinking in the bright sun of the vernal equinox, unknown to us bookish/TV types throughout the long, dreary winter when our only cheer was knowingly discussing who the Yankees were going to beat in the next World Series.

Now "immies" wasn't simply a matter of "playing", any more than are leveraged buy-outs "playing." No, "immies" was, at the risk of overly seeking the universal in the trivial, an experience in the basics of entrepreneurship. These spherical bits of colored glass were bought and sold, traded and bartered. The playing of the games was tangential to the end which was not only who had the most, but who had the best, and ultimately who had the most of the best. What was the best? Aha. Now you see the problem. Future writers of doctoral dissertations pored over these bits of glass seeking the "truth within," the arcane meanings and attractions found within the frosted or smoke-filled glass. The Talmud was not more closely studied or wrung out to arrive at its secret attraction. All to no avail.

But throughout this period of trade, there was the bittersweet realization that this moment was to be, as it was to be for such "swarms," all too short.

We, of course, knew that. I guess the bugs didn't. However, that knowledge caused this "immie" crazed bubble to immediately blow to gigantic proportions. Immies uber alles. Nothing else mattered. Immies night and day. "It don't mean a thing if I ain't got that immie. Give me immie or give me death. I have but one life to give to my immie" I mean it was total absorption. And then. And then. Nothing. Gone. Nada.

History. No, not even history. History assumes a record has been left of some kind indicating that something happened. The immie season ended as if nothing happened. I went to bed one night with images of sugar-plum immies dancing in my head only to awaken the next morning with no recollection of the frenzy of the week before. The tape had been wiped clean.

The entire week had been expunged like a bad dream. And eerily when we, the wheeler dealers of yesterday, the J.P. Morgan wannabes, met to go to school the next morning, no one said a word about the immie. The immie was dead and forgotten.

Huge fortunes were wiped out. Immies that had been stockpiled during the craze, hoarded in a grandiose and monomaniacal attempt to create a monopoly, were immediately and unceremoniously dumped into the garbage. And we, as if on auto pilot, marched to school as if nothing unusual had happened.

For those uninitiated in the art of the immie, a brief description of some of the games might be of some interest. For example, a peewee sized immie was placed a few inches from the curb. A line was draw some six feet from the peewee. If you stood at the line and were able to roll one of your immies so that it struck the peewee, the owner of the peewee paid off, usually from five to ten immies. In another version a cigar or cream cheese box had holes of various dimensions cut into one of its sides at the top so that when the box was placed upside-down on the ground the shooter could try to roll his immie into one of the holes. The smaller hole paid off higher than the larger holes.

See, I told you that the games were incidental to the acquisition. The games were boring. The whole point was to increase your hoard.

At least once during each of our "swarms" an event occurred which seemed to epitomize the various motives which produced this massing of the multitude in the first place: greed and aggression. This was known as the "hot scramble." Without warning one of the mass would move to the center of the street, scream "hot scramble" and simultaneously fling a handful of immies high into the air. These, of course, descended, sometimes on our unprotected heads. But undaunted, the adrenaline masking the pain, the "scramble", indeed, began. We scurried like roaches after the

Immies

Continued from page 8

fallen immies.

The "hot scramble" reached its apex in form and memory when Artie, from the roof of the building across the street from the games, launched hundreds of immies from a height of some sixty feet to rain down on the skulls of us poor schmucks who couldn't decide whether to increase our hoard or avoid a concussion.

But it was the acid test. Those of us who chose to gather the thrown immies, who braved the onslaught and were not punished by the breaking of their bones, learned that the reward was worth the risk and no doubt went on to great careers as captains of industry. Those who decided to gather, to take the risk, but were wounded in the attempt, no doubt had great hesitation and trepidation when making any of life's future decisions. Me, I ran like hell. Avoid pain, is my motto. Play it safe. I never wanted too many marbles anyway. I had no place to store them all. Yes, I thank Artie and immies for teaching me a valuable lesson in life: it may be all right to take a risk, just have a helmet handy.

Rockaway

Continued from page 4

evening I approached the shack. Although the door had a lock, each slab had nothing to hold it but two itty bitty hooks and eyes. Being a skinny kid, I was also, the proud owner of skinny wrists, wrists thin enough to squeeze behind the narrow openings and flip both the hooks from their eyelets. Well, I crawled into the shack and for a nine year old kid with under-developed hormones, the feelings I experienced must have been close to orgasm. All the wonders denied me with just one rotten Milky Way, were now mine. Excess, abundance, riches, affluence... mine.

"What are you doing in there?", shouted the voice from outside. The bubble burst, along with my short career in larceny. But it wasn't the cops, it was worse. It was my sister, Bebe, whose mouth was connected to my mother's ear. Bebe rendered her familiar words, "I'm gonna tell Mamma." And so, to thievery, was added bribery. Three Hershey bars and a pack of Doublemint pacified her for awhile as her words faded in the distance, "You better be home for supper. Mamma's waiting."

I had to hurry. Using my jacket as a sack, I filled it with my favorite candy bars along with two rolls of kite cord. I couldn't carry the soda bottles so I emptied twenty of them and buried each one in the sand. Since each bottle was worth a deposit of two cents, any time I needed a little change, I could literally dig it up. I wrapped my candy cache in a towel and then buried it in the sand under the side porch of the hotel. Two days later, the final irony occurred. The great Karnovsky, eager to improve her domain, had given the green light to expansion. The digging began for the installation of basement apartments along with a row of lockers and showers. Guess where? It was right under the back and side porches. Can you imagine how I felt to see my Hershies, my Baby Ruths, my Mounds, my Butterfingers being licked off those beefy thumbs of five "bullvans" of Polish extraction during their lunch break? As much as I wanted too I couldn't even yell, "They're mine!"

And so, my life of crime came to a tormented end: not because these guys were enjoying the fruits and nuts of my labor, but because my sister ended up with more than I did.

The sunny days were spent at the beach. Mamma would pack a lot of food and lemonade and we'd play in the sand and swim in the ocean. You'd learn to get the feel of the ocean. Sometimes it was bad and angry - the kind of angry you didn't want to tangle with. Then it was calm - the calm that helped you learn to swim. Best of all was when the ocean would play at being angry. It would not want to claim you with its undertow, just bat you around a little. And if it caught you just right, it tossed you "tuchas over teakettle." As you went under you'd tumble swallowing water and sand until it dumped you on the beach gasping for breath. Then you'd end up scooping half the beach out of the ass of your bathing suit. So you quickly learned where they were breaking and you'd either yell, "Over," and let the curl carry you high above it or you'd yell, "Under," and dive into it just before it smashed on top of you and took you under.

On rainy days, it was the porch. We'd play Tag, Blind Man's Bluff, Ringaleveo, Monopoly and Chinese Checkers. Or we'd turn all the rocking chairs upside down and connect them to form a train. Sometimes a grown-up would take us to the movies in Far Rockaway. My favorite place was the penny arcade where everything really was a penny.

In Rockaway, doors were always open. For two months every year, we all lived together, one great community, seeing each other as we really were.

We saw our neighbors in their bathing suits, housecoats, bathrobes and heard them belch, argue, laugh and cry. Lke those sand walls we built, that couldn't hold back the tide, we kids couldn't hold back the years. We, too, grew older.

The one picture I'll always remember was when it was my turn to work in the city and commute every day. My mother would pack a brown bag and as I walked from the rooming house, I would turn to look up. And from the window of Elsie's room, I'd always see a little lady waving to me.

Reminiscing

Rochambeau Avenue Goes To War

By Marvin Rosen Ph.d

3505 Rochambeau Avenue

On those rare occasions, when I find myself in antique stores, I search among the collections of depression glass and faded knit shawls for a warmly remembered residue of childhood. Painted lead soldiers in the early 1940s were available at any Woolworth's for a dime. They were unequaled in simulating the battalions and regiments of America's first line of defense against the Axis—the U.S. Infantry. How many hours did I lie in bed with a ten day dose of the grippe, my boredom relieved only by mock battles of foot soldiers spread precariously across the trenches of germ laden bed linens? To no avail my search. Those momentos of my childhood always seem to elude me, abandoned no doubt on some forgotten scrap heap an eon ago.

I had been home with just such an affliction on that Sunday in December, 1941. I was only in the third grade but already I worried about examinations. I knew there was to be a geography test the next day. Without enthusiasm I tried to memorize the rivers surrounding New York City and the bridges that traversed them. The kitchen Philco droned in the background. Without warning the show was interrupted for a cryptic news bulletin. Some place called Pearl Harbor had been attacked by Japanese bombers. My grandmother also heard the announcement and summoned my parents to come listen. Ships were burning in the harbor. More news would follow later. I struggled to extract our geographic Atlas from the closet—a give-away promotion from the New York Post. Such a tiny country, my mother observed, and so far away. The war, which would undoubtedly ensue, would surely be short-lived. Although I did not understand the significance of that "sneak attack," somehow the bridges into New York City seemed less important.

School the next day buzzed with excitement as teachers and students constantly searched the skies for Jap bombers. P.S. 80 was no different from the rest of the city. One afternoon not long after the outbreak of war, we were sent home on rumors that an armada of attack planes was headed for the Bronx. My mother and grandmother stood by our fifth story bedroom windows, scanning the skies over Rochambeau Avenue. I urged them back to safer rooms to avoid shattering glass.

Gradually Rochambeau Avenue adjusted to the war. An Air Raid Warden squadron was organized and my father volunteered. Most of my friends' fathers did the same. They received white helmets with insignias and gas masks which hung in our hall closet for the duration of the conflict. There were first aid classes and much other planning but the principal activity of the wardens was to organize blackouts. Scheduled on a regular basis, they were rehearsals for the real air raid, should it ever occur. My father never really took his responsibilities seriously. "In case of a raid, follow your warden ...if you can keep up with him."

We grew accustomed to the war news on the radio and at the Tuxedo and Mosholu. In assemblies we sang "Anchors Away", "Off We Go Into The Wild Blue Yonder...", and "Praise The Lord And Pass The Ammunition." We brought quarters to school to purchase Defense Stamps that were pasted in a book at home until we had $18.75 for a Defense Bond (later a War Bond). Dutifully we wound rubber bands into a ball around a cardboard core for the collections on the Avenue. Similarly we peeled the "silver" off chewing gum wrappers to turn in regularly. We brought old 78 inch records to a collection center. They were broken to determine if there was a metal base to aid the war effort. Across my room I strung silhouettes of friendly and enemy aircraft to assist in identification from the ground. The P-40, B-38, B17, B-25, the Zero and Messerschmidt became part of our culture. We drew them in our lined notebooks, propellers whirling, fire spurting from cannons. We hung war maps from the National Geographic. I built the U.S. Lexington, a flattop, from a kit. Insignias from The 1st Army and the Rainbow Division became cherished possessions. Alex, the strapping Super's son was one of the first to serve his country. We saw him proudly strutting in his new Navy blues in front of 3280. We learned to love FDR.

Hitler. We heard our parents speak in hushed voices of places like Auschwitz and Treblinka. My parents learned to use ration books for purchasing sugar and shoes and meat. Such things could also be purchased illegally at a premium on the "black market." Gradually metal toys disappeared from the Woolworth's at Bainbridge, near Webster and on Jerome Avenue. My father had to give up his '38 Chevrolet, when gas was unavailable, and ride the subway to his loft at 7th Avenue and 38th Street. We watched for him at night, coming

Continued page 11

10

Rochambeau

Continued from page 10

from the station at 208th Street carrying a Daily Telegram. The first to spy him from my grandmother's window would shout for my mother to put the gas up on his "hochfleisch."

I passed from childhood to adolescence during the war years. It provided a constant backdrop that shaped my personality. There was no challenging the war. It was natural to support one's flag and country. To do otherwise was considered more than unpatriotic; it was akin to treason. The conviction and execution of the Rosenbergs was not challenged on Rochambeau Avenue. And when the atomic bombs fell to bring the war to a close, Bronxites cheered the successful conclusion of hostilities and return of troops. The devastation to thousands of Japanese civilians was a just and fitting retribution to a warlike and belligerent people. Like thousands of others, my friends and I rushed into the streets cheering and waving flags. It was only later that the repercussions of the bomb were more fully appreciated.

Curiously, my family was relatively untouched by the war.

We knew of no relatives exterminated by the Holocaust; we were too long in this country. There were few members of the family who served. My father's business prospered during the war so that five years after the cessation of hostilities we were able to leave our Bronx apartment for a home in Yonkers. The American dream had been realized.

So what did the war mean to a Bronx boy who left Rochambeau Avenue? It was a time of absolutes. Good was good and bad was bad. God was on the side of the Allies. It was only to be expected that they would emerge victorious and that our enemies would be sorely punished. The war provided the heroes young boys needed and the ideals of honor, patriotism and love of country were firmly ingrained.

Having lived through WWII, it was difficult to challenge Korea or Vietnam. My family and I were to vote Democratic for years after Roosevelt for the Democratic Party seemed synonymous with democracy. Not for many years was a national leader so

Rochambeau Avenue at 206th Street. About 1950

The Bronx County Historical Society Research Library

supported. And for me Rochambeau Avenue and the war merge into a misty collage of school yard, apartment houses, patriotic songs and dozens of brown painted lead soldiers making the world safe for democracy.

Just for laughs...

"Nothing to speak of. Someone left a Bronx Cheer on your voice mail."

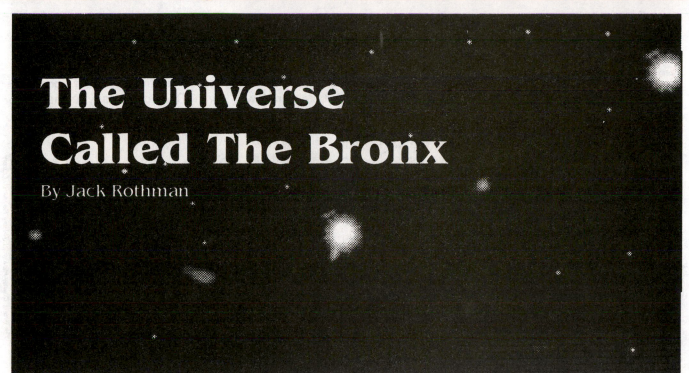

The Universe Called The Bronx

By Jack Rothman

Growing up in the Bronx after WWII there was no universe, no foreign countries, no USA, no New York State. The world was THE BRONX, and your town was either the Grand Concourse, Parkchester, Pelham Parkway, etc. Mine was Hillside Homes (Hillside), located between Boston Post Road and Hicks Street, and between Eastchester Road and Wilson Avenue.

Fall asleep on the 'D' train to the last stop, 205th street. No fears or thoughts about being robbed, mugged, or worse. Run up the stairs and catch the '15A' bus. Speak to some friends and neighbors sitting next to you and before long your home, Hillside, (a five square block, 1500 apartment complex, with 6000 friendly town's people).

We didn't need Jane Fonda's workout video. We had no elevators, but four flights of stairs to walk up and down with groceries, laundry and school books kept us in shape. Groceries were bought at the A&P, and fruits and vegetables at Smilen Bros. 8:00 A.M. Sunday morning was the time for picking up rye bread and rolls, together with jelly donuts and black n' white cookies. Of course, a slice of the rye bread was eaten on the walk home (for energy), and ½ of the cookie as a reward for going to the store.

The Melba theater (RKO movies), the Loew's Post Road (MGM movies), and the bowling alley underground, entertained us. Lee's candy store on Fish Avenue and the candy store on Corsa Avenue sweetened us. Public school was kindergarten and grades one through eight at P.S. 78 and for most of us, high school was Evander Childs. 'Gay' to us meant Mr. Gay, the successful swimming coach. ("Learn to swim or don't graduate.")

"No more teachers, no more books, no more teacher's dirty looks'... and summer time would start with listening to Mel Allen broadcasting Yankee baseball games. The play-ground between Seymour and Fenton Avenues was crowded with children in the wading pool (later used for punchball games). Stickball, softball, and basketball games seemed to be in progress 24 hours a day. Checkers, Chinese checkers and chess games were given out by the person in charge of the playground. They were also returned. We hitchhiked to Orchard Beach, and hours in the calm water cooled us in the daytime. Opened windows cooled us at night. Taking a date to the big city meant taking two buses to Fordham Road, to gaze at the stars on the ceiling of the Loew's Paradise, followed by an ice cream soda downstairs at Krums. Big time shopping was "uptown it's Alexanders."

We laughed, were loved, and lived well. What a fantastic, never boring, memory-filled universe we lived in called THE BRONX.

Evander Childs High School

12

Friends Forever

By Muriel Fine McEvoy

You wouldn't remember me but I remember all of you. I hung out everywhere. I belonged nowhere. I was born on Hoe Ave; P.S. 75 was my school, Susan Lessner my best friend. I lived in Susan's shadow. She was prettier, perkier, and already shaved her legs when I met her. I followed her from childhood, through puberty and well into adulthood. However, if she were to tell our story she would say, she, followed me.

We did everything together, two nondescript Jewish girls from the Bronx. We went from jump-rope, stoop games, dances at Poe Park, to learning to swim at Shorehaven Pool. We laughed, we cried, we fought, we threw our sins into the East River on Yom Kippur, and only she knew what this meant. We watched the neighborhood turn gray and change. We watched our friends leave for undisclosed places with names like Westchester, and Long Island. We clung to each other for support when the gangs came into the neighborhood and were terrified to take the bus to school.

Our junior high school, on Intervale Ave. was all girls. They locked the doors when the bell rang so no one could get in or out (especially the neighborhood boys). We especially feared the "Fordham Baldies Gang." Of course we never actually saw a "Fordham Baldie," but Montrose Mann, a very large tough kid, assured us that they were after us.

One afternoon while watching American Bandstand with Susan and my brother, my apartment caught fire. We barely made it out the door. I could still see my mother's face that day returning home from work, with all the tenants in the street watching the fire. We lost everything we owned. There was no renters' insurance in those days. My father blamed my brother for the fire. He swore he had

to be smoking which was ridiculous. If anyone had been smoking it would have been me. The fireman came; they said it was old faulty wiring. The fire had crept along our cold water flat and turned all our possessions into ashes; it was a blessing in disguise. We were forced to move.

My new neighborhood was 1115 College Ave. I could now tell people that I lived near the Concourse. Things were looking up. My life was changing, the Bronx was changing. My apartment was on the top floor. It was light, it was bright and we barely noticed that the elevator rarely worked. I could see JHS 60 from my window. Susan was distraught. She spent every weekend with me until her parents finally gave up on Bryant Ave and moved to Grand Ave so we could go to high school together. "Best Friends Forever" we'd say. We went to Taft High School.

We met new people, but we felt we had absolutely northing in common with them. We clung to each other for support. Some days we'd cut classes and ride the buses all day. Other days we'd buy sour pickles and sit in the corridor of one of the highrise buildings and dream of a life outside the Bronx. We looked like everyone else and dressed like everyone else, but we had "Hoe Ave. Hearts."

Nevertheless, we hung around Macombs Bowling Alley, necked with a variety of boys under the stars at the Concourse Paradise Theatre, became bolder and took the bus to Pelham Parkway to hob nob with the "real" middle class boys from Columbus H.S.

In my third and fourth year of high school, I became part of an experi-

mental program for the poor. It was called the Coop program. I went to school one week and worked the next, alternating weeks. This was designed for girls like me who had no hope of every going to college. In those days the boys went to college and the girls got married. My father had two bank accounts: one for my brother's college, and one set aside for my wedding. The choices were made for us. It didn't matter that my parents were told by my teachers that "she is college material." My father had other ideas. As it turned out I loved the program and I loved working.

It was like getting out of jail. I was placed by the school in Brooks Brothers in NYC. We were an elite group-the "Coop girls." Where are you all now? We always hung out together, excluding ourselves from the academic types, telling ourselves we were sophisticated and worldly: city girls corrupted by money. By senior year, close to half the class was engaged to be married, including me. Imagine, at 17 we sported diamond rings with tiny stones and we all shared the same dream-getting out of the Bronx!

My dream came true. I made it over the Queens line by marrying a Pelham Parkway prince that later turned into a frog. Susan followed close behind, marrying a frog that turned into a prince, then back again into a frog. I moved twice, she moved twice, both times within blocks of each other. I had children, she went to college. She wanted to be me and I wanted to be her. I sank deeper into suburban life. She dropped out of life, and moved to a farm in Massachusetts.

We tried to hang on to each other but life was sending us in different directions. Susan got divorced twice, then a third time. I finally came out of my 'American Dream' coma and also got divorced. I remarried. We both wondered if there was something toxic in the Bronx water.

I hear from Susan only now and then. Susan will calls me when she is in trouble, or when she's lonely. She calls to tell me no matter what, we will always be "Hoe Ave" girls. I think she's right. It's in the Bronx drinking water.

Life Between Two Parks

By Eda Mittler Pickholtz

In 1940, when I was five, I was lucky to move to apartment 6B at 3957 Gouverneur Avenue, where I lived until I was married in 1957. Gouverneur Avenue was a short street between two parks. I remember an identical 6-story apartment house next door. A large private home on the block had been converted into a synagogue where my father, a CPA, "did the books." This meant that I had to attend Sunday School.

In 1940, we had our choice of apartments, and even a few months free rent. My mother always regretted picking the sixth floor, since she claimed that the heat from the roof descended on us every summer. On the other hand, we were near the clothes lines on the roof. When we first moved in, we had a uniformed elevator man and many beautiful pieces of furniture in our lobby, which were gradually replaced by a self-service elevator and a few pieces of chained-down furniture.

My friend and her family lived in apartment 1C. They actually raised canaries and parakeets right in my friend's bedroom. My friend and her sister had a painted blue ceiling, and whenever they were good, they would have a silver star put up on their "sky." Their mother made wooden Mammy dressing tables, complete with red-and-white checked skirts, white aprons and turbans, large earrings, and their outstretched arms holding a large mirror. They had several "Mammies" in their room, which one month was featured in "House Beautiful" or some other decorating magazine, a "big deal event" for our apartment house. Their mother worked at FAO Schwarz downtown, and would tell us which actors and actresses came in that day to buy toys.

How did we keep busy in those days? Well, indoors we would play many card games, checkers, Chinese checkers, Parcheesi, Monopoly, Dominoes, Pick-up Sticks, Mr. Ree (a who-done-it board game), jacks, etc. When we were teenagers, we played Mah Jong. Outdoors, the girls would play "potsy", jump-rope, jacks. The boys were lucky to have the huge school-yard of P.S. 95 right across from my building for all their ball games. Our New York schools were like fortresses. (When I moved down to Virginia, I always thought the one-level, "genteel" schools here were like toys). Sometimes we broke into two groups. One group would hide in the gardens of the Amalgamated buildings, while the other group would try to find the other. Halloween was always a favorite with us kids going door to door for goodies. We were lucky to have a library in the first floor apartment of a building across the street and up Sedgwick Avenue. My happiest days were in that library choosing a new book to read. My piano lessons were also in that building, with not so happy memories.

We were also collectors. I had a huge comic book collection, a playing card collection with beautiful scenes on the back, and a collection of dixie cup covers with pictures of actors and actresses on them. I was once given signed glossy photographs of the stars because I delivered a package to some movie studio in the Bronx. I wish I had those collections now.

Living between two parks afforded other pleasures. Our Jerome Reservoir Park had a well-trodden wooded path leading to a traditional, old-fashioned concrete-floored playground. Van Cortlandt Park offered much more. We could sled and learn to ski on a tiny hill in the park. We could walk to Van Cortlandt Mansion, ice skate on the lake, watch the Major Deegan being built, and watch the new police recruits take their physical fitness tests on the Broadway end of the park. We could even walk to Riverdale, or take the trolley from 242nd Street to Yonkers, where my father's family lived. In the summer, we could walk a long, long way to swim at Tibbets Brook Park, and return by bus.

In the summer evenings we would bring chairs and sit in front of the schoolyard to catch the breeze supposedly passing between the parks. How did we survive without air-conditioning? The Good Humor and Bungalow Bar trucks helped out. Our neighborhood also had

3951-57 Gouverneur Avenue

"I cash clothes" men, scissors and knife-sharpening men, and milkmen passing through.

Beginning at age twelve, I was able to escape from the hot summers by going to girl scout camp - first as a camper at Camp Laughing Water in Bear Mountain, and then as a C.I.T. and counselor at Camp Andree in Pleasantville, N.Y. You either loved or hated girl scout camp. There was no in-between. I loved the scenery, hikes, singing around the campfire. (Many years later, my daughters hated the bugs, latrines, and chores).

The Concourse Bus played a large part in my life - taking me to Alexander's, the Paradise, the Ascot for foreign films, and Krum's, where a huge hot fudge sundae could be had for around 24¢. There were not many shops in our neighborhood, so the bus would take us to the Jerome

Two Parks

Continued from page 14

Avenue shops when the weather was too messy to walk up the steep hill. Sometimes the bus would take us to a restaurant - always Chinese- where we always ordered chicken chow mein which arrived in a hot covered serving dish heaping with food- unlike today's skimpier portions.

The bus took me to the "old, old" Bronx Science building, and then the merely "old" Bronx Science building. It took me to Hunter College in the Bronx, when it was too cold to walk up the hill and around the reservoir. I imagine I was a geographically undesirable date, since I lived "beyond the subway." Many a cold night my date and I would wait at the Bedford Park Boulevard station for the bus to take us down Mosholu Parkway, past De Witt Clinton H.S., back to my home.

I remember war-time at P.S. 95, especially the air-raid drills, wearing plastic I.D. tags, singing patriotic songs in Assembly. We had many wonderful teachers, such as Mrs. Lapidus, Mr. Levy and Miss Kosky. On the other hand, I learned to hate sewing when Miss Conroy threatened that we would have to "walk down the aisles in our slips" if our graduation dresses weren't finished on time.

We were the last January graduation (1949) at P.S. 95. It was very reassuring to go through eight years of school with basically the same set of 32-36 kids. We recently had an reunion and 14 of us showed up. I couldn't believe that I recognized most of the faces after 44 years!

Grant Avenue

Continued from page 1

Riverdale.

The Concourse was for rich kids, sons and daughters of doctors and accountants. Three blocks east of the Concourse, where we lived, was a different world—for families of firemen, policemen, and hard workers like my dad, who struggled to make a go of it in his own small (very small) manufacturing business.

At P.S. 35 I envied my classmates from the Concourse who came to school wearing coordinated outfits, pretty decorative collars, and cute patent leather shoes. In those days I owned two skirts and four sweaters and blouses to "mix and match." Nothing but sturdy laced shoes were good enough for my feet. And bad weather boots had to be at least three sizes too big "to grow into."

In my family we never went to the hairdresser (in those days we called it the beauty parlor). My mother cut my hair with the aid of a saucepan which she inverted on my head. Clipping around the rim of the pot, she turned me into a dead ringer for the Buster Brown Boy.

The only time my hairstyle changed was for my sister Flo's wedding when I was ten years old. Flo gave me a Toni home perm. I still remember the chemical smell that burned my eyes and nose and excitement of my very first makeover.

Summer evenings on Grant Avenue, neighbors sat on folding chairs, savoring the evening breeze. And I was allowed to stay up late. Playing outdoors at night might have been frightening. Instead it was intoxicating—feeling completely safe in the darkness under the protection of my parents and their friends.

By 9 P.M. I was usually back upstairs waiting for the jingle of the Bungalow Bar ice-cream truck. My father would go downstairs for "combination

Lila Freilicher (1948) on Morris Ave. and 164th St. Fleetwood Theater in background. Movies playing: "Meet Me On Broadway" and Greer Garson & Clark Gable in "Adventure."

cups" of 1/2 ices and 1/2 vanilla ice cream. I remember the special excitement when the flavor of the week was raspberry. Joe, the Bungalow Bar man, came twice each day. If I wanted to buy ice cream during his afternoon stop, I had to yell upstairs to my mother: "Ma! Bungalow Bar is here!" She would wrap coins in a tissue or napkin and launch them out of the window toward my outstretched arms.

Actually my favorite ice cream treat was from the corner candy store. It was a mellow roll—a cylinder of ice cream served on a double cone. The mello roll came wrapped in paper. You placed the roll on the cone, and carefully peeled off the covering.

From my perspective on Grant Avenue, I saw a world divided into friends and enemies. There were two "sides" to our building, separated by the courtyard. On each side was a decorative balustrade—a concrete-covered railing supported with waist high columns- a perfect place for kids pretending to ride a horse. But on weekends and evenings the balustrades became fortesses for the building's opposing forces.

With chairs grouped conversationally in front of "our" balustrade, my mother chatted with her best friends, two sisters, Anna and Rose. I remember Rose best. She had a daughter who was pushed around in a stroller until she was so big that her

Continued on page 16

15

Reminiscing

Grant Avenue

Continued from page 15

legs had to be tucked under so the stroller could move.

My mother's friends spoke in hushed tones about the women who congregated on "the other side." Their self appointed leader was Blossom, a buxom bleached blond broad, queen of the gossips.

Mrs. MacIntyre was the building's ogre. She hated kids and was continually poised to dump a pot of water on our heads if we were too noisy. The danger of this was greater when we were rollerskating. The steel wheels grated on the sidewalks, and the din echoed off the canyon-like walls of the courtyard.

From my parents' bedroom, I could look straight across the courtyard. Mrs. Chinsky was always there looking back at me from that window. I don't believe I ever saw her outdoors. And on those rare occasions when I found her away from her post, I always felt something stable was missing from my life.

Josie, our super, was a mysterious, formidable creature. She wasn't fully human, living as she did amidst the indescribable horrors of the buildings basement. That basement must have been truly awful because we actually bought our own washing machine for the apartment to avoid going down there. And this was an extreme luxury for a family in our circumstances. The few times I did descend below ground I can recall extreme aversion mixed with a sense of amazement that anyone could live in such a place.

Josie did all the work, even though she had a husband. This included collecting the garbage with the dumbwaiter. What strength it must have required to hoist those ropes up and down! And what an odd luxury a dumbwaiter was for such an ordinary building.

My mother was an expert at stove top cooking. The oven was never used for preparing meals. It was used for storage, and on the rare occasion when my mother wanted to bake a cake, it was a monumental task to remove the pots and pans.

Considering this self-imposed limitation, my mother was a pretty good cook—in the Jewish style. But as a child I didn't appreciate foods like sweet and sour soup with flanken, stuffed cabbage, and my mother's "hamburgers"— meat mixed with onion, eggs and matzo meal, formed into patties, rolled in matzo meal and fried. I loathed these mud-colored missiles, amazingly tasteless despite their ingredients. And I remember the joy — years later— of discovering what a real hamburger was.

After that I tried hard to prevent my mother from mixing the meat with other ingredients. "So plain..." she'd lament. Then I would stand over her in a vain attempt to have a hamburger prepared rare. "It's not cooked!" she would cry in alarm.

My grandparents lived two blocks away on Morris Avenue and 163rd Street. They had something in their apartment I coveted—a fascinating and highly practical contraption for drying clothes. It was attached to the ceiling. To hang the clothes, you let it down, and you hoisted it back up again to get it out of the way when you were finished.

Their apartment was just yards away from the Fleetwood, a movie theater known affectionately to us kids as the fleabox, where you could see a double feature and cartoons for a few cents.

Food shopping with my mom was big part of my life in those days, and I fondly remember the stores and retailers on 161st, 165th and 167th Street. There was Hymie, the Butcher, who riveted my attention with his hacking and trimming techniques and Jenny, the chicken plucker who did her work at the back of the butcher shop.

On 165th Street we visited Mrs. Teckel at her haberdashery and notions store. She was a stubby old woman who presided over one of the last places on earth to sell smocks, dress shields and gotkes (long underwear) under one roof.

The only non-Jewish shopkeeper I can remember was Yolanda, the bak-

1113 Grant Avenue

ery lady. Yolanda was at least to me, an exotic woman with a thick foreign accent and long black hair tied tightly into a bun. My favorite treat at her bakery was a vanilla cookie nearly as big as a cake. It had a chocolate circle in the middle which I carefully ate around, savoring the center for last.

By the time I was 12 years old and a student at Jordan L. Mott JHS 22, I was going clothes shopping by myself to avoid fighting with my mother over prices and styles. There was only one department store available to me and that was Alexander's. Luckily there were two branches I could get to by bus: one on the Grand Concourse at Fordham Rd. and the other at 149th Street and Third Avenue (near the Third Ave. "L") an area know as "The Hub."

At Alexander's your money went a long, long way, if you were willing to spend the time sorting through tables piled high with garments. The table method was time consuming especially for shoes—looking for the right style, right color and right size in the big pile. I was 16 years old before I knew you could try on shoes that weren't tied together!

But by then we had moved out of the old neighborhood to Riverdale. Though technically still in the Bronx, Riverdale's proximity to Westchester lent it airs.

In Riverdale, no one ever sat outside to chat on hot summer nights. Keeping yourself in Riverdale was a mark of status. And having lived on Grant Avenue was something to forget. Well, maybe it was for my parents, but not for me— never for me.

Sex and the Single Rail

By Henry Meyerson

When we were teenagers, our roosting spot was on a pipe railing that ran the length of Mosholu Park and , oddly enough was, directly across from our old junior high school-oddly because it would be like parolees deciding to "hang out" in front of Sing-Sing once they were released.

But there we were: every night during the summer, weekends only during the school year. Starting at about 6:30 in the evening we would begin to show up: singly, in pairs, in groups. A trickle at first, then swelling to a stream, and then to a torrent, we would come.

15-19 W. Mosholu Parkway

It was as if every night the Sioux had a powwow with representatives of all their brethren, of all their nations. They all came and formed a mighty river. That was us, a mighty river of adolescence.

Kids from all parts of the Bronx came. From Bainbridge Avenue, from Rochambeau Avenue, we came; from Mosholu Park East and West, we came; from across Jerome Avenue, Gates and Knox Places, we came; from Villa Avenue, from as far away as Creston Avenue and Parkchester, we all came. And why did we come, these hordes, these seekers? No one knows. But it was a hell of a show.

I mean, during a Spring Friday evening we might have had 200 kids

at any one time. Occasionally we also had cops. But they were just there to show the flag, because as one of us said as he was being beaten up by Ray the Bully, "I'm not causing any trouble; I'm going to college." That was us. 200 kids milling aimlessly, ovinely docile and brain-dead, looking for something but too stupid to know what it was, even if we fell over it, all waiting for something else: college, work, marriage, service, death.

Now I think perhaps what we were waiting for was sex, but we couldn't be too sure. So we met like this, on the rail of the park, and we asked each other if it was sex we were looking for and most of us were unsure. But some of us were pretty sure that it was, and they were the first to drop out of school, not being able to understand what education had to do with sex. We also began to wonder if being sexual was incompatible with being educated. And if it was, which would we take? This was a major conundrum.

Sex in the Fifties among thirteen to seventeen year old Jewish middle-class kids from the north Bronx (is this market sufficiently segmented?) was generally in name only: a squeeze here, a hand held there, here a touch, there a feel, kiss, kiss here, hug, hug there, here a fear, there a fear, everywhere a fear, fear. And beside, there was this incredible difficulty of getting through all those crinoline slips girls wore under their dresses. I can't speak for the girls, but for the guys it was like chopping your way through a jungle of gauze. You wished you had brought a machete in order to get through these layers upon layers of

that stupid, ungiving material. Then finally, as you were nearing the target, you got your hand slapped-after at least ten-to-fifteen minutes of hard work. This definitely was not fair. They could be cruel, those Bronx girls.

115 East Mosholu Parkway

3110 Bainbridge Avenue

17

LOST &FOUND

Track down your old friends, neighbors and lost relatives with
THE BRONX TRACKING SERVICE

Did you ever wonder what some of your high school buddies are doing? Where do they live now?

Well, **Back in THE BRONX TRACKING SERVICE** may be able to help you find them and maybe even discover long lost relatives you never know you had. Find the phone numbers and addresses from a database of 70 to 100 million people from all across the U.S. You can find that special old friend who you haven't heard from in years (decades). If you are like most people, as you get older you wonder more about those special friends you've lost touch with over the years. Wouldn't it be great to give them a call to swap stories and reminisce? If you are interested in tracing your genealogy, looking for lost parents, or children, we can help.

**Simply complete the application below—
We'll do the rest.**

THE BRONX TRACKING SERVICE
APPLICATION

Name (Print or Type)

Last _____ First _____ Middle _____

Maiden Name _____

Address (Last know address or general location) _____

_____

City _____ State _____ Zip _____

Approximate date living at above address _____

High School _____ Year graduated _____

Age _____

Requested By:

Address: _____

City _____ State _____ Zip _____

Phone: _____

THE BRONX TRACKING SERVICE
APPLICATION

Name (Print or Type)

Last _____ First _____ Middle _____

Maiden Name _____

Address (Last know address or general location) _____

_____

City _____ State _____ Zip _____

Approximate date living at above address _____

High School _____ Year graduated _____

Age _____

Requested By:

Address: _____

City _____ State _____ Zip _____

Phone: _____

I have enclosed a payment of **$9.95** for each person that I am looking to trace. I understand that I will receive a list of name and addresses and phone numbers for each person from a database of over 70 million names throughout the United States. I further understand that I will have to search through theses names and determine the approximate name that matches the one(s) you are trying to trace.

Missing Persons

MP705 Knox Place, DeKach Ave., **Clinton** '63. Looking for people who remember Kenny Kushin. Call 206-823-4581 or write: 12112 104th NE, Kirkland, WA 98034

MP706 Leslie Naiman from **Evander** '62, CCNY '66, Mosholu Pkwy - I'd love to hear from anyone who remembers me.

MP707 Kingsbridge Road and Reservoir Ave., 1941-1949. The one and only Barracudas SAC and their friends. Stan Getzler would like to hear from you. Phone: 212-787-9026 Fax: 212-873-4302.

MP708 Iris (Kaplan) Samuels, **Taft** '54 & PS 82. Formerly from 1700 Harrison Ave., now in Armonk, NY. Would like to find Rita (Rudich) Kaplan, Joan Austin, Sandra Roth, Mimi (Feinstein) Kaplan, also others from Tremont corner candy store (ex fountain girl) 914-273-8743

MP709 Karen (Gordon) Marrinan, **Evander** '64, JHS 80 '61 & PS 94. Looking for old friends from Gun Hill Road and PS 80. Especially Elaine Schieber. Please write c/o magazine.

MP710 Arthur Spechler, **Morris** '28, retired patent attorney. Presently working with sons as an optician in Cherry Hill, NJ. Would love to hear from old friends or classmates.

MP711 Would like to hear from old friends. **Ridder** '49-'52; **Monroe** '53-'55. Frieda Meyers Tolkov & Jerry Tolkov. 914-476-2399, 104 Hilltop Acres, Yonkers NY 10704

MP712 Prospect JHS 40, Class 7ARIO '41. Where are you Eileen Moriarity of Tiffany St. or anyone in that class? Dolores Isaacson Lessner - still in The Bronx- 718-796-7933

MP713 Howard Nieporent, **Clinton** '55 - Kingsbridge & University - Towers Pharmacy - Strong Street Pharmacist, in Sunrise Florida. Misses "Roz", hitching to "DWC", burning Christmas trees, alternate side parking, the Lone Ranger, his Corvette & GTO, The Kingsbridge Terrace Hill, Ptomaine Toni's onions & tomato hot dog, Kingsbridge movie theatre

MP714 Looking for old friends from Van Buren St. - Anne Barile Liguori, Ronald Previ, Elaine Berlusconi Campbell

MP715 Harold Benzer, **Roosevelt** '45, living in Las Vegas and loving it! Would like to hear from old friends. P.O. Box 12621, E. Las Vegas, NV 89112

MP716 Marie Kovacs, Diane Pera , Warren Lipkin and Sheila (Kotofsky) Lipkin would like to here from you - 407 260-0254 - 517 Faith Terrace, Muitland FL 32751

MP717 I grew up on Bryant Ave. This year will be our 10th Bryant Ave. reunion. We are searching for : Peter Winston or Peter Touissant (nickname Tiny)- we believe he went to Aviation HS. He hung out with Warren Trupin, Butch Lanos, Billy Morrison and Tommy Molloy. Any info please contact Butch Lanos at 914 342-4987.

MP718 Hi! My name is Marc Minick and I would like to hear from Mosholu Pkwy and Evander '68 folks.

MP719 I am searching for our old group from Davidson Ave. We used to play cards, be in the scouts and have great times: Mark Kaplan, Harvey Green, Harvey Rothman and Barbara Simon-my first love.

MP720 My name is Larry Schecter. I lived at 1950 Andrews Ave. in the Bronx. I have a brother Barry. I joined the marines in 1951. Retired in 1975. I am a Sgt. with the Bucks Co. Sheriff's Dept in PA. I hope some one remembers me after all these years.

MP721 Herb Schenk, **Taft** '51, looking for ex-classmates or friends from 165th & Morris-Grant area. Now living in So. FL. Have seen Stu Reich, Marilyn Messenger and had a wonderful dinner recently with Art & Dorothy DeRuve after a 43 year absence. Looking for Larry Schwartz, Myron Cohen, Judy Rydell, Harold Pepper and the "rest of the gang." Call 305 434-2600 day or 305 436-8442 eve.

MP722 I'm looking for Joan Siegel from 825 Gerard Ave. Please contact Rhonda Berman Moskowitz..

MP723 Elena, Diane & Joyce, White Plains Road & Morris Park Ave. looking for friends: Vilma F., Rose R., Frankie N. and Louie B.

MP724 Any Spirals out there from PS 11? Where are you Phillip Greenblat, Jack Plimpton and any others from 1275 Nelson Ave. Last 8th grade graduating class. Like to find Elaine Haber, Diane Wiess and all the old gang. Contact Stephan Selder.

MP725 PS 33 Class of '47. Planning a reunion for 1997. Looking for Barbara Feldberg, Shirley Nelson, Sylvia Grenz, Lila Harris, Royce Goldman, Sheila Call, Audrey Green, Barbara Silverstein, Cecilia Klein, Enid Greennaum, Helene Tiger-Call 718 229-3275

MP726 Mike Gumpel, **Clinton** '64. Would like to hear from old friends from Fordham Rd., Poe Park, Kingsbridge Rd., 180th St. Call 805-639-0430, or E-Mail c/o AOL THE GUMPER

MP727 Anyone attended PS 51, J.K. Paulding JHS '45-48. How about **Morris** HS '48-52. I'm a retired Marine '53-79. Korea to Vietnam. Any Marines out there? Robert Hughes, 2048 S. Ross St, Santa Ana, CA 92707-2715

MP728 Steven Rabinowitz, **Clinton** '61, CCNY (Baruch) '66 - Lou Katz Sq.x HR. Now living in Orinda Ca. Contact at P.O. Box 2083 Orinda, CA 94563

MP729 Looking for **Walton** '61 girls for 35th reunion in 1966. Where are you? Please contact Roberta (Soloff) Seidner 718 884-8634

MP730 Looking for Marilyn (Micky) Brodsky, **Columbus** '59 (8-5), my first love in the late '50's to early 60's while at CCNY. Where is she? What's happened to her? I'd love to talk over old times and the time gone by since. David Trachtman, **Science** '55, CCNY '60.

MP731 1950 **Taft** Graduates Wanted. This was a special group. Contact Sylvia Rapaport 1545 LaVenta Drive, Westlake Village, CA 91361 Office: 818 710-1222 Home: 805 371-9931

MP732 1956 **Roosevelt** Grads - we are planning a 40th reunion. For info call Hal Rosenstein: 516 585-6474 or Nancy (Bologna) Capozi 914 793-4244

MP733 Looking for friends from Andrews Ave. from 1935-1960. Also **Clinton** graduates from '52. Frank Charmatz, Bill Locascio, Jack Hybler, Harry and Roger Messekian, Stan Finkenthal, Buddy Solomon and Paula Bella- where are you?

MP734 Jackie Berner, **Monroe** '57. Looking for old friends. Now living on Long Island. Will there be a reunion in 97?

MP735 Looking for **Evander Childs** Graduates of 1948 Winter. Contact Fran Pryor in Florida: 407 488-3244 (Boca Raton area)

MP736 Tried to get a 25th year reunion for Roosevelt - only 40 people answered- where is everyone from the class of '64. Would like to contact anyone who grew up on 178th St. between the Grand Concourse and Anthony Ave. -1956-64. Is anyone there??

MP737 PS 114 looking for members of Anne Reiter's first 5th, 6th grade opportunity class for a reunion. Write Carol Friedland Berdy: 172 Dorchester, River Edge, NJ 07661.

MP738 Anyone remember me? Sid Morgenstern, **Taft** 1/48. Senior basketball. Would love to hear from anyone Wade Jr. HS '45. Contact 5868 Tooley St., San Diego, CA 92114

MP739 Heather Kaney has been living in Berkely CA for the last 25 yrs. Originally from 2701 Valentine Ave near Kingsbridge, PS 46 '60, Hunter College HS '66. Anyone want to swap memories? 510 525-1795

MP740 Beverly Levy-Sacharow, **Taft** '56. Looking for Shelly (Shirley) Alpertry Finn, Carol Stein, Rita Feinberg- who lived on 174th St and McCombs Rd.

MP741 Taft '56 Anyone out there ever wonder what happened to Rose Kessler - 165th St & Gerard Ave.? Well, she married Lenny Stein of Burnside Ave. & would love to hear from anyone who may remember us.

MP742 Looking for Roberta Trezza {144 St}. I took you to see Blue Denim with Mike & Sandy on your honeymoon night. Sandy Reinitz (Undercliff Ave?) at CCNY you asked your boyfriend if you could date me. Sandy Klinger (Creston Ave.) 1957

MP743 Ethel King Weissman, Monroe '44, looking for classmates and reunion information

MP744 Looking for anyone from JHS 141 in Riverdale, years 1960-65. Call Arnold Brownstein: 305 753-7032

MP745 David Delman (Born Adelman) **Taft** '43, President of that ancient class, would like to hear from mates. Don Croton, et al. And is anyone planning?

MP746 Larry Klein, **Monroe** '59. Father owned Comet Cleaners on Tremont Ave. Living in Florida 407-637-9116. Also hung around club Maxim's 1959-68

MP747 Monroe '58, PS 106, Parkchester people. Stephen Hecht and Mark Hairman are looking for you.

MP748 Brady Ave Gang (Pelham Terrace Bldgs) will have a reunion. Especially looking for Danny Tepper. Have already found Hal Field, Jerry Berman, Dorothy Kimmel, Authur Herman & Ronnie Kashkin. If interested call 502 583 4859

MP749 Dorice Mendelson Baronick, looking for old friends from 2723 Barnes Ave. Remember playing in the hall and back yard, Saturdays at the Allerton theater, Hymies malteds? PS 76 and **Columbus** '50-54. 5735 Marina Dr., Sebastian, FL 32958

MP750 Creston JHS class of Jan. '43: Ted Reich, Sheldon Schwartz, Paul Silverman, Stan Hirsch et al. Write to Bob Rothstein, 13 Rutgers Ct., Rancho Mirage, CA 92270 or call 619 324-9888

MP751 Like to hear from fellow Orchard Beach lifeguards or those who knew us. Would like to know their present whereabouts and how you guys made out. Bob Schweizer

MP752 Linda (Salteberg) November & Sharon (Dranch) Talbot are looking for "that old gang of mine" PS 104, JHS 82, **Taft** '60/61: Plimpton, Nelson, Shakespeare Jesup Avenues between Featherbed & E.L. Grant Hwy. Would like to hear from you.

MP754 Harvey Golden, **Clinton** '54. Living in North Palm Beach, FL for the last 40 years. Would like to hear from any one from De Kalb Ave. 407 845-7272

MP755 Don (Donny) Jacobson would love to hear from old friends. PS 35 '46, PS 70 '48, **Taft** '52, Grant Ave. 165th St., Findlay Ave, Walton Ave. Where are you Saul, Ziggy, Rubert and David? (I don't sell anything) 914 245-2252

MP756 Philip Honig, **Morris** '54. Would be happy to hear from any of the old crowd. I can be reached at 516 889-3332. I promise not to show grandchildren pictures!

MP757 If anyone remembers me, Francine Frank (now Francine Heller), **Taft** '64, please write- I would love to hear from you.

MP758 Anyone out there from Bainbridge Ave/204th St. or St. Brendan's School area from 1950/60. Would love to organize a reunion of old Stawbaum's crowd.

MP759 Charlotte Rudin Winkler: PS11, JHS 82, **Taft** '50 and Myles Winkler: PS 26, JHS 82, **Clinton** '48 looking for Mae Matler, Marley Kreiter, Ronnie Biloon and any other old friends. 516 261-7220

MP760 Nice to be in touch with old friends: Laurels, Ruptured Ducks, JHS 44 '47, **Roosevelt** '50, Benches 176th St/Southern Blvd. - Vivian, Anita, Barbara, Renee, Shelly, Marilyn, Muriel, Ethel, Marty, Truff, Sheldon, Bernice, Artie, Izzy, Paul, etc. Call Edith Miller Black, Potomac, MD 301-299-2961

MP761 Does anyone know a Jewish Orthodox female in NY who is pretty, kind, feminine, health oriented, about 28-38 years old with a sweet wholesome agreeable personality? (preferably never married.) If so, great opportunity for her to meet a special person of high integrity with a depth of understanding and real substance. Please respond and do a "mitzva" (good deed)

MP762 Clara Kerpen and Janet (Levy) Moskowitz are looking for friends from Phelan Place and **Walton** '49. Particularly Ruth Collins, Ruby Wilt, Rose Levitt, Rhonda Schecter, Arlene Soviett. We plan a reunion in 1995.

MP763 Muriel (Orenstein) Newman PS53 & PS 90, **Roosevelt** '36. Maybe someone else is still alive-I hope.

MP764 Jim Smith, Davidson Avenue & 190th St- would like to hear from Rich Halpin, Leo Fox, Fred Suha, John Thomas, Frank Quinn, Steve Hadermyer or any one from the area from 1950-60.

MP765 Now known as Teddy Weiler, formerly Charles Weiler of Pelham Pkwy in the '50s, **Science** '58. Poet and novelist looking for fellow Pelham Pkwyites in the Bay Area, CA.

MP766 My friends called me Red & my brother Mez. Lived on Walton Ave. and 184th St. Belonged to a club called "The Forham Dukes." Went to PS 33 and PS 79. Like to hear from some of my old friends. Living in Tamarac FL now, 305 720-3782 Herman Red Malmid

MP767 PS 79 '30s, **Clinton** '43 or the Bison Basketball team. Call Brother at 718 548-2718. PS 88, EBB, **Taft** '45, The Seltzer Sisters call Muriel at 718 548-2718

MP768 Laurie Ashinoff, **Clinton** '45. 181st St & Ryer Ave. - Creston JHS. Write me P.O. Box 3097, Portsmouth, VA 23701.

MP769 JHS '45 & **Roosevelt** HS '56 Graduates- Please contacct Hal Rosenstein. 516 585-6474 or 516 732-8000

MP770 Where are you Olga Gallo, **Roosevelt** HS '51 or '52. Also remember periodical Publishing House and Belmont Ave. Would love to hear from you. Judith Richman Myers

MP771 JHS 143 Band Class from '62-64. Wondering about each of your paths in life. I know of one tragedy, but no good news. Would love to hear some. Write or call Sherry (Soloman) Platt at 703 978-3025 in Virginia.

MP772 Marvin Abrams, **Roosevelt** '54. Lived at 1841 Marmion Ave. ('46-'60) & 3464 Knox Pl. . Looking for PS 44 guys '50. Dave Karch, anybody who lived in my building, Butch Hoffman, Irving Rothstein, Arthur Alexander. I went to Bronx House Camp every summer.

MP774 Does anybody remember Fulton Ave. and the Y.M.H.A. 1940-48. Also the Cardinals Club. Write Morris Rosenberg, 190 Denver Rd., Paramus, N.J. 07652 201 262-1386

Beverly Lynn Levy, Sacharow, **Taft** '56. Director of the Gerontology Institute of NJ, Editor of Newsletter "Update on Aging", Plans aging conferences for professionals nationwide. Produced over 100 workshops and conferences on aging & health. Produced over 150 Gerontology video tapes (the most extensive video catalog on Gerontology in the world) Also produced 2 fine young men: Brian Evan & Scott Hunter- of course with the help of loving & devoted husband Stan. We also have acquired an adorable daughter-n -law Theresa!

Marion Sternberg Pollack, **Monroe** '56. Substance Awareness Coordinator at Hightstown High, NJ. Won County Counselor of the Year Award.

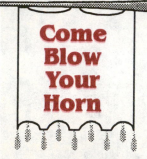

Come Blow Your Horn

Accomplishments
Awards
Businesses
Volunteerism
Works in Progress

David & Phyllis Stolls (maiden name: Muenz) both '65 **Bronx Science** graduates, just celebrated 25 years of marriage. They have a son, Douglas, 24 and daughters Debra, age 23 and Beth, age 18. as well as 9 cats and 2 dogs. Have spent lives traveling worldwide-Africa, Middle East, Asia, Europe, South America-trekking everywhere!

Philip Ettman, **Clinton** '64, is a Professor of Business law and Chair of Dept of Economics & Business at the Westfield State College in Westfield, Mass.

Steven Richards (nee Rabinowitz) of Webb/ Kingsbridge Rd, **Clinton** '61, CCNY (Baruch) '66 is alive and well on a hilltop in Orinda, CA and is a marketing consultant. Contact at P.O.Box 2083, Orinda, CA 94563

Arnold Forman, **Monroe** '52, is the Senior Partner in Forman, Rubin, Richter Certified Public Accountants. Became a CPA in '64. Married 38 years to Ceil Bergman Forman, **Morris** '54 and is also a grandfather of two.

Joel (Iskowitz) Ives, **Monroe** '61, is an architect in New Jersey. Sheryl (Sankel) Ives, **Monroe** '61 is a librarian at the Bronx Science.

Melanie Castagnaro DiGiovanni, Monroe '59 married Robert DiGiovanni, **Columbus** '59 32 years ago. We own a manufacturing security gate and grille company in Brooklyn: Steelcraft Folding Gate Corp. We have 3 grown children and live on Long Island. We would love to hear from anyone in the Bronx.

Married to Ben Dworkis for 43 years. I have 3 daughters, all married and have 7 grandchildren. Former secretary to elementary school principals in Malboro NJ. Retired and living permanently in Boca Raton FL.

Larry Ashinoff, President of Coronet Group Inc. Started 40 years ago - apparel co. that employees 400 people-sell all over the world. Father of 4 great children

Dorothy Kovaly, **Monroe** '59. Married to Joseph Kovaly. Have 3 children. Worked for 4 "fun" summers at Freedomland and now I'm a teacher on the very same spot - Co-op City

Katherine Durkin McCarthy is a special ed teacher at Ridgewood High School. She has 6 children, all college graduates and is also a grandmother of 3!

Mildred Jacobs, **Monroe** '36 married Alfred Jacobs, **Monroe** '36. She has a B.A. from Hunter '40, M.Ed. University of MD. Taught for 25 years in Maryland, has 3 daughters and 10 grandchildren. She now works as a volunteer at the White House.

Gerald (Jerry) Slatin graduated June '54, went to CCNY for 2 yrs (did not graduate). Went to work as a salesperson and have been with General Mills for 27 years. I also became a band leader under the name of Jerry Sands. Presently doing a one-man-band-show. Was in the **Monroe** dance band with Emil Greenberg (teacher and then band leader with Steven Scott.) Morty Westman, trumpet player and Joe Miletti who is now Joey Mills, president and CEO of Steven Scott.

TO PLACE AN AD

Simply fill out the form that appears on the back of each issue of **Back in THE BRONX**.

Please print clearly and legibly- it will help prevent your ad from possibly appearing incorrectly- *Thank you!*

And, as a reminder, if you are a subscriber, the 40 word ad is **FREE!!!**

TO RESPOND TO AN AD

Address your response to:

Back in THE BRONX
Stephen M. Samtur, Box 141 H
Scarsdale, NY 10583

*Be sure to include the number that appears before the ad.(**MP772** for example) and a long, **stamped** envelope so we can mail your letter to the person placing the ad.

TAKE A TRIP DOWN MEMORY LANE WITH EITHER OF THESE GREAT BOOKS!

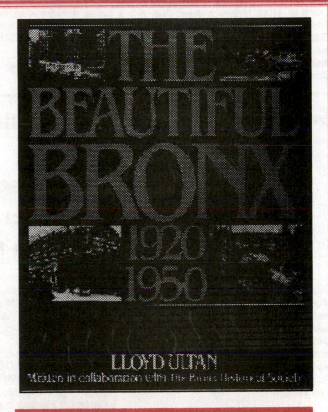

ONLY $25.00

plus $3.95 for shipping and handling

The period from the middle of the 1930's to the middle of the 1960's was a dynamic one in the history of this country. The depths of the Great Depression brought the New Deal to combat economic disaster, and this was followed quickly by the ferment of the Second World War. Peacetime brought great changes in our society, including the movement from the cities to the suburbs and a vast influx of different ethnic groups into the cities. No area was more affected by these changes then **The Bronx**.

Yet, in the midst of this upheaval, The Bronx was also marked by islands of stability and by its continuity with the past. Now that story is told in

The Bronx, It Was Only Yesterday 1935-1965

- Over 200 photos
- Almost every neighborhood represented
- A treasure chest of memories

Take a trip back in time to the glory days and the golden years of the Bronx. Author Lloyd Ultan, a native Bronxite, takes us back to those wonderful years to witness a way of life long passed. 200 rare and beautiful photos take us back to the familiar brick apartment houses, children playing stickball and Potzie, and many other scenes of everyday life that all of us remember fondley. See the long-gone buildings and landmarks, the beautiful Loews Theaters with their magnificent lobbies, the old Yankee Stadium & many other familiar sights.

If you're from the Bronx, you'll find this book to be a treasure chest of memories, and a nostalgic look into your past. Order a copy today! To order, simply turn to the back page of this issue and fill out the order form.

ONLY $25

plus $3.95 for shipping and handling

READER REPLIES

It is vitally important that you fill out the information below. Your input will be essential to the success of this magazine, tailored and inspired by you, the former "Bronxite". We thank you for your participation.

Subscriber? ☐ Yes ☐ No

YOUR NAME _____

ADDRESS _____

CITY _____ STATE _____ ZIP _____ PHONE _____

HIGH SCHOOL ATTENDED _____ YEAR GRADUATED _____

TELL US A LITTLE ABOUT YOURSELF,
(Be sure to include your alma mater, old neighborhood, your best memories about your days in the Bronx, (or anything else you can tell us).

_____

_____

_____

COULD WE SEND A FRIEND A FREE COPY OF BACK IN THE BRONX?

Do you know current or former Bronxites who would like to receive our magazine and reunion information? If you do, we'll be happy to send them a **free** inaugural issue of **Back in THE BRONX.**
Write to Back in The Bronx, Box 141 H, Scarsdale, NY 10583 or call 1-800-7-BRONX 5

Last _____ First _____ Maiden _____
Address _____ City _____ State _____ Zip _____
Phone # ( ) _____ School and year of Graduation _____

Last _____ First _____ Maiden _____
Address _____ City _____ State _____ Zip _____
Phone # ( ) _____ School and year of Graduation _____

Last _____ First _____ Maiden _____
Address _____ City _____ State _____ Zip _____
Phone # ( ) _____ School and year of Graduation _____

Last _____ First _____ Maiden _____
Address _____ City _____ State _____ Zip _____
Phone # ( ) _____ School and year of Graduation _____

COME BLOW YOUR OWN HORN DEPARTMENT

Please tell us about yourself (include your name)—about your accomplishments, awards, titles or works in progress. We're interested in hearing about them. List Below: _____

_____

_____

_____

_____

READER REPLIES

As a subscriber you are entitled to a FREE 40 Word Classified, Missing Persons, Blow Your Own Horn, or Personal Ad. Please write your ad below (if you are not subscribing to our magazine you can still place an ad in the next issue. The cost of an advertisement is 50¢ a word, there is no limit on paid ads).

_____

_____

_____

Is Your Mailing Label Correct?

In order to keep our database current, please correct any errors and place the label and or photocopy with corrections.

Account #	High School	Year Graduated
6817	Roosevelt	1958

SAMPLE

Mary R. Flowers
123 Anystreet Blvd
Anywhere, USA 12345

Change of Address?

If you're planning a move please attach your label corrected with your new address and the date that you will begin receiving mail at that address. This will insure that you don't miss your next issue of **Back in THE BRONX**.

Ordering Information

A Great Gift Idea! In addition to your own subscription, a subscription to **Back in THE BRONX** makes a great and unique gift. Fill in the form below and we'll process the order in time for our next issue. So, order your subscription NOW, and order one for a friend!

YES, I'd like to order the following items:

QTY.

____ 1Yr. (4 ISSUES) Subscription(s) to Back in THE BRONX $19.95
____ 2Yr. (8 ISSUES) Subscription(s) to Back in THE BRONX* .. $29.95   } *FREE John's Menu
____ 3Yr. (12 ISSUES) Subscription(s) to Back in THE BRONX* .. $39.95
____ 4Yr. (16 ISSUES) Subscription(s) to Back in THE BRONX*) .. $49.95
____ The Beautiful Bronx............$25.00 (plus $3.95 S/H) $28.95
____ The Bronx: It Was Only Yesterday...$25.00 (plus $3.95 S/H) $28.95
____ Bronx High School Reunion Weekend Video $29.95
____ SAVE MONEY - BUY 4 FOR JUST $99.00!
____ THE BRONX Tracking Service $9.95
____ I would like to receive all available back issues and have them applied towards my subscription (To date we have at least 12 back issues available - While They Last!)

TOTAL: $ _____

Please fill out completely and include $3.95 for shipping and handling for books only to: **Back in THE BRONX**, Box 141H, Scarsdale, NY 10583

Please Print Clearly ☐ New Subscriber   ☐ Renewal

Name _____

Malden Name _____

Address _____

City _____

State _____ Zip _____

Phone (___) _____

High School _____ Year Grad. _____

☐ Visa ☐ Mastercard ☐ Check ☐ Money Order

No. _____ Expiration Date _____

Signature _____

Back in THE BRONX

Box 141 H, Scarsdale, NY 10583
Phone 914-592-1647 • Fax 914-592-4693

ADDRESS CORRECTION REQUESTED

Volume III   Issue XII

Back in THE BRONX

CELEBRATING THE EXPERIENCE OF GROWING UP AND LIVING IN THE BRONX

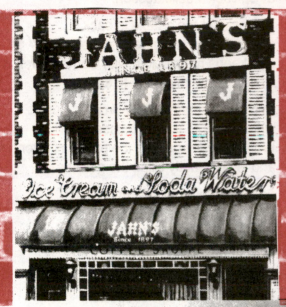

FREEDOM
The World's Largest Entertainment Center
U.S.A.

Sharing Memories of a Special Time... Back In THE BRONX

From the Editors...

CLINTON '61

TAFT '62

This issue of **Back In THE BRONX** is an expanded edition because we are using it as a new updated inaugural issue for those current and former Bronxites who have yet to find out about our magazine.

A few of the stories have deliberately been chosen from previous issues because our subscribers have indicated that they have enjoyed them. Some of you will find them repeats of stories that you may have previously read. Understanding this, we have increased the number of pages in this issue to more than compensate.

An improved inaugural issue should attract more and more Bronxites from all over the United States. This undoubtedly should lead to more (and better) stories about your Bronx of the 40's, 50's, and 60's.

If you have friends, neighbors, or relatives who might be interested in a free inaugural issue of **Back in THE BRONX**, please give us their names and addresses and we will be happy to send it to them. If you wish, they may call our toll free number:

1-800-7 BRONX 5

Sincerely yours,

Stephen M. Samtur &
Susan J. Samtur
Editors

Back in THE BRONX

A number of the photographs in **Back in THE BRONX** are courtesy of and are available from the Bronx Historical Society.

Publishers & Editors:	Stephen M. Samtur	Clinton '61
	Susan H. Samtur	Taft '62
Contributing Editors:	Barbara Fasciani	Roosevelt '65
	Martin Jackson	Science '58
	Sandra Zuckerman	Jefferson '57
	Al Zuckerman	New Utrecht '50
Art & Production:	Ellen Grodjesk	
Printed By:	Trumbell Printing, Trumbell, CT	

Reminiscing
Spivack
By Jay B. Isaacs

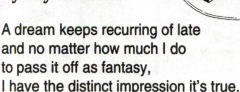

A dream keeps recurring of late
and no matter how much I do
to pass it off as fantasy,
I have the distinct impression it's true.

It takes me back to The Bronx
to a curious obsession
I dream I'm the resident poet
at Spivack's delicatessen.

Spivack set me a table in back
alongside the refrigerator of beer
and keeps me stocked with Corned Beef & Bud,
while I cajole my muse to appear.

And I, the behan of The Bronx
write words to stir the masses,
While Spivack pushes the pastrami & tongue
and is constantly filling the glasses.

And they come by bus and the IRT
from Kingsbridge & Jerome
and every night they stand in line
to hear me read my poem.

Friends tell me to see a shrink.
To rid myself of this obsession.
But I like being the poet in residence
at Spivack's delicatessen.

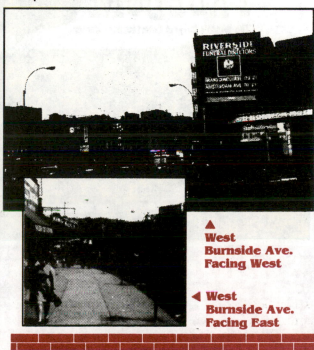

▲ **West Burnside Ave. Facing West**

◄ **West Burnside Ave. Facing East**

Riding the

Both photos: New York Transit Museum Archives, Brooklyn

RAILS

BY ROY H. WEPNER, Bronx Science '64

To grow up in the Bronx in the 1950's and 60's was to revel in the freedom and excitement of riding the subways and elevated trains around the Bronx and to other distant and mysterious destinations.

Beginning around fifth grade, my friends and I would regularly ride the subways to Central Park, museums and Times Square in Manhattan. Once a year, we would even make the endless but exciting trek all the way to Coney Island. It was truly another time and another place. And for those kids lucky enough to get train passes for school, it was like having an endless supply of frequent flyer miles.

The subway map of the Bronx was not unlike a relief map showing the major rivers of the United States. Just as lesser rivers such as the Ohio and the Missouri would merge as they head south into the Mississippi, the subways and Els from the Bronx headed straight south where they came together to form major subway lines leading into Manhattan. Of course, unlike rivers, some of the subway lines crossed. The westerly Jerome Avenue line crossed over to the east side as it headed toward Lexington Avenue in Manhattan, while the D train headed west for its journey downtown along Central Park West. And of course they crossed in the center of the universe — Yankee Stadium.

You were never very far from a subway line in the Bronx. In my old neighborhood, we were always close to the "Woodlawn" train that clattered along Jerome Avenue — perhaps the only mass transit line anywhere named after a cemetery! The Woodlawn-Jerome line was the westernmost train in the Bronx, unless you included the short stretch of the Broadway local that went up to Riverdale (which assumes, of course, that Riverdale is part of the "'real" Bronx). Just as Jerome Avenue split the West Bronx from the East, the trains that ran above it split the night with rattles and screeches which made my bones vibrate.

Of course, riding the Woodlawn-Jerome train was not without its rewards. Surely everyone who rode that train would instinctively look out of the window on the west side of the track as the downtown train descended from the 161st Street station into the tunnel. For about one full second, you could see the inside of Yankee Stadium - for free (unless, of course, you counted the cost of the 15¢ token).

Reminiscing

Riding the Rails

Continued from page 3

My favorite memory of the Jerome Avenue El was the fact that it provided an alternate route to the Polo Grounds, when there still was such a place. Sure, you could get to the Polo Grounds via the D train -it was just one stop beyond Yankee Stadium- but why travel one quick stop on one fast train when there was another way to go which was slower, more complicated and immensely more fun. Specifically, there was a shuttle that ran from the 167th Street station on the Jerome Avenue line over to the Polo Grounds in upper Manhattan. Of course, the first time we tried it, we got off the shuttle at the first stop after 167th Street, only to find that this shuttle actually made an intermediate stop at Sedgwick Avenue. It was the ultimate subway adventure- being stranded at a deserted station which was neither here nor there, with no train likely to come by for what seemed to be hours.

Perhaps the oldest and most certainly the most mysterious train in the Bronx was the old Third Avenue El. Even back in the 60's, the trains on that line were so old that the doors would slide open with a gasp which always sounded like its last. The Third Avenue El was not part of my regular neighborhood turf, but there were occasions when I had to ride it. I dimly recall that when you reached the age when you had to get "working papers", the place you had to go was somewhere off the Third Avenue El. What I remember most about that train was that if you stood at the front of the first car (and there was no other place where a self-respecting subway buff would ride), you could see two or even three stations down the line - they were only a few blocks apart. It was not-quite-rapid transit.

But if the Third Avenue El was the Orient Express of the Bronx, then the D

Subway entrance on E. 138th St. & Grand Concourse

train was the Twentieth Century Limited. The newest and fastest subway in the Bronx, it hurtled past Mosholu Parkway, through my neighborhood, past Yankee Stadium and C.C.N.Y., to exotic destinations like Rockefeller Center, Greenwich Village and- at the end of the line- Coney Island.

From my apartment at 193rd Street, I was actually equidistant from the D train stations at Kingsbridge and Fordham Roads; but I always used the Kingsbridge station, because it provided me with a longer ride downtown.

New York Transit Museum Archives, Brooklyn

The cavernous subway station at Kingsbridge Road was like a wonder of the world to me as a youngster in the 1950's. Since you could enter or leave the station at any of the four corners of the intersection of Kingsbridge and the Grand Concourse, it provided a traffic-free, parent-approved means of crossing the ever-dangerous Concourse without the help of a grown-up. You would simply go down into the station on one corner, sail past the token booth, and come up on any other corner.

I still remember the stairways and corridors- which were long and gloomy even then - that led down from the street to the token booth level. From there, you could continue further down a ramp to the Kingsbridge Road underpass and pick up the No. 20 bus. What always amazed me was that once you bought your token, you actually had to travel *upstairs* to the train level.

Although I suspect the D train never traveled faster than 35 or 40 mph, it always seemed to be barreling along like a rocket during the rush hour, especially when it left Tremont Avenue and arrogantly sailed past landmark stations like Yankee Stadium and the Polo Grounds. But nothing compared to the non-stop stretch from 125th Street to Columbus Circle-three miles at what passed for breakneck speed in the subway system.

I suppose there was probably some crime and violence in the subways in those days. But who could worry about those types of things, when freedom, mobility and adventure beckoned - all for 15¢. I wish my own kids could relive the experience, and I wish I could go along for the ride-in the front car, of course.

What's in a NAME?

Have you ever wondered how some streets got their name?

Grand Concourse facing south towards Fordham Road underpass

Grand Concourse

The idea of this boulevard originated in 1890 with Louis Aloys Rise, an engineer under Louis J. Heintz, Commissioner of Steet Improvements. Ground was broken in 1902 by President Louis Haffen, and it was officially completed in 1909. It ran from East 161st St. up to Mosholu Pkwy, but, later on, a lower section was added down to East 138th St. (which has been called Mott Ave). Eventually the entire stretch became the Grand Boulevard and Councourse in 1927. In 1926, the Gold Star Mothers unsucessfully tried to have the boulevard renamed Memorial Parkway. The Claremont Heights Civic Association also tried to have it renamed Woodrow Wilson Boulevard.

For many years, trees on this thoroughfare carried metal nameplates of Bronxites killed in World War I. When the Independent Subway was constructed under the Concourse, the trees were removed to Pelham Bay Park.

Fordham Road facing east from Jerome Ave

Fordham Road

Considering how ancient is the name of Fordham in Bronx history, this road's name is comparatively new. Originally an Indian path, it became the Kingsbridge Road of Colonial Days (from Marion Ave. to Third Ave.) whereas the length from Jerome Ave. to Marion Ave. was once Highbridge Road.

Around 1850 a railroad station was built near St. John's College (now Fordham) and was given the name of Fordham, as it was on part of the Fordham Grant. The station attracted businesses, and the village of Fordham grew up around it. East Fordham Road and West Fordham Road were widened to become the principal thoroughfare.

Southern Boulevard

Southern Boulevard was a drawing board creation envisioned by the Engineering Dept. of the Annexed District sometime in the 1870's to be a grandiose thoroughfare sweeping up from East 133rd St. and Third Ave., cutting through the wide estates of the Eastern Bronx, bypassing Crotona Park and Bronx Park and terminating at the Botanical Gardens.

A latter-day engineer said its name was first suggested when the countryside was still under the jurisdiction of Westchester County and therefore proposed boulevard was to be the southernmost in the county. Upon annexation in 1874, the name was still applicable to the boulevard originated in the South Bronx. The lower end of Southern Boulevard was settled first and became industrialized early in the 20th century, whereas the upper end, near Hunts Point and running through Bronx Park, was a more attractive residential area.

Excerpts taken from book, *History In Asphalt,* by John McNamara

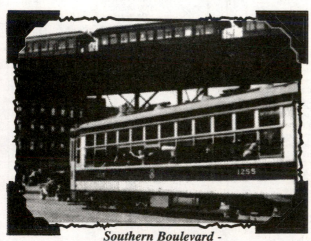

*Southern Boulevard -
(Southern Blvd. & Westchester Ave.)*

There's no place like home.

Bronx Honor Roll
Bronxites Who Have Achieved!

BRONX SCIENCE
Harold Brown
Stokely Carmichael
Leon Cooper (Nobel Prize Winner))
Bobby Darin
Edgar Doctorow
Sheldon Glashow (Nobel Prize Winner)
Russell Hulse (Nobel Prize Winner)
Nita Lowey, Representative
Arno Penzias (Nobel Prize Winner)
William Safire
Melvin Schwartz (Nobel Prize Winner)
Steven Weinberg (Nobel Prize Winner)

CARDINAL HAYES
George Carlin
Rocky Colavito
Kevin Loughery
Regis Philbin

CHRISTOPHER COLUMBUS
Robert Abrams
Anne Bancroft
Christine Jorgenson
Alan Landsburg

DEWITT CLINTON
Don Adams
Nate Archibald
Richard Avedon
James A. Baldwin
Martin Balsam
David Begelman
James Caan
Paddy Chayevsky
George Cukor
Avery Fisher
Arthur Gelb
Judd Hirsch
Robert Hofstadter (Nobel Prize Winner)
Stubby Kaye
Al Kelly
Theodore Kheel
Robert Klein
William Kunstler
Burt Lancaster
Garry Marshall
Jan Murray
Charles Rangel
Richard Rogers
A.M. Rosenthal
Daniel Schorr
Dolph Schayes
Neil Simon
Larry Storch
Marvin Traub
Jimmie Walker
Fats Waller
William Zeckendorf

EVANDER CHILDS
Red Buttons
James Coco
Carl Reiner

MONROE
Jules Feiffer
John Garfield
Hank Greenberg
Ed Kranepool
Leon Lederman (Nobel Physicist)

MORRIS
Angel Cordero
Herman Joseph Muller (Nobel Prize Winner)
Gabe Pressman
E. Colin Powell

ROOSEVELT
June Alyson
Chazz Palminteri

TAFT
Sanford Brown
Eydie Gorme
Stanley Kubrick

WALTON
Bella Abzug
Rosalyn Yalow (Nobel Prize Winner)

OTHER NOTABLES
Joey Adams
Danny Aiello
Alan Alda
Robert Alda
Corazon Aquino
Armand Assante
Herman Badillo
Lauren Bacall
Ellen Barkin
Mario Biaggi
Joey Bishop
Alfred Bloomingdale
Bobby Bonilla
Teresa Brewer
Ralph J. Bunche (Nobel Prize Winner)
George Burns
Cab Calloway
Diahann Carroll
Samuel Clemens
Myron Cohen
Betty Comdon
Cardinal Cooke
Avery Corman
Norman Cousins
Bobby Cremins
Don Criqui
Tony Curtis
Vic Damone
Ossie Davis
Dennis Day
Ruby Dee
Dion DiMucci
John Foster Dulles
Erik Estrada
Fernando Ferrer
Geraldine Ferraro
F. Scott Fitzgerald
Joe Franklin
Arlene Francis
Connie Francis
Frankie Frisch
Edward J. Flynn
Rita Gam
Rudolph Giuliani
Samuel Gompers
Aldolf Green
Richie Guerin
Armand Hammer
Herbert A. Hauptman (Nobel Prize Winner)
David Horowitz
Vladimir Horowitz
George Jessel
Billy Joel
Raoul Julia
John F. Kennedy
Robert Kennedy
Ted Kennedy
Theodore Kheel
Calvin Klein
Edward Koch
Fiorello LaGuardia
Bert Lahr
Jake LaMotta
Louise Lasser

Ralph Lauren
Ron Leibman
Lee Leonard
Joe E. Lewis
Shari Lewis
Hal Linden
Vince Lombardi
Melissa Manchester
John Mariani
Penny Marshall
Willie Mays
Mario Merola
Glenn Miller
Sal Mineo
Hugo Montenegro
Robert Morgenthau
Gary Morton
Paul Muni
Bess Myerson
Gil Noble
Carroll O'Connor
John O'Hara
Charles Osgood
Al Pacino
Jack Palance
Floyd Patterson
Joseph Papp
Joe Pesci
Roberta Peters
Mary Pickford
Ezio Pinza
Edgar Allan Poe
Richard Price
Vincent Price
Charles Nelson Reilly
Rob Reiner
Regina Resnick
Monte Rock III
Franklin D. Roosevelt
Theodore Roosevelt
Billy Rose
Jonas Salk
Isabel Sanford
Marvin Scott
George Segal
Connie Selleca
Sylvia Sidney
Carly Simon
Stanley Simon
Vince Scully
Isaac Bashevis Singer (Nobel Prize Winner)
Curtis Sliwa
Wesley Snipes, Jr.
Cardinal Spellman
Sy Sperling
George Steinbrenner
Henry Stern
Pat Summerall
Renee Taylor
Mother Teresa (Nobel Prize Winner)
U. Thant
Arturo Toscanini
Dan Topping
Leon Trotsky
Lloyd Ultan
Jerry Vale
Bobby Van
Luther Vandross
June Valli
Jackie Vernon
Fran Warren
Del Webb
Vanessa Williams
Herman Wouk

Thanks to Dr. William C. Wolfson and the Bronx Society of Science and Letters

BRONX CELEBRITIES

SPORTS FIGURES

PHIL RIZZUTO
Yankees
Hall of Fame

MICKEY MANTLE
Yankees
Hall of Fame

YOGI BERRA
Yankees
Hall of Fame

WHITEY FORD
Yankees
Hall of Fame

ED KRANPOOL
NY Mets
Monroe HS

POLITICAL

FERNANDO FERRER
Bronx Borough Pres.

ROBERT ABRAMS
Former NYS Attorney General
Former Bronx Borough Pres.
-Columbus HS

NITA LOWEY
Congresswoman
—Bronx Science

G. OLIVER KOPPEL
Former NYS Attorney
General

ENTERTAINERS

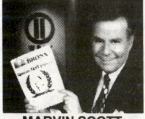

JERRY VALE

RED BUTTONS

ROBERT KLEIN

MARVIN SCOTT

REGIS PHILBIN

JOE FRANKLIN

CARL REINER

DION

JAN MURRAY

DAVID HOROWITZ

GARRY MARSHALL

You're getting closer to home.

Did You Ever Hear of Bonner Place?

By Johanna Hurwitz

The spring day in 1952 when my parents told me that we were moving AWAY from the Bronx was a very happy one for me. It had always seemed that there was something wrong with my Bronx existence. No one in the many books I read (The Little House books by Laura Ingalls Wilder, HEIDI, ANNE OF GREEN GABLES, the Betsy-Tacy books by Maud Hart Lovelace, the BOBBSEY TWINS, NANCY DREW, etc.) lived in walkup apartment houses in the Bronx. No one in the technicolor films I saw at the Fleetwood movie house lived in the Bronx either. So the thought of moving from our cramped apartment on a deadend street called **Bonner Place** (off Morris Ave. between **163rd and 164th Streets**) seemed like a dream come true.

We were moving to a small semi-detached house in Queens, to a community named Sunnyside. Our new subway stop was called Bliss Street. No wonder I thought I was moving to heaven.

I never imagined that years later, I would look back on the Bronx with such nostalgia. What would I like to revisit: My old schools: **P.S.35** on **163rd Street** and **Morris Avenue.** It was a K-6 school with sliding doors on the second floor that when moved could transform the classrooms into an open space to serve as an auditorium for assemblies. The gym, such as it was, was located on the top floor of the building and whenever someone bounced a basketball, bits of plaster automatically fell in the classrooms on the floor below. Next I went to **Jordan L. Mott, JHS 32.** I attended from 1949-52. I was in the first class to go through the three years at this modern development in education. I remember the small model apartment where girls were taught homemaking. We were unliberated and couldn't wait for our turn to wash the floors and scrub the toilet in the darling little tiled bathroom. The toilet was the first I ever saw that didn't have a pull chain with an overhead tank. We also cooked, wearing the aprons and

headcoverings we had spent much of sixth grade producing. We made coleslaw and deviled eggs and learned such useful skills as blending the yellow disk of food coloring into the oleo margarine so it would look like butter. Then we were taught how to line garbage pail using old newspapers (so we could throw out the coleslaw and deviled eggs when the teacher wasn't looking). We learned how to make hospital corners when making a bed because no one then ever dreamed about the future existence of fitted sheets.

However, the best skill I learned in Junior high was touch typing. In that era when computer keyboards weren't even a feature in science fiction stories, I was being prepared for

However, the best skill I learned in Junior high was touch typing.

the work force. I fooled them. I didn't become a secretary. I'm a writer and mastering that keyboard was a big head start in my career.

I remember **Joyce Kilmer Park.** It was my little bit of country, even though the parkman chased us kids off the grass. Still we could see the grass and the trees as we roller skated on the cement walks or dripped Good Humor ice cream pops onto our

Photo courtesy of The Bronx Historical Society Research Library

The Concourse Plaza Hotel, across from JOYCE KILMER PARK.

— Continued on page 9

8

Did You Ever Hear of...

Cont. from page 8

clothing. We oogled the Lorelei statue in the park - it was a memorial to poet Henrich Heine but we girls looked at the bare breasted mermaids and wondered if and when we would look like that.

Bonner Place was near enough to Yankee Stadium that when the Second World War was over and night games were resumed, we could hear the cheering on our street when a homerun was hit. Those were the days when you could count on Joe DiMaggio to hit those long balls with regularity. To encourage women to have an interest in baseball, every Saturday that the Yankees played at home was "Ladies Day". It was only 25¢ for a female to purchase a ticket. The first Saturday that I bought one of those bargain tickets, it was a double header. I didn't understand what was going on during that first trip to the stadium, but it was a lot of fun screaming and cheering with everyone else. And of course, it wasn't long before I learned all the fine points of the game.

But my most precious memory of my corner of the Bronx was the Melrose Branch of the New York Public Library. Located at 910 Morris Avenue, this large Carnegie building became my second home. Our apartment housed six people (my parents, paternal grandmother, sister, brother and myself) and there was little room for privacy or afterschool visitors. The public library took over. My friends and I climbed up the steep steps to the children's room on the second floor almost daily. There we could do our homework together and check out new books. We were only permitted two fiction titles at a time, so the turnover was frequent since I could read a novel in a single evening in those pre-TV days. When I was in fifth grade, the library instituted an after-school reading club for girls. We met bi-

Grand Concourse at 161st Street in 1950. Bronx County Building is on the corner, Franz Sigel Park in background.

Photo courtesy of The Bronx County Historical Society, NYC

weekly and it not only was an entertaining activity, it gave us a chance to see the forbidden third floor of the library building where the custodian's private apartment was located.

Of course, I have other Bronx memories too: **Addie Valins Ice Cream Parlor** on 161st Street, the long dark tunnel that ran under 161st Street and where we would have gone for protection had bombs fallen on the Bronx during the war, and **Franz Siegel Park** which was twice the size of Joyce Kilmer. I remember the local stores like Honig's (we pronounced it Honnicks) candy store and Cushman's bakery, Willie's butcher shop and Zemma's where we could buy fresh produce.

Because I haven't been able to return to Bonner Place by the more traditional modes of transportation: car or subway line, I've found another means. I've devoured all the books set in the Bronx that I can locate: WORLD'S FAIR by

E.L. Doctorow. He's a bit older than I am so his Bronx was slightly different. He writes about the tennis courts on 167th St. and Morris Ave. That's where JHS 22 is located so I know now where they found the land for my old school. Two other books with Bronx settings are THE OLD NEIGHBORHOOD by Avery Korman and SLEEPING ARRANGEMENTS by Laura Cunningham. Laura is a few years younger than me, but she lived in my old neighborhood and even attended P.S.35. After I read her book, I wrote to her and asked if she remembered any of the teachers that I did. I was thrilled that we both had Mrs. Sass. She was such an energetic and enthusiastic woman.

Since my childhood days, I always wanted to be a writer. And in time I began writing children's books for a new generation of readers. I've published 45 books and in them you can find many bits of my Bronx childhood. In ONCE I WAS A PLUM TREE (Morrow, 1980) I actually placed the story in the Bronx of 1947. My Bronx memories are in other books too. Although set in Manhattan, in THE LAW OF GRAVITY (Morrow, 1978), one of the main characters is the son of a library custodian and lives inside the library building. All those games at Yankee Stadium certainly helped me write BASEBALL FEVER (Morrow 1982). There are hundreds of clues to my Bronx childhood scattered through my books. But not too long ago, a child in an Ohio school where I was visiting had a question about THE ADVENTURES OF ALI BABA BERNSTEIN (Morrow 1985). How did you ever make up such a funny name as he wanted to know.

"I guess I'm just clever", I told him.

But you know the truth. There's a piece of my head that's never moved away from the Bronx. ∎

BRONX TRIVIA

1. What Bronx high school has the most (5) Nobel Prize Winners? _____ _____

2. What Cardinal Hayes graduate and television personality had a Bronx street named after him? _____ _____

3. What station is this IRT Jerome Ave train approaching? _____

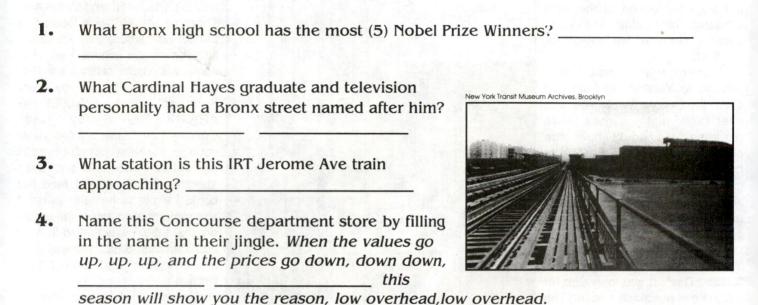

New York Transit Museum Archives, Brooklyn

4. Name this Concourse department store by filling in the name in their jingle. *When the values go up, up, up, and the prices go down, down down,* _____ _____ *this season will show you the reason, low overhead, low overhead.*

5. What was the original name of the sporting goods store located on Fordham Road that since has become Modells? _____

6. What was the nautical nickname of the Art Deco building that is located on the Concourse and 166th St? The _____ Building.

7. The 7th Ave Express train that originated at the South Ferry Station terminated at what Bronx Station? _____

8. What was the name of the Bronx college that initially housed the *Hall of Fame?* _____ _____ _____

9. What was the name of the famous frankfurter stand located on Fordham Road across the street from the Valentine movie theatre? _____

10. What section of the Bronx was 'Custard's Last Stand' located? _____ _____

BRONX TRIVIA

11. In front of what famous Bronx building would you find these monuments?

_____ _____ _____

12. What was the name of the large insurance company that purchased land in the Bronx to build Parkchester?

_____ _____

13. Duke Ellington, R.H. Macy, and George M. Cohan all share a Bronx connection. What is it?

14. How many people did Jahn's 'Kitchen Sink' feed?

_____ to _____

15. What was the most popular chocolate syrup that a Bronxite would use when making a homemade egg cream?   Fox's _____

_____

16. A very popular 1950's Bronx radio jingle advertisement for Saks Quality Furniture included a phone number.
Complete this phone number: *Melrose 5 - 53____ ____*.

17. Complete this Bronx radio advertisement jingle:
"Learn dancing in a hurry with _____ _____"

18. The Bronx has the country's oldest:
a. beer brewery
b. municipal golf course
c. motorcycle racetrack

IT'S EASY! TRY IT!

19. Complete this early 1960's Bronx television & radio jingle:
"Mommy & Daddy take my hand, take me out to _____

20. If you took the D Train from the Concourse in 1954 and traveled to Coney Island how much would you have paid for a token?
a. ten cents
b. fifteen cents
c. twenty cents

You're so close, you can taste it.

Answers on page 25

Reminiscing

GOING TO THE MOVIES

By Henry Meyerson

When my mother took me to the movies, it meant going to Fordham Road. It also meant having to tolerate Alexander's Department Store, but more on that later. To get to Fordham Road meant taking the bus which stopped in front of Charlie's candy store at the corner of Bainbridge and 206th St. The trip took approximately twenty-five minutes and wound through various alien and exotic parts of the north-central Bronx until it got to its final port of call, the corner of Fordham Road and Valentine Ave.

Fordham and the Grand Concourse was to the Bronx as Regents and Oxford Streets are to London, or Saint Michel and Saint Germain are to Paris: the center of window shopping, schmoozing, strolling with no purpose other than to find novelty and stimulation in an otherwise repetitive life. Now we are talking before television, when people were in the streets day or night for reasons of pleasure rather than homelessness or crime, a time when aimless wandering was not necessarily a sign of enui, but an adventure of exploration and of investigating possibilities.

Disembarking from the number 4 bus, we headed west on Fordham Road, passed the jewelry store on the corner of Valentine Avenue, passed the RKO Fordham which might have a Barbara Stanwyck picture playing (I hated Barbara Stanwyck), passed the Lerner Shop, the Fanny Farmer chocolate store, BenHil's, the men's haberdashery, reaching the northeast corner of the Grand Concourse on which stood the London Shoe store, where I would buy my shoes when I was older (at the time I was a

Buster Brown man), and waited for the green light with dozens of other similar people.

On the other side of the Concourse

The Paradise was cavernous by today's standards, large even at that time.

was our immediate objective: Alexander's Department Store. Getting across the Concourse to the

Loews Paradise Theatre. Inner lobby looking west from right promenade

"promised land" was, to paraphrase my guide, worth your life. From my mother's perspective, the buses, trucks, and cars which navigated the Concourse apparently had one objective: to mow down as many pedestrians as possible.

Fortunately, at this crossing the Concourse dipped under Fordham Road so that traversing was generally uneventful. Still, as folk wisdom said, you never knew. Finally, after much trepidation, we arrived at the portals of the Golden City: Alexander's. Named for the son of the owner, this store, which started as a small store on the northwest corner of Fordham and the Concourse selling ladies' stuff, eventually sold so much "stuff" that it gobbled up every other store on the block that sold other "stuff." It became a block-long department store that sold the same "stuff" in one place and under one name. Selling clothing for the lady, the man, and the child, this place was a cornucopia of goodies for the shopper. But for every young Bronx boy who was *schlepped*

Continued on page 13

Movies

Continued from page 12

along by his mother, it became the bane of his existence. I spent many hours sprawled on the floor of the store, or rolling at the feet of unknown hoards of grazers of goods as I slowly went mad with boredom.

When the "shopping spree" was over, and Mom had tried on everything but bought nothing, however, it was time for lunch, so mercifully, we left the store. Recrossing the Concourse, and then Fordham Road itself we found ourselves directly across the street from the RKO Fordham, at the Brighton Cafeteria.

There may have been better places to eat in the world, but not for me. Upon entering, you were given a "passport to the feast", a meal ticket. On the ticket were primed all the prices of the various foods offered at Brighton. Taking a tray and cutlery, you "bellied up" to a chrome tubular shelf in front of a glass case which ran half the length of the restaurant. Behind this steam enshrouded glass case lay the meats, cream pies, sodas, and breads that cause a young glutton's heart to go pitter-patter. The roast beef was my thing; I had a meat tooth. Here was the meat, wrapped around this two-foot-high bone. Standing behind the meat was the carver, who was short, bald and sweating from this proximity to the steamtable, his surgeon's hands were holding a blade the ownership of which would have made D'Artagnian proud. Cut with deft precision, each slice the same thickness as all the others, placed with expert and indifferent care on slices of rye bread, the sandwich was quickly made and lay waiting. But first the meal ticket had to be handed over the countertop, the carver pulling from his apron a metal puncher which, when applied to the ticket, punched out the price of the sandwich. The same procedure was applied to the mashed potatoes, and to the dessert-lemon meringue pie.

The food eaten, my mother and I presented the meal ticket to the cashier at the door who totaled up the costs and took the money. We left, turned left back to the Concourse upon which we headed south until we reached Krum's candy store. There we stocked up on an assortment of sugar replenishment in case we should suddenly go into insulin shock. Exiting Krum's we were now directly across from the Paradise movie theater.

The Paradise was cavernous by today's standards, large even at the time. To a nine-year old kid, the Paradise was overwhelming. Moses at the burning bush, Dame seeing Beatrice in the celestial heavens, Ishmael's first sighting of the whale, seeing Willie Mays play at the Polo Grounds: these were awesome and so was the Paradise.

The outer lobby had Moorish figures in wall niches, tapestries on the walls and carpets on the floor. Roman busts, Grecian urns, and Arabic items adorned the inner lobby. The theatre probably held possibly 1,000 seats among the orchestra and various balconies. The interior walls followed the motif of the lobby: pseudo everything as long as it looked exotic and was painted gold. But the genius of the place was the ceiling. The ceiling was made to resemble the heavens and, I have no doubt, it did. Painted blue, the dark sky darkened with the lights out. With the theater lights out, the celestial dome became lit with hundreds of lights, twinkling and shining as stars in the night sky. Whether it was day or night, the clouds continually rolled by. Whitish, wispy, gentle clouds blew across the huge expanse of ceiling, adding to the dream-like quality of the theatre's presentation. Go to the movies to suspend reality, to get away from life? All right then, we went to the Paradise Theatre and entered the world of illusion as we went through the door.

Photos supplied by the
Theatre Historical Society of America

The Iceman Cometh...Not

By Paul Abramson

Life in the Bronx has changed dramatically during the past fifty or sixty years, and usually not for the better. Much of the South Bronx has been razed, the demographics are completely different, and even the Paradise is now a multiplex. What I choose to write about here is a much smaller deal but which may bring back some old memories.

Up until the early thirties, the iceman was a feature of life in the Bronx. Most homes had an icebox for storing food, with a large compartment where, every few days, a block of ice was inserted. Since ice has a tendency to melt, a drain collected the water and had to be emptied daily. The ice was sold and delivered by an iceman for about 2¢ a pound and generally weighed between 10 and 15 pounds. The appearance of the iceman in the kitchen on a regular basis was an accepted ritual of normal life.

The iceman usually showed up on regular days of the week in a truck containing large coffin-shaped blocks of ice, covered by blankets. The ice was purchased by the iceman from large ice factories located throughout the city; the one in the Bronx was situated at the southern end of the Bronx River. The iceman would unload one of the large blocks of ice on to the street, and then cut it up using an icepick. He would then carry the small blocks of ice up to the houses or apartments using a special set of ice tongs. The remarkable thing was that the

block of ice had been split to exactly fit into the ice compartment of the icebox.

In the Bronx, these icemen were inevitably of Italian extraction, and rumor had it that the routes were protected by the Mafia so that there was no competition. In the summertime,

---

The appearance of the iceman in the kitchen on a regular basis was an accepted ritual of normal life.

small children would gather to watch this operation and receive small pieces of ice as a reward. We were warned, of course, not to suck on the parts of the ice that contained "numonia". The ice was manufactured by an ammonia process, and some of this chemical remained in the ice.

Sometime in the early thirties, something happened. The electric refrigerator appeared, and in spite of the Depression, some of the more affluent people bought them. This, of course, did not bode well for the neighborhood iceman, but most people still had their old iceboxes which were supplied free by the landlord of the apartment house in which they lived. An interesting characteristic of living in those days was that there was a surplus of apartments on the market, due to overbuilding in the twenties, so that in order to attract new tenants, the management of the more expensive apartment houses began to offer electric refrigerators. In order to keep existing tenants, the landlords soon had to replace the old iceboxes with new refrigerators. Signs blossomed on the fronts of buildings (to the dismay of handball players) advertising the fact that all apartments were equipped with new refrigerators. Soon, almost everybody had refrigerators and your friendly neighborhood iceman was doomed. What is truly remarkable is the rapidity with which the iceman vanished. In 1930, the iceman was a normal fixture of everyday life. By 1932, he was gone, except for rare isolated sightings of icemen as late as 1947 in some of the poorer neighborhoods. Today, only people in their sixties and older, even remember the iceman.

For All Those Born Before 1945

We are the survivors!
Consider The Changes We Have Witnessed:

We were born *before* Television, *before* Penicillin, *before* Polio Shots, Frozen Foods, Xerox, Plastic Contact Lenses, Frisbees and the Pill.

We were *before*, Radar, Credit Cards, Split Atoms, Laser Beams and Ballpoint Pens; *before* Pantyhose, Dishwashers, Clothes Dryers, Electric Blankets, Air Conditioners, Drip Dry Clothes and *before* man Walked on the Moon.

We got married first then lived together. How quaint can you be?

In our time, **closets** were for clothes, not for "coming out of". **Bunnies** were small rabbits and rabbits were not Volkswagons. **Designer jeans** were scheming girls named Jean or Jeanne, and having a meaningful relationship meant getting along well with your cousins.

We thought '**fast food**' was what you ate during Lent, and Outer Space was the back of the Paradise Theatre.

We were *before* house-husbands, gay rights, **computer dating,** dual careers and commuter marriages. We were *before* day-car centers, group therapy and nursing homes. We *never heard of* FM radio, tape decks, laser disks, electric typewriters, artificial hearts, word processors, yogurt and guys wearing earrings. For us, '**time sharing**' meant togetherness-not computers or condominiums, a **chip** meant a piece of wood, hardware meant hardware, and **software** wasn't even a word!

In 1940, "Made In Japan" meant junk, and the term '**making out**' meant how you made out on your exam. Pizzas, McDonalds, and instant coffee were unheard of.

We hit the scene when there were 5 and 10¢ stores, where you bought things for five and ten cents. **Krums** and **Jahn's** sold ice cream cones for a nickel or dime. For one nickel you could ride a street car, make a phone call, buy a Pepsi or enough stamps to mail one letter and two postcards. You could buy a **Chevy Coupe** for $600 but who could afford one? Pity too, because gas was 11¢ a gallon!

In our day cigarette smoking was fashionable, grass was mowed, coke was a cold drink and pot was something you cooked in. Rock Music was grandma's lullaby and AIDS were helpers in the principal's office.

We were certainly not *before* the differences between the sexes were discovered but we were surely before the sex change (we made do with what we had). And we were the last generation to be so naive as to think that you needed a husband to have a baby!

No wonder we are so confused and there is such a generation gap today!

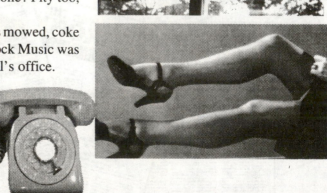

You're pratically there ...turn the page ➡

15

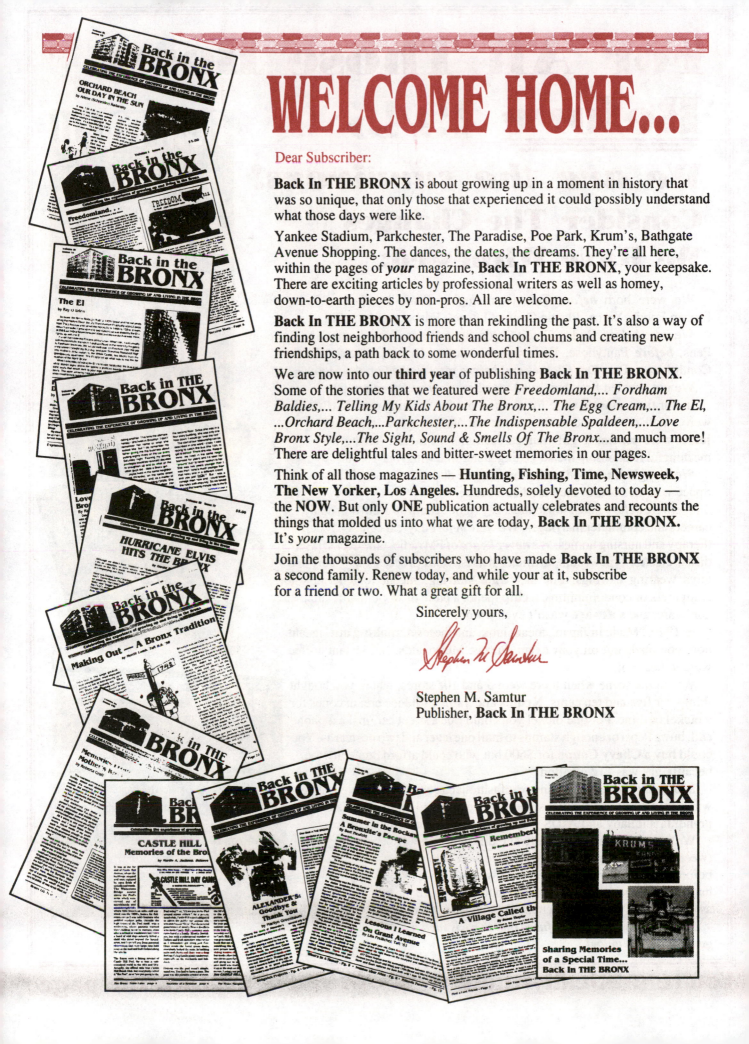

WELCOME HOME...

...WITH Back in THE BRONX

IT'S YOUR MAGAZINE.

Subscribe or Renew Now!

Please fill out the form below to subscribe or renew your subscription to Back in THE BRONX. And while you're at it, think about what a great gift it would be for another Bronxite, a friend and especially, a relative. We'll even acknowledge your gift with a card.

_____ 1 Year subscription(s) to **Back in THE BRONX** - $19.95

_____ 2 Year subscription(s) to **Back in THE BRONX** - $29.95 **($10 Savings)**

_____ 3 Year subscription(s) to **Back in THE BRONX** - $39.95 **($20 Savings)**

_____ (12) Complete set of back issues for just - $39.95 **($20 Savings)**

TOTAL DUE $ _____

FREE JAHN'S MENU

All those who subscribe or renew for _two or more_ years will receive a laminated replica of a vintage JAHN'S MENU.

COLLECTOR'S ITEMS

ALL BACK ISSUES

The complete set (12) of out-of-print back issues of Back in THE BRONX PLUS Jahn's Menu all for just $39.95 (while they last)

Please complete information below and send payment to:

Back in THE BRONX, Box 141H, Scarsdale, NY 10583

❏ New Subscriber ❏ Renewal ❏ Back Issues Requested

Name _____ (Maiden) _____

Address _____

City _____ State _____ Zip _____

Phone # (____) _____

H.S. Attended and Year Graduated _____

METHOD OF PAYMENT:

❏ Check ❏ Visa ❏ MasterCard · Total Amt. Enclosed $ _____

Card No. _____ Expiration Date _____

Use these lines to list the names and addresses of your gift subscriptions

1. Name _____
   Maiden Name _____ _____
   Address _____
   City _____
   State _____ Zip _____
   Phone (____) _____
   High School _____
   Year Graduated _____

2. Name _____
   Maiden Name _____
   Address _____
   City _____
   State _____ Zip _____
   Phone (____) _____
   High School _____
   Year Graduated _____
   List additional addresses on a separate sheet

Reminiscing

The Apartment

By Frank Schmidt

Well, it finally happened. After 54 years, Mom has to leave the apartment in the Bronx. My brothers and I are clearing it out going through dresser drawers and closets that contain the artifacts of that other world we came from. We all grew up in the apartment. It's really all we knew until we went into the Navy. Rumor has it that when we grew too big to pass Dad in the foyer, we had to ship out. And we did, one by one.

The apartment was a fifth floor apartment with two bedrooms, a kitchen, living room, bathroom - and of course, a foyer. Years ago it also had a working dumbwaiter, but that got sealed up as the neighborhood calcified. The apartment picked up the hum of Eastern Boulevard (which became **Bruckner Boulevard)** in the early days, and then picked up the muffled roar of the New England Thruway as the East Bronx underwent renovation. You could see the Whitestone Bridge, and then, later, the Throggs Neck Bridge very clearly from the fifth floor window of the apartment. We grew up with the hum, roar, and view, that only a fifth floor Bronx apartment could provide.

I thought it would be tougher leaving the apartment. But things happened that changed some of the old memories, like getting rid of the old toilet that didn't have a tank, and replacing the old windows that had six frames with new modern windows that had a modern single frame. The biggest change was replacing the old bathroom window that had a frosted surface with an ordinary see-through window. As a kid I used to look at that old bath-

room window on a winter morning and instantly knew from the glare of the bathroom window whether it had snowed during the night. Recently, the elevator was renovated and the old buttons were replaced with new, modern looking buttons. So, the toilet, the windows, the elevator buttons, all that were part of the feeling of the apartment were gone. Takes the sting out of it, I guess.

We're keeping the apartment for the month of September, even though Mom moved out at the end of August. There's still some "stuff" to work through. The secretary in the foyer is a family heirloom and we can't leave it (better to leave the T.V.) and there may be some things still up in the far reaches of the closets that have been hidden for 30 or 40 years. But, on Oct.1st we will be out of the apartment and years of memories, attending **PS71;** playing in the OLA schoolyard; **Pelham Bay Park**; the candy store we called "Garbers;" staying out after dark when we were kids, throwing crayons out of the window to see the sidewalk turn colors when the sun came up; trading comics on the apartment house stairs on a rainy Saturday, taking the garbage down to the mysterious basement; setting up the Christmas train table and tree; keeping things fresh on the fire escape; listening to the sounds in the hall outside of the apartment door after midnight; making snowballs from the slushy snow on the brick windowsill ledge; playing "lavball" with a rolled up sock and ruler in the livingroom/foyer space; falling in love with the girl on the fourth floor-but getting nowhere; going down the stairs two at a time; watching a developing snowstorm

obliterate the boulevard, listening to the caretaker cutting the grass in the Indian museum across the way; lying in bed with the flu listening to "Baby Snooks," and "Captain Midnight," listening to my first rock and roll song: "Earth Angle;" getting dressed for my first dance (St. Helena's, of course...); knocking off half a bottle of J&B with my brother in our old bedroom while we got dressed for our youngest brother's wedding; listening to my mother and father talking late into the night about the war; waiting in the bedroom while Santa Claus came down the fire escape and through the window into the living room; entering the livingroom with the magic of Christmas eve all around me; lying in bed on a Saturday morning with the sun coming through the bedroom window thinking about baseball; listening to Glenn Miller playing "Sleep Lagoon" on the hi-fi in the living room while the curtains blew softly in the summer breeze; listening to Mel Allen and the Yankee games in our bedroom on that old wooden radio; frying Italian sausage in the kitchen on a winter morning; coming up from the street with my cotton gloves all wet from the snow and balls of ice sticking to the cotton; putting on a white shirt and a red tie for the PS71 color guard; coming up from the street all sweaty from a game of ringaleaveo; eating flank steak in the kitchen with my brothers, Mother, Father and Grandma; going to **Bronx Beach** for the day and just looking at the ceiling of the bedroom that I shared with my brothers; all will be pure memory without the apartment.

It had to happen one day

But, maybe it was happening all along...

A Bronx Puzzle

Find the following Street Names, Schools and filler words, then when you're done, the remaining letters spell out a special message. Have Fun!

Conceived and Created by:
Allen Mandel

```
W E G D I R B S G N I K
O H C E L A D R E V I R
T O I A L L I H N U G L
R M L T R E C N E I C S
A E A G E R E Z D S I O
B A T U T P P Y S I G U
C L R S S E L O E R A T
L L U H E L X A S R R H
I I T M H H I N I O E E
N V A E C A C O O N T R
T O C L K M R T N R S N
O P E R R Y O F S D B E
N L D F A R T A I E E D
E U E O P N O T L A W G
N G D R E D N A V E S O
D N A R G R A N D A L L
```

WORD LIST:

BARTOW	KINGSBRIDGE	RANDALL
BRONX	LION	RIVERDALE
CIGAR	LYDIG	SCIENCE
CLINTON	NOISE	SOUTHERN
CROTONA	NORRIS	TAFT
DECATUR	OGDEN	VILLA
EVANDER	PARKCHESTER	WALTON
GUN HILL	PERRY	WEBSTER
GRAND	PELHAM	WESTCHESTER
HOME	PLUG	WHITE PLAINS
HULL	POE	ZEREGA

Answer to Puzzle:
Call up some old friends!

TAKE A TRIP DOWN MEMORY LANE WITH EITHER OF THESE GREAT BOOKS!

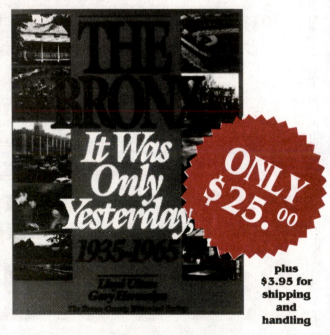

ONLY $25.00 plus $3.95 for shipping and handling

The period from the middle of the 1930's to the middle of the 1960's was a dynamic one in the history of this country. The depths of the Great Depression brought the New Deal to combat economic disaster, and this was followed quickly by the ferment of the Second World War. Peacetime brought great changes in our society, including the movement from the cities to the suburbs and a vast influx of different ethnic groups into the cities. No area was more affected by these changes then **The Bronx**.

Yet, in the midst of this upheaval, The Bronx was also marked by islands of stability and by its continuity with the past. Now that story is told in

The Bronx,
It Was Only Yesterday
1935-1965

Reminiscing

A Place Called GARDEN STREET

By Linda Krell

I would like to take you down memory lane with me, to the forties and fifties, to a street in The Bronx called Garden Street. This is where I spent my childhood. Garden Street was three blocks long. The first block faced the Bronx Zoo. There was a garden across the street from my apartment building. The garden extended the entire block.

Welcome to 702 Garden Street, apartment 6. This is where I lived with my mom, dad, and my older brother, Jack. the year is 1946. Come with me into the living room. We don't have a television, but we have a large console radio. The radio is on and Frank Sinatra is singing. You can hear my mom in the kitchen while she is preparing the traditional Friday night dinner. Let's join her in the kitchen. It is Friday afternoon and my mom is making chicken soup. You can smell the aroma of the chicken roasting in the oven. You can see the challah on the kitchen table and the sabbath candles next to it, ready to be lit at sundown. This is a scene you could see in most Jewish homes all over America.

You don't see a refrigerator because we don't have one. What you will see is an icebox. The ice man would come to our house a few times a week to deliver a huge brick of ice. He would carry the ice on his shoulder up to our apartment an put it in our ice box.

Come along now, the year is 1948. We are getting a new refrigerator. Yippie! We were all so excited. I couldn't wait for the refrigerator to be delivered. I wanted to see what this automatic cooler looked like. My mom couldn't believe that she was finally getting a refrigerator and life would be a little easier.

Now a new year has arrived. It is 1950. My friend Barbara was the first one on the block to get a television set. When my favorite show was on, I would go to her house to watch it. Little by little, our neighbors and friends bought television sets. My mom, brother and I nagged my dad until he finally gave in and bought a new RCA TV. I remember the day it was delivered, we were so happy to have our own entertainment center. Now we could watch in the comfort of our own home.

In the Spring, I would go to the nearby candy store to by an ice cream cone for a

795 Garden Street

dime or an ice cream soda for twenty-five cents.

On a cold December day, mom and I would bundle up really warm and go for a walk to look for the jelly apple man. At times we would find him walking or standing on Prospect Avenue and 181st Street with his cart. He was a friendly elderly man with rosie red cheeks. When I asked for a jelly apple, he would take an apple from his cart, put a stick in it, and then put it into the hot jelly. Boy, was it delectable and it only cost five cents! He also sold fresh coconut for three cents.

Sometimes, my mom would send me to the bakery a few blocks away for a rye bread. I would ask for a fresh rye sliced without seeds; it cost twenty-five cents. As I walked home, I ate a number of slices. When I came home with the bread, my mom looked in the bag, laughed and said, ".What happened to my bread, it shrunk" I confessed that the bread felt so fresh and smelled so good I couldn't resist eating some.

When I got older, my friends and I would walk to Tremont Avenue which was a distance away. We bought a pickle from Charlie's appetizing store. The cost was five cents for a luscious large sour pickle.

On Sundays, my parents would take me to the Deluxe movie theater. It was located on Tremont Avenue near Crotona Avenue. The cost of admission was twenty-five cents for a child and fifty cents for an adult. We would see two films, cartoons, and a newsreel. The newsreel was a narrated account of events from around the world.

My mom never locked the front door of our apartment when I went out to play. My parents would go out for the evening and come home late at night on the subway. They would walk home or take the bus home from the subway in the early morning hours. My mom and dad never feared for their safety.

It was nice taking you down memory lane with me. I enjoyed sharing some of my childhood experiences with you. ∎

724 Garden Street

Back in THE BRONX

Box 141H, Scarsdale, NY 10583

DO YOUR FRIENDS A FAVOR...

Please send a sample issue of Back in THE BRONX with my compliments to my friends.

If YOU enjoy **Back In THE BRONX,** it's likely that some of your friends will enjoy it too.
If you'll send us their names and addresses, we'll gladly send each one of them
a *FREE* sample issue.
So simply *print* their names and addresses on the handy form below, and mail the form to us.
We'll have your friend's free issue in the mail in a jiffy!

Send a sample issue of Back In THE BRONX to the friends I've listed below.

- - - - - - - - - - - - - - - - ✂ - ✂ - - - - - - - -

PLEASE PRINT

Friend's Name _____   Maiden _____

Address _____

City _____   State ____   Zip ____

Phone # (   ) _____

High School _____   Year Graduated _____

Friend's Name _____   Maiden _____

Address _____

City _____   State ____   Zip ____

Phone # (   ) _____

High School _____   Year Graduated _____

*List additional names on a
separate sheet.*

REMEMBER...

DON'T GIVE AWAY YOUR COPY OF BACK IN THE BRONX!

**We will be happy to send any
friends or relatives
their own copy for FREE!!!
Just fill out the form on page 31
or call 1 - 800- 7 BRONX 5
and their copy will be on its way!**

MAIL TO:
Back In THE BRONX, Box 141H, Scarsdale, NY 10583

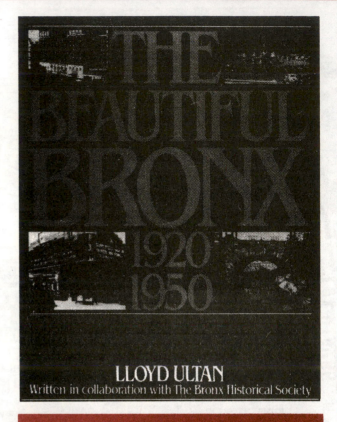

Scrapbook

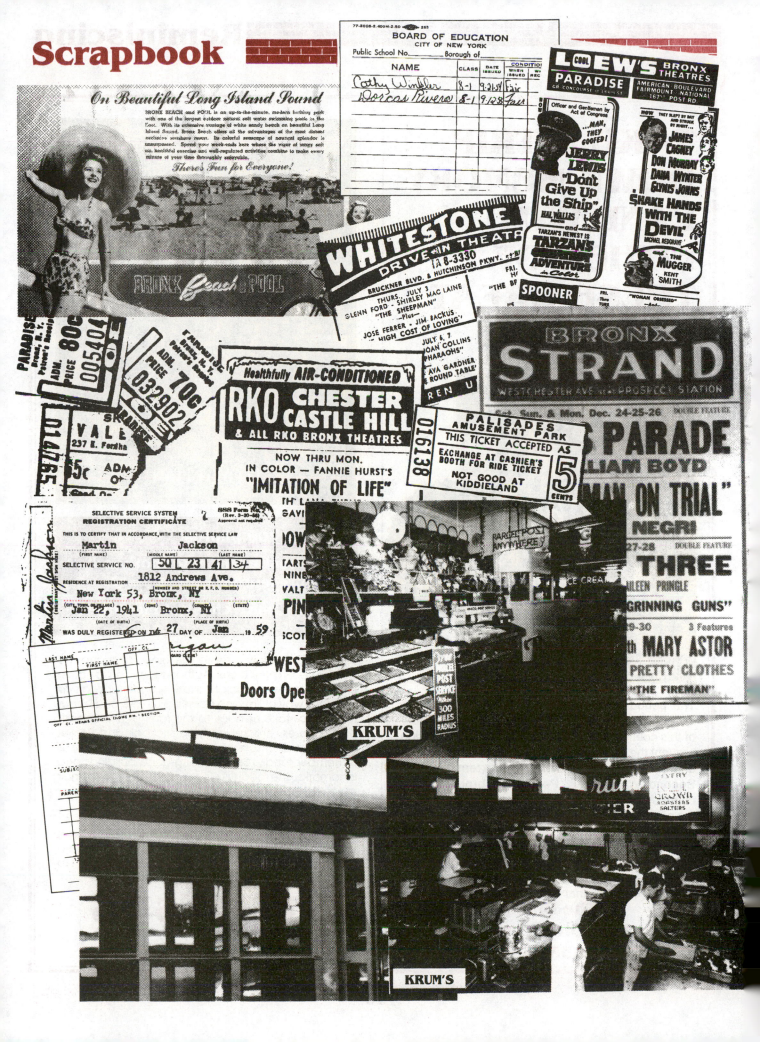

On Beautiful Long Island Sound

BRONX *Beach & POOL*

LOEW'S BRONX THEATRES
PARADISE
GR. CONCOURSE ST. 188TH ST.

...MAN, THEY GOOFED!

JERRY LEWIS "Don't Give Up the Ship"
HAL WALLIS

and
TARZAN'S GREATEST ADVENTURE
in Color

NOW

JAMES CAGNEY
DON MURRAY
DANA WYNTER
GLYNIS JOHNS
SHAKE HANDS WITH THE DEVIL
MICHAEL REDGRAVE

and
THE MUGGER
KENT SMITH

SPOONER

WHITESTONE DRIVE-IN THEATRE
TA 8-3330
Bruckner Blvd. & Hutchinson Pkwy.

THURS., JULY 3
GLENN FORD - SHIRLEY MAC LAINE "THE SHEEPMAN"
— Plus —
JOSE FERRER - JIM BACKUS "HIGH COST OF LOVING"

BRONX STRAND
WESTCHESTER AVE. near PROSPECT STATION

Sun. & Mon., Dec. 24-25-26 DOUBLE FEATURE

PARADE
WILLIAM BOYD

MAN ON TRIAL
NEGRI

Healthfully AIR-CONDITIONED
RKO CHESTER CASTLE HILL
& ALL RKO BRONX THEATRES

NOW THRU MON.
IN COLOR — FANNIE HURST'S
"IMITATION OF LIFE"

PALISADES AMUSEMENT PARK
THIS TICKET ACCEPTED AS
5 CENTS
EXCHANGE AT CASHIER'S BOOTH FOR RIDE TICKET
NOT GOOD AT KIDDIELAND

THREE

"GRINNING GUNS"

3 Features
MARY ASTOR
PRETTY CLOTHES
"THE FIREMAN"

Doors Open

KRUM'S

KRUM'S

BRONX TRIVIA ANSWERS

1. Bronx Science

2. Regis Philbin

3. 161 St. & River Ave

4. Robert Hall

5. Davega

6. Fish

7. 180th St & Bronx Park

8. New York University

9. Gorman's

10. City Island

11. Bronx County Building

12. Metropolitan Life

13. They were all buried in the Woodlawn Cemetary

14. 4 to 6

15. u-bet

16. 00

17. Arthur Murray

18. b (Van Cortlandt Park)

19. Freedomland

20. b

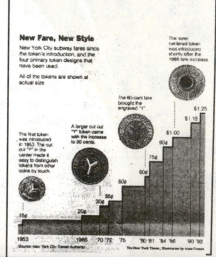

New Fare, New Style

New York City subway fares since the token's introduction, and the four primary token designs that have been used.

All of the tokens are shown at actual size

FOLLOW THE FUN ROAD TO FREEDOMLAND

NEW YORK CITY

25

Did You Attend Any of These Schools?

Taft, Clinton, Monroe, Bronx Science, Roosevelt, Evander, Music & Art, Columbus, Gompers, Stuyvesant, Brooklyn Tech, Bronx Vocational, Industrial Arts, Walton, Dodge, Stevenson, Kennedy, Truman, Hunter, Jane Adams, Tolentine, St. Barnabus, Rice, Fordham Prep, Performing Arts, Cardinal Hayes, Commercial, Spellman, St. Helena, Mt. St. Ursula, St. Raymonds, Manhattan Prep, Aquinas, Bedford Park Academy, and CCNY - or Grew Up In The Bronx

ARE YOU READY FOR A REUNION?

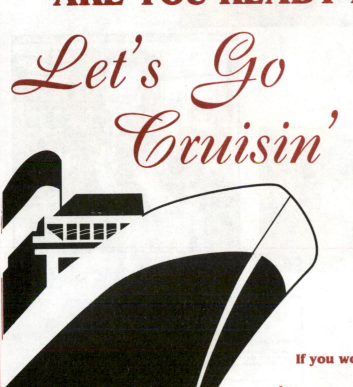

Let's Go Cruisin'

Sometime next year (Date to be decided), **Back in THE BRONX** will sponsor a gala Bronx Reunion Cruise with expectations of over 1,000 in attendance. If you've never been on a cruise or if you've been on many, what better way to go on your next cruise with over 1,000 current and former Bronxites from the 40's, 50's and 60's. In fact, we will not only bring Bronxites together, we will even bring individual schools together.

If you would like us to send you information on
THE BRONX REUNION CRUISE,
please complete the information below and send it to :
Back In THE BRONX, P.O. Box 141H, Scarsdale, NY 10583
or fax it to (914) 592-4893. Should you have any questions,
please call (914) 592-1647.

Name _____

Address _____

City _____ State ____ Zip _____

Telephone: (   ) _____

High School _____ Year of Graduation _____

BRIEF SURVEY
1. Have you ever been on a cruise?   ❑ Yes   How many ____   ❑No
2. Would you Consider attending a Bronx Reunion Cruise? ❑ Yes ❑ No
3. What time of year is best? _____
4. How long should the cruise last? _____ (days)
5. Would you be attending with ❑ Spouse ❑ Friend ❑ Alone
6. What would you enjoy seeing, having, and/or doing on this cruise? _____
_____
_____

26

WHO ARE THEY? ⭐

Can you guess these famous Bronx faces?

A

B

C

D

A. Eydie Gorme
B. Shari Lewis
C. Al Pacino
D. Dion

27

Classifieds

Missing Persons

MP775 Little Barbara from Wednesday night "Shindig" University Ave. If you remember please call Fred 201-991-2181

MP776 Looking for Myrna Landau, Marlene Rosenberg & Barbara Keglovite from Eastburn Ave. Myrna, remember dancing and playing Mahjong at Palace Hotel in Rockaway. Rosanne Frischer would love to know where you girls are.

MP777 Jerry Gross would like to hear from Frank Cavalluzzo to reminisce about old times at the H&M 2nd Mosholu Parkway.

MP778 Where are those guys and gals of Lincoln Dales of the Bronx 50's and PAL. Marty Bond & his wife Tiny, Jimmy Side, Pat McGrath, Carol Woods, Cathy Donnelly, Eileen King, Jerry Collin, Moe Murphy. Call Butch & Bunny Garrison: 717-654 8464 or 717 654 8464. Love to hear & see all.

MP779 Barracudas 1941-1950, Kingsbridge Rd. and Reservoir Ave., looking for old friends plus Charlotte Mayfield of Wallace Ave. Please call Stan Getzler 212 787 9026.

MP780 Marvin Oppenheim of Pelham Parkway Projects - Columbus, 1961 - wants to hear from old friends: Mark & Joel Klein, Raymond Sussman, Robert "Bertie" Puris, Mike Seltzer, Melvin Appelbaum. Call me 212 650 6663.

MP781 Arnold Pollack, **Monroe** '58 is interested in hearing from any old friends from neighborhood, Stratford, Manor, Ward Ave near Watson. Elliot Dietz, Allen Cohen, Eddie Genovese, Joani Donaldson.

MP782 I would enjoy hearing from anyone who knew Carolyn Lebowitz (Cooperman). Remember Jahn's, Krum's, Luhrs? From one who thought the stars were real atop the Loew's paradise. P.S. 79 E.B.B.

MP783 Would like to hear from old friends. Ridder '49-'52, **Monroe** '53-'55. Frieda Meyers Tolkov & Jerry Tolkov. 914 476 2933, 104 Hilltop Acres, Yonkers, NY 10704

MP784 Sidney P. Cohen, **Clinton** '52. Does this name have a familiar ring to it. Please call 800 881 1585

MP785 1956 **Roosevelt** Grads- we are planning a reunion. We have received over 65 names & current addresses. For info call Hal Rosenstein 516 585 6474, or Nanacy (Bologna) Capozi 914 793 4244. Judy Barbanel where are you?

MP786 Stuart Herman, **Clinton** '56 lived and played on Valentine Ave. and Miriam St. Now living in Fort Lauderdale, FL and in the color catalog printing business. Would love to hear from you. Tel: 800 367 2522 or write c/o MegaColor, 1380 SW 8 St., Pompano Beach FL 33069

MP787 East Bronxers! JHS 118. **Roosevelt** HS, Fordham-Belmont-Crotona - 180 St. area. 1940-'44 and earlier. 407 746 9974 or write me (classified #) Anthony Vento

MP788 Bill Penzer, PhD. - shrink in Ft. Lauderdale since '73. Looking for friends from PS 64, Wade, **Taft**, Rockwood St. Cascades. Where are you Lenny Kamil? Will send copy of my book to friends who write. 140 S. University Drive, Plantation, FL 33324

MP789 Joel Weinstein of 181st & Creston, Creston JHS, **Clinton** 1/52 looking for Flicks: Levy, Leicher, Zaretsky, Tils, Siegel, Hecht, Schayes, Berson, Fallick(s), Richter, Lambert, Bergman, Friedlander, Lenderer, Kaye, Beckelman, Krinsky, Krenztel, Woren, Padell, et al. 610 664 8216, 545 Putnam Rd., Merion Station, PA 19066

MP790 Contact, whereabouts, info. sought with, of, about JANE GRABOIS and CRYSTAL LORCH. Seeker: STUART KLIPPER (ex of Parkchester, PS 106, JHS 125, **Monroe**); tel/fax: 612 922 1553, eMail: 2199@topcity.mn.org.

MP791 PS 56 Ms. Fitzpatrick's grade 6 class of 1962 - Capozzi, Scharf, Cohen, Fink, Green, Miller, Frankel, Kalus, Feller, Scher, Sklow, et al. Most of us went from grade 1-6 together. Where are we all now?

MP792 Maiden Name: Geraldine Mintzer (Harry's Daughter) Looking for Barbara & Laura Stevens. Parents Lester & Pearl Stevens 731 Gerard Ave., BX, NY 50's & 60's. Lester had a hardware store

MP793 Fred Auerbach, **Taft** '51-Gerard Ave. & 168th St. and Marilyn (Sharlat) Auerebach of Morris Ave. & 183rd St. Wonder if anyone remembers us. We live in Sarasota, FL. Where are you? 813 365 7679 or Fax 813 366 4522

MP794 Looking for Jackie Bookbinder. She went to **Walton** HS. - I went to **Taft**. I'm living in Northridge, CA for 21 years. Graduated **Taft** 1955. My name is Jeanette (Herstein) Salzman. I lived at 1715 Nelson Ave.

MP795 Were you a member of 9BRI Wade JHS graduating class of Jan 1946. Estelle (Adelman) Laurence and John (Leicher) Bender would love to hear from former classmates. We both graduated from **Taft** in 1948. Let's hear from you.

MP796 Looking for Rosiland Kleinbaum, Morris 1955. Lived on Hunts Point Avenue.

MP797 Happy Birthday Stanley Lofstock (**Evander** '55) from your wife Sandra Jacob (Erasmas '65). Looking for people from either of our graduating classes. Now living in Southern CA 818 880 6808

MP798 Looking for Leonard Goldberg, Willfred Hecker, Daniel Ferstand & Milton (Mousy) Schuss. Please contact the Ritters 407 479 3886. Also looking for twins Frankie & Phillip Coren

MP799 Does anyone know what became of my favorite English/Homeroom teacher Mrs. Levy, at the James **Monroe** Annex. She was a great inspiration to a very shy 13-14 year old, chubby girl. I've never forgotten her.

MP800 P.S. 33 class of '47 is planning a reunion.- please call 718 229 3275. Looking for Audrey Goldman, Sylvia Greaz, Helen Oitiger, Mirum Abolnick, James Cavanugh, John Colross, Francine Davis, William Namos, Marvin Gwortzman, Bari Hoffman, Norm Louy, Phyllis Lipton, Martin Lindonhaum, Robert Uuaics, Robert Kardos, Rich Pilot, Gladys Silverman

MP801 We are looking for **Taft** '48 friends, especially Irene Solomon Stem and Maxine Fisher-to join us at our next reunion. Dolores Stone Altman, Shelia Handshoe Rothman, Maxine Blum Markoff

MP802 Ilene & Jerry Krugman are looking for friends who lived on Popham Ave., Sedgewick Projects, P.S. 109, P.S. 104, P.S. 82 (**Taft** '60) Macombs Bowling Alley, 1961 Laurels Hotel and Bungelows on Sackett LK. Lets Talk! 201 797 8459

MP803 Elaine (Goldman) Vipler would love to hear from old friends from P.S. 70, P.S. 94, JHS 80 '58, **Evander** '61, Hunter '65, 309 East 87 St., NY, NY 10128

MP804 Stuart Speiser, **Clinton** '61-Would like to hear from the guys & gals from Kingsbridge Terrace, Sedgwick Ave., 17068 Dearborn St. Northridge, CA, 91325. 818 886 2520 "Earthquake Survivor"

MP805 "Did you attend PS77 in 1955, '56 and '57 and wonder if you were in the special music class with Mr. Flieshaker and Ms. Shivers? Where are you, Carol Pappemick, Jerrolyn Solomons, Connie the flute player, Sandra Tortorisi, Robert Bratter, Joel Novak, and the rest of the class? I miss you. Please contact me. Donald H. Solomon, 7912 Kingland Drive, Raleigh, NC 27613 home: 919 781 5857, work: 919 821-2000

MP806 Former members Featherbed Lane Presbyterian Church, corner University Ave. and/ or former members University Heights Presbyterian Church, University Ave. & Hall of Fame Terrace. Write Connie Lobody, Box 196, Yarmouth Port, MA 02675

MP807 Sondra Bobbe Nee Kravetz, **Taft** '49, looking for old friends and neighbors. Any King of Clubs guys still around?

MP808 Looking for Dennis Gilbert, Hunts Point neighborhood graduate of the **Bronx High School of Science** about 1955. Contact: Bob Feldman 516 366 2190

MP809 Anyone remember me? Elaine Feingold (now Kramer) P.S. 53, JHS 22, **Taft** '55, 1436 Clay Ave. Please write. Living in St. Louis, Missouri

MP810 Looking for Roberta Trezza. I took you to see Blue Denim with Mike & Sandy on your honeymoon night. Sandy Reinitz (Undercliff Ave.?) At CCNY you asked your boyfriend if you could date me. Sandy Klinger (Creston Ave 1957) 510 933 7257

MP811 **Taft**-who remembers friends from East Mt. Eden Ave. & Topping Ave? Jacky Stolow, Stopsky and Jimmy Stolow are alive & well and would like to hear from you.

MP812 Irv Rubin asks: Anyone from Putnam Place or Gun Hill Road...between Reservoir Oval and Woodlawn Cemetery. Where is the Gang? Already found Paul Barron. Call 201 398 8871

MP813 I want to be a grandma! He's 29, tall, dark, handsome and nice. Really. He lives in N. Westchester. First and last time I'll meddle-Promise! If you have a daughter who may be interested- please respond!

MP814 Where are you Phyllis Reinger, Lei Bowitz? Toasters are looking for you- Phyllis, Arlene, Joan, Carol, Anita, Molly & Elenore. Please contact Eleanore Wertheimer 908 727 3641

MP815 Would like to hear from P.S. 6, 8th grade grads in 1952. Also, Friends on Vyse and 180th. Also friends on Garden St and Southern Blvd. Let's hear from you - Gerry Gafka

MP816 If anyone knows the whereabouts of Barry Herbst (last known - a dentist; Fairfax VA.) Please let me know. D. Stone: 203 882 0736

MP817 Marvin Manis Goldman looking for Arlene (Olly) Smith. Mayfair-Mayflower romance 1948-'53. Unforgettable on Arnow & Barnes Avenue. Without your love letters, could not have endured two years in marines.

MP818 Marilynn (Steckler) Rosenberger, **Science** '64, now from Brooklyn, says "Hi" to all friends, including Danny Fermon and Linda Lustgarten. I'm a mother of eight and musical director for singing star, Ruthi Navon. We perform for Jewish women only.

MP819 Looking for "Mimi" Miriam Rosenthal and all members of James **Monroe** HS class of '46. Write Eugene (Gene) Miller 3306 Startan Ct, Louisville, KY 40220

MP820 Calling any "flyboys", feeders or pressmen from the old American Bank Note Company for the years 1939 - 1942. These were the fellows from the Green Room the Bank Note was on Garrison Ave. and Tiffany St. Drop us a line.

MP821 For transplanted New Yorkers and friends on the West Coast. We hold high school reunions, parades, egg cream drinking contests. Our 10th anniversary reunion this Fall. Our free newsletter - NYAA (New York Alumni Association) P.O. Box 5122 Beverly Hills, CA 90210 (301) 276 8299

MP822 1950 **Taft** graduates wanted. This was a special group. Contact Sylvia Rapaport: 1545 La Venta Drive, Westlake Village, CA 91361. Office: 818 710 1222 Home: 805 371 9931

MP823 Has anyone kept in touch with Debbie Skulsky? Please let me know. Write to Ellen Kremer, 184 Harrison St., New Milford, NJ 07646

MP824 Regina (Schlanger) Elbert & Joan (Hendelman) Efrom are looking for Janice Caporole, Toni Guerro, Marie Perrone, Ruth Hirsch, Joyce Medaglin, Jeannette Denaro, Sally Rosenfeld, Rosemary Sera, Linda Krieger or anyone that remembers us -Class 1954

MP825 **Evander Childs** reunion Jan./June 1945 Classes. Join us Thurs. Oct. 12, 12:00 to 5:00 for a delicious luncheon at the Villa Barone in the Bronx. For more information call Emma Brancati Preza: 718 338 8879

MP 826 Muriel Newman, **Roosevelt** HS, PS 53, PS 90. Stanley Newman, Brooklyn College, **Clinton**, PS 64. Please contact thru Box#

MP827 Anyone from 181st & Ryder Ave. Looking for Harry Witlin, Max Marsoff, Lou Kossof, Bobby Marshal, Hal Gorky

MP828 1940's Rose Janet 1640 Washington Ave., across from the Bronx House. Milton Freedman, my husband, would love to hear from David Offner, Irving Dvorian, Hector Gonzales of **Roosevelt** 1943-45. We live in NJ 201 584 8395.

MP829 Noteworthy! The officers of the senior class of **Evander Childs** HS class of 1945, have, with their spouses, been friends for 50 years! George Green (Pres), Gerald Harrison (V.P.), Seena Stern Silverman (Treas.) Judith (Swimming) and Rita Cohen Grossman (sec.) all send regards on the golden anniversary of our class.

MP830 Looking for anyone who lived on Vyse Ave. and 173rd St in the late 40's and early 50's.

MP831 Seeking Orions and related from the PS 90, '50 era for a June 1996 reunion: Gerald Schwab, Norman Goldman, Stan Turk, Stuart Auerbach, Artie Stem, Paul Marnell, Marty Levy, Noel Frank, Murray Schlifkin, Ron Selinger, Hank Holzer, Artie Warsaw—where are you? Contact Richard Guarascio, 21 Finch Road, New City, NY 10956

MP832 Bud Ruff is looking for Florence Stecker who lived at 107 Elliot Place in the Bronx during the 1940's. Her family consisted of her father, Morris...other family members Ida & Arlene. Any info, no matter how small would be appreciated.

MP833 May Nathanson and Pat Elson (**Taft** '53) looking for Ricky Offsey (**Taft** '53). Would love to get together & hear how the years have treated you. Please call 914 354 4886 evenings.

MP834 Ralph Schlichthernlein, **Evander** '52, looking for Joe Stewart (Paolucci), Fred Romano, Leonore Migliori, Sheila Horowitz, PS113 Jim Zaccaras, Lou Ellen Pepper, Diane, Delores, Elaine, Evelyn Fratarigo, Penfield St., Sonny DiAngelus, Harry Whyte, Artie, Russ, Ruth, Joan, Elaine, Marilyn Andreas.

MP835 Jane (Paxton) Merovick, **Monroe** '38- often think of those wonderful years and our great group! Where are you all? I'm in California. Would love to hear from you.

MP836 St. Joseph's Bathgate Ave., Class of '54. We grew up together for 8 years. Let's have a reunion. Contact John Kuhn, P.O. Box 33, Norwell, MA 02061 or call 617 659 7139

MP837 Looking for Enid (nee Klein) Schoen, who graduated from **Walton** '58, and lived on Tiebout Ave. and 181st Street. Have been looking for her for several years and would like to get in touch with her. Her last known whereabouts in '66 was Yonkers. Please call.

MP838 Elaine Goldstein would like to hear from Jerry Spitzer, Henry Weintraub, Gladys Markowitz, Paul Freeze. Call 516 499 4238

MP839 Hi! Jesse Greenberg (**Monroe** '56). I'm a freelance writer and part time cowboy living in Tucson. Buzzy Mund, Richie Loeser, Dick Bonte, Barb Goldstein, Rose Kriaris, Mick Beattie, Joe Fardella, Sid Goodrich, Bob Angrisani, Ernie Klein, Elissa Kernsweet - anybody interested-write!

MP840 Looking for old friends from Vyse Avenue and 173rd Street in the Bronx. Where are you, Mildred Zimmerman, Estelle Markowitz, Marilyn Karlin? Also, Alex Kalmowitz, Steve Dorfman, Henry Katz, Bernard Silverman? Call Adele 609 983 3303 to remember.

MP841 Members of Scholarship Class, **Clinton** '64 - Reunion- Dr. David Plotkin 201 378 9333

MP842 Eugene Miller, James **Monroe** '46, is looking for old classmates from 1942-'46. Write and relive old memories. Gene Miller, 3306 Startan Ct., Louisville, KY 40220

MP843 Marvin (Paiewsky) Price, **Taft** '59 & PS 82, living in Las Vegas. Looking for old friends, neighbors and classmates - especially Barbara Mathews or Lenny Lawrence, 5760 Hedgeford Ct., Las Vegas, NV 89120 or 702 898 0037

MP844 Sandy Ptalis, **Science** '59, CCNY '62, would like to hear from any of the old gang (male/female) of Gerard Ave., from 153rd St. to 161st St. Lived at 831 Gerard; PS31, JHS 22. Call 914 357 0811

MP845 I lived at 1427 Wilkins Ave., corner of 170th St. from 1932 to 1947. If there's anyone out there, lets hear from you. Eddie Rubinstein, 9015 Ohio Ave., Sun Lakes, Arizona 85248

MP846 Helene (Bookbinder) Scherer, **Walton** '49 and Dorothy (Cooper) Leibowitz, **Evander Childs** '49 are looking for anyone who worked in Camp Eden, Cold Spring, NY in 1948 and '49. Also any H.S. friends who remember us.

MP847 Tina Cohen Reich is looking for old friends who graduated fro PS86 in 1954. Also friends from Webb Ave.: Shelia Cetlin, Rosalind Insler, Eileen Forman

MP848 PS114, skipped 5th grade, we were in Mr. Mulley's 6th grade class when Kennedy was killed. Where is Judy Gostin, Phillip Perlman, Ester Benjamin? Write Gail Goldstein Cerra, 2846C S. Wakefield Street, Arlington, VA 22206

MP849 Looking for grads of JHS98, class of '57 who did not know of recent reunion at Raleigh Hotel, but would like to be on mailing list. Alan Lefkow, Herman Ridder 98 -class of '57, **Bronx Science** '60, lived at 1832 Bryant Ave. (at 176th St.) Now a Director at Consumers Union, Publisher of Consumer Reports magazine.

MP850 Bob Gramacy, **Clinton** '61. Looking for anyone from 182nd St. and Grand Ave., especially Alfred Delgins and Les Litt, Mike, Lee & Richie. Call Bob 818 366 2378

MP851 Marcia Hirsh, PS94 '50, JHS80 '53, **Evander** '57. Would love to hear from anyone who remembers me. I am living in Westchester, NY.

Classifieds

Come Blow Your Horn

Accomplishments
Awards
Businesses
Volunteerism
Works in Progress

Rabbi Stephen H. Pinsky (**Science** '62) is Midwest Regional Director of the Union of American Hebrew Congregations in St. Louis and would love to hear from classmates in the area/or fellow P.S. 81 grads. 314 458 0578

Sylvia Lowry, President of Packaged Parties, Inc, Woodland Hills, California. A Linen Rental and Party Equipment firm shipping nationwide. Full party-planning and consulting service.

Joan Hendelman, **Monroe** '54 will be married 35 years to Hank Efrom. We have 3 daughters and all college graduates and are married. We have 2 grandsons and 1 grandsons and 1 granddaughter. We live in Aberdeen, NJ for 32 years.

Glenda Acker is a Senior Investigator with the Begen County Prosecutor's Office-Special Investigations Squad. Formerly I was a paralegal before becoming a cop. Have also held elected office Board of Education, Oakland, NJ. I am engaged to be married to Ed Rogers, who originally lived on Pelham Parkway and attended **Music & Art**. Our paths crossed many times in the Bronx (Castle Hill Pool, Young Israel, ect.) But it took first marriages and many years to find each other. On 9/29/96 I will become Mrs. Glenda Rogers.

Herb "Woody" Herman, **Clinton** '48, resides in Spring Valley, NY, wife Sarah, children Denise and Eric. Grandchildren Elyssa and Benjamin. General Agent, Allstate Insurance, 1 Penn Plaza, NY. Served U.S. Army Germany. Graduated NYU Brooklyn Law School.

Bob Schuenbacher. Neighborhood-Wakefield/241st White Plains Rd. P.S. 8 '49. **Evander** Swim Team-Orchard Beach Life Guard '53. U.S. Navy '54-58. NYU/SCAF '58-62, Newspaper advertising Career '62 to? Currently New House Newspapers.

Elaine Goldman Vipler. I am the director of Summer Scope, a free camp and teen program advisory service to help families select appropriate summer programs for their children. I am also a reading teacher. Married to Marvin Vipler for 27 years and we have a 23 year old daughter living in Colorado.

Sheila (Fox) Dimond. P.S. 88, JHS 22, **Taft** H.S. - 1330 Morris Ave. (between 169-170th) Queens college-Anthro. Cum laude. Married 37 years to a (gasp) Brooklyn boy. Working at York College as tutor of English as a Second Language. Two married sons, on grandchild and one on the way.

Jeffrey Ballen. Grew up on Hill Ave. & Gun Hill Rd., CCNY 1966, Tufts Dental 1970, Boston U-Grad School-specialist. Lived in Boston 16 years and loved it. Now in California. I remember "pickles in the barrel," "Schweller Rest.", "Curb Ball" and Woodlawn Cemetery, great friends, summer nights and "The Oval" Thanks for the magazine- I love it!

Evelyn Bierman Rothstein is Ed. D. in education, presently an educational consultant working with school districts around the U.S. Author of "Teaching Writing" and other educational books.

Lila Freilicher (**Taft**, '61) is a marketing communications consultant and writer, living in Park Slope, Brooklyn, with her 15 year old daughter. I'd love to hear from anyone who remembers me and from anyone who needs help developing corporate communications or selling products and services through direct mail, catalogs, and newsletters.

Ed Eisenberg Eames (**Science** '48) and Toni Steele Eames (**Taft** '61) of Fresno California received the Maxwell Medallion from the Dog Writer's Association of America for their article describing the rehabilitation of Ed's guide dog, Kirby, following the amputation of Kirby's front leg.

Jesse Greenberg, Creative Director/Sole Writer "The AT&T InfoQuest Center" (55th & Madison). 1 Gold, 2 Silver medals for video-NY Film Festival ('86). Sang/acted on Broadway. Wrote one play and one musical. Produced off broadway. Helped create "Walk America" concept for the March of Dimes, Can ride roundups and flank calves.

Morton H. Floch has become well known in South Florida for HMO Marketing and Operations.

Bernard M. Rubin, President, Royal Management Services- Hotel Management Co. Moved to San Diego area in 1992. Two children, five grandchildren. Offices in NJ and Calf. NJ office 201 587 8777 CA Office 619 752 1693

Stuart Roth. Graduated CCNY 1974, Masters CUNY 1976. Gave commencement address in 1993 to sixth grade graduating class at PS122. Listed in Who's Who. Married childhood sweetheart, Esther Olitsky in 1975. Two great kids: Rachel 14, Ian 11. Working on book about growing up in the Bronx in the 50's & 60's.

Harvey Brandwein, **Taft** '63. *"The National Pastime"* Box 64H, Scarsdale, NY 10583. Promotes baseball card shows, baseball autographs and memorabilia.

Contact some old friends today!!

READER REPLIES

It is vitally important that you fill out the information below. Your input will be essential to the success of this magazine, tailored and inspired by you, the former "Bronxite". We thank you for your participation.

YOUR NAME _____

ADDRESS _____

CITY _____ STATE _____ ZIP _____ PHONE _____

HIGH SCHOOL ATTENDED _____ YEAR GRADUATED _____

TELL US A LITTLE ABOUT YOURSELF,
(Be sure to include your alma mater, old neighborhood, your best memories about your days in the Bronx, (or anything else you can tell us).

_____

_____

_____

COULD WE SEND A FRIEND A FREE COPY OF BACK IN THE BRONX?

Do you know current or former Bronxites who would like to receive our magazine and reunion information? If you do, we'll be happy to send them a **free** inaugural issue of **Back in THE BRONX.**
Write to Back in The Bronx, Box 141 H, Scarsdale, NY 10583 or call 1-800-7-BRONX 5

Last _____ First _____ Maiden _____

Address _____ City _____ State _____ Zip ____

Phone # ( ) _____ School and year of Graduation _____

Last _____ First _____ Maiden _____

Address _____ City _____ State _____ Zip ____

Phone # ( ) _____ School and year of Graduation _____

Last _____ First _____ Maiden _____

Address _____ City _____ State _____ Zip ____

Phone # ( ) _____ School and year of Graduation _____

Last _____ First _____ Maiden _____

Address _____ City _____ State _____ Zip ____

Phone # ( ) _____ School and year of Graduation _____

COME BLOW YOUR OWN HORN DEPARTMENT

Please tell us about yourself (include your name)—about your accomplishments, awards, titles or works in progress. We're interested in hearing about them. List Below. _____

_____

_____

_____

_____

READER REPLIES

As a subscriber you are entitled to a FREE 40 Word Classified, Missing Persons, Blow Your Own Horn, or Personal Ad. Please write your ad below (if you are not subscribing to our magazine you can still place an ad in the next issue. The cost of an advertisement is 50¢ a word, there is no limit on paid ads).

_____

_____

_____

Is Your Mailing Label Correct?

In order to keep our database current, please correct any errors and place the label and or photocopy with corrections.

Account #	High School	Year Graduated
6817	Roosevelt	1958

SAMPLE

Mary R. Flowers
123 Anystreet Blvd.
Anywhere, USA 12345

Change of Address?

If you're planning a move please attach your label corrected with your new address and the date that you will begin receiving mail at that address. This will insure that you don't miss your next issue of **Back in THE BRONX**.

Ordering Information

YES, I'd like to order the following items:

QTY.

____ 1Yr. (4 ISSUES) Subscription(s) to **Back in THE BRONX** $19.95

____ 2Yr. (8 ISSUES) Subscription(s) to **Back in THE BRONX*** .. $29.95   *FREE John's Menu

____ 3Yr. (12 ISSUES) Subscription(s) to **Back in THE BRONX*** .. $39.95

____ 4Yr. (16 ISSUES) Subscription(s) to **Back in THE BRONX*** .. $49.95

____ The Beautiful Bronx...........$25.00 (plus $3.95 S/H) $28.95

____ The Bronx: It Was Only Yesterday..$25.00 (plus $3.95 S/H) $28.95

____ Bronx High School Reunion Weekend Video $29.95

____ SAVE MONEY - BUY 4 FOR JUST $99.00!

____ THE BRONX Tracking Service $9.95

____ I would like to receive all available back issues and have them applied towards my subscription (To date we have at least 12 back issues available - While They Last!)

TOTAL: $ _____

Please fill out completely and include $3.95 for shipping and handling for books only to: **Back in THE BRONX**, Box 141H, Scarsdale, NY 10583

A Great Gift Idea! In addition to your own subscription, a subscription to **Back in THE BRONX** makes a great and unique gift. Fill in the form below and we'll process the order in time for our next issue. So, order your subscription NOW, and order one for a friend!

Please Print Clearly ☐ New Subscriber ☐ Renewal

Name _____

Maiden Name _____

Address _____

City _____

State _____ Zip _____

Phone (____) _____

High School _____ Year Grad. _____

☐ Visa ☐ Mastercard

No. _____ Expiration Date _____

Signature _____

Back in THE BRONX

Box 141 H, Scarsdale, NY 10583
Phone 914-592-1647 • Fax 914-592-4893

ADDRESS CORRECTION REQUESTED

Volume IV   Issue XIII

Back in THE BRONX

CELEBRATING THE EXPERIENCE OF GROWING UP AND LIVING IN THE BRONX

A Look Back At The 50's: Food, Fads and The Bronx

By Judith J. (Goodwin) Yerman, Taft '56

Several years ago I finally made a pilgrimage back to the neighborhood of my youthful, carefree days; back to all the memories that signified my growing-up years. After thirty years of wanting to see the old "hood" again, I was finally back in the Bronx. As the car turned off of the Grand Concourse on to Mt. Eden Avenue, the anticipation and adrenalin came in a rush. There was Lebanon Hospital, taller and larger than I remembered, but still the same landmark that it was back in the 50's. All the small oval parks that dotted Mt. Eden Avenue were still there, just as I had recalled them so many times in my thoughts. I could still

see and smell the tulips that were, one year, donated to the parks, by the Netherlands. The rainbow of color as you looked up Mt. Eden Avenue towards the Concourse stay in my mind still. Claremont Park looked much the same as it had in 1960 when I left the Bronx for California. The majestic stone fortress that surrounded the park was the scene of many childhood games and fantasies. It had withstood the test of time. It was also the scene of my first "bad" crush. Where are you, David Sirota? I mistook his playing tug-of-war with my sweater (and my always landing on my rear) for true love. Mt. Eden Hospital where my tonsils were unwillingly taken from me at age 7, was boarded up and full of graffiti. The private homes in which some of my friends lived in years past were all still there, much the same as I remembered.

315 East Mt. Eden Avenue was gone. I had waited so many years to see it again and all that remained of my childhood dwelling was a bulldozed lot. The rich, red brick walls that we played "Off the Wall" on were gone. The stoop that we used as a stage to sing, "I'm Looking Over a Four Leaf Clover" was gone. The green and yellow elevator inside the vestibule, opposite the bank of mail boxes were gone. The very concrete

1643 Clay Ave., Northwest corner Mt. Eden Ave.

that I had bounced a million Spauldeens, threw jacks, played Potsie had been jackhammered away. The entire block was gone. Where are you Shirley Rubnitz, Marilyn Juda and Ruthie Charles? One summer we had collected about $11.00 for the Infantile Paralysis Foundation. The Bronx Home News wrote a minuscule article of this accomplishment. It could have been a million dollars. We were thrilled.

So much flooded back in the hour I sat and looked at the street. We had moved to Mt. Eden Avenue when I was five, just in time to start school at P.S. 70. The ancient ruin of a building provided the best of beginning educations. Sunk below the street, with a wire fence all around it, was the playground where we would congregate at recess, The "jelly apple" man who

Continued on page 8

Mt. Eden Ave. East of Jerome

From the Editors...

CLINTON '61

Some Bronx old-timers have asked why aren't there more Bronx stories from the decades of the 30's and 40's? This issue should give you what you wanted, dumb-waiter and all. As always, if you want more stories about your generation and/or neighborhood, start the ball rolling by submitting YOUR story. When it is printed, it encourages others to do the same. It really becomes contagious - if you catch my drift.

TAFT '62

The last issue of **Back In THE BRONX** that we sent was very-well received. Over 60,000 were mailed and with a pass-along of three or four, we probably reached over 200,000. As a result, we have substantially increased our Bronx database of names. So if you have a friend, neighbor, or relative who might be interested in a free inaugural issue of **Back In THE BRONX**, please give us their name and address and we will be happy to send one out. Any requests can also be made through our toll free number:

1-800-7 BRONX 5.

Stephen M. Samtur

Susan J. Samtur

StephenM. Samtur &
Susan J. Samtur
Editors

Back in THE BRONX

A number of the photographs in **Back in THE BRONX** are courtesy of and are available from the Bronx Historical Society.

Publishers & Editors:	Stephen M. Samtur	Clinton '61
	Susan H. Samtur	Taft '62
Contributing Editors:	Barbara Fasciani	Roosevelt '65
	Martin Jackson	Science '58
	Sandra Zuckerman	Jefferson '57
	Al Zuckerman	New Utrecht '50
Art & Production:	Ellen Grodjesk	
Printed By:	Trumbell Printing, Trumbell, CT	

Reminiscing

A Hair Raising Experience

By Frank Schmidt

Sunday night, 1954- St. Helena's dance in the Bronx. Lovely, lovely girls here and Parkchester sweethearts have come by the dozen. That pretty one over there, she is a doll and I'm going to ask her to dance as soon as a slow one comes up. Monsignor Scanlon is on the stage—reading but watching, "Make room for the Holy Ghost." (He's watching allright). I can't get that close even if she says yes. OK, here goes. "Dance?" (my God, she said yes!) Smells like flowers. Hair like silk. Heaven on earth (The Platters say so) Very close. Too close. Something is wrong. The worst has happened! My chewing gum is stuck in her hair! What can I do? The song's half over. She doesn't suspect a thing. Gotta chew it off or let it dangle when the dance is over. Chew it out. The only way. The song will be over soon. She must think I'm weird. Acting very strange—chew, chew, it's my only hope. The song will be over in a minute. Only a little to go. Chew! It's over. We part. Her hair looks pretty good. And I have a mouth full of gum and hair. Beautiful; brunette hair and Juicy Fruit. But I made it. Back to the side lines with the guys. What a story! They have to believe me- just look in my mouth. But another fantasy botched. Can't ask her again. She's bound to find out. There's got to be a hole in her hair. So much for chewing and dancing my way to romance. Wonder if she ever found out. Are you there? I'm the culprit. I admit it. I never chew and dance anymore. But I would ask you dance again—chewless of course.

Why Leave Out The Thirties?

By Herbert Gitlin, Clinton '37

It's hard to recall. The faces are blurred , the events shadowy, and the places all too often misplaced or out of order. Well, that's the way it was until BACK IN THE BRONX ARRIVED.

Suddenly, names like Seymour Rosenblatt, guard of the 1936 football team came before me; Guy Segatt, the quarterback. Then " Pop " Jahoda, our loving caring coach. I had tried out for the football team each season and each season, it was a sprained ankle or knee. Finally it dawned upon me that being manager was much safer.

Events began to stand out more than people and I began to relive a vital part of my life. Bringing me into the world in 1918 on the fifth floor of 1398 Clay Ave. was in itself quite an accomplishment for the doctor who was paid $2 for climbing the five flights. My father took one look at me and said "No more," but I became the apple of his eye. As for my mother, her one and only could do no wrong.

My father was an operator on ladies' coats and he was told to get out of the " shop " or become consumptive. So, he opened a candy store on 199th St. and Jerome Ave. I had to go to the 200th St. IRT station to pick up the newspapers because there was no delivery to us in the "boondocks." There was also no business; so while my mother stayed in the store, my father went downtown and sold light bulbs floor-to-floor.

I went to P. S. 42 and my teacher, whose name escapes me, wore three pairs of glasses. It always amazed me how they all stayed on at the same time. Business grew and we moved to 169th St. and Sheridan Ave. just off the Grand Concourse where my father opened his second store and I went to P.S.46 on Walton and 170th St.

For years I was convinced that I was the only kid in Bronx who was lucky enough to go to summer camp. Well, it was not just any summer camp.

1256 Clay Ave., E 169th St.

It had to be the best and from 1925 to 1929 it was Green Mountain Camp in Brandon Vt. where I learned the basics that stood up for me the rest of my life.

P.S. 90 was built and I went there for a year and then graduated in 1932 from P.S. 53 to enter De Witt Clinton in

Mosholu Parkway

it's new building on Mosholu Parkway. I saw the beautiful Grand Concourse torn up for the Independent Subway.

Names like the Luxor Theater

brought memories of Saturday afternoon in the pool hall above the theater where we waited for the baseball scores and did our little betting. Krum's and the Paradise brought back vivid memories of the football team cutting class on Friday to see the show and returning to school in time for practice.

Being tall, it was easy to pass for being older and I joined Club Kiat, on Jerome Ave and Kingsbridge Road. This was the era of coach-lined walls, dimly lit rooms and the peabody dance. We visited other clubs and had dance contests and couldn't wait for the summer and the Albany Night Boat that went only a short way up the Hudson.

In my senior year, the entire football team took "drawing" not because it was easy or we wanted to be artists but because the teacher, who was just out of training, was absolutely gorgeous. She was built the way all women should be built and her shoulder length blond hair swished in rhythm with her hips. We gave a her a bad time.

So one day she said, "O.K. wise guys, lets see what you have learned." She drew a white chalk line across the entire top of the blackboard, then down the side, along the bottom and up to the top where she started. Then she took a piece of red chalk and drew a red solid circle in the lower right hand corner.

She stood backand asked each of us. "what do you see?" Of course, yours truly as well as every other student thought it was some kind of a gag and played along, answering, "the red dot." A victorious smile filled her face as she asked, "Doesn't any one of you see the big frame?"

Since that time I have always been able to see the big picture as well as remembering a beautiful young lady who must be 77 by now and who helped me learn a valuable lesson.

Reminiscing

Flashbacks From Featherbed Lane

By Robert Schoolsky

I submit the following for your interest. Someone passed along a copy of your publication to me and I read it with great interest.

Reading your publication for the first time reminded me of my first therapy session; pulling dim images up from my toes. Some were painful but many joyful. My earliest memories are of my family's root years in the West Bronx beginning on Featherbed Lane, jumping to W. 176th Street, leaping to Anderson Avenue in Highbridge.

My mother, Marie Schoolsky (nee Berkowitz) now lives in Denver. She helped fill some of the name gaps. We lived at 65 Featherbed Lane across from the hospital and dreams of childhood were often filled with images of the terminally ill patients being wheeled out to enjoy the sunny weather.

It was a gentler time back in the late 30's. Men wore fedoras. Women, veiled hats of every size and description. Featherbed Lane was a typical Bronx neighborhood of small merchants where a four year old could go shopping and bring back the correct change.

New York's finest patrolled the streets in long, heavy blue melton overcoats but once in a while a green and white squad car came on the scene. Sanitation men, called white wings, swept the curbs which often contained horse droppings since ice (not everyone had the new refrigerators with the round coil compressor on top), milk and vegetables were still delivered by horse wagon. A sure sign of spring was the arrival of the pony photographer offering a free ride if you bought a picture of your offspring. An organ grinder was a frequent visitor, his monkey picking up the coins tossed from apartment windows.

We were weekly regulars at Dubin's Kosher delicatessen and the local appetizing emporium. Sol's Infant and Children's shop outfitted my brother Sandy and me until we were old enough for Rogers Peet and Barneys. We kept returning for Sol's each spring for our camp outfits.

The neighborhood had miniature town square at the base of the hill going up to University Avenue. It was dominated by the Public National Bank. Later, the square would be the sight of war bond drives where my mother and other women in the neighborhood, in their blue and gold AWVS overseas caps, collected funds for the men in uniform.

Number 65 was a well-maintained building with a pleasing, trim forecourt and the familiar marble tiled lobby. Mail was delivered twice a day. Above the mailbox was a gilt framed box which carried the week's schedule for the Park Plaza theater up on University ave. The building had no elevator but no one seemed to mind the walk to the upper floors. The small apartments had glass French doors on some of the rooms.

Top floor dumbwaiter at 343 Crimmins Ave.

Tiny kitchens came complete with dumbwaiters for the garbage. I vividly remember sitting on the oilcloth floor in the morning listening to the CBS 8:00 A.M. news, rebroadcasting the ravings of a man named Hitler. I was fascinated but preferred the soothing Midwest accent of William L. Shirer.

The lobby boasted a single apartment perched atop a small circular flight of three or four steps with a polished brass bannister. A doctor's office at one time, the family in residence had a daughter named Natalie who took me to school at P.S. 104 one day when my Mother was giving birth to my brother. It was a thrill for a three year old. I've been in love with older women ever since.

80 Featherbed Lane & Jessup Ave.

Up on Macombs Road, the other, longer route to University Avenue was Saul's candy store where one could feast on an ice cream sandwich made of a ball of chocolate or vanilla between two large round "wine crackers." It cost a nickel. Mello-Rolls, with sprinkles were a must. When we moved to 74 West 176th St. part of my chores was picking up a "Forward" and "Morning Journal" for my Grandfather, Simon Berkowitz. He lived with us throughout our nomadic tour of the Bronx.

Our move, a few blocks north, was due to my entering P.S. 82, across

Macombs Junior High School

176th St. The steep hill was ideal for belly whopping in the winter. I looked foward to each Saturday. My father, Ben, would take me along on his weekly routine. First came a nod to his single vanity: a visit to the barbershop next door to the Park Plaza theater for

Continued on page 5

4

Featherbed Lane

Continued from page 4

a manicure which removed the grime embedded in his fingernails from his work, sorting and grading rags in Brooklyn.

The double feature at the Park Plaza was next. We sat in the balcony and if we were early we could enjoy live music from the golden organ in the pit. Who needed Radio City!

Park Plaza Theater

Down below, in the orchestra section, were the young of the neighborhood sans parents. They were carefully watched over by a buxom, white clad "matron" equipped with a flashlight weighing at least ten pounds. These Amazons could wield these weapons with careful aim to inflict the most pain. I am firmly convinced most of them were retired prison guards. When matrons were not on duty, you begged an adult to buy your ticket to gain entry.

After the movie my father and I dodged the trolley cars on University Avenue to cross over to Hahns, the German ice cream parlor for our weekly banana splits. We perched on highback wire chairs at the zinc counter watching the construction of this creamy delight—half a banana sliced lengthwise, scoop each of chocolate, vanilla and strawberry ice cream, chocolate, vanilla and strawberry syrups, crushed nuts, whipped cream

and a cherry. Cost? - 15¢. No charge for the seltzer.

Malteds were special treats. Each slowly poured from its icy metal container in a steady lava flow, They held at least two full glasses with secure metal bases with curved handles. South of Hahns was the grocery store that caused a commotion when it became the first in the neighborhood to install a freezer to carry Mr. BirdsEye's frozen peas and carrots.

I clearly remember the Park Plaza on a Sunday afternoon in December watching the Maltese Falcon. At the point that Bogart was telling Mary Astor, "You're good kid, really good," yellow lettering started to appear on the bottom of the screen ordering, "All military personal return to your base. All leaves are cancelled!" The message was repeated throughout the rest of the picture. It wasn't until I returned home that I learned about a place called Pearl Harbor. My life long love affair with the radio and news started at that moment.

My mother and father were celebrating Bongard's wedding anniversary that night at Leon and Eddie's and I remembered their saying Manhattan was like New Year's eve. I guess everyone sensed that our safe, peaceful world was coming to an end.

We got visual confirmation of the change later that week when a truck rolled up to a concrete traffic island on University Avenue depositing an armed sentry with a metal pot, webbed ammunition belt and combat leggings. He guarded a man-hole cover shielding the flow of drinking water from Macombs Dam aqueduct. The post was manned 24 hours a day in all weather well into the war, protecting our water.

And what water! It ran cold and sweet from the tap. My other grandfather, Issac Schoolsky, when visiting us from Brooklyn, delayed any hellos or greetings until he drank his fill from the kitchen sink. Remembering the sulphur-like water at his Flatbush home I understood his excited quaffing of something we took for granted.

Slowly the boys who were playing softball and stickball in the street and school yards began to disappear. Many never returned. The school yard and the Park Plaza became the focal points for bond drives. We had meatless Tuesdays and got used to rationing cards, points and rationing stickers in the corner of car windshields.

We saved everything. Newspapers, scrap metal, tin cans were bundled and recycled long before we heard the phrase. Cooking fat was accumulated in cans. You received ration coupons when you brought them to the butcher. Nylons became liquid assets. A youngster in the Bronx became a power in the neighborhood when he got a supply of Fleer's Double Bubble gum. The pink squares were coin of the realm.

Lucky Strike Green went to war. Everyone had saving stamp books and you pasted stamps in the books. On sale in movie theaters, post offices and banks, a filled book of stamps was traded for a war bond. Slackers, draft dodgers, hoarders and black market profiteers were detested public enemies, worse than Dillinger.

Change of schools meant another shift for the Schoolsky tribe and we moved to Anderson Avenue when I was in Third Grade. Our new neighborhood was centered on Woodycrest Avenue and 167th St. But, the main artery for those of us who lived in the towering group of red brick apartments at the foot of Anderson Avenue was the long alley behind the buildings.

Here mothers strolled sunning their babies. Girls skipped rope and double dutched. Boys played Slug against the wall. The chalk outlines of Potsy contests lingered until the next rainfall.

Buses were our main means of transportation, riding down to 161st Street to Jerome Avenue or IND lines. We also enjoyed the benefits of the little known shuttle stop on Anderson Avenue that ran between Jerome Avenue and the Polo Grounds at 155th Street in Manhattan.

When I graduated in 1948, the big

Continued on page 6

Reminiscing

Featherbed Lane

Continued from page 5

song at the prom was Vaughn Monroe's "Dance Ballerina, Dance." "The Old Lamplighter" was another big hit along with, "You Came A Long Way From St. Louis." I delivered orders for Tunick's meat market and when our Mother wasn't home, my brother and I had lunch in Schwab's candy store and luncheonette. Reflecting the times, the candy store sold single cigarettes for those on tight budgets. My brother and I built a very profitable business taking neighbor's washes to the new machines that were placed in the basement of 1185. We charged a nickel for the services.

Most important, Anderson Avenue was the place were I first met Bernice (Bunny) Blane (orignially Bluestein) nee Rosenberg. Little did we know that she would become the center of my life, my significant "other" to this very day. Other names that I recall were the Faces family and the Seidenstocks.

The memories of the late '40's come easier: The blizzard of '47 when we

Macombs Rd & Featherbed Lane

cursed the elements because it shut down the city when the schools were closed anyway, making sure we boarded the first car of the Jerome Avenue El to "drive" the train downtown, rushing to the window of the El when the train came out of the South Bronx tunnel to briefly catch a view of

the ball game at the stadium, envying those who lived in the apartments overlooking the stadium who could watch the game for nothing, The mournful howl of the El in the distance when our windows where open on a warm night. Finally in 1949 we joined the throngs flocking to suburbia and moved to Elmont. I never graduated from Clinton which was my dream to follow in Jerry Bongard's footsteps.

Years earlier, back on Featherbed Lane, as a diversion for our Sunday trips up to "tar beach," my father, Lou Bongard and the rest of our friends decided to build a huge kite. It stood over eight feet tall and was wider than anyone's arm span. It had a long rag tail and was weeks in construction.

We all looked foward to the coming Sunday when the kite would be flown for the first time.

The big day arrived. True to its promise, the wind took it easily. It was a memorable sight as it climbed higher and higher in the sky, a grand sight. Suddenly, the string snapped and the kite, free from its tether, began to float south. We watched it go over 170th Street and follow the track of the El. It slowly got dimmer and dimmer until we finally lost sight of it over Yankee Stadium. I cried for a long time for that kite. Now it's only a memory. Just one of the things that happened, "Back in The Bronx," a memory floating in the mist of time.

The Mouse That Roared

By Peter Picciano

Little League baseball hadn't yet come to the Bronx neighborhoods. The P.A.L. and Parks Department provided kids with competitive sports. Because most of my friends were older, I always seemed to be outclassed and rarely got a chance to play. Coaches back then weren't required to play everyone. Playing on a team with my older brother meant that his uniform was always dirty and mine was always clean.

One Sunday afternoon, my father came to our game that was being played adjacent to Yankee Stadium. The Yankees were playing and the game was a sellout. My pop urged (coerced) the coach to put me in to pinch hit. I finally got my chance. The first pitch whizzed by my head. Helmets were not worn in the 50's. The next pitch was straight down the middle and I swung and hit a line drive triple over the centerfielder's head and at that very moment, someone in Yankee Stadium must have hit a homer, because 60,000 fans roared.

To this day I like to believe that they were cheering for me. I know my dad was!

A Quiet Evening In The Bronx

by Saul Lindenbaum

As I left the Ward theater, a little after 6 P.M., I was surprised and delighted to find that it was snowing. I turned left onto Westchester Avenue just as a train rumbled overhead on the elevated tracks. It was the Pelham Bay local, headed uptown, having just pulled out of the Elder Avenue station. I hoped that my father had been on that train. He often came home early on Friday evenings, so that we could have a Shabbos (now we call it Shabbat, but in those days I had never heard of the modern Israeli Sephardic pronunciation of Hebrew) dinner together: my mother, my father, my sister and I.

After walking just a few steps I turned left again onto Boynton Avenue, and began to ascend the gentle hill toward Watson Avenue. Boynton was a nice street, on which five and six story apartment buildings coexisted comfortably with private homes. There were quite a few trees on this section of Boynton Avenue, big ones, too, which made it somewhat unusual for our neighborhood.

As I walked up Boynton, my mind was more on the movies I had just seen than on the snow. Even back then in elementary school, I loved the movies. And I often went there alone, on Friday afternoons when it was too cold even for our sports-minded crowd, to play touch football in the gutter in front of 1105 Elder (our favorite "playing field"), or to slap box (our homage to the Golden Gloves) on the corner of Elder and Watson near Sadie's Luncheonette, our favorite hangout. My grandfather Trost had a barber shop on Watson Avenue, and whenever he put a poster in the window advertising the current double bill at the Ward theater, he received one ticket that was stamped for a 20% reduction. Since the normal price of admission at that time was 15 cents, that meant that I could get in for 12 cents. Believe it or not, it made a difference in being

University Ave in the Highbridge Section

able to go.

The movies I had seen that afternoon made a strong impression on me. One was 'Taproots,' a film about the Civil War. (Many years later I made the mistake of watching it on television. It was terrible, and I've never repeated that mistake again.) I don't remember the name of the other film, but it was a documentary about the exploration of the Arctic Circle and the North Pole. I think that it involved Admiral Byrd. There were spectacular aerial shots of the seemingly endless fields of ice and snow, and remarkable scenes of men in rubber suits diving in the icy waters of the Arctic Ocean- in Technicolor, I may add, as was 'Taproots.' Everything I saw that day was new to me, and the film about the Arctic had, I think, put me into a very dreamy state of mind.

At any rate, I walked up Boynton Avenue daydreaming about heroes and adventurers of the past and present. I was also thinking about the delicious roast chicken dinner, preceded of course by chopped chicken livers and chicken soup, that awaited at home. Then, I knew, we would settle down in front of our new television set (a Traveller, with push buttons no less!) to watch the latest episode of Ralph Bellamy in 'Man Against Crime.' Later I would drift off to sleep on the Castro Convertible while my father watched the Friday night fights.

Lost in these thoughts, I paid little attention to the snow. But when I reached Watson Avenue, and crossed it towards Zimmie's candy store, I was greeted by a remarkable scene. The snow was now falling thickly, in large, soft flakes. All of the stores on Watson Avenue, a street that was usually crowded with people and cars, were closed, and the only light was from the large streets lamps, in the glow of which the snow floated down in a steady, almost hypnotic stream. It was quiet, too. There was not a soul in sight nor a car to be heard, with the snow creating that special hush that feels, in some way, beyond silence. The combination of the snow, the silence and the anticipation of the evening ahead, produced a feeling of contentment and well-being as satisfying as any I have ever known.

I lived on Elder Avenue for the first 21 years of my life. It was a fine place to grow up, and much of what made it so good were the many children who were my friend, some of whom remain my friends to this very day. Perhaps it was the contrast with the usually busy street scene that impressed me so much that evening, or perhaps it was something else, which even now I find hard to define. But that startling impression of the silent snow transfixed me then, and transfixes me still, eventhough more than 40 years have passed.

7

Reminiscing

Looking Back
Continued from page 1

stood outside of school with his cart and the wonderful tastes and aroma of "jelly shoe leather" and "jelly marsh-mallows". The three grocery stores and the two candy stores that surrounded my little world sprung to mind; the Devil Dogs and the penny candy (my favorite was always those little tin plates of sugary confection that you ate with the smallest of spoons), "Classic" comics, egg creams, cherry Cokes, and Mello-Rolls. Having to wear those terrible cotton stockings so we wouldn't freeze to death. How I hated those. No matter what the weather, we would leave our houses, and roll the hose down to resemble a very bulky pair of anklets. The A&P was built and it was a whole new world. It was no longer necessary to go from the butcher, green grocer and to the grocery store for food.

Having graduated from P.S. 70 where I was a Lieutenant Hall Monitor in the 6th grade (and wore my maroon and gray badge so proudly), manning the doors that swung to and fro near Principal Morris Scherer's office, I started Wade Junior High School the following September (J.H.S. 117). Where are you Carol Pinsky, Deanna Nayer, Rita Shiftman, Stan Greenberg, Barbara Raskin, Mel Aarons and The Nappi twins?

J.H.S. 117—Wade—the more formative years. We would walk home from school, stop at one of the two delis on Mr. Eden Avenue for French fries. They were always hot and perfectly crisp, in a brown paper bag dripping grease. We tossed as much ketchup as we could in to the bag in order to coat every piece of potato. We could use the subway and the buses now. We could ride to Fordham Road and Alexander's. There was a coffee shop right near Alexander's, on the Fordham Road side, where one day after exhausting ourselves shopping, we stopped for a Coke. Coming out of Carol's coffee shop on this warm summer day, my best friend, Iris (who was and will forever be my best

friend) were met with a sudden, heavy downpour. I had Peds on inside my sandals. Almost 40 years later, we both still remember my offering her one Ped so her feet (foot?) would not get wet.

We could look in the National Shoe Store windows and have Chow Mein sandwiches on a hamburger bun at Woolworth's on Fordham Road and Valentine Avenue. There are days that I still long for that silly Chow Mein sandwich. We had "make out" parties in the finished basements of friend's homes; tentative, shy and very sweet. Audrey Goldenberg, who lived on Townsend Avenue and I ate cans of Heinz spaghetti every day for lunch for a solid school year. Marianne Cuminale introduced me to dry Italian Salami, and I would beg to trade sandwiches with her.

One summer, my brother was an usher at the Surrey Theater on Mt. Eden. I would go with him each Saturday and sit through a double feature three or four times, clutching my box of Jordan Almonds (10¢) and wait for him to finish his shift. I think I saw, "D.O.A." two dozen times. They held it over at the Surrey for several weeks. We would also foray down to the Mt. Eden theater, sit in the balcony, and find all our neighborhood buddies. The best pizza I remember was at a small Italian restaurant where Mt. Eden Avenue joined Featherbed Lane. I wish I could remember the name of the place.

In 1953, I entered Taft H.S. which was a short walk across Claremont

Park from Mt. Eden Avenue. Life in H.S. in the 50's was one big adventure after another. Poodle skirts, and sugar-starched crinolines, white bucks (with just the proper amount of dirt and grime on them), cardigan sweaters that we wore buttoned up the back, with little Peter Pan collars of lace or leather. Pizza and more pizza. One couldn't get enough pizza in those days (and there is many a day when I sit here working in sunny Southern California that I long for a "real" Bronx pizza). I also long for "real" Bronx Chinese food and knishes and chicken salami and rye bread and bialys and corned beef that melts in your mouth; for the sight of the Good Humor man or the Bungalow Bar truck that stopped each day on the corner of Mt. Eden and Clay Avenues.

I long for a walk with my dad up the Concourse to Krum's for a hot fudge sundae or a trip to Yankee Stadium or the Polo Grounds, even though I am now an LA Dodgers fan (I know ...traitor). I want to go back and re-live the days of working on the Yearbook Staff at Taft in my senior year. I wonder where all my Yearbook pals are. The class of '56 graduated and we all went our separate ways as often happens; me to C.C.N.Y. and, ultimately, to Los Angeles, CA.

As I sat in the car, parked across the street from 315 E. Mt. Eden Avenue, sniffling back tears, I felt a bit like Dorothy finally having returned to Kansas. Despite what Thomas Wolff once said, you can go home again.

William H. Taft High School, 1950

8

Bronx Honor Roll
Bronxites Who Have Achieved!

BRONX SCIENCE

Harold Brown
Stokely Carmichael
Leon Cooper (Nobel Prize Winner))
Bobby Darin
Edgar Doctorow
Sheldon Glashow (Nobel Prize Winner)
Russell Hulse (Nobel Prize Winner)
Nita Lowey, Representative
Arno Penzias (Nobel Prize Winner)
William Safire
Melvin Schwartz (Nobel Prize Winner)
Steven Weinberg (Nobel Prize Winner)

CARDINAL HAYES

George Carlin
Rocky Colavito
Kevin Loughery
Regis Philbin

CHRISTOPHER COLUMBUS

Robert Abrams
Anne Bancroft
Christine Jorgenson
Alan Landsburg
Martin Scorcese*

DEWITT CLINTON

Don Adams
Nate Archibald
Richard Avedon
James A. Baldwin
Martin Balsam
David Begelman
James Caan
Paddy Chayevsky
George Cukor
Avery Fisher
Arthur Gelb
Judd Hirsch
Robert Hofstadter (Nobel Prize Winner)
Stubby Kaye
Al Kelly
Theodore Kheel
Robert Klein
William Kunstler
Burt Lancaster
Garry Marshall
Jan Murray
Charles Rangel
Richard Rogers
A.M. Rosenthal
Daniel Schorr
Dolph Schayes
Neil Simon
Larry Storch
Marvin Traub
Jimmie Walker
Fats Waller
William Zeckendorf

EVANDER CHILDS

Red Buttons
James Coco
Carl Reiner

MONROE

Jules Feiffer
John Garfield
Hank Greenberg
Ed Kranepool
Leon Lederman (Nobel Physicist)

MORRIS

Angel Cordero
Herman Joseph Muller (Nobel Prize Winner)
Gabe Pressman
E. Colin Powell

ROOSEVELT

June Alyson
Chazz Palminteri

TAFT

Sanford Brown
Eydie Gorme
Stanley Kubrick
Mal Z. Lawrence*

WALTON

Bella Abzug
Rosalyn Yalow (Nobel Prize Winner)

OTHER NOTABLES

Joey Adams
Danny Aiello
Alan Alda
Robert Alda
Corazon Aquino
Armand Assante
Herman Badillo
Lauren Bacall
Ellen Barkin
Mario Biaggi
Joey Bishop
Alfred Bloomingdale
Bobby Bonilla
Teresa Brewer
Ralph J. Bunche (Nobel Prize Winner)
George Burns
Cab Calloway
Diahann Carroll
Carmen Cavallaro*
Samuel Clemens
Myron Cohen
Betty Comdon
Cardinal Cooke
Avery Corman
Norman Cousins
Bobby Cremins
Don Criqui
Tony Curtis
Vic Damone
Ossie Davis
Dennis Day
Ruby Dee
Robert DeNiro*
Dion DiMucci
Art Donovan*
John Foster Dulles
Erik Estrada
Fernando Ferrer
Geraldine Ferraro
F. Scott Fitzgerald
Joe Franklin
Arlene Francis
Connie Francis
Frankie Frisch
Edward J. Flynn
Rita Gam
Rudolph Giuliani
Samuel Gompers
Aldolf Green
Richie Guerin
Armand Hammer
Herbert A. Hauptman (Nobel Prize Winner)
David Horowitz
Vladimir Horowitz
George Jessel
Billy Joel
Raoul Julia
John F. Kennedy
Robert Kennedy
Ted Kennedy
Theodore Kheel
Calvin Klein
Edward Koch
Fiorello LaGuardia
Bert Lahr
Jake LaMotta
Louise Lasser

Ralph Lauren
Ron Leibman
Lee Leonard
Joe E. Lewis
Shari Lewis
Hal Linden
Vince Lombardi
Melissa Manchester
John Mariani
Penny Marshall
Willie Mays
Mario Merola
Glenn Miller
Sal Mineo
Hugo Montenegro
Robert Morgenthau
Gary Morton
Paul Muni
Bess Myerson
Gil Noble
Carroll O'Connor
John O'Hara
Charles Osgood
Al Pacino
Jack Palance
Floyd Patterson
Joseph Papp
Joe Pesci
Roberta Peters
Mary Pickford
Ezio Pinza
Edgar Allan Poe
Richard Price
Vincent Price
Tito Puente*
Charles Nelson Reilly
Rob Reiner
Regina Resnick
Victor Riesel*
Monte Rock III
Franklin D. Roosevelt
Theodore Roosevelt
Billy Rose
Jonas Salk
Isabel Sanford
Marvin Scott
George Segal
Connie Selleca
Sylvia Sidney
Carly Simon
Stanley Simon
Vince Scully
Isaac Bashevis Singer (Nobel Prize Winner)
Curtis Sliwa
Wesley Snipes, Jr.
Cardinal Spellman
Sy Sperling
George Steinbrenner
Henry Stern
Pat Summerall
Renee Taylor
Mother Teresa (Nobel Prize Winner)
U. Thant
Arturo Toscanini
Dan Topping
Leon Trotsky
Lloyd Ultan
Jerry Vale
Bobby Van
Luther Vandross
June Valli
Jackie Vernon
Fran Warren
Del Webb
Vanessa Williams
Herman Wouk

Thanks to Dr. William C. Wolfson and the Bonx Society of Science and Letters

A Streetcar To Hell Gate?

By Richard T. Turner

St. Ann's and 3rd Ave.

135th Street between Brook and St. Ann's Avenues was home to a great swarm of young rapscallions in 1934, and Artie and I, the pair of us just ten years old, were among them. Now some were bad and some were worse, but my pal Artie was the worst; a first-class holy terror who could figure out more ways to get me into trouble than... well, let me give you, for example, the sweltering Bronx - summer day when he very nearly got me killed—not once, but twice. That Artie never did things by halves!

The misadventure began when he decreed that we should go for a swim in the East River, at the foot of 134th Street. I had no objection to that part; swimming on a day hot enough to bubble the tar roofs of the tenements was always a swell idea. But the question was, how should we get there? I wanted to walk, but Artie said, "Are you crazy? That's way too friggin' far. We'll grab a hitch on a trolley."

If I'd known then what I was going to know a few minutes later, I never would have agreed. But who knew? "Okay, okay," I said. "We'll hitch."

So we hitched. Easy to do, as all red-blooded Bronxites know. At the rear of the streetcar is a ledge tailored to the size of a hooligan foot, and a few feet above it, a cord pulley cut to the size of a hooligan hand. Simple, therefore, to stand on the ledge and hang on to the pulley. Simple, that is, if there are no cops around, and things aren't moving too quickly. On the other hand, if the speed of the trolley is about to fling you off anyway, and then suddenly a policeman appears on the scene—well, my friend, you've got trouble.

That's just what happened. We were racketing down the hill between Cypress Avenue and the river, the trolley lurching from side to side, the steel wheels striking sparks against the tracks, picking up speed, faster, faster, and when Artie shouted, "Oh jeez— there's a cop on the corner." So now I had a choice: I could jump off and take a chance on killing myself, or I could ride to the corner and

get nabbed by a "brass buttons, blue coat." Who knew? Maybe this one could "catch a nanny goat."

I jumped, and hit the cobblestones hard. I rolled, bounced, popped, crackled and snapped. Oh, Lord, every bone in my body must be broken. I was bleeding all over and I was — as Cary Grant says in "Gunga Din" —"A tower of pain." But at least I wasn't nabbed.

An then? And then here comes Artie back from the corner, laughing fit to die, shaking his head pityingly. "Oh, man, you are dumb! Did you really believe that crap about the cop? Oh, are you dumb!"

At this point I should have walked away from him and never looked back. But I guess he was right. I guess I was dumb. Besides, I had blood dripping from my elbows, knees, ankles, ears and other less public parts. I figured a swim in the East River would clean me up and cool me off. Besides, I'd be safe in the river. My grandmother used to tell me, "If you're born to hang, you'll never drown"— and I figured I was born too hang. If only I'd known...

We made our way, Artie in leaps and bounds, I in limps and groans, to the old pier that jutted far into the water at the bottom of 134th Street. To the right of the wharf, as you faced it, was a somewhat sandy, mostly rocky beach. Nah, come to think of it, it couldn't properly be called a beach because the water which lapped it was alive with raw sewage and only the Bronx Breaststoke would serve to give you swimming room. I'll never know why we didn't die of diphtheria—unless it's true that only the good die young. In any case, the poor people of the southeast Bronx were not given to fine distinctions. As long as you stayed between the shore and the far end of the pier, you were, if not safe, at least in no immediate danger. On the other hand, if you ventured beyond the wooden pilings, there was a roiling current waiting to suck you into the maelstrom of Hell Gate, which, every summer, as certain as the ebb and flow of the

Continued on page 11

10

Hell Gate

Continued from page 10

**535 St. Ann's Ave.
and E. 149th St.**

tides, would claim a few men, women and children.

Now, Artie and I swam there many times before and were well aware of the danger, but on this day...well...what can I say...Artie felt like gambling, and the two of us very nearly cashed in our chips.

We went out too far and the current snatched us. Before we could holler "Help" we were on our way to Hell Gate. We swam as hard as ten-year-old arms and legs could pump, but were getting nowhere at all. It was obvious to anyone watching that unless something miraculous happened in a hurry, our names were going to appear in the obit column of the next day's Bronx Home News.

Well, in the words of dear old grandma, we weren't meant to drown. Out of nowhere, came a rickety rowboat manned by two old codgers out for a day's fishing. They reached out and plucked us by the hair from otherwise certain death.

We dried off—the cobblestone-blood completely washed away now, and even the bumps and bruises felt better—and it was time to go home. "Come on," says Artie, "we'll grab a hitch."

"Are you crazy? After what you did to me on the way here?"

"Ah, that was just a joke. Come on—don't be so dumb."

Talk about a rock and a hard place; I'm dumb if I do and I'm dumb if I don't. So I guess I'm dumb.

We hitched home.

Schoolyard Anxiety

By Frank Schmidt

Schoolyard basketball. Three on three. Winners stays up. Some pretty *BIC's sitting on the bench, watching and holding our jackets (we, the Gladiators). I'm 6 feet tall now, in good shape, but where was it then? I was too short, too light, and I had sciatica. Useless under the backboard and all the time they watched. Who knew their secret language? Was a good jump shot a virile thing? Did testosterone flow with a drive to the basket? Had to look good. No sneakers then. A layup with leather soles was a dance. The inevitable slide next to the bench was a statement. And if a layup went in, it was Clint Eastwood and Marlon Brando rolled up in a moment of glory. Did they notice? What were they whispering about? Does winning six or seven games in a row mean a movie date? We were very much kings and paupers then. Royalty through passing. Dribble your way to fame. Candy store notoriety will surely come to those who stay on the court. They watched us, and we watched them. And I jumped, but didn't jump. Sciatica. Not today! Not with them watching! Drive and slide. That's it. Drive and slide near the bench. It will be as good as the rebound that can't happen. Sciatica! Sixteen years old with sciatica in the schoolyard. Drive and slide. Thank God I'm not wearing sneakers. Can't drive and slide with sneakers. Near the bench. Hook shot! In. She's smiling. I'm sweating. It's 45° out and I'm sweating. But she's smiling. Drive and slide. Hold my jacket for one more game. We won.

***Bronx Irish Catholic**

RATES PER PERSON

Category	Deck	Accomodations	Per Person- Double Occupancy
5	Main	Inside, Twin/King	$389
7	Main	Outside, Twin/King	$439

*Single Occupancy .... 200% of double occupancy rate

Third and Fourth passenger in cabin with:
Two Full Paying Passengers .... $199.00 per person

Taxes $84.50 per person (Additional)

Air add-on and transfers are available at an extra low cost.

CANCELLATION PENALTIES:

61 days prior to departure (up to April 27, 1996).......... No Penalty (Full Refund)

60 to 30 days prior to departure (April 28 - May 28, 1996).......... $100 per person

29 to 4 days prior to departure (May 29 - June 24, 1996) .... $200 per person

3 to 0 days prior to departure .... No Refund

We strongly recommend that you buy cancellation insurance at $39.00 per person.

Category 7 Stateroom

Passport or Birth Certificate
with photo I.D. is required
for proof of citizenship.

- -

Fill out and send this Reservation Form and Deposit Check To: **Back In THE BRONX, Box 141H, Scarsdale, NY 10583; or Fax (914) 592-4893**

Please reserve a room in Category # _____ on the **BRONX REUNION CRUISE** on June 28, 1996, for which I enclose my deposit of $200.00 per person and make check payable to: ***BRONX REUNION CRUISE.***

Payment: ❑ Money Order   ❑ Check   ❑ VISA   ❑ MasterCard

Account # _____ Exp. Date._____

Signature: _____

Check One: ❑ M/M   ❑ Ms.   ❑ Mr.   ❑ Mrs.

Name (Print) _____

Address _____

City _____ State _____ Zip _____

Home Phone: _____ Business Phone _____

High School _____ Year Graduated _____

Section of the Bronx that you grew up in: _____
_____

❑ I (We) will need air from (Name of City/Airport) _____

❑ I (We) will not need air.

I (We) wish ❑   Do not wish ❑   to purchase cancellation insurance.

❑ *I would be willing to share a cabin with a single person. (On request only).

Back In THE
BRONX

Reminiscing

The Old Neighborhood

By Stanley Glasser, Clinton '54

Why is it the older I get the less I remember? The answer to that is simply explained as the "aging process." What I can't explain, is the total recall I seem to have when I think of my old neighborhood.

I grew up on Elliot Place around the corner from 170th Street. Sitting here I begin to realize that a person could live his whole life never having to leave the old neighborhood. Yet when it was time to leave, just 1/2 block away on Jerome Avenue stood **Schwartz's Funeral Home**, proving my point.

Sure you think your neighborhood was nicer, but did it have the **Zenith Theater** where you and your friends could go in at noon, and come out at five after having seen two features, three cartoons, a race, coming attractions, a serial, etc., plus everyone got a free comic book? The matron in her white uniform and flashlight had the disposition of today's meter maid.

So what if the **Luxor Theater** didn't have fake stars in its ceiling, it had Sol the usher who'd let you in free. With Pauline's Vegetarian, two luncheonettes, a Chinese restaurant and an automat, one never traveled far for fine dining. Am I dating myself if I remind you that the Dollar Savings Bank rtight off Walton Avenue used to be a two story Horn and Harddart complete with the lion heads that spit hot coffee for a nickel?

Can any of us forget the culture shock we experienced when going to our first Chinese restaurant out of the Bronx? Plates rattled; people spoke in normal tones and the waiters wrote down your order on a pad. I remember a meal at the **Concourse Gardens** restaurant as being a religious experience. You walked on carpeted floors and never spoke above a whisper. Our wizened waiter could take 10 orders without a notepad and never brought out the wrong dish (as long as all 10 people ordered chow mein).

And speaking of culture shock, I remember my confusion in college Sociology class years later, when the professor lectured on coldness of N.Y. neighborhoods. What planet was he from? I never sat down to supper without a neighbor dropping in to see what was in the pot.

Education was courtesy of **PS 64**. Not the **PS 64** of recent vintage where an alumni dinner was held in Queens out of fear, but the PS 64 where each spring we were marched to Roosevelt Gardens Apartments on the Concourse to see the Tulip displays circling the fountains. The PS 64 of Yo-Yo championships and ink wells with pen nibs (there I go dating myself again). It is in the same schoolyard I distinguished myself in, as lieutenant of the teachers entrance monitors, until I got into a fight with the captain, whose mother, Mrs. Moskowitz taught at the school. Go explain nepotism to a 10 year old. We were at war then, and I was proud that I was one of the only kids whose father was in the service. It's tough to make 10 year olds understand why Mom's unhappy that her husband was one of the few lucky Dads who got drafted and shipped overseas. Show and Tell gave me a chance to show off the great souvenirs Dad sent home. In the meantime, we bought in our pennies and were given war stamps to paste into our victory books. We practiced our air raid drills sitting in the hallway floors and we listened to out mayor tell our moms to "bring their fat cans down to the market." War can be a great experience for a 10 year old when it's being fought thousands of miles away.

The pharmacy on 170th Street was the place you went when you got something in your eye. The service was free and professional. I sometimes wonder why we never considered our doctor qualified enough to solve that problem. Perhaps we felt he was too busy. After all, he was a general practitioner which meant he did everything himself from delivering babies to removing tonsils to making housecalls-no easy task when you considered we lived on the 5th floor of a walk-up building.

On the corner of Walton Avenue and 170th Street stood a shoe store. Alongside the brick wall of that store, each morning, the cleaning woman gathered. They came by bus from the East Bronx with their pails and their rags and sat on their pails in what today might be politely called a "shape-up"; 300 years ago it might be likened to a slave auction, and they waited. If a housewife needed someone to do a heavy cleaning job that day, she went to the corner and picked out a woman to clean. By one o'clock, if you weren't picked, you took your pail and got back on the bus to go home. I passed that scene every day on my way to school and never saw it for the painful horror it was.

Morrisania Hospital was a few blocks from my house. I can't remember the exact epidemic, but I vividly remember the hours of waiting with my family on a long line as it snaked its way around the block waiting for a shot. They hoped this shot would work against the disease. I say "hoped" because I remember another epidemic as a child where we had no shot to ward it off. Our mothers sewed little sacks that we wore on strings around our necks and the sacks were filled with camphor. I don't know if it worked or not, but not one case of moth bite death was reported in the Bronx that year. Sitting through a double feature though was quite a chore when everyone had a camphor sack around the neck.

O.K., still not convinced that my neighborhood was the best? I didn't want to rub your nose in it, but...

Picture a hot sticky day in July. Too hot for stickball, or immies, or Johnny-on-the-Pony. One short blast past Jerome Avenue, and you were at the "ice plant". There, right on the loading dock was this big mound of "SNOW". It was our secret, and we never told anyone about it until now. But you wouldn't believe me when I told you that my neighborhood was the greatest.

SNOWBALL FIGHTS IN JULY—ONLY IN THE BRONX!

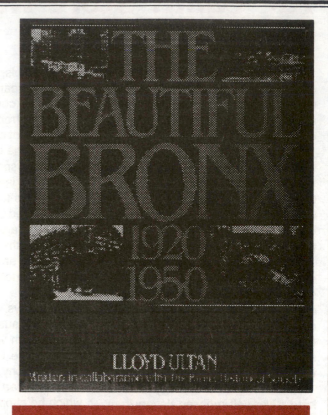

The Candy Store Was The Hub

By Herbert Gitlin, Clinton '37

Long before ice cream parlors, chain drug stores, and everybody's having a phone, the neighborhood Candy Store was the center of activity.

At the beginning, there were what was commonly called, "dry stores." With the advent of the soda fountain, they became "wet stores." My parents had both, and I became a integral part of life in the Bronx through the Candy Store.

My parents' first store on 199th street and Jerome Ave. was a dry store with oiled floors, dark stained candy cases and toys on one side; cigars and cigarettes were on the other. The newspaper stand was outside and was brought in at night or when it rained.

In those days everybody worked hard; it was self imposed slavery from 5:00 A.M. to midnight because every possible sale was a penny earned. I was too young to fully understand what was going on, but there were always men congregating in the store after I came home from P.S. 46.

My mother was a beautiful woman so who could blame the delivery men from "schmoozing" with her when they were finished with their morning deliveries. Dad was downtown selling light bulbs from floor-to-floor trying to make ends meet. "The Daily News," "The Times," "The Herald Tribune," "The World" and the scandal sheet, "The Mirror," were the papers of the day.

When I was ten, my parents opened a second store on 169th street between Sheridan Ave. and the Concourse and this was where my real education began. I went to P.S. 64, 90 and graduated from 53 in Jan. 1932 before entering Clinton.

Each day, after school, I helped out in the store while the gang was playing stickball around the corner. Since this was a "wet" store with a 16 foot soda fountain and seating for six

in fixed stools, I became good at making egg creams, ice cream sodas, malts and could adeptly scoop ice cream out from the 5 gallon containers to fill pint size cartons with all the flavors of the day.

The newspaper stand was still outside but cigars were now displayed under glass-topped counters with reserve closed boxes stored in humidified cases against the wall. The two phone booths were inside and I was constantly answering the phone to call any of the tenants who lived in the building.

Saturdays were especially interesting because I was in the store before noon when the delivery men would come for their usual morning meeting. Tony, the iceman, had shoulders as broad as the slab of ice from which he chopped out the 25¢ piece that he carried upstairs to the waiting tenant. The rubber blanket across his back resembled a serape.

The milkman, leaving his horse and wagon, soon followed with his two metal containers filled with milk bottles. The cream was always on top and we had to shake the bottle before pouring. They were two welcome visitors every morning.

The trucker who delivered fruit and vegetables and another who delivered groceries also joined the iceman and the milkman in the rear of the store to swap stories. Tony was a braggart and prone to exaggerate about his food consumption. My father and the other three constantly baited him and on this particular day, a bet was made that Tony couldn't eat a small stalk of banana which was procured from the fruit store.

"The Mirror" was called and sent a reporter and photographer to cover this unlikely feat, arriving when Tony appeared to be half-way through the stalk. My father had not only taken off the first two rows but, being a good samaritan, supplied the thick malts,

as he said, "to help wash down the bananas." The speed of peeling and eating began to slow down and Tony was well into the last row.

The thick malts didn't seem to help the bananas which became more and more difficult to swallow. Tony's eyes were beginning to bulge and a pause was agreed on for Tony to get a second wind or a second stomach, if he could find one. By this time the store was full of cheering neighbors yelling "ONE MORE, TONY!"

He finished the last row and the actual count was 56 bananas but "The Mirror," with pictures and a lead headline, said, MAN EATS WHOLE STALK OF BANANAS.

The candy store became an attraction, and the story grew with each repetition, until I heard somebody say that Tony, the iceman, ate 250 bananas.

With all the candy at my disposal, the only thing I ever ate was frozen MilkyWays. Breyers ice cream was the finest and I made the best ice cream sodas with syrup first, a shot of milk and a stream of fine soda to raise the foam, then the ice cream and finally the soda to fill the glass; the price was 10¢.

All my friends envied me as I stood behind the fountain with my apron, making two sodas at a time. We knew everyone by their first name and it was common practice for the customer to say "put it on my bill," which was settled weekly, after pay day.

The punch board was a big attraction with winnings as high as $100 and as low as 10¢. The choices ranged from $1 to 10¢. There were about 200 picks so the storekeeper could make a 20% profit when the entire board was sold.

Life in the Candy Store trained me for the world and I have always been grateful to my parents for allowing me to share their experiences and dedication to the community.

Longfellow Avenue

by Helene Dunkelblau

Longfellow Avenue was a festival of sound and color, a city cavern, a valley of brick and cement, where I spent the magic summer days of my childhood during the 1950s. School was out, and this block-long universe would come alive, as every kid in the world poured onto the street to move, run, play — to do all the things that children do everywhere on their summer vacation.

Mornings would begin softly on a shadowed sidewalk where three little card sharks engaged themselves in a fierce game of pinochle against the cool wall of Mr. Smith's building. Somehow the pleasure of this play always seemed to wane just in time for the arrival of the sun on our block. First its rays would tickle the roofs of the tenements across the street with a golden layer. Then, always taking its own time, it would creep down the side of the buildings, leisurely painting the walls with light, until finally one whole side of our brick valley would miraculously change color! This must have been some work of magic, for the sun never failed to draw kids of all ages out of their apartments down into the street in time for the completion of the visual transformation.

The sun would fill our world with energy of the new day, and we were ready for play. Stoopball and stickball in the gutter, slug against the wall, potsy and jumprope for the girls — kids moved in and out of intricate kaleidoscope patterns in time to the random rhythms of rubber balls slamming and popping, and shouts and chants of young voices. The activity would go on and on, building to a fever pitch, until, as though by some prior plan, our block would be punctuated by a chorus of motherly voices calling from the windows, "C'mon in, time for lunch!" leaving our concrete valley suddenly empty and still.

All through the noon "time out" the sun would keep its steady course, sliding across the street, filling it with light, to make way for activities suitable to a summer afternoon. In fact, an unassuming traveller who might happen upon Longfellow Avenue at this time of day would probably think he stumbled into some kind of carnival, where, depending on the current fad of the week, spinning hula hoops, roller derbies, bicycle races or a world series tournament in sandlot baseball made up the main attractions. And if this inadvertent visitor decided to stay for a while longer, he would probably be treated to a symphony of sounds rising from the loudspeakers on the trucks that brought the whip or the rocker, from the jingling of the bells of Bungalow Bar, or from the cry of the man who sold the candied apples and marshmallows, all complementing the movement on the street.

Toward the end of the afternoon, the sun would prepare the last of its performance and rapidly conquer each crevice and corner of Longfellow Avenue with its heat. It was always at this time that a most interesting ritual occurred. All at once, as if on cue, a line of perpetually knitting mothers sitting by the curbside in their aquamarine beach chairs would suddenly arise, and in one great centipedic movement, slide their chairs and their belongings towards the building wall

994 E. 172nd St. & Longfellow Ave.

in pursuit of the afternoon's last bit of shade.

When the sun was finally satisfied with its day's work, it would take its leave, coaxing happily exhausted children and frantic mothers back into their buildings to prepare for the dinner meal. A little later, however, the gentle gray of the evening hour would draw everyone out again for one last chance at play. This time it was a quick game of running or hide-and-seek, under the loving and watchful eyes of the fathers finally home from work.

And as darkness would approach, turning the chunk of sky that could be seen between the building tops a slowly deepening blue, life on Longfellow Avenue was put to bed for the night, making a perfect end to a perfect childhood summer day.

1102 Longfellow Ave. & Westchester Ave.

Another Bronxite Remembers Ed Carmel

Dear Susan and Steve,

When I received your publication in the mail and I flipped to page 18 and saw an article about my old friend, Edward Ha Carmeli, A.K.A Ed Carmel. He and I were neighbors for a short time at Co-op City. I had moved there along with my wife and son, Eric in 1972 planning to remain for many years to come. About that time my son Myles was born. I made the acquaintance of my neighbor Ed and his Mom and Dad. Ed rarely came out of his apartment and when he did it was usually at night. He exercised by walking down the hall using crutches. One evening I came off the elevator and observed this large gentleman slowly negotiating the hallway. We exchanged pleasantries and we agreed to meet in the near future.

Well, very soon afterward, I answered the doorbell and there's Ed, in a wheelchair, at my door. With some maneuvering, we got him into the livingroom and there he stayed for several hours regaling us with stories about his life as a "curiosity" in the circus and then with more intimate details of his everyday encounters with the "ladies" who were fascinated with his potential manhood! He was quite risque about these encounters and he had a great sense of humor. My son Eric (now 26 and a police officer NYPD Precinct 19 on Manhattan) had no end of enjoyment "riding his size 36 foot". Ed was truly a "gentle giant". His mom signed the "Baby Book" with the family name Hacameli. Unfortunately, she died, and soon after, Ed also passed away. He had been hospitalized for a long time, but we did not know how serious it was. We left Co-op City by 1974 and moved to Long Island. Ed's dad returned to Israel and that was the last I heard of him till I saw your article. Ed subscribed to Variety newspaper and shortly after his death I found it in my mailbox. I still have the issue and wrapper in remembrance of a truly unique human being.

I can recall the time Ed had tickets to see a show. I can't remember the name of the show but I do remember the time we had getting him into our two-door Cutless Oldsmobile and the looks on people's faces when we pulled up to the theater and eventually got him out. The show was not very memorable, but being with Ed was. I remember him with warmth, love and a sadness that he could not have lived longer to enrich more people's lives with his humor and zest for life.

I regret I did not take any photographs of Ed, but at the time I wanted to make him feel at ease and be accepted as a fellow human being and not as a "freak" which so many viewed him as. Because of that sensitivity, I denied myself the pleasure of having photographs to enhance the memories of Ed and of his parents.

Thank you for including Ed in one of your magazine stories and allowing me the privilege of remembering Ed when we were back in the Bronx.

Sincerely,

Gregory Keith Tobkes

Reminiscing

Bronxite Ed Carmel Could Be The World's TALLEST Man

Reprinted From Bronx Westchester Magazine, January, 1958

By Robert C. Roman, Associate Editor

Just a few giant steps from Tremont and University Avenues lives Ed Carmel a young man who claims: "I'm the tallest man who ever walked the face of the Earth." Ed, who weighed 16 pounds at birth, now stands a shade over 8 feet 9 inches and weighs over 450 pounds. "At my last check-up the doctor said that I grew about one-quarter of an inch last year, and, who knows, maybe I've gained one-quarter of a ton!"

The son of Isaac and Miriam (Pines) Ha Carmel, he was brought to the United States as an extra large two-year old ("the doctor picked me up and slapped me, so I slapped him right back!") from Tel Aviv Israel, where he was born some twenty-eight years ago. "When I grew a bit, my father gave me blocks to play with," Ed recalls. "Six blocks to my left-hand were . . . And trains, too— the New York Central, the Pennsylvania . . ." His father, an insurance salesman for Metropolitan Life , is 5'6", his mother, a secretary for the National Women's League of the Theological Seminary of America, is 5'5". But Ed's grandfather Isadore Carmelotzky, a rabbi in Warsaw, Poland, was 7'5" and known as the tallest rabbi in the world. When Ed entered kindergarten, he was already taller than his teacher, and all through grade school (at eleven he was 6 feet tall) and high school (he was well over 7 feet when he graduated) he towered over everyone else. When the basketball coach at the Bronx's William Howard Taft High School saw him he supposedly proclaimed "I've got the beginning of a championship team right there (pointing at Ed)"

"I stopped playing when my head kept hitting the rim of the baskets," Ed recalls, reflecting upon his brief basketball days. "My favorite memory of Taft was a fine teacher and person, Mrs. Greenwald, who was very helpful to me."

He was elected vice-president of the freshman class, was almost unanimously elected Class Giant, and left college after two years to enter show business. He began nightclub work and called himself "The World's Tallest Comic-Poet." He also did extensive radio and television work as a folk singer, disc jockey, and in commercials. Because Ed has one of the lowest voices in the United States, he has recorded the bass parts in numerous commercials. He has also made two recordings; "The Happy Giant" and "The Good Giant".

Brief experience as a wrestler ("I'd play the part of a monster, while my opponent died of fright") and appearances as a giant on scores of television shows, including those of Wendy Barrie, Robert Montgomery, Art Linkletter, Gary Moore, Perry Como, Dean Martin and Steve Allen and gave him a chance to do some comedy routines and helped to bring him to the attention of Hal Eagles, a man who assembles unusual people for circuses, carnivals, fairs and other theatrical enterprises.

Ed was hired to replace Ted Evans (a mere 8'6" inches), who had died, as the giant for the Ringling Bros. Barnum and Bailey Circus (they billed me as "The Tallest Man on Earth"). He thus began a happy association and an assignment ("from the end of March to the middle of May") which he has held for eight years. He loves this work. "I love children," he says. "It gives me a great deal of satisfaction to see them marvel at me and the other sideshow attractions".

Ed has also appeared in five films. He did a bit role in Alfred Hitchcock's "North By Northwest," did larger parts in three low-budgeters, "Trouble Makers," "I was a Nazi," and "50,000 B.C.," but was most noticeable American International's "The Brain That Wouldn't Die," made in 1962. He played the monster finally set free from a mad doctor's lab who escapes and sets fire to the building where he has held for eight years. He loves the doctor, and thereby ends the suffering of the doctor's other victims. He also was hired to plug another TV chiller. "I had to dress as the Frankenstein monster and walk around giving out shrunken heads," he recalls. "Then I had to lug a coffin on my back around town. It had a mummy hanging out of it. Delightful, wasn't it?" He has no

Continued page 19

LOST &FOUND

Track down your old friends, neighbors and lost relatives with
THE BRONX TRACKING SERVICE

Did you ever wonder what some of your high school buddies are doing? Where do they live now?

Well, **Back in THE BRONX TRACKING SERVICE** may be able to help you find them and maybe even discover long lost relatives you never knew you had. Find the phone numbers and addresses from a database of 70 to 100 million people from all across the U.S. You can find that special old friend who you haven't heard from in years (decades). If you are like most people, as you get older you wonder more about those special friends you've lost touch with over the years. Wouldn't it be great to give them a call to swap stories and reminisce? If you are interested in tracing your genealogy, looking for lost parents, or children, we can help.

Mail the completed form and $9.95 for each person you want tracked to: Back In THE BRONX, Box 141H, Scarsdale, NY 10583

THE BRONX TRACKING SERVICE
APPLICATION

Name (Print or Type)

Last _____ First _____ Middle _____

Maiden Name _____

Address (Last know address or general location)

_____

City _____ State _____ Zip _____

Approximate date living at above address _____

High School _____ Year graduated _____

Age _____

Requested By:

Address: _____

City _____ State _____ Zip _____

Phone: _____

THE BRONX TRACKING SERVICE
APPLICATION

Name (Print or Type)

Last _____ First _____ Middle _____

Maiden Name _____

Address (Last know address or general location)

_____

City _____ State _____ Zip _____

Approximate date living at above address _____

High School _____ Year graduated _____

Age _____

Requested By:

Address: _____

City _____ State _____ Zip _____

Phone: _____

I understand that I will receive a list of name and addresses and phone numbers for each person from a database of over 80 million names throughout the United States. I further understand that I will have to search through theses names and determine the approximate name that matches the one(s) I am trying to trace.

Classifieds

Missing Persons

MP852 Hal Brayton, PS 73, **Taft** '52 Anybody from Anderson Avenue still around? Would like to hear from you. 9100 So. Dadeland Blvd, Miami FL 33156-7866.

MP853 Anyone having information about the whereabouts of Sidney Schnitzer please contact Muriel Bernstein, 212 679 1632. Last known address: Philadelphia, sister Millie, AA in WWII.

MP854 Judy (Hilda) Kugler, **Morris** '46 and Bronx House married 44 years to Sam Kimbarow (Kimbarofsky) of Witkins Ave. Live in San Diego. Call and say hello: 619 286 0514.

MP855 Looking for Jan '53 graduates of **Monroe** who went to CCNY.

MP856 Maryann Gill Salvaggio, lived on So. Blvd near Tiffany Street. **Dodge** '57 grad Would love to have reunion. Anybody who remebers me, love to hear from you.

MP857 Eileen Savit would love to re-connect with Olga Cavaliere, Slyvia Braverman, Alma Burgos, Gloria Bershatsky, Gladys Marquez, Betty Berenson, Norma Forzano and **Morovians** in Atlanta GA area.

MP858 Jeanette Meshel Kalb says hello to all who remember her from PS86 and **Evander**. Married 45 years, 2 grandchildren. Lives in Syracuse. Often thinks about the good old days.

MP859 Chris Bohlmann would love to hear from other **Taft** grads of 1960. Live in Houston now. Any **Taft** reunion coming up?. Can be reached at 102676.3347@compuserve.com

MP860 Ricky Wilson, Noel Colon and the gang from Jack's Candy Store on 167th St. and Walton. Where are you? Contact me, Lew Kilb, Box 223, Shelter Island, NY 11964.

MP861 Mel Schwartz, PS44 '52; **Bronx Science** '55 says hello and hopes to hear from neighborhood or school friends at: POB 22082, San Diego, CA 92192.

MP862 Bonita Bunnie Rubenstein, **Taft** '58 is looking to find Sheila Goodman Miskind. Would like to reminisce on old times.

MP863 Claudia Patrone who graduated from **Saint Francis Xavier** in 1952 and from **Thomas Aquinas** in '56 would like to hear from any classmates. Address correspondance to: Claudia (Patrone) Perri, 60 Acrelane, Hicksville, NY 11801.

MP864 Where are you **Creston Jr. High** class of '49? Neil LePow would like to find: David Raspler, Leontaro Rosenburg also Morris Ave's Arthur Broder, Harvey Gezman, Marilyn Sacks, Alan Levin, Bruce Levine and Harold Ashor.

MP865 Would like to know what happened to classmates and friends of Albert Acierno, PS78 '56, **Evander Childs** '60. Now living in and around Hillside Homes.

MP866 Jay Gould—where are you? Clay Avenue, **Clinton**, left high school in '39. All the boys are wondering where you are, call me: 310 822 8961—Nick.

MP867 Irwin A. Ziser is looking for members of "New Vous Deu", Arnie "Mo" Moses, Lou Mauriello, Sy Benson, Bob Brown etc.

MP868 Leon (Louis in yearbook) Lebensbaum. Curly hair (long gone)- would like to hear from **Monroe** '40 classmates. I now live in Plainview, LI with a Condo in Delray Beach.

MP869 Mike Glick, Morris Avenue & 196 St, **Clinton** '69. Looking for the whereabouts of Bennett Rubin, Steve Greenburg, Gary Jacoby. He also attended PS86 '54 & J.H.S.

MP870 Garden Street/Grote Street/PS32 - JHS45/TRHS '50-60. Where are you?

MP871 Eleanore (Bloom) Surkis is looking for Joan Broder Goldman, **Taft** '55. She lived at 1188 Grand Concourse, then in Yonkers. Would love to hear from her or anyone else in my class. I now live in Manhattan.

MP872 Jerry Shapiro, D.O.B. 10/6/41, lived at 1660 Topping Ave (corner 173rd St.) until Aug '55. Now living at: 4207 Michelangelo Ave., Woodland Hills, CA 91364. Would love to hear from old friends.

MP873 Myles V. Lynk, PS3, PS44, JHS 123 and **Morris** HS '66, would love to hear from old friends. A lawyer in Washington D.C., I am President elect of D.C. Bar. I am often in NYC on business— so please get in touch! 202 862 1047.

MP874 Carole (Swettow) Lane is looking for friends from Valentine Avenue, PS85, EBB, **Walton**, Hunter College. Especially Nancy Unger, Joyce Gould, Sandy Moskowitz, Geri Weiss, Joel Levy, Philip Levine, Bobby Glatter, Carol Weinstein. You can contact me at: 38 Wallace Dr., Chestnut Ridge, NY 10977 or call 914 735 7928.

MP875 Howard Pincus, **Taft** '61 is a Captain with American Airlines living in Grass Valley, Ca. Would like to hear from some old friends. 916 272 9098.

MP876 Hi! My name is Leo Zornow, **Clinton** '48. Living on Fulton Ave- across from Crotona Park. Attended the Bronx Y. Norman Pearl- are you out there? If so, get in touch!

MP877 Henry Herschaft, **Taft** '57, is a Senior Vice President at Smith Barney, 1 Penn Plaza, NYC, NY (fromerly of Marcy Place, Marlboro, NJ and Atlanta GA- now back in NYC. Married and have 2 adult children. Looking for Fred Stern and Alice Colton. 212 643 5700.

MP878 Looking for classmates that graduated from PS76 in '57 and **Evander Childs** HS in '61 who lived in the Burke Ave neighborhood. Write to: Joe Sagaria at this classified number and relive old memories.

MP879 Where is Gladys Barver and Sue SLade (June '48 **Taft**) Myrna Bernstein (Feb '48 **Taft**) and Beverly Bennett ('48 **Walton**) It has been too long! Sue Lynn (nee Helen "Sue" Goldman) Ft. Lauderdale, FL 305 472 1779 (phone& fax).

MP880 The gang from 167th St. and Grant Ave (Flyod Rosenburg, Ken Rosenburg, Howie Nestler, Marv Gettinger, Marty Fleishman) If your out there, contact Les Levine at: 407 452-7726.

MP881 Gary S. Schreibman- Hunter (Bronx) Tan Delt Pledge Class Fall '57...Looking for members of my pledge class for annual reunion with other TanDelt Alumni. Call me at: 914 362 1187.

MP882 Pearl and Marlene, **E.B.B. Jr. High School**, 1946-49 looking for fellow "Assorted Nuts" 516-496-3554 or 718 776 7992.

MP883 Gary Glenn, **Clinton** '64, **Creston JHS**, PS86 would like to hear from old friends. Grew up at 2928 Jerome Ave & 2700 Grand Concourse.

MP884 Linda Sussman (now Hunt) PS46, EBB, **Walton** '59 then Hunter would like to find friends who climbed the "mountain" on Creston Ave, played hide-n-go-seek and ring-o-leevio on summer nights, who played "skully" and "Potsy" and skated in the street.

MP885 John Cullen (**Dubois** '60 & **Fordham University** '65) Vice President Estate Planning Unit at Citibank. Grew up in Highbridge- married Carol O'Brien from Noonan Plaza at 168 St. on Nelson Ave. Moved up to Mosholu Pkwy to Riverdale and now live in Eastchester. Would like to hear from old friends.

MP886 Robert Kaplan from Gates Place and Mosholu Pkwy. Is there anybody out there who lived in this area from 1944 to 1967? How about the Candy Store on Moshlu and Jerome Avenue? Schweller's and the Cafeteria? PS80? I went to **Clinton.** Graduated '62 and went to PS95.

MP887 **Evander** Grads '46. AnnLee Goldfarb Stein would love to hear from anyone from class of '46 or from **Walton** and 183rd.

MP888 Ronald Furman would like to hear from old friends that knew him from hangouts in the Bronx, PS95, **Clinton**. Some are: Linda Olson, Bobby Gonzales, Dolores & Lorraine Petrullo, Eddie Small, Eddie Gerwin, and Linda Lee Solomon. Call 305 944 8420.

MP889 Looking for Jimmy McKiernan & The Gang from Perrer's Candy Store on Cauldwell Ave & 160th Strett. Also the gang that hung out at Charles Candy Store, Moshulu Pky & Webster Ave during the late 1950's.

MP890 Don Wachs **Clinton** '48 is living in California. Would love to hear from friends that knew me and my wife, Dolores Laura Brooks, **Taft** '52. Call us at 818 882 5516 or write 22317 Golden Canyon Circle, Chatsworth, CA 91311.

MP891 Robert Silverstein, Knox Place- DeWitt **Clinton**, tennis team, visual ads squad, I am in the medical supply field.

MP892 Carol Siegel Wurcel is looking for Dave Feinstein, **Clinton** '62. Shorehaven, 92nd St. Y and Parkchester. Also interested in hearing from JHS 125 (Mr. Broady's class '60) classmates and **Monroe** '63 classmates.

MP893 Elaine Goldstein, from Vyse Ave. is looking for Al Gerbs & Irv Siegel. Important to know whereabuts of Al Gerbs from Longfellow Ave. Call 516 499 4238.

MP894 Leonard Grossman from Parkchester, JHS127 '57, **Monroe** '60 is looking for old friends. Call 212 877 4917—especially Paul Dickstein & Paul Koch.

MP895 Shelly Alpert Finn where are you? Your bobsey twin Beverly Lew Sacharow is looking for you. Wondering where the h___ are you and how've you been.

MP896 **Monroe** '30 photo editor, Herb Hillman, now living in Box 135, Whitingham, VT 05361 wants to know- anyone else alive from those ancient days?

MP897 Judy (Fischer) Reiter and Alene (Friedman) Gottlieb are looking for Leslie Michaelson, formally from 1560 Metropolitan Ave in Parkchester. PS106 '54, JHS127 '56, before she moved to Forest Hills.

MP898 Jerry Manius is looking to hear from Ethan, Paul, Phil, Lenny and any other PS104 classmates of the early '50s. 201 235 6706.

MP899 Our old gang is looking for Annette Abolofia and Irving Candiotti from the 170th St. area. Annette taught us to dance and Irving was just so funny! (1952-55) Contact Bunny and Herb Rogers: 914 359 7695.

MP900 Hello all you graduates of 1957 **Evander Childs** HS—how about a reunion. Hello Marcia Hirsh, I remember you. Richard Denet, Yonkers NY.

MP901 Anyone out there from **Evander** 1960? Charlie Moschitta, 11 Hunterdow Ave, Spotswood, NJ 08884.

MP902 Bob Bonchick, PS97, PS113, **Clinton** '53. Looking for classmates and for neighbors from Eastchester Road area. Living down in S. Florida. Retired from IBM.

MP 903 Looking for Joel Gimpelson, **Bronx Science** '59, NYU '63. He graduated some time in '65. Contact Sandy Klein: 908 235 7827 or write: Box 6136 Bridgewater NJ 08807.

MP904 Where are the kids from Home Street who played with Manny and Margie Short in the early fourties. Please write to Madaline Short Pino, 2232 Fitzgerald Ave., Los Angeles, CA 90040. Also Rosie and Josie, Claire's friends are you there?

MP905 Looking for Joan Rappaprt of Gun Hill Road. Remembering Summer '47, Cold Spring Rd., Monticello. Call Sy Lask 212 206 6570.

MP906 The Jewish Service Center provides life sustaining Jewish enrichment services for the Bronx Jewish poor/elderly. Individuals who wish to support this effort should contact: Asher Moskowitz, Director, Jewish Service Center, 2432 Grand Concourse, Room 502, Bronx, NY 10458 or call: 718 363 7900.

MP907 Norman Shapiro is looking for Robert Dresner who attended PS67 around '39-'40. Call: 818 886 9797.

MP908 Looking for guys and girls that hung out on rubber legs. Vyse Avenue Candy Store: Ronnie, Patty, Bobbie, Vinnie or anyone else—found 18 girl friends in the last 3 years, looking for more! call: 908 679 3648.

MP909 Looking for: Joseph Untermeyer. He is living in Fla. We knew him Back in The Bronx! Please contact: Artie and Leah Weingarten at: 407 391 0227. Lots of memories to relive!

MP910 Hoping to hear from **Taft** '47 grads. any plans for a 50th anniversary reunion? Bernie Stonz 212 245 8662.

MP911 Jim Stolow, **Taft** '58 can be found in Bellrose Queens, NY.

MP912 Jay Citron, **Taft** '65. Living and working at the Crazy Horse Memorial, the world's largest mountain carving, 17 miles from Mt. Rushmore,-in the beautiful Black Hills of South Dakota. Would love to hear from my friends (PS70, **Wade**, **Taft**) You know who you are!! God bless Jason Magida, long live Roosevelt Gardens. Eddie Kirshbaum, meet me at Lou Zaklins- I'll buy you some black high-top converse. Laura Nyro-Please write me, we all love your album dedicated to Native Americans. Cousin Wendy & Helene, please write me. Joseph Rabinowitz, please contact me. I miss you. Address: Ave of the Chiefs, Crazy Horse, S.D. 57730-9506.

MP913 Club Hylo, East Bronx (1930-42) Where are you and 23 others? Roy Ross, Mack Baron, Jack Dobkin, Ben Marks, Milt Cutler, etc. Roy Ross.

MP914 Ralph Fried, where are you? The Apes+G+S Players are looking for you! You too, Annette Friedman. Call Marty: 201 471 1850.

MP915 Looking for Virginia Voltuoa and Harriet Weinstein. Originally from Pelham Pkwy area. We were 3 Musketeers in JHS135 (Earth Science) What were the names of our horses? Please contact Janice Ackerman, the 3rd Musketeer.

MP916 If you remeber Mr. Rich, Mrs. Rosen, Mrs. Davidoff and were at PS70 in the early 60's, would like to hear from you. Eric Aronowitz, 126 Lafayette Pl., South Plainfield, NJ 07080. (908) 755-2096.

MP917 Yonkel- where are you? You were "All school yard" Remember Tiger, Pete the Greek, Fat Boy, Zonch, Schloime & Arty? Arty wants to see you. Please call: days 212 789 2407 weekends 718 548 5486.

MP918 Help me locate old friends from the E. Bronx. We all lived on Union Avenue. Lois Freeman, **Walton**; Regina Droisen, **Morris**; Doris Auerbach, **Taft**.

MP919 Mel Turner of Sheridan Ave., **Taft** '60 and Leone Rosner of Gun Hill Road, **Evander** '60. Looking for guys from Levines candy store or Moe's Luncheonnette. Call: 718 830 3607.

MP920 Looking for Howie Muchnick Steve Silverstein, **Clinton** '61. Call 305 233 8419, Mitch Cohen.

MP921 PS6, **Evander** '42, 178th & Bryant Ave. Looking for Bucky-Eugene Rosenkrante, Herbie, The Bandleader, Freddie Cowan, Jeanette Schact, Helen Sirota, Sam Silver, Seymour Schwimmer, Irv Katz and the **Evander** A.S.V. Gang.

MP922 Would be interested to know how many people from the Bronx live in Dutchess County.

MP923 Bennet Abramson, **Clinton** '56, Creston JHS '79, PS28, Anthony Ave, 179 St. Looking for old friends, living in Hartsdale, Westchester, NY. Call 914 725 7112. Presently coaching High School Girls Basketball & Softball at Ardsley HS.

MP924 Elliot Satinoff looking for friends from Hillside Homes, 1953-64 Ira Rubin, Kenny Price, Jill Kaplay, Joan Friedfurther, Marvin Kraus, Paul Ridder, Phil Brodrie, call 813 784 8338.

MP925 Bud Rosner, Gun Hill Rd. & Putnam Pl. looking for a reunion with PS94 and PS80 pals. Remember Max's candy store? Call me: 212 836 1810 or 516 783 5205.

MP926 Richard Wolfe played soccer, drew class buttons, lived on Stevenson Place and prior at 178 St. (Echo Park), where is Burton Green? (Cousin to John Garfield).

MP927 Looking for neighbors of Harrison Avenue-between Tremont and Burnside, especially Shelly Rubinstein and PS26, JHS82 crowd and for 1886, 1878 and 1898 Harrison reunion and stoop ball game.

MP928 Love to hear from my classmates from PS6 class of '60. Also from my friends from Longfellow Ave (Ralph Steinberg, Ira Kanis, Ira Kofsky, Barton Ward, Joel Ainnowitz and Norris Insler).

MP929 Where is Joan Gordin Lazarwitz? Where are Ben Forsyth, Pat & Jerry Rosencrantz, Rima Winchester? 201 839 3177.

MP930 I would like to hear from any friends who remember JHS44, PS92 and **Clinton** '58. Mel "Moose" Schwab. Also any of the guys who worked as an usher at the Paradise Theater.

MP931 Carol Block, 15 Featherbed Lane, younger sister of Nancy. Friends: Lew (Howie) Cohen, Lenny Leibowitz & Dave Fenster would love to hear from you. Also any other friends from **Science**, **Taft** and the Ballparks!

MP932 Kathie Carr, Anderson Ave, **Taft**. Would like to renew old friendships. Call me in Ft. Lauderdale: 305 721 2172.

MP933 Looking for Roz Israel, **Monroe** '60; Pat D'Alto, **Monroe** '61-2. Remer..ber Bobby LaFontaine? Call me, Marcia Golden Levy, **Monroe** '60: 516 822 4828.

21

Classifieds

MP934 Looking for anyone from Washington Ave. From Claremont Pkwy to Tremont Ave. Anyone to PS4 '45-54? How about Bryant Ave? Would love to hear from you.

MP935 Perry Rothenberg, **Taft** '60, Real Estate Broker, Founder Creative Leasing Concepts, Tribeca's Best Realtors- Commercial, Retail, Industrial, Building Sales, Lofts. Management our specialty. Manhattan located: 8 Harrison Street, 2nd floor, NYC 10013 or call 212 431 1338.

MP936 Phyllis (Bodker) Pincus is looking fro Grand Ave (Fordham Rd) guys and gals: Doris Kornbluth, Ira & Carol Garber, Howie Marlin, Mel Silverman, Joan Manning, Carol Gantwag, Carol Schneider (Kingsbridge Rd) 1940's-50's. Found Adrienne (Friedman) Teitlebaum in Fla. I'm in Long Island, NY.

MP937 Fran Pitlevnick Farber, **Ridder** '54, **Monroe** '57 is looking for anyone who hung around Murray & Jack's on 174 St. Especially Teddy Rosenberg "Moe" Edeiglass.

MP938 Lenny Fegarsky, Murray Katz, Fred Kasbarian, Mike Pappas, Frank Morea, Stan Berfas, Ronnie Smith, Enrigne Torres, Ira Reiss, Goodman Twins, Fulton Ave 1956 crowd. Respond to Model: 1 800 484 7070 ext1819.

MP939 I would love to hear from Neil Zern & Gene Epstein, both **Clinton** '64 grads. Must find Hernan Rodriguez, **Clinton** '62- from 177 St & Davidson Ave. Last seen in Miami in 1980 or 81 on a Harley. May be in Calif. Contact Howie & Ella Gottlies: 305 680 6502 (Fla).

MP940 Stanley Jeshiva, **Taft** graduate '58, would like to hear from old friends from Sheridan Ave., Gene Josephs, David Price, David Bienstock, Joseph Massa. Call: 914 961 2120.

MP941 Elaine Feldman Friedman, **Columbus** '52. Looking for Arline Heller and Genny Schwimmer Feldman for "old times sake!"

MP942 Herb Rukin of W. Tremont & Phelan Place would like to hear from the crowd from Crown Pizza, PS109, 1st graduating class of PS82, **Taft** '60-61. Contact: Box 9335, Lowell MA 01854 or call 508 970 1558.

MP943 Sal Gallo of Morgan Ave., **Columbus** '61, JHS 135 '55, would like to hear from: Andy or Nicky DeStefano, Bob Santoro or Lou Bombace. Please call 914 769 8999.

MP944 Barracudas 1941-1950, Kingsbridge Rd. and Reservoir Ave., looking for old friends plus Charlotte Neufeld of Wallace Ave. Please call Stan Getzier 212 787 9026.

MP945 Frank & Dorothy Schmidt (Beatty), **Clinton** '52 - '56 and **Preston** '55 - '59. Tony's candystore on Middletown Rd and St. Helena's dances on Sunday nights. Married 35 years after hanging out in PLA schoolyard with romantic voyages to Loew's American. 39 years at 50 Steiner Drive, Mahopac, NY 10541. Tel 914 628 2888.

MP946 My name is Geraldine Mintzer. I lived at 3434, Knox Place, Apt. 5G. My name is Marvin Abrams and I lived at 3464, Knox Place, Apt. 2B. Do you know us? Or remember us? We would like to hear from you.

MP947 In search of Harriet Feder or Doris Salzman, Roosevelt '47. Both lived on University Ave.

MP948 Looking for old friend Roberta (Bobbie) Bologh, married name Goodman, last address was in New Jersey. Contact Maxine Weiner, 1204-B, Westlake Blvd., Westlake Village, CA 91361 or call 805 495 7295.

MP949 PS114, JHS22 and **Taft**. We were in Mrs. Wahrsinger's fifth grade class when Kennedy was shot. My father was "Big Murray" at Murray's on 161 St & Walton. Any old friends contact Jeff Emmer at 914 725 7706.

MP950 Seymour Moskowitz, 1254 Grant Ave., **Taft**, City College, Cutis Wright Engineer. Any information please contact Archie Krauss.

MP951 Tom Capozzi, **Clinton** '59, JHS80 '56, would like to hear from any friends, especially those who hung out on Mosholu Pkwy by JHS80. Call 718 351 3838 or write to 88 New Dorp Plaza, Staten Island, NY 10306.

MP952 Parchester 1941-54, PS106, Herman Ritter JHS, **Monroe** June '54. Where are you Ed Weinstein, Mike Starr, Robert Dunn, Frank Kahn? Would love to hear from you and reminisce.

MP953 1947-52 Jerome Ave, DeKalb Ave, Mosolu Pkwy, 208 St, PS80, Candy Stores (3) Van Cortland park, David Marcus Theater, Stickball, Touch Football, Katz Deli. Jay Rosen, Howard Koorhan, Steven Stein, Joyce buckholtz, Patti Krohn, Helene Kornbluth, Barbara Goodman, Geo Feinberg- where are you? Contact Jay Rosen.

MP954 1956 **Roosevelt** grads-we are planning a reunion. We have revieved over 65 names & current addresses. For info call Hal Rosenstein 516 585 5474 or Nancy (Bologna) Capozi 914 793 4244. Judy Barbanel where are you?

MP955 Frank Blum, **Clinton** '53, Rockaway Beach, 59th Street, where are all the dancers: Boggy, Rich, Howie, Shelly, Stan, et al. **Morris, Walton**, Creston Ave., Bob Hughes, Alan Levin, Stuart Ives, Joel Margolin, Stanley Wolfe- my basketball partner. 3 sewer stickball anyone?

MP956 I am looking for graduates of **Taft**, Jan. '53. I live in Westchester. Call me at 914 941 8569 evenings. Elaine Herzfeld Fast.

MP957 Seymour Bailis, lived on Wilson Ave., (Hillside Homes) graduated PS78 '43, **Evander Childs** '47, NYU '51. Camp Eden '47, '48, '49. Korean War took me to St. Lois. I'd love to hear from any old friends. 314 432 6620.

MP958 Shorehaven, poems by Gayl Teller, illustration by Joyce Muller. The Leibowitz sisters remember Doc, the Follies, Harry Bruce and dancing under the stars, the salt-eater pool, the sports and tournaments, friends and family. A National Leauge American PEN Women Poetry Winner. $19.95 + $5.00 postage and handeling. Mellen Poetry Press, PO Box 450, Lewiston, NY 14092.

MP959 Ridder '54-57, **Roosevelt** '57-'60: Appreciate help locating teacher's graves.

MP960 PS104 graduates '66, anyone remember Mrs. Alexander, Unger and especially Mrs. Hoffman. Also friends from Sedgewick Projects. Would love to hear from you—Arnold Kerbis.

MP961 Those from PS26 Class of Milton Pascal, from about 1941, lets write, talk or get drunk together. Only those living need reply. Call Douglas Buck at 212 697 7333.

MP962 Herb Gitlin, **Clinton** '36, would like to hear from any of the following: Ray Cohen, Joe D'Addario, Abe Golub, Milt Jurow, Arthur Klein, Bernie Kitman, Irving Linderbaum, Saul Madel, "Red" McAvey, Irv Moser, Al Schneider, Harold Shenker, Harold Tietz. 141 Columbia Drive, Rancho Mirage CA 92270.

MP963 Club Windsor, mid 1940's to early 1950's, Gun Hill Rd., Putnam Place, Kings College Place, Reservoir Oval, Maxies Candy Store. It was the best of times, feeling nostalgic? Guys & Gals contact us: Mel Flax & Irwin Margolin at: 914 779 9737.

MP964 Mickey and Marion (Price) Davies are looking for old friends. Please call 908 393 1455 or khxg43a@prodigy.com or write us at 266 Amherst Avenue, Colonia, NJ 07067.

MP965 Jerry Hait, **Clinton** '62, looking for David Alan Goldstein, **Science** '62 who lived at 2701 Valentine Ave. Also looking for Linda Haberman, **Walton** '63 or others from the old gang (that hung out on Valentine & 196th St).

MP966 Looking for all our friends from the Sedgwick Progects 1955-62. Also Eddie Cicchetti, **Taft** '59 from Sheridan Ave. Maddy and Nat Pearl are still together.

MP967 Agnes (Oliveri)Mattera, **Evander** '56 , married 38 years to Tony Mattera of Edson Ave. Anyone remember Jimmy's candy store- Baychester Ave. Dyre Ave Train (Dinky) Station also any Baychester boys around? Love to hear from you.

MP968 Gay people who grew up around 161st - 170th Streets, Grand Concourse vicinity in the 1950's and 60's. Let's get together and compare notes about before/after coming out. Jerry Harris 201 333 8657.

MP969 Looking for classmates! Graduates of PS4 love to touch base with someone from that time. Call or write and make my day!

MP970 Taft '53. Is there anyone out there from Sheridan Ave 162-165 Streets? Anyone remember "The Flames" Bob Rubinstern, Katonah, NY 914 232 8350.

MP971 Artie Tiger, Bob Greenstein, feel like bowling tonight at Jerome Ave. Lanes? Pig in a molier chart, mist coming through the fog. Love to hear from you. Hal (in Chicago) 708 398 6423.

MP972 I am looking for anyone who graduated JHS40 (Prospect Ave) Ms. Flynn's class, June 1944. Home phone number, evenings preferred: 718 549 2067. Herbert Schlamowitz, **Monroe** '47.

MP973 Catherine or brother Michael O'Sillivan formally of Brook Ave, last known Kay lived behind Alexander's. Madekine Perroni of Louise DiStasio from "Little Italy". Write: Sid Tush, 978 W. Main St. Nanticoke, PA 18634-4011. Tel: 717 735 0955.

MP974 Trudi & Stanley Weiner, **Taft** '53 have moved to Aventura Forida where they have bought a business called AVLI: American Video Language Institute.

MP975 If anyone knows the wherabouts of a Sydney Rubenstein last known locations was Gary Indiana or Paul Uhny of Philadelphia, PA—please contact Edward Schiller, 5 Juniper Lane, Ridgefield CT 06877.

MP976 Artie Kauffman (Al) Burnside and Creston Ave. Married Vanna 1955 Grand Concourse, moved to Maryland in '67. Drop us a line to: 232 Glyndon Drive, Reisterstown, MD 21136.

MP977 I lived on Echo Place, went to PS28 and Creston JHS '44-47, played trumpet and watched Adolph Shayes play. Norman, Stanley, Bernie, Jerry are you there?

MP978 John Wyberanee, Roosevelt '62. Marmion Ave. Looking for any of the guys or classmates that hung out at Morris' candy store or school back in the 50's - 60'. Especially Angelo M. , Andy C. Seymour S., Alan D etc. 1111 Midland Ave, Bronxville, NY tel: 914 961 3495.

MP979 Would like to hear from Roberta Feinstein Heller, **Evander** '54, Hunter '58; Joanna Schreiber Heller, Hunter '58; Lester McClung of Prospect Ave and 164 St. Call Ethel Schwartz Bock, **Evander** '54, Hunter '58 tel: 212 724 2158.

MP980 Judith Schneider Veder Scheinbach of Marble Hill Progects '55-65 looking for friends from PS122 '55, JHS7 & 143 '56-58, **Walton** '61, **Hunter** '65. Marsha Cohen, Dona Godia, Helene Keshner, Helen Schloss, Charlette Ross, Mariel Gordon.

MP981 Cold Spring Village, Monticello 50's & 60's would like to hear from anyone who was at Cold Spring Village during the summers of 1950-60. Please call Neil and Arlyn (Herz) Kanowsky at 954 726 0903 or write 1713 Coral Ave, No. Lauderdale, Fl 33068.

MP982 Would love to hear from old high school buddy, Louie Perillo, **Clinton**. For that matter, anyone from **Clinton** '49 graduating class who might remember me. Write to: Dan Mangieri, 5319 Baybrook Dr., Houston TX 77062.

MP983 Would like to know if there is going to be a reunion for class of '57 for **Roosevelt**. Michael Flanagan, 512 Barkridge Trail, Burleson, TX 76028.

MP984 Where is the old gang from Hughes Ave between 179th & 180th. Woould like to hear from the Cosia's, Gross's, Conicelli's, Ferranti's, Puglieses's. Lets Reminice. —Frank Pernice.

MP985 Gail (Neuman) Harmon, **Taft** '64 is living in Pittsburg for 17 years Would love to hear from former friends and classmates. Graduated CCNY '68, M.Gd '92 Univ. of Pittsburg, October 1995 Divorce, Meditaion, training. Presently Prospam Coordinator/Counselor Community College of Allegheny County.

MP986 Interested in finding whereabouts of the gang from Vyse Ave and 172 St: Marvin Antman, Eddie Manfreno, Vinnie McKeever, Burt - Call"Twinny" 914 352 7980.

MP987 PS7 50 year reunion, January 1947 class looking for Dante Rivetti, Ronald Smith, George Bauer, John and Harris Maebeth, Former Dorothy Thonhorst, Judith Kahlman, Camille Lauretano, Mary Bauer, Maureen O'Connell, Geraldine Fitzgerald and Sonia Nagerian. Call Bob Eisinger at 914 356 8222.

MP988 Charlotte Dashkin and Rose Kroin— where are they?

MP989 Muriel Littman Fishbein would love to hear from friends from Mosholu Pkwy, PS80 '49, **Evander** '53. Have been in touch with many. Please call 718 423 7051.

MP990 Howard Harmetz '63 & Roni Greenberg '63 Roosevelt, married with children- love to hear from anyone who remembers us. Also the Fairmont Pl. Group. 482 S. Main St. Chesire CT 06410.

MP991 Marvin Moskowitz is interested in hearing from old friends, Bernice Ruderman, Lila Kessler and Natalie Bochner. Also any old musicians from JHS 44 and **Clinton**. Call 908 246 8600.

MP992 Don Seiden, PS96, JHS135, **Monroe** '65, Pelham Parkway, Allerton Ave., Columbus HS. Now living in Bend, OR via Berkeley, CA. any old friends still remember? Johnny-on-a-pony, stoop ball, skelly? Please call me at: 541 383 2566.

MP993 How about a PS8 Moshulu Pkwy class of '62 reunion? Remember Mrs. Wellman; Kleinsingers, Berkson? Write Gary Brook at 8 Camino Estreuas, Placitas, NM 87043.

MP994 Looking for Thea-Toby Goldstein of Spotford Ave- Hunt's Point Area. Also Pat Bogad of **Morris** High '53-4. Those who would like to attend or help make a huge reunion, please contact me. Target date1997 or 98.

MP995 Charles Ardolini would like to hear from twins Ann and Frances Wildau who lived at 2835 Bainbridge Ave. Call: 301 776 5266.

MP996 Teddy Weiler, **Science** '58, formerly Charles Theodore Weiler, performance poet, San Francisco, would like to hear from anybody from the Pelham Parkway Area in the '50s. Call 415 398 9545.

MP998 Looking for old friends from 193 St. and Marion Ave., Bainbridge Ave. The Shonogans, the Cartwells, Peter Haas. Call 518-584-2188 or write John V. Healy, 101 State , Saratoga Springs, NY 12866.

MP999 Where are you Linda Triano, Cecilia Cohen, grads of PS56? Phyllis Carpenella from the Ducky gang? Is anyone still in the old neighborhood? Love to hear. Get in touch.

MP1000 **Dodge** HS, Class of '57 where are you? Ann Higgins Chickory and Ruth McAlister Johnson. Would love to hear from you. Ruth Jahnson, 7 Stevens Pl., Chesren, NY 16918.

MP1001 Tony Pandolfo, **Monroe** '65. After 35 years as an administrator at Montefiore Medical Center moved to the University of Concinnati Medical Center. Looking to hear from friends, graduates and former teamates. Call 513 469 1251.

MP1002 Dorothy Weinstock, **Roosevelt** '62, married Edward Rubin, **Roosevelt** '60. Now living in South Florida. Remember Garden St., E. 180th St., Prospect Ave.? Looking for old friends, neighbors, classmates.

MP1003 Looking for missing friends from 50's on Willis Ave and St. Pius. Call Pete Cullen: 516 785 1223.

MP1004 **Evander Childs** Class of '56- Anything planned? 40 year reunion this year. PS78, Shirley Hillman- where are you? Contact Anne Fletcher at 617 937 0598.

MP1005 Our crowd was from the Poe Park area, some names: Kanata, Sullivan Dever, Elms Joyce Kennedy, Lynch, McCarthy, Foy, Staunton, Kelly, Harmon, Gardner, McGovern, St. John, Smith, Campbell. Please write.

Contact Some Old Friends TODAY!

Classifieds

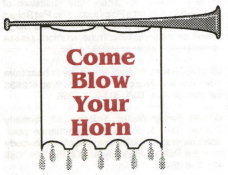

Come Blow Your Horn

Accomplishments
Awards
Businesses
Volunteerism
Works in Progress

Muriel Bernstein, retired as V.P. of Chemical Co in Precast Concrete. Now director of marketing for engineering co. in NYC. Widow, 2 children, lawyer & artist/chef, V.P. of mid-Manhattan Democratic Club, Trustee Murray Hill Comm.

Jim Molinaro has been working in Rockland County for past 50 years as a Real Estate Broker (Century 21). Builder and appraiser. I have been president of Ind. Fee Appraisers, Rockland Bd. of Realtors and MLS.

Helene Dunkelblau is presently a teacher trainer in a nationally recognized Chinese bilingual program based at Seward Park HS. I received my doctorate from NYU in (Chinese) bilingual education. My husband and I spent the 1993-94 academic year in Shanghai, China teaching at a teachers college. I began my study of Chinese at James **Monroe** HS.

Barbara Moss Fortson is the Mother of 1 Doctor and 1 Art Director. She was Assist. to the Editor and Special Projects for Women's Seminars and television award show for 8yrs for Ladies' Home Journal. Retired to Atlanta, resumed working after much volunteer work and now an Exec. Asst. to General Manager of Rich's Dept. Store. Widowed in '89, Grandmother of 4.

Al Macovski is presently Prof. of Engineering & Radiology at Stanford University, Endowed Canon Chair, member National Academy of Science- Nat. Academy of Engineering, Inst. of Medicine. Fello - Inst. Elect & Electronics Eng., Optical Soc. of Auer, Auer Heart Assoc. over 130 issued patients, Nobel Prize Nominator.

Steven W. Kalt, L.U.T.C.F., a former Bronxite is now working and residing in Westchester is offering financial planning and insurance services to other former Bronxites. Complete line of Insurance Products through many companies, with competitive rates. Call 914 428 4095.

Neil Lepow, B.S., M.A., NYU class of '80. Living in central Florida. 35 years International Distributor of Optical Supplies.

My name is Betty Relihan McBauly. My accomplishment in life is raising 6 children as a single parent. And great children. This is also my award. I went to work and now I'm retired and getting on with life.

Mitchell Marks is a Certified Public Accountant, Chairman of Prestige Packaging Inc- an investment Company, President of a Philadelphia based manufacturing company.

Ann Haber Stanton has put one ex-husband and 2 sons thru law school and am serenely settled in the Black Hills of So. Dakota where I have the distinction of being a Certified Medical Transcirptionist Proofreader at our hospital. I am editor of our Synagogue's Bulletin, have my own electrolysis business and some where still find the time to teach Medical Terminology & Transcription. Every now and then, I have come home to NY for a knish, some decent rye bread, and to touch my feet on home base. Still hoping for Mr. Right. Write to find me!

Eleanor Surkis, Boston University '59 B.S., Columbia University MA '61, worked as clinical audiologist for many years, presently working in pharmaceutical sales. Married, one son who is on the way to medical school, volunteer for American Cancer Society for 10 years, on Board of Directrors in my Co-op.

Al Mindes lived in 2150 Creston Ave, across from PS79. I am a Certified Public Accountant practicing in New York. All my Bronx memories were great.

Marv Goldberg is (modestly speaking) a world-renowned expert on 1950's Rythm & Blues music and have written articles and album liners notes for 25 years. There's also a book on the Ink Spots (which desperately needs a publisher). In my spare time, I'm a systems analyst for CitiBank.

David Kaplinsky graduated from Pratt University with a degree in Industrial Design. Moved thru the corporate ladder designing for Lowey, Deskey, Ideal Toys, CBS Toys and finally V.P. of design for Galoob Toys in San Fransico. Now retired due to heart transplant in '90 and enjoying my second chance! Married and halve 2 beautiful children.

Sandra Bobbe has 3 children, 6 granchildren and is retired after being a Special Ed Teacher, Editor & Publisher of a weekly publication, Team Leader/Medical Assistant for Mental Health & Substance Abuse program.

Tell Us About Yourself!

Elinor and Irving Steinbrechor, married 36 years. Have 2 daughters ages 25 and 29. I am a housewife and secretary for an Insurance Broker in Hicksville, NY. Irving is a computer technician for NYNEX. He played sax, clarinet and flute in the James **Monroe** band and now is first clarinet with NASSAU Community College Classical Orchestra and plays clarinet with the Seaford Community Band.

Eugene Eddstein, B.S., Math, CCNY (P.B.K., Cum Laude) '60, MS, Statistics, NYU '66. Director, Engineering, Northrop Brumman Data Systems & Services Div.

Marc Furman is currently Director of Construction Organization for the United Brotherhood of Carpenters working in Washington D.C. and Portland OR.

Larry Starr is married 36 years, with 2 daughters, one living in Queens and the other in Tucson with her husband. Have been involved with childhood Bronx friends through the "Royal Reunion" over the past 10-12 years, a group of friends from PS95 '45. Recently moved to Tucson, selling medical equipment business in NY for a new career- opening an ice cream cafe, a new concept in ice cream parlors, with wife and daughter-Jahn's watch out!

Esther Goldberg Youngermann went into the army from the Bronx. Ret Lt, Col, Int, president now of Textiles firm in Oregon with N.Y. ties and resources.

Ellen Himelfarb, **Walton** '61, is owner of the Anxiety Control Center. The center specializes in stress, anxiety and phobias. She is married and has two children. Please drop into the Center at 2070 Central Park Ave, Yonkers, NY to say hello.

Sue (Helen Goldman) Lynn, **Taft** June '48. Freelance writer, former director "Florida Children's Wear Guild", past year managing editor "Florida Design" writes travel for Southeast Travel Professional & columns for weekly publication "Miami Today."

Ray Sandusky is an Associate Director of Pharmacy at the Brookdale Hospital and Medical Center in Brooklyn.

Henry Herschaft: Senior Vice President/Financial Consultant at Smith Barney, NYC. Formerly Nat. Product Manager for Shearson Lehman Bros., NYC. Past member Industrial Development & Zoning Boards of Marlboro, NJ.

Eugene R. Johnson. I am the Executive Director of the Children's Home of Jefferson County. A residential institution for abused and neglected youth. Married to Arda (Vargas) Johnson for 30 years. Two children, one grandaughter. Grew up in Hunt's Point worked five years in Bismarck, North Dakota. 3 Years at United Church of Christ Mission for Native Americans.

Linda Sussman Hunt teaches English literature at Ohio University. My specializations are 19th century fiction and women's literature. I'm divorced, have a 26 yr. old son and am going with an English prof. from Brooklyn.

Nadine Wagner Caul, JHS60 '58, **Columbus** '61 is a caseworker in Suffolk County dealing with abused children. I have 3 children and became a grandmother for the first time.

Irving Greenberg retired 1988. Returned to Nassau Community College and became the oldest graduate in May '92. Member of 1932 Football Team undefeated untied unscored upon in regular sched. Played scoreless tie in charity depression game.

Thomas J. Palmieri, M.D.: **Fordham Prep** '56, is in practice as a Hand Surgeon in New Hyde Park, Long Island, NY. He is the Physician in Charge of Hand Surgery at the Long Island Jewish Medical Center in New Hyde park. He is also an Associate Professor of Clinical Surgery at the Albert Einstein College of Medicine. Tom resides in Brookville, NY and has two adult daughters.

Carol O'Brien married John Cullen in '64, childhood sweethearts. Lived in Highbridge, raised 3 great kids, boy 28 and twin girls 20 in college now. Presently live in Eastchester. John is Trust Officer and V.P. at Citibank Headquarters at 53rd & Lexington Ave. NYC. Carol works for White Plains School District. Still remain friends with lots of people from Highbridge. We were active in Sacred Heart Parish.

Bennett Tobias is married with one child and is President of B.T. Design Inc. which manufactures fashion accessories for stores in the U.S. and all over the world.

Vivien Gordon Lax grew up 3235 Grand Concourse, recieved Bachelors from **Hunter** Cbx Campus '59, Masters **SUNY Stony Brook** '72. Married for 35 years to Bert Lax (**Taft** '53, **Hunter** '57) 3 great children. Now an avid skier, tennis player, traveler, former teacher and now President and Founder of Energy Rate Analysis Inc. a utility bill consulting corp. Bert retired this year as Principal of PS221 in Queens.

Barbara Kuntz Glass is a R.N. Bellvue Hosp., married an Erasmian from Flatbush, who is now a dentist, after a hiatus returned to school. B.A. Ramapo College, M.A. English from Rutgers, one son- Brad. Have done writing for magazines and now work in husband's dental office.

Ann Lee Stein worked in Garment Center for 10 years. Had 2 great kids and then went on to own personnel agency. Now retired and living in New Jersey. Grad. of **Evander Childs** '46.

Phyllis Berman Fisher, C.A.D.C. private practice, Center for Addiction Recovery and Education. Nationally recognized speaker on Eating Disorders and other addictions. Widowed, 3 sons- all married, 2 grandsons. Would like to hear from old friends or others in this area.

Stanley Pargman has been living in Florida for the last 26 years. Married to Joy, going on 30 years, 2 children Kimberly and Brett. I am Senior Vice President of Oppenheimer & Co. and also represent football players as their agent playing in NFL.

Ronald Furman has worked for Metro-Dade County (Civil Service) in the '70s and '80s primarily recreation for handicapped. Since '91 I have been Activity Director for Gumenick Center, N. Miami Beach, Florida.

Leonard Grossman taught at PS102 for 24 years, twin daughters born in '72, married Martin Jackson's sister.

Robert Kobinson, Doctor of Public Health, V.C. Berkeley '83, presently Assoc. Director for Program Development, Office On Smoking and Health Centers for Disease Control and Prevention (D.C.) Director of African American Studies, Adelphi University '69-76. Any members of **Morris High School** track team or orchestra out there and listening?

Richard Denet was in the Navy for 2 years, got out '60. Started working for a company in Mt. Vernon, after 5 years they moved. I started woking for the Housing Authority after 10 years switched to the Board of Education. Twentyone years later almost ready to retire.

Gregory Tobkes, Teacher **Science**, JHS194, married 27 years (same woman) 2 sons- Eric 27 NYPD 19th Precint in Manhattan, Myes 24 businessman. House, 4 cars, 3 iguanas, 2 cats, lots of plants. Lived in Co-op City and Ed Carmel was my neighbor.

Fil Capria at age 19 joined Navel Reserve. Got a job with New York Telephone pushed up my active duty , went active for 3 years 1965-68, came back from Country went back to N.Y.Tel still with them- 31 years.

Anna Sheppard collects dolls, thimbles, makes dolls and crafts, love to have fun with family and friends, cooking, baking and anything to make people feel comfortable around my house and to keep family always smiling.

Gerald Killenberger, 32 years member of N.Y. Fire Dept. Chief of Staff, Manhattan Bureau of Fire Investigators, Fire Marshals. Active in community, Boy Scouts, Fire Company (VP), Ambulance, Church etc. Grandparents to Lindsey Elizabeth, Ryan Peter, Kaitlyn Marie, Parents to Elizabeth 34, Dorothy 30 and Edward 25.

Robert Mantel, my work background is in the legitimate theatre and sports complex (MSG). I'm a Mason, I do charity work when possible, play golf as often as possible. Planning to move to Arizona.

Patrick Inniss, Phd '94 NYU School of Social Work, MSW, Hunter College '75, BA Hunter '68.

Bernie Weissman, class '33 A.K.A. George Wyle, married Gertrude Kornbloth in 1938. Living in California since '46. Composed many songs including theme song for Gilliean's Island and Xmas hit "Most Wonderful Time of the Year".

Marty (Blackie) Finucane operates Marty's Place a Bar & Grill at Main St. Cairo NY 12413, 125 miles north of the Bronx, 35 miles from Albany. I've been here 5 years 6 months. Enjoying the country life.

Mel Silverman taught school in the Bronx for 2 1/2 years (JHS145 & JHS123) for the last 18 years I have been working for Johnson & Johnson in the dental field. I am an Executive Key Account Manager. I have a G.A. & M.A. from CCNY. Married with 2 children.

Norm Kailo, active realtor in Wayne NJ and Delray Beach FL. Past President NJ Ass'n. of Realtors & Director of Nat'l Assoc. of Realtors, Director of YM-YWHA of Wayne NJ. Author, speaker, consultant and innovator in real estate. Will be married to Marylin Waldman of Andrews Ave. for 50 years in 3/96. Served US Army Air Corps on Tinian & in India & China '42-45.

Freddie Glass served in US Army '64-66 Vietnam, correction officer Bronx House of Detention 1970-92. Retired. Still live in the Bronx.

Edwin F. Scherb works for the NYCTA and coordinates the maintenance activity of the Kingsbridge bus garage on 218th & Broadway.

Sonia Helfendt Love worked for the NYC Board of Ed for 25 years, retired and went into my own business- designing and manufacturing womens clothes, this was done while living in Merrick Long Island. Retired to Florida in Sept. 1995 with my husband who I met when I was 15 years old. Have 2 daughters and 3 grandchildren- who all live in Florida.

Sandi E. Cooper, **Science** '53, now Chair, University Faculty Senate CUNY and Prof. of History, City (Summa) '57, NYU PhD '57, mother and grandmother.

Wilfred Alverio '60 **Roosevelt**, '61-68 Wallstreet Clerk, '68-'70 US Army (Europe) '70-72 Hunter College graduate '75 graduate of Rutgers Univ. law School. Teaching '78 to present at George Washington H.S. (Manhattan) and South Bronx Leadership Academy. 2 children 16 & 18, wife Daisy, beautiful borough of Manhattan Comm. College Dean and now professor, own 2nd home in the Bronx (234th & Kingsbridge).

Michael A. Lewis Esq., Brooklyn Law School '64, NYU '61, **Columbus** '57 now living in Westchester.

Victor Levenson, Chiropractor practicing in Long Beach, LI past 28 years, Board Eligible Chiropractic Orthopedist, married 25 years, 2 children: Jennifer 21- Boston University, Jeffrey 23-Univ. of Mass.

Herbert Rukin, Director of Nutritional Services (Healthcare) Publications on serving pureed foods to the elderly and people with swallowing disorders.

Sandy Flanzenbaum, Engineer, now retired, married Marcy Peristein in Sept 1959. Have 3 sons & 1 grandson with another on the way. Lived at 2161 Barnes Ave after marriage and moved to Long Island in 12/68. Spent 2 years in California and 2 years in Japan courtesy of US Air Force, 1952 to '56. Graduated NYU Engineering '60. Graduated "State Tech" in Brooklyn '51.

Classifieds

Diane Cohen (Gorowitz) and Allan Cohen grew up on Elder Ave. with a gang of 9 guys and 5 girls. Where are they now? Allan (the boy across the street) became my husband of 33 years. Growing up with "the gang" he became a correction officer and kept our friends out! I became a legalized bookie working for off-track betting. We have 2 married sons and one grandchild with more to come. We look to our future with pride.

Peter Picciano , **Hayes** '57, is President of Woodcrafters Inc. A Bronx based architectural woodworking firm. He still resides in the Bronx with his wife of 20 years, Eileen Matthews Picciano, 3 sons and 1 daughter.

Michael Grafinkel, Chemical Engineer, contributed chapter in major reference on industrial operations. Now operate my own financial services company specializing in buying privtely held notes backed by real estate.

Philip Honig, Senior Partner in a regional Long Island CPA firm. Married to Dianne Robbins, **Taft** '55, 2 married children and 2 1/2 grandchildren.

Joel Ehrlich is currently Senior Vice President of Marvel Entertainment (Spider Man, Hulk, X-Men etc.) in New York. I previously was a V.P. Group publisher of Modern Bride, HealthyKids and American Baby.

Fred Weiner is now retired from NYC Police. Now engaged in supporting a small Jewish Community still in SUBA even the USA Government does not appreciate.

Fran Faberalter, Attorney at Law, Member of the Englewood City Council, Member of the National Board of Trustees, American Civil Liberties Union (ACLU).

Ethel Schwartz Bock, Advisor and Executive Assistant at Robert Louis Stevenson School since 1975. Two sons: Jeffrey 29- Director of the Synagogue Space, David 26- living in Albany and getting College degree.

Tell us about yourself!

Judith Veder, School Counselor at **Walton**- I "went home again" was English Teacher, 2 sons, one trying to get an academy award in L.A., the other in Albany SUNY, always writing, never published, searching for old acquaintances with whom to reminisce.

Gail Neuman Harmon, CCNY '68, received M.Ed. Psychology in Education '92, University of Pittsburg, Oct '95- trained as a divorce mediator. Presently I am a program coordinator/counselor for Community College of Allegheny County. Would love to hear from old friends and classmates.

Marvin Silver, accomplished owning one of the largest Fashion and Commercial Photography Studios in NY. (Married one of the beautiful models) retired in 1991, now own a large party goods store with my son and daughter in Wappingers Falls, NY.

Fredrick Schneider is a Graphic Designer and Illustrator (have been since H.S. graduation) Run Graphic Design Studio in Western Mass and teach (Professor: Art Institute of Boston) Married 20 years, 2 children: boys 15&11.

Helen Cademy she is a graduate of Cooper Union Civil Engineering was a charter member of Society of Women Engineers. I was an Electrical/Reliability engineer for Defense Dept. for 35 years in top secret work.

Father Hohn Brinn was ordained a Priest on June 2, 1962 by Francis Cardinal Spellman at St. Patrick's Cathedral and assigned to the parish of St. Peter in Liberty, NY. After serving as Associate Pastor for 18 years, Terence Cardinal Cooke appointed Fr. Brinn pastor of St. Martin's church on March 4th 1983. In Jan. 1994 Cardinal O'Connor asked Father Brinn to be Pastor of the Parish of St. Mary in downtown Poughkeepskie, where he continues to minister.

Daniel Mangieri retired from NASA in 1989 after 34 years of federal Service. Continued Engineering career in Aerospace as Deputy Director of Test & Verifation on Space Station Project. After 5 more years retired in 1994. Enjoyed traveling & watching 5 grandchildren frowing up. Travels include: Egypt, Scotland, Germany, Austria, Switzerland and of course NY every year or so.

Mitchell Marks, old neighborhood Andrews Ave., (University & Tremont Area) Macombs Jr. HS (PS82) **Taft**, graduated from Bronx Campus of Hunter College, worked at Alexanders on Fordham & Concourse, worked at J.S. Krum.

My name is Bob Cohen, from Bayside HS (**Monroe** '54) I served in the US Marines '56 and '57. I've owned my plumbing business (in NY and FL) for the past 35 years. I'm the proud father of 2 children and the proud grandfather of 2 granddaughters.

B. Kravette (Me) 2 children, 1 girl and 1 boy. My daughter is a Jr. 3rd year as they call it at the University of Virginia, she is 20. My son is in Jr. High and is 12 years old. I teach in NJ and hold a B.A. from Queens College and a M.A. in Communications from William Paterson College of NJ.

Norman Valle, currently Director General, International Advertising Associates (advertisers, Agencies, Media) Only global partnership of its kind.

Raymond Carioscia, Director of Human Resources past 24 years for Nationwide Distribution Co. based in Scarsdale.

Judith Rosenkrantz Tager. BA degree (music major) Barnard '55, MHOL (Masters in Human Development & Learning) with major in Counseling from University of N.C, Charlotte '79. Careers: Teaching, counseling, bookkeeping (for husband) salesperson to buyers of regional apparel market. President of Charlotte Hadassah.

Howard Kaplan (in chronological order) Made two documentary short films - both won Flaherty Film Awards- one won First Prize at the Venice Film Festival. Wrote and illustrated "The Dragon from the Bronx", published by Putnam, married an Israeli Sargent, father of two Yeshiva "bochers"

Carol Seskin became Registered Nurse while 3 daughters were young children. Married 33 yrs to Bob Seskin, **Science** '60. Did hospital nursing, managed pediatric office for 12 years. Returned to college (Ramapo '94) for degree in Psychology & Gerontology and now am manager of large Senior Center in Pearl River, NY.

READER REPLIES

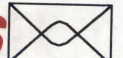

It is vitally important that you fill out the information below. Your input will be essential to the success of this magazine, tailored and inspired by you, the former "Bronxite". We thank you for your participation.

Subscriber? ❑ **Yes**   ❑ **No**

YOUR NAME _____

ADDRESS _____

CITY _____ STATE _____ ZIP _____ PHONE _____

HIGH SCHOOL ATTENDED _____ YEAR GRADUATED _____

TELL US A LITTLE ABOUT YOURSELF,

(Be sure to include your alma mater, old neighborhood, your best memories about your days in the Bronx, (or anything else you can tell us).

_____

_____

COULD WE SEND A FRIEND A FREE COPY OF BACK IN THE BRONX?

Do you know current or former Bronxites who would like to receive our magazine and reunion information? If you do, we'll be happy to send them a **free** inaugural issue of **Back in THE BRONX**.
Write to Back in The Bronx, Box 141 H, Scarsdale, NY 10583 or call 1-800-7-BRONX 5

Last _____ First _____ Maiden _____
Address _____ City _____ State _____ Zip _____
Phone # ( ) _____ School and year of Graduation _____

Last _____ First _____ Maiden _____
Address _____ City _____ State _____ Zip _____
Phone # ( ) _____ School and year of Graduation _____

Last _____ First _____ Maiden _____
Address _____ City _____ State _____ Zip _____
Phone # ( ) _____ School and year of Graduation _____

Last _____ First _____ Maiden _____
Address _____ City _____ State _____ Zip _____
Phone # ( ) _____ School and year of Graduation _____

COME BLOW YOUR OWN HORN DEPARTMENT

Please tell us about yourself (include your name)—about your accomplishments, awards, titles or works in progress. We're interested in hearing about them. List Below. _____

_____

_____

_____

_____

READER REPLIES

As a subscriber you are entitled to a FREE 40 Word Classified, Missing Persons, Blow Your Own Horn, or Personal Ad. Please write your ad below (if you are not subscribing to our magazine you can still place an ad in the next issue. The cost of an advertisement is 50¢ a word, there is no limit on paid ads).

_____

_____

_____

Is Your Mailing Label Correct?

In order to keep our database current, please correct any errors and place the label and or photocopy with corrections.

Account #	High School	Year Graduated
6817	Roosevelt	1958

Mary R. Flowers
123 Anystreet Blvd.
Anywhere, USA 12345

SAMPLE

Change of Address?

If you're planning a move please attach your label corrected with your new address and the date that you will begin receiving mail at that address. This will insure that you don't miss your next issue of **Back in THE BRONX**.

Ordering Information

A Great Gift Idea! In addition to your own subscription, a subscription to **Back in THE BRONX** makes a great and unique gift. Fill in the form below and we'll process the order in time for our next issue. So, order your subscription NOW, and order one for a friend!

YES, I'd like to order the following items:

QTY.

____ 1Yr. (4 ISSUES) Subscription(s) to **Back in THE BRONX** $19.95
____ 2Yr. (8 ISSUES) Subscription(s) to **Back in THE BRONX*** .. $29.95
____ 3Yr. (12 ISSUES) Subscription(s) to **Back in THE BRONX*** .. $39.95   *FREE Jahn's Menu
____ 4Yr. (16 ISSUES) Subscription(s) to **Back in THE BRONX*** .. $49.95
____ The Beautiful Bronx...........$25.00 (plus $3.95 S/H) $28.95
____ The Bronx: It Was Only Yesterday..$25.00 (plus $3.95 S/H) $28.95
____ Bronx High School Reunion Weekend Video $29.95
____ SAVE MONEY - BUY 4 FOR JUST $99.00!
____ THE BRONX Tracking Service $9.95
_____ I would like to receive all available back issues and have them applied towards my subscription *(To date we have at least 12 back issues available - While They Last!)*

TOTAL: $ _____

Please fill out completely and include $3.95 for shipping and handling for books only to: **Back in THE BRONX**, Box 141H, Scarsdale, NY 10583

Please Print Clearly ☐ New Subscriber ☐ Renewal

Name _____

Maiden Name _____

Address _____

City _____

State _____ Zip _____

Phone (_____) _____

High School _____ Year Grad. _____

☐ Visa ☐ Mastercard ☐ Check ☐ Money Order

No. _____ Expiration Date _____

Signature _____

Back in THE BRONX

Box 141 H, Scarsdale, NY 10583
Phone 914-592-1647 • Fax 914-592-4893
ADDRESS CORRECTION REQUESTED

Volume IV   Issue XIV

Back in THE BRONX

CELEBRATING THE EXPERIENCE OF GROWING UP AND LIVING IN THE BRONX

Shorehaven

WHAT GREAT MEMORIES!

By Arlene (Schneider) Radansky, Taft '54

For several summers my friends and I went to Shorehaven Beach Club, a haven for teenagers, as well as adults and children. The adults and children stayed close to the pool. The teenagers sought out a separate area, on a grassy strip, away from the noise of the children.

The summer most memorable to me was my last summer there, when I was sixteen years old. Boys were the number one topic of conversation. We would talk about them on the bus coming and going. The Club had its own bus. This made it possible to get there, since we lived across the Bronx at Nelson Ave and 172nd St. We had to walk to PS82 at Macombs Road to

get the bus, but that was all right, since we talked about boys along the way. When we got to the gates of Shorehaven and showed our passes to get in, our first glances around were to see which boys were in view. Teenagers have one-track minds.

How early in the morning we arrived determined whether or not we saw the tide coming in from the Sound. If it was, there would be a strong ammonia smell that out-did the chlorine smell of the pool. But we knew it would only last a short time, so it was tolerable.

To the right of the entrance were the locker rooms. The ladies' section was very large and went on for what

seemed forever. After the first year, we knew to reserve a locker room in a convenient location a year in advance. For the price of $75 per summer each, three of us shared a small cubicle which contained a bench, a shelf above it, and hooks on the walls on which to leave our clothes. It had a dutch door so that we could talk to others while changing. The smell of dampness never left this area.

When we left the locker rooms, we would continue on, past the pool, to our special area. We would always find a batch of teenagers there.

There was a speaker over which music would play all day long. I remember Billy Eckstine singing, "From The Bottom Of My Heart Dear, I Apologize." Now that was music!

There were several sports that girls could participate in, but our favorite was preening for the boys. This could be done while playing tennis, volley ball, shuffleboard, or while swimming. But always, we were watching out of the corner of our eyes for - you're right- boys.

Shorehaven Beach Club, a haven for teenagers, as well as adults and children.

On Wednesday nights Shorehaven had square dancing. Since there was a late bus to take us home, we would usually attend. On Wednesday afternoons we would spend a couple of hours in the locker room area, showering, setting our hair, and putting on nail polish. Then we

Continued on page 8

Patriotism On the Bronx Front - Pg. 6 • Growing Up With Mah-jongg - Pg. 12

From the Editors...

CLINTON '61

Much has happened since the last time we published. We now have over 10,000 subscribers to **Back In THE BRONX**. Subscribers are coming from referrals, gift subscriptions, and the publicity that has been generated with a front-page (Metro Section) New York Times article that appeared on February 12. Not only did it appear in New York, it was carried all over the United States as well as in Canada. For those who didn't get a chance to read it, this issue will give you a chance to see it, as well as read a letter from a Bronxite mentioned in the story.

It appears that a major publisher will be printing our just completed book about the Bronx in the 40's, 50's, and 60's. As soon as we get an official commitment, we will pass this information on to our readers. We are very excited about this development.

We are also happy to report that WLIW Channel 21's nostalgic television program entitled **NEW YORK THE WAY IT WAS: THE BRONX** will air several times during the month of August 1996 (beginning the week of 8/5) on Channel 21 which is carried by most cable carriers in the NY Tri-State area. Channel 21 will also broadcasts as a UHF television signal throughout the same viewing area for people who don't have cable. It reaches 18 million homes!

TAFT '62

The one hour program contains the voices of many ordinary Bronxites and those of the following celebrities: Colin Powell, Phil Rizzuto, Dion DiMucci, Shari Lewis, Robert Klein, Red Buttons, Mavin Scott, Judd Hirsch, Ed Kranpool, Geraldine Ferraro, and Mal Z. Lawrence.

The program will air in three acts. The basic content of each act is as follows:

ACT I   The power of memory, in particular, the nostalgia and significance of having grown up in the Bronx, general apartment life stories from around the Bronx, the year-round activities played on the roof, living in Parkchester, on the Grand Concourse or in Riverdale, the NY Yankees during Ruth and Gehrig years.

ACT II   Stickball was king, street games, riding our bicycles throughout the Bronx, the public schools we went to, singing on the street corners, getting in trouble, the significance of the church and the temple in the community, anecdotes about working and community life, the NY Yankees during the 40's and early 50's.

ACT III   Movie theatres, the Loew's Paradise, going to Krum's, music and dancing at El Tropicana and the Hunts Point Palace, family and fun and stories from the Botanical Gardens, the Bronx Zoo and other Bronx parks, summertime fun at Orchard Beach, Shorehaven and the Castle Hill Pool, Freedomland stories, the NY Yankees of the 50's and early 60's, closing lines about what our memories of growing up in the Bronx means to our lives today.

As always, if you have a friend, neighbor, or relative who might be interested in **Back In THE BRONX**, please give us their name and address and we will be happy to send them a free copy. Any requests can also be made through our toll free number:

1-800-7 BRONX 5.

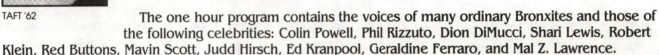

CHECK OUT OUR INTERNET ADDRESS:
http://www.inter-net.com/bronx

Stephen M. Samtur &
Susan J. Samtur
Editors

Back in THE BRONX

A number of the photographs in **Back in THE BRONX** are courtesy of and are available from the Bronx Historical Society.

Publishers & Editors:	Stephen M. Samtur	Clinton '61
	Susan H. Samtur	Taft '62
Contributing Editors:	Barbara Fasciani	Roosevelt '65
	Martin Jackson	Science '58
	Sandra Zuckerman	Jefferson '57
	Al Zuckerman	New Utrecht '50
Art & Production:	Ellen Grodjesk	
Printed By:	Trumbell Printing, Trumbell, CT	

I Married TWO Bronx High School of Science Graduates!!

By Ellen Rothman

The other day at breakfast I glanced through your magazine **Back In THE BRONX,** and enjoyed seeing the photos of Jahn's ice cream parlor and Paradise Theater. Having always considered myself a Bronx girl, I was surprised to turn the magazine over to find that it was addressed to my husband, Bronx High School of Science, Class of '52. "Oh," I exclaimed, "I almost forgot you're a Bronx Science Graduate too." "What do you mean *too?*" my husband, the NYU dentist asked. I said, "Fred (my ex-husband) also graduated from Bronx Science." "Oh," he said smiling, "So you marry only Bronx Science graduates!" I grinned and thought to myself that he's right and my high school sorority sisters would be proud of me.

I can remember what it was like dating when I attended Columbus HS on Astor Avenue in the Bronx. It was a very innocent time; there was no confusion for a Jewish middle-class girl from the Bronx. We lived the original phrase, "just say no." It was a time before the pill, before legal abortions, before traveling to Europe or living on your own, before unmarried girls had any of the options they now have.

We formed a sorority in high school. Actually we were eight girls who met in a basement of Ronnie Klar's house. My best friend Marion Bleir joined. We decided on a Greek name and each of us chipped in $3.00 so we could make up gold pins with Greek letters to wear on a neck chain. Meeting eligible college guys in the Bronx ment going to frats or to house parties which all seemed to have the Greek letters Kappa in them. You wouldn't want to go to these alone and ruin your "reputation," hence the formation of the "high school sorority." There was safety in travelling in a group. My dad knew exactly what I was up to. Every Friday before I was ready to leave to meet the other sisters he'd say "be careful." I knew he ment not just crossing the street. It was a reaffirmation of all the silent scripts my parents had planted in my mind through the years.

The really rich college boys belonged to Zeta Beta Tau or ZBT (Zillions, Billions, Trillions) in an elaborate house on Andrews Ave. near the NYU Heights campus. We never got invited there. Instead, I remember descending into a cave-like basement structure near Fordam Road. Once inside, there was always a large dark room with couches along the wall, couches that, in another life, had belonged to some guy's mother and even she had decided the slipcovers had become too worn. The music played on a hi fi with 33 1/3 speed records. The sounds of Johnny Mathis' "In the Still of the Night" filled the air. Through the night some lucky sisters got asked to dance; other remained on the couch talking to each other pretending it really didn't matter and they didn't care. After dancing, some drifted into other rooms while others just gave their phone numbers out hoping to upgrade to a Saturday night date. It was always very dark and every guy said he was either a pre-med or an engineering student. I had my qualifications: no glasses or corduroy pants. At the end of the evening we took the City Island bus home. We got off at White Plains Rd and Pelham Pkwy in front of the Globe Theater still complaining about what a waste of time it had been, about what jerks the guys were and still trying to decide where we could go next Friday.

If you had a date, it was always Saturday night and you dressed for it. I had a black sheath dress, black peau de soie pumps and a faux pearl necklace which I thought was very sophisticated and stylish. Except for a date who took me to the Peppermint Lounge in New York City by train, we usually stayed local. If a guy from Brooklyn dated a Bronx girl, it meant she was something special. Most times girls from the Bronx were GU—"Geographically Undesirable" to Brooklyn guys.

Dating usually meant going bowling or going to the movies. The movies in the Bronx meant the Loew's Paradise. I remember the beautiful

Continued on page 18

3

The Metro Section

The New York Times

"The Cuddies"

8-16-'41

ABOVE LEFT
The cover of Back in the Bronx, a kind of resource guide for finding former New Yorkers.

ABOVE
Stanley Getzler, bottom row left, is a stockbroker who was friends with . . .

LEFT
. . . Lenore Simon, top row left. Now a California artist, Ms. Simon shared Mr. Getzler's sled in the borough's bygone days.

Going Back To the Borough

Former Bronx Residents Reunite in Myriad Ways

By RACHEL L. SWARNS

Before the Cross-Bronx Expressway ripped through the old Jewish neighborhoods, and before Spanish replaced Yiddish as the lilting chatter of Old World grandmothers, there were Rosanne and Myrna, Myrna and Rosanne, the inseparable duo of Eastburn Avenue.

As little girls they crunched on five-cent sour pickles, choked on bootleg cigarettes and swiveled their skinny schoolgirl hips to "Rock Around the Clock," the best of friends in the Tremont section of the Bronx in the 1950's.

But as young women they were swept apart by the 1960's suburban exodus that emptied their neighborhood of working-class Jewish families. And when they started searching for each other decades later, the hunt turned up only dead ends. Their community had simply vanished, pulling up its businesses, its temples, its people, its roots, and leaving for the suburbs and beyond.

Last year, after months of hopelessly poring through New York phone books, Rosanne Gordon decided to try something new: she placed a classified advertisement in a historical magazine that helps to reunite people who once lived in the Bronx.

"Looking for Myrna Landau, Marlene Rosenberg and Barbara Keglovitz from Eastburn Avenue," wrote Mrs. Gordon, a 53-year-old legal secretary who now lives in Spring Valley, N.Y., in the ad that appeared in the September issue of Back to the Bronx. "Myrna, remember dancing and playing mah-jongg at the Palace Hotel in Rockaway?"

A stunned Barbara Keglovitz, now Barbara Colozze, read Mrs. Gordon's ad in Chester, N.Y. She had an 18-year-old address for Myrna in California. And so it was that on Dec. 24, 1995, Myrna Landau, now Myrna Abramowicz, received an unexpected letter.

"I started reading and I burst into tears," said Mrs. Abramowicz, now a 52-year-old real estate broker in Napa, Calif., who called Mrs. Gordon first thing Christmas Day. "My childhood had just sort of disappeared because I had not been able to keep in contact with these people. It was like 35 years had gone and all of a sudden, there was a huge gap in my life.

"Now, Rosanne and I, we're talking on the phone every week, giggling about the same things we used to, talking about the men in our lives," said Mrs. Abramowicz, who plans to fly to New York in April to visit her old friend. "It's as if we never left Eastburn Avenue."

Across the country, former New Yorkers who were part of the suburban exodus from New York City of previous decades are trying to reconnect to communities they never thought they would miss. And in finding old friends and reliving old memo-

Continued on Page B4

Ex-Bronx Residents Go Back to the Borough

Continued From Page B1

ries through periodicals and other vehicles like the Internet, they are rediscovering lost parts of themselves.

In Corona, Queens, church newsletters connect people who have moved to such distant places as North Carolina and Georgia.

On Staten Island, a column called "Inside Out" in The Staten Island Advance often reunites expatriates living in New Jersey and on Long Island.

In Los Angeles, an annual newsletter called The Eagle — modeled after the one-time Brooklyn newspaper of the same name — also runs a classified section to reunite former residents of Brooklyn and other boroughs.

And on the Internet, a Bronx mailing list connects former neighbors, high school classmates and others who describe how their Bronx memories still bring them comfort.

"My best friend often goes back to 2042 Morris Avenue when she can't sleep," wrote Sharon Chernoff, a 48-year-old social worker who left the Bronx in 1968, in a recent E-mail letter.

"In her mind, she walks up the flight of stairs, noting all the apartments on each landing and recalling who lived in them — then she finally makes it to her apartment on the top floor and walks through the rooms as if it were yesterday," wrote Ms. Chernoff, who now lives in Visalia, Calif. "This relaxes her and helps her to sleep. I, too, have tried to do this and find some measure of comfort in 'going back home.' "

But back in the 1950's and 1960's, when thousands of Jews, Irish and Italians were leaving the Bronx, many thought they would never look back. They were taxi drivers and janitors, mailmen and small businessmen, struggling their way out of the working class and determined to live in quieter suburbs. Many also fled fearful of the growing numbers of blacks and Hispanics, many of them much poorer, who were moving in.

The result: The Tremont section of the Bronx, which was 95 percent white and overwhelmingly working-class in 1960, was transformed into a mostly poor community that was 88 percent Hispanic and black by 1980, according to census data analyzed by William Bosworth, an associate professor of political science at Lehman College.

Now as the decades have passed and their Bronx accents faded into ordinary New Yorkese, many expatriates from the borough have found themselves longing for the past. With children grown and friends scattered, they have found themselves lonely and isolated in anonymous suburbs, nostalgic for the days when one city block seemed to encompass the whole world.

In those days, calling a friend meant shouting from an apartment window, not using the telephone. Fun was a 25-cent movie at the Loew's Paradise Theater, where the stars twinkled in the movie-house ceiling and fat goldfish wiggled in the gurgling fountains. A trip from East to West Bronx was an adventure then, and a trip "downtown" — to Manhattan — often involved wearing a tie.

"Leaving the city to become middle class seemed so desirable in the 1950's that people didn't have time to think through what kind of changes in life style it would bring," said Steven Gregory, an assistant professor of anthropology at New York

University who has studied the impact of movement on social networks in communities like East Elmhurst and Corona, Queens.

"What it meant was severing ties with a culture of the block, a small-scale, face-to-face culture with long-term networks of family and friends," Mr. Gregory said. "By reconnecting with that memory, that shared experience and those people, they feel they're becoming whole again."

Nearly 1,000 people have turned to Back in the Bronx to find old friends over the last four years. The publisher, Stephen Samtur, who left the Bronx for Yonkers in 1972, says about 200 have been reunited.

Stanley Getzler, who moved to Manhattan in 1956 and became a successful stockbroker, found Lenore Simon, the little girl who used to share his sled on snowy afternoons as they careered down Kingsbridge Road. Mrs. Simon, 67, now works as an artist in San Diego, Calif.

And Jackie Stopsky, who moved to Dumont, N.J., in 1964 and became the executive director of a trade association, found Enid Boyarsky, the little girl who used to accompany her to the old Alexanders' Department Store on Fordham Road. Mrs.

Stoop-sitting, only this time the stoop is the Internet.

Boyarsky, 60, now works as a sales representative for a vitamin company and lives in Ardsley in Westchester County.

In November, the two women met at a restaurant for the first time in 32 years. They talked for so long that the waiters had to ask them to leave at closing time.

"We couldn't stop reminiscing," Mrs. Stopsky, 61, said. "When I hear her voice, I close my eyes and I'm 14 years old all over again."

It is a memory world they return to, sugar-coated and sepia-toned, and largely free of the painful recollections of Bronx life. Some people simply forget the families of five crowded into one-bedroom apartments, the ethnic rivalries among Irish, Jewish and Italian neighborhoods, and the unpleasant circumstances that surrounded the endings of some friendships.

One man, who placed an advertisement in Back in the Bronx searching for his old sweetheart, found her only to discover that she was still bitter about their breakup 40 years ago.

And perhaps the greatest irony of all is that while many Bronx expatriates eagerly travel back in time, they rarely visit their former borough. For many, the Bronx is an alien and forbidding place filled with strangers who look and speak differently than they do. Over and over again, the old-timers repeat the mantra: The good old days are gone.

But Mr. Samtur, the 52-year-old publisher of Back in the Bronx, says he believes the good old days continue even now, and that his magazine will still meet a need for the coming generations. A physical education teacher in the Bronx schools until 1980, he said he has seen today's children teetering on mounds of snow, screaming with joy.

"The buildings may be gone and the faces may look different," Mr. Samtur said, "but the feelings are still the same."

Jackie Stopsky, left, and Enid Boyarsky, reunited through a feature in Back to the Bronx, met recently in Dumont, N.J. Nearly 1,000 people have turned to the newspaper over the last four years to retrace the steps of old friends.

Chris Maynard for The New York Times

My Heart Never Left the Bronx

Jacqueline Stolow Stopsky, Taft 1952

A phone call from "The New York Times." It must be someone soliciting for a subscription. It must be a wrong number. No, they said, they want to know about my reunion with a long-lost friend and the publication Back In THE BRONX.

Let's start at the beginning.

I have subscribed to **Back In THE BRONX** for about 2 years and have enjoyed reading the "personals" although my name had never appeared. No one was looking for me. I decided to place an ad which read "Jacky Stolow Stopsky and Jim Stolow are alive and well. Would like to hear from old friends." The first contacts were for my brother Jimmy. He was reunited with the "guys" he played basketball with in Claremont Park on East Mt. Eden Avenue... Harvey Wasserman, Marshall Bloom, Marvin Berger. A letter came from someone living in California who knew Jimmy. A call from Carol Ball who lived on Topping Avenue and knew Jimmy. No one was looking for me... yet.

About two weeks after that issue came out, I received a letter in the mail. Enid Hochwald Boyarsky was my friend from the time we were kids. Our parents were friends... way, way back in the Bronx. Our mothers had a Saturday afternoon Mah Jongg game. Of course, the "kids" had to find something with which to amuse themselves while their mothers played Mah Jongg. If we could afford it, we went to the Loew's Paradise. If we had no money, we spent hours in Alexander's hat department trying on hats and pretending to be movie stars. After all, we were only 12 or 13 years old and pretending was close to being "the real thing." Enid Hochwald Boyarsky wrote in part ... "Glad you're alive and well. Please call me as soon as you can."

I did. We met. It was wonderful.

Then, came the call from The NY Times. Rachel Swarns said she wanted to do a feature article on **Back In THE BRONX** and specifically on reunions. Excited? I was overwhelmed! She interviewed me and then called my friend Enid and interviewed her. We were going to be celebrities... our 15 minutes of fame.

I guess she interviewed other people ... but for Enid Hochwald Boyarsky and Jacky Stolow Stopsky, this was our big hurrah. The Metro section published on February 12. I got calls from four people I hadn't seen or heard from in about twenty years.

It just seems that as we grow older, we want to remember fondly all the good things in our past. Rachel Swarns asked me why it was important for me to find old friends. I said nostalgia is what made the TV show "Brooklyn Bridge" so wonderful. That program and its realistic set looked like everybodys apartment house ... whether it was in the Bronx or in Brooklyn. It was *my* house at 315 East Mt. Eden Avenue.

It's that same good nostalgic feeling when we "connect" with our past. We remember the secret things we did and the places we went that we thought our parents did not know about. Who remembers being told that mothers had eyes in back of their heads and could see us no matter where we were? I smoked my first cigarette in a friend's bathroom when her parents weren't home. Her mother knew, and I found out later that my mother knew too. We couldn't figure out how they did. Eyes in the backs of their heads. I now live in Dumont, New Jersey. Have been married to the same wonderful husband since 1952. We have two great sons and the most brilliant, beautiful four year old grandaughter. Yes, I'm alive and well and would love to hear from you. ∎

Going Back To the Borough
Former Bronx Residents Reunite in Myriad Ways

Patriotism On The Bronx Front In The Korean War

By Michael Bobkoff

Michael Bobkoff is curriculum chairman for liberal arts and humanities at Westchester Community College in NY. His father was the owner of Bobkoff's department store.

On June 25, 1950, the arrived forces of communist North Korea, led by about 100 Russian-made tanks, crossed the 38th parallel in a massive surprise attack on South Korea.

For the next three years, until a truce was finally signed at Panmunjom on July 27, 1953 to end the Korean War, United States and other United Nations forces battled the North Korean and Chinese Communists.

My friends and I were Bronx second graders on that June day when the war started, and we were thrilled and proud because the American Military again defeat an evil enemy. We were, after all, totally caught up in the post-World War II national pride and military self-confidence fostered by Army parades down the Grand Concourse and by comic books and films.

Those parades on Memorial Day in the late forties had been the high point of our year. The soldiers marched north on the Concourse all the way from the Yankee Stadium area to Edgar Allan Poe Park.

We waited expectantly at Poe Park, standing on tip-toes and jostling each other for position, as we picked up the first distant sounds of the approaching drums. Then, where the Concourse emerges from beneath the Fordham Road overpass, the huge brown wave appeared, led by a color guard of four flag-bearing soldiers. So wide was this brown sea, so prestigious was this ever-extending brown tongue emerging from the mouth of the tunnel, that we concluded that the entire U.S. Army must be right there.

Suddenly concerned, we wondered who was guarding the rest of the country.

Just as baseball players sometimes toss baseballs to kids in the stands, some soldiers threw spent bullet shells to children along the parade route. These trophies were more valuable to us than any baseball card, more desirable even than an Imperial yo-yo, which cost $1.

Parades and comic books feed a second grader's enthusiasm.

Our military enthusiasm was equally fueled by the comic books that we bought each week at a drug store on Kingsbridge Road. In the early part of the Korean War, the comic books were still fighting World War II. Huge German Tigre tanks were incapacitated by clever G.I. foot soldiers; large squadrons of Japanese Zeros were decimated by far fewer American fighter planes. Once in a while, an American was killed.

Soon, the Messerschmitts became MIG's, black German crosses turned into red Russian stars and Asian faces belonged to new uniforms. The message we received for our dime was still the same: The American military was both just and invincible.

War films conveyed a similar message. Not even popular television such as "Howdy Doody"; "Tom Corbett, Space Cadet," or "Captain Video," introduced by the rousing Flying Dutchman Overture of Richard Wagner, appealed to us as much as those films.

The RKO-Fordham was our favorite theater, and we went there nearly every Saturday.

We never knew that it was possible to find out the starting time of a film and thus see it from the beginning. As a result, nearly every Saturday afternoon we paid a quarter, arrived somewhere during the film, watched the end of it, then the next film, then a cartoon, serial, newsreel and coming attractions before finally seeing the beginning of the original film.

One time, absolutely by chance, of course, we arrived at the very beginning of a war film. American anti-aircraft gunners were rushing to their battle stations as two Japanese planes menaced from above. This was good. Clearly, there would be plenty of action in this film. But to the Americans surprise — and to our great disappointment — the planes did not attack. Instead, they dipped their wings in a strange salute and flew off.

The Americans soon learned that the war had just ended. For us, this was not good. It did not matter what the rest of the film might be about. We were so let down, we left the theater

Patriotism
Continued from page 6

immediately and went to play punchball in Poe Park.

A few occurrences chipped away at the idol of war that we kids worshipped, nudged it a bit but couldn't topple it.

At Public School 46, for example, we began to have air-raid drills. We crouched under our sturdy, brown wood desks, our personal protection against A-bombs. Because of two very bad Americans, we learned the Russians did have A-bombs.

At school, we also received dog tags with our names and addresses on them, the very same tags our heroes, the G.I.'s had in the comics and films.

I still have mine. Our teacher never told us why we needed them, but we understood that if the North Koreans or the Chinese or the Russians bombed our school, our mothers would want to identify us. Strangely, though, mothers themselves never got dog tags.

Soon yellow and black air-raid shelter signs appeared and proliferated throughout our neighborhood. There was one in the basement of our apartment building on the south side of Poe park. My mother explained that we would have to go there if we got bombed, but someone else added that the radiation would kill us anyway.

Those foreboding situations not withstanding, my two best friends and I hurried down Valentine Ave. to the RKO-Fordham one Saturday afternoon to see the latest war movie. The film was the best we had ever seen.

It filled us with such patriotic fervor, such desire to be a soldier, that we rushed out of the theater, made a sharp right turn, and ran in our Keds and PF canvas sneakers one block west on Fordham Rd. to the Concourse where two identical recruiting stations faced each other, like guards on each side of the Concourse overpass.

Gateways to the nation's wars. When we arrived there after our dash from the RKO we entered hesitantly and respectfully as we would a church. One represented the U.S. Navy and

the Marine Corps, the other Army and Air Force.

The amused officers in both stations gave each of us a handful of glossy brochures and we rushed home to look at them.

Opposite the elevator in my building were rows of mailboxes for the tenants. Too young to have my own key, I would always stop and peek through the holes of our mailbox to see if we had mail. Standing in front of the mailboxes, a tiny, grey-haired, well dressed woman was crying uncontrollably.

I had never seen a grown-up cry before. Her tall son stood next to her and stared at an open letter. "I never thought I'd be drafted," I heard him say as I entered the elevator, my recruiting brochures tightly clutched in my hand. "I never thought I'd be drafted."

The doors shut and I ascended to my apartment, where my room waited with its toy-soldier collection, war comics stacked near my bed and carefully built plastic models of the laser jet fighters. ∎

Underage in the Bronx
By Frank Schmidt

There was the time when we figured that we would pull off a major coup. Paulie's folks were out for the evening and his house was free. We'd order a keg of beer from the local distributer and ask the Parkchester girls to drop in (imports, if you will.. we were in Pelham Bay, but Parkchester girls were oh so cute.) Nothing to it. Charlie would make the call to the distributor because he sounded good on the phone. The keg would be delivered to Paulie's house and we would have a party. The Parkchester sweethearts would be invited from the infamous Parkchester "Oval." It took a pretty good party to get them on the train and "hoof it" to Pelham Bay. But what the heck, the keg of beer would make the difference. Charlie will make the call. "This is Mr. Blah Blab, I would like to have a keg of beer delivered to blah blab blah." Charlie was real steady. How could anyone question his resonating voice? (he was our Walter Cronkite..) It looked like a great evening ahead. Summertime and beer and the girls from Parkchester. Who cares if we were sixteen? We were beer drinking vets anyway. Holy Name meetings assured that.

Charlie makes the call.. He really sounds good. He orders the keg. The guy on ther other end of the phone, at the last minute asks Charlie his age. Just a formality.. Charlie says eighteen. (Eighteen? That's too close..) Sounds fishy to the distributor. He says to Charlie, "Is your father home?" Charlie says "Yes" and looks at Chick. The distributor says, "Put your father on." Charlie hands the phone to Chick. The guy on the other end of the phone says to Chick, "How old is your son?" Chick says "Eighteen." The distributer quickly asks Chick, "How old are you?" Chick says, "twenty one."

Party's over folks... Cancel the call to Parkchester.

Now it's just another summer evening hanging out on the corner. What an evening it could have been...∎

Reminiscing

Shorehaven
Continued from page 1

would put on our "square dance outfits," usually poodle skirts and two piece matching sweater sets on which our initials were embroidered. Shorehaven supplied music and a caller, and we had a great time, especially if we met someone "interesting."

On Saturday nights there would be a vaudeville-type act, which usually included a comedian. That summer I saw Myron Cohen do his impression of two old men meeting on a street corner (he played both parts), and Buddy Hackett doing his Chinese waiter routine. They were great.

The following summer I started working and never went back to Shorehaven, but the memories will live on forever. It was a wonderful part of my past. ■

Shorehaven circa 1950

Remembering...SHOREHAVEN BEACH CLUB

By Joan Altman Schmulson

Going to Shorehaven, located at the end of Sound View Avenue, was where I enjoyed the best summers of my teenage life; especially after going to two all girl schools: E.B.B. and Walton H.S. - the social life at Shorehaven was wonderful and I met and dated many boys from there. I have only the best of memories when I think about Shorehaven.

- Wednesday night squaredances
- Saturday night social dancing
- Moonlight swims
- The sundeck
- Largest salt water pool in the East
- Miss Shorehaven contest
- Ping pong, shuffleboard, paddleball, handball, tennis & volleyball tournaments, Swimming races
- Season passes with a new picture each year
- Leo, the cafeteria and cherry cokes
- Barbecues in the back near the sound
- Lockers, showers and gorgeous life guards
- Snack bar and baby bar and baby pool
- The field house

- Card tables and mah jong
- Chair bins and roller skating
- Mini petting zoo and playground
- Indoor four wall courts
- Big diving board in the middle of the pool where the lifeguards put on a show at the end of each summer
- Singing "There is No Haven Like Shorehaven" at the Shorehaven Follies
- Mrs. Goodstein who always came once a year to say hello to all the members
- Doctor Goodstein who always said, "As long as there is a Goodstein alive, there will always be a Shorehaven." (Unfortunately, Phil, his son, was a "Badstein.")
- The bandstand, the good shows and great entertainers
- The plants and flowers we all took home at the end of the season
- The Fisano brothers who kept the grounds clean and who made sure everyone behaved
- The summer one of the Fisano brothers shaved his head
- Dance lessons and exercises

More Shorehaven? See ad MP 1089 on page 25 **8**

REVISED

Bronx Honor Roll
Bronxites Who Have Achieved!

BRONX SCIENCE
Harold Brown
Stokely Carmichael
Leon Cooper (Nobel Prize Winner))
Bobby Darin
Edgar Doctorow
Sheldon Glashow (Nobel Prize Winner)
Jeff Greenfield
Russell Hulse (Nobel Prize Winner)
Ronald Lauder
Nita Lowey, Representative
Arno Penzias (Nobel Prize Winner)
William Safire
Melvin Schwartz (Nobel Prize Winner)
Steven Weinberg (Nobel Prize Winner)

CARDINAL HAYES
George Carlin
Rocky Colavito
Kevin Loughery
Regis Philbin

CHRISTOPHER COLUMBUS
Robert Abrams
Anne Bancroft
Christine Jorgenson
Alan Landsburg

DEWITT CLINTON
Don Adams
Nate Archibald
Richard Avedon
James A. Baldwin
Martin Balsam
David Begelman
James Caan
Paddy Chayevsky
George Cukor
Avery Fisher
Arthur Gelb
Judd Hirsch
Robert Hofstadter (Nobel Prize Winner)
Stubby Kaye
Al Kelly
Theodore Kheel
Robert Klein
William Kunstler
Burt Lancaster
Garry Marshall
Jan Murray
Basil Paterson
Charles Rangel
Richard Rogers
A.M. Rosenthal
Daniel Schorr
Dolph Schayes
Neil Simon
Larry Storch
Marvin Traub
Jimmie Walker
Fats Waller
William Zeckendorf

EVANDER CHILDS
Red Buttons
James Coco
Mercer Ellington
Carl Reiner

MONROE
Jules Pfeiffer
John Garfield
Hank Greenberg
Ed Kranepool
Leon Lederman (Nobel Physicist)

MORRIS
Angel Cordero
Herman Joseph Muller (Nobel Prize Winner)
Gabe Pressman
E. Colin Powell

ROOSEVELT
June Alyson
Chazz Palminteri

TAFT
Sanford Brown
Eydie Gorme
Stanley Kubrick
Mal Z. Lawrence

WALTON
Bella Abzug
Gertrude Elion (Nobel Prize Winner)
Rosalyn Yalow (Nobel Prize Winner)

OTHER NOTABLES
Joey Adams
Danny Aiello
Robert Alda
Corazon Aquino
Armand Assante
Herman Badillo
Lauren Bacall
Ellen Barkin
Mario Biaggi
Joey Bishop
Alfred Bloomingdale
Bobby Bonilla
Teresa Brewer
Ralph J. Bunche (Nobel Prize Winner)
George Burns
Cab Calloway
Diahann Carroll
Carmen Cavallaro
Samuel Clemens
Myron Cohen
Betty Comden
Cardinal Cooke
Avery Corman
Norman Cousins
Bobby Cremins
Don Criqui
Tony Curtis
Ossie Davis
Dennis Day
Ruby Dee
Robert DeNiro
Dion DiMucci
Art Donovan
John Foster Dulles
Erik Estrada
Fernando Ferrer
Geraldine Ferraro
F. Scott Fitzgerald
Art Fleming
Joe Franklin
Arlene Francis
Frankie Frisch
Edward J. Flynn
Rita Gam
Stan Getz
Rudolph Giuliani
Samuel Gompers
Aldolf Green
Richie Guerin
Steve Gutman
Armand Hammer
Moss Hart
Herbert A. Hauptman (Nobel Prize Winner)
David Horowitz
Vladimir Horowitz
Irving Howe
George Jessel
Billy Joel
Raoul Julia
John F. Kennedy
Robert Kennedy
Ted Kennedy
Theodore Kheel
Calvin Klein
Edward Koch
Fiorello LaGuardia
Bert Lahr
Jake LaMotta
Louise Lasser
Ralph Lauren
Ron Leibman
Lee Leonard
Joe E. Lewis
Shari Lewis
Hal Linden

Vince Lombardi
Melissa Manchester
John Mariani
Penny Marshall
Willie Mays
John McSherry
George Meany
Mario Merola
Glenn Miller
Sal Mineo
Hugo Montenegro
Robert Morgenthau
Gary Morton
Richard Mulligan
Paul Muni
Bess Myerson
Gil Noble
Carroll O'Connor
John O'Hara
Charles Osgood
Al Pacino
Jack Palance
Floyd Patterson
Joseph Papp
Joe Pesci
Roberta Peters
Mary Pickford
Ezio Pinza
Edgar Allan Poe
Seymour Posner
Richard Price
Vincent Price
Tito Puente
Charles Nelson Reilly
Rob Reiner
Regina Resnick
Victor Riesel
Edward G. Robinson
Monte Rock III
Franklin D. Roosevelt
Theodore Roosevelt
Billy Rose
Howard Safir
Jonas Salk
Isabel Sanford
Martin Scorcese
Marvin Scott
George Segal
Connie Selleca
Jose Serrano
Sylvia Sidney
Carly Simon
Stanley Simon
Vince Scully
Isaac Bashevis Singer (Nobel Prize Winner)
Curtis Sliwa
Wesley Snipes, Jr.
Cardinal Spellman
Sy Sperling
George Steinbrenner
Henry Stern
Pat Summerall
Renee Taylor
Mother Teresa (Nobel Prize Winner)
U. Thant
Arturo Toscanini
Dan Topping
Leon Trotsky
Lloyd Ultan
Jerry Vale
Bobby Van
Luther Vandross
June Valli
Jackie Vernon
Fran Warren
Del Webb
Jerry Weintraub
Vanessa Williams
Herman Wouk
Vic Ziegel

Thanks to Dr. William C. Wolfson and the Bonx Society of Science and Letters

9

Reminiscing

Jackson Avenue— "A True Melting Pot"

By Chet Wargocki, Morris '43

Starting from the Jackson Avenue station, the El structure headed north via Westchester Avenue up to Prospect Ave, and westward again over the Westchester Avenue trolley line down to Third Avenue (The Hub) eastward toward Prospect Avenue again, and south down to 149th Street. This was the area where I grew up.

We had Greeks, Polish, Irish, Germans, Jews, Italians, Blacks, Hispanics and others who gravitated to this area of the South Bronx during the 20's and 30's and well into the 40's. Most were apartment dwellers with a smattering of private homes interspersed here and there. We were exposed to many diverse sounds, smells, and sights. At times you could hear the clippity-clop of horses' hooves as they trotted over the pavements, as well as the blacksmith's hammer beating down on white-hot horse shoes.

You could bring home groceries from a Kosher deli, goodies from the appetizer sidewalk stand or shop. Italian delicatessens, Casselli and Larosa located 152nd Street off Jackson Ave, provided pungent smells from their many varieties of cheeses, salamies, etc. We had German bakeries, and the greatest Jewish bakery of it's day, Hecht's, near the corner of Wales Ave. Hecht's had several portly sisters who were uncanny in their ability to cut the exact weight of rye bread that you requested from the formidable 4-pounders. Brun's ice cream parlor was located at the foot of the uptown side of the Jackson Avenue station. If your clothes needed tailoring, cleaning and pressing, these were available, so were shoemakers, a Chinese laundry, candy stores, houseware stores and an early version of an A&P. Garages with vacancies were not rare either. Automobiles were not permitted overnight parking on the streets and during the day, traffic was light to moderate-allowing for many street

The Silver Top Cafe, Jackson Avene, Southward, 1960's

games to be played with little interruption. Unfortunately, there were no well manicured parks to play in, the nearest being St. Mary's Park bounded on the north by 149th Street and the south by St. Mary's Street.

It is in this same vicinity there were synagogues which were more commonly referred to as "shuls." Baptist churches too. There were Catholic churches that were well attended. The Italians frequented St. Roch's, the Irish populated St. Anselm's, and the Polish faithfully walked to St. Adalbert's— a distant two miles away. For movies, the first-rate theaters were to be found in "The Hub" section of the Bronx with the National showing Warner Brothers' films and the Royal featuring R.K.O. pictures. Scattered throughout this neighborhood were many "second-rate" movie houses: the Lewis, the Congress, Arcadia, Melrose, Bronx Opera House, Oceola, Prospect, Empire, Loew's Victory and the RKO Franklin.

There was a "Cigar store," a shoe-shine parlor with a hat blocker in attendance, and saloons aplenty: The Silver Top Cafe (formerly Mike's), Boyle's, and around the corner from

St. Roch's, and Oleary's. Down on Third Ave., you could easily lose yourself in the multitude of busy shops where you could have visited Adam Flannagan's, Hearns, Pisers, Royal Furniture, Vim's, Davega's, Howard's, and the greatest concentration of five and dime stores. We had Woolworth's, McCrory's, H.L. Green, and Kresge's located between 151st and 149th Streets. You could eat in a Chinese restaurant for 35¢, go bowling, or skate in the streets without fear of being run over.

If you were inclined to take up boxing, you could visit Gleason's gym right next to the Rex Theatre. Meat packing houses dotted Westchester Ave. down close to Brook Ave. If you wanted fresh killed poultry, the Union Ave. shopping district off the Prospect Ave. station had Kosher meat markets with regular deliveries of still warm slain chicken or ducks where you could get them "flicked" for a few pennies. There were dairy stores that sold tub butter, measure of sour cream, eggs, cheeses of all kinds plus other dairy products.

For the economy minded, Robert Hall set up shop on Concord Ave. and

Jackson Avenue

Continued from page 10

150th St. St. Mary's park offered band concerts in their gazebos from the highest point in the park plus a playground for youngsters. Handball courts were set up along with tennis courts at no charge and in the 40's two baseball diamonds were established which got a lot of attention from both players and viewers, especially on Saturday and Sunday. St Mary's Park in the summer offered performances of comedy and drama courtesy of the Parks' Department. A large and long van would open it's side panels to produce a stage. You had to bring your own stool or bench for seating. Take a walk to the northwest and you had the public library. If you needed dry goods, shops were within easy reach. If you needed a softball, bat, hockey stick or a Spaulding (Spaldeen), "Cheap Albert's" was the place to go on Westchester Ave. A good place to cool off for 15¢ was the Prospect Pool near the Intervale Station. Transportation was no problem should you wish to visit Palisades Park in New Jersey. Trolley Cars with liberal transfer policies got you to 125th St. with a ferry across the Hudson River to Ft. Lee for only 5¢. The same mode of transport took you to Classon Point, an amusement park in the Bronx, Pelham Bay Park, Orchard Beach, City Island, Singer's Beach, German Beach, the Bronx Zoo, with it's Botanical Gardens. What was lacking?

As on winded his or her way up to his or her apartment, you could detect the fact that Mr. Fox had returned from his appetizer shop, or Mrs. Murphy's was preparing that stew or baking breads, or the unmistakable smell of Polish kielbasa in the pot, and the ever-pervasive odor of Italian cooking. This truly was a melting pot of nationalities. We hardly ever made the papers because people got along with each other just fine. This is not to say that we lived in a paradise, but it was relatively crime free in those days. Doors were kept open in the apartment houses to better catch a hallway draft during sultry days, while some brave souls slept on fire escapes or roof tops to catch whatever breeze existed. Few homes had fans, let alone air-conditioning. That came in the movie houses who first introduced it into wide spread use. Drop-outs were in the minority and so were college graduates. Helping with the family expenses was foremost on children's minds. Apartment house dwellers were a common sight when they brought down their folding chairs or benches to sit on outside to

We hardly ever made the papers because people got along with each other just fine.

enjoy the sun even on chilly days.

Produce stores were many, supplemented by horse-drawn wagons who fell prey to many an adventurous lad who hitched a ride to snare a 'tater or two. Drug stores in the neighborhood not only offered pharmacies but they also were the place for developing and printing film from your bellows or box camera. If you had something in your eye, or had splinters that were hard to remove, the pharmacist was happy to oblige you. Siegel's was such a drug store at the foot of the station. You had only to walk a bit north of the station to a florist, or an appliance store but if you needed to pick up that hot record, you walked down to the Hub and got your disc for about 37¢ with a packet of needles going for about 5¢. There was Lebanon Hospital that bordered on Trinity and Cauldwell Avenue. Lincoln Hospital was southward on Jackson Avenue. Empty lots were numerous in those days as they afforded some sandlot baseball or softball if they had some measure of evenness to play on. Streets were scenes for touch football and roller hockey as well as numerous slap ball games. These same lots were used for building campfires to roast those purloined 'taters or "mickies." The carnival came around each year and set up on these sites and were a great source of amusement with their games of chance, rides with calliope music, merry-go-round, ferris wheel, brite lights and refreshments. Like many neighborhoods in those days, coal deliveries by way of coal chutes were common; milk wagons and laundry wagons were still horse drawn not to mention movie houses that advertised its coming features with two large billboards leaning one against the other. Once in a while, this form of transport took its toll when the sight of a dead or dying horse made you turn away.

Merchants of all kinds knocked on your door trying to sell you meats, beauty products, subscriptions, insurance, policies, clothes, haircuts, etc. Back yards were the scene of some would-be singers trying to earn a few coins for their efforts. There were men soliciting your money for hooking up your clothes line and pulley, and buying used clothing. Occasionally from St. Roch's a parade would form and up Jackson Ave.

Our particular apartment house had a wonderful landlady who afforded her tenants awnings with which to cover windows that faced the setting sun. What a luxury! What a thrill to get the refrigerator that replaced "Tony's" 15¢ ice. Most laundry was done at home with boiling drums of water, starch for the collars, and ironing. Only special clothes were sent to the Chinese laundry.

Shoe stores offered a comic book, sponge ball, or paddle and ball with every purchase of sneakers or shoes. The "egg-cream" was a favorite at Miller's candy store as we perused the comic book rack much to the annoyance of the owner.

There is so much more to relate as this was such a wonderful neighborhood to grow up in. We lacked for nothing. It was a great time in our young lives. It was Jackson Avenue, a true melting pot in the South Bronx. ■

Reminiscing

Growing Up With Mah-jongg

By Stuart Roth

It was the late fifties and early sixties and their names were Ruth, Rita, Rozzie, Phyllis, Harriet, Pauline, and Mary. They were all housewives who had many things in common, one of which was a passion for the game of Mah-jongg. My family and I lived in the Marble Hill Housing Project

Marble Hill Projects, 1968

in the Bronx, an 11 building complex built in the early 1950's with public funds by the New York City Housing Authority There were similar versions built in Manhattan, Brooklyn, and Queens,. All of us simply called it "The Projects." You may have heard the term used before by Whoopi Goldberg in many of her comedy routines. We were lower middle class families, whose fathers worked mostly in blue collar professions, (mine drove a Yellow Taxi), and whose mothers stayed home and raised the kids and took care of the house. These were simple times. Front doors were rarely locked and the biggest crime was kids playing football on the grass island in the middle of "the projects."

If you happened to be the house that hosted the Mah-jongg game for

the evening, there was a whirlwind of activity during the afternoon. There was vacuuming to be done, floors to be washed, books and magazines to be put in their proper places, lest the hostess be accused of not having a "clean house." My mother always cleaned the house but it seemed to me that the effort on "Mah-jongg nights" was much more focused. If you were the oldest child in that house, many of those chores fell on you. I was the oldest and had to take out the folding bridge table, and the four folding chairs from the closet, move the coffee table in the living room out of the way, and setup the table and the chairs. By the way, if you were wondering, of course we had plastic slip covers on all the Living Room furniture. If your family was not fortunate enough to have a second television in a bedroom, you couldn't watch T.V. that night. If your father had a choice, he worked late, went bowling, or went out with his friends that night. Unfortunately, we kids did not have that option.

Four of my friends' moms would show up around 8:30 PM and they would play until around midnight. The approved dress code was a "duster" with large front buttons, two side pockets, usually purchased at Alexander's on Fordham Road in the Bronx. Shoes were open toed slippers of leather, or most likely vinyl and usually pink, green or blue. A small change purse weighted down one duster pocket and might contain a pack of cigarettes for those who smoked. My earliest memories of the Mah-jongg games were the shouts of "one Bam," "two Crak,"

"Soap," "Dragon" and, the always dreaded, "Mah-jongg." These cries stayed in our ears and subconscious well into the night. The end of game was particularly noisy. This was when the tiles were dumped from racks, similar to Scrabble racks and then all the tiles were mixed around to be picked for the next game. The layout of the apartment itself made it almost impossible to sleep during a Mah-jongg game when the women were slamming down their tiles. As if the noise of the game itself wasn't enough, the conversation amongst the moms was endless. The topics covered every subject under the sun, but very rarely touched on politics. If you really listened intently from our bedroom, you heard the latest gossip about every so-and-so in the building. All the mom's in my mother's game were high school grads, almost no one had attended college. For the most part, I would say they were very happy with their respective lives. Money, or the lack thereof, was always a concern, but there was a roof

---

My earliest memories of the Mah-jongg games were the shouts of "one Bam," "two Crak," "Soap," "Dragon" and, the always dreaded, "Mah-jongg."

---

over our heads and food on the table, and Mah-jongg.

Perhaps one of the most interesting aspects of being the house that hosted the game, was the rare appearance of a bakery cake, candies (M and M's), peanuts, and certain kinds of soda purchased just for the "Mah-jongg" moms. It was forbidden to touch any of the above, until the appearance of the first guest mom. The "goodies," as we kids called them,

Mah-jongg

Continued from page 12

were placed strategically around the living room in "crystal" candy dishes that were used only for this special occasion. If you were really lucky, and the moms didn't eat all the goodies, your mom let you have the leftovers the next day after school.

One event related to the game itself occurred annually. This was the arrival of the new National Mah-jongg League Card. Members received it in the mail prior to its availability in the local card shop. The rooms would wait each day by the mailboxes, in the lobby of the apartment buildings for the card's arrival. As soon as one of the moms received the card, a game would be convened for that evening, "no matter what." The first person to win a game using the new card would be the "celebrity" all evening long. The talk for the rest of the night would be about all the new hands.

The other special event I remember was the purchase of a new Mah-jongg set by a game participant. This was cause for a major celebration in the group. The new set was examined and carefully unpacked, so as not to damage a single tile. Even though each mom usually had her own set, the new set was used no matter whose house the game was being played in. The tiles were either made of very hard plastic or, if you could afford it, the set was made of "ivory."

The invitation to a particular Mah-jongg game was very important in the Mah-jongg social strata of the building in which you lived. Players were ranked as really good players, middle range, and beginners. The games at all levels tended to be "closed" to outsiders. Some moms played in several different games, during the week, while others played in the same game every week. If you got invited to the "special" game, you made every effort to participate. Failure to do so, would probably mean you would not be invited again, even if there was an

opening on a particular night. The continuity of a particular group over many years, was very typical. The stakes were relatively small, with none of the moms losing or winning more than a dollar and change each evening. In some of these groups money was set aside from each game, maybe a quarter, and was saved for an outing later in the year. My mom's group always managed to see a Broadway show, from the "pishka" money.

Many years have passed since I last heard the tiles and the shouts. All the families moved away and some of the moms got into new games where they now lived. Unfortunately for the moms who remained, the games were never quite the same. My mom and her friends used Mah-jongg to freeze time and cultivate life-long friendships. Although I poke fun at their passion, I have come to realize how important the game was not only to the moms but to me personally. How else would I have learned about life and how else would I have ever tasted Strawberry Short Cake?

Thanks mom. I love you. ∎

The invitation to a particular Mah-jongg game was very important in the Mah-jongg social strata of the building in which you lived.

Back in THE BRONX

IT'S YOUR MAGAZINE.

Subscribe or Renew Now!

Please fill out the form below to subscribe or renew your subscription to Back in THE BRONX. And while you're at it, think about what a great gift it would be for another Bronxite, a friend and especially, a relative. We'll even acknowledge your gift with a card.

____ 1 Year subscription(s) to **Back in THE BRONX** - $19.95

____ 2 Year subscription(s) to **Back in THE BRONX** - $29.95 **($10 Savings)**

____ 3 Year subscription(s) to **Back in THE BRONX** - $39.95 **($20 Savings)**

____ (12) Complete set of back issues for just - $39.95 **($20 Savings)**

TOTAL DUE $ _____

FREE JAHN'S MENU

All those who subscribe or renew for *two or more* years will receive a laminated replica of a vintage **JAHN'S MENU.**

COLLECTOR'S ITEMS

ALL BACK ISSUES

The complete set (12) of out-of-print back issues of **Back in THE BRONX** *PLUS* Jahn's Menu all for just $39.95 **(while they last)**

Please complete information below and send payment to:

Back in THE BRONX, Box 141H, Scarsdale, NY 10583

❑ New Subscriber   ❑ Renewal   ❑ Back Issues Requested

Name _____ (Maiden) _____

Address _____

City _____ State _____ Zip _____

Phone # (_____) _____

H.S. Attended and Year Graduated _____

METHOD OF PAYMENT:

❑ Check ❑ Visa ❑ MasterCard   Total Amt. Enclosed $ _____

Card No. _____ Expiration Date _____

Use these lines to list the names and addresses of your gift subscriptions

1. Name _____
   Maiden Name _____
   Address _____
   City _____
   State _____ Zip _____
   Phone (_____) _____
   High School _____
   Year Graduated _____

2. Name _____
   Maiden Name _____
   Address _____
   City _____
   State _____ Zip _____
   Phone (_____) _____
   High School _____
   Year Graduated _____

   List additional addresses on a separate sheet

Walking Distance From Heaven

By Stan Friedman, Science '55

I don't know if I ever fully appreciated living within walking distance from heaven. I remember the many times, in the late 1940's and early 1950's, starting out from my apartment on Findlay Avenue and 165th Street and making the trek to the Grand Concourse, going through Joyce Kilmer Park, passing the Concourse Plaza Hotel. Then, down 161st Street toward Jerome Avenue, feeling the anticipation of the excitement that awaited me. Just being in the vicinity of Yankee Stadium promised adventure.

Usually, having started my journey after school, it would be about the 6th or 7th inning by the time I arrived at the ballpark. The gatekeepers were understanding of both the passions and limited finances of youngsters such as myself and, considering that it was already just about time for the "7th inning stretch," generously "looked the other way" when we "sneaked in." Then came the delicate task of locating a vacant seat, preferably one of the expensive boxes near the field, while at the same time avoiding the unwanted attention of the ushers.

It didn't matter whom the Yankees were playing, we just knew the Bronx Bombers would win. It seemed a distortion of destiny whenever they lost. After all, could there possibly be any better ballplayers in the world than Jerry Coleman, Billy Johnson, Johnny Lindell, Joe DiMaggio, Charlie Keller, Yogi Berra, Ed Lopat, Vic Rashi, Phil Rizzuto, Allie Reynolds?

Yet, even more exciting was collecting their autographs. In those days, there were no autograph signing sessions for a fee! It's not likely that any player would have been taken seriously if he charged for his autograph. Most were happy to sign your book or sepia-tinted picture card and chat with you. Collected autographs were never sold, although duplicates might be traded for a needed one. I have so many fond memories of my "adventures" and of the lengths we went to getting autographs.

Jerry Coleman used to "thin out" the crowd of youngsters following him by running up towards the Bronx County Courthouse. Those that were able to keep up with him were rewarded with a signing and some conversation.

Bobby Brown (later the President of the American League) was always busy, when not playing, studying his medical texts (he later became a physician; it's interesting that his roommate was Yogi Berra, who was usually busy studying his comic books). So, to please his fans, Bobby's mother would stand outside the stadium after a game and hand out, to those aware of who she was, slips of paper which he had already signed.

The thrill of spotting Joe DiMaggio! To avoid the mobs seeking him, Joltin' Joe would often wait until most of the autograph seekers and other fans had already gone before leaving the stadium. By the way, statistics don't tell the full story. I don't think I've ever seen a more graceful outfielder in my life. He made the most difficult plays look easy AND graceful. Thinking of him now, reminds me of the time when, waiting outside Yankee Stadium after an All Star Game (or was it a World Series game?), I spotted Dom DiMaggio (a great player in his own right) in the crowd, waiting for his brother. He was gracious and accommodating, and I valued his autograph for many years.

I still enjoy baseball and, having since lived in a number of cities across the country, have rooted for several other teams. Yet, nothing will ever compare with or replace the innocent, yet exciting memories of ...

...the Bronx Bombers and "The House That Ruth Built."

SUMMER "RUNNER"

By Anne Flatcher, Evander '56

In the Fall of '57, I was a sophomore at Hunter College and had just spent the summer working in Alexander's Department Store. I was a "runner" in the refund department. Remember us? You would bring your ticketless returns to the Refund department and we would "run" from department to department trying to locate the manager so he or she could "identify" the article and write down the necessary numbers and the price. That is where I first learned that without a ticket you had to accept the current sale price. It was also the beginning of a long retail career which culminated twenty years later when I opened my first store. BUT, the training that I received, and the "schlepping" that I did throughout Alexander's, was an experience I shall never forget. After all, I got to meet all the young hand-

> **Did anyone have it better than I? I think not! Hunter College by day, Alexander's by night. Orchard Beach on the weekends**

some male buyers, assistant managers, stock boys, etc. I remember one evening "bumping" into Ralph Lauren near the men's department. (I really did run) I hate to mention this but .... he was not a looker...not somebody you would turn around and look at twice. But I was and am tall, (haven't shrunk yet) so my first impression of Ralph was the top of his wavy brown head. Guess what? I should have looked again! So much for hindsight. If my memory serves me correctly, Mr. Ivan was manager of the refund department on the third floor. Since the store closed at nine o'clock and we wouldn't accept any returns after 8:45 p.m. (my last run), needless to say, there was

ALWAYS that one customer who complained loudly that she had waited for an hour in line and couldn't come back the next day.

So there I was learning the difference between the wholesale and regular price and the markdown price from the sale price from the promo price. So what is a "shicksa" doing in a place like this? Who better to learn retail from, than Alexander Farkas? Well, as it happened, that year Mr. Farkas decided that in the interest of promoting camaraderie among his employees, Alexander's was to sponsor a variety show at the Concourse Plaza. All employees were encouraged to try-out and I was one of the first. I believe there was a theme but it escapes me at the moment. Having danced for many years (Babe Landers school of dance) and being a frustrated Rockette, I became part of the chorus (the Alexander girls) that was choreographed by a professional dancer. Also, I had a cameo part in one of the store scenes. I was one of two "freeze models" who appeared in the mock window scene, with our backs to the audience until the end of the skit when suddenly, without warning, we turned around. The audience gasped so I guessed we were a hit. Shortly after the show I was promoted to salesgirl (as we were called) in the accessories department where I learned how to sell, inventory stock, write tickets and all that "good retail

Continued on page 18

17

Reminiscing

Summer "Runner"

Continued from page 17

stuff." I was no longer running, but then I was no longer "bumping" into the opposite sex. (a taboo word in those days). The accessories department was too close to the jewelry department and too far away from menswear. Alas! I never saw Ralph again but it must have been love at first sight because I contributed to his success years later as I stood in a Polo store paying retail for that little horse.

Did anyone have it better than I? I think not! Hunter College by day, Alexander's by night. Orchard Beach (section 15) on the weekends! The Whitestone Drive-In on Saturday night! And "belly bombs" at the White Castle afterwards. By day, I met young, intelligent, Jewish boys, a few veterans (Korean War) who attended college under the G.I. bill and a few Italians, (John Falco where are you?). By night, in particular Friday night (Saturday night was "date night") I caroused at the local hangouts in search of Irish American lads. So where did a tall, skinny, BIC (Bronx Irish Catholic) go to meet Gentile boys? Blondell's on Tremont Avenue that's where! Blondell's, the home away from home for almost every Irishman in the East Bronx. Or, perhaps one would go to the Inwood Lounge in the West Bronx for starters. In the back room of Blondell's on a Friday night was the largest assemblance of khaki pants, white shirts and TIES, I ever saw. A retailers dream! Or was it a Brooks Brothers dream? If you were lucky enough to get past Vinnie Simpson at the door, then you walked into a packed bar, five to ten deep and were served by Ray Montgomery. Loud music, screaming voices, thick smoke, guys on the prowl, and giggling girls contributed to the ambiance. The front room was filled with regulars (serious drinkers) and the back room was reserved for the college crowd. In three years, the only time I wandered into the back room was to use the ladies room which was always an "at risk" venture. After midnight, some of the older crowd shifted down the street, to Roda's for more beer on tap with the added attraction of juicy hamburgers. Most of the time I arrived with and went home with my friends except on those rare occasions when I thought I had met Mr. Wonderful. (And I did ONCE). Standing on the corner after midnight waiting for the last bus to take us home, we never worried about being abducted, seized, kidnapped or the like. Occasionally, a group of guys drove by, whistled and asked if we wanted a ride home. Of course, we declined. As we emerged from the bus on Boston Road and Eastchester Road, still chattering away about who was with whom and...did you see the way she was dressed? and... did you see her flirting with...., we never worried about the late hour. How could we be in any danger?. This was "our neighborhood." (Hillside Homes). We were as innocent as the times. And still, I can't help wondering aloud, "Did anyone have it better than we? I think not!" ∎

I Married Two...

Continued from page 3

gold leaf chandeliers and live goldfish in plaster ponds in the lobby. I sat in the semi-darkness of the theater glancing at the constellations in the ceiling wondering if he'd put his arm around the back of the chair and then slide it onto my breast for a quick moment. I tried not to move and held awkward neck and back positions for hours.

We went home by bus. "Do you want to come up?" I asked knowing I was being forward but hoping not to have the evening end. The apartment was dark; we went into the living room. The sofa and chairs were covered in clear plastic slipcovers. A tree with plastic leaves reflected in the floor to ceiling mirror with gold sconces on either side. Wall-to-wall carpet covered the living room and hall area. I was lucky there were some peanuts and raisins in a dish left over from the Tuesday night mah-jongg party my mother hosted. I put on the TV tuning to a late night movie knowing full well we weren't going to watch it. We sat together talking more about our lives, our friends and our interests. Somehow our conversation always got around to the biology of human needs and male urges. I could hear the little voice telling me, "be careful." We maintained a thin line between lust and purity. The TV had long since gone to black and white static

when the station stopped broadcasting but we never noticed. In the midst of the soft moans, creaking sofa, sighing and muffled giggles, came the sound of banging on the wall. It was a return to reality. Time to button my blouse and straighten my skirt. It was my parents' way of saying enough already. I understood. He understood. We were good kids and we said good night. I went to bed with a smile on my face. He didn't wear glasses or have corduroy pants and of course, best of all, I found out he was a Bronx High School Graduate. ∎

GOOD OLD GEORGE, THE HAVEN MAVEN

By Richard T. Turner, Morris '42

169 Alexander Avenue

If you grew up around 138th Street and Alexander Avenue in the 1930s, then surely you remember George, the old gaffer who owned and operated The Haven, perhaps the most appropriately named movie house in the history of filmdom. For it truly was a haven for us ragamuffins who inhabited the south Bronx in those good old days. It was place to escape the grit and grime of daily living and to be, for a while, an explorer of lost worlds, a fighting ace shooting the enemy from the sky, or a soldier

> **THE HAVEN, PERHAPS THE MOST APPROPRIATELY NAMED MOVIE HOUSE IN THE HISTORY OF FILMDOM**

trekking across the sands of Morocco with the French Foreign Legion. And it was George who made all these dreams possible. For George was (and in fond memory still is) an unsung hero — a public-spirited benefactor of the human race as represented by the legions of dirty-faced, snotty-nosed, holes-in-their-shoes tatterdemalions of Mott Haven. And so I am moved to write this tribute to him now, these many years later. We begin by easing ourselves into the scene: It's 1935, a Saturday morning ...

... a Saturday morning, and even though my brother Mattie and I are early, we still find ourselves at the end of a long line waiting to get into the Haven. It's always like this on Saturday; every boy in the south Bronx is here.

There are two reasons for this: First, the Haven never shows any sissy movies; no Shirley Temple, no Jane Withers, no Fred Astaire and Ginger Rogers. Second, while the price of admission is supposed to be five cents

apiece, it is possible —with a sad enough song and dance —to get George to let you in two for a nickel. That way, you have the extra five cents to buy candy— from George.

George doesn't really care; he owns the Haven, and he gets all the nickels one way or another before the day is done. I guess he just likes the routine, which goes something like this:

With downcast eyes and a catch in my voice I say, "Hi, George. My brudder and me have only five cents. Can you let us in?"

"G'wan, get outta here. You know it's a nickel each."

"Yeah, but my mudder had only five cents to give us. Can't you please let us in? We have to find out what happens to Jungle Jim." If Mattie can force a tear or two at this point, so much the better.

Now George goes into his act. He puts on his best W.C. Fields rasp and speaks to all the other kids on line:

"Listen to this, my little chickadees. These two boys say their momma gave them only one nickel for the two of them. Is that enough to break your heart? They want me to let them in two for five. What do you say?"

Now the other kids — most of whom are going to give George the same line as Mattie and I — shout, "Yeah, yeah, let dem in. Dere holdin' up de woiks."

So George lets us in — and Mattie and I duck inside to find good seats about halfway down the aisle. We have our lunch with us, of course, because we'll be here for hours. At the Haven you get your money's worth: Three features like "Lives of a Bengal Lancer," "Little Caesar," and "Public Enemy," followed by at least one serial (right now, as you know, it's "Jungle Jim"), then a couple of "Felix the Cat" cartoons, a travelogue or two, and a newsreel.

When the seats are all filled and the doors all closed, the projectionist climbs up to the booth to begin the show.

The projectionist?.
You know. George.
... and so we thank you George, wherever you are. ∎

East 138th Street

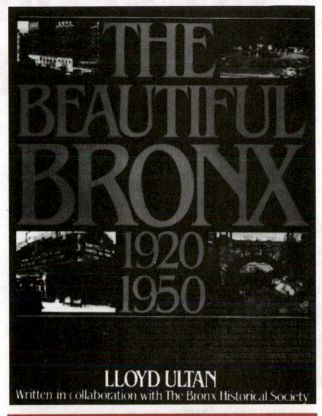

The Games of Youth

By Robert B. O'Connell, Clinton '38

Long before a growing boy learns "there is nothing like a dame" there is the time when he believes there is nothing like a *game*. And, from ages 10 to 14, love of a game prevented my learning to play the piano, caused me to meet and argue with Mayor Fiorello H. LaGuardia, and kept me from meeting newly elected President Franklin Delano Roosevelt.

The time was the early 1930's. The place: West 207th St. between Bainbridge and Perry Aves., which contained St. Brendan's School, and between Hull and Decatur Aves., where there was P.S. 56.

The game was stickball, played in the classic manner, in the center of a street, with a broomstick, preferably one fatter at the end where the broom was attached, and with a Spaulding, never called a "Spauldeen" by any of us then.

Spauldings, smallish and made of pink-rubber, were the balls of choice, for they were livelier, fit pitchers' needs better, and, carried further when hit squarely.

But Spauldings, which we bought one—at-a-time at the candy store on the northwest corner of 206th St. and Bainbridge Ave., cost a staggering 15¢ apiece, and had the nasty habit of splitting into perfect halves when caught on the seam by the end of the stick.

That was a princely sum during the Depression, since it cost only 15¢ on a Saturday to go to the Mosholu Theater on 204th St. or to the Bedford on Webster Ave., both offering a double feature, short subjects, a serial, and a newsreel.

The substitute ball just cost five cents, but it was larger, heavier, less responsive to the "English" pitchers put on it to deceive batters, and didn't carry as far when hit solidly. Further, it was possessed of its own nasty trait.

It often cracked or broke tapered broomsticks at their weak spots.

So there were agonizing sessions over which ball to play with, the Spaulding winning whenever we could add pennies and nickels and reach 15¢, or scrounge up the rarely discarded beer bottles, which had a two-cent return deposit, or quart-sized soda bottles, each good for five cents.

Three men to a side was the minimum—a pitcher, an infielder, and an outfielder, with each side providing a courtesy catcher. At times, we could muster a full six, provide our own catcher, and add another infielder and outfielder. Because of parked cars, telephone poles, hedges, and trees, ground rules were complicated and their interpretation a source of continual argument.

The games started right after school, lasted until dark or a summons from home called them, and were played in every season except winter.

My mother, whose small hands couldn't stretch an octave on the keyboard, had waited for my hands to grow before teaching me to play the piano.

Unhappily, this came at age 10, the very age at which stickball became my consuming passion.

Within months, my anguished pleas to be released to play

Mayor Fiorella LaGuardia (front row, second from left) at dedication of the Westchester Ave. Bridge 1938.

stickball caused her to decide that piano would never take root in my heart, and she yielded.

Daily, the games went on, played with an intensity and an excitement that I still retain, and led to my temporarily reviving the game here in suburban New Jersey some 25 years

ago. But also daily, complaints poured into the 52nd Precinct, on Webster Ave. and Mosholu Parkway. As a consequence, sometimes hourly, a police car swung into 207th St., scattering us down alleys or into a vacant lot, the game resuming as the police car, creeping slowly up the street, cleared the other end of the block.

Ordinary cars bothered us not at all. At the cry "car," we drifted to the sides of the street, waited for the intruder to pass, then drifted back to our positions.

However, one day a long, black car glided into our playing area, freezing us in our tracks without evoking the customary cry. For this was the menacing car of gangster movies, or the haughty vehicle of the Depression-era comedies ridiculing the rich, a formal chauffeur-driven limousine, out of which stepped Mayor LaGuardia.

Stunned, yet still ready to scram at a moment's notice, we waited as the five-foot-tall Mayor advanced. (Later, upon entering high school, I was only four-foot eleven.)

"Boys," he squeaked, in the high, scratchy voice we knew from radio and the newsreels, "I want to talk to you."

It was his practice, he said, to take time each week to visit police precincts in various parts of the city, and to read the blotters to determine the level of criminality.

To his surprise, he had learned

Continued on page 22

21

Reminiscing

Games of Youth
Continued from page 21

that the crime wave in the 52nd was "boys playing stickball on 207th St." He then sternly detailed the huge number of complaints, and the amount of police time involved.

"Oh, Mayor, it's all her fault!" we cried in unison, pointing to a private red-brick house with a small privet

265 East 207 Street

hedge in its front yard. "The lady who lives there yells at us all the time, and keeps the ball whenever it lands on her property."

LaGuardia asked why we didn't play in the nearby lot, looking directly at me, possibly because I was closest to him in size. "It was too hilly, too rough, too small, and only good for roasting 'Mickies'." Why didn't we play in the newly finished playground near P. S. 80 on the Parkway? "Couldn't pitch on the gravel; it was too small; and for little kids!" Faced with such unshatterable logic, and murmuring sympathetically that he would see what could be done, the Mayor climbed back into his limo, and departed.

The next afternoon, in the middle of a hot inning, a police car edged into 207th St., and, as we moved toward our escape routes, stopped dead in the middle of the street.

Ignoring us completely, two cops got out, opened the trunk, removed a heavy metal sign, the first of its kind we had ever seen, wheeled it on its base, and left it there.

As the patrol car drove on, we read in wonder that 207th St. had been declared a play street and was not open to "through traffic" during certain hours on weekdays, other hours on weekends.

In the meantime, the patrol car reached the Perry Ave. end of the block. There, the cops placed an identical sign.

Stickball may have altered the course of my life.

At that time, my grandmother was co-leader of Tammany Hall's famed Osceola Club, a Democratic headquarters in Manhattan.

The very nature of her role in organizing and getting out the vote meant she was well-known to Governors Smith and Roosevelt, to Mayors Walker and LaGuardia, to U. S. Senators and Congressmen.

And so, after Roosevelt was elected President, she was on the list of party officials invited to the President's family home in Hyde Park, New York, to receive his personal thanks.

Each invitee was permitted to bring a guest to meet the President; and

---

Stickball may have altered the course of my life.

---

my grandmother, for obscure reasons, possibly political (singling out one party contributor might offend all others), possibly out of family pride (the President would surely notice her clean-faced, well-mannered grandson), chose me.

The problem was that very Saturday was the day on which the annual stickball championship of 207th St. was to be decided.

The date and rules had been set in concrete. No excuses allowed—not sickness, dental appointments, parents' demands, vacations, and no last-minute substitutions from other teams, or ringers. Play with what you had—or forfeit. Only torrential rain at game time, could change the date. (It's a miracle we all didn't read for the law.)

As the pitcher for my team, a pitcher who could also hit "the long ball," I was begged, with all the fervor young boys could summon, not to let the team down.

The argument raged over a change of date, but there was no give. "Tough" was the opponents' rejoinder.

I also raged in my home, other parents wisely staying out of it. My mother was on my side, "Let Bobby play. You know what it means to him."

My father, having grown up in a home in which politics approached religion, argued with incredulity, "Isabel, the boy has the chance of a lifetime, to meet the President. Do you realize what that could mean to him in the future?"

Furthermore, he knew with dismay what his mother's reaction would be; it came memorably when my mother and I carried the day.

"I tell you, Arthur," my grandmother thundered, "by the time that boy is sixteen, he'll either be in a jail—or be a communist."

We won the championship. I can't play the piano. I have never been in jail, nor have I ever been a communist. My grandmother never forgave me. But I still carry the magic of "the game" within me to this day. ∎

[Author's Note: LaGuardia's limo surfaced during Mayor Koch's Administration when it was removed from storage for restoration and the Mayor's use. Controversy arose almost immediately, and the public's opinion was solicited. I wrote in favor. But the cost, which united do-gooders, who claimed better uses for the money, and political opponents, who did not want Koch to don LaGuardia's symbolic mantle, doomed the project.]

Missing Persons

MP1006 Reunion PS77. Graduating class '56. Were you in the special music class with Mr. Fleishaker and Ms. Shever? We are having a reunion and are looking for all members of the class who have not been found, including Sandra Tortonicci, Connie Utila, Jack Max, Samuel Webber, Leona Faber, Robert Piasonti, Leslie Kurtz. Please call 919 781 5857 or write to: 7912 Kingsland Drive, Raleigh, North Carolina 27613.

MP1007 Looking for Noonan Plaza gang. Morty Smithline, George Brokin, Nick Sciliano, Robby Gotsegan. From Bobbie and Stan Tuerk 908 536 4086.

MP1008 Stan Friedman, PS53, JHS22, **Bronx Science** '55. Findlay Avenue & 165th St. Ed Greengrass, Morton Winner, Authur & George Bressler, Harry Falber, Harold Skurnick. Love to hear from old friends. Call 813 938 1509 or write 1007 Caravel Court, Tarpan Srings, FL 34689.

MP1009 Jerry Resnick is seeking the whereabouts of classmates who graduated with him from PS50 in '51 (Mrs. Stahl's class) and JHS98 in '54 (Ms. Dolan-official class teacher).

MP1010 Dennis Over, 245 E. 236th St., Woodlawn, PS19, Grad '55. Would like to hear from old friends. Please call 516 261 0991

MP1011 I am looking for Rosemary & Ruthann Yrongman. My name is Ronny Stretch. My phone number is 718 225 2918. Please call before 9 a.m. - 6 p.m.

MP1012 Fat Ralph Gentile from 189th St. and Arthur Ave. Call or write me. Played ball at PS57. 201 335 6020

MP1013 Anyone from the South Bronx listening? St. Jerome'sPparish, PS43, Wilton JHS, **Dodge** '56. Some folks I'd like to hear from: Irene Hall, Elaine Wilson, Tom Clark, and othres whose names I can't remember.

MP1014 Anyone from Hunts Point, PS60 or 48 between '50-'54. Please call Arline (Sesky) 201 843 1414 (9:00-5:00) or 201 837 6796 after 6:00. If anyone found Rosalind Kleinbaum please call.

MP1015 Edward Tierney would like to hear from John or Kevin McCann and Jackie (Lee) or (Yee) who's father had a chinese food take-out store. They lived on Willis Ave. & 140th St. in the 40's and 50's. Call 407 225 3772.

MP1016 Irene Dorsky of Knox Place, where are you? This is your date for the JHS80, 9th grade graduation dance in '55. Are you still playing the trombone? Please call Donald Santamaria at 519 693 1039.

MP1017 Lois (Mandel) Myers looking for friends from Valentine Avenue, PS115, E.B.B., **Roosevelt '67**. Parents (Sam & Lenore) owned Mandel's Grocery on E. 184th St. Call 718 652 1570.

MP1018 Looking for my friends- we swam for **Evander's** fabulous Boys Swim Team, under Coach Mr. Gay in the early 60's. Mr Stern's homeroom class, and the rain-soaked football game at Randalls Island as **Evander** trounced Stuyvesant, with Ronnie Bianche (my pal) making some fabulous receptions in '61. Call John Binenbaum at 718 225 2011.

MP1019 Tom McConnell, Our Lady of Mercy '63, **Roosevelt** '68 would like to hear from old friends from St. James Park, Poe Park, school and neighborhood. Joe Borelli, Chris Langdoo, Steve Burns, where are you?

MP1020 Our group that grew up in Tremont Ave. area and LaFontaine Ave. (179th St.) are looking for Alfredo Giovani Casseiri. He was a fire fighter out west before going to college. Think he graduated from University of Florida and was in the Coast Guard. Any leads would be appreciated—Stella Dukas.

MP1021 Anyone from Band at PS45 during the time of Mr. Ingerman and Agelo Patri 1939-'42, please call John Pagliaro, drummer, at 407 467 9993. Would also like to hear from friends & customers of J&J Pagliaro Grocery, 187th & Crotona Ave.

MP1022 Looking for Elaine Greenberg, Anita Levine, Irwin Jay Solomon et. al. **Evander** '45, Brooklyn College and the old Bronx neighborhood friends. I've relocated to Southern California. The Bronx, Great Neck, Manhattan to Southern CA. Write to Barbara c/o this number.

MP1023 Ray Crapo (Hayes '54) a former teacher and Assistant Principal at **Evander** was President of the Bronx County Historical Society for 11 years. He now teaches both computer and health care management graduate level courses as an adjunct professor at Long Island University.

MP1024 Where is the crew from the Crosstown Diner in Throgs Neck? Jiggs, Red, Philly, '56-'57. Also anyone from E.178th St. and Southern Blvd. area.

MP1025 Barbara Fritz McCrum, Highbridge '41 to '60-Some of the best years of my life. Sacred Heart, Lowey Park, Ogden Theater. Does anyone remember "Anything for Thanksgiving." It must have been just a NYC thing. I loved the old days!

MP1026 Looking for friends of Sylvia (Dorin) **Roosevelt** '53, Hunter '57 and Arnold (Sheikowitz) Sherman, Wade '46, **Clinton** '48, CCNY '52. Write 155 Wailea Ike Ol. #10, Maui, HI 96753 or call 808 874 8742

MP1027 Denise Carusos Bendo would like to hear from former **Walton** '61 classmates: Pat Jones, Barbara Pegues, Lourdes Rivera and Maria Santana. Call 914 668 3420.

MP81028 Sol Silverstein is looking for Sam Boshes, Milty Feder, Henry Cohen, Buddy Witte, Harry Kleinman. Please call 305 653 2147 or write 130 NE 202 Terrace, N. Miami Beach, FL 33179

MP1029 Warren Tockerman would really appreciate hearing from all my friends living around 182nd & Concourse, PS115, Creston JHS '79 & **Clinton.** Would also enjoy having a reunion of my 6th grade class from PS115. Office: 908 671 4450. Home: 908 671 4141

MP1030 Lewis Aaronson formerly of Tyron Ave. & Wilkens Ave. Allan Kaplan would like to get in touch with you. Frank & Tony Forte of Crotona Park. Call 516 981 3413.

MP1031 Where are you Gloria Goldberg, Selma Scopp, Phyllis Friedman, Bunny, Murial Weinberg & Joan Dalugoff? It's been so many years. I'm Harriet Schwartz Bisordi, now living in SW Fla. I'd love to hear from you and the bunch of guys we knew & loved. I lived on Vyse Ave. between 172nd & Jennings until '54-5.

MP1032 Bernie Messinger would like to find a school chum from PS4. Her name was Marcia Bacher and she lived on 3rd Ave. and 174th St. If you know her whereabouts, please call me at 914 356 6784.

MP1033 Where are you Rochelle Stein, Helene Toledo, Royce Goldman, Myrna Rohhbot? Call 305 868 4823.

MP1034 W231st St. & Broadway. Love to hear from any of the Kingsdale Mice that played football with Sid Chayevsky in the early 1940's. Red Randles 516 653 6579.

MP1035 Gloria Hirsh, PS94 '49, JHS80 '52, **Evander** '56. Would like to hear from anyone who remembers me. I live in New York City.

MP1036 Barney Stopsky, **Monroe** '49. Who remembers Evergreen Ave. and Luigi's on Westchester. Where is the gang of guys from Watson & Boyton Aves? Would like to hear from you.

MP1037 Rick Herman. Grew up on Hull Ave. and Gun Hill Rd. Seeking friends from PS94, JHS80 '57-'59. Remember Sam's, the oval stickball, Skully, Loew's Paradise, David Marcus Theatres, Orchard Beach, Pleasantville Day Camp and the Yankees!

MP1038 Samuel B. Zinder, PS86 '48, Claflin Ave., **Clinton** '52. Anyone out there who remembers me?

MP1039 Seeking contact with Karon Gilbert, PS70, JHS117, **Music & Art** '64, Sarah Lawrence College. I believe she grew up on Teller or Morris Ave. Please call Michael Steinberg at 212 535 2401.

MP1040 Mike Werner, **Evander** '58. Grew up in the Eastchester Projects (Burke Ave.) Attended PS121, JHS13, **Evander**, Bronx Community College and CUNY. AA, BA, MA. Married 21 years to a Yonkers girl, two sons and I am a Material Management Specialist for the USPS in Philadelphia.

MP1041 PS4 class of '54 and **Roosevelt** '54. Murray's Sugar Bolw on Claremont Pkwy., Bronx House, YMHA on Fulton, Manny Grossman's Luncheonette. Anybody out there? Sammy Shikora, 1E Hemlock Dr. #157, Bayshore, NY 11706. Phone 516 666 7904.

Classifieds

MP1042 PS73 class of '39, **Clinton** Swim Team '42-'43. Anybody still alive? August Kellermann would like to hear from you.

MP1043 Merrily Pallas Mitnick, PS102 '54, JHS125 '57, **Science** '60, Queens College '64. Happily married Stan from GardenView. Currently Assistant Principal of CS150. Willing to share their experience with my students. Email: smitnick@1x.netcom.com

MP1044 The Isalene family counseling network. Helping people in the Bronx since 1981. Video therapy. Sam Coloman, family counselor and coordinator. Call 718 543 6151 for a brochure.

MP1045 Mel Tiger PS48 '47, **Science** '51. Remembers Temple Beth Elohim, Doley's Candystore, Furgatch's Deli, Kitzel Park, Loew's Pooner, Loews Blvd., Star Theater, pennies on trolly tracks, Hunts Point trolley, marbles, stickball, curb ball, candied apples. Lets hear from you.

MP1046 Anyone who graduated in '52 from Cathedral, or who worked for WEED TV in the 50's, and is reading this, please write and we can reminisce about "the good 'ole days."

MP1047 Hey, where's all the guys from Crotona Park East? We hung out at the candy store and played in the big park (we called it that). Remember the Indian Rock. Fred Weiner would like to hear from you.

MP1048 Fellow **Taftites & Clintonites** (circa '55) living in the San Diego area, please contact Evelyn Schwartz Luner or Len Luner at 16029 Cross Fox Ct., Poway, CA 92064 or Email us at: eluner@aol.com

MP1049 Old friends where are you? Bruce Fitell PS114 and 1275 Edward L. Grant Hwy, Walter Rubin **Taft** '64, Cliff Forstadt **Taft** '64. Anyone know Cyrill Cohen- prettiest girl on Anderson Ave? Write: Billy Birken, 302 Davie Road, Carrboro, NC 27510

MP1050 Susan (Rosenthal) Martin, **Walton** '58. Now at 720 Eagle Ave., Longwood, FL 32750. Phone: 407 260 5536. Looking for Joanne (Greenwald) Schoenfeld and Carol (Davidowitz) Kahn? Possibly both in Rochester, NY. or anyone who knew me. Reunions? Please contact me!

MP1051 Estelle Sherer (Hecht/Goldberg) is looking for Gloria Schein (Pincus), Ruth Wolfe (Hockstadt) and Gertrude Margolin - **Roosevelt** '46. Write to me at 6 Abbey Lane, Delray Beach, FL 33446.

MP1052 I would love to hear from Judy Berger, **Taft** '59. Myrna Cohen is looking for you. Call 212 876 6640.

MP1053 Richard Cohen, Townsend Ave., PS64, JHS117, **Music and Art** '54, married Maxine (Micki) Schwimmer, JHS22, **Taft** '63. Looking for old friends. 718 631 1770 or 212 602 0647

MP1054 Seeking Roy Cohen from Wilkins Ave. who moved to California. Please contact Howard Weinberg at 718 343 9859.

MP1055 Lee Bandh would like to find Florence Blumberg. She has a sister Clara and a brother who is a dentist. She graduated High School around '36.

MP1056 Anyone remember Lily Piccarelli, Albie Hoffman from 171st and 3rd? A cute alter boy from Our Lady of Victory- Jimmy? Met him again on Webster Ave. & 174th St.- but I was just married. Call Elaine Demaria at 201 927 6905.

MP1057 Gloria (Katz) Nelson is looking for Diane Ackerman from Marcy Place and Rochelle Sandler. I am looking for friends who went to PS64 from '45-'51, Wade 117 from '51-54, **Taft** '54-57. You can contact me at: 718 884 6684 or write 3800 Waldo Ave., Apt9G, Bronx, NY 10463.

MP1058 Vinny Restiro, PS89 '41-49 is looking for Wilma Mitchelle born 6/23/35. She attended PS89, **Columbus** '54 and lived with family, sister Jean, at NY Blind Institute on Pelham Pkway. Friends were Virginia & Ruth Adeirs. Please contact me at 516 728 6312

MP1059 Alicia Veras, **St. Helena's** '58 has 4 children, 7 grandchildren and her son Richard will become a priest on May 11th. He will say his first mass on May 12th in St. Helena's. Alicia is married and runs a surgeon's practice.

MP1060 Would love to contact Louie Coli, **Columbus** '41. How are you Louie? Edward Wasp would like to hear from you.

MP1061 1948 Jan/June **Columbus** Grads- Claire DeLafuente would like a 50 year reunion. I lived at 2455 Cruger Ave. (at Mace) Now in Phila. Any old members of Club America from Allerton, Olinville, Mace Aves.?

MP1062 Andrea Stone, **Columbus** '73 and Stephen Zuckerman, **Science** '71 looking for classmates. Also looking for anyone who knew Stones (Bernie, Milton, Rita, Derwin, Joe and kids) from S. Boulevard, Stebbins Ave., St. John in '30s-'50s.

MP1063 Mosholu-Montefiore Community Center, 3450 Dekalb Ave., Gun Hill Rd., Bronx 10467. We're still here and quite busy. If you played basketball as a young adult here or were involved in our other programs, drop us a line. Let us know where you're living so we can keep you informed about life in this part of the Bronx. Send it attention: Don Bluestone.

MP1064 To Stanley Adler, who lived on Knox Place was in the Air Force with Artie Goldstein. Get in touch with Arthur Goldstein in Tamaral, FL in Kings Point. 954 720 5040.

MP1065 Looking for Howie Sobel, PS102, JHS127, **Monroe** '62, also Diane Greenfield, Davidson Ave, **Taft** and her blond twin friends. Found Jeff Sandman, Sue Ellen Wilder and the Parkchester "Shuff" gang. Contact Ron Frank, P.O. Box 843, Katonah NY 10536.

MP1066 Gary Wasserman, Manida St, E231st, **Evander** '58 and Diane Wain, Arthur Ave., Murdock Ave., St. Gabe's '61 are alive and well in Albany, NY. Is there anyone out there? Call 518 785 8128.

MP1067 Cold Spring Village, Monticello 50's & 60's would like to hear from anyone who was at Cold Spring Village during the summers of 1950-60. Please call Neil and Allyn (Herz) Kanowsky at 954 726 0903 or write 1713 Coral Ave., No. Lauderdale, Fl 33068.

MP1068 Looking for Sherman Ave. friends '38: Shirley Levy, Millie Danowitz, Rosalie Lake, Bernie Levine, Bernard Loomis. Contact Seymour Sobel 203 661 0500 or 212 444 6000

MP1069 Sandy Bergman would like to hear from old friends. Westside, Eastside, Highbridge, PS11, **Clinton**, Wilkins Ave., Boston Rd., Nelson Ave., and Ogden Ave.

MP1070 Anyone having information about Irene Schreck, Fran Lupensky, Sherman Kimmel -last known address was Pelham Pkwy. Please contact Martin Herman at 800 345 0009.

MP1071 Howard Muchnick, **Clinton** '61 is looking for old friends from Davidson and Grand Ave and 181st St. and Creston JHS. Also looking for Steven Silverstein and Norman Abramson. Call 416 322 6613.

MP1072 Friends looking for reunion with Bonnie Rena Weiss. She lived on Sedgwick Ave, attended PS91, JHS115, **Walton** '52 and NYU. Brother-Robert, From Elayne, Laurel, Marcia, Ruth, Helene and Sandra. 212 861 1715.

MP1073 2929 Bainbridge Ave.- anyone knowing present whereabouts of members of the Donar family residing at the above address during the 1950's. Please calll A.W. Lyons at 516 352 2131.

MP1074 Mitch Badler, **Clinton** '48, retired from corporate PR, now a newsletter publisher. Looking for anyone from "Clinton News" 1946-48 era. Also other **Clintonites** with remembrances of those days. Anyone know what happened to Les Alberts, Bernie Lloyd?

MP1075 Members of the class of 1956, **Bronx Science**. Our 40th reunion will take place on June 23rd at The American Festival Cafe, Rockerfeller Center, 2pm. For more info contact: R.I. Glazer at 201 767 8119

MP1076 Helene Lynn (Glaser) Tobkes, **Taft** '61 is interested in contacting old friends from the 1955-60's time period. Please write: 251 Peters Ave, East Meadow, NY 11554-1528

MP1077 Steve (Horny) Hornstein, **Clinton** '62 looking for the guys or gals from Gerard or Walton Aves near Yankee Stadium: Roy, 3 Dannys, Steve E, Tommy. Call 201 763 5712 or write 91 Oakville Ave, Maplewood, NJ 07040.

MP1078 Jack Rosendale would like to hear from Diane Ferrara (Maiden Name) or Marie Furme or 2558 Grand Concourse 40's-50's. Please cal 718 835 4550 with any information.

MP1079 Looking for lost classmates from **Roosevelt** '53-'54, PS45 and friends from 185th St. & Southern Blvd.

MP1080 Howard Cooperman, Deputy Director, U.S. Customs Service, S. Florida. M. Cooperman, Chairperson, Reading Dept., Broward Cty, School Bd.

MP1081 Ethel Knig Weissman, **Monroe** '44, PS6 '40, looking for classmates, friends and reunion information.

MP1082 Stanley Reinhart, PS90 & PS53 graduated Public School '36. Maybe someone else is still alive out there! I hope- please write.

MP1083 Ethel (Allison) Perrino is looking for old friends from the East Bronx: Eleanore (Rauchelle) Walderman, Gladys Hladik, Eleanore Watson, Martin & Lois Kuch. **Roosevelt** '40

MP1084 Residents Hillside Homes in 50's. **Evander Childs** Graduates '56, PS78 '52. June '96 is 40th anniversary of HS graduation. Edith Lipman, Vita Dinen, Adele Zingarelli, Susan Kavesh, Barbara Bashark, Billy Andrews, Jay Strum, Warren Gluckman, Joyce Kleinman and Joyce Epstein.

MP1085 Looking for Rita DeMario from Washington Ave. Call your friend Rose at 914 428 1387. Anyone out there from or near 2023 Monterey Ave.

MP1086 Walter Bruckner, PS28, PS117, **Taft** '53. Living in Orange County, CA. Would like to hear from old friends. Please call 800 779 2506.

MP1087 Anybody seen Larry Gordon, Marble Hill Projects, PS122, JHS143, **Clinton.** If you have information please contact me: Les Klein (a.k.a. Leslie Klein)

MP1088 Trying to locate Irving Mamber of Pelham Pkwy. Last know address was Phoenix AZ. My name is Howie Pooler, 99 Rochelle St, City Island, NY 10464. Phone: 718 885 2288.

MP1089 SHOREHAVEN, by Gayl (Leibowitz) Teller. Illustrated by Joyce (Leibowitz) Muller. Recapture the days of Shorehaven Beach Club. Order from Mellen Press, P.O. Box 450, Lewiston, NY 14092-0450. $19.95 + 5 handling.

MP1090 PS46 graduates, **Walton** '46 graduate who lived at 2670 Valentine Ave. Father was a barber on E. Kingsbridge Rd. Mother (Frieda) was a dressmaker. Husband Ralph Kravtz is looking for Marty Sokol or Jerry Sokol.

MP1091 Mona Hollander, Briggs Ave., **Walton** 59, Hunter '63 is looking for any old playmates. Especially Joel Shofel, Mike Helft, Aaron Gold, Ocky Cohen, Hal Kleinman, Steve Sunderland, Howard Ubel. Would love to reunite! 212 772 6797.

MP1092 How about a PS8 Moshulu Pkwy class of '62 reunion? Remember Mrs. Wellman, Heinsingers, Berkson? Write Gary Brooks at 8 Camino A Las Esterllas, Placitas NM 87043-804

MP1093 Bob Crema is looking for friends from the 50's -60's from 196th St. and Jerome Ave. Danny McCarthy, "Chickie" Martin "Swede" Bobby Nilson, John McKeon. Make my day- please contact me: 914 362 8142.

MP1094 Looking to find: Evelyn Tanzer, **Taft** '46 and 4 **Monrovians** from '46. Laura Klein, Thelma Rothman, Ruth Hayden, Ethel Rosenberg. Contact Arlene Goldberg Rubinstein at 516 569 4935.

MP1095 Father Duffy Squires, Knights of Columbus honors Ken McLaughlin on his 50th Anniversary. Meet old friends and pay tribute to a special person. June 21st at Fordham University. For info call Kof C at 914 237 2747.

MP1096 Where are you? Members and friends of Club Paragon...Holland Ave. mid '30s, Eischel sisters, Holland Ave., call or write Murray Schneider, 688 Dickens Ave., Franklin Square, NY 11010 or call 516 481 7547. Clare and Moe Blatman from the Bronx and Spring Valley.

MP1097 Would like to find the whereabouts of Naomi Nacht fro PS53 '40-'43. Also any class- mates from that time frame. Contact Vito at 718 892 1209

MP1098 Klipper, **Monroe** '58 would like to talk with K. Lipper. I thought this might be a good way to contact my semi-eponym call 612 922 1553 or Email 2199@topcity.mn.org

MP1099 Joan (Desberg) Greenberg, PS86 was a cheerleader at **Evander** '50 and lived at 2709 Webb Ave. Living in L.A. and still close with Phyllis Jagoda, Marie Pantusco and Diane Levy.

MP1100 Bronx Tomboy would be interested in hearing from **Morris** grads. Now living in Florida. Several of us would like to form a **Morris** Club. My brother and I (Larry & Ellie Meshibosh) grew up on E. 170th St.- Freeman St. Sta. Call 954 452 3733.

MO1101 Looking for Peter O. Flood, **Clinton** '45, lost track of when he went to Korea, last known address: 730 E. 178th St. anyone who knows/ knew him please call me. "Rosie O'Grady" 914 472 0968.

MP1102 PS86 '48. **Clinton** '52. Claflin Ave between Kingsbridge Rd and Reservoir Ave. Sam Zinder 516 883 6226.

MP1103 Joe Puglieses looking for old friends from The Normandy, 170th St. and Walton Ave. and surrounding areas of Townsend Ave. and Mr. Eden Ave. Miss all the old friends- please call 516 884 4202 or write 1520 3rd St., W. Babylon, NY 11704.

M1104 Where are all the "Clip-ette's?" **Taft** '54. Call Edie 718 969 3419.

MP1105 Elliot Malis, **Clinton** '50 is looking for Friends from Grand Concourse and 182nd St. Lived on Creston Ave. between 181st & 182nd St. Lets get together, call 407 241 7311.

MP1106 Where are the Monroe Ave. Comets? Are any of you in Florida? If so, contact Whitey Lerner for old times sake.

MP1107 Wanted! Former classmates and friends of Marilyn Heller. **Taft** '49 and CCNY '53. Contact Marilyn Heller Wittenstein 1114 Solly Pl., Philadelphia, PA 19111.

MP1108 If there is anyone who graduated **Evander** '66- it's our 30th anniversary and would like to get together to discuss fond memories, please write to Mary (Unger) Zolfo c/o this magazine.

MP1109 St. Josephs, Bathgate Ave., Class of '55. It's been a long time. Let's renew old friendships. Contact Robert Iulo, 29A - E 34th St., Bayonne, NY 07002.

MP1110 Looking for fellow "Assorted Nuts" E.B.B.JHS '47-'49. Anyone knowing the whereabouts of: Joan Wolther, Phyllis Hafter, Shirley Blitz, Roslyn Grossman, Carol Edwards, Joan O'Grady, Ruth Jarmus, Joan Leopold, Angelica Mercurio. Please call Pearl 516 496 3554 or Marlene 718 776 7992 or Elly 914 761 4443.

MP1111 Where are all the **Morrisites** from '50- '55. Judy and Irv want to know.

MP1112 Would be great to hear from the Pelham Pkwy. crew. We would hang out by 2220 Wallace Ave, go to **Columbus** & play cards.

MP1113 Tom Farrelly was raised on 198th St and Pond Place. As expected, I never really made much of myself, but I'm still alive and well in the Bronx.

MP1114 Joel Buckstein attended PS33 '49'-'54. Looking for old friends- call 212 255 8400 especially Robert Stone, David Rubinstein. I grew up at 2564 Creston Ave. Want to relive some old memories.

MP1115 Lois Zittzer (Gerstein), **Taft** '56 lived on Selwyn Ave, now living in Flushing Queens, NY. Have 2 children-daughter 30 and son 25. Looking for Bunny, Manly, Ellen, Gail from PS70, Wade and **Taft**. Call 718 961 1953.

MP1116 Reuben Gutoff, **Clinton** '44 is looking for Gerald Cooper- class valedictorian and Marceline Horowitz -first crush. Also friends from Saxon Ave and Van Cortland Park South on the fence. Write 190 East 72nd. St, NY 10021 or call 212 734 9873.

MP1117 Joseph G. Masterson, PS65 '49 on 141st St, PS37 (Clark JH '52) and Central Commercial High '55, lived at 338 St. Ann's Ave, hung out with the Shamrocks (would like to hear from any of them) worked on Wall St. Was ordained a Baptist Minister in '59, now Pastor of church in Lancaster, TX. father of 5 and grandfather of 9. Love music, walking, fishing and reading. Going to Ireland this summer.

MP1118 Toby Brestin Heilbrunn, Wyatt St., **Monroe** '56, NYU is seeking Celina Berkowitz, Renee Farber, Judy Lesser, George Horowitz, Joan Greenberger and others. Living in Woodstock selling real estate. Divorced. 914 679 5438.

MP1119 Joan Ganis Kranitz would appreciate any info that might lead to the whereabouts of either twin- Myra or Barbara Klinger, **Bronx Science** '54. Please call collect: 513 885 2006.

Classifieds

MP1120 Mary Makein, PS46 '52. Would love to hear from former Briggs Ave friends: Beatrice, Roberta, Jack and John. Where are you? Lets meet at the Bronx Home News Store.

MP1121 Would love to hear from former Bronxites living in the Kansas City Metropolitan area.

MP1122 Thanks Emma for a great reunion! **Evander** '45 Judy & Sol.

MP1123 Looking for PS33 '47 grads: James Cavanaugh, Norm Leoy, Bari Hoffman, William NoMaso, Betty Suhr, Herman Jaeger, Audrey Goldman, Barbara Silverstein, Gladys Silverman, Sam Maniello, Francine Davis. Call 718 229 3275

MP1124 Looking desperately for my high school best friend. I miss her dearly- Janice Kitover lived on Post Ave. We also attended PS44 '64.

MP1125 Attention! If you lived in 1145 Boynton Ave and are between the ages of 48-56, I would love to see you again. Maria Golden Levy 516 822 4828.

MP1126 Marcia Altabet (Katz), PS26, 82, **Science** '65. Would love to hear from old friends, neighbors or classmates from Loring Place, Burnside Ave, University Ave. area.

MP1127 Joe Green, **Bronx Science** '55 (Joe Greenberg in the yearbook-Loring Tyson in the Senior Show) is retired and living in So. Calif. Any **Science** '55 classmates out here? Call 805 583 4082.

MP1128 Richard Wald is searching for members of JHS82 '56. Especially Miss Sheridan's class 9-1. Contact him at 718 868 1215 or 1210 Cornaga Ave, Far Rockaway, NY 11691

MP1129 Judy (Levy) Fischer would love to hear from classmates and friends from Crotona Park East, PS61, Ridder and **Morris** '62. As would my husband, Peter Fischer- friends from Mohegan Ave and **Stuyvesant** '60. Home #: 203 261 7841

MP1130 Looking for Julie Katz, **Clinton** '53. Weightlifter.

MP1131 George Thompson, PS87, PS68, **Clinton** '48. Ford broker, Santa Monica Calif. Lived on Bruner Ave. in Wakefield Section looking for friends from that area: Billy Ticho, DePugh Brothers, Rinaldi Bros.

MP1132 Dear Cookie (a.k.a Karen Wachtler) a good friend would love to hear from you if you're out there. Let me know. Call Toby at 914 833 3159.

MP1133 Hoody (Hilda) Kugler, **Morris** '46 and Bronx House, Married 44 years to Sam Kimbarow (Kimbarofsky) of Wilkins Ave. We live in San Diego. Call and say hello: 619 286 0154.

MP1134 JHS123 '56 is looking for Herb Landes. We had a lovely reunion about 5 years ago. The old Hebrew class missed you! You should have graduated **Stuyvesant** in '59 with Sukenick who's now in Texas.

MP1135 Mario Tolisono of 137th St and also of Ward Ave. Where are you? Baseball guys-The Hawks- Ray McClosky & the gang, Jose Betancount, Mickey Ryan, etc. Remember the egg creams and cherry cokes at Chubby's? Remember Chubby's daughter? Please get in touch!

MP1136 Where's everyone who was from Burnside & Andrews in the 40's and 50's. Where is the Messikian Bros., Jack Hubler, Rochelle Bloom, Bill Locascio, Frank Charmatz, Stan Finkental, Elena Rabine, Helen Kaplan, Sandra Goodman, Sylvan Curiel wants to know.

MP1137 Bob Minsky lived at 3440 Fish Ave., Hillside Homes from 1937-52 attended **Evander** from '48-52, PS78 from '40-'48. I'd really love to hear from the old crowd. Write: 1002 Curtis St., Port St. Lucie, FL 34983.

MP1138 Jerry Tennenbaum would like to hear from Margaret Zaroff of Olinville Ave., who met him at Camp Kinderland. Write Jerry at 85 Lutz Dr., Valley Stream, NY 11580.

MP1139 The Denizens of Popham Ave 174-176th St, circa '46-'54. Fax Irwin 954 427 1210 or Gary 407 369 8876 or mail Gary Linderman at 6043 Golf Villas Dr., Boynton Bch. FL 33437.

MP1140 Lois Zittzer (Gerstein) **Taft** '56, lived on Selwyn Ave. has two children-daughter 30, son 25. Looking for classmates: Bunny, Nancy, Ellen & Gail. PS70, Wade and **Taft**. Call 718 961 1953. Now living in Flushing Queens.

MP1141 Marvin Feinsmith is searching for Marty Holtzman from Walton Ave- my best friend from age 6-14, when we moved to L.A. and I lost contact with him forever.

MP1142 Don Van Raalte, **Monroe** '52, Fox St and 167th St., 3rd Ave and 173rd St. To talk about the Bronx or the NYC Teachers Pension Plan on which I am writing a book chronicling 33 years of experiences working for educators call me at 914 347 5352.

MP1143 Attention **Herman Ridder** JHS98 class of '54. Looking for names and addresses of former drama class members (Ms. Reibel & Ms. Rothstein's class) for a possible reunion. Write to Adolf Klainberg, 39 Great Jones St., Apt 4, New York, NY 10012-1136.

Contact Some Old Friends TODAY!

READER REPLIES

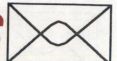

It is vitally important that you fill out the information below. Your input will be essential to the success of this magazine, tailored and inspired by you, the former "Bronxite". We thank you for your participation.

Subscriber? ❑ Yes ❑ No

YOUR NAME _____

ADDRESS _____

CITY _____ STATE _____ ZIP _____ PHONE _____

HIGH SCHOOL ATTENDED _____ YEAR GRADUATED _____

TELL US A LITTLE ABOUT YOURSELF,

(Be sure to include your alma mater, old neighborhood, your best memories about your days in the Bronx, (or anything else you can tell us).

_____

_____

_____

COULD WE SEND A FRIEND A FREE COPY OF BACK IN THE BRONX?

Do you know current or former Bronxites who would like to receive our magazine and reunion information? If you do, we'll be happy to send them a **free** inaugural issue of **Back in THE BRONX.**
Write to Back in The Bronx, Box 141 H, Scarsdale, NY 10583 or call 1-800-7-BRONX 5

Last	First	Maiden
Address	City	State — Zip
Phone # ( )	School and year of Graduation	

Last	First	Maiden
Address	City	State — Zip
Phone # ( )	School and year of Graduation	

Last	First	Maiden
Address	City	State — Zip
Phone # ( )	School and year of Graduation	

Last	First	Maiden
Address	City	State — Zip
Phone # ( )	School and year of Graduation	

COME BLOW YOUR OWN HORN DEPARTMENT

Please tell us about yourself (include your name)—about your accomplishments, awards, titles or works in progress. We're interested in hearing about them. List Below. _____

_____

_____

_____

_____

READER REPLIES

As a subscriber you are entitled to a FREE 40 Word Classified, Missing Persons, Blow Your Own Horn, or Personal Ad. Please write your ad below (if you are not subscribing to our magazine you can still place an ad in the next issue. The cost of an advertisement is 50¢ a word, there is no limit on paid ads).

_____

_____

_____

Is Your Mailing Label Correct?

In order to keep our database current, please correct any errors and place the label and or photocopy with corrections.

Account #	High School	Year Graduated
6817	Roosevelt	1958

Mary R. Flowers
123 Anystreet Blvd.
Anywhere, USA 12345

Change of Address?

If you're planning a move please attach your label corrected with your new address and the date that you will begin receiving mail at that address. This will insure that you don't miss your next issue of **Back in THE BRONX**.

Ordering Information

A Great Gift Idea! In addition to your own subscription, a subscription to **Back in THE BRONX** makes a great and unique gift. Fill in the form below and we'll process the order in time for our next issue. So, order your subscription NOW, and order one for a friend!

YES, I'd like to order the following items:

QTY.

___ 1Yr. (4 ISSUES) Subscription(s) to **Back in THE BRONX** $19.95
___ 2Yr. (8 ISSUES) Subscription(s) to **Back in THE BRONX*** $29.95
___ 3Yr. (12 ISSUES) Subscription(s) to **Back in THE BRONX*** .... $39.95   } *FREE Jahn's Menu
___ 4Yr. (16 ISSUES) Subscription(s) to **Back in THE BRONX*** $49.95
___ The Beautiful Bronx...........$25.00 (plus $3.95 S/H) $28.95
___ The Bronx: It Was Only Yesterday.....$25.00 (plus $3.95 S/H) $28.95
___ Bronx High School Reunion Weekend Video $29.95
___ SAVE MONEY - BUY 4 FOR JUST $99.00!
___ THE BRONX Tracking Service $9.95
___ COMPLETE HARDBOUND SET of all 16 past issues..$49.95 (plus $4.95 S/H)
      Order Now and receive a Jahn's menu & vintage Krum's photos from the 40's-50's for FREE!! $54.90
___ I would like to receive all available back issues and have them applied towards my subscription
      (To date we have 16 back issues available - While They Last!)

Please fill out completely and include shipping and handling where applicable for books only to: **Back in THE BRONX**, Box 141H, Scarsdale, NY 10583

TOTAL: $ _____

Please Print Clearly ☐ New Subscriber ☐ Renewal

Name _____

Maiden Name _____

Address _____

City _____

State _____ Zip _____

Phone (_____) _____

High School _____ Year Grad. _____

☐ AMERICAN EXPRESS ☐ MasterCard ☐ VISA ☐ Check ☐ Money Order

No. _____ Expiration Date _____

Signature _____

Back in THE
BRONX
Box 141 H, Scarsdale, NY 10583
Phone 914-592-1647 • Fax 914-592-4893

ADDRESS CORRECTION REQUESTED

Volume IV   Issue XV

Back in THE BRONX

CELEBRATING THE EXPERIENCE OF GROWING UP AND LIVING IN THE BRONX

Britain's answer to Marilyn Monroe

By Al Ramrus

Your "Bronx Honor Roll" is a terrific feature, even it tends to overshadow one's own accomplishments, especially after I read the names of all those Nobel Prize winners from my alma mater, the **Bronx High School of Science.** Just the same, though I have never won a Nobel Prize, and have no immediate plans to do so, I take some consolation in the thought that Nobel or no Nobel, I came within an inch of making Bronx history.

Here's how it all happened: After going through **P.S. 80, Bronx Science** and CCNY, and then a two-year stint as a police reporter in Canada, I returned to New York in 1956 at 26 and landed a writing job with a then comparatively unknown TV newsman, Mike Wallace. Our local "Nightbeat" show, with its karate interview style, swiftly went network where, to spice up the mix which leaned heavily toward guests like Frank Lloyd Wright and Adlai Stevenson, we also hooked Diana Dors. For those too young or too ancient to remember, Ms. Dors was an almost illegally blond actress fanfared by the media as

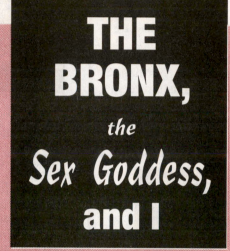

THE
BRONX,
the
Sex Goddess,
and I

Ms. Diana Dors

"Britain's answer to Marilyn Monroe."

Smart, unaffected, with a sense of humor about her steamy public image, Ms. Dors glided into our ABC studio for a Sunday morning taping, wearing a black evening dress that appeared to be having a good time clinging to its owner. Wallace, as usual, noticed something interesting but normally too personal for polite conversation: Diana didn't shave her long, well-shaped legs. Under the studio lights, they almost gleamed with a silken blond down.

"How come?" Mike asked her, fortunately off-camera. "I like them that way," she smiled.

I decided I liked them that way, too.

After the taping, I quickly volunteered to escort Diana back to her hotel in our rented limousine. And as the chauffeur hooked a sharp right onto Central Park West, she swayed up against me, her perfume drifted straight to the primitive centers of my brain, and I caught a flash, like summer lightening, of lush upper thigh.

Knowing that she was flying

Continued on page 6

Corners - Pg. 3 • The Nickel Palace - Pg. 5 • Allerton Coops - Pg. 11

1

From the Editors...

CLINTON '61

TAFT '62

This issue of **Back In THE BRONX** has been expanded to include many subscriber ads that weren't able to be placed in our last issue. We've also included a very large *Come Blow Your Horn* section this issue.

We hope that you were among the millions of viewers in the tri-state area and some parts of Florida fortunate to catch WLIW's presentation of *New York The Way It Was: The Bronx.* What did you think of their one-hour retrospective of the borough in the decades of the 30's, 40's, 50's, and 60's? Marty Jackson, a good friend and our Contributing Editor, was asked to do a review for us as he has done for many publications including The *New York Times.* His review can be found next to this editorial.

Do you have, or do you know anyone who has old Bronx menus such as those from Krum's, Addie Vailin's, Rushmeyers, Luhrs, etc., etc., etc.? We would like to borrow (or make copies) so we can share these fond memories with our subscribers. Okay, you may not all have old menus but everyone has a favorite candy store. Tell us about it so we can include it in our book. Simply complete the information that is on page 16.

As always, if you have friends, neighbors, relatives who might be interested in **Back In THE BRONX,** please give us their names and addresses and we will be happy to send them a free copy. Any requests may also be made through our toll free number: **1-800-7 BRONX 5.**

Sincerely,

Stephen M. Samtur
Susan J. Samtur

Back in THE BRONX

A number of the photographs in **Back in THE BRONX** are courtesy of and are available from the Bronx Historical Society.

Publishers & Editors:	Stephen M. Samtur	Clinton '61
	Susan H. Samtur	Taft '62
Contributing Editors:	Barbara Fasciani	Roosevelt '65
	Martin Jackson	Science '58
	Sandra Zuckerman	Jefferson '57
	Al Zuckerman	New Utrecht '50
Art & Production:	Ellen Grodjesk	
Printed By:	Trumbell Printing, Trumbell, CT	

New York The Way It Was: THE BRONX

WLIW - Aug. 6, 1996

By Martin A. Jackson

I'm sitting here with my "Bronx" baseball hat, with Dion on tape singing about the New York streets, and on my bookshelf are most of the books published in the last two decades about the Bronx. My copy of Lloyd Ultan's <u>Beautiful Bronx</u> is pitifully worn and dog-eared from hard use. So what did I think of WLIW's Bronx program? I liked it, naturally. But then, WLIW could have played the Bronx Tourist Board's video of Bronx attractions or rerun <u>Marty,</u> and I would have liked that too. The question really is, did WLIW contribute anything new to Bronx fans like me? Did this latest installment of the *New York The Way It Was* series measure up to the high standards of those preceding, and did it capture the special flavor and aroma of the Bronx streets during the 40's, 50's and 60's?

To answer this question I have to think somewhat harder. It's not enough to show some old films of the Grand Concourse or have Robert Klein make some sharp Bronx jokes. We all know, after all, that the Paradise had stars on the ceiling and that kids played stickball in the middle of the streets, and that candy stores made egg creams. For the couple of million of us who actually lived through those years in the Bronx, it was more than egg creams and the Concourse that made the experience so long lasting and so difficult to recapture in words. Here is where the magical power of the moving image comes into its own. By skipping over the barrier of words and fragmented memory, the films and still photos so skillfully arranged by director Roman Brygadere have the potential to bring those times to fitful life. Did he succeed?

I think for the most part, the venture is a rousing success, and Brygadere deserves our applause. Perhaps his outsider's perspective (he's from Long Island) helped Brygadere hone in on the essentials, and weave together the varied strands into a whole that makes sense even to Bronx veterans. There are the street stories and the bittersweet memories

Continued on page 21

THE CORNER

By Fred Baruchin, Ed.D.
Roosevelt '50

No way **Mt. Eden** or **Longfellow Avenues**. Not you either **Rochambeau, Elder, Hughes, Boynton, Walton**, or the others. You were nice places to visit occasionally, drive through, or date someone from. But there was only one Bronx center of the universe in the forties and fifties. And that was the southeast corner of **Belmont Avenue** and **179th Street**, in front of Herman's grocery store.

The corner was neutral turf where we celebrated good times and bad.

As we poured out of our apartment houses we invariably turned toward the corner, where we'd socialize, discuss, argue, commiserate, or just hang around. Herman was the original "chop buster," which doesn't mean he ran a butcher component to his store. Whenever one of us entered, we'd be greeted with the Yiddish revelation, "Seh failt dir a klepke in kopp" ("You've got a screw loose in your head.")

The barrel of sour pickles— the real McCoy —sustained us for a nickel each. And the pay phone booth inside allowed us to develop and maintain our love lives in private. When we'd come back from a Saturday night movie, we'd awaken the massive cat sleeping in the window of the darkened store. Then we'd draw a piece of string across the outside of the window causing the cat to chase it. The more he chased, the more boxes and cans he knocked over until the window display was in disarray. When Herman opened the next day he could be heard to exclaim, "What's the matter with you, you crazy cat?"

Herman and some of the guys

Mario Caputo was the de facto captain of the corner. When a "Spaldeen" was hit down the sewer, he'd authorize its retrieval. When he said, "All right, we'll let Freddy get this one," I walked ten feet tall.

It was on the corner that Mario probably saved Herman's life. Herman had came out indicating he was going home to lie down because of a vicious pain across his abdomen. Whereupon Mario rushed him instead to **Fordham Hospital** where Herman underwent emergency surgery for a ruptured appendix.

Mario's father, a friendly, diminutive man, always wore a hat and smoked what he called "Guinea Stinker" cigars. They were gnarled, coiled, pungent chunks of what appeared to be black rope. And it was one morning when he was alone on the corner that I lit up with him. We stood man to man enjoying our cigars. I became a man at the age of fifteen that day. And with manhood came the subsequent wisdom never to try one of those things again.

The corner was neutral turf where we celebrated good times and bad. We convened there for the trip to

Goveneur's Island to attend Albie Sherman's posthumous receipt of the Distinguished Service Medal. His heroism in Korea saved fellow soldiers' lives but cost him his. And we commiserated when the local priest compassionately refused the donation which had been collected in Albie's memory, because Catholic masses couldn't be said for Jewish dead.

On summer and spring evenings, the harmonies of four guys singing on the opposite corner entertained everyone. And one Saturday, we watched a football-field-sized limo arrive to pick up Freddy Milano to transport him to the Dick Clark show. Dion and the Belmonts were on their way.

Around on the **Belmont** side was a brick wall and a fire escape ladder for the apartments above Herman's store. We played basketball through the first rung of the ladder, "Down the River" against the wall, "Box Ball" in front of it, and pitched pennies to it. There was always something to do.

Ralph Costello and Albie Sherman

In the fall, football activity moved us into the street in the form of "Two Hand Touch." The ball was a "Daily News" folded vertically and rolled up tightly, with rubber bands at the ends.

Continued on page 10

3

STRANGERS IN PARADISE

By Toby (Solomon) Cohen
Evander '57

While we wereliving at 1219 Adee Avenue in the **Eastchester projects**, my Dad, Bob Solomon, was manager of the **Loew's Paradise** Theatre on **Fordham Road**. Several years later he was promoted to district manager of all the Loew's Theatres in New York City. But to me that wasn't as prestigious as his tenure at the Paradise. My dates never knew! I would tell my dad that should he see me enter the theatre with a date he is NOT to acknowledge my presence. We had to tell "Louie" the doorman/ticket taker the same thing. I wanted the fellas I dated to pay the full price of two tickets. After the movie started I would walk out to see my father. Daddy didn't approve of my tactics, but he went along with our secret.

People used to ask me what my dad did as manager of the theatre. After all, the public would see managers standing or walking through the lobbies. As he once said to me, "if the theatre is clean, the bathrooms are clean and the paper supplies are adequate and everything works, the air-conditioning or heating is comfortable, the concession counter moves along quickly and sound and picture of the movie are perfect, the seats are clean and comfortable, the ushers are neatly dressed in their ironed uniforms (and sometimes a hat), and they speak clearly and politely and if you can find your lost umbrella and you had no hassle in your life for few hours- then that's the theatre manager doing his job.

After all, you were in "Paradise" for only a few hours!

On Saturday afternoon in 1956 I answered our home phone to hear a man ask for Bob Solomon. My dad finished his conversation and then asked me if I ever heard of a fellow named, "Moondog?" I excitedly replied, "Sure...why?" My father said that was the person who had just called. Alan Freed alias "Moondog". It seems that Alan Freed was to do a promotional gig at the Paradise. I immediately called everyone I knew.

My dad also arranged backstage visits to the Rock 'N Roll groups playing in many theatres in the Bronx. Through my dad's connections I was able to meet and interview the 50's groups up close and personal for the **Evander Child's** newspaper. **Evander** even held it's graduation in the Paradise Theatre.

As I read Back In THE BRONX, I realize that none of us were "Strangers in Paradise"

TERMS NO LONGER HEARD:

- Do you want to sit in the loge.
- Oh, this is where I came in!
- Stop hitting me, the matron is coming.
- "B" movie.
- Smoking section.
- Newsreels.

4

The Nickel Palace

City Island Avenue
Photo Courtesy of Bronx Historical Society

City Island Bridge
Photo by Eugene Vinogradov

by Nancy (Pooler) Malanga

Remember the Nickel Palace? Sure you do. Just let your memory go back to the summertime of the 1950's. You just spent the day at **Orchard Beach** swimming, sunning and having fun. You walked from Orchard Beach all the way to **City Island**. You were hot, thirsty and hungry and when you reached the **City Island Bridge** there it was just over the bridge on the left THE NICKEL PALACE.

I was there waiting for you. I served you hot dogs with five year old sauerkraut (I think that sauerkraut was left floating in that hot water since I was born but you loved it) and ice cold root beer from that big root beer barrel. Many of you hung around outside the little hot dog stand but some of you would come in and sit at the booths and play the juke box. Do some of you remember that if you didn't have any money for a hot dog and a drink, Mr. Goldsmith, who owned the little stand would ask in his heavy Russian accent, "You want a hot dog and a drink?" You would tell him you had only bus fare but you got your food and drink and he told you to pay him next time. And you always did. You used to come in droves. And when the **City Island** bus finally came, you all piled on and we would usually see you the next day. I worked at The Nickel Palace every summer during my high

Summertime was the best. Everyone from the Bronx came to City Island

school years. Some of us used to call it "Goldies" after Mr. Goldsmith. Of course he didn't know this, at least I don't think so.

I grew up on **City Island**. What a great place to live.

Summertime was the best. Everyone from the Bronx came to **City Island**. At that time most of the "big" restaurants were at the other end of the Island and of course the "Penny Arcade." Remember?

We all went to High School off the Island. Many of us went to **Columbus** High School at Pelham Parkway. Sometimes we were late because the bridge was up to let boats pass and it would be announced over the loud speaker at school that the **City Island** bus is late because of the bridge. Some of my "off the Island friends" would tell me that we were late not because the bridge was up but because we were out digging for clams. Thus, we were called the "Clam Diggers."

We also had our "candy store" in which to hang out. In my early teens we hung out at, you guessed it, The Nickel Palace ("Goldies"). Someone always had a nickel to play the jukebox and if it wasn't crowded Mr. G. would let us dance. We sat in those booths for hours and sometimes Mr. G. would tell us to leave if he had paying customers.

I live in Virginia now and when I go to visit my mother and brother (who still live there) as I cross the **City Island Bridge** (especially in the summer), childhood memories start coming back and the fun I had growing up.

But that's what **City Island** does to you, you never forget. It's the greatest little place in the Bronx!!!! ∎

Reminiscing

Sex Goddess
Continued from page 1

back to London soon, I worked up my nerve and asked, "What're your plans for the rest of the day?"

"I have none," she said.

"Why don't we take the limo out to Mike's place in Sneden's Landing, up the Hudson. It's beautiful out there."

"Sounds wonderful," she purred. "First let me get into something more comfortable."

Mike Wallace interviewing Diana Dors

Arriving at her suite in the Sherry Netherlands Hotel, Diana slipped into the bedroom while I waited in the sitting room. My mind raced. Screw driving out to Wallace's place, I thought. Nothing interesting could happen there. For the day to end successfully, I first had to entertain this wondrous creature. I had to show her a good time. Having no credit cards and only a few bucks in my pocket. And then it came to me. I would take Diana Dors to a place, something told me, she had never seen before. I would take her up to the Bronx and show her the Old Neighborhood.

Pacing, I imagined the two of us tooling up the **Grand Concourse** in the long, low Cadillac. Maybe I'd spot an old girlfriend or two, intense intellectuals addicted to classic foreign films, standing in front of the **Ascot Theater**, and I'd casually introduce them to Diana Dors. After such a moment, a guy could die smiling.

But topping that, I saw the limo finally arriving at **Moshulu Parkway**, where some of my buddies, at least those who hadn't married and moved away, might either be sitting on the park railing or playing ball in the **P.S. 80** schoolyard. I pictured myself telling the chauffeur, "Stop right here," and while all the neighbors gaped from their windows, I would exit the limo with Diana Dors on my arm, and introduce her to all the guys. And after schmoozing with them for a while, I'd take Diana over to **Schweller's Deli** on **Jerome Avenue,** for a Hebrew National and a knish.

The more I thought about it, the better it sounded. As a kid, I may have been just so-so at schoolyard basketball or touch football, and nothing could get me to stand in front of a baseball rocketing off a bat and screaming at my head at 200 mph. But now, today, I would make up for it all. With Diana Dors, the Ultimate Shiksa, at my side, I was going to make Bronx history. I was going to step into the realms of Bronx Myth and Legend.

With Diana Dors, the Ultimate Shiksa, at my side, I was going to make Bronx history. I was going to ascend into realms of Bronx Myth and Legend.

But first I had to make sure the stage was set. I grabbed the hotel phone and called my Bronx buddy, Pikey, who, teachers at **Clinton** had predicted, would someday wind up digging ditches or on welfare. (He'd eventually become a division president at the Dail-Purex Corporation. So much for **DeWitt Clinton**.)

"Pikey's not here," his father said over the phone. "He's probably wasting time somewhere."

"Could you please find him for me, Mr. Schultz?" I asked. "It's very important. Tell him to tell all the guys, I'm coming up there with Diana Dors."

"Whose doors?"

"No, no. Diana Dors."

"So nu, who is Diana Dors?"

"Don't worry. Just tell him. Pikey will know."

At that moment, Diana emerged from the bedroom. She had changed into tailored slacks and a sleeveless something, revealing creamy shoulders, "I know this sounds like a bad movie," she grinned, the kind of grin that made you feel she was peering right into your deepest thoughts. "But would you help me with these buttons up the back?"

Would I help her? I'd have hurled myself out of the window if she asked. Standing close, I managed, after a few minutes, to secure three or four buttons. Diana grabbed a jacket and we headed for the door. I thought of saying I was taking her to the Bronx instead of to Wallace's place in Sneden's Landing, but decided it would be better to surprise her. Suddenly, the phone shrilled. "Oh, damn," she muttered. "Just give me a minute."

She rushed back into the bedroom and before she closed the door behind her, I couldn't help overhearing that it was a call from London. Some guy. Then I remembered, the gossip columns had been buzzing about Diana's love life. Trouble with an ex-husband. Or with a boyfriend. Or maybe both. That's okay, I told myself. I'll make her forget every trouble she ever had.

Five minutes passed. Then ten, thirty, forty. Through the wall, I could hear her muffled voice. Still on the phone to London. I flipped on the TV and sat watching some Sunday afternoon cultural show. "I should get up and leave." After all, a man should have some pride. But the phone calls weren't Diana's fault. Besides, I had

Continued on page 10

6

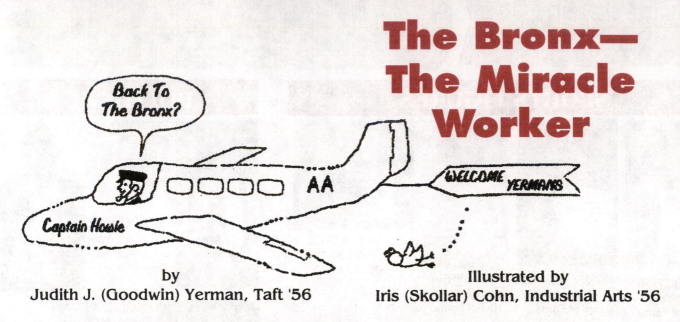
The Bronx— The Miracle Worker

by
Judith J. (Goodwin) Yerman, Taft '56

Illustrated by
Iris (Skollar) Cohn, Industrial Arts '56

Miracles don't happen only on 34th Street.
They happen because of being raised in a very special part of New York; the Bronx.

It is still a small world, no matter where you go...even if you were born and raised in the Bronx. When my article, "A Look Back At The 50's: Food, Fads and The Bronx" appeared in Volume III, Issue XIII, I looked forward with great anticipation to hearing from some old friends.. The collective experiences of growing up in the Bronx still draw people together. Instead, I have made some new friends.

In the middle of March 1996, my husband, my brother-in-law and I returned to Newburgh, NY to attend the funeral of my husband's older brother. It was an extremely haphazard trip, leaving California with very little advance notice and flying cross country for a sad family event. The next three days were as expected... grievous. Our dear friends, Iris (Skollar) Cohn (Industrial Arts— 1956) and her darling husband, Mort, drove from Commack, NY to Newburgh to visit us on the last day of our three day whirlwind trip. We were leaving very early the next morning for California. We needed a quiet dinner the night before our return home.

In the cozy dining room at 'Cosimo's on Union', in Newburgh, NY, we relaxed a bit and looked at the menu. We were all catching up on news and chit-chatting. As people tend to do, we were half listening to a conversation at the table adjoining ours, when my brother-in-law, thought he heard the words, **Back in THE BRONX**. Not being sure, he "ssshed" us and kept listening. He heard correctly. A couple sitting opposite a gentleman by himself was engaged in a discussion about **Back in THE BRONX**. It was impossible not to strike up a conversation with these people. The stereotypical loudness, harshness and unfriendly demeanor often credited to New Yorkers vanished instantly. There was an immediate Bronx rapport as we talked. "Where do you live?" What schools did you go to?"

"What are you doing in Newburgh?" "What sort of job do you have?" No coincidence, you say? Of course not. We were, after all, in New York. Nothing terribly strange about Bronxites meeting one another in NY, except that the gentleman sitting opposite the couple went to **Taft High School** and now lived in Grass Valley, California. We all laughed about coincidences until it became even more fortuitous. As questions popped back and forth between our tables, we found out that the Grass Valley, California resident and **Taft** High School graduate was an American Airlines Captain. We asked when he had arrived and when was he due to fly out again. He told us his flight was in the morning at 9:00 for Chicago's O'Hare. We gasped. That was our flight. After a good laugh and some head shaking, he told us to stop by the cockpit when we boarded the plane in the morning and say "hi."

Walking out on the tarmac at Stewart-Warner Field in Newburgh, NY (no jet ways there yet, folks) and up the steep roll-away steps, we were met at the door of the plane by our new found friend. His smiling face and easy disposition were such a pleasant sight after the last few days. He welcomed us aboard, introduced us to his flight crew, who immediately became indulgent and friendly and seated us in First Class. Our new friend, the Captain, began his warm up speech, indicating that he was ready to push back the plane, start to taxi out to the runway and take off. Weather, flying altitude and expected arrival time to Chicago behind him, he concluded his welcome with, "And I want to extend a very warm welcome to my friends, the Yermans, formerly of the Bronx." His crew was very attentive and amiable throughout the flight and the touchdown was perfect. We really hated the fact that we were changing planes in

Continued on page 13

BRONX CELEBRITIES

SPORTS FIGURES

WHITEY FORD
Yankees
Hall of Fame

PHIL RIZZUTO
Yankees
Hall of Fame

MICKEY MANTLE
Yankees
Hall of Fame

YOGI BERRA
Yankees
Hall of Fame

ED KRANPOOL
NY Mets
Monroe HS

ART DONOVAN
Baltimore Colts
Football Hall of Fame

We applaud
these former
Bronxites
and their many
accomplishments

POLITICAL

FERNANDO
FERRER
Bronx
Borough
Pres.

NITA LOWEY
Congress-
woman
Bronx Science

ROBERT ABRAMS
Former NYS
    Attorney General
Former Bronx Borough Pres.
Columbus HS

G. OLIVER
KOPPEL
Former NYS
Attorney General

ENTERTAINERS

JOE FRANKLIN

MARVIN SCOTT

REGIS PHILBIN

GARRY
MARSHALL

JERRY
VALE

CARL
REINER

JAN MURRAY

RED BUTTONS

DION

ROBERT
KLEIN

MAL Z.
LAWRENCE

DAVID HOROWITZ

CURTIS
SLIWA

DANNY AIELLO

Bronx Honor Roll
Bronxites Who Have Achieved!

BRONX SCIENCE
Harold Brown
Stokely Carmichael
Leon Cooper (Nobel Prize Winner))
Bobby Darin
Edggar Doctorow
Sheldon Glashow (Nobel Prize Winner)
Jeff Greenfield*
Russell Hulse (Nobel Prize Winner)
Ronald Lauder*
Nita Lowey, Representative
Arno Penzias (Nobel Prize Winner)
William Safire
Melvin Schwartz (Nobel Prize Winner)
Steven Weinberg (Nobel Prize Winner)

CARDINAL HAYES
George Carlin
Rocky Colavito
Kevin Loughery
Regis Philbin

CHRISTOPHER COLUMBUS
Robert Abrams
Anne Bancroft
Christine Jorgenson
Alan Landsburg

DEWITT CLINTON
Don Adams
Nate Archibald
Richard Avedon
James A. Baldwin
Martin Balsam
David Begelman
James Caan
Paddy Chayevsky
George Cukor
Avery Fisher
Arthur Gelb
Judd Hirsch
Robert Hofstadter (Nobel Prize Winner)
Stubby Kaye
Al Kelly
Theodore Kheel
Robert Klein
William Kunstler
Burt Lancaster
Garry Marshall
Jan Murray
Charles Rangel
Richard Rogers
A.M. Rosenthal
Daniel Schorr
Dolph Schayes
Neil Simon
Larry Storch
Marvin Traub
Jimmie Walker
Fats Waller
William Zeckendorf

EVANDER CHILDS
Red Buttons
James Coco
Carl Reiner

MONROE
Jules Pfeiffer
John Garfield
Hank Greenberg
Ed Kranepool
Leon Lederman (Nobel Physicist)

MORRIS
Angel Cordero
Herman Joseph Muller (Nobel Prize Winner)
Gabe Pressman
E. Colin Powell

ROOSEVELT
June Alyson
Chazz Palminteri

TAFT
Sanford Brown
Eydie Gorme
Stanley Kubrick

Mal Z. Lawrence
WALTON
Bella Abzug
Gertrude Elion (Nobel Prize Winner)*
Rosalyn Yalow (Nobel Prize Winner)

OTHER NOTABLES
Joey Adams
Danny Aiello
Robert Alda
Corazon Aquino
Armand Assante
Herman Badillo
Lauren Bacall
Ellen Barkin
Mario Biaggi
Joey Bishop
Alfred Bloomingdale
Bobby Bonilla
Teresa Brewer
"Cousin Brucie"
Ralph J. Bunche (Nobel Prize Winner)
George Burns
Cab Calloway
Diahann Carroll
Carmen Cavallaro
Samuel Clemens
Myron Cohen
Betty Comdon
Cardinal Cooke
Avery Corman
Norman Cousins
Bobby Cremins
Don Criqui
Tony Curtis
Ossie Davis
Dennis Day
Ruby Dee
Robert DeNiro
Dion DiMucci
Art Donovan
John Foster Dulles
Erik Estrada
Fernando Ferrer
Geraldine Ferraro
F. Scott Fitzgerald
Art Fleming
Joe Franklin
Arlene Francis
Connie Francis
Frankie Frisch
Edward J. Flynn
Rita Gam
Stan Getz
Rudolph Giuliani
Samuel Gompers
Aldolf Green
Richie Guerin
Armand Hammer
Moss Hart
Herbert A. Hauptman (Nobel Prize Winner)
David Horowitz
Vladimir Horowitz
Irving Howe
George Jessel
Billy Joel
Raoul Julia
John F. Kennedy
Robert Kennedy
Ted Kennedy
Theodore Kheel
Calvin Klein
Edward Koch
Fiorello LaGuardia
Bert Lahr
Jake LaMotta
Louise Lasser
Ralph Lauren
Ron Leibman
Lee Leonard
Joe E. Lewis
Shari Lewis

Hal Linden
Vince Lombardi
Melissa Manchester
John Mariani
Penny Marshall
Willie Mays
John McSherry
George Meany
Mario Merola
Glenn Miller
Sal Mineo
Hugo Montenegro
Robert Morgenthau
Gary Morton
Richard Mulligan
Paul Muni
Bess Myerson
Gil Noble
Carroll O'Connor
John O'Hara
Charles Osgood
Al Pacino
Jack Palance
Floyd Patterson
Joseph Papp
Joe Pesci
Roberta Peters
Mary Pickford
Ezio Pinza
Edgar Allan Poe
Richard Price
Vincent Price
Tito Puente
Charles Nelson Reilly
Rob Reiner
Regina Resnick
Victor Riesel
Edward G. Robinson
Monte Rock III
Franklin D. Roosevelt
Theodore Roosevelt
Billy Rose
Howard Safir
Jonas Salk
Isabel Sanford
Martin Scorcese
Marvin Scott
George Segal
Connie Selleca
Jose Serrano
Sylviá Sidney
Carly Simon
Stanley Simon
Vince Scully
Isaac Bashevis Singer (Nobel Prize Winner)
Curtis Sliwa
Wesley Snipes, Jr.
Cardinal Spellman
Sy Sperling
George Steinbrenner
Henry Stern
Pat Summerall
Renee Taylor
Mother Teresa (Nobel Prize Winner)
U. Thant
Arturo Toscanini
Dan Topping
Leon Trotsky
Lloyd Ultan
Jerry Vale
Bobby Van
Luther Vandross
June Valli
Jackie Vernon
Fran Warren
Del Webb
Jerry Weintraub
Vanessa Williams
Herman Wouk

Thanks to Dr. William C. Wolfson and the Bonx Society of Science and Letters

Reminiscing

Corners

Continued from page 3

It spiraled like a top on clothesline passes to criss-crossing receivers.

The corner was the takeoff point on Saturday mornings for the long, one-block walk up to **Tremont Avenue** and the **Deluxe Theatre**. Several hundred kids would behave through a double feature, cartoon, Movietone News, a chapter, and the "Funny Races." A box of Jujubes lasted the show, and was preferred by Ralph Costello, Mel Dener, and me. Occasionally, we even paid for them. Buddy Hirsh and Mac Maglione were the "Good and Plenty" kids. Mario preferred Sugar Babies. Mounds Bars and frozen Milky Ways provided support service.

Other days, the trek up to **Tremont** was for a long walk or to **Singer** and **Bernstein's** bakery for their phenomenal onion rolls, bialys, rye bread or danish.

Nothing was sacred as we discussed everything on that corner: girls; the similarities between Italians and Jews; whether Senator Joe McCarthy's nervous laugh derived from a psychosis; whether Mel Ott could hit so many homers in a stadium which didn't have the Polo Grounds short right field line; Carl Furillo's bullet throws; Mickey and Willie; the future of this new gadget called "Univac"; Joe D's grace in centerfield; do the ends ever justify the means?; how to tell whether a lens was for near or far-sightedness; boating at City island; whether Dupont #7 gave a better car shine than Turtle Wax; and pretty girls. The corner was essentially a male bastion, but not totally so. It was a place for truth, humor, beauty, goodness, and loyalty.

The light from those days and nights on the corner probably enhances the universe somewhere, somehow. And the myriad memories of those good times ripple through our brains consciously sometimes, subconsciously always. We are better people now for what we were then. Today they speak of values. But if they really want to know what those are, all they need do is look back at the corner. ∎

Sex Goddess

Continued from page 6

invested so much time already, what were another few minutes...if she and I finally got into that limo waiting downstairs? With a world class Sex Goddess like her, I would (the words had a certain ring and bore repeating) ride into Bronx Myth and Legend, Maybe someday a bronze plaque, with my likeness, commemorating the event would be laid in the **Moshulu Parkway** sidewalk.

At last, Diana emerged once more from the other room. I could see that the emotional marathon calls from across the Atlantic had drained and wilted her. She was in no mood now for the Bronx or anything else, not even a knish, "I'm afraid almost the whole day is shot," she said. "And now it's so late. Will you forgive me? Maybe some other time."

"No problem," I said, realizing there would be, after all, no bronze plaques with my likeness on **Moshulu Parkway.**

After a few more awkward pleasantries, I shook her hand, said goodbye, and left, Downstairs, I told the waiting chauffeur that we wouldn't need the car anymore.

"Okay," he said, "but I usually get a tip."

I dug into my pocket and found a $10-bill, all I had. I gave the bill to the driver who peered at it as if it were a hair in his soup. Then, without a coin or subway token to my name, I trudged through a cold and windy Manhattan all the way back to my apartment, from 59th and Fifth to 99th and Riverside Drive.

Early the next morning, Pikey phoned from the Bronx. "I got your message, and I was waiting and waiting," he said. "What happened?"

"Do you have to know everything?" I said mysteriously, sensing that his feverish imagination would far outstrip the reality.

Sometimes, I wonder whether Sheldon Glashow or Steven Weinberg, two of **Bronx Science's** Nobel laureates...I hope they won't mind if I call them Shelly and Stevie because, after all, we did go to the same school...sometimes I wonder if Shelly or Stevie would've traded a Nobel Prize, or at least a piece of it, for a day with Diana Dors. Probably not.

But you never know. ∎

Diana Dors has a laugh with Mike Wallace.

The Allerton Coops As I Remember Them

By Sam Goldman

On a beautiful, sunny November Saturday, two years ago, 500 former "Coopniks" gathered in the auditorium of Aging in America on **Pelham Parkway** for another reunion. Once again the old comrades hugged and kissed, sang old labor songs, and shared memories of the May Day Parades, the protests, the Young Pioneer League and their political heroes, Earl Browder and Elizabeth Gurley Flynn.

A few miles north of this reunion site, the Coops, a 700 unit Tudor-style complex still stands on **Bronx Park East** between **Allerton Avenue** and **Arnow**. From a distance, when the sunlight shines on it, it looks the same, but it isn't and never will be. Like the now discredited idealism that the former inhabitants shared, the physical beauty and glorious spirit of the Coops has disintegrated. But politics aside, I often find myself reminiscing about my childhood, playing around the climbing ivy buildings, the fresh smell from the gardens, the coolness of the fountain waters that shot out of stone structures to keep the flowers looking brisk. I remember Lugovey, the proud gardener who, from dawn to dusk, was tending the gardens in the three courtyards. And who could forget Tony Caballero, who protected these gardens, sometimes wearing a full, policeman's uniform including as club and gun? I feared but respected him, especially when he shouted his traditional "Get oudda da court!"

I often think about our sessions on the benches on the **Barker Avenue** side. On summer nights people would sit there as late as 3.00 a.m. Yes, they talked about what was read in the

A view of the first house from Bronx Park in the late 1930's.
Photo credit: Sonya Ackerman

"Daily Worker" and the "Morning Freihelt," but also, "Who was a better baseball player, Ted Williams or Joe DiMaggio?"

On the **Bronx Park East side**, there was our self-made ballfield in the park. I remember an abandoned greenhouse in the outfield. If the bat-

The Columbus H.S. contingent of the American Student Union steps off in a May Day Parade.

ter hit a ball into it, it was an automatic home run. The glass pane had to break of course.

I remember walking through farms to get to **Columbus** High School, the smell of hay, even though there were

no cows or horses around. I cherish my memories of the many clubs we had in the Coops. Some were political, some were scientific, some were athletic and some were social. My faded blue jacket indicated that I was a "VICEROY." We all had our own clubrooms In the basements of the Coops. We all felt that we belonged. There was a special spiritual force that made those years of living in the coops, marvelous ones that could never return.

> There was a special spiritual force that made those years of living in the coops, marvelous ones that could never return.

The Coops Reunion Committee now helps present residents of the Coops in various ways. When the Committee meets, they still call each other Comrade although their political views vary. With the cooperation of interim **Columbus** Principal, Jerry Garfin, a former Coopnik himself, The Committee presents a college scholarship to all worthy senior students who now live In the Coops. ∎

"Say Good-bye to Those Oldies but Goodies?" — Not Me.

By Linda Comac

It's Friday night. The car radio is tuned to CBS-FM. The Flamingos are singing, "I only have eyes for you." Suddenly, I'm 19 years old again. **Walton Avenue** is still the hub of my universe and that universe is the Bronx.

As always, music has the power to transport me to another time and place. My journey takes me back to my youth, back to a time before Vietnam, Watergate, and the woman's movement raised our consciousness and made us aware of injustice, corruption, and the torment that choice carries with it. It was a simpler time. A time when sights, sounds, and smells were enough to fill and fulfill me.

Back in the fifties and sixties, all my senses truly savored the Bronx: The sight of tree-lined streets, the statue in the center of **Joyce Kilmer Park**; the corner train stations...; the smells of Kosher delis, Italian pizzerias and Chinese restaurants and especially that pungent after-the rain smell only city streets can have...; the sounds of "I cash clothes"; the knife-sharpener's bell and even the clop clop of hooves when the fruit and vegetable man's horse-drawn cart came around.

My memories seem to involve sounds more than anything else. For me, growing up in the Bronx is synonymous with the rumble of the **#4 Woodlawn-Jerome IRT**. It's the sound of traffic on the **Grand Concourse** on summer nights when the windows were open—bus brakes and hurrying taxis (the kind with pull-down seats behind the driver). It's the shouts of "Saloogi" when someone swiped my belongings, the sound of balls bouncing on pavement to the tune of "A, my name is Alice." It's the sound of the crowds at **Yankee Stadium**-football and baseball fans, and periodically, Jehovah's Witnesses. It's the sound of the Irish Brothers at mass on Sunday mornings in their residence

at **All Hallows** across the street from me.

Life in the Bronx played a distinctive melody full of vigor. Now whenever I think about the Bronx, "I can hear music, sweet, sweet music," the kind before the rock got hard and

Cousin Brucie then...

...and now

computers took over this "new age."

My earliest musical memory is of walking, arms linked with either Janet Rosoff or Helaine Pollack and singing "Schlemiel, Schlemozzle, Hasenfeffer Incorporated" Why? I don't know why anymore than I know how to spell it, but away we skipped up the path in **Joyce Kilmer Park** that led from **Walton Avenue** and **165th** St. to the water fountain.

Later, when this girl changed "from bobby socks to stockings" and started "changing her baby toys for boys," another musical interlude was provided by a boy whose name I've forgotten. He sang "Silhouettes on the Shade" to me at the Henry Kaufman Camp Grounds in Pearl River, New York, where the **Concourse** "Y" sent

us to day camp. I was a member of that "Y" for a couple of years—swimming with Toby Peyofsky, drama with Susan Rose, and something called "club." When I wasn't at the "Y", I was at **P.S. 114** where Mrs. Warsinger and her pitch pipe introduced scores of Bronxites to the joys of singing and where Murray Periah (now called the "foremost Mozart interpreter today") or Arlene Blumenreich was likely to accompany us on the piano.

I remember, too, my sister Tema (**Hunter H.S**. '59) screaming to the gyrations of Elvis Presley. That's when she and I weren't fighting over whether she'd watch the *Peggy Lee Show* or I'd watch *Father Knows Best*. I must add that I was also fighting with my grandmother who wanted to watch that "nice Jewish boy"— Eddie Fisher.

I laughed at Presley's first performances on *The Ed Sullivan Show* and thought my sister was a little ditzy. Nonetheless, the depth of her feeling won her a charm bracelet replete with hound dog, hotel, guitar, and shoes (not quite blue suede, of course—just phoney silver) in the *Daily News* "Why I love Elvis" contest. Then the King went into the army and my sister put away her 78's for other things.

Years later, Elvis's implied sexuality was supplanted by overt lyrics. Among the earliest of those was "Wouldn't it be nice if we were both in bed together?" I remember listening to that song one evening with a group of other CITs from Woodlane Country Day Camp. Although Woodlane was

Continued on page 15

Bronx Miracle...

Continued from page 7

Chicago to continue our trip on to Los Angeles. We exchanged business cards as we were leaving and told him that if he were ever in the Southern California area that we would love to have dinner with him. We thanked him for the kindness extended to us, for his friendly manner and for his thoughtfulness. In a certain way, he had made a very difficult trip more pleasant than he will ever know.

Several days after my arrival home, I spoke by phone with Iris Cohn who had been at dinner with us the night we overheard the **Back in THE BRONX** conversation. She had just received her issue of **Back in THE BRONX**, and, laughingly said into the phone, "look at Page 20, the classifieds, the middle column...the one in black print." I pulled my magazine off the shelf in my office. There it was, the last of the coincidences. I had necessarily overlooked it because I did not recognize the name at the time I received my issue. A small, teary smile crossed my face as I read: "MP875 Howard Pincus, Taft '61 is a Captain with American Airlines living in Grass Valley, Ca. Would like to hear from some old friends (followed by his telephone number). It was our "Captain Howie" as we have taken to referring to him. Coincidence or design? No matter which, it served as proof that Bronxites, whether present or past still retain that sense of being very special. Captain Pincus tells me that he may be visiting California this summer. We look forward to sharing with him the hospitality he so graciously showed to us. Thanks, "Captain Howie" once again. I hope you find many, many of your old friends and know with certainty that you have made new ones in California. May all your trips be "Heavy" and all of your touchdowns be perfect. You have shared a very benevolent part of yourself with us.

I received a long, handwritten letter from Stan Greene (formerly Stan

Continued on page 17

Corners
By Frank Schmidt

It was always a corner, hardly ever in the middle of the block. Something about hanging out on the corner was implicit. Maybe a natural law of some kind controlled us. But corners were always first. Corners were dimension rich. The crowd could split and distribute itself between the two walls that intersected at the corner! Guys on one side, girls on the other, and then maybe couples on one side (those going steady..) and the non-attached on the other side. Corners were handy. One side would provide the doorways that the attached required for privacy. The other side would provide the brick wall that supported a game of king/queen.

Corners gave the best view. Knowing who was coming down the block was critical to behavior, especially for those in the doorways. One never knew whose Mom or Dad was coming down the street. Corners could save you. Once, when the guys (for whatever reason..) were cursing up a storm, my Dad, having just parked the car, came walking toward the corner. I was the other other side. He really "laid into" the guys for their language. He never knew I was part of the gang because I was around the corner.

I had a crash on a girl, but she always seemed to be on the other side of the corner. We were all hanging out together, but she was always on the other side, where the doorways were-never got around the corner with the right timing. Timing was so important a quick move around the corner to the other side, then say something. Timing had to be perfect. Words had to be right. Corner had to be open for the move. But either the corner was too crowded or the timing was lousy. The corner controlled the move. Corners ruled.

Corners gave us shelter. The wind couldn't come from both directions at once. We crowded into the lee side of a corner on a cold, windy afternoon or evening. Corners had mailboxes. Mailboxes were our podiums. Lean against a mailbox and you became a focal point. No one ignored the words of anyone leaning against a mailbox.

"Meet you on the corner." This was perfectly natural. Corners were perfect for meeting someone. Nobody ever planned to meet anybody in the middle of the block. It had to be a corner. Corners had character, provided the geography neccesary to identify a place to hang out. Corners were innocent, yet they demanded respect. We had our corner, but there were many others, plenty of others. And each corner triggered an image of who hung out there. Corners were the congnitive hook. Corners were pivotal psychological triggers in our teenage imagery. Corners were boundry markers, demarcation points, landmarks, territorial points of reference. "He's down the corner." It's right around the corner, you can't miss it."

The corners are still there. But I think they've lost their meaning. Cyberspace is replacing real space. Corners are reality. The world is becoming virtual. One can't hang out on virtual corners.

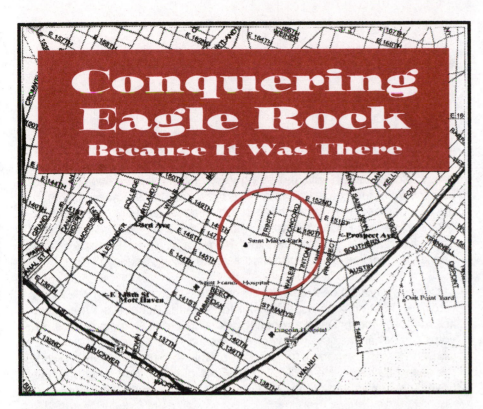

Conquering Eagle Rock
Because It Was There

By Ed Handibode

The northernmost boundary of **St. Mary's Park** ends at E. 149th St. in the Beautiful Bronx. The avenues running into 149th St. at this point include **St. Ann's Ave., Eagle Ave., Cauldwell Ave.,** etc. Sitting majestically in the park is a massive rock which must date back to the ice age. It seemed every bit of thirty feet high although its right side sloped evenly to grade level, making climbing relatively easy. On its left side the rock is cleft, and the fissure runs all the way to the ground. The cleavage seemed five or six feet wide. I've never determined whether Eagle Rock has taken its name because of its proximity to **Eagle Avenue** or the rock had been named first.

It was a brisk October day in 1940 when four young Bronxites, one of whom was my brother Dick, ventured atop this monolith. No sooner had we arrived when Don Kerr, the most daring of the foursome, did a standing broad jump across the opening, followed, after some hesitation, by his twin brother, Jim. Both insisted that if I was to remain their "blood brother," I would have to follow suit. The thought of the thirty foot drop was too unpleasant and I didn't dare the leap. Man's greatest enemy, fear, had won out. I rationalized my failure. They were each a year older than I was, and a body could develop a lot of ability in a year's time. But then they baited my brother, Dick. He, thirteen months younger than I, having celebrated his eighth birthday the day before, leaped the precipice in a heartbeat. Now I had three of them goading me. I was still unable to measure up, however, and walked slowly down the slope with the certainty I would never be a man. I definitely had not "seized the day."

Ten years elapsed. I joined the Army at the height of the Korean conflict thinking I might take a bullet for my country. Perhaps this would be my redemption. Alas! I didn't get shot. I didn't even see combat. I would just have to carry the failure at Eagle Rock for a lifetime.

Upon discharge from the Army, I went to work in the construction trades. Even the fact that I could "walk steel" did not seem to let me off the hook from my failure on that October afternoon in my ninth year of life.

Some years later I took the test for the NYC Fire Department. One of the requirements during the physical examination was to do a standing broad jump of six feet minimum. This was accomplished at ground level, however, and could not have redeemed me at Eagle Rock. I went on to a long fire fighting career during which I had some hair-raising experiences. I seemed to have the need to make an obvious display of courage. Even promotion to the rank of Captain couldn't wipe out my blighted past.

Ten years ago I worked overtime in a firehouse I hadn't worked in before and, lo and behold, Eagle Rock was only three blocks away. I decided I would visit the site that very day. The opportunity arose when we responded to a stove fire about 11:00 AM. It wasn't of serious consequence, and we finished the job within thirty minutes. Taking advantage of my position as the Captain, I told the other firefighters we would be stopping at Eagle Rock before returning to quarters.

As we stood near the rock I was both amused and surprised to notice it's height was only about twelve feet. Yielding to nostalgia, I screwed up my courage and told the others all the sordid details of the "Bad Day At Eagle Rock." I must confess the opening in the rock was smaller too, and, at the prompting of the others, I walked up and stepped across the "chasm." One of the firefighters offered to go the fire truck and obtain a tape measure, "just for the hell of it." Dare I measure this? What need was there, after all, to know the precise measurement? Wasn't it enough to know that I could step over it? The others insisted the measurement be made and then absolutely refused to reveal to me the "tale of the tape." They gleefully told me I would have to carry this uncertainty with me the remainder of my days, unless I decided to return to the scene with a ruler on my day off. We laughed about the incident, on an off, for the remainder of the work day. Some of them might have had their own "eagle rock" in the past. The release the laughter brought felt especially good for hadn't I conquered Eagle Rock after all? And it had only taken me forty-five years. ■

Oldies But Goodies

Continued from page 12

in Westchester, my days at the camp are a Bronx memory, a memory of the many Bronxites I met who expanded my horizons, literally and figuratively. Linda Moskowitz of **Elliot Place** became my first friend from "beyond the Great Divide"—**167th** Street. Until high school, the east and west borders of my life were **Gerard Avenue** and the **Grand Concourse;** the north and south borders were 161 St. and **167 St.** There were, however, occasional forays to **Mullaley Park** for swinging or sliding in spring and fall, and running through the sprinkler in summer.

Although the Beatles had invaded America, I was listening to my older cousin's Chet Baker records long before Baker was "discovered" by the yuppies of the 80s and 90s. To get Baker albums at that time, I had to order them from **"Spinning Disc"** next to **Alexander's** on **Fordham Road** and the **Grand Concourse.**

The first LP I ever bought was, however, purchased at **Music and Art** on the south side of **161 St.** The store by the same name on the north side of the street was where we bought Nancy Drew books and school supplies. My first LP was soon followed by a Tommy Sands album and the soundtrack of *Palm Springs Weekend* on which—I tell you no lies—Troy Donahue actually sings. *Boss, man.* I first saw Troy Donahue with the fires of Parrish raging behind him on the bigger-than-life screen of the **Earl** on 161 St. I also bought my first 45 because of Troy Donahue—"Al di La" from the flick *Rome Adventure.* I paid 99¢ at **Music and Art** for that record.

Troy Donahue may have been the "man of my dreams," but "men" did not play a part in my real life until I was in

my senior year of high school. In Mrs. Friedman's French class at **Taft** H.S., I sat behind Allen Burdowski whose blazers, crew neck sweaters, and saxophone playing inspired one heck of a crush. Music seemed to surround us. From the earliest days of listening to him play with **Taft's** band to our prom night at the Plaza Hotel followed by Neil Sedaka's singing at Jack Silverman's International through **Hunter's** orientation weekend at the Tamarack.

Dion in '61

Dion today

Summer nights were spent sitting on the black iron railing around the **Joyce Kilmer Park** at 161st St., listening to someone's transistor bemoaning, "Hot town, summer in the city, back of your neck getting dirty and gritty." Or "You didn't have to be so nice, I would have loved you anyway" or "I only have eyes for you."

Bob came from **Sheridan Avenue** and introduced me to a whole other "crowd"—Howie Lewengrub and that kid who imitated sportscasters all the time and, of course, Richie Sherwin.

On our first date, "The Bej," as Bob was known, took me to my first hockey game—at the "old Garden." Later he would take me to movies at the **Earl or Loew's 167 St.** then we'd rush home to catch the Rangers' game on T.V. Once, we even went to an "art" movie at the **Lido** on the **Grand Concourse** near **Fordham.** And once, we went to a semi-porn flick, "Carmen, Baby," at a theater on **Jerome** and **Fordham.** (Bizet never meant it *that* way.) But classical music wasn't really our thing. We dated to the tune of "Pretty baby, now that I've found you stay and let me love you, baby."

But then Bob "brought me down," tossing me aside for another **Hunter** co-ed.

But...the "beat went on," and the music of my dates continued—harmony and discord alike. Among the highlights of my dating years were concerts at **Fordham's Rose Hall** campus, sitting on the bleachers for— what—$2? I saw Sammy Davis and Trini Lopez in concerts that must have rocked the entire Bronx. I also saw The Association there. "Cherish is a word I use to describe all the feelings that I have hiding here inside."

There were others—the boy in the apartment next door who enlisted in the air force when his "lottery number" turned out to be a seven. And the boy from **901 Walton Avenue** who often shared the park railing with me .

So many names, so many faces, so many songs seasoned my Bronx days. Although the sounds of the Bronx are only a memory today, I listen still—and often—to the songs of my past, allowing them to evoke memories that sometimes seem more real than reality.

"Those were the days, my friend, we thought they'd never end." But youth passes. Relationships end. Neighborhoods decay. Only the beat goes on. Hear it? Just close your eyes. Listen to the music and join me as I journey back to the Bronx. ∎

Candy-Store Sol's School of Hard Knocks

Richard T. Turner, Morris '42

Did I learn my P's and Q's in the Bronx? You bet I did. First at **P.S. 43 (Brown Place and 135th Street)** where Miss Singer, my fourth grade teacher, taught me that "Birds Of A Feather Flock Together." Then at **Clark Junior High School (145th Street, near Willis Avenue)** where Mr. Cohen, my math teacher, taught me that "All Work Is Noble." And finally, at **Morris High School (Boston Road and 166th Street)** where Mr. Bonheure, my French teacher, taught me that "Idle Hands Are The Devil's Tools."

Good precepts all, and isn't it funny how things like that stick in the mind? But not so funny, not funny at all, was the lesson I learned from another kind of teacher, a disciplinarian whose domain was not a classroom, but a candy store. His lesson was simple, direct, painful — and I never forgot it. We'll call him Sol, though after all these years, I'm not sure that was his name.

Maybe you'll remember him if I tell you that his candy store was located at the bottom of a long hill, where **Longwood and Spofford Avenues** came together. I'm going back to 1932 now. Do you recall the place? It was exactly like a thousand other candy stores in the Bronx — newsstand just outside the sliding window that opened into the soda fountain. Inside were stools along the counter where you could have your egg cream (or a vanilla malted if you were flush). Then, toward the back were the penny-candy case filled with licorice, caramels, peppermints, butterscotch, sour balls and enough other goodies to tempt even a rosy-cheeked, eight-year-old choir boy to a life of crime.

Well, they did. They tempted me. Tempted me into a career as a Master Criminal: short and brutal. Start to finish it lasted just under three minutes, and when it was over, I swore that if ever I could walk again, I would walk on the side of the angels.

The affair began when the Great Depression forced my family to move from New Jersey to the Bronx, swirling rowdydow of Dutch Schullz and

His lesson was simple, direct, painful— and I never forgot it.

Continued on page 17

TELL US ABOUT YOUR FAVORITE BRONX CANDY STORE(S) AND WE'LL ADD AN EXTRA ISSUE ONTO YOUR SUBSCRIPTION! INCLUDE A PHOTO AND RECEIVE 3 ADDITIONAL ISSUES!

NAME OF STORE: _____

LOCATION (intersection or cross streets) _____

_____

APPROXIMATE YEAR /YEAR(S) THERE: _____

NAME OF OWNER (or person running store): _____

_____

To receive an Extra issue, you MUST be a subscriber and complete the information below: (Non-subscribers may also contribute)

Subscriber's Name: _____

Subscriber's Address: _____

City _____ State ____ Zip _____

Phone # ( ) _____ Subscribers Account # _____

Describe store and any endearing stories and/or recollections of store or owner. Indicate the cost of items that you purchased, the uniqueness of the server, and/or the specialties that you enjoyed: (attach additional sheet if necessary)

_____

_____

_____

_____

_____

_____

_____

_____

Candy Store
Continued from page 16

his mob. Before I'd been there a week, I had figured out the scam: eat or be eaten. And when I learned that every kid within twenty blocks was ripping off Sol's candy store, I figured, *why not me?*

Just amble in and help yourself to two penny candies. Slip one in your pocket, pay for the other and amble out again. It's easy as stealing pennies off a dead man's eyes. The young neighborhood brigands had been doing it for years without ever getting caught: one piece at a time, slow but sure. But it was too slow for me. Shoot the works! Go for broke! That was my style — the last of the eight-year-old blue-chip gamblers.

So on a balmy summer day, I stroll into Sol's wearing a pair of knickers tailored by the fates for just this occasion. Over time, a small hole in each pocket has grown larger and larger until now there are no pockets; anything that goes in falls straight to the baggy knees.

I sidle up to the candy counter and case the joint. Sol and a salesman are deep in conversation at the soda fountain. As far as I can tell, neither is paying any attention to me. So ... is the hand faster than the eye? Now you see it, now you don't. In a matter of seconds I have filled each leg of my knickers with Mary Janes, Baby Ruths, Bubble Gum, Bits O' Honey, and every other kind of candy known to God, man, or covetous child. Then, waving a long licorice stick in my hand as a kind of diversionary banner, I shuffle over to Sol, hand him a penny, and ease on out the door. My life of crime has begun and just as quickly is over.

Did Sol see me stuffing my pockets? Was it the salesman? Who knows? I know only that when I am about twenty feet from the scene of the crime, the door crashes open and Sol comes charging out like a wounded water buffalo. Grabbing me by the ankles, he flips me upside down and shakes me till every last piece of candy is fanned out on the concrete like a

ragamuffin's dream of heaven, then slams me to the sidewalk. "You little son of a @^#$%&," he says, "Don't you ever come near my store again." He smashes a huge, angry fist against my right thigh. Crunch! Then the left. Crunch! I have charley horses like no other charley horses in recorded history. And pain — *oy, the* pain!

But it was worth it. I had just received a lesson in the best Institute of Learning the Bronx had to offer — Candy-Store Sol's School of Hard Knocks — and it was one I would never forget.

So I thank you, Sol, wherever you are. My classroom teachers had given me much, and I thank them for it, but it was you who taught me the one most important lesson of them all: Crime Does Not Pay!!! ■

Bronx Miracle...
Continued from page 7

Greenberg **Taft** '53) of Spring Valley, N.Y.. I mentioned him in my article as one of the friends that I would love to hear from again. This Stan Greene turned out to not be the one I was looking for, a curious, coincidental mystery. He knew everyone that lived in my apartment building and no one that attended school with me. His best friend was the brother of a good friend of mine when we lived at **315 E. Mr. Eden Avenue**. Looking again in my PS 70 autograph album, the handwriting of "Stan Greenberg" still matched the handwriting of Stan Greene. The page on which he had written was wedged between pages that were autographed by two people that he knew well, Gail (Goldie) Savage and Shirley Rubnitz (and, if you two are around, please let me hear from you!). I replied to his letter with photocopies of the autograph, yearbook pictures and explanations. Please solve the mystery, Stan. While you are not the Stan Greenberg I mentioned, you are most definitely someone that I knew back in the Bronx.

One evening I received a wonderful phone call from Jim Wiley of Santa Monica, California (**Clinton** '47). He had just read my article and called to talk. We reminisced a bit about the good old days in the Bronx. It was a laugh and tear-filled conversation. He is a retired writer for television enjoying the good life in sunny Southern Ca. We promised to call one another and get together when we found ourselves in the neighborhood.

I have not yet heard from any of my old friends, but I feel as if I have found three new ones. It does not happen every day that strangers are brought together because of the place in which they once lived.

I could not, in all good conscience, conclude this tale without mentioning Arty Morgenstern (**Taft** and Aviation High School- 956) of Granada Hills, California. We grew up together (along with Iris Skollar Cohn) and have been in and out of touch over the years. We have renewed this friendship via computers and E-Mail on a weekly basis and talk on the telephone when time permits. Iris Cohn and Arty have remained in touch all these years. I guess I owe them, at the very least, a word of gratitude for seeing that we have all kept in touch over this span of time besides, he was extremely upset about not being mentioned in the past article.

It is miracle enough that two childhood friends have maintained contact (mostly by "real-time" mail) for over 36 years, at a distance of 3,000 miles. It is with extreme pride that we have both worked together on this little "miracle." ■

Judith J. Goodwin Yerman, Taft '56, lives in Alta Loma, CA, and owns a small desktop publishing company. Her poetry has been published by Blue Mountain Arts of Boulder, CO. Married for 35 years she has one 27 year old son, Jay. I can be reached at jjyerman@sprynet.com.

Iris Skollar Cohn, Industrial Arts '56, has lived for many years in Commack, N.Y. and working for Majestic Greeting Card Company on Long Island. She is married 30 yrs and has two sons, Steve, 27 and Dan, 25.

18

Yes, There IS life West of the Grand Concourse!

By Les Neumann
Clinton '65

West 232nd Sreet

What gives? I just received your latest issue of **Back in THE BRONX**, and I am deeply wounded. For those of you who thought that there was no life west of the **Grand Concourse** you are sadly mistaken.

There were those of us who lived down the hill from **Riverdale** (which to this day shares the same zip code) and had a life very similar to those of you up the other hill going towards **Fordham Road**. I grew up on **232nd Street** and **Kingsbridge Avenue**, the Bronx. We had all the amenities, 6 candy stores, 2 butchers (one kosher, one not), the fruit store, the fish store, **Shelvyn Bakery, Progress TV, Dan** and **Joe's Barber Shop, Loeshers Deli, Woolworth's, Grand Union** and **A&P, Thom McAnn, Williams' Funeral Home, McGlynn's Market, Luhrs Soda Shoppe, Hy's Eating Place,** the Diner, PS7, the **VFW Hall, the Drum and Bugle Corps, Gaelic Park, Sugar Ray Robinson's house, Fanny Farmer** (more important was the empty lot next to it), **horseshoe hill** (for roller skating), **Kelton's Pool and Ice Skating Rink,** the **RKO** and **Dale** movie theaters, the **Little League Field, Stella D'Oro,** the **Broadway IRT,** the #1 bus to **Clinton,** and on and on. All this was between **231st** and **Broadway** and **238th** and **Broadway**...the Bronx.

The ethnic makeup was simple: Irish and Jewish. We all went to **PS7**. I was the second or third class to go on to **JHS 143**. Some of my friends went to 141. We all went to **Clinton, Walton or Science** (**Clinton** for me, class of '65). I remember standing in front of the Italian Bakery waiting for the bus that took us to **Clinton**. Since we were the beginning, or the end of the line (depending on your perspective), the driver could sit and have a cup of coffee and ignore us for as long as possible. When the driver finally got brave enough to open the doors, the mad rush began. Sure we could have gotten on in an orderly fashion, what fun would that have been? Although we all had bus passes, we never showed them; that was the least of his problems. As the bus started to fill, guys were getting on from the back door as well as the front. Others were being passed through the windows or over the top of the throng. About half way through the loading process, the driver would start to think about closing the doors; he knew how long the process would take. There was no violence, no fights, but rather a chaotic ritual. When the bus finally left, the morning choruses of "what does you father do for a living?" "Nothing, he's a bus driver," began. Every morn-ing, the chants, like a religious service, took place.

Games of choice were stickball, football and basketball in the **PS7** schoolyard, king/queen, box baseball, hit the penny, curb ball (aka stoopball), ring-a-levio, hide and seek (summers only), johnny-on-the-pony, punch ball, nok hockey (in **PS7** after school program), ping pong, pool, sprinklers (again, summer only) and the outdoor movie shown on the side of the school (our version of the drive-in) and of course, potsy. So you see we had a life, a darn good one.

The major shopping excursion also included the trip to **Alexander's**. I once got a very sharp gold jacket with leather pocket and collar trim that was the envy of every kid I saw. I got the jacket for the high holidays, matched with a pair of black pants from **Robert Hall**, black shoes from **Thom McAnn**, white shirt from **Alexander's** and black tie (a hand-me-down from my dad). I remember losing my brother in Alexander's one year when he hid in one of the bargain bins. After shopping, there was the "thank God it's over" reward: the trip to either **Krum's** or **Jahn's**. Either one made it almost bearable. My first memory of the **Loew's Paradise** was during Passover when my mother took my brother and me to see "The Ten Commandments." I also thought the stars were real. So what of it?

I also remember when **Alexander's** got a parking lot. When my dad realized that five hundred cars were trying to get into fifty-car lot, we began to explore the new phenom-enon, the Cross County Shopping Center. What a change!

Tuesdays and Thursdays before Hebrew school I got 35¢, fifteen each way for the bus and the other five for a Devil Dog. Most times I walked the four miles home to save the fifteen cents. Don't tell. Ours was the generation just before drugs, but not before drinking. Sex was mysterious but not unheard of. None of us had cars but we always managed to get around. We got WINS, WMCA and WABC when they played real music. There is lots to know about the West Bronx, the forgotten Bronx. ∎

"Jake the Pickle Man"

By Rosalind Cohen Owitz

Anyone growing up in the vicinity of **Jennings Steet** had to know about "crazy" Jake the pickle man. His stand was located in the middle of the market.

I lived at **1500 Boston Post Rd.**, which was at the corner of **Boston Rd. and Wilkins Ave.** from the mid '30's to 1954. My mother would go shopping at the **Jenning Street Market** and would try to buy pickles and sauerkraut from Jake. Because my mother had black hair and black eyes, Jake thought she was a gypsy and would not sell her anything. He would yell at her to put on earrings and go tell fortunes. Everytime she passed his stand, he would yell "fortune teller go away!" Everyone would laugh. Embarrassed she would cross the street never to pass his stand again. My mother was born in Austria, and come to think of it, she did look like a gypsy. So what is Friday night and roast chicken without a green vegetable (a sour pickle) or Sunday night- deli franks without sauerkraut?

My mother then sent my older sister Lena (Libby) to Jake's. My sister who was very fat, would stand on line (and there was always a line), when Jake and his wife saw her, they would shout at her to go away. They would yell "She doesn't need pickles, she is fat enough!"

That left me, because I was small and thin. So every Friday after school, carrying a jar and a quarter, I would go down **Wilkens Ave.** The trip to **Jennings St. Market** should have taken only 15 minutes, but it took me an hour. Sometimes Aleene Kaplan who lived in the same building, joined me. At every stoop there were some games you could join in. (Where are you Doris Kramer and Little Billie?) You could stop and play jump rope, jacks, double dutch, cut out dolls, etc. Half way down **Wilkins Ave.** you could watch the boys play stickball. (Where are you Frankie and your sister Lena?)

When I finally reached Jake's, it was almost closing time. When Jake saw me he would always smile and give me a small sour pickle to eat on my way home. I would watch his wife dipping her diamonds in the pickle barrels and then dream she lost a ring and then I would dive into the barrel and eat all the pickles until I found her ring.

Instead of taking **Wilkins Ave.** home, I would round the corner and go to **Charlotte Street** where there were more games and different friends.

About 15 years ago the "New York Daily News" in their color-photo section ran a story about famous pickle stands in New York. Sure enough they had a story about Jake. At the end of the story it said Jake was mysteriously shot. I guess he refused to sell someone pickles and that person wouldn't take no for an answer. ∎

Editors' Note:

Deja Vu(?) Does Jake remind anyone out there of "Seinfeld's Soup Nazi"? It occurs to us that there is a parallel to be drawn here. Just as the "Soup Nazi" chooses whom he favors with his soup and/or bread, Jake chose his "favorites" and his "victims"; just as Jake made his rules in his place, so the "Soup Nazi" makes his rules - and just as arbitrarily. Could these two men possibly be related? Hmm ....

N.Y. The Way It Was... THE BRONX

Continued from page 2

provided by folks such as Colin Powell, Judd Hirsch, Red Buttons and Robert Klein as well as several non-public figures whose Bronx fables are no less important. The common theme for these interviewees is the joy they all take in reliving, even momentarily, a pretty nice time in their lives. Jon DiMucci might win MVP award for his tough and funny stories of Arthur Avenue and Bronx Park, but Colin Powell scores high too for recalling his days on Kelly Street. Marvin Scott has the pictures to bolster his claim that he actually <u>did</u> get into the girls' gym class at Taft High School and Shari Lewis (minus Lampchop) retells the glories of Parkchester with great vigor. All those on camera indeed smile

and shine with youthful light as they stroll down memory lane, and that enthusiasm crosses the barrier of the TV screen.

The home movies and the snapshot are great, of course. Who wouldn't want another look at Krum's candy counter, or a glimpse of Alexander's sales floor on a busy day? Somebody with foresight took a camera aboard the Woodlawn Jerome subway as it rattled along Jerome Avenue one day in the 50's, and that film is pure gold today. Of course many people recorded their own families and friends in great moments of Bronx life: the visits to the Zoo, the bar mitzvah, the dance at St. Raymond's, graduation from high school or the day the new car arrived. These

once-private scenes are the stuff of history today and WLIW has done laudable work in unearthing these family treasures.

Perhaps there is a bit too much baseball in the program and those long pitches from WLIW are tough to take. On the premier screening on Aug. 6, the pleas for membership contributions were just about as long as the film itself. Later airings should be more watchable and you can always get an unbroken video of your own (WLIW is selling the entire series on VHS).

To readers of **Back In THE BRONX**, this WLIW production is a necessary addition to their video collection. Don't worry about the little blemishes or the missing neighborhoods, *New York The Way It Was: The Bronx* is a pure joy and shouldn't be missed. ∎

Reminiscing

by Irwin M. Kaufman

When I'd tell my mother I was going out, she didn't have to ask, "Out where?" It was understood that "out" meant the playground. The playground was the gathering place for many of the residents living in the neighborhood bounded by **College and Morris Avenues** and **166th and 167th** Streets. It was my home away from home during the Forties and early Fifties.

Located next door to a tennis court, which would later become the home of **P.S. 22**, the playground was probably no different from other such places around the city. Built above street level, it contained an assortment of play equipment for kids of all ages: swings, monkey bars, slides see-saws, and a basketball court that served as a wading pool during the hot summer months and an ice skating rink in winter. Handball courts, shuffle board and paddle tennis were also available. Punch ball, dodge ball, touch football, and any other activity that could be thought of, took place in a large open area. Benches were conveniently located around the playground where the men played chess and checkers and the women kept a watchful eye on the toddlers.

The guys I hung out with were at that stage of life where sports took on more importance than girls. We spent most of our time keeping our raging testosterone levels in check by playing basketball whenever we could. During winter we played on the ice in the wading pool, skillfully avoiding the ice skaters until chased by the playground director.

The basketballs we played with (and footballs, too) were laced and leather-covered with an inflatable rubber bladder inside. The bladders of some of those balls had been patched and re-patched so often that the balls had become misshapen—so much so that at times it became difficult to tell the basketballs from the footballs.

When the basketball court was unavailable, we played punch ball, chasing after fly balls while carefully maneuvering around people and playground paraphernalia. When we weren't chasing a ball, we chased each other in a form of tag called "ring-a-leaveeo."

We kept ourselves from becoming bored by inventing daring ways to challenge each other, like leaping from a swing as it reached the highest point in its forward arc. Some guys would walk around the wading pool atop the wrought iron fence like a high wire acrobat. And there was always one guy who would stand at the very top of the monkey bars and drop to the ground between the pipes.

We found tamer things to do, of course. Card games like "war" and "knucks" occupied our time. When we could afford to buy baseball cards and comic books, we played poker using them as chips. We had other ways of gambling with those baseball cards as well: pitching them, flipping them and matching them. Had

The Playground

there been a way to use them in a slot machine we'd have done that, too.

While we gambled away our baseball cards and comic books, the older guys, those who worked during the week, played high-stakes handball on weekends. The singles and doubles matches were usually played with a "Spaldeen." But when the games really got serious, they played with a small, hard black ball and wore soft leather gloves. Some of my friends were good enough to be picked to play in those games. Others were lucky enough to make a few cents running errands to the grocery store across from the playground on **Morris Avenue** to buy sodas for the players and spectators.

When **P.S. 22** was built, we got a place to play where we didn't have to contend with stuff meant for

little kids or with people sitting on benches. Some of the guys were working after school by then either at the neighborhood stores or delivering the Home News. We had our own weekend softball and basketball tournaments using real money as the stakes instead of baseball cards and comic books.

Shortly after I graduated from **Taft** High School my folks moved to **Bronxwood** and **Allerton Avenues** I found I'd outgrown the playground by that time and was ready to move on to yet another of life's many stages four years at City College. I have no regrets about having grown up in the Bronx except that I wish I'd saved those baseball cards and comic books. But then again, who knew that someday they'd be valuable?

Dear Mr. Bobkoff,

Judging by the dates in your recent article, "Patriotism on the Bronx Front in the Korean War" in <u>Back in the Bronx,</u> you have about six years on me. However, your article brought back vivid memories of my own Bronx boyhood in the Highbridge section. I, too had collections of toy soldiers, war comics and scads of plastic model planes and battleships.

What prompted me to write was the photo of your father's store, which brought back one of my best memories of all. It was a cold fall evening, in 1966, I believe, when I was a college freshman. I went up to Fordham Road to buy a new pair of Levi's; it was worth the trip, since the stores around there had such good prices and had much more in stock than those in my neighborhood. I headed for Bobkoff's, as I had done several times before, and picked out a pair of the olive-green jeans that happened to be in style that year. I was also pleased that I could find my exact size, which not many stores carried (a chubby waist and very short inseam). A middleaged gentleman working the sales floor asked if he could help me with anything else, such as a belt. He pointed to a rack of really good-looking, western-style leather belts, and I couldn't resist. I took my purchases to the register; the total came to something like $8.50. (it's tempting to long for those low prices while blocking out the fact that my after-school job paid $1.25 an hour!) I was disappointed and embarrassed when I realized that I had but $7.00 in my wallet, and about 47 cents in change — 20 cents of which I would need to catch the "D" train home. I apologized to the cashier and asked him to take back the belt because I did not have enough money.

The man who had just assisted me asked what was wrong. I explained the problem, and he told the cashier to put the belt back in the bag. He asked me how much I could pay, and I counted out $7.27, explaining that I needed 20 cents for the train. He put the 27 cents back in my hand, and said, "Hang on to this; you might need to take a bus from the subway stop, or get a cup of coffee. It's cold out tonight". He then took the handwritten green receipt pad from the cashier, changed the amount to $7.00 with his pencil, and marked it "Special". I stammered out something about returning some other time with the money, but he dismissed that idea with a wave of his hand, saying, "No, son; this is your special price". Still amazed, I thanked him profusely as I left.

I don't know if this kind man was your father, but, since he had the authority to change a price (actually, make a gift of a fine belt) on the spot, I think maybe he was. Time has blurred my recollection of what he looked like, so I won't attempt a description, but the memory of that simple but uncommon act of kindness will stay with me forever.

Time and circumstances took me away from the Bronx and clothes-shopping on Fordham Road, but not before I made some return trips to Bobkoff's and many recommendations to my friends that they should do so. However, I know that the kind man in the store wasn't just thinking of good business practice; I was a total stranger and he had no assurance at all that he would ever see me again. Blessings on that beautiful man!

Sincerely,
George Morris

Editors Note:

We regret that several errors in Michael Bobkoff's piece on the Korean War in the last issue affected meaning. For example, "arrived forces" in line one should have been "armed forces" and "laser jet fighters" in the final line should have been "latest jet fighters."

Classifieds

Missing Persons

MP1144 Ron Friedman, **Clinton** '58, Hunter '62, Phi Sigma Delta, 197th St & Bainbridge Ave, 182 St & Grand Ave , Creston Jr. H.S.; Wants old friends to contact him at 516/536/9598.

MP1145 I'm interested in collecting anecdotes about Bronx Jewish doctors for an article that I'm writing. If you have a good one to share write to Michael Nevins, 808 Arcadia Place, River Vale, NJ 07675

MP1146 Delfin Alyarez would like to hear from any of the old gang - 40's, 50's, 60's who lived in 859 & 863 Southern Blvd. Call 305/771/8743.

MP1147 Former residents of Sherman Alley (more properly known as Sherman Ave), an area bounded by Grand Concourse on the west, 167th on the north, College Ave on the east and 165th on the south...in the 30's and WWII years...who can recall the Sector Sentinel, the hometown newspaper with a circulation of 300, to every "boy" in the service 1941-1946... who played basketball, touch football and softball in PS 90 playground. Contact Stan Kagan PO Box 441, Caldwell, NJ 07006- 201/226/4486.

MP1148 Howard Dohrman looking for George T. and Frank P. **Evander** and Parkchester 1944-1948. Call 813/784/2029.

MP1149 Reward - '56 **Roosevelt** graduates - we need current addresses and/or phone numbers for: Rosemarie Gariano, Josephine Savino, Diane Vitucci, Rosemarie Vasano, Isabell Federella, Rhoda Ginsberg, Elaine Slepp, Joanna Paesano, Flora LeDuca, Elaine Meneghel, Lucille Salemi, Margaret Bruni, Barbara Domashefsky, Anna Devita. We need your help please call Hal Rosenstein at 516/585/ 6474 or Nancy Cappozzi at 914/365/2176. '56 **Roosevelt** Graduates Reunion - October 12, 1996 for more info call Hal Rosenstein at 516/585/6474 or Nancy Cappozzi at 914/365/2176.

MP1150 Barney Stone is interested in hearing from the gang from Pop's candy Store on Burnside Ave & the boys from Boy Scout Troop 175 that met at PS28 on Tremont Ave. Call **304/787/320?** or send E-mail to BSTONE2494@aol.com

MP1151 Seriously seeking my best friend, Barbara Scheele, from Belmont Ave. in 1954. Also looking for Mary Ann Pavigilanti, Lenny Landis, Stanley and others from our group —Joan Szanto

MP1152 Attention **Morris** HS grads Class of '45. Eleanor Gianni (now Abbate) and Evelyn Salamone (now Vasika) would love to hear from Charlotte Joyce, Rosie Greenstein and Peter DelBene. Write Eleanor Abbate 230 Calhoun Ave, Bronx, NY 10465

MP1153 PS 56 Ms. Fitzpatrick's grade 6 class of 1962 - Cohen, Fink, Green, Holt, Frankel, Miller, Scharf, Narcisso, Feller, Kalus, Purdu, Scher, Skow, Zornitsky, et.al. Most of us went through 1-6 together. Where are we now?

MP1154 Looking for **Evander Childs** H.S. Graduates of West Bronx - Cecil Heider Rappaport - Renee Albert Getz - Irving Perry from Burke Ave. - Julia Wolfson from Holland Ave. Contact Shirley Applebaum Small at 407/737/5066 (Florida).

MP1155 Looking for painting/drawings by my grandfather, William R. Shoemaker who lived in the Bronx 1920-1945. He gave them to friends and to pay bills during the Depression. No one in the family has one. Please contact Dan Ryan, 1905 Sunny Slope Rd., Bridgewater N.J. 08807.

MP1156 Looking for John Donnelly (J.D.) from Valentine Ave & Fordham Rd., Bronx. Last heard, a butcher. Call the Fordham girls : Kathy & Carole: 914/255/7957.

MP1157 Arlene Kaye Richards, PS 94 '41, E.B.B. '43, **Evander** Jan. '46. Looking for Shirley (Bamfi) Kemelhar, Joan Weiss, Roslyn Greenberg, Delores Ferro, Jacqueline Harris, Lois Mandell, Muriel Hornik. Please call 516/626/9566.

MP1158 Thelma Rosen is still looking for Greta Finkelstein, Linda Weiss, Arline Herskowitz and anyone who still has their mother's dishes from "Dish Night" at the Freeman Theatre. Desperately trying to put a set together! Thelma Rosen Kimble 656 Beach St., Costa Mesa, Ca. 92627 June '49 Graduate.

MP1159 Harriet Lefkowitz from Macombs Rd. moved to Gloversville circa 1950. Please contact Harvery Rosenberg 2350 Water's Edge Blvd., Columbus, OH 43209.

MP1160 Looking for Vinnie Vignali from 1155 Woodycrest Ave. graduated Samuel Gompers 1955/56. Write: Sarah (Hickey) Carroll-3006 LaSalle Ave., Bronx, NY 10461.

MP1161 CCNY, Wilde '52 Seeking Laura Chesluk, Rhoda Buchholz, Rita Kantor, Arthur Yellin and Florence Tendler for next reunion. We are all alive and well (almost all, anyway). call us in Westport, Ct 203/255/4450. Shelia Handshoe Rothman.

MP1162 Looking for old friends from Montgomery Ave. such as Roy & Jay Siegal, Phil Rothstein (Father owned the deli on University Ave.), Jay Burton, Vinnie & Chuckie Volturo, etc. I lived at 1793 Montgomery Ave. Would love to hear from you. Phyllis Lerner 100-22 Bellamy Loop, Bronx, NY 10475.

MP1163 David Toperosky, **Monroe** '63 & Wileen Schneiderman Toperosky, **Monroe** '64 are looking for old friends from the neighborhood. We'd love to hear from you! 22436 N.E. 18th St., Redmond, WA 98053 206/868/3852.

MP1164 Ellen Schatz (now Wolf) of Clay Avenue & **Taft** '45 would enjoy hearing from Bill Kortrey, Joan D., Dorothy D., **Taft** girlfriends , Louise Donner, Judith Riccio, Florence Kephart.

MP1165 Billy Hayden - **Roosevelt** '58 Love to hear from classmates JHS 44-55 & crowd from Tremont and Prospect, Pines Restaurant, Eddie Snitzsky, Eddie Gallo, & Barbara Gruceski, & friends from Loew's Paradise 56-58, now running a Bed & Breakfast in Bath, Maine. Call 207/443/6069 or 800/516/4578.

MP1166 Jerry Graff - Circa 1949 **Monroe** H.S., lived & played Beach Ave. & E. Tremont near Taylor Ave. & Thierot Ave., kept in touch with Jerry Cohen, Bernie Fass & Ed Kammerer. Would love to hear from old friends. Married to Marilyn Krammerer - **Monroe** H.S. Jerry Graff 1730 Sweetbay, Toms River, NJ, 08755 - 908/914/0497.

MP1167 Where are you? Members and friends of Club Paragon - Holland Ave, mid 1930's - Eischel sisters, Holland Ave. Call or write Murray Schneider 688 Dickens Ave, Franklin Square, NY 11010 - 516/481/ 7547. Clara and Moe Blatman from Bronx and Spring Valley.

MP1168 Adeaide Vitiello - **Walton** '52 Would love to reminisce with my classmates. I live in Lodi, NJ - 15 min from GWB, through my high school years, I lived at 156th St. then East Tremont in the Bronx. Adelaide Seaton 92 First St., Lodi, NJ 07644.

MP1169 Jim (Mack) McNally , **Dodge** '55, St. Jerome '51. Love to hear from South Bronx 136/137 St. Willis Ave - crowd or **Dodge** alumni (Seig, Tom Brennan, Bob Crossen, Mary Walsh etc.) Lost track of all but Jack Kinahan. Joined Army '56; stayed in Detroit. Married 33 years, two grown kids. 810/754/3039.

MP1170 Tetard JHS Grads Bert Reisman is interested in hearing from his students. Also I am seeking news from Barracuda Jrs. from Kingsbridge Road area. Bert Reisman 3 Regina Rd., Monsey, NY, 10952 914 /352/3013.

MP1171 Where are you now? Jack Samonsky, Elinor Shulmon, Stanley Glossman, Marty Sconlon, Stanley Lewis, Dave Selmon, Bunky, Richard Strom, Luis Romero, Monarchs Baseball Team: Fred Barnes, Paul Boland, Abe Goland, Jerry Geisler, Leo Solomon, Eddie Vasquez, Jermy Ortiz, Steve McGee, Joe Mancello, Lester Skulnick, Andy Luperillo, Lenny Stark, Eli Stark, Herb Krystal, daniel Elber, Harvey Brass, Stall Bros, Phil Drucker, Muscrella Bros., Barry Wagner, Jerry Wagner, Abe Rodriguez, Berny Bonilla, Ballas Bros., Neil Fidler, Marty Rothstein. Contact Jerry Toplitsky - 12 Charles Lane, Pomona, NY 10970

MP1172 Looking for Phyllis Koeppell (last known address Washington Ave, Brooklyn) and Joan Sigman - camp friends from Camp Naticook 1948-1956. Do you know them? Can you help me find them? Gale Holtz Golden, Burlington, Vermont, 802/864/0757.

MP1173 I'm George Stone 178 & Bryons PS 64, **Evander**, Berlin, neighborhood bum, Jewish boy who owned a Harley, Stardust Ballroomer, hacked a few years out of West Farms. Retired in San Fernando Valley, Los Angeles. Love to hear from some old West Farmites. George Stone - 8811 Canoga Ave. #116, Canoga Pk., CA 91304

MP1174 Wanted: Sidney Grosfeld of 1141 Elder Ave. Rumored to be in Florida . Three dolphins looking for a reunion: Saul L., Gerry W., Joe M. Please get in touch: Saul Lindenbaum 4307 Roundnoll Rd, Baldwin MD, 21013

MP1175 Dave Bohlmann would like to hear from friends of PS 107 class of '50 & **Gompers** H.S class of '54. Presently living at 12334 Grove Meadow, Stafford, TX 77477

MP1176 Murry Salad, where are you? Lived on Lowell St. in the Bronx. Married and heard he lived in Manhattan 165th St. Crowd would like to know how you can be reached - Emily Mordeci 30 The Rise, Congers NY 10920 914/268/7605.

MP1177 Dorothy Hull Purcell and Sylvia San Severino Mohola would like to hear from graduates of 1937. St. John chrysostom School on Hoe Ave.- Contact Sylvia Mottola 8887 ASW 95 Lane Ocala, FL 34481.

MP1178 Does anyone know the whereabouts of Rose Gorshovski (maiden name) and Selma Gerstenzang who lived on University Ave. and moved to Florida in the 40's also Pearl Spielman Dambrot contact Sanford Falk PO Box 475 Hewlett NY 11557.

MP1179 Charles Moravec would love to hear from any of the persons listed below or from anyone residing on Marcy or Elliot Place between Jerome Ave and the Concourse from 1940 to 1950: Marilyn Avreen, Jack Barush, Dorothy Behrens, Anita Levinson, Arthur Musen, Ann Edson (Ne Rabin). Contact Charles Moravec 43-70 Kissena Blvd. Apt 27K, Flushing NY 11355 718/461/3477.

MP1180 I would be very happy to find Rita Alter, Beatrice Greenberg, Sylvia Aponte, Gladys Benjamin and Doris Brown - All friends from the old Kelly St. neighborhood. Contact Marilyn Powell Berns 22181 Apache Dr., Lake Forest, CA, 92630 714/768/9410.

MP1181 Looking for Joey Ergas 1267 Grant Ave. Bronx lived there 1940's- 1960's. Call Archie Krauss 30 Daley Pl., Lynbrook, NY 11563.

MP1182 Howard Sherman, M.D. **Clinton** '52, CCNY '56- USAF Md Corp -Looking for Jessup Ave guys, 1940's & 1950's; PS 104, JHS82 - Phil & Harry's Candy Store - Where are you Sy Levy, Eddie Wersa, Richie Cohen, Jerry Weinberg, Seth Sheiner, Jill Felsen, Jack Hand. Please contact me at 7701 Wurzbach Rd #1001, San Antonio, TX 78229 210/615/3787.

MP1183 Looking for **Walton** '61 Graduates Planning 35th Reunion on Sunday, October 13th. I have 100+ names & current addresses. For info call Roberta (Soloff) Seidner 718/884/8634. Looking for Steve & Laura Kahn from Shorehaven Beach Club. Also Judy Katonah from 182nd & Grand Ave. & Barbara Billitchy from Davidson Ave. Would love to hear from you! Call Roberta (Soloff) Seidner 718/884/8634.

MP1184 Prewar WWII remember the 'BENCHES', Macy's Pool Room, the Park Plaza Theater on University Ave.? Remember 'Jake' Badler and Myra, Buddy Barovick (now 74, bald and fat) and Lenore, Claire Wolfe, the Linn Twins, Sedran, Ravinett, etal. Write Buddy at the internet, (BUDDY_B@WOW.com)

MP1185 I am Herb Crane: Went to PS 70 graduated 1932. Looking for Leo Golberg, Henry Weintraub - Anyone who remembers me. Contact me at 11246 Cloverleaf Circle, Boca Raton, FL 33428 407/487/7948.

MP1186 Anyone remember me? Arlene Fox (now Cohen) PS 33, 1950 E.B.B, 1953 **Walton,** 1956 Jacqueline Berg, Barbara Johnson, where are you? Contact me at 91 Elm Dr., Levittown, NY 11756

MP1187 Where are you Bernie Feldman - graduate of **Taft** HS? Carol Marcus would love to hear from you. Remember 'Moon River'? Contact me at 10865 Deborah Dr., Potomac MD 20854.

MP1188 Interested in locating people who lived in or near the Amalgamated section who attended PS 95 in the mid 1950's. Also 1958 **Clinton** grads. Call Rich Hantman 201/334/9167.

MP1189 Anita (Friedman) Frohmann Spector will complete her PhD degree in Management/Adminstration December 1996. I have been accepted into "Who's Who in the East" and am currently a Buyer at Colgate Palmolive Company. I am married and have one son and two stepchildren.

MP1190 Where are all you uyse guys (178th) Walt Samey, Bobby Bloom, Morty Gold, Al Goldstein, Marky Hoppy. Anyone heard from Whippets (Wilken Ave) Izzy, Teddy C. Johnny. Write Paddy Farrell 240 Peterson St, Brentwood, NY 11717.

MP1191 Looking for a Beatrice. Betrice (Bebe) Metzger, whither? From over the bakery on Katonah Ave. in Woodlawn. Thence to Edson Ave in Wakefield, and since lost. Now? You, **Walton** High School '57 (?). Me, **Iona Prep**, then West Point, Then away, burdened. You, dark ringlets, skin of porcelain, eyes that flashed of Cuba. Ah silenciosa! Does anyone know of this Beatrice? There was a Missing Persons in the Jahn's issue. MP260. It referred to a **Walton** High School reunion, class of '58. Perhaps they could assist. Jim Ryan, 535 Cathedral Pkwy., NYC 10025 212/316/6009.

MP1192 1/51 **Walton** Grad. Eunice (Hayes/ Marolda) Wexler. Lived at Kingsbridge Terrace. Also went to PS86 & Hunter. Looking for Joan Cavaliere, Barbara (Maisie Neiderman, Dorine Silverman, Irene Lee or anyone from schools or neighborhood. Now live N. Broward County, FL.

MP1193 Would like to hear from anyone who remembers me or my family (1940-60) from corner candy store and old neighborhood at 1490 Crotona Park East and Wilkins Ave. David Hochstein, 1945 East 38th St., Brooklyn NY 11234.

MP1194 Where are you my friends from **Taft** 6/50. Lost contact with everyone - would love to hear from someone. Contact me, Joan Goodstein, Bryer, P.O. Box 282, Westbury NY 11590.

MP1196 Seeking information on the Eichel sisters (Anna, Frieda, Lilian, Blanche) who lived at 2535 Holland Ave. during the late '30s and 40's. Contact Milton Klein at 423/584/4565.

Classifieds

MP1197 Marilyn (Gitelson) Levy, **Taft** '53, PS82. Lived on Nelson Ave. Looking for old friends: Rita Basin, Janice Wolff, Ann Rose Levine, Arlene Kohl, Marilyn Potasnick, Edna Fisher, Stan Jaffee. I am now residing in Delray Beach FL.

MP1198 Sue Goldstein (nee Lax) is wondering what happened to all of you who grew up in the '40s and '50s on that great little street called DeVoe Terrace?

MP1199 Would like to hear from any survivors of NYU Heights graduates of '43 or Tau Delta Phi members of '43. -Bernie (Lazarus) Layne, 931 Tulip Ct., Marco Island, FL 33937.

MP1200 Westchesterites (or out-of-towners) renew old aquaintances- phone Shelia Furmansky Kerper 914/923/3168. PS93-77, **Monroe** '57, CCNY (uptown) '55. Married 40 years to Lester Kerper, Brooklyn Tech, Brooklyn College.

MP1201 If you are out there Andrea Oberlander-Arnow Ave., Gayle Baker, Scott Towers, David Kagen-PS28, Ian Karasic- I hope you are well. Call Howie Harris at 201/860/7091 (office).

MP1202 Where are the "Golden Dragons" of Eastburn Ave? Lenny Hillsenrad, Arthur Factor, Arthur Posner, Marvin Lew, Marvin Rosen, Stanley Friedberg, Stuart Robinson, Charley Woolf, Billy Epstein, Martin Gordon.

MP1203 Bobbie Fiarman would like to contact some of my childhood friends from PS26, PS82 and **Taft**: Sheila Bloom, Marilyn Miner, Marilyn Luttinger, Lenore Gross, Marilyn Klausner, Stephanie Lang. All from Phelan Place in the Bronx. Irwin Fiarman would like to hear from anyone he knew from his childhood days in the Bronx, PS6 and **Roosevelt** as well as **Hunter** College: George Ahearn and Seymour Zwieback. Bobbie Fiarman 23 Crosswick Rd., Willinburo, NJ 08046 609/877/9492.

MP1204 Anyone who remembers "Smileys" on W. 162nd & Woodycrest Ave. Anyone from Woodycrest Home and anyone from the Jr. Rebels (who hung out on Summit Ave.) PS73 & **Taft**. Write me: Cecilia (Cecil) Boyce 437 W. Oak Ave, Wildwood NJ 08260.

MP1205 Where are you: Sherman Golomb, Sheldon Morgenstern, Danny Diamond? I found Sonny Sturman in Calf. Contact Leona Bayles Brauser (**Taft** 1/48) 7841 Afton Villa Ct., Boca Raton FL 33433.

MP1206 Louise Ubanka- lived near Webster Ave and 175th St. Graduated **Roosevelt** '41. Marie Simon also graduated **Roosevelt** in '41.

MP1207 Arlene Goldberg Rubinstein, **Monroe** '46. Would like to hear from Thelma Rothman, Ruth Hayden, Layra Klein, Evelyn Tanzer (**Taft**), Blanche Kaufman (Longfellow Ave.) Call 516/569/4935 evenings.

MP1208 Remember East 182nd St. between Crotona Ave. and Southern Blvd. during the forties? Where are you Gloria Kershaw, Rosemary Barbella, Mitzie Munz, Seymour Scharf, "The Dusters?" Remember JHS118, Joyce Nicosia, Felix Miele? Contact Charlotte Ramsaur through this Classified #.

MP1209 Ronnie Levine-PS31, PS73, **Hunter** High '56, NYU '60. Grew up at 711 Walton Ave. (bet. 153 &158 Sts.) in the shadow of the Yankee Stadium. Memories anyone? Call 516/658/7543.

MP1210 Jerry Bleich, did your dream of earning $10,000 a year come true? — Nettie

MP2111 Sandi Denowitz Reich would like to hear from old friends. PS82 '63, **Taft** '66. Call 602/951/2869.

MP1212 Looking for Ellen Lichtschein of 1895 Morris Ave. Please contact Eric Klass, 1140 N. Clark St., #301, Los Angeles, CA 90069.

MP1213 Looking for Stephen Kinsler, formerly of 975 Walton Ave., **Taft** '60, CCNY '64.

MP1214 Beverly Levy Sacharow- your bobsey twin Shelley Alpert Finn found and lost you. Please write: 193 Regents Park, Westport CT 06880 or fax 203/256/8109. I would love to see you and catch-up!

MP1215 Bobby Finz, **Taft** '66 would love to hear from old friends. If you hung out on 170th St. or played hoops at Mullally Park or if you have any Murray Zinovay stories. Call 914/357/5311.

MP1216 Looking for info on Demetrios (Jim) Kambosos. He lived on 81 West 182nd St, his Father Gus owned a shoe repair shop on Burnside Ave. (near Concourse) Grad. **Clinton** '50-51. Contact Mary DiCesare Heaven at 510/886/6956.

MP1217 Gladys Stern Amoroso would like to hear from you if you were from Hunts Point Section, Hoe Ave., Aldus St etc. I am a retired registered nurse.

MP1218 Does anyone remember Celia Zucker, **Monroe** 1/'44 or Bill Vevy Getman, **Monroe** '35? We now live in Forest Hills, Queens. 718/263/7779. We lived on Kelly St. (Manor Ave.) and 173rd & Vyse Ave., respectively. Please call or write.

MP1219 Does any graduate of the Class of '56 at PS103 remember Mrs. Murphy and the paint closet? This **Evander** grad '60 would love to hear from any of you. Maurisa Fisher Solomon can be reached at 914/429/1004, Fax 914/354/9636. 17 Hidden Valley Dr., Suffern, NY 10901.

MP1220 Does anyone from Beach, Taylor, Theriot or Leland Avenues remember Arline Bronstein: PS102, Ridder, **Monroe**, Hunter College? Please write to Arline Weisberg, 22520-3, Jeffrey Mark Court, Chatsworth, CA 91311.

MP1221 Looking for Gregory Rhodes, son of George Rhodes, Music Director of Sammy Davis Jr. Lived in Highbridge and went to **Cardinal Hayes** HS around 1970, worked in PS11 Community Center.

MP1222 Roxanne Gross Zimet looking for **Waltonites**, Iris haida, Barbara Buck, Joan Becker, Maurice Prince, Clea Nerenberg. Also Olinville JHS '40 RA grads. Email Roxygolf@AOL.com or call 407/495/0312.

MP1223 Pelham Bay & Burke Ave. Renunion. "Growing up in the 50's and 60's" Saturday, Oct. 5, 1996 at the Eastwood Manor. Cocktail hour 7:00pm-8:00pm, Dinner and Dance 8:00pm to 1:00am. $65 per person. For more info contact Joe Mineo 203/778/8141 Home or work 718/579/6919.

MP1224 Luciano Siracusano from "The Harvard House" 1981 LaFontaine Ave. 1940's-50's. In sales for 30 years. Now an independent assoc. of PrePaid Legal Services, Inc. Is there anyone out there from the Harvard House?

MP1225 Beverly Rosenblett Broth, **Monroe** '49 married that Marine who is now listed in Who's Who in the South-SouthEast. Bev is President of Sarasota Camera Exchange & Video Center, Vice President of Art & Frame of Sarasota. She has 4 daughters, 7 grandsons. She would love to hear from the BIOGA's or Centaur's. Or anyone else that remembers Bev & Ray.

MP1226 Victor MacDougall served in WWII from 1942-45. With the 5th Air Force in the Pacific. Then worked for NY Telecom (34 years) retired to Fla. in 1981. Now doing Senior Citzens Problems with Nursing Homes.

MP1227 Hallandale Symphonic Pops Concerts, Maestro Barry Volkman 1996-7 season: Nov. 10 Dec 15. Jan 19, feb. 23, Mar. 23 @ 7:30 pm. Call 954/454/3721 or write HSP, PO Box 2544 Hallandale FL 33009. Tickets at $10 and $9. Discounted for Seniors.

MP1228 Barry Berger lived on Gates Place in the '60s. where are you now? Does anyone know? Call Carol Madison Feldman in Florida 954/741/2246 or write 9756 NW 41 St., Sunrise, FL 33351.

MP1229 Fran Kornspan Cagner, PS94 '54, JHS80 '57, **Evander** '60 is looking for Al Mandel, Eddie Schulman, Phyllis Young, Barbara Ruderman, Andrea Jacobs, Barbara Muttelson, also any old friends from Rochambeau Gardens. Would love to hear from neighborhood and school friends. Call 914/354/4587.

MP1230 Former Bronxite members of "Club Slap You" who also graduated from **Wade, Creston, Taft or Hunter**, where are you? Maiden name: Rose Gorshovsky, Pearl Spielman, Ruth Eisenstat, Janet Runenstern. Call or write Sandy Falk 516/374/4154. Po Box 475 Hewlett NY 11557-0475.

MP1231 Nathan Drut's daughter, Marcia, **Music & Art** '60, is looking for his students at PS80 and JHS115 to warm his 85 year young heart.

MP1232 Wendy Citron Krassner, **Taft** '67 is looking for Helaine Haber, Sheryl Berman, Judy Gerdinand, Sharon Bottman, Bruce Schultz, and anyone else growing up or near Macomb's Rd. and 174th St. Please call me and leave message 301/230/7200 Ext. 254.

MP1233 Looking for my best friend Joan Broder Goldman, **Taft** '55. Lived at 1188 Gr. Concourse. Went to Jordan Mott JHS, Hunter College. Any information (or if you were a June '55 **Taft** grad) Please contact me: Eleanore Bloom Surkis.

MP1234 Looking for **Roosevelt** graduates '59, '60 & '61 members of baseball team plus others. 40th class reunion in year 2000. Please contact Wilfred Alverio, **Roosevelt** '60 at 914/354/5010. 129 E. Willow Tree Rd., Spring Valley, NY 10977.

MP1235 Mike Esposito lived on Valentine Ave & 199th St. went to Immaculate Conception, **Clinton** '59. Spent teen years on Fordham Rd. "Lou Jacks" Any one remember? I would love to hear from you. Joanne Petricola 516/427/8419.

MP1236 Charlie Bosco would like to hear from guys & gals from Boynton to Bronx River, late 40s to early 50s. Irene Abrevaya, Edith Trempski, Bunny Innerfeldt, Marsha Pat Carter, Big Gladys, little Gladys, Elayne, Larry (Peewee) Goldberg, Joe Nazzaro, Phil Cuirio. 516/732/4560.

MP1237 Robin Bloom, PS70 '59, **Wade** '62, **Science** '65 and Cherl Katz, PS70 '59, **Wade** '61, **Taft** '64 are looking for old friends for a reunion.

MP1238 Marv Levine **Clinton** '47, of Hughes Ave. Near 179th St. from 1940 to early 50's would like to hear from my old friends from that unique and lively neighborhood. Write 27 LaCumbre Circle, Santa Barbara, CA 93105. 805/682/1772.

MP1239 Carl M. Dimedio seeks the whereabouts of WWII soldier (surname) Abramowitz. Assigned 909th Air Force Engineers Camoflage Unit. Mitchell Field Air Force Base. Long Island, NY in 1943. Abramowitz was married on base. I was his best man. Where are you? Write or call 718/824/6849.

MP1240 Allan Jeffrey Katz, **Evander** '61. 3604 Bx. Blvd. H: Low Deliso, Henry Alviti (Yonkers) Rich Cohen, Rich Kerns, Francis Bosco, Gerald Segal, Bobby Taglew, Lew Weinberta, Bobby B. Call 516/599/2178. Allan Katz, E. Rockaway, NY.

MP1241 Bob Klein, 1738 University Ave., PS82-School Yard- Tony's Poolhall, University Ave., & 176th St, **Clinton** '61, Friends from **Taft**, Vietnam, then home again. Live in Newburgh area. I work in NY. Have 3 sons. If you remember call 914/562/7756.

MP1242 John Simpson, **Monroe** '63 is looking for Barry Weiss & Herbie Crow from 1057 Faile St.

MP1243 Diana Rappoport Markowitz, Helen Jacobs Fishman, Sylvia Tanenbaum Fenmore (**Evander** '40/'50) would like to hear from our old friends from the Barnes Ave? Wallace Ave. Mayfair/Mayflower crowd. Call Sylvia: 718/261/4061 or fax 718/261/4062.

MP1244 Anyone from PS6, the 6-1 class, class of '62, James Morgan, Warren Silverstein, Melissa Ressler, Mark Liff, Pamela Hyman, Jackie Hessel, both Stephanies, Ellen and anyone else. Contact Neal Unruch 201/361/1172. Would love to see all of you again.

MP1245 What happened to all the people from St John Ave., Fox St. and Southern Blvd? Has anybody seen Rubin Feldman or Issy Eskenazi? Joe and Phyllis Vosk live nearby in Raleigh. Dave Halpern, **Morris** '42 would like to hear from you. write to 1417 Wensford Court, Raleigh, NC 27615. 919/847/9686.

MP1246 Rich McDermott, **Columbus** '60, would love to hear from anyone late 50s CCHS: Marie Muccio, Marilyn Schauer, Margie Seltzer (I had a crush on you). Carolyn Stern (You too!) Stuart Warner, Chorus/Melody singers et. al. 516/579/5788.

MP1247 Bob Laemel, **Clinton** '56, University of Bridgeport '60 is looking for Mel Klein, UB graduate. Call 407/287/9664.

MP1248 John P. Dillon, teacher and Alumni of **St. Simon Stock School** and former teacher at PS38, IS151 is a contact person for SSS Alumni. Call 718/367/0453.

MP1249 Esther Levine would love to hear from old friends who lived on Franklin Ave/ Maples Ave. or attended PS63, 55, **Roosevelt** '53.

MP1250 Hey! Where are all the guys and gals from Boston Post Rd. & Wilkins Ave? Went to PS61, Herman Ridder and **Morris**. My first crush was on Julie Weintrop- where are you? —Fred Weiner 212/673/5073.

MP1251 Marvin Flack, **Evander** '37 "Tempus Fugits" seeking Saul Rosenechs, Walter Rosen, **Clinton** '37-'38 & Irving Yasny, **Clinton** '37-'38. Shock me and contact me (or their friends) I'm happily married and living in Fla. 453 Golden River Dr., West Palm Beach, FL 33411-2427.

MP1252 Hillside Homes '35-'67. PS78 '39, **Evander** '43. Now Nathalie (nee Rockower) Meltzer-Ellman. Now upstate, NY. Would enjoy hearing from you! 9 Groo St., Middletown, NY 10940.

MP1253 Connie Tuzeo McHugh is looking for anyone who graduated in '56 from **St Rita's Elementary** on College Ave. (i.e. J. Schettino, J. Johnson, C. Petrolzullo, C. Fitzferald, M. Middleton) Call 210/835/9134.

MP1254 Did WWII kill us all off? **Bx Voc HS** '42- electric wiring. or PS44 (Farragut JHS) 1936-39 Marmion & 175th. Irv Kermish: 510/836/4036 or fax 510/832/5279. Anybody?

MP1255 760 Grand Concourse!! 1950s - 60s. Steve Heimoff looking for his buddies. Sat morning touch football, stickball, slug! Feldman's Drug Store. Shorehaven. We grew up together, but I lost you. Paul, Ricky, Stevie, Donald, Jimmy and Irwin and other pals. Call 510/893/7479.

MP1256 Norma Lippe Brecher, **Walton** '59. Resided at 2700 Gr. Concourse. Would love to hear from any old friends who knew me. Sandy Martin, Barbara Banks, Elissa Friedlander, Sandy Klinger, Abby Schwartzberg- where are you?

MP1257 Anyone from Bronx YMHA '58-69 or Creston Ave and 184th St. Would love to hear from you. Frenchy, Irene M., Francine B., Larry Lang., Walter Sklar, Gary Weiner- where are you? Mark Z. 305/670/9921.

MP1258 Tommy Cronin, 621 Manida St & Hunts Point, St. Athaniasus, Fox St. Don of Tim (Tiru) Loretta (Meegan) 4228 Hillale, Mt. St. Michael, **Evander** '65, Mabstoa '65. Living on Cape Cod. Would like to hear from old friends. 508/945/9352.

Classifieds

MP1259 Hello! Anyone left out ther that remembers Red Letter Day from **Monroe** class of '37? I'm married 51 years, have 3 sons and 6 grandchildren. Living in Hartsdale and working as a Fiduciary. Call Seymour Scharf 914/328/0128.

MP1260 Diane Pomerantz (nee Lowenstein/Lowe) PS11 '52. **Music & Art** '56, Hunter College '60. Lived at 1425 University Ave. Would like to hear from anyone who remembers me- Linda Sigal, Mel Dubner, Maddy Berman. 407/642/8554.

MP1261 Mike Werner, **Evander** '58. Grew up in the Eastchester Projects (Burke Ave.) Attended PS121, JHS113, **Evander**, Bronx Community College and CCNY, AA, BA, MA. Married 21 years to a Yonkers girl, two sons and I am a Material Management Specialist for the USPS in Philadelphia. 215/321/6742.

MP1262 Diana (Rappoport) Markowitz, Helen (Jacobs) Fishman, Sylvia (Tanenbaum) Fenmore - **Evander** '49-'50 - would like to hear from old friends from the Barnes Ave/Wallace Ave. Mayfair/ Mayflower crowd. Call Sylvia: 718/261/4062.

MP1263 198th St. - Valentine Ave., Grand Concourse, looking for some of The old guys and gals 40's and 50's. PS 46, **Clinton**, Miriam St. gang also contact Joe Ricevuto 35-65 86th Apt 3A, Jackson Hgts, NY 11372

MP1264 Mike and Faye (Moskowitz) Strongwater still living in the Bronx. Looking for Pearl Oberstein from Boston Road. Also Vivian Messinger, Sid & Lorraine Weinberg - Would love to hear from you... revive old friendships- we'd love it. Call 718/601/9072.

MP1265 JHS '82 class SPI '51 Dr. Saul Scherzer would enjoy hearing from classmates and how life turned out for them, especially Elaine Klinger. PO Box 3035, Westport CT 06880

MP1266 Looking for people who knew Jeff Fields or his cousin Joel, PS67, JHS113 and **Clinton** '64. Contact Joel 407/364/9563.

MP1267 Gang of Sheridan Ave, 165th St. where are you? Vincent Dixon, Bernie Cavanaugh, Jimmy Clemons, Eddie Molloy, Buddy Lazarus, Wally Ives, Abe Kalkstein, Rose dePalma, Jack & Edna Fishbone, Bernie Leifkowitz, Muriel Rabin, Henry Welinsky. Call Richard Ferris 212/757/2180.

MP1268 Beulah Bright (**Walton** '59) would like to hear from Barbara (Gigi) Cuadra or Vernia Hawkins - How is life treating you? Contact Beulah Bright Johnson 2907 Kingsbridge Terrace #6B, New York, NY 10463 718/884/9704.

MP1269 Looking for Cornelia & Gloria Vitale (Mace Ave) Anita Colonna (Yates Ave), Eddie Atlas, Richard Brunner (Bros Pharmacy Gun Hill Rd) Myrna Rosenberg, Michelle Solarz, S. Howard Gorfinkel. Contact Charlotte Kobert Rossen 3955 Paseo Grande, Moraga, CA 94556

MP1270 Looking for my Union Ave. South Bronx friends. Lois Freeman-**Hunter**, Doris Auerbach-**Taft**, Regina Droisen-**Morris**, Frances Wein Friedman, Israel Rosenweig, Marmion Ave-**Roosevelt**, Marvin Abrams-Prospect Ave, **Monroe**. Contact Sohia Helfendt Love 954/436/1087.

MP1271 Russell (Rusty) Marrapodi - Went to PS45 '47-'49. Would like to hear from people who knew me from school & friends from Cambreleng Ave., Beaumont Ave., Belmont Ave. & all of Fordham's Little Italy at 187th St. in the Bronx . Write to 658 N. Hayden Dr., Tuscon, AZ. 85710.

MP1272 Carl Salzinger 1016 Bryant Ave PS75 '42. would like to hear from old friends. Moved to Cleveland, OH from the old neighborhood in 1942. Call 216/449/1199 or write 6561 Vallevista Dr, Mayfield Hts, OH 44124.

MP1273 Fordham-Belmont Area 40-44 PS118 **Roosevelt**, Drake Academy. Last flyer caught many old friends. Let's expand the list and share it. Anthony Vento 104221 Muirfield Rd., Boynton Bch, FL 33436 407/736/1100.

MP1274 Jerry Fineman looking for "old' good friends Harold "Whitey" Stegman, Charles Starkman & Joel Brooks- **Clinton** '47 & Dominick "Bosco" Lubcano PS82 '44. Contact me at 73 Hilary Circle, New Rochelle, NY 10804

MP1275 My name is Thelma "Grubert" Rosenblatt. I lived at 1104 Elder Ave. Do you know me? Or remember me? I would like to hear from you. Call me at 954/570/6212.

MP1276 Fran Lipensky Cohen is looking for the last 8th grade graduates from PS6 '52. I would love to hear from you. Also looking for Phylis Commodore, Claudia Meyers, K Phyllis Greenstein from Longfellow Ave.

MP1277 Joe Henrt (**Science** '46) and Bob Bagar (**Fordam Prep**) are interested in hearing from Bob Hamlisch (**Science**), Armen Burgujian (**Clinton**), Sylvester Cangemi (**Roosevelt**), Roy Rothemund (JHS '79) Al Gannon (Hates) and 187th St gang. Write 553 Ludlow Ave, Cinti, OH 45220

MP1278 Are there any former piano students of my Dad, Dr. Aloys Kremer, who lived at St. James Park in the 30's and 40's. Write to Jacqueline Kremer at 400 East 50th St., NY, NY 10009. My father was a well known teacher.

MP1279 **Clinton** '45 - Anyone around from 181st & Ryer or Anthony Ave. Please contact Larry Ashinoff 804/488/4441 or Fax 804/488/0166. Virginia Beach, VA.

MP1280 Dennis Kaplan, Phelan Place (University Heights) is looking for long ago friends Cossy, Gogs, Blacky, Shecky, Dicky, Val, Louie Grippo or any classmates PS26 '40-46. Call 212/686/4630 or Fax 212/684/3889.

MP1281 Looking for Danny & Harry Klein twins also Marty K. from Pop's poolroom on Boston Rd & grad class 1948 central commercial would love to hear from anyone who remembers Rozzy Coohen 1500 Boston Rd. Now living in Florida 941/945/4140.

MP1282 Roana Cohan nee Schechter looking for David Rand. We both graduated **Monroe** 1/'50. I'm in Boca Raton, FL and currently meeting with ladies from **Monroe** '50-52. Write to me at 5690 Coach house Circle #E, Boca Raton, FL 33486.

MP1283 Where are the Clip-ettes from Wade JHS., **Taft** '54 & Cappy's Candy Store. Call Edie 718/969/3419.

MP1284 Linda Diamond would like to hear from old friends and classmates from Bainbridge Ave., JHS80 '52 and **Evander** '55. Write Linda Diamond Scharf 427 Golden Isles Dr. Apt 14D, Hallandale, FL 33007

MP1285 Margaret Lorenz (May). Where are all the kids from Bersteins Candy Store on Whitlock Ave during the 1930's Virginia Hart Marion, Elliott Campbell Scott and Annette. Remember St. Octavious School graduated 1934. Remember Sr. deSales? Kids from 183 St and Webster Ave.?

MP1286 Anyone near the Port St. Lucie, FL area that would like to get in touch with me- **Monroe** '60—Ginny. Write Virginia Levy: 32 Lake Vista Trail (207), Port St. Lucie, FL 34952.

MP1287 Late 50's looking for Lewis Perkowski & Jerry Habib from Southern Blvd. in South Bronx. Also for Eddie O'Connell from Undercliff Ave. late 50's thru 60's. Write Phil Growick 129 Pioneer Drive, West Hartford, CT 86117 or call 203/232/1149.

MP1288 Al Restivo, **Evander** '54 looking for classmates from Mrs. Mazzorana's Homeroom (342). Also anyone who was in Class of 50 at PS76. Love to hear from you. 818/952/1969.

MP1289 Eileen Grossman looking for Shelly Goldfarb, Alice Gortz, Jenny Holender, Pearl Greenstein, Sheila and Gail Dinerstein - love to hear from you . Write 225 East 93rd St., NY, NY 10128.

MP1290 Columbus '57. Looking for Jerry Giangrasso, Michael E. Borruso, Steve Schoen, Dr. Richard Cunningham. Lived on Holland Ave. Contact Barry S. Beyer 516/595/1298.

MP1291 We are "**Back in The Bronx**" at PS64. Giving back to great underprivileged kids. This "alumni group" attended 64-117 **Taft** in the '40's and '50's. Join us -it's a rewarding experience. Suzanne Berne, Rhoda Boxer, Helen Schwartz, Rose Vaena, Suzanne Menache, Lenore Levenson, Beverly Tucker. Contact Helen Miller: 221 Broadfield Rd., New Rochelle, NY 10804.

MP1292 Enid Samuels, PS73 '42-43, looking for gals & guys from Gerard Walton Ave. or Highbridge section. Played tennis at Mullaly Park. Now living in Arizona.

MP1293 Ellen (Levine/Schottland) Estrin, PS67 '56, JHS98 '59, **Hunter** '66. Would love to hear from former classmates and from old friends from Daly Ave. 201/575/8715.

MP1294 Jim Healy would like to hear from Bill Taylor & any others from **St. Simon Stock** during the '40's. I lived at 2172 Ryer Ave. Contact me at 3413 Rockhaven Circle, Atlanta, GA 30324. 404/237/7198.

MP1295 Marilyn (Salomon) Harris is looking for Linda Zucker and other friends from PS64, JHS117 and **Taft** '65. Susan Stern, I lost your address. Please write 173 Carrollwood Drive, Tarrytown NY 10591.

MP1296 Art Stalling out there? Where are you Glenda Silverman? Did you stay at 72? Do Ballet? Irving Karp & Morty Klein & Paul Marin & Jerry Presser, gang at College Doc did any of you survive Korea & Willy Pop & the Senator & Irv 1 Tooth? —Arthur Finn, Box 3784 Beverly Hills, CA 90212. Email: A6F306@sprinet.com

MP1297 Hi! Margie Mackenzie (Alias Klein) grew up on University Ave. and 197th St., Roosevelt '66, JHS143, PS86. **Roosevelt** Where is everybody? Contact me at 9 Waterside Ct, Germantown, MD 20874.

MP1298 Nancy Vicari & Nunzio Vicari. She was born Sept. 2 1965. He was born in March 1967. Last heard was living in Long Island. Mother's nickname: Cookie, Stepfather Bill. Call Patti 718 /829/0369.

MP1299 Looking for 1947 graduates of **Samuel Gompers Voc.** HS Especially those from the electrical group ie. Vincent Bertolini, Charles Bauer, Leon Meyerson, Stanley Straus, Robert Schwartzman, Walter Weems & many others. Let's get together and have a reunion. Ernie Seiderman- 17 Ravenwood Dr, Fletcher, NC 28732.

MP1300 PS6 (K-8) Class of '50 (Daly Ave until '57) The moon hit your eye like a big pizza pie and your beautiful dark eyes adorned me, but I was far to shy to respond. You were very (sigh!) handsome "I scorpioni" leader. I was the "Class Brain" a tall, fair, model/dancer, thin brunette. Remember? Call Trudy M.: 212/691/9807.

MP1301 Vincent Restivo , PS89 ('41-49) is looking for Wilma Mitchell, born 6/23/35. She attended PS89 '49-'50. Lived with family, sister Jean at NY Blind Institute on Pelham Pkwy. Friends were Ruth and Virginia Adair. Please contact me at 516/725/0971.

MP1302 Phyllis Goldberg Goetz, 2075 Morris Ave, is searching for old friends; PS79 '50, JHS115 '53, **Walton** '56, CCNY '60. Phone or write 24 Roe Circle, Monroe, NY 914/783/6154; or Email: pgoetz@rhqvm19.vnet.ibm.com

MP1303 Love to hear from people who also attended PS28, Wade JHS, **Taft** '60, CCNY '65, especially Judy Shorten, Leslie Sass, Artie Flink. Lived on Anthony Ave. and East 174th St. Now in San Francisco— Herb Levine 375 28th Ave., San Francisco, CA 94121

MP1304 Minnie Gelman Rimland, **Columbus** '43. would like to hear from friends from Columbus and Pelham Pkwy.

MP1305 Officers of Senior Class, **Evander** '56- Where are You? We found Linda Smalline, but where are: Ron Previ, President; Brenda Vogel, Secretary; Jan List, Treasurer; Dina Shpiro, Historian. We're planning a 40th year reunion and we need to locate you. Contact Anne Fletcher Price, **Evander** '56, 325 Place Lane, Woburn, MA 01801. 671/937/0598.

MP1306 Anybody out there from the SP Class of JHS115, EBB who graduated about 1953? I'm Rhoda (Simon) Block and I used to be the runt of the class with the thick glasses. Please contact me at 714/770/4277 or Email: Century2@apc.net

MP1307 There will be a 50th reunion of the 1947 graduating class of **Hunter College.** The reunion is to be held on May 10, 1997 at the Sheraton Hotel and Towers, Seventh Ave. and 53rd St, NYC. Anyone interested in obtaining additional information should contact Evelyn Hersh at 516/421/0625, or the Alumni Assoc. of **Hunter College**, 695 Park Ave., NYC 212/772/4087.

MP1308 Attention **Clinton** baseball players from years of '52-'54. Lets get together. Contact Mike DiMaggio at 914/628/9086.

MP1309 Where is Bernie Fox, **Roosevelt** '53? Elaine Barkin of EBB remembers exercising at my house and then eating chocolate pudding.

MP1310 Paul Narson of 173rd St off Croes hung out at Nick's Candy Store would like to hear from old friends.

MP1311 Marvin Rinder (now Matt Rinder) Grew up on Grant Ave. PS90, **Taft** '51. Looking for old friends: Ruth Goldberg, Ronnie Beck, Hal Kritelman, Richie Zeitlen, Fran, Richie, and Morty. Where are you? Call 619/486/0556.

MP1312 Looking for Artie Crames, Louie Schwartz and Marcia Tabachow (Girard Ave) I am Myron Liberman. Call me at 505/344/7869.

MP1313 Nancy (Hirsch) Crandall: PS54, JHS56, **Bronx Science** '59, Hunter (uptown) '63. Love is the greatest the 2nd time around...Doug and I celebrated our 3rd anniversary on the "**Back In THE BRONX Cruise**." Fantastic!! Would have loved to have seen more people from the schools on 205th and the Concourse.

MP1314 Miron Moskowitz, former Bronxite, Andrews Ave., PS26, JHS82, **Roosevelt**. Turned screenwriter. Needs help in getting read by WGA agents and/or producers and directors. 593A Wren Song Rd., Yardley, PA 19067.

MP1315 Pat Mundy (Zimmerman) PS86 '48, **Walton** '53. Lived on Kingsbridge Rd and Sedgwick. Looking for Anne Morrow, Paul Ulrich, Howard & Harold Sweitzer, Ivan Tarnopow, Paul Von Austron & Buzzy (Eugene Lowe).

MP1316 Earnie Seiderman is looking for 1947 graduates of Samuel Gompers Voc. HS. Especially those from the electrical group i.e.: Vincent Bertolino, Charles Bauer, Leon Meyerson, Stanley Straus, Robert Schwartzman, Walter Weems and many others. Let's get together & have a reunion!

MP1317 Dolores Goldberg Ungerleider is looking for old friends from Morris Ave. between Burnside and 181st St. Graduated PS79, EBBJHS and **Walton** '49. Now residing in Central NJ 609/395/0229.

Classifieds

Come Blow Your Horn

Bennett Gottlib moved from the Bronx to Bayside Queens in 1960. Attended the **NY School of Printing** graduated in '64. Entered the Navy in '66-'70, served a tour of duty in Vietnam abroad an Ammunition Ship. Entered Polyclinic Hospital School of Radiologic Technology in '71, and today is the Administrative Director of Radiology at Hempstead General Hospital. Dabbled in Magic as a hobby and has performed at numerous clubs on Long Island and appeared 8 years in a row at Harrah's Marina in Atlantic City on New Years Eve.

Barney Stone owns a tax service in Beaver, West Virginia. Married with 3 kids. Email me at: Bstone2494@AOL.com

Peter Foley is VP of Sales for Viking Freight Inc., San Jose, CA. Living in Pleasanton, CA. Went to **Cardinal Hayes** HS. Lived on Marion Ave. Big Yankee Fan!

Murray Gross married Ann Weishaus on 9/8/40. Joined National Guard and then the Army '38. Was sent to Guadalcanal 1/'42 as part of the 1st Marine Div., became 2nd Lt. returned to US 3/'43. Remained with 244th C.A. until Disability Retirement in 1/1/45.

Martin Dubbs graduated Chiropractic School in '54. Earned a degree of Dr. of Chiropractic. Served in U.S. Army '54-'56. Became Master Electrician in NYC in '60 and went into business as Electrician. Retired in '89. Became Pawn Broker in '93. Married to JoAnne in '78. 4 Children.

Ron Friedman, **Clinton** '58, Hunter '62. Was Sec. Treasurer, Soc. Director of Phi Sigma Delta Frat. US Army '64-'66. Lived in England for 14 yrs. 2 children- Anthony & Danielle who are university ready in England. Been a parole officer for 6yrs. Marrying Lynn Sherinski- a loving, intelligent, sensitive, friend for life.

Michael Nevins just published a book "The Jewish Doctor" - a history of Jewish physicians throughout history. Publisher: Jason Aronson.

Herb Dicker graduated JHS98 Herman **Ridder** in Jan. '45, Graduated NYU School of Commerce in '58 with a BS in Accounting.

Martin Dubbs was President of Town Hall University Theater in Eastchester, NY. Starred in many productions over the years. Had leads in Guys & Dolls, Prisoner of 2nd Ave, 40 carats and many others.

Naomi Schildwachter Herron, married 52 years, has 3 children and 4 grandsons. My Bachelors Degree is from NYU, Masters from Montclair State University. Retired from NJ School System. Presently supervising student teachers for Hood College.

Pasquale D. Mattioli entered US Airforce '48, in Japan June 25, 1950, went to Korea instead of USA (had bags packed). Discharged Oct. '53. Feb. '55 entered NYC Police Dept. Left Aug. 31 '81. Retired 4 times.

Bill Hayden, **Roosevelt** '58, had been residing in Merrick LI and employed at American Airlines for 30 years, retired June 1 '95. Now running a Bed & Breakfast in Bath Maine. Call 203/443/6069 or 800/516/4578

Murray C. Schneider, **Evander** '35, Eagle Scout, ScoutMaster, NYU "35-'42, Army Service '42-'46, 1st St. Infantry. Ran my own insurance agency for 40 yrs., past president of Kiwanis, past president, currently on Board of Directors Ranachqua Foundation, Inc. which sent thousands of needy Boy Scouts to summer camp over the years and still do. Wife, Florence is Treasurer of Brandeis University Womens Committee, women raise funds to flood library with books.

Barbara Demaio, Diplomate in Social Work, Dir. of Social Work, Rockland Cty Dept. of Hospitals over 20 yrs. 2 sons- Antonio & Damon, 2 grandchildren- John & Valerie.

Jerry Toplitsky is retired as a Senior Project Coordinator with the NYC Transit Authority after 33 years. I now live in Rockland County with my wife Sally, who is also an ex-Bronxite. Jules Bernstein was born on Simpson St. (next to 41st Pct. "Fort Apache), lived Alous St., Hoe Ave (1005) PS75, **Monroe** '44, 5th Air Force (Pacific), Pratt Institute Grad, NY Ad Agency (owned) Art/Creative Director. Old Bethpage, LI, Retired to Florida.

Emily Mordeci moved to Hull Ave/Gun Hill Rd. Married Sam Israel and had 4 children. Owned luncheonette on 204th St between Perry Ave and Hull Ave. Moved to Rockland Cty. Bought our own home. Sam owned dry cleaners and Emily worked for Burlington Industries & Rockland Cty offices. Now have 8 grandchildren and spend our winters in FL.

Marilyn Powell Berns, Bachelors Degree from State University College of Buffalo. Masters Degree from State University of NY at Buffalo. Taught elementary school for 27 years. Raised 2 daughters. Retired in June of '95 as a bilingual teacher in Santa Ana, Ca.

Charles Moravec was a member of the football and track team at City College, an Inter-Collegiate wrestling champion and most important was inducted to the Pershing Rifles (an honorary fraternity of the ROTC) Between graduation and the present I held many administrative positions in numerous industries, including construction and shipbuilding. I was a Major League Scout for the Pittsburgh Pirates, Cincy Reds and St. Louis cards. For 15 years I managed City Championship Baseball teams. I was president of the Rego Park Democratic Club as well as the Flushing branch of the AARP. Currently I am not married nor have any children.

Donna Carter Berusch, PS76. Pre-school teacher to Principal. Now corporate CEO. Was in China representing the USA in early childhood education.

Herbert Birnbaum lived in the **Hunts Point** section of the Bronx. After college I moved to Lynbrook, got married, served in the Army, graduated from Brooklyn Law School, went to work as a clerk in NYC Council. Retired after 30 yrs. as Head of Council Legal Division. Moved to Binghamton for 15 yrs. Now in Ft. Lauderdale area 7 yrs. Volunteer arbitrator in Juvenile Court. On Board of Directors of Condo Assoc.

Muriel (Oreustein) Newman worked for the OPA. Raised 3 sons for 19 yrs. and went back into the work force at Creedmoor Psychiatric Center. Retired to FL in '84.

Sol Schoenback-NYU '39, CBS staff '32-'37, Philadelphia Orchestra '37-'57, A.V.S '44-'46. Settlement Music School Ex. Director '57-81-Retired.

Herb Crane, Pace University '40. Started Crane's Autoleasing in Great Neck, NY and Apple & Eve Inc, Roslyn, NY. Past President of NY State Car & Truck Leasing Assoc. Past Pres. Bayside Jewish Center, Active Past Member of Pine Hollow Country Club Present Active Member of Boca Wood Country Club- Boca Raton, FL.

Judith Taylor Dimmerman was a Buyer Accessories for 700 stores. I've been widowed for 20 yrs. There are many Bronxites I would like to hear from.

John Bredehoft was in the Marines from '51-'53, then joined the NYPD in '55 and retired in '90. Almost 36 years. Moved to Boca Raton in '93. Married almost 40 yrs. to Viola (nee Struhar) have three sons and one daughter. Was President of Pelham Bay Little League for 8 yrs. (member for 25 yrs.)

Irving Kupin is a CPA since '57. Private practice in NYC, now in semi-retirement. Specializing in taxes, estates & trusts and estate planning and specialized audits.

Howard "Howie" Harris, **Clinton** '73. A VP for Facilities Planning for Bankers Trust Co, NY. Member of Professional Bowlers Tour, resident pro at Manalapan Country Lanes, Manazapan, NJ. Married 16 yrs to Terry and have a great son, Justin.

Sandi Denowitz Reich is the owner of a water purification company with her husband Stuart, who is a **Taft** '60 graduate.

Jean Radlein Goetz, **Columbus** '63, Miss Bronx '64 and Carl Goetz, Jr., **Clinton** '61, Ft. Schuyler Maritime College '65 and CCNY (MBA) '70. July '96 married 30 years, 2 girls, one married with grandson on the way. Moved to FL four yrs. ago to open franchise business, Express Personal Services- have 2 offices- Ft. Lauderdale & Boca Raton. In the South Fla. Business Journal we were rated in the top 25 women owned businesses & top 25 personnel companies in South Fla. (for Dade, Broward & Palm Beach Counties) for '95. Any old acquaintances give us a call: 954/721/2429.

Vivian Johnson (Lindros) lived 7 years in Brooklyn, worked in office and War factory WWII. Built our own home in Ramsey, NJ., raised four children there, moved to Colorado in '76.

Chuck Rapoport (I.C. Rapoport) writes for "Law & Order" TV Drama. (Wed. 10pm-NBC)

Fran Kornsoan Cagner graduated **Bronx Community College** in '63, CW Post '65-BS in Medical Technology. Currently Service Rep. for a major laboratory co.

Tina Zucker Getman is an Administrative Assistant and Editor. I became an accomplished Desktop Publishing Computer Expert. I now write lots of short stories, my husband's war memoir, as well as my memories of life in the Bronx.

Luciano Siracusano just started his own business as an Independent Associate of Pre-Paid Legal Services. 3 grown children: Gina, Luciano III, Michael. Wife Louise, 1 granddaughter- Alexa Marie and 2 more on the way.

Marvin Levine, **Clinton**, L.I.U., Brooklyn Law. Practiced law in NY and Calf. Retired after 22 yrs. an Attorney for County of Santa Barbara. Now the easy life!

Terry Chayefsky, **Evander** '44, got his Masters degree at Mercy College '68, Herbert Lehman College '72. Taught in Westchester School Dist. Moved to NYC. Just wrote a book that is coming out this fall called "Acting in Prime Time."

Dolores Goldberg Ungerleider is married with 2 sons. She is a retired Secretary and is now teaching Craft courses in local HS and Adult Communities in Monroe Township, NJ.

Louis Hemmerdinger, **Taft** '52, Columbia BS & MS in Mechanical Engineering. Worked for Grumann 36 yrs. and retired in '94. Playing some golf & stockmarket. Married 29 yrs, 3 sons: MIT, Cornell and last is pre-med at Duke. Awards from NASA, Grumman & Soc. of Mechanical Engineers. Just finished video for my 40th reunion at Columbia.

Fred Weiner is retired from NYC Police Dept. does Humanitarian work in Cuba with remnents of Jewish community.

David Gerteman has a Masters Degree, New School for Social Research (Sociology Major) '74; on the Board of Trustees of Congregation Beth-El, Norwalk, CT; Co-Chairman of the Cultural and Continuing Ed Committee of Congregation Beth-El. Helped build a new Synagogue, Temple Sholom in Greenwhich, CT in '90. Lived in Greenwhich for 14 yrs. Married 25 yrs to a Bronx girl. Miss the old Bronx of the 50s & 60s.

Jay Weitz, **Fordham University** Coll. of Phamacy '51, Regional Sales Director Lederle labs Pharm. Co, Early retirement '91; Pres. Prof. Med. Comm. Inc. a pharmaceutical co/physician meeting co.

Jerome Kass is a writer of TV movies and plays. I'm represented in "Who's Who In America," "Who's Who in the Words," "Who's Who in the West," and "Who's Who in Entertainment."

Norma Lippe Brecher, **Walton** '59, married 33 yrs. to Richard Brecher, **Science** '58, 1 daughter - Tara-21 yrs. old. Careers as a Dental Hygienist, Photostylist, film producer & Sales. Lived in FL for 14 yrs and presently live in Northern CA.

Roger Bernstein, **Monroe** '57. Has been married to former Sandi Bell of Wontagh, NY for 31 yrs. They have 2 grown sons. Have lived in Nassau County for the past 30 yrs- we are moving to Delray Beach, FL July 1, 1996.

Lillian Stafinsky Stern- during WWII I was a volunteer in the NY Police Corps. , I was a School Aide in JHS101. My hobbies are knitting, crocheting, etc. I also have made several porcelain dolls.

Jerry Resnick is currently completing his 35th yr. in Public School Education. I have been a High School Principal since '84. I served 10 yrs as a Science Dept Chairman in Sheephead Bay HS in Brooklyn I'm a graduate of NYU '61 BA and attended NYU with a MA in '62.

Harold Bohlin, member of Fordham Bedford Community Coalition and Fordham Bedford Homeowners Assoc., Treasurer of AARP Parkchester 453 chapter. Served 20 yrs as Church Council Member Fordham Lutheran Church- 4 yrs as President. Presently President of Board of Kenwood Gardens, Clearwater, FL.

Beulah Barght Johnson, mother of 2 daughters. Presently **Principal of PS107, Bronx.**

Carl B. Salzinger, BS, MS Ohio St. Univ., Vice President Research & Development. Owner of a Laminating Company which was sold to a major company. Now retired and spend winters in South Palm Beach, FL and summers in Cleveland suburb, Mayfield Heightd, OH.

Jerry Fineman graduated University of Tampa '51, US Army '51-53, Professional Baseball '53-'54. Toy business '55 to present. Married to Rhonda with 4 children and 2 grandchildren (1 more on the way!)

James Healy was an Industrial Psychologist and is now retired. He has a second home in Amsterdam, Holland and he lives there in the Spring and Fall.

Sidney Beickel went into the Army in '43. Married in '42, has 2 sons, 4 grandchildren and has the greatest wife ever! Plays golf and racquetball to this day. Captain of the greatest basketball team in the **Bronx: "Delhi AC"**

Thomas DeGaglia, Life Service Award, Lifeguard of NYC Swim Club '64, US Navy '67-'69. Married JoAnne Cappuccio at Holy Family on Castle Hill Ave and the reception was at Tardi's. Started a Wall St. career in '67 at Bocke & Co. Began present job on 11/17/69 with Lehamn Bros. Worked my way to Sr. Vice President- Equity Finances.

Wilma Kuhn, **Taft** '68, NYU '72. I'm divorced, childless, 5'6" blond who wishes to rewed. Co-op owner in Manhattan- I still take the **#4 Woodlawn-Jerome** to see my mother. I am looking for a Bronx reared professional man (**Bx Science** '60-'65 preferred (who can remember his not-so-square roots.)

Classifieds

Quentin DeSantis is a retired Detective NYPD. He has been disabled by Agent Orange- but now in remission. I am a widower with 3 college children.

Louis Blazquez received his BS (physics) and MA (teaching) from Fairleigh Dickinson. I just celebrated my 16th wedding anniversary. I have 1 daughter (13 yrs old) and I have been teaching in Flaggstaff almost 20 yrs. I passed my 3rd degree black belt test in June '95. I was in "Who's Who of Teaching."

Herb Levine Graduated CCNY Phi Beta Kappa, Magna Cum Laude. Proudest "accomplishments" have to do with having 2 great children, working in the (disability) civil rights movement, trying always to make my life a "work in progress."

Abby B. Bergman, currently School Principal. Earned doctorate from Columbia University, have written 5 books for Prentice-Hall one new one in the works on the principalship. Married Rose Rosenburg from **Cruger Ave**. have 1 son studying International Marketing in England. Still love to visit the Zoo and the Botanical Gardens.

Paul Narson from 173rd St. & Croes Ave is now living in Queen. Sales Rep for the Glass Depot, won the companies Presidentail Citation Award for Community Service. Vice President of the Queens Chapter #32 of the Vietnams Veterans of America.

Myron Liberman lived in Alburquerqe, NM 25 yrs. Instructor in a Community College. has 4 great kids, divorced and approaching retirement.

Pat Zimmerman Mundy was the first female Director of Human Resources for Merch & Co., Inc.

Arlene Lax Wechsler, PS88, PS64, JHS117, **Taft**, CCNY. Director for Long Island Center for Short Term Psychotherapy, 230 Hilton Ave., Garden City. 516/565-2600. Married over 40 yrs to Harvey. 3 married children, 7 grandchildren.

James Tanner is a Petroleum Geologist for the CA State Land Commission in the offshore oil and gas leasing unit in Long Beach, CA. I am a Vestry candidate for my church, St. Thomas of Canterbury in Long Beach.

Tell Us About Yourself!

Ann McGowan is published in Popular Photography- interview and photos. Received Lord Grenfel Medal for photography and Kodak award. Studied with Martha Graham and performed modern ballet and later Irish dance setting. Presently doing Argentine Tango (demonstrate for Sandra Cameron) and design and sell tango shoes. Presently an undergraduate student at Hunter College, in the Honors program.

Barbara Kamenetsley Gildin **Ridder** '78 Returned to school (Adelphi) for BS & PD. Taught at Parkwest HS, was Dean at Norman Thomas HS. My daughter is an MD in So. Cal. My son works for Disney's Buena Vista Home Video. So here I am! Still keep up with many **Ridder** friends.

Richard Wald is a supervisor in Child Support Enforcement at Manhattan Family Court. He is married and has a 22 yr. old daughter and 20 yr. old son. Earned a BA in Political Science from Brooklyn College and a MS in Library & Information Science from Pratt Institute. He is also a member of MENSA.

John Pagliaro, BS from NYU- Executive Mgt. Consultant, Author, Lecturer, Faculty St. Joseph V, Philadelphia, Consultant to US State Dept., Flood Marketing Inst. Now retired.

Art Fitzpatrick, **Roosevelt** '60. Lived at 4578 Park Ave. & 189th St & Washington Ave. Now live in Ransomville, NY. He is a Safety Director for an Interstate Trucking Co.

Tony Natelli, **Taft** '55. A consultant to many major record companies is responsible for picking songs for over 100 compact disks over the past 5 years for artists such as: Frank Sinatra, Doris Day, Johnny Mathis, Four Aces, Buddy Greco, Tony Bennett, Tills Bros. Louis Armstrong, Billie Holiday, Sarah Vaughan, Andy Williams, Franki Laine, Jerry Vale (a Bronx boy!), Rosemary Clooney, Dinah Shore, Harry James, Sammy Davis, Peggy Lee and scores of other.

George A. Kief, passed the CPA exam and was in corporate accounting until retirement in '81. Served in the US Army from '43-'46. Served in the Italian campaign and Europe in '55.

Norman Rosner- VP with Merrill Lynch- still working!

Charles Bruno spent 23 yrs. in US Army Dec '42-Sept '74. Retired in Camp Darby, Italy Sept. '74. Did not look for a second career. Just do what I want, when I want. Think alot about the old blocks- 141st & 3rd Ave.

Melvin Tiger, Board Certified Internist in private practice, named top doc by Philadelphia Magazine 2x, proudest of wife who retuned to school for a PsyD and 3 children who are great people.

Samuel Goldman, Teacher in **Riverdale**. Married Iselene Goldman, married 35 yrs. Master Degree in Education, **Hunter College**. MS Guidance, Manhattan College. Initiated the Iselene Family Counseling Network '81. Interests: Videotherapy, filmmaking (documentaries), writing. Daughter, Marianne -engaged to James McNamara, Jr.

Ed Apelzin retired as Director of Liability Claims in a large California based insurance Co. Served in Credit Union Loan Services Board. US Army '51-53. Officer in JWV, Bnai Brith and Sons in retirement. Wife, Doris (40 yrs.) a retired RN. Much traveling- including several Elder hostels.

Richard Reinstein, after WWII was a member of the first Veterans Club at **Taft**. Ed Gelfard and a bunch of good people should remember. Was involved in Boy Scouting (Frontier District, Bronx Council) Awarded Silver Beaver. Presently enjoying life in Baltimore. Retired and would enjoy hearing from anyone who remembers me: 6813 Timberlane Rd., Baltimore, MD 21209.

Fred Weiner served USAF '60-63, NYC Police Dept. '73-93. Son, Jonathan, now with NYCPD less than 5 yrs. and is a Sgt. Now I'm doing humanitarian work in Cuba with the remnants of the Jewish community.

Billie Lederman Bauman, a Jewish princess from Pelham Pkwy- I'm Not!! This November I completed my 16th NYC Marathon out of my total of 19 marathons (including Boston'83, Phil. '82, Moscow '83) Despite hitting the big 50 last April, I look foward to a long running career.

William Birkin took 2 PhD in English history from the University of North Carolina at Chapel Hill '77. Have published a number of scholar articles over the years and I am looking foward to teaching an Elder hoste class this summer. Also contributing medica biographies to the New DNB, to be published by Oxford Univ. Press in 2004. Married to Jane Adams of Kernersville, NC since '76 No children-except our cats Jasper Caswell. We rent a small brick house and enjoy mowing the lawn, tending our flower and feeding all sorts of wild bird. I wor fulltime in the cataloging Dept. of Dav Library on UNC Chapel Hill campus.

Mel Gerard & Annette Newburger married 52 yrs, have 3 sons (all sucessful professionals) Mel- WWII Pacific Theater, formed and operated Engineering (CCNY) Company 30 yrs. Both Mel & Annette organizationally active in community 45 yrs in Executive roles. Enjoy travel.

Elaine Palmgrew Demaria (Blondy) was married at 17 yrs old, on 4th of July '52. Has 3 daughters and 8 grandchildren. Got GED Diploma at age 47. Presently attending Dover Business College in Parsippany NJ. Been divorced 9 yrs. Can't find any men to compare with NYC men- still looking.

Andrea Stone, National Reporter for USA Today. Stephen Zuckerman, Principal Research Assoc. for the Urban Institute Health Policy Center. They have one son, Alex Ston Zuckerman and live in Washington DC.

Larry Starr (Freiman) now retired in Tucson AZ since Sept '94 with his wife Judy of 36 yrs. Recently purchased a "2001 Flavors plus Potatoes Cafe" franchise and will be opening in April. Married daughter, Michele will also be involved in business. Would love to hear from Bronxites that lived in 3871 or 3881 Sedgwick Ave. Graduated PS95 '47, **Clinton** '51.

Vinny Restivo graduated from **Mt. St. Michael** '53, Iona '57 and **Hunter College** '63 with a MA.

Edward J. Wasp was a recipient of the Elmer A. Sperry Award '81 in "Recognition of a Distinguished Engineering Contribution to the Advancement of the Art of Transportation." BS ChE Cooper Union '45, MS ChE NYU '47, MS Math University of Pittsburg '60, BMC University of Calf. SF '68, MBA Golden Gate University '73.

Walter J. Senior is married 35 yrs to Bronx girl, Pat Crowley. They have 3 children. Retired NYFD in '83. Owner of Crestwood Auto Body Inc. Pat graduated Sacred Heart Academy '59.

Eugene (Gene) Miller, **Monroe** '56 would love to hear from old classmates. Retired after 30 yrs at Jewish Hospital, Louisville KY as Chief Pharmacist. Former yrs around 80th St & Mapes Abe. Write: Gene Miller, 4306 Startan Ct., Louisville KY 40220

George Jochum retired Educator was secondary principal in Rochland County for 13 yrs, graduated from **Fordham** '57, Columbia TC '59, Nova Southwestern '80. Now in Florida half the year and the other half in Mahwah NJ.

Mac Weinstein Kasdan, PS95, **Evander** 70. Working as a Med Tech in Charlottesville VA. Married since '93 to Steve (from Brooklyn) have one child, Ian. We live in Waynesboro in the Shenandoah Valley.

Tony Pandolpho grew up on Freeman St., Remember Southern Blvd. Spooner, Star Ad Blvd. Theater, Stickball, Kick the Can and the friendship of my High School Football teamates. Married Majorette Laura Costa at age 21 and have 2 children. Worked at **Montefiore** for 23 yrs.

George Wyle graduated **Monroe** '33, now living in Calif. Conductor and Arranger for top TV shows- including Andy Williams, Flip Wilson, David Copperfield and many others.

Diane (nee Ackerman) Schneeweis, **Taft** '57 and Hal Schneeweis, **Clinton** '56 celebrated their 35th wedding anniversary in June. Hal retired as a Colonel from the US Army and is an Executive with the Pacific Gas & Electric Co. Diane is a CPA firm administrator in Marin County CA. They reside in the San Francisco Bay area and would welcome hearing from old friends.

Rita Stollman Radest graduated from PS4 '43, **Roosevelt** '47, Hunter College '51. Married to Howard Radest. Got my MA from **Hunter** in '55.

Jeff Smolen graduated **Clinton** '64, went to New Paltz State for 2 quarters, graduated Pace College in '69. I am a career Civil Service Employee having obtained the rank of Supervising Investigator for NYS-DOT. I celebrated 25 yrs of service in '94 and am looking foward to retirement in 5 yrs.

Stanley Reinhart, Aerospace Aero Engineer, Republic Aviation in Farmingdale Long Island, 17 yrs then Hughes Helicopters- Culver City CA, McDonnell Douglas Helicopter-Culver City CA & Mesa Ariz. Israel Aircraft Corp. LOD, Israel-Locheed Aircraft -Edwards Airbase CA & Englin. Air Base - Ft. Walton Beach Fla. etc. etc. etc.

Norton Stein **Columbus** '45, married 46 yrs to Diana Blitz. Son, David a government Defense Analyst, Washington DC. Daughter, Perri is married to Mario Procida and have 4 children. Perri is VP of TV Sales at NBC-New York.

Lenore Pomonick Drogin-Sculptor, Jeweler, Freelance Model Maker. Worked at American Museum of Natural History in the Exhibition Dept as an Artist and Designer for 16 yrs. ('65-'81) Presently experiencing mid-life readjustment.

Leslie Klein- proudly working in elementary school in Upper Manhattan facing my elementary school PS122xas an Integrator of Computer Technology. My wife of 16 yrs, Gail and my 2 children, Doug-14 and Allison -12 are major accomplishments.

Irwin B. Miller, Acting Principal at a High School in Manhattan. last 14 yrs I have been Subject Supervisor of Phys. Ed at Indian Hills HS, NJ. Was selected as a member of the US Basketball team to the Israeli Maccabai Games in '52. Served in Korea in the Army. Wife Paula and 3 grown children are all through college.

The "Liptons" run the finest Kosher style deli-restaurant in Las Vegas. All the food is prepared daily on premises. When you are in Vegas, give us a try! Best regards from former Bronxites.

Stuart Klipper, artist (photography), explorer, writer. Solo exhibition at MoMA, etc. Twice a Guggenheim Fellow, etc. Widely traveled both domestic (all 50 states) and global (esp. Polar regions) 4x to Antarctica, once under sail. In Minneapolis since '70. Single.

Iris Cohn Skollar, published artist of childrens book, greeting cards (Norcross-Majestic) Youngest son, Dan, directed his 1st feature film at age 21 "Eyes Beyond Seeing", I was very involved as Asst. to Director, make-up and craft services. The film was shown at Tribecka in NYC- Disney Studio in CA and at the Commack Multiplex in Suffolk County.

Joan Desberg Greenberg has written various sitcoms (One Day at a Time- Maude, etc.) Just taking it easy mostly now. Would love to hear from anyone who remembers me. My daughter Faye and her husband David - they work together. He is a composer and arranger and she is a lyracist. My husband Jules, is a percussionist.

Ida Bastini Vellone's biggest accomplishment is getting through 38 yrs of marriage to my still wonderful husband Joe, having raised 3 great daughters who are now married and have given me 5 terrific grandchildren.

Toby Brestin Heilbrunn, **Monroe**, elected to Woodstock Town Council, Advertising Director of the Woodstock Journal.

Helene M. Weintraub Fish, Educational Programming at Jefferson County Jail, Optometric Technician for Northern NYS Prisons, graduated Hunter College & Hebrew Union College. Married Dr. Louis R. Fish and have 2 sons: one a Physician Asst. and the other a Bank Manager. Reside in Watertown NY.

Do You Recognize Anyone?

Classifieds

Mario Tolisano, currently President & Owner of Ciprietti Tolisano Associates, Inc. A Development & Construction Mat. firm located in Eastchester NY. Formerly President of TM SEBCO Development Corp., a development firm responsible for the construction of over 3,000 apartments in the **Hunts Point** Aldus section of the South Bronx during the South Bronx Rennaisance between the '70-'80s.

Richard Kolbliney, appears in "Whos Who in the East." "Whos Who in American Education," Consultant for the Wall Street Journal-classroom edition; College Advisory Consultant, Writer of curriculum guides, Middle Ages Longmen, Inc., Human Rights AFT, Black Studios UFT, Censorship Newsweek Magazine. Developed School University Partnerships Middlebury College, Williams College. Past President Social Studies Teachers NUC.

Shirely Franklin Pachtman attended Hunter College and became Lab Tech. Married in '48 and have 5 children- one is a MD, Lawyer, Teacher, Public Health and a Mother. I have 2 grandchildren. Taught med terminology, anatomy etc. to students in public health field. Presently writing my autobiography (not for publication). Retired to Boca Raton in '86. This is utopia. Travel during the summers- have been to Europe many times.

Bob Drews started in the mailroom at Helmsley Spear Real Estate in '65. Retired at the age of 46 in '93 from London-Leeds RealEstate in NY as Executive VP. Was VP on NY Building Owners and Managers Association. Director of the Institute of Real Estate Mgmnt. Director of the Management Committee of the Real Estate Board of NY I credit my success to what I learned on the streets of the Bronx. Bob Lessa, where are you buddy? Call 904/446/3444.

Jerry Resnick, Principal of Clara Barton HS, Brooklyn '84. Have been a Science Educator since '61 and a Supervisor since '72. Past President of National Science Association, Author of numerous articles, Co-author of currently used NYS Regents Biology Syllabus. Married with 3 children.

Harriet Schwartz and Ed Bisordi have been married 39 yrs. He is my best friend and my true love. Naturally he's from the Bronx (**Allerton Ave & Wallace**) We had a successful business in NY until '92 when we moved to Cape Coral, FL. where we now have a wonderful group of NY friends. I'm lucky and happy to say I have maintained friendship with at least 3 friends since my pre-teen yrs: Anna Smolik-Slezack, Ida Altibet-Moreno-Reple, and Roslyn Cohen-Owitz. I am now interested in ceramics, fabric painting, decorating and travel.

Ralph H. Schaeffer graduated Pace "College/Institute" now University. I am a Tax Accountant, married with 2 children and a Grandfather, WWII Veteran. Still working. Attended **Ridder** Reunion. My sister, Ida Schaeffer won a Shirley Temple Doll Contest by the "Daily Mirror" in '35. She now lives in Charleston SC.

Robert Hughes, **Morris** '52, joined the Marines. Was in Korea '53, Vietnam '66-'67,'68'69. Served in Japan, Taiwan, Phillipines, Okinawa, Hawaii. Retired in '79. Working in Calf. as a CAL/OSHA Safety Engineer. Any Marines out there?

Why Don't You Tell Us About You?

TO PLACE AN AD

Simply fill out the form that appears on the back of each issue of **Back in THE BRONX.**

Please print clearly and legibly- it will help prevent your ad from possibly appearing incorrectly- *Thank you!*

And, as a reminder, if you are a subscriber, the 40 word ad is **FREE!!!**

TO RESPOND TO AN AD

Address your response to:

Back in THE BRONX
Stephen M. Samtur, Box 141 H
Scarsdale, NY 10583

*Be sure to include the number that appears before the ad.(**MP842** for example) and a long, **stamped** envelope so we can mail your letter to the person placing the ad.

READER REPLIES ✉

It is vitally important that you fill out the information below. Your input will be essential to the success of this magazine, tailored and inspired by you, the former "Bronxite". We thank you for your participation.

Subscriber? ☐ Yes ☐ No

YOUR NAME _____

ADDRESS _____

CITY _____ STATE _____ ZIP _____ PHONE _____

HIGH SCHOOL ATTENDED _____ YEAR GRADUATED _____

TELL US A LITTLE ABOUT YOURSELF,

Be sure to include your alma mater, old neighborhood, your best memories about your days in the Bronx, (or anything else you can tell us).

_____

_____

_____

- -

COULD WE SEND A FRIEND A FREE COPY OF BACK IN THE BRONX?

Do you know current or former Bronxites who would like to receive our magazine and reunion information? If you do, we'll be happy to send them a free inaugural issue of Back in THE BRONX. Write to Back in The Bronx, Box 141 H, Scarsdale, NY 10583 or call 1-800-7-BRONX 5

Last	First	Maiden	
Address	City	State	Zip
Phone # ( )	School and year of Graduation		
Last	First	Maiden	
Address	City	State	Zip
Phone # ( )	School and year of Graduation		
Last	First	Maiden	
Address	City	State	Zip
Phone # ( )	School and year of Graduation		
Last	First	Maiden	
Address	City	State	Zip
Phone # ( )	School and year of Graduation		

SOME BLOW YOUR OWN HORN DEPARTMENT

Please tell us about yourself (include your name)—about your accomplishments, awards, titles or works in progress. We're interested in hearing about them. List Below. _____

_____

_____

_____

35

READER REPLIES

As a subscriber you are entitled to a FREE 40 Word Classified, Missing Persons, Blow Your Own Horn, or Personal Ad. Please write your ad below (if you are not subscribing to our magazine you can still place an ad in the next issue. The cost of an advertisement is 50¢ a word, there is no limit on paid ads).

_____

_____

_____

Is Your Mailing Label Correct?

In order to keep our database current, please correct any errors and place the label and or photocopy with corrections.

Account #	High School	Year Graduated
6817	Roosevelt	1958

Mary R. Flowers
123 Anystreet Blvd.
Anywhere, USA 12345

Change of Address?

If you're planning a move please attach your label corrected with your new address and the date that you will begin receiving mail at that address. This will insure that you don't miss your next issue of **Back in THE BRONX**.

Ordering Information

A Great Gift Idea! In addition to your own subscription, a subscription to **Back in THE BRONX** makes a great and unique gift. Fill in the form below and we'll process the order in time for our next issue. So, order your subscription NOW, and order one for a friend!

YES, I'd like to order the following items:

QTY.

___ 1Yr. (4 ISSUES) Subscription(s) to **Back in THE BRONX** $19.95
___ 2Yr. (8 ISSUES) Subscription(s) to **Back in THE BRONX*** .... $29.95 } *FREE Jahn's Menu
___ 3Yr. (12 ISSUES) Subscription(s) to **Back in THE BRONX*** $39.95
___ 4Yr. (16 ISSUES) Subscription(s) to **Back in THE BRONX*** $49.95
___ The Beautiful Bronx...........$25.00 (plus $3.95 S/H) $28.95
___ The Bronx: It Was Only Yesterday....$25.00 (plus $3.95 S/H) $28.95
___ Bronx High School Reunion Weekend Video $29.95
___ SAVE MONEY - BUY 4 FOR JUST $99.00!
___ **THE BRONX** Tracking Service $9.95
___ **COMPLETE HARDBOUND SET of all 16 past issues**..$49.95 (plus $4.95 S/H)
        Order Now and receive a Jahn's menu & vintage Krum's photos from the 40's-50's for FREE!! $54.90
___ I would like to receive all available back issues and have them applied towards my subscription
        (To date we have 16 back issues available - While They Last!)

Please fill out completely and include shipping and handling where applicable **TOTAL: $** _____
for books only to: **Back in THE BRONX**, Box 141H, Scarsdale, NY 10583

Please Print Clearly ☐ New Subscriber ☐ Renewal

Name _____
Maiden Name _____
Address _____
City _____
State _____ Zip _____
Phone (_____) _____
High School _____ Year Grad. _____

☐ AMEX ☐ MasterCard ☐ VISA ☐ Check ☐ Money Order
No. _____ Expiration Date _____

Signature _____

Back in THE BRONX

Box 141 H, Scarsdale, NY 10583
Phone 914-592-1647 • Fax 914-592-4893

ADDRESS CORRECTION REQUESTED

Volume IV   Issue XVI

Back in THE BRONX

CELEBRATING THE EXPERIENCE OF GROWING UP AND LIVING IN THE BRONX

You CAN Go Home Again!

By Carol Baskin Rothenstein, Monroe '59

It was October, a sunny Sunday afternoon. As we drove forward from **Longfellow** and **174 St.** towards Boynton Avenue, I was going back in time, to when life seemed simpler: when Eisenhower was in the White House and White Castle meant hamburgers, not fairy tales; when the Yankees ruled baseball, not the South; when coke meant soda and not drugs; and to when I was a girl growing up in The Bronx.

I am now in my 50s - that was then in the '50s :...decades ago and only yesterday.

Have you ever sought to retrieve your childhood by driving down the streets you played on, past the schools you went to or the house you grew up in? Have you ever dreamed of going back into that house and revisiting the memories held there? I was recently able to do just that and want to share the journey with you.

My husband and I live near Boston and were spending a weekend in Manhattan with friends, also former New Yorkers. We decided to spend Sunday morning in the lower East Side buying pickles and bialys on Essex St. and reaching for our roots eating borscht at Ratners. Foods do that to people. We immersed ourselves in the sights, sounds and smells of another time and imagined our grandparents or parents walking beside us. We then drove uptown to Zabar's for more food and that was it .... we were hooked. We decided to detour via the **Bruckner Expressway** to return to

1253 Boynton Avenue

the past rather than to go directly to the New England Thruway and the present.

We lived at **1253 Boynton Avenue** from 1943 to 1960 in one of those brick semi-attached houses. **P.S.77** was two blocks around the corner, **Monroe High School** was at the top end of the street and down the hill was the El, the **Elder Avenue** train stop along **Westchester Avenue**. The neighborhood is still the same, but the neighbors are different. We were mostly Jewish along with Italian and Greek families; they are mostly Hispanic along with African American families.

1534 Westchester Ave & W. Boynton Ave

Continued on page 6

From the Editors...

CLINTON '61

TAFT '62

Congratulations to the Yankees for bringing the World Series back to the Bronx where it belongs. For those readers who aren't Yankee fans, somewhere you must have waxed nostalgic at all the attention being focused on our favorite borough. The Samturs have a fond attachment to the Stadium because we both worked there in the 50's and 60's as do our two sons who are working there today (see accompanying story). What better way for parents to relive their youth than by watching their kids enjoy the experience of working at Yankee Stadium during the World Series!

With this issue we will have completed four years of publishing **Back In THE BRONX**. To celebrate this milestone, we have printed a **hardbound** book containing *all* sixteen past issues. Additionally, each book includes a 1950's laminated menu from **Jahn's**. It is a gift that every current and former Bronxite will want to own. To order, see page 18.

As always, if you have friends, neighbors, relatives who might be interested in **Back In THE BRONX**, please give us their names and addresses and we will be happy to send them a free copy. Any requests may also be made through our toll free no.:

1-800-7-BRONX-5.

Sincerely,

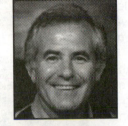

Stephen M. Samtur

Susan J. Samtur

CHECK OUT OUR INTERNET ADDRESS:
http://www.inter-net.com/bronx

Back in THE BRONX

A number of the photographs in **Back in THE BRONX** are courtesy of and are available from the Bronx Historical Society.

Publishers & Editors:	Stephen M. Samtur	Clinton '61
	Susan H. Samtur	Taft '62
Contributing Editors:	Barbara Fasciani	Roosevelt '65
	Martin Jackson	Science '58
	Sandra Zuckerman	Jefferson '57
	Al Zuckerman	New Utrecht '50
Art & Production:	Ellen Grodjesk	
Printed By:	Trumbell Printing, Trumbell, CT	

Reprinted from Daily News • Sunday, October 27, 1996

They kin really vend beer, eats

By JANE FURSE, Daily News Staff Writer

The Samtur family is vending royalty at Yankee Stadium.

Four members of the family have worked as vendors, a tradition that began 39 years ago when Stephen Samtur donned his cap and lugged hot dogs, peanuts and beer through the stands.

"The best thing to sell was beer. Generally you got to sell beer when you had more seniority. The worst was the souvenirs. Those went very slowly," said Samtur, 53, who grew up in University Heights in the Bronx and quit the vending racket when he became a teacher at **Taft** High School after graduating from City College.

Stephen and his wife, Susan, 51, still take pride in their connection to the Yanks and their deep roots in the Bronx.

"When you grow up in the Bronx, you develop a certain streetwise ability," said Susan, who grew up near Claremont Park "We call it being hungry."

The Samturs, who live in Scarsdale and have four sons, have parlayed their Bronxbred street wisdom into a successful publishing business.

Stephen is editor of "Back In THE BRONX," a magazine for past and present borough residents. Susan is the self-proclaimed "Coupon Queen." Her book, "Cashing in at the Checkout," has sold more than 1 million copies.

From 1957 to 1967, Stephen developed the art of slicing open a can of Knickerbocker with three swift pulls of his kegliner. Now, the beer his 19 year-old son, Mark, is hawking comes in pre-packaged cups.

Mark Samtur, a junior at the University of Hartford and the second of the Samturs' four sons, will take home more money than did his dad. Stephen made about $25 a game. Mark generally pulls in $50 to $60 during a game and expects $100 a game during the World Series.

In Susan Samtur's day, women were forbidden to work the stands, but she ran concession counters at Yankee and Shea stadiums while attending City College in the early 1960s.

"I could barely see over the counter," said Susan, who doesn't quite reach 5 feet.

"About 50 times a day somebody would say, 'Hey, are you standing in a hole?'"

She said working the games made her feel 10 feet tall, though.

The Samturs, who met at City College, saw all the greats perform and "sort of grew up with Mickey Mantle."

They saw no-hitters pitched by the Dodgers' Sandy Koufax and the Phillies' Jim Bunning and saw Met Jimmy Piersall hit his 100th home run and run the bases backward.

Two weeks ago, Susan drove another son, Michael, 16, to the Stadium for his vending gig.

The memories came flooding back.

"It was like a dream come true to be working at Yankee Stadium. When you get there, a few hours before the game, there is a certain excitement," she said.

"When I dropped him off, the same energy was there. You feel it, watching them cleaning the field, wiping off the seats. You feel like an insider," she said. ■

Flo Levy, Where Are You?

by Marty Goldstein, Roosevelt '55

Flo Levy, where are you? I never told you that I love you.

It's been 40 years and a few lifetimes since I last saw you, on the benches, across the street from 1700 Crotona Park East. Black hair, red lips, creamy skin and a smile that could melt stone.

You were gorgeous, I never had a chance.

Pudgy and 16, I was a good Jewish boy. Smart, funny, responsible, and loudly shy. I could never approach you. You were this Jewish angel, high above my rank: in the crowd. You always went with the most important guy on the block.

I always knew how to dance, and all the girls liked to dance with me, but I don't think we ever danced together. Certainly not anything slow. I just wasn't secure enough (dear God, why not?) to try to fish or grind with you. Lindys, bops and cha-chas only.

You wore those white shirts and black skirts and leather belts much wider than the two inch garrison I wore with my dungarees. I can still see you sitting there, your collar up, and all of Crotona Park behind you. I get drunk on the image. You were beautiful. I loved you.

Were we in school together? I can't remember. Maybe not. I went to JHS 44 and then to Roosevelt High. You went to Herman Ridder JHS, didn't you? After that, who knows?

I married Judy. Remember pretty Judy? We had a dozen or so great years, and two wonderful sons, but we couldn't survive the 60's, and we divorced after 17 years of marriage. That was almost 20 years ago... other lifetimes...

Anyway, I became a not-so-straight, not-so-pudgy, successful entrepreneur (pardon my French).

After 4 years at Pratt Institute and 10 years as an art director in NYC, I started my own business. Eighteen years later (about the same length as my marriage), I sold it for lots of money and retired young(ish). Now, I lie in my hammock in Westchester and I think of you.

Where are you? Where did you go? Gone with the neighborhood and my optimistic youth.

Gone with size 32 pants. Rich but elusive memories... more lifetimes...

Too special to lead an ordinary, uneventful life, I imagine you in the best of all possible worlds. Happily married, family, career, the works. These last 56 years tell me that life is not easy, and happiness can be hard to find, but my memories are bits of old dreams and fantasies, warm and comfortable like the inside of my worn shoebox with the duotone cowboy post cards and soda bottle caps and decoder rings. They're the stuff of childhood and don't always mirror reality.

But, boy oh boy, they make wonderful daydreams, Just like you.

And now, (with The Moonglows singing in the background), this teenage fairytale swims into my mind again, reminding me of all those longings, so long ago, in those endless summers, on the benches, in Crotona Park.

The Fountain in Crotona Park near Tremont and Arthur Aves, circa 1920.
Photo courtesy of the Bronx County Historical Society, NYC

So on the off chance that you read this letter, don't answer it. (Not that you were rushing to do so).

In my mind, you'll never change, never show the cracks that appear in the walls we spend our lives building.

Forever Flo, forever beautiful, forever young. I will love you till I die. ♥

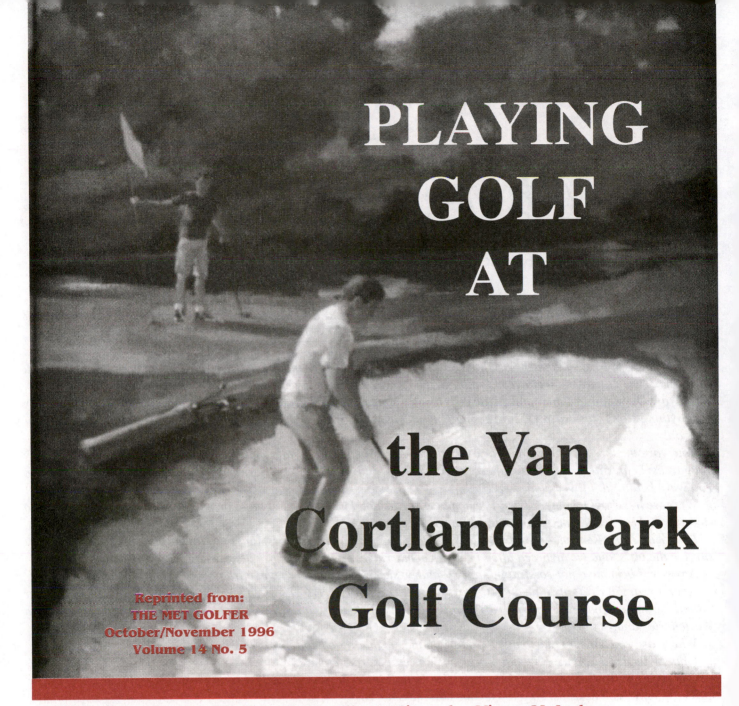

PLAYING GOLF AT the Van Cortlandt Park Golf Course

Reprinted from:
THE MET GOLFER
October/November 1996
Volume 14 No. 5

Story by Paul S. Levy • Illustrations by Vince McIndoe

I grew up in the 1950s in the very north Bronx, in a 10th floor apartment on **Van Cortlandt Park South**, immediately east of Broadway, close to the Major Deegan Expressway-and overlooking the last four holes of the **Van Cortlandt Park Golf Course.**

These were the holes which were severed from the course in the mid-1950s, when the **Deegan** and **New York State Thruway** pushed north. They were known as the "hill holes" and were best-suited to billy goats.

In fact, before golf carts arrived at **Van Cortlandt**, many golfers finished their rounds on the 14th green.

The terrain worked well for me and my buddies because it meant few golfers ever disturbed our play. This was just as well because when we started out playing we enjoyed a special status at **Van Cortlandt**: "sneak on." Every day we'd clamber onto the course through gaps in the fence which bordered my street. When the Parks Department personnel responsible for maintaining the hill holes and keeping the likes of us off the course—the "Parkies"—wired one gap shut, we'd just use another. Failing that, I resorted to the wire cutters I carried. Such was my growing addiction to this curious game.

I don't know why I got into golf. Perhaps the landscape took hold of me. It wasn't hard, after all, for a street kid from the Bronx to find comfort in the soft green colors, the rolling fairways, and the solitude and quiet of it all. Years later, when was in my senior year at **Bronx Science**, I even found a spot in the rock cliff by the 18th fairway where I could lie back

on a bed of leaves and read my newly discovered and much-loved Greek tragedies. The city wasn't all bad.

Each season we started to play as soon as the snow began to melt in March. Anticipating the start of a new season, each day I'd watch from my window as the 16th green, about 300 yards away, gradually revealed itself. As the season went on, I came to know when the Parkies would cut the fairways and greens, aerate them, fertilize them, or generally patrol. This was my turf, so to speak, my practice area. I'd spend entire afternoons here, until my sister would hang a towel from her window to signal that dinner was ready. It took me minutes to get home.

My two main golf buddies were Lou Rosenberg and Joey Newman. Joey lived closer than Lou so he was my daily companion. Lou lived over near **Mosholu Golf Course**, where we'd play with Blair Netburn, a chubby guy who played on the **DeWitt Clinton High School** golf team and could hit it a mile. Lou talked about things like, "pronation" and how he dreamed of copying Gene Littler's swing—the purest swing on the Tour, Lou said. What did I know?

We set about teaching each other how to play: No cheap criticisms, lots of mutual support, endless competition. We had a great teacher: "Sam Snead on Golf." If we wanted to know how to grip the club, chip, putt, drive or whatever, we looked it up. The book was chock full of pictures so sometimes we'd stand out on the 16th fairway, one eye peeled for lurking Parkies, comparing things like our "position through the hitting area" with that of Slammin' Sammy Snead.

I did have one teacher other than Sam, Lou, and Joey. His name was Jack—I never found out his last name —and he was a wiry little guy in his 30s, built like Corey Pavin, his fingers and nails cracked and stained with grease: Jack was an auto mechanic. He also was the first scratch golfer I ever met. He played in dungarees and a tee-shirt, but he walked like an ath-

lete and his swing was perfect, the movements all fluid and smooth. In correcting my myriad swing flaws he

A towel from the window was a signal that dinner was ready.

always knew what to say but never said much. Jack liked to practice his putting on the 15th green and one night as the sun fell behind the 17th hole and we squinted to see the lines of our putts, he made three 60-footers in a row. I will never forget seeing that little guy with his pock-marked face shrieking and squirming in an otherworldly way. Then last June, on Sunningdale's sharply-pitched seventh green, at about the same time in the evening, I did the same thing, but with my daughter Charlotte at my side. It was an eerie feeling, and I immediately thought of Jack.

Van Cortlandt has always been a busy place, and it was hard to get in a full round. On weekends I'd get up at 4:30 in the morning, make a few sandwiches, then meet Joey at around five. We'd walk about a mile to the **Van Cortlandt** Lake Boat House to sign up, getting there around 5:30, long after the crazies had gotten the

best tee times and had gone back to sleep in their cars. We'd tee off some time between seven and eight.

The rounds were excruciatingly slow. As bad as we were, most of our playing partners were much worse, and it often was after two-o'clock in the afternoon by the time we trudged home. After playing the 18th hole I'd try to play back up the 15th hole and then leave by one of my personalized holes in the fence. Public links golf— lugging a bag to, from, and around the golf course, starting at 5 a.m. and getting home at 2 p.m.—Wasn't easy. But what should I have expected for just $1.25 per round? And besides, it was then that I first learned all about the beauty and peacefulness of late-afternoon naps.

The pace grew even worse when we had to look for lost balls. At **Van Cortlandt** you *really* searched for your ball before declaring it lost, not because of the penalty strokes (heck, **Van Cortlandt** players didn't even have handicaps), but because it cost so much to replace it. Even today I get nervous twitches when a Sunningdale buddy abandons a new Titleist after only a brief search.

We often stopped playing just to look for balls. The pickings were pretty fair in a swamp that bordered the 15th green and 16th and 18th fairways. We needed balls for practice as well, as **Van Cortlandt** didn't have a range where you could hit a bucket. What it had instead was amazing. Not far from the first tee was a firm, grassless bank that overlooked the lake that skirted the 14th hole. If you had an ample supply of balls you could warm up by hitting them into or over the lake. In either event, they were gone forever. But we had to warm up; Sam Snead told us to!

This crazy game gradually started to yield a bit. I broke 100, then 90, and then, in my freshman year at high school, I broke 80, with not one professional lesson along the way. Who could afford it? But as my game was improving, another tough challenge had risen

continued on page 22

Home Again

Continued from page 1

The first stop was where Evy (Baker Lang, **Monroe** '54) grew up: 1690 Longfellow Avenue. It was a large apartment house, connected to and surrounded by other apartment houses. Her eyes found the windows to her apartment and her thoughts found their voice. Then we found our way to my neighborhood as we drove past **Monroe**, down Boynton Avenue

1253 Boynton Avenue

to 1253 - my home. It felt just like that .... as if I was going home, like Emily in "Our Town" expecting to see her family appear before her one more time. What happened next wasn't magic, but it was magical.

We stood outside the house, my husband and I, as I recounted again how I played stoop ball on the steps and potsie on the sidewalk. Joe took pictures of the house so that I could show my family that it still exists. Then without realizing it, I was climbing on the porch as I used to, standing on the ledge, grasping the wrought iron railing and going from one end to the other - and he took another picture.

It was the same, but different. Feel-

ings, images and echoes rapidly crystallized and then slowly blurred, much as when you look through a kaleidoscope. The trance had begun, time was suspended and I was a child again.

Reality suddenly appeared in the form of the woman looking out from her (my) living room window at this stranger who was climbing all around her (my) porch. In a few moments she opened the entrance door and I explained my behavior and apologized for the intrusion. She smiled as I spoke and seemed pleased to know how important this house was to someone else and then she beckoned me in. She actually asked if I would like to go through the house and I thought my heart would burst. You see, for years it had been my hope, my desire, my intention to be able to do just that; in my reverie it would be an Hispanic family that would take me in and there she was. As Hillel said, " .... and if not now, then when?"

As we walked into the small entrance hallway that separated our home from the neighbor's apartment upstairs, I was transported to another time, in the same place. We walked into the living room and the kaleidoscope turned. Their plants and furniture disappeared and there was my upright piano on one wall, our 12" television set along another wall and my father sitting at the front window watching the comings and goings of people outside. As we walked down the hallway the woman's husband came out and greeted us warmly as she explained to him who we were. This man and this woman, whose names I don't even know, were like two angels walking gently beside me.

Then we were in my bedroom, originally shared with my two older sisters

and then mine alone after each one married. There were the pictures from <u>Photoplay</u> scotchtaped on the wall over my bed: Tab Hunter, Tony Curtis, Montgomery Clift, and there was my roll-top desk which stored my secret treasures. It was all there but oh, so much smaller. How did the six of us live in such tiny rooms? When did all this shrink to such Lilliputian size? How was this possible?

How did the six of us live in such tiny rooms? When did all this shrink to such Lilliputian size? How was this possible?

I turned around and there was the kitchen and eating area, the heart of our house. And there I was cleaning the front of the refrigerator again for my mother and there she was, humming softly to herself.

Without warning I heard someone crying and she couldn't stop. The man put his arm around me and told me that it was OK, that he understood because he too had gone back to his original home in Puerto Rico.

We walked past my brother's and my parents' bedrooms and then the bathroom. The physical tour took only about twenty minutes; the emotional tour encompassed part of my lifetime and will take forever to process.

Like many of you I have traveled to different areas by now and have been awed by various sights and experiences. But it was <u>this</u> trip that touched the most primal parts of my being and for which I am most grateful.

P.S. In all the years I lived there, and even through the course of this visit, I had never noticed the beautiful brickwork design on the house. It wasn't until I looked back at the picture that was taken that afternoon that this intricate pattern came into my awareness. Sometimes the blind spots of things right in front of us can be transformed into things of beauty, just as in a kaleidoscope. ■

Woodlawn Express

By Margo Nash

Life started to improve as the **Woodlawn** Express rumbled north through the West Bronx. I was on my way to see my cousin.

The West Bronx was magical to me back in the 1950's. It seemed like such a happy place. On the **Woodlawn** Express, in those days, when you emerged from the tunnel into the daylight, you got a peek into **Yankee Stadium** and for a few glorious seconds got a free look at the packed stands and the players on the field.

As the train headed up the line, it passed the backs of apartment buildings strung with wash. I imagined the cozy lives inside those apartments, mothers bustling in shiny walled kitchens, fathers in the undershirts at kitchen tables, reaching for the food or seltzer bottles, kids coming up for lunch and going down again.

West 176th St. and Jerome Avenue
Photo courtesey of Bronc Historical Society

My Aunt Rose, my Uncle Harry and my cousins, Judy and Debby lived in the **Mosholu Parkway** section of the Bronx, just before the end of the **Jerome Avenue** line.

As the Woodlawn train drew closer to **Mosholu Parkway**, the view from the elevated train got better and better. Even the names of the stations improved and changed from numbered streets to names like **Fordham Road** and **Kingsbridge Avenue**. By **Bedford Park Boulevard** you saw fewer and fewer apartment buildings, more and more blue sky, more green. It was the beginning, I thought, of the country.

When I got off the train, I descended into the world of **Jerome Avenue**, a two block stretch under the El, lined with stores. Both sides of the Avenue were usually packed with people pushing shopping carts, going in and out of vegetable stands, the dairy store, the supermarkets, stopping in for curtains, corsets, schnaps, whitefish, chatting with store owners who were also their neighbors. The street's four delicatessens—we didn't call them deli's then-were all busy.

I would pass **Schweller's Bakery**, the barber shop with the stripes outside, the Irish bar, and the candy store where my cousin Judy and I would go out for egg creams at night. Rounding the corner to **DeKalb Avenue**, I passed assorted apartment buildings, each with a touch of grandness, a courtyard, a lion, steps, granite spheres, wrought iron fences, pillars, mirrors in the lobby.

The block, like the neighborhood, was mostly Jewish. It felt like a village. People understood one another here. But in love they weren't.

Continued on page 22

Bronx Movies

"REAL to REEL"

By Martin A. Jackson

The Bronx is no stranger to American movies. In the earliest years of the medium, around the turn of the century, silent movies were shot on the streets of the Bronx and even in special studios built on the open lands of that northern borough. Edison himself established a movies studio in the 1900s, and later on, the Biograph Studios on **175th Street** were host to Chaplin, Pickford and Fairbanks. The master himself, D.W. Griffith, shot a few silents around the Bronx, which offered rugged woods and quaint farms for backgrounds. Griffith went as far north as **Fort Schuyler** to make a movie about the American Revolution.

Several movies overt the years have featured the borough as a central character, most notably in "Marty" (1955) or in "I Like It Like That" (1995)... films that manage to capture something of the special flavor of the Bronx while not ignoring the gritty reality. True, there have been the infamous works that have tarnished the reputation of our part of the city, items like "Wolfen" (1981), in which the Bronx is the hellish locale for a fantasy about wild wolves devouring people. More famous even, in this negative sense, is "Fort Apache, The Bronx" into the folklore of America and made the Bronx a synonym for urban disaster. "The Seven Ups" (1979), another police movie, took the Bronx for its locale too; Bronx people will not recognize their borough very well in this shoot-em-up.

AIR-CONDITIONED

PALACE Theatre

1603 UNIONPORT RD.   TA 3-4140

An Affair to Remember

"marty"

WHITESTONE BRIDGE
DRIVE-IN THEATRE
TA 8-3330
BRUCKNER BLVD. & HUTCHINSON PKWY. •, BRONX, N. Y.

"Raging Bull"

"Bonfire of the Vanities"

CHILDREN UNDER 12 FREE!

At times, though, the Bronx has been kindly treated by moviemakers. Foremost among these affectionate portrayals of the Bronx remains "Marty", the classic tale of the Bronx butcher who finds true love at the **Stardust Ballroom** on **Southern Boulevard** under the **El**. When Ernest Borgnine gave his Oscar winning performance in '55, the Bronx was still a comfortable middle-class community, at least in the popular vision. The days of burning buildings and gang wars still lay in the future, and director Delbert Mann painted a lovely portrait of a close-knit Italian community in his movie. Bronxites were thrilled to be on the big screen, and in such a successful movie at that and the dialogue became cliche... teenagers all over the Bronx asked, "So wadda ya wanna do tonight, Marty?" And responded universally, "I dunno Angie, wadda you wanna do?" It's still possible to get a glimpse of the old Bronx in **Marty**: the **Arthur Avenue** market, the **West Farms** neighborhood and assorted streets are captured forever on film.

Philip Kaufman's, "The Wanderers" (1979) has the virtue of being shot on the real streets of the Bronx, and it nicely captures the tone of Richard Price's novel. The slightly surreal story of Bronx teenagers in the 1960's, "The Wanderers" will stir up memories of high schools and changing times for those who lived through those

8

Bronx Movies

"REAL to REEL"

years. All former Bronxites will recall the familiar terror inspired by leather-coated gangs with terrifying reputations, every neighborhood had one. In this case, the gang is the **Fordham Baldies**, probably mythical but certainly well discussed in candy stores and schoolyards around the Bronx for many years.

In the 1980s, the Bronx continued to fascinate certain filmmakers. Tony Bill directed the very strange **"Five Corners"** with John Turturro as the psychotic Bronx guy who throws his mother out the window. Jodie Foster also starred in this film, which got little reward at the box office but has developed a cult following in the years since. It, too, was made on the real streets of the Bronx and while it won't reflect everybody's experience (I hope) it does recreate a time and place with some accuracy.

Recently there has been **"A Bronx Tale"** 1993, Robert DeNiro's adaptation of a successful stage performance by Chaz Palminterri. Palminterri, a product of the Italian neighborhood around **Arthur Avenue**, painted a vivid portrait of his childhood and the characters who lived around him. With Palminterri in the lead role as the local mob boss, **"A Bronx Tale"** is swift and often brutal, but it has a ring of truth about it. Sadly, the movie was shot on location in Queens... a plausible substitute for the Bronx for out-of-towners, but it won't fool the natives.

Even more implausible was **"Rumble in the Bronx"** (1995), a Jackie Chan martial arts thriller. Somehow the producers felt that the

word "Bronx" in the title would improve sales around the world (and they were probably right) but then why didn't they shoot in the Bronx? Instead, **"Rumble in the Bronx"** is filmed in Vancouver, British Columbia, a lovely city but hardly a stand-in for the Bronx. The Bronx, for example, does not have snow-capped mountains nor a sweeping harbor, both of which appear prominently in **"Rumble in the Bronx"**. Still, it's a good action film and Chan fans will probably overlook the inaccuracy. In the same vain, but even more, was **"The Bronx War"** (1990), a movie about Latin gangs, drugs and violence. This purports to give us a glimpse into modern Bronx life, while it manages some exciting moments, it has little to do with the real Bronx.

More realistic was **"I Like It Like That"** (1995), a bright comedy about contemporary life in the Bronx. There are some sad and honest views of the Bronx Latin community, but overall this is an upbeat and colorful movie with fine performances. ■

9

REVISED

Bronx Honor Roll
Bronxites Who Have Achieved!

BRONX SCIENCE
Harold Brown
Stokely Carmichael
Leon Cooper (Nobel Prize Winner))
Bobby Darin
Eddgar Doctorow
Sheldon Glashow (Nobel Prize Winner)
Jeff Greenfield*
Russell Hulse (Nobel Prize Winner)
Ronald Lauder
Nita Lowey, Representative
Arno Penzias (Nobel Prize Winner)
William Safire
Melvin Schwartz (Nobel Prize Winner)
Steven Weinberg (Nobel Prize Winner)

CARDINAL HAYES
George Carlin
Rocky Colavito
Kevin Loughery
Regis Philbin

CHRISTOPHER COLUMBUS
Robert Abrams
Anne Bancroft
Christine Jorgenson
Alan Landsburg

DEWITT CLINTON
Don Adams
Nate Archibald
Richard Avedon
James A. Baldwin
Martin Balsam
David Begelman
James Caan
Paddy Chayevsky
George Cukor
Avery Fisher
Arthur Gelb
Judd Hirsch
Robert Hofstadter (Nobel Prize Winner)
Stubby Kaye
Al Kelly
Theodore Kheel
Robert Klein
William Kunstler
Burt Lancaster
Garry Marshall
Jan Murray
Basil Paterson*
Charles Rangel
Richard Rogers
A.M. Rosenthal
Daniel Schorr
Dolph Schayes
Neil Simon
Larry Storch
Marvin Traub
Jimmie Walker
Fats Waller
William Zeckendorf

EVANDER CHILDS
Red Buttons
James Coco
Carl Reiner

MONROE
Jules Pfeiffer
John Garfield
Hank Greenberg
Ed Kranepool
Leon Lederman (Nobel Physicist)

MORRIS
Angel Cordero
Herman Joseph Muller (Nobel Prize Winner)
Gabe Pressman
E. Colin Powell

ROOSEVELT
June Alyson
Chazz Palminteri

TAFT
Sanford Brown
Eydie Gorme
Stanley Kubrick
Mal Z. Lawrence

WALTON
Bella Abzug
Gertrude Elion (Nobel Prize Winner)
Rosalyn Yalow (Nobel Prize Winner)

OTHER NOTABLES
Joey Adams
Danny Aiello
Robert Alda
Corazon Aquino
Armand Assante
Herman Badillo
Lauren Bacall
Ellen Barkin
Mario Biaggi
Joey Bishop
Alfred Bloomingdale
Bobby Bonilla
Teresa Brewer
Ralph J. Bunche (Nobel Prize Winner)
George Burns
Cab Calloway
Diahann Carroll
Carmen Cavallaro
Samuel Clemens
Myron Cohen
Betty Comdon
Cardinal Cooke
Avery Corman
Norman Cousins
Bobby Cremins
Don Criqui
Tony Curtis
Ossie Davis
Dennis Day
Ruby Dee
Robert DeNiro
Dion DiMucci
Art Donovan
John Foster Dulles
Erik Estrada
Fernando Ferrer
Geraldine Ferraro
F. Scott Fitzgerald
Art Fleming
Joe Franklin
Arlene Francis
Connie Francis
Frankie Frisch
Edward J. Flynn
Rita Gam
Stan Getz
Rudolph Giuliani
Samuel Gompers
Aldolf Green
Richie Guerin
Armand Hammer
Moss Hart
Herbert A. Hauptman (Nobel Prize Winner)
David Horowitz
Vladimir Horowitz
Irving Howe
George Jessel
Billy Joel
Raoul Julia
John F. Kennedy
Robert Kennedy
Ted Kennedy
Theodore Kheel
Calvin Klein
Edward Koch
Fiorello LaGuardia
Bert Lahr
Jake LaMotta
Louise Lasser
Ralph Lauren
Ron Leibman
Lee Leonard
Joe E. Lewis
Shari Lewis
Hal Linden

Vince Lombardi
Melissa Manchester
John Mariani
Penny Marshall
Willie Mays
John McSherry
George Meany
Mario Merola
Glenn Miller
Sal Mineo
Hugo Montenegro
Robert Morgenthau
Gary Morton
Richard Mulligan
Paul Muni
Bess Myerson
Gil Noble
Carroll O'Connor
John O'Hara
Charles Osgood
Al Pacino
Jack Palance
Floyd Patterson
Joseph Papp
Joe Pesci
Roberta Peters
Mary Pickford
Ezio Pinza
Edgar Allan Poe
Seymour Posner*
Richard Price
Vincent Price
Tito Puente
Charles Nelson Reilly
Rob Reiner
Regina Resnick
Victor Riesel
Edward G. Robinson
Monte Rock III
Franklin D. Roosevelt
Theodore Roosevelt
Billy Rose
Howard Safir
Jonas Salk
Isabel Sanford
Martin Scorcese
Marvin Scott
George Segal
Connie Selleca
Jose Serrano
Sylvia Sidney
Carly Simon
Stanley Simon
Vince Scully
Isaac Bashevis Singer (Nobel Prize Winner)
Curtis Sliwa
Wesley Snipes, Jr.
Cardinal Spellman
Sy Sperling
George Steinbrenner
Henry Stern
Pat Summerall
Renee Taylor
Mother Teresa (Nobel Prize Winner)
U. Thant
Arturo Toscanini
Dan Topping
Leon Trotsky
Lloyd Ultan
Jerry Vale
Bobby Van
Luther Vandross
June Valli
Jackie Vernon
Fran Warren
Del Webb
Jerry Weintraub
Vanessa Williams
Herman Wouk

Thanks to Dr. William C. Wolfson and the Bonx Society of Science and Letters

BRONX CELEBRITIES

SPORTS FIGURES

PHIL RIZZUTO
Yankees
Hall of Fame

MICKEY MANTLE
Yankees
Hall of Fame

YOGI BERRA
Yankees
Hall of Fame

WHITEY FORD
Yankees
Hall of Fame

ED KRANPOOL
NY Mets
Monroe HS

ART DONOVAN
Baltimore Colts
Football Hall of Fame

> **We applaud these former Bronxites and their many accomplishments**

POLITICAL

FERNANDO FERRER
Bronx Borough Pres.

NITA LOWEY
Congress-woman
Bronx Science

ROBERT ABRAMS
Former NYS Attorney General
Former Bronx Borough Pres.
Columbus HS

G. OLIVER KOPPEL
Former NYS Attorney General

GENERAL COLIN POWELL
Former Chief of Staff

ENTERTAINERS

JOE FRANKLIN

MARVIN SCOTT

REGIS PHILBIN

GARRY MARSHALL

JERRY VALE

CARL REINER

JAN MURRAY

RED BUTTONS

DION

DANNY AIELLO

ROBERT KLEIN

MAL Z. LAWRENCE

DAVID HOROWITZ

CURTIS SLIWA

11

How I Became A Bat Boy
"Being in the right place, at the right time"

By Richard J. McCabe

I was born and raised in the **Tremont** section of the Bronx, where I lived for 28 years. While growing up, I developed a great love for the game of baseball. As a small child, my father would take me to **Fordham University** Campus and hit fungoes to me, and one day a grounder hit a rut and hit me in the eye. Needless to say, I was gun-shy for a long time thereafter. My Father was a Yankee fan and would take my Mother and I to games where we would sit in the bleachers, who could afford Grandstand or Box Seats. I remember the great play of Joe DiMaggio who played the outfield with such grace!!! I also remember the 1950 World Series (Yanks vs. Phillies). My Father and I got to the stadium at 5:00 a.m. to wait for a bleacher seat—which we were lucky enough to get! In the Spring of '51, I saw an ad in the news that read: "Giants vs. Reds, Polo Grounds this Saturday...etc." I asked my father to take me to see these New York Giants. He did, reluctantly (remember...he was a Yankee fan). At about the fourth inning where Ewell Balckwell and Clint "Hondo Hurricane" Hartung were in a 0 - 0 duel. It was at this time I realized I was falling hopelessly in love with these "Giants." I did not want to hurt my father's feelings, but eventually he understood. After all, everybody can't be a Yankee fan.

In order to have carfare to take the **"D"** train to the Polo Grounds as often as possible, I took a job delivering meats two days a week. Most of the gate personnel were very understanding with us kids and let us in about the 7th inning. One game stands out in my mind, the Giants vs. Dodgers game because I had such a "fever" in my mind about seeing this game that me and another "regular" climbed up the left

field wall outside the ballpark, which was about 30 feet high in order to enter the grandstand. Later, I realized how stupid we were- we could've been killed.

We "regulars" were taught the "ropes" by, of all people, a 13 year old girl!! She showed us how to get autographs, how to set up a scrapbook and where to wait for the Home and Visiting players. I became a real "Pro" in a short period of time thanks to here assistance. I amassed a HUGE collection of baseball and football autographs. The thought of becoming a Batboy never entered my

12

Bat Boy...
Continued from page 12

mind— that was reserved for people who knew "people." The miracle of "Being in the Right Place at the Right Time" happened during the latter part of Sept. 1953 with about 13 games left in the season. I was standing outside the Polo grounds, in the street, when a man came out of the Giants Clubhouse. He called me over and requested that I run an errand— to go to the Luncheonette in the Projects and get him a sandwich. When I returned with his sandwich he offered me the change of a $5.00 bill (about $3.75) as a tip. I told him, I

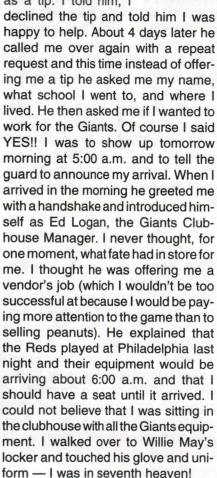

The author, Richard McCabe

declined the tip and told him I was happy to help. About 4 days later he called me over again with a repeat request and this time instead of offering me a tip he asked me my name, what school I went to, and where I lived. He then asked me if I wanted to work for the Giants. Of course I said YES!! I was to show up tomorrow morning at 5:00 a.m. and to tell the guard to announce my arrival. When I arrived in the morning he greeted me with a handshake and introduced himself as Ed Logan, the Giants Clubhouse Manager. I never thought, for one moment, what fate had in store for me. I thought he was offering me a vendor's job (which I wouldn't be too successful at because I would be paying more attention to the game than to selling peanuts). He explained that the Reds played at Philadelphia last night and their equipment would be arriving about 6:00 a.m. and that I should have a seat until it arrived. I could not believe that I was sitting in the clubhouse with all the Giants equipment. I walked over to Willie May's locker and touched his glove and uniform — I was in seventh heaven!

Mr. Logan emerged from the rear

of the clubhouse and informed me that the Red's equipment had arrived and that we had work to do. I was introduced to the man to be my new boss, "Little Pete" who was the Yankees' Assistant clubhouse manager, who worked the Giants visiting team clubhouse when the Yankees were on the road. When I asked "Little Pete" what my job was going to be, he looked at me and said in an aggravated way, "You are going to be a batboy— is that alright with you?" I nearly went into cardiac arrest! Then he said, "let's get going, we have alot of work to do." Little Pete explained that in each of the Red's trunks there were 6 trays each belonging to a player. He said the Rookies were to use the cubicles on the upper level. The first tray I picked up was Ted Kluszewski, the star, first cubicle, downstairs.

I worked there the very last part of 1953, all of 1954 and 1955. The players are like most people you meet — some are very nice, some don't bother with anybody and some are demanding pains in the _____! There were players that I held a special fondness for because they took an interest in getting to know me personally. They were Roy Campanella, Stan Musial, Del Crandal, Del Rice and Robin Roberts.

It is hard to describe the feeling

of excitement on the field, in the heat of a tight game, especially in the World Series. Even during the regular season the players are very serious about winning. If a team loses there is no fooling around in the clubhouse. Just shower, dress and depart.

I particularly enjoyed playing with the players in batting practice after my work was done. I remember sitting on the **155th St.** subway platform after a long night on the field waiting for the **"D"** train to the **Tremont station** at 11:30 p.m. laden down with broken bats for the kids in my neighborhood. Now that I look back- I realize that I must have given away a fortune in memorabilia.

I kept in contact with my old mentor, Ed Logan, who passed away in May 1995 at 83 years of age. The Logan family were baseball in New York for many years. Fred Logan, Ed's father was clubhouse manager in New York in 1896. He hired the old Yankee clubhouse manager, Pete Sheehy "Big Pete" right off the street in 1927. As a young boy, Ed Logan started working with his father in the clubhouse in 1931 and took over 1947 when his dad passed away. Ed retired in 1980 after 49 years in the clubhouse. He was a wonderful man, and I'll miss him dearly. I'll conclude by saying that being in the right place at the right time created a miracle for me! ∎

June 2, 1955 Polo Grounds
Theodore Kluszewski- runner
Walter Post:- #28
Wesley Westrum- catcher
Richard McCabe(#32)- batboy
Photo courtesy of the National Baseball Library & Archive photo collection

Reminiscing

MARVELOUS MARBLE HILL

Arlene Jacks

Marble Hill was one of those places you would drive by and probably not even take notice of. To most "outsider," it was just a group of eleven buildings, all looking pretty much the same, nothing special or out of the ordinary. To us, it was the whole world. And what a world it was!

I was one of the "lucky'" who was privileged enough to call **Marble Hill** home for the first twenty years of my life. In fact, I moved there with my family at the tender age of five months when both the projects and I were in our infancy. Built upon swampland in the section of the west Bronx closely bordering Manhattan, this young group of middle income families was treated to just about every form of recreation and entertainment the Bronx had to offer.

The interior of the RKO Marble Hill on Broadway near 232nd St.

Photo courtesy of The Bronx County Historical Society

If a movie was on our agenda, we could choose between the **RKO** or the **Dale**, both within walking distance, which was major selling point to parents with kids who were too young to travel by bus alone or to drive. It was at the **Dale** (which I believe still exists) that I experienced sitting through "West Side Story" with my friends - twice! (We were still in tears when we reached our front door!). On those occasions when we were feeling a little bit more athletic, the local bowling alley was just a stone's throw away as was both **Van Cortlandt** and **Inwood** parks.

Many of my fondest childhood memories occurred within the project's very parameters. There was that famous plot of grass known as the "big circle" which seemed to be the center of all life in **Marble Hill**. In the wintertime, after a big snowfall, it would freeze over and become one giant ice skating rink. And, it is here we stood every July 4th, twirling our sparklers until dark when you could no longer see bodies, only hundreds of tiny flickering lights. This was also the route of John, the ice cream man, who, along with his little white truck filled with dry ice, lazily traveled the neighborhood selling his goods. We all loved John!

Then there was our ever-faithful flagpole. It was here that on that fateful day back in November of 1963, the half-staffed flag confirmed to a bewildered seventh grader the reality of what she hoped was only an ugly rumor.

Visiting family members and friends were always amazed that we were able to sleep midst the roar of the **IRT** as it rumbled by, almost touching distance from our windows. I was never aware of any such disturbance. In fact, the first time I noticed any noise discomfort was when finally we moved to Westchester county. For weeks I struggled to fall asleep at night...the silence was absolutely deafening!

Halloween was a special day at **Marble Hill**. We never strayed any further than out own building. Each one had at least fourteen floors (some had fifteen) and there were ten apartments on every floor. By the time we covered floors one through six, we had almost filled our trick-or-treat bags with candy. And, in those days, we never had to have our moms inspect any of it. Razor blades and the like were unthinkable back then.

My friends and I didn't even own keys to our apartments...it just wasn't necessary. I don't ever recall my parents locking our front door. Boy, how times have changed!

"Calling" your neighbor didn't necessarily mean picking up the telephone. All it took was a knock on the kitchen steampipe for windows to fly open and for conversation to be in full swing! It was of no consequence that most tenants in the general vicinity got to overhear the whole thing. It kind of added to the charm. There were few secrets in **Marble Hill.**

While most of us experience at least four seasons, the residents of **Marble Hill** enjoyed a few additional ones. There was hula-hoop season, kite-flying season and the most popular of all...marble season. (How apt, considering our namesake, that is). When, how and by whom it started each year was always a mystery. Nevertheless, one morning we would just awaken to throngs of kids on hands and knees vying for that all important little ball of glass which, to us, at the time, was worth more than gold.

Every neighborhood had its candy store. Ours was directly across **225th** street and housed one of the most colorful characters I've ever met. Who could forget old "Rosie", the proprietor? She had this nasty habit of yelling at us if she suspected that we went to her competitor first before stopping at her place for our precious goodies. Somehow, I always believed that deep down, a truly loving heart beat within good old Rosie,

You know, so many of us grew up blaming our parents for whatever shortcomings we felt they had while rearing us. They were either too strict, too lenient, too overbearing, not caring enough, etc. Whatever the beef, there's one thing that stands out in my mind as my parents' crowning achievement - raising my sister and me in a place, where kids could still be kids and encounter all of life's experiences in a safe and loving environment.

Thanks Mom & Dad! And thank _you_, **Marble Hill**! You were the greatest! ■

14

At Play on the Flats of Vanny

By Tom McGowan

My world was defined by **Broadway**. The apartment we lived in was on the west side of it, at **246th Street**, 2 blocks after the end of the **IRT 7th Avenue El**. **Van Cortlandt Park** was on the east. It had many names, **Van Cortlandt, The Park, Vanny**. A huge city park, bigger than its cousin, Central Park, in Manhattan. More wild and varied. A lake—to boat and skate on. A railroad — the better to flatten pennies under the wheels of passing trains. A swamp for getting wet and dirty and seeing ducks, snakes, even hugh turtles. Two caves, a granite mountain, two graveyards. The flats for ball games, trails to hike and run, horse stables and pony rides, a spring, huge trees, and occasional fox, some bums and vagrants in rags, an occasional pervert or pedophile, playgrounds with monkey bars, see saws, hugh swings. Yes and more. A place for sport, fun and secrets.

The **Van Cortlandt Mansion** was the centerpiece. Built in the colonial era. A place were George Washington slept. Heavy stone walls, broad plank floors laid on huge beams. The main house for extensive farms. A place of beauty and grace and remembrance of things past.

The park was a gathering place for diverse groups. Irish hurlers, Jamaican cricket players. The Manhattan college baseball team. Hoards, no, thundering herds of high school cross country runners. The old timers playing baseball by the mansion, still playing on Saturdays, invited me to pick up a mitt last time I stopped by. Men well past their prime that had more than a passing interest in the game. Hitting virtually every ball pitched, how can that be? The faithful Boys of Fall.

The **Van Cortlandt Aerodrome**, a model plane buff called it. Claimed it held that title at one point in time. You see, on the West side of **Broadway,** a block down from the flats was **Seymour Brown's Hobby Shop**. Many was the time I glued my face to the multipane windows, looking at the planes, **HO trains** and other (almost) unattainable toys. Even a working model stationary steam engine, which not a boy in the entire neighborhood would ever find under a Christmas tree.

Seymour's trade was primarily older men with money, buying big toys. Their planes had 6' wingspans, large gas engines and 10" propellers. And, if you can believe it in 1964, many of their best planes were radio controlled.

Tom McGowan in 1962, standing in front of 6065 Broadway

Sam McGowan, Tom's son on top of Granite Mtn. looking south over the Flats towards Broadway. 1995

Before the time of transistors. When one of them hit the ground unexpectedly, grown men were known to cry. My rig was a "Ranger 49" with a Pee Wee .029 engine. Free flight, no con-trols. Balsa wood, glue and a bit of paint. Hard to start for a kid. Awful hard. Gas it up, connect the big dry cell battery to the glow plug, spin the prop, hope, if it caught, that it did not cut your hand. The normal routine: Brap. Braap. Brap. Braaaaaa-ppppp. Brap. But this day was different. A middle aged black man, one of the plane buffs, took an interest. Filled the tank to the top. Connected two dry cells in series to the glow plug. A few twirls of the prop. Brapp. Brappp. Braaap. Braaapaa-ppaaaaaaaaaaa, finally started, feverishly tuning the needle valve to get the mixture right, then the few step run and toss of the plane into the air, due north, in line with the flats and parallel with Broadway. A slight breeze blowing south. The Ranger 49 climbed. And climbed. And climbed until it was hard to see. Heading due north, with me running after it. Running as hard as I could, lungs hurting. When would it run out of gas? Would it crash in the trees? Can I keep it in sight? Keep running. Keep it in sight. Further north, a mile now. On the other side, just short of the horse stables, the plane landed. Not gracefully, but in one piece. A miracle. Back I go, walking and running. Upon my return the men shared in my glory, pleased that such a simple machine could do such a thing. Glad for a good ending for a boy with a plane. Perhaps recalling the simple pleasures of their youth.

Weeks later, at the hobby shop, I'm perusing the stocks of balsa wood, brass tube and copper wire, and Seymour, the owner, talking to a customer says, hey, weren't you the kid with the Ranger 49 that flew that day.... and I got to spend a moment in the adult limelight. ∎

Westchester Square

Tremont Ave West of Westchester Square
Photo courtesy of Bronx County Historical Society Research Library

By Joan (Caniell) Del Monte

The odd thing about **Westchester Square** is, it actually is a triangle. My parents sent me to **Sacred Heart School** on **Zerega Avenue**, which meant I had to cross **Westchester Square** every day, where **Westchester** and **Tremont Avenues** met in the Northeast Bronx.

The base of the triangle was the elevated station for the **IRT Pelham Bay**, the clatter of trains and buses beneath to take people out to **Fort Schuyler**. Two blocks up Westchester Avenue, under the El, was **St. Peter's** church, rough cut fieldstone, one of the earliest buildings in

A Kenmar shop celebrates its grand opening in the '50s
Photo courtesy of the Bronx County Historical Society Research Library - Max Levine Collection

the Bronx. And its cemetery! We dared each other to go in.

On one side of the triangle, underneath the El station, was the **Little Smoke Shop,** ten by ten feet, walls strung with clothes-pinned magazines, a wooden bench outside heaped precariously with the Times, the News, the Mirror, and the

Journal American, with a metal ashtray on top for the change, and inside the store a glass case of cigarettes and candy bars.

And on the same side was "**The Square,**" that wonderful neon moviehouse where I fell in love with Paul Henreid as he pursued Maureen O'Hara in "The Spanish Main". I stayed to see that movie three times and my parents called the police because they thought I'd been kidnapped.

And between the two was **Jack's Diner**. After the school dance late at night, they served toasted lemon pound cake covered with a scoop of melting vanilla ice cream.

The other side of the triangle was notable for a **Woolworth's**, a treasure house. First there was a huge candy counter where my mother bought chocolate bridge mix, and I bought wax lips with a few drops of sweet colored liquid inside. My other favorite was multicolored candy droplets which you bit off what looked like adding machine tape. Then there was a lunch counter along one wall where they served tulip sundaes and melted cheese sandwiches. And in the back of the store were pencil boxes and lined loose leaf paper and barrettes to wear in your hair. And canaries! Poor woebegone canaries, singing hopelessly in their cages in a corner.

And in the middle of this urban triangle, the public library, oak checkout desk, children's room up linoleum stairs and wonderful windowseats next to yellow leaded glass windows. To this day I'm a sucker for windowseats. Outside, one side of the building was a disreputable portico, shabby men, and forbidden toilets, and on the other side, a minuscule triangular park, brown grass around a memorial to the great war and that's where you got the **Tremont Avenue** trolley and it took an hour-and-a-half to rattle to **Sedgewick Avenue** at the other end of the run.

And there was a creek that came in from Eastchester Bay and went to **Westchester Square**, it was lined with stinky black mud and discarded oil cans, and we smoked punks, between the lumber yard and the gas station. I caught killey fish in jars with string around the mouths and bread on the inside. I put the jar on the radiator in the living room and the fish committed suicide by jumping onto the carpet.

I graduated from eighth grade at **Sacred Heart** in 1945. In 1990 the school fundraiser mailed me an appeal at my forty-five year old grammar school address. I had long since left the Bronx. I had graduated from Columbia and from UCLA, lived in Europe; I had another

Westchester Square in the late 1930's. The elevated structure along Westchester Ave. carries the Lexington Ave Pelham Bay Local.
Photo courtesy of The Bronx Historical Society, NYC

name, and I washed up on the other side of the country; however, I still got the school appeal.

You see, my parents still lived there, in the apartment house they moved into when they married. They forwarded the school appeal to me. ∎

MONDAY AT THE MOVIES

The lobby of the Loew's Grand Theatre on Fordham Road and Jerome Ave in 1927.
Photo cortesy of The Bronx County Historical Society, NYC

by Molly Adele (Silverman) Ellowis, Evander, June 1948)

The Monday afternoons I spent at the movies with my mother were among the happiest days of my childhood. Every Monday, my mother waited for me to come home from school; and as soon as I did, we left for the **Loew's Grand.**

In the post-depression days, the movies gave a much needed lift to our hearts and spirits. We were lucky because we had a pass, thanks to my mother's sister Pearl, who worked in the movie industry. One of her perks was a weekly pass to the **Grand**. Valid only on weekdays, all we had to do was present it at the box office. A hole was punched in the ticket and we were admitted. We defected, only rarely, to see a film at the **Fordham** or the **Valentine**, but Mondays were always reserved for the **Grand**.

I remember seeing an early Lana Turner film there. Her hair was still brown. As we watched, a word leapt onto the screen: "pregnant." The next thing I knew, my mother had me firmly by the hand and we quickly exited. The transition from the mysterious and wonderful darkness of the theater to the bright daylight of the real world was always startling. This time it was shocking — I didn't understand why we had left before the end of the movie. Bewildered, I looked to her for an answer, but my mother wasn't talking. In my mind, I questioned her action, but I knew enough to remain silent. I was eight, old enough to know that pregnancy and birth were not subjects my mother would discuss with me. These mysteries re-

mained, subjects my friends and I would whisper about. Our information came from books which we hid, and pamphlets which we burned in the kitchen sink immediately after reading them.

Only one word can describe the transformation from my world of home and school to the wider world of the movies: magic. My love of movies extended to reading movie magazines, cutting out photographs of my favorite actors and lovingly pasting them into scrapbooks. I also collected glossy black and white stills which my Aunt provided, courtesy of MGM. I was enchanted by the make-believe world which the big screen provided. Travel, adventure, humor, mystery and what I liked best, romance, all were mirrored, expanded and glamorized by the images on the screen.

Movies were also scary. The evil cackle of Snow White's step-mother reverberated in my mind for years, thanks to Disney's expertise and my mother's quite accurate imitation. Images of voodoo dolls, Frankenstein's monster, Dracula, and other assorted Hollywood evil-doers, returned to me in the form of nightmares. Mostly though, movies took me to places and worlds far away from my everyday life. History and fantasy, future worlds and exotic lands, became mine.

There was also a secret activity in which I engaged, protected by the darkness and the anonymity of being among many in the movie house: the marvelous release of crying during a movie where no one could see my tears. And there were many occasions to cry. Heartbreak on the screen was common and quickly internalized as I wept with and for the suffering players, who, to me were quite real. The cathartic effect was wonderful and no matter how sad I was during the process, it resulted in my feeling part of something larger than my life and its limits of place and childhood. I still love to go to the movies, but nothing has replaced those I saw with my mother at the **Loew's Grand**.

The Loew's Grand Theatre in 1928.
Photo courtesy of Bronx County Historical Society, NYC

The stories of your life have now been published.

All the priceless memories of The Bronx have been bound up for you in this book.

Now you can really go back in the Bronx...right back to the very first issue and start enjoying every story and article, every moment that we have gathered with over **165 stories** including countless **vintage photographs** and about your Bronx in the 30's, 40's, 50's and 60's.

Shop at **Alexander's**, spoon a sundae at **Krum's**. A date in the **Paradise** or a day at **Orchard Beach**. Dancing in **Poe Park** or cheering at **Yankee Stadium**.

This wasn't your life, it IS your life because all those formative years are what made us what we are today. The ups and downs, the hopes and dreams...it's all there for you to keep forever.

You can also locate friends and classmates through our **1000+** classifieds advertisements.

All these wonderful priceless memories now have a wonderful price. Four years in the making, this finely **bound book** of the complete **16 issues** can now be yours for just $49.95. If you order another for a friend, you'll save $9.90(shipping and handling) (2 for $99).

As an extra bonus, with every order, you will receive two collector's items. A laminated replica of a 1950's Jahn's menu, plus pictures of the interior of Krum's taken in the 40's - 50's.

Please be aware that **this is only available through Back In THE BRONX** Also, be aware, that though this book makes these wonderful days and memories last, this great offer **will not** because supply is limited and we know from past experience that the demand will be great.

So don't delay. Fill out the request form or call toll-free **1 800 7BRONX5** to charge your order. And every order comes with a **30 day-money-back guarantee**. That's how confident we feel about this offer.

Why is this the deal of a lifetime? Because it's **your** lifetime.

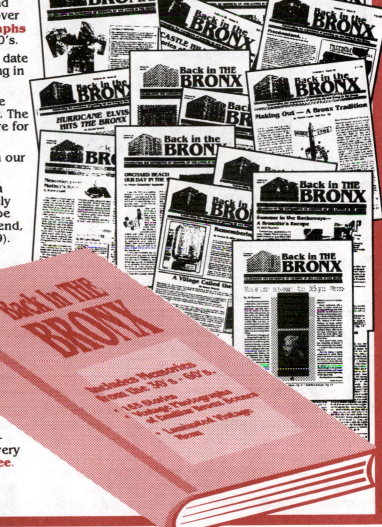

Free Jahn's menu for all those ordering now!

It's Your Magazine. Subscribe (Reorder) Now!

Please fill out the form below to subscribe to (reorder) Back in THE BRONX. And don't forget, whether you subscribe (reorder) for three, two or even one year, we'll send a friend or relative, free of charge, a one year subscription, acknowledging your gift with a card.

_____ 1 Year subscription(s) to **Back in THE BRONX** - **$19.95**

_____ 2 Year subscription(s) to **Back in THE BRONX** - **$29.95 ($10 Savings)**

_____ 3 Year subscription(s) to **Back in THE BRONX** - **$39.95 ($20 Savings)**

_____ (12) Complete set of back issues for just **$39.95 ($20 Savings)**

TOTAL DUE $ _____

FREE JAHN'S MENU

All those who subscribe (reorder) for *two or more* years will receive a laminated replica of a 1950's vintage JAHN'S MENU.

COLLECTOR'S ITEMS
ALL BACK ISSUES

The complete set (12) of out-of-print back issues of **Back in THE BRONX** *PLUS* Jahn's Menu all for just **$39.95 (while they last)**

Please complete information below and send payment to:

Back in THE BRONX, Box 141H, Scarsdale, NY 10583

☐ New Subscriber   ☐ Renewal   ☐ Back Issues Requested

Name _____ (Maiden) _____

Address _____

City _____ State _____ Zip _____

Phone # (_____) _____

H.S. Attended /Year Grad. _____

METHOD OF PAYMENT: ☐ Check

☐ VISA   ☐ MasterCard   ☐ AMERICAN EXPRESS   Total Amt. Enclosed $ _____

Card No. _____ Expiration Date _____

Use this box to enter the name and address of the friend or relative you want to recieve the FREE one year subscription to **Back In THE BRONX**. They will receive a card with your name as the gift-giver. Offer is not valid on subscriptions purchased before Dec. 31,1996. Valid from Jan. 1, 1997 to March 15, 1997

Name _____

Maiden Name _____

Address _____

City _____ State _____ Zip _____

(_____) _____

Phone Number _____

High School _____ Graduated -year

P.S. 93 DEJA VU IN THE BRONX

by Stanley I. Cohen

Earlier this year all the local networks and newspapers ran a headline story about a five year old kindergarten child who brought a loaded handgun to school. The principal disarmed the child. The community, upon learning that the gun was loaded and cocked, went into a state of shock. The child was suspended, which, we are told, is *standard practice* in such cases. Furthermore, the story continued, the whole incident is under investigation by the local school board, the Board of Education, and the police department. This incident took place at **PS93** in the Bronx. Forty-seven years ago another child brought a handgun to **PS93**. I was that child, and there were standard practices in those days too.

In the 30's and the 40's **PS93** was the last building in the Bronx. From there you crossed **Story Avenue**, where as kindergartners and first-graders, we visited the farms. Beyond that there were the swamps of Soundview and the **Bronx River**, where the fishing boats motored on their way to and from the East River. I never found out where they went from there, or what they caught, but you could wave to the people on the boats at the landing a few blocks away at **River Avenue**.

To go to **PS93**, from my house, on **Evergreen Avenue**, you had to cross two major thoroughfares. **Watson Avenue** had no traffic lights, and probably not much traffic either, but there was always a (green Ford) police car patrolling there. One block further was **Eastern Boulevard** which had been rebuilt by the WPA for the World's Fair of 1939. I can't remember if it had been renamed **Bruckner Boulevard** yet, but I had seen President Roosevelt passing there, in an open car waving to the cheering crowd, on his way to open the Fair. There was a traffic light on the corner of **Elder Avenue** and the **Boulevard**, and every kid's ambition was to become a crossing guard (or monitor, as we called them then).

Mr. George Lewis, the principal, was a tall, quiet, and stern man whose cold blue eyes could cool the heat of any wayward urchin. The assistant principal, Miss Powers, whose voice raised in anger, threatened the very foundation of that solid building. To a large extent we were kept in line, lest we be sent to confront that formidable lady. Rarely, were two visits with her required. For a serious offense the harshest punishment was dealt. Your parents would receive a directive to come to school, early in the morning, having to take a half day off from work, for a meeting with Miss Powers. The worst part was that you, the perpetrator, the accused, and soon to be defendant, had to deliver the summons home to your parents. Those meetings were not conversations. Miss Powers did all the talking.

She spelled out the nature of the transgression, the rules of the realm, and dictated the judgement and the punishment.

The year was 1942, the War had just begun, people were distracted from the ordinary work-a-day news releases, and it is unlikely that it was important enough news that a child had brought a gun into **PS93**. My recollection is that it must have been a very serious offense. I had been

DejaVu in the Bronx

Continued from page 20

caught "red-handed," and had to bring home the note. My father took the half-day off and went to face the ominous "Powerhouse." The repercussions of that meeting must have been felt throughout the neighborhood. My report card for that term, which, preserved to this day by my parents, is still warm. Only World War II, could have kept it off the front page of **The Bronx Home News.**

I had a book entitled, "The Macy's Handy Book for Boys," by Jack Becholdt, which was an adventure in astonishing projects. They ran the gamut from building a camping cooksite, with a clay stove and charcoal broil recipes to the construction of a pseudo-television set and theater.

One of the chapters, "Slings, Guns, and Targets," had directions for an elastic target gun. I must have thought, how "swell" it would be to have a gun, just like the boys in the army. I made the gun of pieces of an orange crate, and a rubber band. I painted the handle in red and white stripes, and on the barrel painted blue, I inscribed "Nazi Schmeisser." The ammunition was one-inch linoleum squares, which could be slung-shot a long way. I was proud to have such a formidable weapon. I could emulate our soldiers, and knockdown enemies, real and imagined. What better place could there be to show off such a treasure than the boys' schoolyard of **PS93**.

I hid the piece, under my jacket, I loaded my ammunition, and went off, across **Watson Avenue**, to **Elder Avenue**, across the **Boulevard**, to meet the enemy. In the schoolyard, my fantasy came true. I was the hero and center of attraction. I loaded the gun. An ominous hush descended on the crowd. I took aim at the enemy. The linoleum square shot off the end of the gun, scaled into the air, over the fence, into the enemy's camp; the girls' schoolyard.

The missile struck a little red-headed girl in the middle of her forehead. She shrieked, began to cry, and held her breath until she turned blue and fell down. The teacher on yard duty ran over to her. All the index fingers on the girls' side pointed to the boys' yard. I turned and saw what Moses must have seen as the Red Sea parted. Miss Powers charged through the masses in our yard, demanding to the know the identity of the assassin. Her bellows admonished the crowd that the heinous act was on the level of a Nazi war crime. Not a single finger was pointed at me. The crowd merely backed off, leaving me alone, with the "Lord High Executioner," in the middle of the ring of accusation.

The rest of the story fades into a blur. The *standard practice* was immediately invoked. The note went home, and my father was summoned. The events of that night, the next day, and the following night have been blocked out along with some of my more painful memories of Marine Corps Boot Camp, many years later, during another war.

My punishment was reflected on my report card:

Works and plays well with other	**U** for unsatisfactory
Respects the rights of others	**U** for unsatisfactory
Practices good health habits	**U** for unsatisfactory

My overall conduct grade was not filled in. I can only surmise that D for failing was not low enough. The net effect of the punishment was humiliation, not notoriety. I was held up as a bad and dangerous example.

I never received any more **U**'s in any area of deportment.

My one brush with THE authority was enough. The power and the presence of Miss Powers, had the situation at **PS93** well in hand. Her influence was recognized by the community as the power to be reckoned with. **PS93** was her turf. The police, the Board of Education, and even Mayor LaGuardia, were off limits at **PS93**.

Quixotic illusions were relegated to fantasy games in the empty lots between the tenement buildings. I never again brought a weapon to school. ■

Reminiscing

Golf

Continued from page 5

up to test my mettle. When I was 13 my folks had bought me a half-set of "no-name" clubs that were so poorly made I even lusted over an old, wooden-shafted 5-iron I once had a chance to use. It was when I was in high school that I decided I needed a proper set of clubs.

I decided that MacGregor Tourneys were the clubs for me and did what every young boy would do: I asked my Dad for the money—$164. Did he ever laugh! He proceeded to tell me about his milk route during the Depression, about his tour of duty in the New York City Fire Department, and about his father the painter (as in walls). As he talked I sensed the money for the clubs would not be forthcoming, but I just didn't believe he'd turn me down. He did.

But he also did me the best favor any father ever did for a son. If I wanted those clubs, he told me, I would have to *earn* the money to buy them. I took a job after school delivering leaflets to each and every individual apartment in our housing project, the **Amalgamated**, which had about 14 five- to 12-story buildings. I slipped tens of thousands of sheets of paper under thousands of apartment doors. After about five months, I had my $164.

My Dad was elated when I told him. "When are we going to buy the clubs?" he said.

"What do you mean 'we'?" I replied. On a cold, damp day in March of '62, I took the **Sedgwick Ave** bus to the **D train** and then the **D train** downtown to Chambers Street, where I bought my Tourneys. I came home the same way. The snow had melted so out I went to 16 and swung away. That night I slept with my new clubs. Today, the too-stiff, too-heavy irons are in my garage and the woods, refinished twice, are in my locker at Sunningdale. I expect to have them 'till I die.

Golf almost ended for me in my first year at college. I'd captained the **Bronx Science** team and made the varsity squad at Lehigh University. In May of 1966 we were facing a match at Cornell, a few hundred miles away. I had a final exam the day after, and when I mentioned this to the coach he told me to get my priorities in order. I did. I quit the team then and there and didn't pick up a club seriously until 1986, when my wife and I joined Sunningdale. I still wonder whether I'd have gotten even better, but the time was well spent building a family and a career.

In some ways, not that much has changed since my Bronx childhood. I still live across the street from my favorite golf course, only now the course is Sunningdale. I live opposite its 13th green and every spring I can watch as the snow slowly disappears from it, just as I did so long ago with No. 16 at **Van Cortlandt**. And every evening I can walk outside and feel the cool night air rising from the fairways. Thomas Wolfe said "You can't go home again," but I feel as though that's *exactly* what I've done. It's been a great trip. ∎

Paul Levy is a founding general partner in the New York investment firm of Joseph Littlejohn & Levy and resides opposite Sunningdale Country Club with his wife and two daughters.

> **Today, the too-stiff, too-heavy irons are in my garage and the woods, refinished twice, are in my locker at Sunningdale. I expect to have them 'till I die.**

Woodlawn Express

Continued from page 7

during the day and evening.

But the big fun was at night while my Aunt and Uncle listened to Baby Snooks or Phil Harris and Alice Faye or some other radio show. Judy and I lay in bed giggling, telling jokes, playing geography or actors and actresses. Rose would come in and yell at us and then we'd giggle some more and fall asleep. On **DeKalb Avenue** life was ment to be enjoyed. In this house I knew the meaning of a happy childhood and my cousin was my joy in life and the best friend that I ever had.

One particular visit to this charmed block stands out in my mind. When I reached apartment 5D my cousin was there to greet me. "Hi Ya!', she said.

Judy was doubled jointed, skinny and moved in three different directions at the same time like a rubber band.

Her mother brought a malted milk machine to make her fatter. It didn't work. This was another reason I believe she led a charmed life.

She always had something special to tell me when I arrived. This time she pulled me into her bedroom. "C'mere, wait'll you see this," she whispered, her eyes bulging, her eyebrows raised and her lips pursed together in a tight little "o".

At the age of 14 my cousin made a discovery in her bedroom. If

Continued on page 23

> **On DeKalb Avenue life was meant to be enjoyed. In this house I knew the meaning of a happy childhood and my cousin was my joy in life and the best friend that I ever had.**

Woodlawn Express

Continued from page 22

you stuck your head out of the window looked left and waited long enough, you could see a man in one of the apartments in the next building peeing.

Judy knew his schedule.

Would he appear? I couldn't believe we would see such a thing. But sure enough, as we peered with our two heads turned left, protruding ever so slightly from apartment 5D, the man showed up. We could not see his head. But we saw everything else.

For Judy who had spent her sub teen years pouring through the magazines and postcards thought to be hidden in my Uncle Harry's bottom drawer, the new discovery was only a gradual advance in her knowledge. But I was horrified.

Judy's friends Joyce and Susan would be joining us for an afternoon of mah jongg. We would take out my Aunt's beautiful hand painted ivory tiles from their blue velvet case and sat like middle aged women at the card table, matching tiles and dipping our hands into candy bowls to snare candy kisses and M&Ms.

Joyce and Susan were big girls, my age, but more developed. They wore dungarees that looked just right around their developing hips and thighs. They wore saddle shoes. Joyce and Susan were peppy and fun.

But I wasn't. My life over in the eastern part of the Bronx was more lonely. My father had left my mother and I never saw him. I stayed home from school alot. I just wasn't able to laugh as much as my cousin and her friends.

Judy took her friends Joyce and Susan into her bedroom to display her latest discovery, the peeing man. I sat down on the sofa to read an Archie comic and about Veronica, the beautiful brunette with the bangs everyone was jealous of. My cousin would tell me that day I wasn't much fun anymore. The **Woodlawn Express** was leaving me behind. ■

Turning Back the Clock

By Carol D. Pellach (nee Gitterman)

I delve into my memory, hoping I can find,
The symbols of my childhood, deep inside my mind.
I see a street all tree-lined and a place called Echo Park,
An El train where it's fun to ride and walk home after dark.

On Sunday Dad comes up the stairs with fragrant fresh-baked rye,
There's onion rolls and charlotte russe and
eggs for Mom to fry.
The "Herald Tribune's 'neath his arm with sections piled galore,
Now we've got the Comics page, so who could ask for more?

We had no phone 'til I was six and then we had just one,
Back then, Ma Bell owned telephones and each one weighed a ton.
The day a man came to our house and brought a telephone,
Around our number were the words, "wait for the dial tone."

Our first T.V. was a console with doors,
a 19 inch black & white set,
I was in the Second Grade- How lucky can you get!
Some programs that we watched back then were fifteen minutes
long, Like soap operas or shows in which somebody sang a song.
At 5:30 p.m., each day, we wouldn't miss "Howdy Doody,"
And then, at six, we'd sit and watch our friend, "Rootie Kazootie."

Records only had one speed- 'to big, they spun real fast,
The lyrics all were pure and clean, in songs, back in the past.

When you needed cereal, vegetables, fruit and more,
They didn't have a supermarket- just a grocery store.
The grocer was just like a friend- he knew us all by name,
He'd bring the food up to our house
when very bad weather came.
Then there was a fruit wagon, just around 2 o' clock,
We knew it by its horse's hooves,
when they clomped down the block.

And when the heavy rains came down and your umbrella broke,
The street umbrella man fixed it up- now, fixing it's a joke.

In summertime I heard a voice say, "I cash, I cash clothes,"

Winter sounds were banging pipes, when angry tenants froze.

Now when I look back upon those Bronx days of my past,

I wish I *could* turn back the clock
and make those good times last.

Missing Persons

MP1318 I would be interested to hear from anyone! So many places starting on **Jennings St, Intervale Ave, Charlotte St, Wilkens Ave., 174 St.**, etc. Curious about my brother Jack's friends. I'm in Cherry Hill, NJ (609) 424-4375. Mary (Levy) Glatt.

MP1319 Evelyn Grubman. Please write to Hinde (Harriet) Schutzman Friedman of Codor's Shul #45. Already in contact with May & Annette. Trying to reach Beaty. Let's have the reunion that we were planning so many years ago. Hinde Friedman 6818 Chippewa Dr. Balt. MD 21209-1435.

MP1320 Fond memories of Izzy's Candy Store on **Nelson Ave.** at **169th St. Highbridge** '50-'56. **Walton** '55. Anna's "King of Siam" and Sally's "Busy Bee". Were you there? Many thanks to whomever for introduction to "Back In THE BRONX." Pat Cosby 5271 Pro's Dr. West Chester, OH 45069.

MP1321 Hi- It's Porky NKA Liz Garibaldi. Please call daytime: (212) 593-9454.

MP1322 Officers of the Senior Class, **Evander** '56. Where are you? We found Linda Smalline but where are: Ron Previ, Pres., Brenda Vogel, Secretary, Jan List, Treasurer, Dina Shapiro, Historian. We're planning a 40th Reunion and want to locate you. Contact: Vinnie Bucci, Woodlawn, P.O. Box 53, Bronx, NY 10470.

MP1323 Dorothy Clacer Wildhagen-**Roosevelt** '59: Read my poems "The Eighth of July: Poetry by Dorcas" The Christopher Publishing House, Hanover MA 02339. FAX: (617) 826-5556.

MP1324 Would like to locate Lowell Sherman of **Knox Pl. Mosholu Pkwy**, Bronx 1930-1950+. It has been 50 years. Arnold Weber, 5 Chestnut Lane, Woodbury, NY 11797 (516)921-6199.

MP1325 Cheryl Stallon and Gail Randell, both live in South Florida. We are looking for anyone from **J.H.S. 80** '62-'65 and **Evander** '65 - '68. Please call Cheryl at (954) 349-8670.

MP1326 Dianne Kopperman Podell (**P.S. 64, Wade, Taft** '48). Wondering about Alice Cocheres, Selena Teller, (Diane Podell, 12 Cumberland St., Jericho NY 11753.

MP1327 Bonnie Bienthen, Bernice Aks now. **Roosevelt**, Jan '45. Nostalgic for sexy/exciting days of the past. Would so enjoy hearing from anyone & everyone with whom I have lost contact with. Bernice Aks, 10 Crest Rd., E. Brunswick, NJ 08816. (908) 238-0203.

MP1328 Frank Regensburg looking for "Assorted Nuts," **Concourse & 198th St.**-Geo & Sara Altman's Candy Store—Poe Park dancing crowd? Also would like to hear from **Fordham & Davidson** Crowd. Marders Candy Store. Write: 2639 Sunset Lane, Finksburg, MD 21048 or call (410) 833-0357.

MP1329 **Clason Pointers.** There must be some of us out there. Still alive and not in Prison! Remember the Beach Theatre? Larry's?, Dirty Ruby's? **Holy Cross School? Academy Gardens**? 1950'S -1960'S. Write P. Oragoo, 2100 Miramonte St., #15, San Leandro, CA 94578.

MP1330 Marcel "Mickey" Singleton would like to hear from friends and former classmates from **P.S. 53** in '64 or '65 and **J.H.S. 22** '66 or '67. The Value Engineering Alliance, 478 Putnam Ave., Cambridge, MA 02139. (617)492-1252. E-MAIL: marcelvea@aol.com

MP1331 Looking for friends of Sylvia (Dorin) **Roosevelt** '57 and Arnold (Sheikowitz) Sherman, **Wade** '46, **Clinton** '48, CCNY '52. Write 155 Wailea Ike Pl. #10, Maui, HI 96753. (808)874-8742.

MP1332 Jerry Tennenbaum would like to hear from Margaret Zaroff of **Olinville Ave** who met him at Camp Kinderland. Write: 85 Lutz Dr., Valley Stream, NY 11580.

MP1333 Looking for the class of June **Evander** '52. Especially Thelma (who went to Cornell and never wrote), Rhoda B. Harvey, Judy, Phil, Zelda, Fran, Irene D., Claudia, Penelope Drinkwater, Rozie Lee, Marcia, Rosevita, Joyce, et. al. Contact: Dolores (The Human Noise Maker) Rivellino, 20532 Pacific Coast Hwy., Malib, CA (310) 456-5376.

MP1334 Where are my old pals from **P.S. 11** last graduating class of 8th grade '56, then **Taft**? Belonged to a club called "Spirals". My name: Steve Seider I lived at **1275 Nelson Ave**. Please call: (602) 661-1694, Scottsdale, AZ

MP1335 Looking for Mary Ann Crawford, **Science** '61. Please call Ellen Tafel Scheinbach at: (718) 796-6898.

MP1336 Would enjoy hearing from **Taft** '53 classmates. David Kassoy 2832 Angelo Dr., Los Angeles, CA 90077 (310) 276-7362.

MP1337 Lou Blasquez from 164th St and Anderson Ave., **Sacred Heart** '64, **Cardinal Spellman** '68. Passed his 3rd Degree Black Belt Test: P.O. Box 18637, Munds Park, AZ 86017. 72520.1617@compuserve.com

MP1338 Seeking whereabouts of Barbara Rosenbluth Mark. father-Joe, mother-Selma, brother-Gilbert. Lost contact with her after a visit to E. Orange, NJ in 1960(?) and she moved to Queens: Contact Eileen Lazarus: (803) 705-5097.

MP1339 **Oval Boys**-Ducky Boys. Those times together are eternal. Where are you now? Remember me? Bob Wiemers! 3241 Perry Ave at corner of 207 St. Let's Chit chat! Bob Wiemers. 98 Wallace Ave., Buffalo, NY 14214.

MP1340 Marie Tancredi Russo, 224th St. looking for Marie Grieco, Geraldine Carroll (St. Francis), Bonita Militello, **Evander**. Husband Carmine (Charlie) Russo, **Rosewood St., White Plains Rd.** Looking for Ralph Palces. (540) 678-8802. P.O. Box 3192, Winchester, VA 22604-2392.

MP1341 Looking for twins Betty & Minna Hocky/ Graduated **Walton** and Brooklyn College together. Twins Greta & Hedy Strauss of **Riverdale** and **Walton** H.S. Ruth Gotfried, 6269 Pointe Regal Circle, Delray Beach, FL 33484 (561) 637-3245.

MP1342 Burt Halpern, **Clinton** '46, **Kingsbridge**. Past 30 years in Israel. Operating P.R. Office in Tel Aviv, FAX: 972.3.5225126. TEL: 5241532/6042677. Diane Prussak (nee), **Walton** '48.

MP1343 Hello, Judy Dardick (maiden name) are you out there? Friends are looking for you. Call: Celia Schuchtman (Brown) (301) 299-4597.

MP1344 I grew up in the Bronx right outside of **Parkchester. Monroe** '60. Would love to hear from anyone near Pt. St. Lucie, FL. Write: Ginny and maybe we can do lunch. Virginia Levy, 32 Lake Vista Trail, Unit 207, Pt. St. Lucie, FL 34952

MP1345 Looking for those who were 10, 11, 12 on 12/7/41 who played stickball, softball, football 2-hand touch and tackling. All done at **P.S. 45, 85, French Charlies Trojon Field, Van Cortlandt Pk.** Our group mostly went in services in late 1946 for original G.I benefits. R. Friscia, One Bloomindale #618, Bloomindale, IL 60108.

MP1346 I was known as Johnny De Gag; name is Johnny DeGablin. I am looking for the friends I hung out with on **214th St.** in Bronx. Want to contact a person who was my best friend, Joe (Black) Spordone. Anyone who remembers me, who hung out with me, from any of the neighborhoods, call me at (415)359-0214.

MP1347 Florence Ramm Lagergren, P.S. 68- knew Tony (MP 967) Mattera- were in same class. Where is Bunny Reichert, Jean DeVito, Josephine O'Brien, Ruth Horowitz, Nancy Hannon? Graduated in '50. Florence Lagergren, 4715 Upland Dr. Alexandria, VA 22310-1344.

Classifieds

MP1348 Looking for old classmates from **Walton** '53 - Mr. Roth's mike squad- Any reunions in Boston area? I'm Bea Montes, now Bea De Muinck Keizer. Beatrice De Muinck Keizer, 9 Marlboro St., Belmont, CA 02178.

MP1349 Anyone from **Highbridge? Woodycrest Ave.**?, especially Vinnie Vignali, Joanie O'Connell. Remember 1155, Sam & Lou's, Schwabe's, Dave's, **Yankee Stadium**. So many wonderful memories. Would love to hear from any of you. —Sarah Hickey Carroll, 3006 La Salle Ave., Bronx, NY 10461

MP1350 Roberta (Votava) Verhoye, **St. Helena's** '61. We're having our 35th anniversary Class Reunion October 5th, 1996. Where are you Nancy Baldi, Lorraine Flair, Carol Kavanagh and Margaret Zamot? Would like to hear from you. Please call (201) 868-6885.

MP1351 1945 to 1965 were the Judaean years for me—travelling daily visiting Y.J. clubs. I am Sy Alper, the leader who recruited the members. Those days may be gone, but memories, etc. last..and lots more! Sy Alper, c/o Palmach, Box 529, Yonkers, NY 10702

MP1352 Alan Zimmerman, **Morris** '53, desperately seeking my old flame, Harriet Klapper, **Morris** '52 or '53, who lived on Barretto St., and other **Morris** graduates of that era. After 40 years in the news business, retired to Guilford, CT. Call (203) 453-3533 or E-Mail 102431.3312@ Compuserve.com

MP1353 Help! I've been isolated in Texas for too long! I need to hear from some old friends. Y'all write: Ginger Dorlini Foster, 3620 Harwood Ct., Bedford, TX 76021-2309.

MP1354 Isaac from Brooklyn looking for Hilda Graber, childhood friend. Would be great to hear from you. Call (516) 626-1647

MP1355 Barry Jacobs is looking to locate George Popp and Eddie Beane. We lived on **Kingsbridge Terrace**. (619) 673-1144.

MP1356 Stanley Kramer would love to hear from any old friends, **P.S. 64, Creston J.H., Evander** & CCNY '45. Currently living in Huntington, on Long Island. I am in the phone book. Stanley Kramer, 30 Renwick Ave., Hunt. Sta., NY 11743

MP1357 Harron Kelner, **Roosevelt** '46. First name was different. If you recognize the last, you'll know who I am! Lived on **Walton** Ave. Alexander "Allie" Roth, are you there? Saul Marlieb? If you knew me please call in California (818)882-6948 or Fax (818)709-0948.

MP1358 Judy (Bjoze) Nabavian would like to hear from **Taft** '58 friends, especially those in Dramatic English & The Traveling Players. Also anyone who remembers me from CCNY & **Undercliff Ave.** 1940-'62. (914) 268-7454.

MP1359 Alan H. Kimbarow, **Sedgwick Houses/Co-Op City, Truman** '78 graduate. If you know my parents, Hoody & Sam, your children may know me! Hope to hear from anyone who knew me. (516)433-5861.

MP1360 Girls of **Eagle Ave.**: Mary Whalen, Jeannie Trickler, Stella Donahue, Gloria LaRoche, Carol Whitholm.—Richie Moss would love to hear from you. (954)771-8933, or write 4687 N.E. 18th Ave., Ft. Lauderdale, FL 33334.

MP1361 Phil Sacks, lived **Honeywell Ave., P.S. 67, P.S. 6**, Killers Candy Store- last Yonkers—where are you? Contact Richie Levchuck. 4 Chassyl Rd., Commack, NY 11725-4804

MP1362 Catherine Johnson from **Sacred Heart** moved to Kalamazoo, Michigan in1940. Would love to hear from Pat Lombard, Betty Hawe, Joan Reilly, Loretta Fritch, Rita McHugh, Ed Curzon, Behrens Twins, and John Counihan. Now living in Brooklyn. (718)854-6348. Call me!

MP1363 Looking for my past: Vicki Frank from **Mosholu Pkwy.**, Rita Rosenzweig, Miriam Rodriguez, Marty Seiden, Marv Kidder— Ken Schaeffer would enjoy hearing from or about you. Please write P.O. Box 491401, Ft. Lauderdale, FL 33349.

MP1364 Old friends from **135th St.**, between **Brook & St. Ann's Ave**. Do these names sound familiar? Gattuso, Logan, Gavigan, Reynolds, Sansalone, Zubicky, Gordon. Contact me, Bunny Havel (nee) Cunningham, 5900 21 St. N., St. Petersburg, FL 33714. (813) 525-8988.

MP1365 Arthur Cohen, **Intervale Ave,** Textile '52, Best Man at our wedding, Oct. 23, 1955. Irving Borensweig, **Simpson St., P.S. 20**, Double Bar Mitzvah, May 1947. Would love to hear from you. Neil & Sylvia Bechinsky (360)671-3236, Bellingham, WA.

MP1366 Mitzi (Feldstein) Smith would like to hear from friends from **Marcy Place, P.S. 64, JHS 22** and **Taft**. Still see five Darlenes. Where are the rest of you? Mitzi Smith, 22 Joseph Lane, Bardinia, NY 10954.

MP1367 (MP) Try to find—Gil Goldstein, John Tomaino, Irv Figenbaum. Best friends in the 50's. Contact Jerry Halpern (505)293-8740 or write 7601 Palo Duro N.E., Albuquerque, NM 87110

MP1368 Looking to hear from anyone on **Andrews Ave. & 176th St.**, especially Irv Cordova & Harriet Satler; or anyone else remembering Charley Ludwin, **Taft** '59, **JHS '82**, '56. Write: 9 Acorn Circle, #201 Balitmore, MD 21286 Call: (410)821-9006

MP1369 For all the guys who played stickball in **P.S. 78** school yard...shoot pool at Charle **Shultz** on **Boston Rd.**, hung out on **214th St.**...Love to hear from you. Andy Loiacono (954) 966-0787 (Ft. Lauderdale, FL)

MP1370 Tom McEntee looking for Richie Schwarz, who moved from **Quimby** and **Castle Hill** to Queens in '55. Father- Arthur; Mother-Eleanor; Sister-Carol. Any leads (since '56)? Please write: 2020 Beech Ave. #A-15, Nashville, TN 37204, or call collect (615) 292-2512.

MP1371 The girls from **200th St. & Decatur Ave.** Circa 1957 Gerry, Eileen, Barbara, Mary, Judy, Witty...Artie would like hearing from you and hopes you are all well. Have not become a dirty old man. Arthur W. Prior, 1088 Ott Lane, N. Merrick, NY 11566. Call: (516)485-1891

MP1372 **Boynton Ave., Watson Ave.**, Rich's Deli, Schaefer's Pool Room, **Bronx River Ave.**, Mr. D's Candy Store. **Monroe** '57 Would like to hear from old friends. Edward (Eddie) Kanterman (910) 852-2396.

MP1373 Norma Cohen looking for anyone from **Manida St., Hunt's Point Ave., JHS 60, Morris** '53. Anyone living in California? I've been a Santa Barbaran for 40 years. Miss old Bronx friends. Phone (805) 967-4996 or Fax (805)683-3654.

MP1374 Hope to find any, or all of (from **PS 121**): Gerry Gayer, Barbara Schlossman, Janet Gaio, Kenny Anderson, Gregory Cole, Barbara Schwartz, Henry Weiss, Allan Feinstein. Write Norman Abramowitz at 849 W. Mulberrt St., Louisville, KY 80027. Or call: (303)666-9395.

MP1375 Sylvia Finkelman Jacobs: Would like to contact some of my childhood friends: Ethel Heitzner Cinnamon and Evelyn Reiter Guttenplan. The Bronx was the best place to grow up. So many places to go and things to see. Never tired of Zoo or Yankee Stadium! Write: 7 Plymouth-A, West palm Beach, FL 33417-1642

MP1376 Anyone remembering Barbara Dlck **(PS 104)** from 1465 Wilson Ave, I'd like to hear from you. My mother died in 1958 and my memories are fuzzy. Please call (718) 476-7600.

MP1377 Where are Marcia Rhea Posner, Barbara Sklar and Leona Katz? Francine Buchman and Marjorie Schloss are looking for you for a reunion, along with Sandra Herskowitz. Write Marjorie Schloss Stern, 11 Westminster Dr., Pearl River, NY 10965-2841 or call: (914) 735-9057.

MP1378 Phyllis Weinstein, Rita Gorsky, Judy Cohen, Janice Levinson are looking for lost **Waltonites** from 1953. Please contact Janice at 800-233-2526. Also looking for **Morris Ave.** girls around **Burnside Ave.** Does anyone know whereabouts of Ann Sternberg who moved to NJ?

MP1379 Lived at **55 East 190th St.** Looking for any girls from the Tri-Dels from **Schiff Center** on **Valentine Ave.** or any of the Clubs we hung at with. Call Sandy Lippman (516)889-3032 Eves. Let's talk!

MP1380 Shikokoans- It's our 50th Anniversary, I think! Best wishes. Raymond McCann, 883 Amaryllis Ave., Oradell, NJ 07649.

MP1381 Paula Mandel and Yonis Family lived **183rd St.** and **Morris Ave.** Paula's birthday 12/31. **PS 79, JHS 115, Walton,** Clinton, Hunter grads. Joan Fundiller (Gould) looking for you all. Please call (516) 295-0928 or Florida #: (561)966-0170.

MP1382 Clason- Pointers-Holy Cross-1940. Who remembers Fuelner's Farm Mobile-Library-Truck-Any Spagnuolos-Graff -Montalto's-Patty McPherson ? Patricia Manz - Lived Conn. 25 years - now in Ventura County, Calif. 278 Henry Dr., Newbury Park, CA 91320.

MP1383 Did you know Dr. Abraham Bellwin, General Practitioner, in the Bronx who died in 1954? I'm especially interested in finding a photo of him. Write: Dr. Marian Kaplan Shapiro, 17 Lantern Lane, Lexington MA 02173 or call: (617) 862-3728

MP1384 Looking for old friends from **Creston Ave.; PS 79; EBB & Roosevelt.** I graduated High School in 1962. Lived on **Creston Ave.** 7/44 to 8/65 (182nd). Would love to talk. Call me (516) 499-6310-Arleen Chester Wartley.

MP1385 Larry Klein, **Monroe** '59- Father owned **Comet Cleaners** on **Tremont Ave.** Would like to hear from old friends. I live in Florida. (561) 496-2311.

MP1386 I really would like to hear from my friends from **College, Morris Ave., Findlay Ave. 167th St.** : Jackie Michaels, Francine Heckler, Phyllis Romanoff, Sandra Itkin, Selma Boritzer & Sheila Cohen. We all went to **PS 53** and then onto **Taft.** All 1952 graduates. "The Best Years of Our Lives." Thank you. Sheila Schneider (Shelly Segelman) (201) 843-7181.

MP138 Marshall Blaufarb, **Morris** '55 is alive and kicking out here in California. His wife, Ellen Schalkinger Blaufarb, **Monroe** '57, still resides with him. Judy & Irv Larry & Ellie Meshibosh await your call at (707) 746-5048.

MP1388 Abrams, Gloria (married name "Troy") graduated **JHS 98** '50, **Walton** '53- Anyone knowing whereabouts please call Sarah Bricker Schriebman at (813) 937-6669. Gloria, where are you?

MP1389 Looking for anyone who hung out at the University Ave. Projects 1965-69. Also anyone who knew the Schwartz's on **Jesup Ave.** (Janet, Robin, Barbara, Stewart). Barbara Schwartz Robbins, 4523 N.W. 26th Place, Boca Raton, FL 33434

MP1390 Karen Greenberg (presently Karen Numme), **PS 26, JHS 82, Taft 50 W.Tremont.** Looking for anyone that remembers me. Contact: K. Numme, P.O. Box 29314, Los Angeles, CA 90029.

MP1391 Does anyone remember **Clason Point, Soundview Ave., O'Brien Ave.,** Beach Theater, Higg's Boatyard, etc.? Margaret Hayes Sudol. Box 202, North Salem, NY 10560

MP1392 Diana (Rappaport) Markowitz, Helen (Jacobs) Fishman, Sylvia (Tanenbaum) Penmore, **Evander** '49/'50, would like to hear from our old friends from the **Barnes Ave./Wallace Ave.**, **Mayfair/Mayflower** crowd. Call Sylvia (718) 261-4061 or Fax: (718)261-4062.

MP1393 Looking for men and women who lived near **Brook Ave.** and **St. Paul's Place-**Finks Candy Store- Kaplan's Grocery and Pool Room just South of St. Paul's Pl. and **Brook Ave.** during years 1938-42. Write Jack Climan 9521 Sunrise Lakes Blvd.,Sunrise, FL 33322 or call: (954)748-1621

MP1394 Rita Stein, sister of Maxie, Apt. 4C at **2018 Belmont Ave.**, contact Fred Baruchin (Apt. 3C) at (516) 932-9512. Our family would live to hear from you.

MP1395 Rosemary Laverty lived on Cedar Ave. near **Fordham Road** in the 1940's with her sisters. This was in the **St. Nicholas of Tolentine** Parish. Where is she? Call Bob Hennessy at (212) 628-9151.

MP1396 Looking for Selma & Harold Stein. We went to **Bronx House** at the same time. S. Kinzer, 328 Mockingbird Dr., Cranbury, NJ 08512.

MP1397 Looking for Arlene Goldstein & Gail Zimmer 1956 graduates of **Evander** H.S. & **PS 46.** Thea (Schwamenau) Sittenfeld. Write: Thea Schwamenau Sittenfeld, P.O., Box 1066, Naples, FL 34102 or call (941) 434-0035.

MP1398 Milton & Phyllis (Bley) Chernack would love to hear from all old friends. (212) 245-4169.

MP1399 William Hirsch, Howard Fruckman, Arthur Rose, neighbors Hillside Homes, **PS 78, Evander Childs,** surrounding area, REUNION, Feb. 23, 1996. My name, Carol Friedman-Lefkowitz. Anxious to hear from you (305) 932-3498; (561) 637-7359 We have 100's of people coming. Please call even if you just think you know us.

MP1400 Florence Falkenberg, now Tannenbaum, would like to hear from Freddie Sidransky who attended **Taft** in the mid 40's. 85 Lutz Dr., Valley Stream, NY 11580.

MP1401 Elaine Goldstein wants to know where are you now- Alfred Gerbs, Bobby Sass, Elaine Haber **(Vyse Ave)**, Sheila Beagle, Larry Goldberg & Lorraine Bernstein? From **174th St.:** Sammy Levine -Prince & Pauper-Bobby Strome.

MP1402 Brenda Bachman Wangel looking for old friends from East & West Bx. **Monroe** '58. Pat Hedges, Andrea Carco, Vivian Harrison, Stan Kotler, Jeff Hirshhorn, Barbara & Rochelle Frost. Call me (718) 738-4448.

MP1403 Harriet Hammer Hecht Minde, **PS 94, JHS 80, Evander** '54, NYU '58, Rutgers '84, residing in Manalapan, NJ for 30 years, would love to hear from childhood friends who grew up on **212th St., Bainbridge** and **Rochambeau** Aves Call (908) 446-7126.

MP1404 Looking for Carol & Susan Goldberg. They were my neighbors at **132 W. 169th St., Highbridge** - Apt. 3A and I lived in Apt. 1-D, then 3C. If anyone out there knows their whereabouts, please contact- Spencer Field, (908) 889-8733.

MP1405 Roseann (Albrino) Reichenbach - **St. Helena's Business HS** '65. Looking for all former classmates esp. Beverly Smith, Sheila Collins, Adele Fiorillo, Fran Gaetano, Marty Ryan, Ann Golia, Jerry Kroner, Lorraine LaBianca, & Bob Marion. Write 11 Spurwoods Lane, Farmindale, NY 11738. (516) 654-0486.

MP1406 Bob Balma, **Clinton** '61, would like to hear from teammates of the middle 1950's "Comets", baseball team, **Wilder Ave.**, Bronx. My wife of 30 years and I live on Long Island, NY. We have two daughters and one grandson. Robert Balma, 760 Nicolls Rd., Deer Park, NY 11729 Call (516)667-4452.

MP1407 Looking for Naomi (Normi) Rosenthal. Lived at 219 E. 196th St. Married "Jack". Call Paulette Stern (nee Littman), (201) 263-0150 or Fax: (201)263-4005.

MP1408 Tommy Cronin, 621 **Manida St., Hunts Point, St. Althaniasus, Fox St.**, son of Tim (TWU) Loretta (Meegan) **4228 Hill Ave., Mt. St. Michael, Evander** '65, MABSTOA '65 - '92. Living on Cape Cod. Please call: (508) 945-9352.

MP1409 If you have any recollections or memorabilia of the New York, Westchester & Boston Railway, which ran through the Bronx until 1937, or were or knew an employee, please call Michael R. Weinman at (610) 525-9950, or write c/o PTSI Transportation, 1062 Lancaster Ave., Bryn Mawr, PA 19010-1570.

MP1410 Anyone living around **Prospect Ave. & 176th St.** or **Fairmont Place**, I'd love to hear from you to share memories. I moved away in 1955. aka Jerry Mandel. Write 8744 Double Eagle Dr., L.V.,NV 89117

MP1411 Are there any former piano students of my Dad, Dr. Aloys Kremer, who lived at **St. James Park** in the 30's and 40's. Write to Jacqueline Kremer at 400 East 20th St., New York, NY 10009. My father was a well-known teacher.

MP1412 Honey Rand (nee Helen Kleir) **Monroe** '51. Looking for anyone who remembers me and my sister, Pepi, widow of Al Rand, also of **Manor Ave.** Living in Delray Beach 8 yrs. (561) 495-2692.

MP1413 Marty Blumenthal, **Roosevelt** '45, and Rosalie Feinberg, **Evander** '46 would like to hear from anyone who remembers us. **PS 44**, Gerald Hurwitz, Doris Band, Hazel Fox, Jerry Schusser, Dave Singer, Irving Beller. P.O. Box 278, Dumont, NJ 07628.

MP1414 Looking for Danny & Harry Klein twins; also Marty K. from Pop's poolroom on **Boston Rd.** & grad. class 1948 Central Commercial. Would love to hear from anyone who remembers Rozy Cohen, **1500 Boston Rd**. Now living in Florida. (941) 945-4140.

MP1415 Anyone see Vinny Rizzo from **Garden St.** & **182nd**.; Anthony Rapini, Anthony Ritucci, Ralph Basil, all from **Fordham Section** of the Bx. Joan Picca from **Throgs Neck**, class of '49 **PS 45 JHS.** Dom Panepinto, Mario Giampaulo, Ralph Volpe (Willie Mays). Anyone know or see Margie Mazza Caminati, Josephine Franz Petracola, Lefty Moes Candy Store P.S.32 crowd of '47, '48, '49. Hopp, Morgase, John Rippolo, Joe Petrolla, Phil the Greek Provotaris, Rusty from **Cambreleng Ave. & 187 St.** Skinhead Cheech Naccarello, Tony Cavigliano, Vinny Rex, Tom Toal. Contact: Russell (Rusty) Marrapodi, 658 N. Hayden Dr., Tuscan, AZ 85710.

MP1416 **Shorehaven** lovers, come reminisce about the pool, the dancing, the sports, and meet some old friends as Gayl Teller reads from her book, "SHOREHAVEN." Sunday, Jan. 5th, 7pm, Mid-Island Y, 45 Manetto Hill Rd., Plainview (516)822-3535, Ext. 346, L.I.E Exit 45, left, 5 lights.

MP1417 Here are names from long ago past...If still alive, please contact Murray C. Schneider, 688 Dickens Ave., Franklin Sq., NY 11010. (516) 481-7547: Ella Austreich, Evander '35, "The Varsity Drag!.. From Delta Sigma Tau.. Leo Hornigstein, Dave Krenz, Bruce Dardick, and from Camp Ranachqua 1930's...Aaron Schwartz.

MP1418 Bert (Buddy) Sugarman and former Ruth Malinick looking for friends from **Mosholu Pkwy.** and **Walton 181st** areas. If you remember us, call (415) 586-5591. Bert, **Clinton** '38, Ruth **Roosevelt** '40.

MP1419 Ethel King, **PS 6**, 1940, **Monroe** 1944, **178th St., Bryant Ave.174th St.**, looking for friends and schoolmates. Anyone who remembers Manny's Candy Store, Frank's Barbershop, playing jacks on the stoop steps. Contact:Ethel Weissman (King),1348 Stanley Lane, Schenect ,NY 12309

MP1420 Looking for Laurie Horvath, friends of Mike & Edie Nelson, Sid & Iris Cohen. Remember me from Camp Hosiery. Living now in New City, NY. Would love to hear from you. Stephen Bass,10 Scenic Vista Dr, New City, NY 10956-1332

MP1421 Brought up on Ward Ave. 1937-52, **PS 77** & **Monroe.** Would like to hear from Ron Kurtz, Norman Gandelman, Ted Putterman, Mickey Polite, Demas Bros., Brooks Bros., Gerald Kalb, Saundra Segan, Phyllis Kramer, Temple Emanuel Crowd. Contact Arnold Forman, 4972 Poseidon Way, Oceanside, CA 92056-7416.

MP1422 Chris Bohlmann, **Taft** '60, currently living in Houston area, would like to hear from some of the other 2,000 graduates of the class of 1960. Anyone aware of a class reunion coming? Can be contacted at CRBohlmann@aol.com.

MP1423 Stan Grayson who grew up at **1731 Harrison Ave.** (near **P.S. 82/Park Plaza Theater**) from 1944-54 and graduated from Music & Art, **PS 82/PS 26** is looking for old friends and classmates to reminisce. Write Stanley at: 24 Harding Pkwy., Mt. Vernon, NY 10552-1914

MP1424 1950's-Steve M (**Daly Ave.**) still dreams about Marie G. (**Hoe Ave.**) Please write: 15 Franklin Rd., Scarsdale, NY 10583-7509.

MP1425 Where is the gang from **Longfellow** between **172nd & Jennings** 1953-61? Graduated **Ridder** 1960. Also from **Wallace Ave.** between **Lydig & Brad**, graduated **Columbus** '63. My name was Estelle Wiener. Sisters Marcia & Elsa. Estelle Celoski, 11 Donovan Ave., Carteret, NJ 07008

MP1426 I am looking for Grace Smith, or any graduate of PS 78, Bx '48, '49, **Hillside Homes** friends. Live in Florida. Reunion Feb. 23, 1997. **Evander** '52-53. Call Carol Friedman Lefkowitz (407) 637-7359) or write132 Waterford F, Delray, FL 33446.

MP1427 Roberta Davidoff, **Monroe** '53, married to Sergei Kanevsky, **Taft** '50, for 39 years. We have lived in Jackson Hts., Puerto Rico and for the past 29 years, in Manalapan, NJ. Three children and three grandchildren. Looking for fellow graduates and guys from the "Kingsmen." Roberta Davidoff Kanevsky, 7 Clinton Dr., Manalapan, NJ 07726. Call (908)431-0723.

MP1428 Jerry Schwartz **PS 94, Clinton** '46, **Tryon Ave.** looking for Jerry Silver, Arnie Sternberg, Gloria Seckler, Ann Goldman, Sondra Zimmerman,all from around **Reservoir Oval** or anybody who remembers me. 3560 S.W.Sunset Trace Circle, Palm City, FL 34990 (561) 781-2172.

MP1429 If at first I didn't succeed....Trying again to find people who knew me from the Amalgamated 1954 **PS 95** grad & **Clinton** '58 grad. Richard Hantman, (201) 334-9167, Fax #(201)335-9113.

MP1430 Hey Guys..still looking for you! **196th St. Jerome Ave.** '43-'62. Also **St. James Park, Jerome Ave.** Dan McCarthy, Bob (Swede) Nillson. Chickie Martin, Mike Driscoll, Al D Orio, Jim Moccio. Call (914)362-8142.

MP1431 Seeking my best friend, Eve Ingenito, from **PS 68** (1966-70) Please call Laura Carbonaro Warner at (718) 324-8821.

MP1432 Would love to hear from SIOGAS (Success Is Our Greatest Aim), Mimi, Naomi, Renee, Vivian, Sandy & Elaine, & Mohawks (Vyse Ave.) & Ticonderogas. Let's get together and party-Class of '51, **Monroe.** Phone Evelyn (516) 261-5382.

MP1433 Seeking **Dodge** '57 grad friends. Where are you? Frenchie, Shirley, Rose G., Marcia N. Winnie, Tina C., Carol P. Eileen, Barbara G.? Would love to hear from you. Maryann (Gill) Salvaggio, 20 Highview Dr., Salisbury Mills, NY 12577 Call (914) 496-9692.

MP1434 Harvey (Lucky) Baidowsky, **Roosevelt** '57 and Barbara Ann Sklar **Roosevelt** '58 - married (gasp..) 34 years- searching for old friends who used to hang around **179th St.** and **Southern Blvd;** and for Mrs. Mildred Fox, math teacher. Please call (201) 943-1890.

MP1435 Delfin (Bobby) Alvarez would like to hear from any of the old gang who lived in **859, 863 Southern Blvd.** Please write: 231 N.W. 52nd Ct., Ft. Lauderdale, FL 33309-3234.

MP1436 Looking for people who knew Jeff Fields who lived on **Bronx Park South** and **Daly Ave.** in the 50's. He went to **PS 67**, JHS 118, **Roosevelt** '59. Contact Joel (407) 364-9563. Write to: 9810-5 Pineapple Tree Dr., Boynton Beach, FL 33436.

MP1437 Rosalyn Resnick: Family name is Goldin. I am presently single. I am self-employed with my own business. Looking for anyone who remembers me from the Bronx. Write: 3840 Greystone Ave., Bronx, NY 10463.

MP1438 Eileen Lazarus Brenner looking for an old friend, Barbara Rosenbluth of **West 170th St.** & **University Ave.** Married Herbert Marks in the 50's. Contact me at: 103 Vincent St., Bluffton, SC 29910.

MP1439 Looking for Claire Davis Wyman- lived **Pelham Pkwy.** Ida Levy-Children Morty & Florence; lived near **Vyse Ave.** late 30's early 40's. Hilda Wolin-husband Jack, sons Alan & Barry, & sister-in-law Yetta Seltzer. Please call Ida Werbowsky (908) 363-7012 or Irwin Werbowsky (516)266-2771.

MP1440 Mark J. Adler, formerly of Pgh., PA, has just moved to Jacksonville, FL. Any Bronxites living in JAX area please call to reminisce. (904)564-2491

MP1441 Anybody remember Donny Gaon, Jack Matalon, Matty Orlando, Fred Cohen, **Jordan L. Mott** 1950/51/52. We are still all good friends living in NYC. Would like to hear from anybody that went to school with us. Call Don or Jack at (212) 564-3838.

MP1442 Remember me? Maxine Pomerance (now Falk). Would love to hear from you, **Monroe** Jan 1944. **Faile St., Aldus St., Grand Ave., Hull Ave.,** Mt. Vernon Coop, Paramus, now Rockland County (914)356-4783

MP1443 Where are you Ellen Feldschneider, Michelle Green, Alicia Shatsky, Sheila Baskin, Janet Handelman from PS 76, **Bronxwood & Adee Ave.**,1958 grads. Remember Mrs. Cooper? Anita Cohen Sternberg Silverman, 19874 Dinner ey Dr., Boca Raton, FL 33498.

MP1444 Anyone from 500 Southern Blvd. (149th St)? I went to **PS 25**. Miss Scherr 6th Grade teacher. Lived at 500 during WWII years, 40's,50's. Living in Florida. Don Blau (954)786-7740.

MP1445 Barbara Rosenthal, Sarah "Candy" Cashman, Joan Wesp, **Evander** "Red Knee Socks" sorority members, Toby Cedar, where are you? Contact Barbara Unger-Sakano.101 Parkside Dr. , Suffern, NY 10901 or call 914) 357-1683.

MP1446 Would like to contact any old buddies from **Evander** or **Hillside Homes** & **Wilson Post**. If anyone remembers Weinstein's Majestic Bungalow Colony, contact me, Howard Groder, 23 Homestead Terr. Scotch Plains, NJ 07076

MP1447 Celina Berkowitz & Renee Farber Weiss, please call Toby Brestin Heilbrunn (914) 679-5438. Would also love to hear from those who grew up on Wyatt St.

MP1448 Roy & Lillian Glassberg Schlachter, **Monroe** '53 & '54 looking for Edgar Storm, John Gsell, Ralph Sirico, Morty Kallman, Ronie Wasserman, Phyllis Battiste, Arthur Soller, Bernie Zuckerman & other dear friends. E-mail: LILSCHLACH@AOL.com

MP1449 Looking for the **Thieriot Ave.** Co-op girls from the 60's: Estelle Knipple, Janet Cohen, Ann Waxman, etc. Looking for reunion with **Archer St.** boys. Contact Don Metscher, 20 South Lane, New City, New York 10956, or call (212)723-7266.

MP1450 Would love to hear from anyone who might remember me? Doris Langer of **Vyse Ave.**, and Vivian (Zina) Solokoff of Ave. **St. John,** where are you? Contact: Roberta (Bobbie) Verman Cohen 878 Rudder Way, Annapolis, MD 21401 (410)266-1681.

MP1451 Lee Evans (Ely Levine) where are you today? Mildred Zimmerman you are still missing **(173rd & Vyse Ave.)** Call Adele Goldstein (609)988-3699.

MP1452 **E. 174th & Vyse Ave.**-Chester Deli Corner (1958-1962)-looking for Susan Hill, Marcia Broth, Seena Weiss, Judy Lynn, Thelma Horowitz, Elliot & Arlene, Lester Baer, David Myron, Barry Fierst, Carole Winokor- Contact Billy Roth, 1721 Spruce Ridge Ln., Las Vegas, NV 89115 (702)459-3423.

MP1453 Remember us? Rhoda Rubin **(Townsend Ave., PS 64, Wade JHS)** and Donna Meshibosh **(Monroe Ave., PS 70, Wade** JHS). Would love to hear from you. Write: 5317 Tennis Ln.,Delray Beach, FL 33484-6649

MP1454 James Tanner, grew up in **Eastchester Gardens** 1953-1971, **PS 121**, **JHS 135, Evander** '65, **Bx. Comm. College** & Hunter College. Looking to hear from former neighbors & schoolmates. Write: 4031 E. 4TH St., Long Beach, CA 90814-2846 or call (310) 590-5250.

MP1455 Lois Frischer (Baruch) **Taft** '63, would love to hear from Marcia Feldman (Luftig) from **Mt. Eden** & **Grand Concourse.** Anybody else who remembers Shelly's Luncheonette, the Library on **Selwyn** and me, please write: 22 Underwood Rd., Monsey, NJ 10952.

MP1456 Wanted: 1960 **James Monroe** Year Book.Will pay $50. Call Evenings (914) 676-3203

MP1457 Richard Janowitz, **Taft** '54, where are you? Call Joel Lerner, (914) 794-5793.

MP1458 Frank Benedetto PS 90 '49, **Gompers** '53, lived at **166th St.** & **Morris Ave.** I work as doorman Caesar's Casino, Atlantic City. Stop by and say hello!

MP1459 Harriet Terdiman (Pravda) **PS 26, 82, Taft** '58, **Hunter College** '62, would love to hear from old friends from **Loring Place, Andrews Ave., Popham Pl., Harrison, Davidson Ave. Burnside area.** Please write: 28 Douglas Terr.,Woodcliff Lake , NJ 07675. or call (201) 391-8008.

MP1460 Martha (Byer) White and Roseline (Shebitz) Glazer are looking for Arlene Perlmutter. Please call 1-800-54-LATCH.

MP1461 Mimi Wiener Morrow lived in **Hillside Homes** early '50's, **PS78, Evander** '55. Would love to hear from old friends. Now living in Seattle Call (206) 644-4253.

MP1462 Harold & Myrtle (Ball) Mangels celebrating 52nd Anniversary & wondering about old friends & neighbors at **2188 Creston Ave.** & environs. PS 79 '33, **Evander** '36, NY Naval Cadets U.S.N. (Ret.) Living in Jacksonville Beach, FL Write: 904 16th Ave. N., Jax Beach., FL 32250

MP1463 **Marcy Place & Gr. Concourse,** **PS 88** & Vic. The war years: WWII, Korea! Might be interesting to get together- What do you think M-F call Ron White (203) 245-0657, or drop a line 103 Bishop Ln., Madison, CT 06443.

MP1464 Westchesterites (or out-of-towners) renew old acquaintances- Phone Sheila Furmansky Kerper (914) 923-3168, **PS 93/77**, **Monroe** '51, CCNY (uptown) '55. Married 40 years to Lester Kerper, Brooklyn Tech, Brooklyn College.

MP1465 Cathy McDonald, **Tremont Ave.** (Father was a bus driver) where are you? Also, Elaine Slepp where are you? Harriet Hyman Meltzer (619)340-1572 and/or (212)447-0045. Please leave message.

Classifieds

MP1466 Arthur M. Driscoll (Chick), where are you? Jake passed away 10 years ago. No contact with you since White Fathers, NY (formerly of Logan Ave). Contact Bill Padula, 2088 S. San Ray, Green Valley, AZ 85614-1425. Anyone: Alice?

MP1467-Once Little Sara "Hirsch" Berlan- remembers many classmates and neighborhood friends. Bust St., Anthony Ave., **Burnside Ave.**, and beyond. PS 28 '48, EBB '51, **Walton '54**. 516-889-4548, Long Beach NY.

MP1468 Bubby S, Casey S, Dave L, Sheldon L, Burt K and any other Eagles or Emanons from **University Ave.** benches. We are looking for you-contact Irwin (Goldy) Goldberg- (954)720-9231 or Stanley (Ray) Raderman (407)995-7574 Seeking **Macombs Jr. HS (PS 82)** students for 2nd reunion in Boca Raton, FL Call I. Goldberg(954)720-9231, or S. Raderman (407)995-7574

MP1469 Reunion-Class of 1947 - **PS 33** Bronx-Looking for the following: Miriam Abolnick, Donald Baida, Stan Brownstein, James Cavanaugh, Francine Davis, Wm. De Masi, Richard Gaudy, Audrey Goldman, Royce Goldman, Barbara Greenstein, Paul Greenwald, Sylvia Grenz, Phillip Haas, George Higham, Barbie Hoffman, Herman Jaeger, Norm Levy, Marty Lindenbaum, Sammi Maniello, Wm. McDonald, Robertt Munies, Raymond Nielson, Jackie Phillips, Robert Rosenberg, Mel Rubin, Mickey Schugkagol, Ronnie Schiff, Martin Schwartz, Gladys Silverman, Barbara Silverstein, Helene Tiger, Constance Winters-Please call (718)229-3237 for further information

MP1470 Gail (Fedol) Lowenthal has been living in the Chicago area for 30 years but have great memories of growing up in the Bronx. Would love to hear from lost friends.

MP1471 Am looking for **Monroe '45** graduates. Bert Gottesman for one, was never notified of any reunions. Lenore Greenberg, 5120 N. Avenida Primera, Tucson AZ 85704)

MP1472 Where are you Larry Wolfe (Wolfie)? Formerly of **1634 Popham Ave.** Remember sleigh riding "the steps" down to **Undercliff Ave**? We were crazy to do it. **The Park Plaza** + 100 Cartoons + dbl features. In by 10 and out by 5. Steve Galkin, 123 E. Elm St., Greenwich, CT 06830.

MP1473 Love to hear from old school or neighborhood friends. **PS '63**, graduated '47, **Prospect JHS '39, Morris '42, CCNY '49**. Lived on **Jennings/Prospect Vyse/ 179**. Please call (919)408-0072-Seymour Lerman, 6 Burnwood Pl., Chapel Hill NC 27514

MP1474 Ned Viseltear looking for the old gang from Kappy's on **Walton & 176th.** Let's get in touch and maybe throw a reunion. Call or E-Mail me at 212-838-0768 or NedVee. @aol.com. Let's do it. The clock is running!

MP1475 Fred Romano looking for friends **Burke & Holland** 1940's, **PS 113**, SP's classes1947-49. **Evander '53. Burke & Paulding** early 1950's and Iona '56. Drop a note with phone # P.O. Box 194, Eastchester, NY 10709.

MP1476 Lenore ("Leni" Goldman) Simon from **PS 46 & PS 86** who remembers playing "books" by the schoolyard, "ping pong" after school, hanging out at **Strong Street** Park off **University Ave**, rollerskating around the **Reservoir**? E-Mail: simonesque@ AOL.com, or write 3862 Mt Acadia Blvd. San Diego CA 92111

MP1477 Mattie Carruthers of **Morris HS** moved north (northeast Bronx off Boston Rd). Where are you now?You worked for Jacobi Hospital-Sylvia Baxter Weather. (203)797-9034.

MP1478 Would like to contact old Dudes from **St. Ann's 141 St.** Joe Feretta, Peter Crilly, Con Dolan, John O'Niel, Johnny Dormer, Jimmy Deeneen, Larry Wiendoff, Jimmy Barry, Mike Fogerty. Anyone knowing anything, please call Kelly (914) 735-7298, Otto (516)887-0898.

MP1479 Carole Frank (Kriegsman) living in Massapequa Park are looking for Eileen Becarelli and Heddi Rosenberg/Brier. Please call me at (516)541-7281.

MP1480 Looking for the guys and girls who hung out in Lefty Moes Candy Store in 1948-49 thru the 50's and also the guys and girls from Jerrys on **183 & Beaumont Ave**- Rusty Marrapodi - 658 N. Hayden Dr., Tucson AZ 85710 call (520)721-0105

MP1481 Does the I.D.Y.C. mean anything to you? Does Miss Sheridan's class 9-1 (1956) mean anything to you? If so —then you're the one's we're looking for. Contact Joyce (Klein) Barbara (Novick), Sandy (Altschul).Sandy Altschul Juskowitz, 169 Huntley Dr., Hartsdale NY 10530.

MP1482 If you want to get in touch with Irene Dranow who attended **PS 26, JHS 82,** and Performing Arts, please call me at (516)462-6581. I'd love to hear from you! Irene Dranpw Blaymore, 27 Stonehurst Lane, Dix Hills, NY 11746.

MP1483 Trying to locate Dorothy Shore from **Mohegan Ave**, later to Brooklyn and then California; also Benny Goodman from Daly Ave. Please write Arthur Williams, Box 13391, Hauppauge NY 11788.

MP1484 Where are you? Looking for Gilda Diamond from **Boston Rd**, Pat Miller (now Commens), Arlene Damsky. I would love to hear from you. Please call Pearl Oberstein (now Fleischman) (201)387-9178.

MP1485 Who remembers Harrlette (Kaminsky) Jordan, **21 W. Mosholu Pkwy**.1941-'53, **PS 80**, EBB, **Evander** - call (301)443-6480 or e-mail HJ19Q@NIH.GOV

MP1486 Roosevelt '48 -40th Reunion - Send information +(maiden name) of classmates to: Jana Raphael 56 So. Parker Dr., Monsey NY 10952. Where's: Vicky Acosta, Fern Heringer, Susan Thomases, Peggy Caspers, Cecilia Neff, Sandra Harris, Carol Siegel, Judith Rubin, Audrie Sherman, Doris Crockwell?

MP1487 Officers of senior Class, **Evander '56** - Where are you? We found Linda Smalline, but where are: Ron Previ, President; Brenda Vogel, Secretary; Jan List, Treasurer; Dina Shapiro, Historian. We're planning a 40th year reunion and we need to locate you. Contact Anne Fletcher Price, **Evander '56**, 325 Place Lane, Woburn MA 01801 (617)937-0598.

MP1488 **Evander '56** will hold a reunion luncheon on Saturday, April 5, 1997. Contact Vinnie Bucci : (914)423-4491.

MP1489 Searching for Ralph Yanowitz **DeWitt Clinton '45, PS 80,** U.S. Navy. He lived at 30 or **33 E. 208th St**, Bronx. Dr. Aaron S. Greenwald, 300 E. 56th STt.-Apt. 4K, New York, NY 10022.

MP1490 Thea (Schwamenau) Sittenfeld **Evander '56** is looking for Arlene Goldstein & George Camarinos, Gail Zimmer **PS 46** and **Evander '56** or any other **Evander '56** grads. Write Thea at: Box 1066, Naples FL 34102.

MP1491 Dennis Daniels from Gun Hill & Decatur Ave. **PS 94, JHS 80 ('58), Clinton '61** Married Renee Steiner from **Andrews Ave.** Looking for old friends - drop us a note 1825 Country Club No., St Petersburg Fl 33710.

MP1492 Looking for Isobel Moss, Florence Drucker, Blossom Yanko. Would love to see Ida Barenbaum (Gootzait) call (718)225-4255.

MP1493 Looking for Scorpions', Freeman St 'Y' Scout Troop 247, mid 40's-50's Remember Jackie Rodriquez, Gene Norman, Larry Fagin, and Mel Klein? We're in contact with Larry Mesinbush, Walter Cherry, and others. Where are you? Call (407)645-4324 or write: 2305 Middleton Ave. Winter Park, FL 32792

MP1494 Need help-Looking for a book called *Throggs Neck Memories* by John McNamara. Call Mike at 914-623-5024.

MP1495 Jerry Levine is looking for the gang from **Longfellow/Bryant Aves**. & 173rd St; **PS 50, Herman Ridder, JHS 98 (1948)**, left **Gompers** in 1950 to join the US Army. Also the bunch that hung out at the park-Bryant & 175th St. We were the "Black Orchids". Write: P.O. Box 911, Farmingdale NJ 07727.

MP1496 Ridder 54-57, Roosevelt 57-60: Appreciate help locating teacher's graves. Maury Englander, 43 Fifth Ave, New York, NY 10003.

MP1497 Len Chasen, **PS 83, Columbus '63** is a principal in the Virgin Islands' CPA firm, Brammer, Chasen, O'Neil & DeLuca, P.C., and has lived in the Virgin Islands almost 30 years, with his Karen. Let's hear from old friends.

MP1498 Allan Jeffrey Katz **3604 Bronx Blvd, Evander '61**. Hi to Gerald, Lou Peluso, Lewis Weinberg, Rich Cohen, Red, Henry and Mike Alvito of Yonkers, Bobby B., Richard, Snowball. 67 Denton Ave, Rockaway NY 11518.

MP1499 Evander '50 graduate looking for Edward Carr, fellow graduate or John F. Byrnes, NYC policeman probably retired. Herb Fuchs, 117 Boston Post Rd., #221, Waterford, CT 06385 (203)366-5211.

MP1500 Alpha Mu Phi, CCNY, looking for Bob Posner, Eddie Magrab, other missing charter members. 1994 NY reunion included Herbie, Harvey, Barney, Mike, Sid, Kurt, Abe, Al, Hal, Louie Moishe. Call Mike Stone at 407-369-1602, or write 5188 E. Europa Dr., Boynton Bch FL 33437.

MP1501 *SKULLY™* That <u>street game</u> you loved as a kid! Now a big, colorful, vinyl game board. Check or money order, **$22.95 (includes s/h)** to: Stone Communications, P O Box 585, Buffalo NY 14215. Created by Joann Liggio Steinmetz.

MP1502 Desperately seeking "cookie". Marcia Cashman Heller and Gloria Fox Moskowitz would love to find our **James Monroe HS** friend Anita "Cookie" Kleinberg, married to Morey Lerman. Have pictures and enjoy reminiscing. . Marcia: (516)868-2182. Gloria: (201)837-8713.

MP1503 Former Bronx Boy Scouts! I collect the history of the Bronx Boy Scouting and Ranachqua Lodge. I want your photographs, patches, neckerchiefs, newsletters, programs, certificates and other documents. Will copy and return originals or purchase if preferred. David Malatzky, 2332 Holland Ave, Bronx NY 10467; E-mail: DMALATZKY @AOL.COM.

MP1504 Taft '62, Barry Cashman would like to hear from old friends from the Bronx "Y", Mosholu Day Camp. Living in Boca Raton, Florida last 25 years, retired from BellSouth after 32 years, now working for a internet Service Provider, (cashman @gate.net)

MP1505 Clinton '38; **P.S. 80** '34; earlier St. Brendan's, **P.S 56**. lived on **Mosholu Pkwy, Bainbridge, Perry Aves.**, Seeking: Pearl and Shirley Bienstock, Patsy McCool, Ruth Walsh, John Littlejohn, Morris Dein, Whitey Kleinsmith, Joe Spencer, Bill Mellin, Bob Ford, and others. Call Bob O'Connell (908) 647-3298

CORRECTION
1043 Merrily Pallas Mitnick, **PS102** '54, JHS125 '57, **Science** '60, Queens College '64. Married Stan from Garden View. Currently Asst. Principal of CS150. Email: ixnetcom.com

Come Blow Your Horn

Leatrice Isler Bell married Stanley Bell in '52 and are still honeymooners after raising 4 children. They have 4 grandchildren. After working as a model, dental assistant and for ABC-TV in the Kinescope Dept., raised our family and returned to business as Director of Sales in the Hotel Industry which led to Catering for Hotels. My friend of longest standing remains close since before we entered kindergarten at PS39.

Burton Dornfest, PhD '60 (NYU), Professor Med. Schools, 30 years at Downstate Med Ctr. (Brooklyn). Currently retired, but teaches as adjunct professor at Einstein Med. School, CUNY Bio-Med Program, Articles in Hematology, Teaching Gross Anatomy. Married, wife-Eviline, 2 sons-Michael & Barry.

Russell Marrapodi graduated PS45 in '49.

Went into the US Navy '51. Worked for Bronx District Attorney for 25 years. Wife, Carol, passed away Dec. 1 '86. Alone since. Have two daughters-both teachers.

Arnold Weber, Director International Sales, US Military Affiliation involving 30 countries.

Jerry Halpern have written "The Boy Who Tends to Sheep, Mistakes You Say? The man, the wood, the crucifer and the truth." CEO of wedding invitation printing company. Married 35yrs. with 4 children and 4 grandchildren.

Joe Weinstein, **Monroe** Swim Team '41-'45.

Barry Bealick, PS104, Macombs JHS #82, **Clinton**. At **Clinton** he was in journalism and lead features editor on the Clinton News. Grew up in Sedgwick Houses "56-'70, bldg. 140. Left the Bronx in '69 to attend and graduate from Syracuse University (Dual bachelors: Journalism & Economics) Worked and lived in Long Island from '73-'90. Now resides in White Plains. Brother-Howard.

John Collins, Navy WWII, NYPD Harbor Unit. Hobart & Wm Smith Colleges- 12 straight NCAA Div III Lacrosse Champs (Admin-asst). Now retired in Geneva, NY.

Jayne Schorr McMahon moved to Florida

to open a new office for "Western International Media". This year will be married 20 years and have 2 great sons: Frank (15) & Eric (6).

Harris Semegram, Director of Credit for large consumer products company. Obtained Certified Credit Executive designation. Resides in NW Bergen County with a wonderful wife and two great sons.

Marie Tancredi Russo lived on LI Suffolk County for 36 years. Worked for the County of Suffolk and is now retired. AAS Accounting Suffolk Community College. BS Accounting CW Post. Married with 2 children who are college grads. Spouse, Charlie, 2 years, college NWA Airline Maintenance Supervisor,

John DeGallia, formerly of 214th St. Lived in LA for 10 years. Moved to Bay area SF in '77. Worked for City of SF as plumber for 15 yrs. Now retired and living in the town of Pacifica and plan to build on 11.6 acres of land to spend my golden years. Lived in the Bronx until '67.

Ruth Zemlowitz Gotfried-retired Administrator, Passaic County Board of Social Services. 3 children- 6 grandchildren-widowed.

Nancy M. Cozine is the recipient of a

Classifieds

President George Bush "Point of Light" award and was invited to the White House for ceremonies in 1992 as the founder of SHARE, an organization responsible for collecting and moving over 60 tons of food donated by Long Islanders to the families of Long Island military personnel sent to the Persian Gulf for Desert Shield/Storm. She was also named a Newsday "Volunteer of the Year" that same year, in addition to "Woman of the Year" by Islip Town Women's Services, and was identified as a Channel 2 News "Homefront Hero." Professionally, I have received numerous awards from the New York State School Public Relations Association for achievements in educated journalism.

Barry Jacob, M.D., Board Certified Surgeon, Nutrition Expert who developed an American Medical Assoc. certified course: Nutrition for Prevention Medicine and in 1996 was a featured speaker on nutrition with C. Everett Koop, MD the former Surgeon General of the U.S. at the World Congress on contemporary therapies in medicine.

Allan Brown graduated **Taft** in '63 and went into the US Air Force until '66. where he then went to work for Pan American Airways as an A&P aircraft mechanic . In '91 the company closed down. He then put together I.C. motors for robots and medical purposes.

Al Shapp has just been elected President of the North Miami Beach Condo Home Owners Association.

Andrew Loiacono was fascinated in hair dressing, but never would think about it with the guys I hung around with...I never would have heard the end of it. So after I moved to South Florida I endured & now own 13 hair salons in the So. FL area along with my 2 sons and 2 daughters.

I am Abby, the 4 year old daughter of Ira Siegal, **Columbus** '66. Daddy loves his life as an intellectual property attorney in Los Angeles. However, he can't wait to take me to the Bronx Zoo, Yankee Stadium and Orchard Beach.

Norman Abramowitz taught High School Physical Education in NYC for 9 years. Now he is a Systems Analyst in Colorado and coaches girls youth soccer.

Sidney Brickell, WWII VET '43-'46. Wed in '42 and has 2 sons and 4 grandchildren and have a great wife of 54 years. Loves to play golf and racquetball to this day. Captain of the greatest basketball team in the Bronx "Delhis"- the finest group of fellows ever assembled. Champions at PS67 cc 3 years.

Sylvia Finkelman Jacobs attended **Hunter College**. Quit to get married. Lived in the Spring Valley area for 35 years. Graduated from Empire State College in '82. Taught at various religious schools for 35 years. After graduation worked as an accountant in NYC. Presently I am teaching again, and volunteer to teach adults.

Patricia Manz Menona earned a scholarship to Business College. Sec'y to Treas., General Foods, Sec'y to Supt. of Schools, Conn., retired from IBM as an Executive Secretary. Now volunteer as teachers ass't for the 4th grade. I also teach English to non-English speaking people. Have twin grandchildren (boy & girl) in Conn., and 2 grandsons here in California.

Marian Kaplun Shapiro received a Masters Doctorate at Harvard and practices as a psychologist and have written 1 book, Second Childhood (Norton '89) and have published many articles in her field, plus much poetry. Biggest accomplishment: building a wonderful, rich, warmth-filled life, both personally & professionally.

Renee N. Shields went to Queens College (BA, MS in Ed) St. John's University (30-ABD). Married Joel F. Shields in '56 (div. '73) Have 1 son and 1 daughter. Taught English at **Taft** (very briefly) L.I.C.H.S. & JHS (South Jamaica) Retired.

Eleanor Prinz, MA in '56 and started teaching science. I taught at **JHS54** from '54 to '70 at **Morris**. In '76 I was transferred to **Truman** HS where I taught until '91. I am now retired and still living in the Bronx.

Evelyn Giniger Hottman just retired from 10 years of producing and hosting a weekly TV talk show called "Better With Age". I also founded and direct a Senior Group 14 years old for which I received "Humanitarian of the Year Award." My TV show is a national "OWL Award" recipient. I write an editorial page as well.

Jack Climan is the father of 3 sons in Bronx, 2 from **Science**. Sandy Climan was valedictorian in '74 - Adlai graduated from **Evander** as above my "Claim to Fame", moved to Gunther Ave - Boston Post Rd. near Co-op City & Freedomland. Active in Jewish Center of Violet park, commander-Jewish war veterans, choir leader in synagogue.

Charlotte Frank nee Kizner graduated **City College** '50, **Hunter College** M.S.Ed '66, Teacher **PS62**. Bronx Math Teacher IS 131

Bronx curr. Supervisor Dist 12, Exec.Direct-Curr& Inst.- NYC BD of Ed Livingston St. Brooklyn. Now VP McGraw-Hill.

Rosalyn (Goldin) Resnick, **Evander** '57, has her own business and is presently single.

William (Vevy) Getman, **Monroe** '35, WWII decorated. Was top typesetter, investments. Now enjoying cultural pursuits and celebrating Silver Anniversary with second-time-around- (the best) wife, Tina!

William Ferstenfeld is currently Executive Administrator of Pennsylvania's largest synagogue- 1800 families.

Richard Sullivan graduated from **Fordham** '38. Three years overseas in Army WWII. Graduated from **Fordham Law** in '48. Practiced law in Manhattan. Married Julia A. Monahan. Moved to Washington DC-Chief Counsel Congressional Committee for 32 years, Committee on Public Works and Transportation, House of Representatives. Attended Harvard Business School and Kennedy School of Government Program for Senior Managers in Government class of 1976. Now a consultant in Washington DC. Seven children, four grandchildren.

Larry Kolber, songwriter-two hits #1 "I Love how you love me" Bobby Vinton (sold 1 million) "Patches" Dicky Lee. Two #1 country hits "Yes Mr. Peters" and "Yellow Bandana." Fifty seven songs recorded by artists including Patti Page, Billy Eckstein, June Valli, Neil Sedaka, Wayne Newton, Hank Williams Jr. "I learned how to rhyme 'neath the Morris Avenue sign"

Martin Blumenthal married Rosalie Feinberg, **Evander** '46 have 3 children and 7 grandchildren, CPA in NJ. In business with my son, Rosalie works at and teaches ceramics. I'm interested in all sports, play tennis and winter in Florida.

Sheldon Silverstein graduated **City College** and is Chief Financial Officer of Fuller Tool Company and Sarafay Krauss Silverstein graduated NYU and recently retired as an elementary school teacher.

Bert Sugarman moved to SF '78 to be with his new granddaughter. Member Board of Trustees and teach 10th grade in Synagogue. Past Commander Jewish War Veterans for the State of Calif. volunteer at local VA hospital as well as at travelers aid at SF intl. airport. Active member of Masonic Shrine.

William Kent wrote "The Smart Money" Doubleday '72, December '96 will publish "What Your Doctor Doesn't Know Can Kill You" Now writing, "I Never Left the Bronx."

Selma (Sally) Fleher Jaffe moved from Riverdale to Florida 10 yrs ago. Reunited with a childhood friend Helen Platkin (from the Bronx)

Arnold Forman, father of 2 super people. Married almost 40 years to Cecile Bergman, Morris '55, 3 grandchildren. Semi-retired CPA. Living in Oceanside CA. Past & current activities: Chabad - on various boards of any civic charitable organizations. Left the Bronx '52. Never looked back, but miss it. The world has been good to a kid off the streets.

Mildred Gill Spitz, widowed since '86. Have 3 wonderful daughters around the country: Michigan, New Jersey and California. I've been a secretary most of my life, most recently with LA School District. Now live in Newbury Park, CA.

Loretta Strahl Anaguost graduated Brooklyn College '80, summa cum with Honors in Educations, BA, Masters '82. MS Humanities, Brooklyn College, Summa Cum. Won Awards: Alpha Sigma Lambda '80. Kappa Delta Pi '80. Scholarship award Jewish Foundation for the Education of Woman '80. Special Bacca laureate degree program for adults, writing for Public Relations firm, editing, woman's magazines, Educator NYC public schools, writer, married 26 years, 3 children.

Mark L. Haiman, **Monroe** '58 is a retired Colonel US Marine Corps, living in Carlsbad, CA at (619)729-2845.

Sergi Kanevsky, **Taft** '50, Sheridan Avenue and 172nd St. Member of the "Kingsmen". CCNY '55 Engineering, CCNY '57 Masters, P.E. Remembers night center at **Taft**. Waiting outside dances on Saturdays to pick up girls.

Roslyn Wilkin nee Cooperman graduated **Taft** '46. Grew up on College Ave & 170th St. Married, 2 daughters and 3 grandchildren. Started Health Care Agency in '74. Now have 7 offices throughout NY.

Myna Skoller, **Taft** '59. Owner of "Designer Resale" best consignment shop in NYC.

Howard D. Kibel is currently a Professor of Psychiatry, New York Medical College.

Mrs. Dorothy M. Wildhagen - 1970 Metropolitan Life Camera Club Class B - 2nd Pl. Award for slide competition and First Runner up for "Slide of the Year" Award for slide entitled "Two Alone". Club is a member of the Photographic Society of America. I am publishing a collection of my poems "The Eighth of July: Poetry by Dorcas" - The Christopher Publishing House, Hanover MA 02339 - write to CPH or look for in stores Fall '96.

I am interested in any Bronxites who are interested in building a substantial second income in their spare time- no investment and inventory. Call Luciano (718)796-8153

Stan Grayson is currently Vice President Associate Media Planning/Buying Director at ODB Needham Worldwide Advertising. He resides in Westchester (Fleetwood) with his wife of 33 years. He has 2 children- a son who is getting his Doctorate in Clinical Neuro psychology and a married daughter who would like to become a physicians assistant.

SHOREHAVEN by Gayl (Leibowitz) Teller. Illustrated by Joyce (Leibowitz) Muller. Recapture the days of Shorehaven Beach Club. Order from Mellen Press, POBox 450, Lewiston, NY 14092-0450. $19.95 +$5 shipping/handling.

Samuel Goldman- Teacher and Family Counselor in Riverdale. Married 36 years to Isalene Silensky-Goldman. MS Degree in Education, Hunter College, MS Guidance, Manhattan College. Initiated "The Isalene Family Counseling Network" '81. Interests: Videotherapy, Filmmaking, (documentaries), writing. Daughter, Melanie recently married James McNamara, Jr.

Nicholas Petera presently a Senior Quality Assurance Engineer with the Hughes Defense Communications Company (formally Magnavox Electronics Company), in Fort Wayne, IN. Have worked in the military smart electronics business for the past 40 yrs with various government contractors. My wife and I live on a small farm in Indiana outside of Fort Wayne and enjoy the peacefulness. Over the years I have achieved certifications as an Engineering Technician, a Quality Auditor, Associate Welding Inspector, Welding Educator and hold a Professional Engineers License with Bachelors Degree in Quality Assurance/Quality Control.

Sol Liebowitz, NYU Heights, NYU Medical School, New York Eye&Ear Infirmary (ophthalmology)

Leah Wallach, **Ridder** '55, **Industrial Arts**, married 35 yrs to Dr. Saul Scherzer. 2 children: one is an Account Exec. with major US bank; and the other is a doctor. 2 granddaughters. Graduated FIT and designed girls dresses, Briarcliff College BS, Art Ed, Fairfield University MA, Career Counseling Consultant facilitating Career Transition workshops. Paint, sew and design ceramics. Travel extensively.

Bonnie Maser Graser presently teaches at MS118, 8th grade special education and is finishing her second Masters in Gerontology.

Giacinta Liggio Pompa graduated from **Hunter** in '33 - Math Major. Then attended Drakes Business School for Accounting. Did clerical work until '38 when I began working for HRS- City of NY. Married in '56, left the agency. Then worked as an accounting clerk until '62 when we moved to Florida. We travelled to Europe. I worked for the State of FL as a Social Worker and later as a Supervisor. Left in '94 to care for my invalid husband. '78 I began working for a CPA as very satisfying. Retired 12/95.

William Roth left NYC in '64 to Los Angeles, went to Viet Nam '64 to '66. Married '66 raised 3 kids, moved to Las Vegas '77. Because Dealer, have worked in different Casinos in different positions thru the years. Presently Craps table at Treasure Island, swing shift.

Howard Groder graduated Cornell '55, CW Post MS, University Bologna MD, practice of gynecology past 19 years in New Jersey. Married with 2 daughters: Shari 28 and Erika 22, both single and working. Wife, Elenore, is school psychologist in NJ.

Barbara Unger Sakano published 5 books of poetry and has won several awards. Often writes about the Bronx. Many prize-winning poems and short stories. I have written about the Bronx of the 30's, 40's and 50's.

Richard Kobliner appears in "Whos Who in the east," "Who's Who in American Education," Consultant for the Wall Street Journal-classroom edition; College Advisory Consultant, Writer of curriculum guides, Middle Ages Longmen, Inc., Human Rights AFT, Black Studies UFT, Censorship Newsweek Magazine. Developed School University Partnerships Middlebury College, Williams College. Past President Social Studies Teachers NYC.

Norma R. Axelrad appeared in 2 Gilbert & Sullivan Operettas. NYU for Main Early Childhood Educ. Taught Kindergarten for 33.5 yrs. from '50 to '57 acted in the Walton Community Theatre, photography, music, ballet, theatre, birding and reading. Currently

Classifieds

a Volunteer at the Museum of Natural History. Have been retired since 3/81.

Eileen Lazarus Brenner Grew up in the West Bronx- Highbridge section. Attended **PS11** on Ogden Ave and then taught there from 1969-'68. Retired after 35 years.

Irene Dranon Blaymore - one of her biggest accomplishments had everything to do with the Bronx. She always wanted to be a comedienne, so at age 40 she entered a stand-up comedy contest for the "Funniest Person on LI". She came in 2nd out of 52 contestants and got tremendous Newsday and Channel 12 coverage. What was my routine about? I made jokes about growing up in the Bronx and how it compares to living in Dix Hills today!

Ruby Polonetsky married Peter Schrimmer from CCNY '56. They have 2 children: one is a NYC HS Science teacher, and one is a practicing PhD Clinical Psychologist. Husband, engineer, recently took early retirement, she is an elementary school teacher my districts teacher of the yr. for 1996. Have been local teachers assoc. President, member of Connecticut Educ. Assn's PR Commission Science & Math. Elem. Coord on difficult yrs, very active on all levels of school district and state education committees, study groups and causes. Trustee coordinated scholarship drives. Won fellowship for MS in Special. Educ. Teaching computer skills to ele. students.

Carol Frank Kriegsman , **Monroe** '60 is a secretary and her husband Stanly works for Kinney Parking as Director of Security & Audits & Vice President.

Russ Marrapodi worked in Bronx DA office '60-'85. Married in '67, have twin daughters, wife deceased in '86. Man of the Year, Father of the Year '94. B'way stores, class president **PS45**, '49 graduating class, Navy vet, ran for Assemblyman in Westchester in '77. Retired to Tucson AZ in '85.

Joel Leichter went to PS70, **Wade JHS117** and **Clinton.** Went to CCNY and then Denver University. Graduated from DU:BSME '58. Have 3 children and one grandchild. Office # (212)922-0800 x134

Sylvia Baxter Weather graduated from **Morris** '53, lived at 762-64 Cauldwell Ave, now 60 yrs. old and working for Dept. of Justice. Married '56 and is the mother of 3 and stepmother of 5. Have 19 grandchildren!

Lenore (Leni) Goldman Simon - thanks to Naomi Reba I learned about Washington Irving HS where I could major in art- it became my strongest-and only- addiction. I continued on to Cooper Union and am still practicing my craft: Etching. I have been lucky enough to have been awarded 8 grants via the California Arts Council thanks to my husband Robert for taking us to San Diego and as an added plus we have 3 great children!

Dr. Richard E. Wainerdi is President and CEO of the Texas Medical Center in Houston.

READER REPLIES

It is vitally important that you fill out the information below. Your input will be essential to the success of this magazine, tailored and inspired by you, the former "Bronxite". We thank you for your participation.

Subscriber? ☐ Yes ☐ No

YOUR NAME _____

ADDRESS _____

CITY _____ STAT E _____ ZIP _____ PHONE _____

HIGH SCHOOL ATTENDED _____ YEAR GRADUATED _____

TELL US A LITTLE ABOUT YOURSELF:
(Be sure to include your alma mater, old neighborhood, your best memories about your days in THE BRONX, (or anything else you can tell us).

_____

_____

_____

- -

COULD WE SEND A FRIEND A FREE COPY OF BACK IN THE BRONX?
Do you know current or former Bronxites who would like to receive our magazine and reunion information? If you do, we'll be happy to send them a **free** inaugural issue of **Back in THE BRONX**.
Write to Back in The Bronx, Box 141 H, Scarsdale, NY 10583 or call 1-800-7-BRONX 5

Last _____ First _____ Maiden _____

Address _____ City _____ State _____ Zip _____

Phone # ( ) _____ School and year of Graduation _____

Last _____ First _____ Maiden _____

Address _____ City _____ State _____ Zip _____

Phone # ( ) _____ School and year of Graduation _____

Last _____ First _____ Maiden _____

Address _____ City _____ State _____ Zip _____

Phone # ( ) _____ School and year of Graduation _____

Last _____ First _____ Maiden _____

Address _____ City _____ State _____ Zip _____

Phone # ( ) _____ School and year of Graduation _____

COME BLOW YOUR OWN HORN DEPARTMENT
Please tell us about yourself (include your name)—about your accomplishments, awards, titles or works in progress. We're interested in hearing about them. List Below. _____

_____

_____

_____

_____

READER REPLIES

As a subscriber you are entitled to a **FREE 40 Word Classified, Missing Persons, Blow Your Own Horn, or Personal Ad.** Please write your ad below (if you are not subscribing to our magazine you can still place an ad in the next issue. The cost of an advertisement is 50¢ a word, there is no limit on paid ads).

_____

_____

_____

Is Your Mailing Label Correct?

In order to keep our database current, please correct any errors and place the label and or photocopy with corrections.

Account #	High School	Year Graduated
6817	Roosevelt	1958

Mary R. Flowers
123 Anystreet Blvd.
Anywhere, USA 12345

Change of Address?

If you're planning a move please attach your label corrected with your new address and the date that you will begin receiving mail at that address. This will insure that you don't miss your next issue of **Back in THE BRONX.**

Ordering Information

A Great Gift Idea! In addition to your own subscription, a subscription to **Back in THE BRONX** makes a great and unique gift. Fill in the form below and we'll process the order in time for our next issue. So, order your subscription NOW, and order one for a friend!

YES, I'd like to order the following items:

QTY.

___ 1Yr. (4 ISSUES) Subscription(s) to **Back in THE BRONX** $19.95
___ 2Yr. (8 ISSUES) Subscription(s) to **Back in THE BRONX*** $29.95
___ 3Yr. (12 ISSUES) Subscription(s) to **Back in THE BRONX*** } *FREE Jahn's Menu $39.95
___ 4Yr. (16 ISSUES) Subscription(s) to **Back in THE BRONX*** $49.95
___ The Beautiful Bronx...........$25.00 (plus $3.95 S/H) $28.95
___ The Bronx: It Was Only Yesterday.....$25.00 (plus $3.95 S/H) $28.95
___ Bronx High School Reunion Weekend Video $29.95
___ SAVE MONEY - BUY 4 FOR JUST $99.00!
___ THE BRONX Tracking Service $9.95
___ COMPLETE HARDBOUND SET of all 16 past issues..$49.95 (plus $4.95 S/H)
    Order Now and receive a Jahn's menu & vintage Krum's photos from the 40's-50's for FREE!! $54.90
___ I would like to receive all available back issues and have them applied towards my subscription
    (To date we have 16 back issues available - While They Last!)

Please fill out completely and include shipping and handling where applicable **TOTAL: $** _____
for books only to: **Back in THE BRONX**, Box 141H, Scarsdale, NY 10583

Please Print Clearly ❑ New Subscriber ❑ Renewal

Name _____

Maiden Name _____

Address _____

City _____

State _____ Zip _____

Phone (_____) _____

High School _____ Year Grad. _____

❑ AMERICAN   ❑ ⬭   ❑ VISA   ❑ Check   ❑ Money Order

No. _____ Expiration Date _____

Signature _____

Back in THE BRONX

Box 141 H, Scarsdale, NY 10583
Phone 914-592-1647 • Fax 914-592-4893

ADDRESS CORRECTION REQUESTED